AMERICA

AMERICA

A NARRATIVE HISTORY

THIRD EDITION

VOLUME II

GEORGE BROWN TINDALL
with
DAVID E. SHI

W · W · NORTON & COMPANY · NEW YORK · LONDON

FOR BRUCE AND SUSAN
AND FOR BLAIR

———————————

FOR JASON AND
JESSICA

Since this page cannot legibly accommodate all the copyright notices, the
Credits section beginning on page A54 constitutes an extension of this
copyright page.

*The text of this book is composed in Caledonia, with display type set in
Torino Roman. Composition by Com Com, Inc. Manufacturing by R. R.
Donnelley. Book design by Antonina Krass.*

Library of Congress Cataloging-in-Publication Data

Tindall, George Brown.
America: a narrative history/George Brown Tindall.—3rd ed.
p.   cm.
Bibliography: p. 000
Includes index.

ISBN 0–393–96151–6 Vol. II pb.

1. United States—History.   I. Shi, David E.   II. Title.
E178.1.T55   1988
973—dc19   87-23174

W. W. Norton & Company, Inc., 500 Fifth Avenue,
New York, N.Y. 10110
W. W. Norton & Company Ltd., 10 Coptic Street, London WC1A 1PU

3 4 5 6 7 8 9 0

CONTENTS

MAPS

PREFACE

The warm reception instructors have accorded two editions of *America: A Narrative History* suggests that the book's purpose remains valid: to offer an introductory narrative history of America—a narrative alive with character, augmented with analysis and social texture, and propelled by the energy of great events. The format continues to be unique in its field: *America* is designed to be read. Its attractive, single-column page remains uncluttered by distracting inserts, portfolios, or other interruptions to the story. It also remains the only text that students can purchase without breaking the bank and carry around without breaking the back.

This third edition of *America* features a co-author with George Tindall—David Shi. The British novelist Evelyn Waugh once observed that he "could never understand how two men can write a book together; to me that's like three people getting together to have a baby." To be sure, joint authorship is a distinctive and occasionally awkward enterprise, but we have discovered that it is not nearly as cumbersome as Waugh thought. Our collaboration affords the chance to combine our qualities of writers and teachers with our interests as historians to broaden and enrich the narrative. By discussing new research and reading and reworking each other's drafts, we learned much from one another. Among other things, we confirmed a shared commitment to recount American history with as much wit and wisdom as we can muster, and to tell the story of national development so as to encompass the wide spectrum of human endeavor: social and economic, cultural and spiritual, political and military.

The most salient theme of this new edition is embodied in a question posed over two hundred years ago by J. Hector St. John de Crèvecoeur, a transplanted French farmer: "What then is the American, this new man?" Crèvecoeur, who arrived in the colonies in 1759, married an American woman, and settled on a New York farm, went on to explain in *Letters from an American Farmer* that in America "individuals of all nations are melted into a new race of men, whose labors and posterity will one day cause great changes in the world." Fifty years later the transcendental philosopher-poet Ralph Waldo Emerson addressed the same point when he wrote in his journal that in America, this "asylum of all nations, the energy of Irish, Germans, Swedes, Poles and Cossacks, and all the European tribes—of the Africans and of the Polynesians, will construct a new race . . . as vigorous as the new Europe which came out of the smelting pot of the Dark Ages."

These statements express a shared truth: from its inception America has been an ambitious effort to create a pluralist society. The United States has welcomed more people from other places than any other country in history, and the process of absorbing such a multicultural population has given American life its roiling energy. The lofty social aim of American civilization is expressed in the official motto of the United States, *e pluribus unum*—"one out of many."

Yet the national motto has rarely described the reality. Americans have prided themselves on their ability to fashion what one New York mayor called a "gorgeous mosaic," an integration of different ethnic groups and cultural backgrounds. But in fact the United States has never become the mythic "melting pot" envisioned by Crèvecoeur, Emerson, and others. Instead, peoples from the four corners of the globe have converged to form a richly diverse—and often fractious, too often violent—society held tenuously together by a shared commitment to democratic principles, economic opportunity, religious freedom, and the rule of law.

From the Revolutionary era to the 1990s, the nation's politicians, preachers, and pundits have debated the effects of America's quest for unity through diversity. This quest is a prominent thread running through the pages of this edition. It surfaces in discussions of the backgrounds and folkways of the colonists, in accounts of the waves of "new" immigration in the late nineteenth and late twentieth centuries and the nativist prejudices they aroused, in descriptions of the tangled skein of legislation affecting immigrants and refugees, and in data detailing recent trends in immigration and ethnic diversity. Few students, we suspect, realize that immigrants were responsible for one-third of the population growth of the United States in the 1980s, or that fully 80 percent of the newcomers were from Asia and Latin America.

To describe the remarkable "peopling of America," this edition of *America* highlights biography. From Anne Hutchinson and John

Winthrop through Sojourner Truth, Mary Elizabeth Lease, and Martin Luther King, Jr., brief biographies integrated throughout the narrative give students a more textured feel for the character and personality of key figures. And in fresh treatments of female slaves, women workers at the Lowell mills, women on the frontier and on the social fronts of foreign wars, this third edition of *America* offers enhanced discussions of women's lives and their contributions to American history.

Our collaboration for this edition benefited greatly from the insights and suggestions of many people. The following scholars provided close readings of the manuscript at various stages: Albert Broussard (Texas A & M University), Janet Coryell (Auburn University), Charles Eagles (University of Mississippi), Peter R. Knights (York University), Phillip L. Osborne (United States Air Force Academy), David Parker (Southwest Missouri State University), Malcolm Rohrbough (University of Iowa), and Daniel B. Thorp (Virginia Polytechnic Institute and State University). Copyeditor Debra Makay employed a falcon's eye and historical sensibility in polishing the manuscript, and Kristin Prevallet showed remarkable energy in gathering material for illustrations. Linda Sellars (University of North Carolina) updated the bibliographies originally prepared by Gary Freeze (Erskine College) and revised for the second edition by David Parker. Steve Forman, our steadfast editor at W. W. Norton, remains a pillar of insight and patience. An accomplished wordsmith with a certain historical flourish himself, he pruned our prose without bruising our pride and in the process gave enhanced meaning to the term discretion. We are confident that this edition of *America* is the better for the assistance provided by all of these people.

—George B. Tindall
Chapel Hill, North Carolina

—David E. Shi
Davidson, North Carolina

AMERICA

18 ⌀

RECONSTRUCTION:
NORTH AND SOUTH

THE WAR'S AFTERMATH

In the spring of 1865 the cruel war was over, a war that saw more men killed than in all other American wars before Vietnam combined. At the frightful cost of 620,000 lives and the destruction of the southern economy and much of its landscape, American nationalism emerged triumphant, and some 4 million slaves emerged free. Ratification of the Thirteenth Amendment in December 1865 abolished slavery throughout the Union. But peace had come only on the battlefields. "Cannon conquer," recognized a northern editor, "but they do not necessarily convert." Now the North faced the task of "reconstructing" a ravaged and resentful South. A few northerners thought the task was relatively simple. The Boston poet and professor James Russell Lowell wrote a friend in April 1865: "I worry a little about reconstruction, but am inclined to think that matters will very much settle themselves." He was wrong. An array of difficult issues confronted northern politicians. Should the Confederate leaders be tried for treason? How were new governments to be formed? How and at whose expense was the South's economy to be rebuilt? What was to be done with the freed slaves? Were they to be given land? social equality? education? voting rights? Such complex questions required sober reflection and careful planning, but policymakers did not have the luxury of time or the benefits of consensus.

DEVELOPMENT IN THE NORTH   To some Americans the Civil War had been more truly a social revolution than the War of Independence,

In celebration of victory, Union forces parade down Pennsylvania Avenue, Washington, D.C., in the Grand Review, May 1865.

for it reduced the once-dominant power of planter agrarians in the national councils and elevated that of the "captains of industry." It is easy to exaggerate the profundity of this change, but government did become subtly more friendly to businessmen and unfriendly to those who would probe into their activities. The wartime Republican Congress had delivered on the major platform promises of 1860, which had cemented the allegiance of northeastern businessmen and western farmers to the party of free labor.

In the absence of southern members, Congress during the war had passed the Morrill Tariff, which brought the average level of duties up to about double what it had been on the eve of conflict. The National Banking Act created a uniform system of banking and bank-note currency, and helped to finance the war. Congress also passed legislation guaranteeing that the first transcontinental railroad would run along a north-central route from Omaha to Sacramento, and donated public lands and public bonds to ensure its financing. In the Homestead Act of 1862, moreover, Congress voted free homesteads of 160 acres to actual settlers who occupied the land for five years, and in the Morrill Land Grant Act of the same year conveyed to each state 30,000 acres of public land per member of Congress from the state, the proceeds from the sale of which went to colleges of "agriculture and mechanic arts." Such measures helped stimulate the North's economy in the years after the Civil War.

DEVASTATION IN THE SOUTH   The South, where most of the fighting had occurred, offered a sharp contrast to the victorious North. Along the path of the army led by General Sherman, one observer reported in 1866, the countryside still "looked for many miles like a broad black streak of ruin and desolation." Columbia, South Carolina, said another witness, was "a wilderness of ruins," Charleston a place of "vacant houses, of widowed women, of rotting wharves, of deserted warehouses, of weed-wild gardens, of miles of grass-grown streets, of acres of pitiful and voiceless barrenness." In the valley of Tennessee, a British visitor reported: "The trail of war is visible . . . in burnt-up gin houses, ruined bridges, mills, and factories." The border states of Missouri and Kentucky had experienced a guerrilla war which lapsed into postwar anarchy perpetrated by marauding bands of bushwhackers turned bank robbers, such as the notorious James boys, Frank and Jesse.

Throughout the South, property values had collapsed. Confederate bonds and money became worthless; railroads and rolling stock were damaged or destroyed. Stores of cotton that had escaped destruction were seized as Confederate property or in forfeit of federal taxes. Emancipation at one stroke wiped out perhaps $4 billion invested in human flesh and left the labor system in disarray. The great age of expansion in the cotton market was over. Not until 1879 would the cotton crop again equal the record crop of 1860; tobacco production did not regain its prewar level until 1880; the sugar crop of

Virginia's Capitol, designed by Thomas Jefferson, looms over the ruins of Richmond, April 1865.

Louisiana not until 1893; and the old rice industry of the tidewater and the hemp industry of the Kentucky Blue Grass never regained their prewar status.

LEGALLY FREE, SOCIALLY BOUND   The newly freed slaves suffered most of all. According to Frederick Douglass, the black abolitionist, the former slave remained dependent: "He had neither money, property, nor friends. He was free from the old plantation, but he had nothing but the dusty road under his feet. He was free from the old quarter that once gave him shelter, but a slave to the rains of summer and the frosts of winter. He was turned loose, naked, hungry, and destitute to the open sky."

A few northerners argued that what the ex-slaves needed most was their own land. But even dedicated abolitionists in large part shrank from endorsing measures of land reform that might have given the freed slaves more self-support and independence. Citizenship and legal rights were one thing, wholesale confiscation and land distribution quite another. Instead of land or material help the freed slaves more often got advice and moral platitudes.

In 1865 Representative George Julian of Indiana and Senator Charles Sumner of Massachusetts proposed to give freed slaves forty-acre homesteads carved out of rebel lands taken under the Confiscation Act of 1862. But their plan for outright grants was replaced by a program of rentals since, under the law, confiscation

According to a former Confederate general, recently freed blacks had "nothing but freedom."

The Freedmen's Bureau set up schools such as this throughout the former Confederate states.

was effective only for the lifetime of the offender. Discussions of land distribution, however, fueled rumors that freedmen would get "forty acres and a mule," a slogan that swept the South at the end of the war. Its source remains unknown, but the aspirations which gave rise to it are clear enough. As one black man in Mississippi put it: "Gib us our own land and we take care ourselves; but widout land, de ole massas can hire us or starve us, as dey please." More lands were seized as "abandoned lands" under an act of 1864, and for default on the direct taxes that Congress had levied early in the war, than under the Confiscation Act. The most conspicuous example of confiscation was the estate of Robert E. Lee and the Custis family, which became Arlington National Cemetery, but larger amounts were taken in the South Carolina Sea Islands and elsewhere. Some of these lands were sold to freedmen, some to Yankee speculators.

THE FREEDMEN'S BUREAU   On March 3, 1865, Congress set up within the War Department the Bureau of Refugees, Freedmen, and Abandoned Lands, to provide "such issues of provisions, clothing, and fuel" as might be needed to relieve "destitute and suffering refugees and freedmen and their wives and children." The Freedmen's Bureau would also take over abandoned and confiscated land for rental in forty-acre tracts to "loyal refugees and freedmen," who might buy the land at a fair price within three years. But the amount of such lands was limited. Under General Oliver O. Howard as commissioner, and assistant commissioners in each state of the former Confederacy, agents were entrusted with negotiating labor contracts (something new for both freedmen and planters), providing medical care, and setting up schools, often in cooperation with northern agencies like the American Missionary Association and the Freedmen's Aid Society. The bureau had its own courts to deal with labor disputes and land titles, and its agents were further authorized to supervise trials involving Negroes in other courts.

This was as far as Congress would go. Beyond such temporary relief measures, no program of reconstruction ever incorporated much more than constitutional and legal rights for freedmen. These were important in themselves, of course, but the extent to which even these should go was very uncertain, to be settled more by the course of events than by any clear-cut commitment to equality.

The Battle Over Reconstruction

The problem of reconstructing the South arose first at the very beginning of the Civil War, when the western counties of Virginia refused to go along with secession. In 1861 a loyal state government of Virginia was proclaimed at Wheeling and this government in turn consented to the formation of a new state called West Virginia, duly if irregularly admitted to the Union in 1863. The loyal government of Virginia then carried on from Alexandria, its reach limited to that part of the state which the Union controlled. As Union forces advanced into the South, Lincoln in 1862 named military governors for Tennessee, Arkansas, and Louisiana. By the end of the following year he had formulated a plan for regular governments in those states and any others that might qualify.

LINCOLN'S PLAN AND CONGRESS'S RESPONSE   Acting under his pardon power, President Lincoln issued on December 8, 1863, a Proclamation of Amnesty and Reconstruction under which any rebel state could form a Union government whenever a number equal to 10 percent of those who had voted in 1860 took an oath of allegiance to the Constitution and the Union, and had received a presidential pardon. Participants also had to swear support for laws and proclamations dealing with emancipation. Certain groups, however, were excluded from the pardon: civil and diplomatic officers of the Confederacy; senior officers of the Confederate army and navy; judges, congressmen, and military officers of the United States who had left their posts to aid the rebellion; and those accused of failure to treat captured Negro soldiers and their officers as prisoners of war. Under this plan loyal governments appeared in Tennessee, Arkansas, and

Louisiana, but Congress recognized them neither by representation nor in counting the electoral votes of 1864.

In the absence of any specific provisions for reconstruction in the Constitution, politicians disagreed as to where authority properly rested. Lincoln claimed the right to direct reconstruction under the clause that set forth the presidential pardon power, and also under the constitutional obligation of the United States to guarantee each state a republican form of government. Republican congressmen, however, argued that this obligation implied a power of Congress to act.

A few conservative and most moderate Republicans supported Lincoln's program of immediate restoration. A small but influential group known as Radical Republicans, however, favored a sweeping transformation of southern society based on granting freedmen full-fledged citizenship. The Radicals also maintained that Congress, not the president, should supervise the reconstruction program. To this end they helped pass in 1864 the Wade-Davis Bill, sponsored by Senator Benjamin Wade of Ohio and Representative Henry Winter Davis of Maryland, which proposed much more stringent requirements than Lincoln had. In contrast to Lincoln's 10 percent plan, the Wade-Davis Bill required that a majority of white male citizens declare their allegiance and that only those who could take an "iron-clad" oath (required of federal officials since 1862) attesting to their *past* loyalty could vote or serve in the state constitutional conventions. The conventions, moreover, would have to abolish slavery, exclude from political rights high-ranking civil and military officers of the Confederacy, and repudiate debts incurred "under the sanction of the usurping power."

Passed during the closing day of the session, the bill was subjected to a pocket veto by Lincoln, who refused to sign it but issued an artful statement that he would accept any state which preferred to present itself under the congressional plan. The sponsors responded with the Wade-Davis Manifesto, which accused the president, among other sins, of usurping power and attempting to use readmitted states to ensure his reelection.

Lincoln's last public words on reconstruction came in his final public address, on April 11, 1865. Speaking from the White House balcony, he pronounced the theoretical question of whether the Confederate states were in the Union "bad as the basis of a controversy, and good for nothing at all—a mere pernicious abstraction." These states were simply "out of their proper practical relation with the Union," and the object was to get them "into their proper practical relation." It would be easier to do this by merely ignoring the abstract issue: "Finding themselves safely at home, it would be utterly immaterial whether they had been abroad." At a cabinet meeting on April 14, Lincoln proposed to get state governments in operation before Congress met in December. He was reported to have said that there were men in Congress who, if their motives were good, were nevertheless impracticable, and who possessed feelings of hate and vindictiveness in which he did not sympathize and could not participate. He wanted "no persecution, no bloody work," no radical restructuring of southern social and economic life.

THE ASSASSINATION OF LINCOLN   That evening Lincoln went to Ford's Theater and his rendezvous with death. Shot by John Wilkes Booth, a crazed actor and Confederate zealot who thought he was doing something for the South, the president died the next morning. Accomplices had also targeted Vice-President Johnson and Secretary of State Seward. Seward and four others, including his son, were victims of severe but not fatal stab wounds. Johnson escaped injury, however, because his chosen assassin got cold feet and wound up tipsy in the barroom of Johnson's hotel.

Martyred in the hour of victory, Lincoln entered into the national mythology even while the funeral train took its mournful burden north to New York and westward home to Springfield. The nation extracted a full measure of vengeance from the conspirators. Pursued into Virginia, Booth was trapped and shot in a burning barn. His last words were: "Tell Mother I die for my country. I thought I did for the best." Three of Booth's collaborators were brought to trial by a military commission and hanged, along with the woman at whose boardinghouse they had plotted. Against her the court had no credible evidence of complicity. Three others got life sentences, including a Maryland doctor who set the leg Booth had broken when he jumped to the stage. All were eventually pardoned by President Johnson, except one who died in prison. The doctor achieved lasting fame by making common a once obscure expression. His name was Mudd. Apart from those cases, however, there was only one other execution in the aftermath of war: Henry Wirz, who commanded the infamous prison at Andersonville, Georgia, where Union prisoners were probably more the victims of war conditions than of deliberate cruelty.

JOHNSON'S PLAN   Lincoln's death suddenly elevated to the White House Andrew Johnson of Tennessee, a man whose state was still in legal limbo and whose party affiliation was unclear. He was a War Democrat who had been put on the Union ticket in 1864 as a gesture of unity. Of humble origins like Lincoln, Johnson had moved as a youth from his birthplace in Raleigh, North Carolina, to Greeneville, Tennessee, where he became proprietor of a tailor shop. Self-educated with the help of his wife, he had made himself into an effective orator of the rough-and-tumble school, served as mayor, congressman, governor, and senator, then as military governor of Tennessee before he became vice-president. In the process he had become an advocate of the small farmers against the privileges of the large planters. He also shared the racial attitudes of most white yeomen. "Damn the negroes," he exclaimed to a friend during the war, "I am fighting those traitorous aristocrats, their masters." Scrupulously honest but often tactless, Johnson was an unyielding character. After visiting the White House, the English writer Charles Dickens noted that the stern Johnson displayed great commitment but no "genial sunlight."

Some of the Radicals at first thought Johnson, unlike Lincoln, to be one of them—an illusion created by Johnson's gift for strong language. He had, for example, once asserted that treason "must be made infamous and traitors must be impoverished." Ben Wade was carried away with admiration. "Johnson, we have faith in you," he promised. "By the gods, there will be no trouble now in running this government." But Wade would soon find him as untrustworthy as Lincoln, if for different reasons. Johnson's very loyalty to the Union sprang from a strict adherence to the Constitution. Given to dogmatic abstractions which were alien to Lincoln's temperament, he nevertheless arrived by a different route at similar objectives. The states should be brought back into their proper relation to the Union not by ignoring as a pernicious abstraction the theoretical question of their status, but because the states and the Union were indestructible. And like many other whites, he found it hard to accept the growing Radical movement toward suffrage for blacks. By May 1865 he was saying "there is no such thing as reconstruction. Those States

Andrew Johnson.

have not gone out of the Union. Therefore reconstruction is unnecessary."

Johnson's plan to restore the Union thus closely resembled Lincoln's. A new Proclamation of Amnesty (May 1865) added to those Lincoln excluded from pardon everybody with taxable property worth more than $20,000. These wealthy planters, bankers, and merchants were the people Johnson believed had led the South into secession. But special applications for pardon might be made by those in the excluded groups, and before the year was out Johnson had issued some 13,000 such pardons. In every case Johnson ruled that pardon, whether by general amnesty or special clemency, restored one's property rights in land. He defined as "confiscated" only lands already sold under court decree. This applied to lands set aside by order of General Sherman, who had allocated for the exclusive use of freed Negroes a coastal strip thirty miles wide from Charleston south to the St. John's River in Florida.

Johnson's rulings nipped in the bud an experiment in land distribution that had barely begun. More than seventy years later one freedman, born a slave in Orange County, North Carolina, spoke bluntly of his dashed hopes: "Lincoln got the praise for freeing us, but did he do it? He give us freedom without giving us any chance to live to ourselves and we still had to depend on the southern white man for work, food and clothing, and he held us through our necessity and want in a state of servitude but little better than slavery." A South Carolina Land Commission, established by the Radical state government in 1869, distributed lands to more than 5,000 black families. One black community in the up-country, Promised Land, still retains its identity more than a century later, an obscure reminder of what might have been.

On the same day that Johnson announced his amnesty program, he issued another proclamation which applied to his native state of North Carolina, and within six more weeks came further edicts for the other rebel states not already organized by Lincoln. In each a native Unionist became provisional governor with authority to call a convention elected by loyal voters. Lincoln's 10 percent requirement was omitted. Johnson called upon the conventions to invalidate the secession ordinances, abolish slavery, and repudiate all debts incurred to aid the Confederacy. Each state, moreover, was to ratify the Thirteenth Amendment. Lincoln had privately advised the governor of Louisiana to consider a grant of suffrage to some blacks, "the very intelligent and those who have fought gallantly in our ranks." In his final public address he endorsed a limited black suffrage. Johnson repeated Lincoln's advice. He reminded the provisional governor of Mississippi, for example, that the state conventions might "with perfect safety" extend suffrage to blacks with education or with military service so as to "disarm the adversary"—the adversary being "radicals who are wild upon Negro franchise."

The state conventions for the most part met Johnson's requirements, although South Carolina and Mississippi did not repudiate their debt and the new Mississippi legislature refused to ratify the Thirteenth Amendment. Presidential agents sent south reported back for the most part "that the mass of thinking men of the south accept the present situation of affairs in good faith." But Carl Schurz of Missouri found "an *utter absence of national feeling* . . . and a desire to preserve slavery . . . as much and as long as possible." The discrepancy between the two reports is perhaps only apparent: southern whites accepted the situation because they thought so little had changed after all. Emboldened by Johnson's indulgence they ignored his counsels of expediency. Suggestions of Negro suffrage were scarcely raised in the conventions, and promptly squelched when they were.

SOUTHERN INTRANSIGENCE   When Congress met in December 1865, for the first time since the end of the war, it had only to accept the accomplished fact that state governments were functioning in the South. But there was the rub. The new governments were remarkably like the old. Southern voters had acted with extreme disregard of northern feelings. Among the new members presenting themselves were Georgia's Alexander H. Stephens, ex–vice-president of the Confederacy, now claiming a seat in the Senate, four Confederate generals, eight colonels, six cabinet members, and a host of lesser rebels. That many of them had counseled delay in secession, like Stephens, or actually opposed it until it happened, made little difference given the temper of the times. The Congress forthwith excluded from the roll call and denied seats to all members from the eleven former Confederate states. It was too much to expect, after four bloody years, that Unionists would welcome ex-Confederates like prodigal sons.

Furthermore, the new southern legislatures, in passing repressive black codes, regulating the freedom of blacks, demonstrated that they intended to preserve slavery as nearly as possible. The codes extended to blacks certain rights they had not hitherto enjoyed, but universally set them aside as a separate caste subject to special restraints. Details varied from state to state, but some provisions were common. Existing marriages, including common-law marriages, were recognized, and testimony of Negroes was accepted in legal cases involving Negroes—and in six states, in all cases. Blacks

Slavery Is Dead (?) *Thomas Nast's cartoon suggests that, in 1866, slavery was only legally dead.*

could hold property. They could sue and be sued in the courts. On the other hand Negroes could not own farm lands in Mississippi or city lots in South Carolina. In some states they could not carry firearms without a license to do so.

The codes' labor provisions confirmed suspicions that whites were seeking to preserve the slave labor system. Blacks were required to enter into annual labor contracts, with provision for punishment in case of violation. Dependent children were subject to compulsory apprenticeship and corporal punishment by masters. Vagrants were punished with severe fines and could be sold into private service if unable to pay. To many people it indeed seemed that slavery was on the way back in another guise. The new Mississippi penal code virtually said so: "All penal and criminal laws now in force describing the mode of punishment of crimes and misdemeanors committed by slaves, free negroes, or mulattoes are hereby reenacted, and decreed to be in full force against all freedmen, free negroes and mulattoes."

Faced with such evidence of southern intransigence, moderate Republicans drifted more and more toward Radical views. Having excluded southern members, the new Congress set up a Joint Committee on Reconstruction, with nine members from the House and six from the Senate, to gather evidence and submit proposals. Headed by the moderate Senator William Pitt Fessenden, the committee fell under greater Radical influence as a parade of witnesses testified to the rebels' impenitence. Initiative on the committee fell to determined Radicals who knew what they wanted: Ben Wade of Ohio, George W. Julian of Indiana—and most conspicuously of all, Thaddeus Stevens of Pennsylvania and Charles Sumner of Massachusetts.

THE RADICALS Their motivations were mixed, and perhaps little purpose is served in attempting to sort them out. Purity of motive is rare in an imperfect world. Most Radicals had been connected with the antislavery cause. While one could be hostile to both slavery and blacks, many whites approached the question of Negro rights with a humanitarian impulse. Few could escape the bitterness bred by the long and bloody war, however, or remain unaware of the partisan advantage that would come to the Republican party from Negro suffrage. But the party of Union and freedom, after all, could best guarantee the fruits of victory, they reasoned, and Negro suffrage could best guarantee Negro rights.

The growing conflict of opinion over reconstruction policy brought about an inversion in constitutional reasoning. Secessionists—and Johnson—were now arguing that their states had in fact remained in the Union, and some Radicals were contriving arguments that they had left the Union after all. Stevens argued that the Confederate states were now conquered provinces, subject to the absolute will of the victors. Sumner maintained that the southern states, by their pretended acts of secession, had in effect committed suicide and

Two leading Radicals: Senator Charles Sumner (left) *and Representative Thaddeus Stevens.*

reverted to the status of unorganized territories subject to the will of Congress. But few ever took such ideas seriously. Republicans converged instead on the "forfeited-rights theory," later embodied in the report of the Joint Committee on Reconstruction. This held that the states as entities continued to exist, but by the acts of secession and war had forfeited "all civil and political rights under the constitution." And Congress was the proper authority to determine conditions under which such rights might be restored.

JOHNSON'S BATTLE WITH CONGRESS A long year of political battling remained, however, before this idea triumphed. By the end of 1865, Radical views had gained a majority in Congress, if one not yet large enough to override presidential vetoes. But the critical year 1866 saw the gradual waning of Johnson's power and influence; much of this was self-induced. Johnson first challenged Congress in February 1866, when he vetoed a bill to extend the life of the Freedmen's Bureau. The measure, he said, assumed that wartime conditions still existed, whereas the country had returned "to a state of peace and industry." No longer valid as a war measure, the bill violated the Constitution in several ways. It made the federal government responsible for the care of indigents. It was passed by a Congress in which eleven states were denied seats. And it used vague language in defining the "civil rights and immunities" of Negroes. The Congress soon moved to correct that particular defect, but for the time being Johnson's prestige remained sufficiently intact that the Senate upheld his veto.

Three days after the veto, however, Johnson undermined his already weakening prestige with a gross assault on Radical leaders during an impromptu speech. The Joint Committee on Reconstruction, he charged, was "an irresponsible central directory" which had repudiated the principle of an indestructible Union and accepted the legality of secession by entertaining conquered-province and state-suicide theories. From that point forward moderate Republicans backed away from a president who had opened himself to counterattack. He was "an alien enemy of a foreign state," Stevens declared. Sumner called him "an insolent drunken brute"—and Johnson was open to the charge because of an incident at his vice-presidential inauguration. Weakened by illness at the time, he had taken a belt of brandy to get him through the ceremony and, under the influence of fever and alcohol, had become incoherent.

In mid-March 1866 Congress passed the Civil Rights Act. A response to the black codes, this bill declared that "all persons born in the United States and not subject to any foreign power, excluding Indians not taxed," were citizens entitled to "full and equal benefit of all laws." The grant of citizenship to native-born blacks, Johnson fumed, went beyond anything formerly held to be within the scope of federal power. It would, moreover, "foment discord among the races." This time, on April 9, 1866, Congress overrode the presidential veto. On July 16 it enacted a revised Bureau Bill, again overriding a veto. From that point on Johnson steadily lost both public and political support.

THE FOURTEENTH AMENDMENT   To remove all doubt about the constitutionality of the new Civil Rights Act, which was justified as implementing freedom under the Thirteenth Amendment, the Joint Committee recommended a new amendment which passed Congress on June 16, 1866, and was ratified by July 28, 1868. The Fourteenth Amendment, however, went far beyond the Civil Rights Act. It merits close scrutiny because of its broad impact on subsequent laws and litigation.

The first section asserted four principles: it reaffirmed state and federal citizenship for persons born or naturalized in the United States, and it forbade any *state* (the word "state" was important in later litigation) to abridge the "privileges and immunities" of citizens, to deprive any *person* (again an important term) of life, liberty, or property without "due process of law," or to deny any person "the equal protection of the laws." The last three of these clauses have been the subject of long and involved lawsuits resulting in applica-

Extract Const. Amend. *Referring to the recently ratified Fourteenth Amendment, Uncle Sam advises the president in this cartoon, "Now, ANDY, take it right down. More you Look at it, worse you'll Like it."*

tions not widely, if at all, foreseen at the time. The "due-process clause" has come to mean that state as well as federal power is subject to the Bill of Rights, and it has been used to protect corporations, as legal "persons," from "unreasonable" regulation by the states. Other provisions of the amendment had less far-reaching effect. One section specified that the debt of the United States "shall not be questioned," but declared "illegal and void" all debts contracted in aid of the rebellion. Another section specified the power of Congress to pass laws enforcing the amendment.

Johnson's home state was among the first to ratify. In Tennessee, which had harbored probably more Unionists than any other Confederate state, the government had fallen under Radical control. The state's governor, in reporting the results to the secretary of the Senate, added: "Give my respects to the dead dog of the White House." His words afford a fair sample of the growing acrimony on both sides of the reconstruction debates. In May and July bloody race riots in Memphis and New Orleans added fuel to the flames. Both incidents amounted to indiscriminate massacres of blacks by local police and white mobs. The carnage, Radicals argued, was the natural fruit of Johnson's policy. "Witness Memphis, witness New Orleans," Sumner cried. "Who can doubt that the President is the author of these tragedies?"

RECONSTRUCTING THE SOUTH

THE TRIUMPH OF CONGRESSIONAL RECONSTRUCTION   As 1866 drew to an end, the congressional elections promised to be a referendum on the growing split between Johnson and the Radicals. In August Johnson's friends staged a National Union Convention in Philadelphia. Men from Massachusetts and South Carolina marched down the aisle arm in arm to symbolize national reconciliation. The Radicals countered with a convention of their own and organized a congressional campaign committee to coordinate their propaganda.

Johnson responded with a speaking tour of the Midwest, a "swing around the circle," which turned into an undignified shouting contest between Johnson and his critics. Subjected to attacks on his integrity, Johnson responded in kind. In Cleveland he described the Radicals as "factious, domineering, tyrannical" men, and he foolishly exchanged hot-tempered insults with a heckler. At another stop, while Johnson was speaking from an observation car, the engineer mistakenly pulled the train out of the station, making the president appear quite the fool. Johnson may have been, as Secretary Seward claimed, the best stump speaker in the country. The trouble was, as another cabinet officer responded, the presi-

*This cartoon appeared at the time of the 1866
congressional elections. It shows "King Andy I"
approving the execution of Radical leaders in Congress.*

dent ought not to be a stump speaker. It tended to confirm his
image as a "ludicrous boor" and "drunken imbecile," which Radical papers projected. When the returns of the congressional elections came in, the Republicans had well over a two-thirds majority
in each house, a comfortable margin with which to override any
presidential vetoes.

The Congress in fact enacted a new program even before new
members took office. Two acts passed in January 1867 extended the
suffrage to African-Americans in the District of Columbia and the
territories. Another law provided that the new Congress would convene on March 4 instead of the following December, depriving
Johnson of a breathing spell. On March 2, 1867, two days before the
old Congress expired, it passed three basic laws of congressional
reconstruction over Johnson's vetoes: the Military Reconstruction
Act, the Command of the Army Act (an amendment to an army
appropriation), and the Tenure of Office Act.

The first of the three acts prescribed new conditions under which
the formation of southern state governments should begin all over

again. The other two sought to block obstruction by the president. The Command of the Army Act required that all orders from the commander-in-chief go through the headquarters of the general of the army, then Ulysses S. Grant, who could not be reassigned outside Washington without the consent of the Senate. The Radicals had faith in Grant, who was already leaning their way. The Tenure of Office Act required the consent of the Senate for the president to remove any officeholder whose appointment the Senate had to confirm in the first place. The purpose of at least some congressmen was to retain Secretary of War Edwin M. Stanton, the one Radical sympathizer in Johnson's cabinet, but an ambiguity crept into the wording of the act. Cabinet officers, it said, should serve during the term of the president who appointed them—and Lincoln had appointed Stanton, although, to be sure, Johnson was serving out Lincoln's term.

The Military Reconstruction Act, often hailed or denounced as the triumphant victory of "Radical" Reconstruction, actually represented a compromise that fell short of a thoroughgoing radicalism. As first reported from the Reconstruction Committee by Thaddeus Stevens, it would have given military commanders in the South ultimate control over law enforcement and would have left open indefinitely the terms of future restoration. More moderate elements, however, pushed through the "Blaine Amendment," which scrapped the prolonged national control under which Radicals hoped to put through the far more revolutionary program of reducing the rebel states to territories, plus programs of land confiscation and education. With the Blaine Amendment in place the Reconstruction program boiled down to little more than a requirement that southern states accept black suffrage and ratify the Fourteenth Amendment. Years later Albion W. Tourgée, after a career as a "carpetbagger" in North Carolina, wrote: "Republicans gave the ballot to men without homes, money, education, or security, and then told them to use it to protect themselves. . . . It was cheap patriotism, cheap philanthropy, cheap success!"

The act began with a pronouncement that "no legal state governments or adequate protection for life and property now exists in the rebel States. . . ." One state, Tennessee, which had ratified the Fourteenth Amendment, was exempted from the application of the act. The other ten were divided into five military districts, and the commanding officer of each was authorized to keep order and protect the "rights of persons and property." To that end he might use military tribunals in place of civil courts when he judged it necessary. The Johnson governments remained intact for the time being, but new constitutions were to be framed "in conformity with the Constitution of the United States," in conventions elected by male citizens twenty-one and older "of whatever race, color, or previous condition." Each state constitution had to provide the same universal male suffrage. Then, once the constitution was ratified by a majority of voters and accepted by Congress, and once the state legislature had ratified the Fourteenth Amendment, and once the amendment became part of the Constitution, any given state would be entitled to representation in Congress once again. Persons excluded from officeholding by the proposed amendment were also excluded from participation in the process.

Johnson reluctantly appointed military commanders under the act, but the situation remained uncertain for a time. Some people expected the Supreme Court to strike down the act, and for the time being no machinery existed for the new elections. Congress quickly remedied that on March 23, 1867, with the Second Reconstruction Act, which directed the commanders to register for voting all adult males who swore they were qualified. A Third Reconstruction Act, passed on July 19, directed registrars to go beyond the loyalty oath and determine each person's eligibility to take it, and also authorized district commanders to remove and replace officeholders of any existing "so-called state" or division thereof. Before the end of 1867 new elections had been held in all the states but Texas.

Having clipped the president's wings, the Republican Congress moved a year later to safeguard its program from possible interference by the Supreme Court, which in a series of decisions had shown a readiness to question certain actions related to Reconstruction. With the Court considering *Ex parte McCardle,* the case of a Vicksburg editor arrested for criticizing the administration of the Fourth Military District who now sought release under the Habeas Corpus Act of 1867, Congress acted. On March 27, 1868, it simply removed the power of the Supreme Court to review cases arising under the law, which Congress clearly had the right to do under its power to define the Court's appellate jurisdiction. The Court accepted this curtailment on the same day it affirmed the principle of an "indestructible union" in *Texas v. White* (1868). In that case it also asserted the right of Congress to reframe state governments.

THE IMPEACHMENT AND TRIAL OF JOHNSON   Congress's move to restrain the Supreme Court preceded by just a few days the opening arguments in the trial of the president in the Senate on an impeachment brought in by the House. Johnson, though hostile to the congressional program, had gone through the motions required of him. He continued, however, to pardon former Confederates in wholesale lots and replaced several district commanders whose Radical sympathies offended him. He and his cabinet members, moreover, largely ignored the Test Oath Act of 1862 by naming former Confederates to post offices and other federal positions. Nevertheless a lengthy investigation by the House Judiciary Committee, extending through most of the year 1867, had failed to convince the House that grounds for impeachment existed.

Johnson himself provided the occasion for impeachment when he deliberately violated the Tenure of Office Act in order to test its constitutionality in the courts. Secretary of War Edwin M. Stanton had become a thorn in the president's side, refusing to resign despite his disagreements with the president's reconstruction policy. On August 12, 1867, during a congressional recess, Johnson suspended Stanton and named General Grant in his place. Grant's political stance was ambiguous at the time, but his acceptance implied cooperation with Johnson. When the Senate refused to confirm Johnson's action, however, Grant returned the office to Stanton. The president thereupon named General Lorenzo Thomas as secretary of war after a futile effort to interest General William T. Sherman. Three days later, on February 24, 1868, the House voted impeachment, to be followed by specific charges. In due course a special committee of seven brought in its report.

Of the eleven articles of impeachment, eight focused on the charge that he had unlawfully removed Stanton and had failed to give the Senate the name of a successor. Article 9 accused the president of issuing orders in violation of the Command of the Army Act. The last two in effect charged him with criticizing Congress by "inflammatory and scandalous harangues" and by claiming that the Congress was not legally valid without southern representatives. But Article 11 accused Johnson of "unlawfully devising and contriving" to violate the Reconstruction Acts, contrary to his obligation to execute the laws. At the least, Johnson had tried to obstruct Congress's will while observing the letter of the law.

The Senate trial opened on March 5 and continued until May 26, with Chief Justice Salmon P. Chase presiding. Seven managers from the House, including Thaddeus Stevens and Benjamin F. Butler, directed the prosecution. The president was spared the humiliation of a personal appearance. His defense counsel shrewdly insisted on narrowing the trial to questions that would be indictable offenses under the law, and steered the questions away from Johnson's manifest wish to frustrate the will of Congress. Such questions, they contended, were purely political in nature. In the end enough Republican senators joined their pro-Johnson colleagues to prevent conviction. On May 16 the crucial vote came on Article 9: 35 votes guilty and 19 not guilty, one vote short of the two-thirds needed to

House of Representatives managers of the impeachment proceedings and trial of Andrew Johnson. Among them were Benjamin Butler (R-Mass., seated left) and Thaddeus Stevens (R-Pa., seated with cane).

convict. The trial then adjourned for a week. Reconvening on May 26, the Senate voted on Articles 2 and 3 by the same division, 35 to 19. Thereupon the Senate dissolved the tribunal.

In a parliamentary system Johnson probably would have been removed as leader of the government long before then. But by deciding the case on the narrowest grounds, the Senate made it unlikely that any future president could ever be removed except for the gravest offenses, and almost surely not for flouting the will of Congress in his execution of the laws. Impeachment of Johnson was in the end a great political mistake, for the failure to remove the president was damaging to Radical morale and support. Nevertheless the Radical cause did gain something. To blunt the opposition, Johnson agreed not to obstruct the process of Reconstruction, named a secretary of war who was committed to enforcing the new laws, and sent to Congress the new Radical constitutions of Arkansas and South Carolina. Thereafter his obstruction ceased and Radical Reconstruction began in earnest.

REPUBLICAN RULE IN THE SOUTH   In June 1868 Congress agreed that seven states had met the conditions for readmission, all but Virginia, Mississippi, and Texas. Congress rescinded Georgia's admission, however, when the state legislature expelled twenty-eight black members on the pretext that the state constitution had failed to specify their eligibility, and seated some former Confederate leaders. The military commander of Georgia then forced the legislature to reseat the Negro members and remove the Confederates, and the state was compelled to ratify the Fifteenth Amendment before being admitted in July 1870. Mississippi, Texas, and Virginia had returned earlier in 1870, under the added requirement that they too ratify the Fifteenth Amendment. This amendment, submitted to the states in 1869, ratified in 1870, forbade the states to deny any person the vote on grounds of race, color, or previous condition of servitude.

Long before the new governments were established, Republican groups began to spring up in the South, chiefly sponsored by the Union League, founded at Philadelphia in 1862 to promote support for the Union. Emissaries of the league enrolled African-Americans and loyal whites, initiated them into the secrets and rituals of the order, and instructed them "in their rights and duties." The league emphasized the display of such symbols as the Bible, the flag, the Constitution, and the Declaration of Independence. Agents of the Freedmen's Bureau, northern missionaries, teachers, and soldiers aided the cause and spread its influence. When the time came for political action, they were ready. In October 1867, for instance, on the eve of South Carolina's choice of convention delegates, the league reported eighty-eight chapters, which claimed to have enrolled almost every adult black male in the state.

BLACKS IN SOUTHERN POLITICS   The new role of African-Americans in politics caused the most controversy, then and afterward. If largely illiterate and inexperienced in the rudiments of politics, they were little different from millions of whites enfranchised in the age of Jackson or immigrants herded to the polls by political bosses in New York and other cities after the war. Some freedmen frankly confessed their disadvantages. Beverly Nash, a black delegate in the South Carolina convention of 1868, told his colleagues: "I believe, my friends and fellow-citizens, we are not prepared for this suffrage. But we can learn. Give a man tools and let him commence to use them, and in time he will learn a trade. So it is with voting."

Several hundred black delegates participated in the statewide political conventions. Most had been selected by local political meetings or by churches, fraternal societies, Union Leagues, and black army units, although a few simply appointed themselves. "Some bring credentials," explained a North Carolina black leader, "others had as much as they could to bring themselves, having to escape from their homes stealthily at night" to avoid white assaults. The African-American delegates "ranged all colors and apparently all conditions," but free mulattoes from the cities played the most prominent roles. At Louisiana's Republican state convention, for instance, nineteen of the twenty black delegates had been born free.

By 1867, however, former slaves began to gain political influence, and this led to debates that revealed emerging tensions within the black community. Some southern blacks resented the presence of northern brethren while others complained that few ex-slaves were represented in leadership positions. Northern blacks and the southern free black elite, most of whom were urban dwellers, tended to oppose efforts to confiscate and redistribute land to the rural freedmen, and many insisted that political equality did not mean social equality. As an Alabama black leader stressed, "We do not ask that the ignorant and degraded shall be put on a social equality with the refined and intelligent." In general, however, unity rather than dissension prevailed, and blacks focused on common concerns such as full equality under the law.

Brought suddenly into politics in times that tried the most skilled of statesmen, many African-Americans nevertheless served with distinction. Yet the derisive label "black Reconstruction" used by later critics exaggerates black political influence, which was limited mainly to voting, and overlooks the large numbers of white Republicans, especially in the mountain areas of the upper South. Only one of the new conventions, South Carolina's, had a black majority, 76 to 41. Louisiana's was evenly divided racially, and in only two other conventions were more than 20 percent of the members black: Florida's, with 40 percent, and Virginia's, with 24 percent. The Texas convention was only 10 percent black, and North Carolina's, 11 percent—but that did not stop a white newspaper from calling it a body consisting of "baboons, monkeys, mules . . . and other jackasses."

In the new state governments, any African-American participation was a novelty. Although some 600 blacks—most of them former slaves—served as state legislators, no black man was ever elected governor and few served as judges, although in Louisiana Pinckney B. S. Pinchback, a northern black and former Union soldier, won the office of lieutenant-governor and served as acting governor when the white governor was indicted for corruption. Several blacks were elected lieutenant-governors, state treasurers, or secretaries of state. There were two black senators in Congress, Hiram Revels and Blanche K. Bruce, both Mississippi natives who had been educated in the North, and fourteen black members of the House during

A lithograph depicting five of the major black political figures of the Reconstruction period: Revels (top left) and Bruce (center) served in the U.S. Senate, Rainey (bottom left), Lynch (bottom right), and Rapier (top right) in the House of Representatives.

Reconstruction. Among these were some of the ablest congressmen of the time. African-Americans served in every state legislature, and in South Carolina they made up a majority in both houses for two years.

CARPETBAGGERS AND SCALAWAGS   The top positions in southern state governments went for the most part to white Republicans, whom the opposition whites soon labeled "carpetbaggers" and "scalawags," depending on their place of birth. The opportunists who allegedly rushed south with all their belongings in carpetbags to grab the political spoils were more often than not Union veterans who had arrived as early as 1865 or 1866, drawn south by the hope of economic opportunity and by other attractions that many of them had seen in Union service. Many were teachers, social workers, or preachers animated by a missionary impulse. Albion W. Tourgée, for instance, a badly wounded Union veteran, moved to North Carolina in 1865, seeking a milder climate for reasons of health. He invested

$5,000 in a nursery, and promptly lost it. He would have needed a fine crystal ball indeed to see two years in advance the chance for political office under the Radical program. As it turned out, he served in the state constitutional convention of 1868 and later as a state judge.

The "scalawags," or native white Republicans, were even more reviled and misrepresented. A jaundiced editor of a Nashville paper called them the "merest trash that could be collected in a civilized community, of no personal credit or social responsibility." Most "scalawags" had opposed secession, forming a Unionist majority in many mountain counties as far south as Georgia and Alabama, and especially in the hills of eastern Tennessee. Among the "scalawags" were several distinguished figures, including former Confederate general James A. Longstreet, who decided after Appomattox that the Old South must change its ways. He became a successful cotton broker in New Orleans, joined the Republican party, and supported the Radical Reconstruction program. Other "scalawags" were former Whigs who found the Republican party's economic program of industrial and commercial expansion in keeping with Henry Clay's earlier "American System." Unionists, whether Whig or Democratic before the war, and even some secessionists, agreed with Georgia's Confederate governor and later Democratic senator: "The statesman like the businessman should take a practical view of questions as they arise." For the time a practical view dictated joining the Republicans. Mississippi's James L. Alcorn, wealthy planter and former Whig, was among the prominent whites who joined the Republicans in the hope of moderating Radical policies. Such men were ready to concede black suffrage in the hope of influencing African-American voters. Alcorn became the first Republican governor of Mississippi.

THE REPUBLICAN RECORD The new state constitutions were objectionable to adherents of the old order more because of their origins than because of their contents, excepting their provisions for black suffrage and civil rights. Otherwise the documents were in keeping with other state constitutions of the day, their provisions often drawn from the basic laws of northern states. Most remained in effect for some years after the end of Radical control, and later constitutions incorporated many of their features. Conspicuous among Radical innovations were such steps toward greater democracy as requiring universal manhood suffrage, reapportioning legislatures more nearly according to population, and making more state offices elective.

Given the hostile circumstances under which the Radical governments operated, their achievements are remarkable. For the first time in most of the South they established state school systems, however inadequate and ill-supported at first. The testimony is almost universal that African-Americans eagerly sought education for themselves and their children. Some 600,000 black pupils were in southern schools by 1877. State governments under the Radicals also gave more attention than ever before to poor relief and to public institutions for the disadvantaged and handicapped: orphanages, asylums, and institutions for the deaf, dumb, and blind of both races. Public roads, bridges, and buildings were repaired or rebuilt. Blacks achieved new rights and opportunities that would never again be taken away, at least in principle: equality before the law, and the right to own property, carry on business, enter professions, attend schools, and learn to read and write.

Yet several of these Republican regimes also practiced unparalleled corruption. Public money and public credit were often voted to privately owned corporations, especially railroads, under conditions which invited influence peddling. But governmental subsidies—especially for transportation—were common before and after Reconstruction (and still are), and the extension of public aid had general support among all elements, including the Radicals and their enemies. Contracts were let at absurd prices and public officials took their cut. Taxes and public debt rose in every state. Yet the figures of taxation and debt hardly constitute an unqualified indictment of Radical governments, since they then faced unusual and inflated costs for the physical reconstruction of public works in the South. Most states, moreover, had to float loans at outrageous discounts, sometimes at 50–75 percent of face value, because of uncertain conditions.

Nor, for that matter, were the breaches of public morality limited to the South or to Republicans. The Democratic Tweed Ring at the time was robbing New York City of more than $75 million, while the Republican "Gas Ring" in Philadelphia was lining its pockets. In national politics a number of scandals plagued the Grant administration (1869–1877). Corruption was neither invented by the Radical regimes, nor did it die with them. Louisiana's "carpetbag" governor recognized as much: "Why," he said, "down here everybody is demoralized. Corruption is the fashion." In three years Louisiana's printing bill ran to $1.5 million, about half of which went to a newspaper belonging to the young governor, who left office with a tidy nest egg and settled down to a long life as a planter. But a later Democratic state treasurer decamped for Tegucigalpa in 1890 with the accounts over $1 million short, far outstripping the governor's record or anybody else's. About the same time Mississippi's Democratic state treasurer was found to have embezzled over $315,000.

During Republican rule in Mississippi, on the other hand, there was no evidence of major corruption.

WHITE TERROR   The case of Mississippi strongly suggests that whites were hostile to Republican regimes less because of their corruption than their inclusion of blacks. Most white southerners remained unreconstructed, so conditioned by slavery that they were unable to conceive of blacks as citizens or even free agents. In some places hostility to the new regimes took on the form of white terror.

The prototype of terrorist groups was the Ku Klux Klan, first organized in 1866 by some young men of Pulaski, Tennessee, as a social club with the costumes, secret ritual, and mumbo-jumbo common to fraternal groups. At first a group of Merry Andrews devoted to practical jokes, the founders eventually realized, as two of them wrote in a later account, that they "had evoked a spirit from 'the vasty deep' [which] would not down at their bidding." Pranks turned into intimidation of blacks and white Republicans, and the KKK and imitators like Louisiana's Knights of the White Camellia spread rapidly across the South in answer to the Union League. Klansman rode about the countryside hiding under masks and robes, spreading horrendous rumors, issuing threats, harassing African-

This Thomas Nast cartoon chides the Ku Klux Klan and the White League for promoting conditions "worse than slavery" for southern blacks after the Civil War.

Americans, and occasionally running amok in violence and destruction. "Typically the Klan was a reactionary and racist crusade against equal rights which sought to overthrow the most democratic society or government the South had yet known," wrote one historian. During its brief career it "whipped, shot, hanged, robbed, raped, and otherwise outraged Negroes and Republicans across the South in the name of preserving white civilization."

Klansmen focused their terror on prominent Republicans, black and white. In Mississippi they killed a black Republican leader in front of his family. Three white "scalawag" Republicans were murdered in Georgia in 1870. That same year an armed mob of whites assaulted a Republican political rally in Alabama, killing four blacks and wounding fifty-four. In South Carolina the Klan was especially active. Virtually the entire white male population of York County joined the Klan, and they were responsible for eleven murders and hundreds of whippings. In 1871 some 500 masked men laid siege to the Union County jail and eventually lynched eight black prisoners. Although most Klansmen were poor farmers and tradesmen, middle-class whites—planters, merchants, bankers, lawyers, doctors, even ministers—also joined the group and participated in its brutalities.

Congress struck back with three Enforcement Acts (1870–1871) to protect Negro voters. The first of these measures levied penalties on persons who interfered with any citizen's right to vote. A second placed the election of congressmen under surveillance by federal election supervisors and marshals. The third (the Ku Klux Klan Act) outlawed the characteristic activities of the Klan—forming conspiracies, wearing disguises, resisting officers, and intimidating officials—and authorized the president to suspend habeas corpus where necessary to suppress "armed combinations." President Grant, in October 1871, singled out nine counties in up-country South Carolina as an example, suspended habeas corpus, and pursued mass prosecutions which brought an abrupt halt to the Klan outrages. Elsewhere the Justice Department carried out a campaign of prosecution on a smaller scale, while a congressional committee gathered testimony on Klan activity which ran to twelve volumes. The program of federal enforcement broke the back of the Klan, whose outrages declined steadily as conservative southerners resorted to more subtle methods.

CONSERVATIVE RESURGENCE   The Klan's impact on politics varied from state to state. In the upper South it played only a modest role in facilitating a Democratic resurgence. But in the Deep South, Klan violence and intimidation had some effect. In Georgia, for instance, Republicans virtually quit campaigning and voting. Throughout the

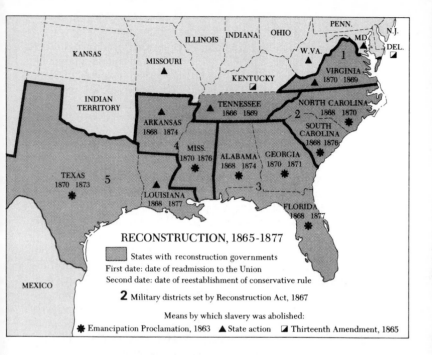

RECONSTRUCTION, 1865-1877

☐ States with reconstruction governments
First date: date of readmission to the Union
Second date: date of reestablishment of conservative rule

2 Military districts set by Reconstruction Act, 1867

Means by which slavery was abolished:
✳ Emancipation Proclamation, 1863 ▲ State action ◪ Thirteenth Amendment, 1865

South the activities of the Klan weakened black and Republican morale, and in the North they encouraged a growing weariness with the whole southern question. "The plain truth is," noted the New York *Herald,* "the North has got tired of the Negro."

Americans had other fish to fry anyway. Western expansion, Indian wars, economic growth, and political controversy over the tariff and the currency distracted attention from southern outrages. Republican control in the South gradually loosened as "Conservative" parties—Democrats used that name to mollify former Whigs—mobilized the white vote. Scalawags, and many carpetbaggers, drifted away from the Radical ranks under pressure from their white neighbors. Few of them had joined the Republicans out of concern for black rights in the first place. And where persuasion failed to work, Democrats were willing to use chicanery. As one enthusiastic Democrat boasted, "the white and black Republicans may outvote us, but we can outcount them."

Republican control collapsed in Virginia and Tennessee as early as 1869, in Georgia and North Carolina in 1870, although North Carolina had a Republican governor until 1876. Reconstruction lasted longest in the Deep South states with the heaviest Negro population, where whites abandoned Klan masks for barefaced intimidation in paramilitary groups like the Mississippi Rifle Club and the South

Carolina Red Shirts. By 1876 Radical regimes survived only in Louisiana, South Carolina, and Florida, and these all collapsed after the elections of that year. Later the last carpetbag governor of South Carolina explained that "the uneducated negro was too weak, no matter what his numbers, to cope with the whites."

THE GRANT YEARS

GRANT'S ELECTION   Ulysses S. Grant, who presided over this fiasco, brought to the presidency less political experience than any man who ever occupied the office, except perhaps Zachary Taylor, and perhaps less political judgment than any other. But in 1868 the rank-and-file voter could be expected to support "the Lion of Vicksburg" because of his record as a war leader. Both parties wooed him, but his falling-out with President Johnson pushed him toward the Republicans and built trust in him among the Radicals. They were, as Thad Stevens said, ready to "let him into the church." Impeachment proceedings were still in progress when the Republicans gathered in Chicago to name their candidate. Grant was the unanimous choice. The platform endorsed the Reconstruction policy of Congress, congratulating the country on the "assured success" of the program. One plank cautiously defended Negro suffrage as a necessity in the South, but a matter each northern state should settle for itself. Another urged payment of the national debt "in the utmost good faith to all creditors," which meant in gold. More important than the platform were the great expectations of a soldier-president and his slogan: "Let us have peace."

The Democrats took opposite positions on both Reconstruction and the debt. The Republican Congress, the platform charged, instead of restoring the Union had "so far as in its power, dissolved it, and subjected ten states, in the time of profound peace, to military despotism and Negro supremacy." As to the public debt, the party endorsed Representative George H. Pendleton's "Ohio idea" that since most bonds had been bought with depreciated greenbacks, they should be paid off in greenbacks unless they specified payment in gold. With no conspicuously available candidate in sight, the convention turned to Horatio Seymour, war governor of New York and chairman of the convention. His friends had to hustle him out of the hall to prevent his withdrawal. The Democrats made a closer race of it than showed up in the electoral vote. Eight states, including New York and New Jersey, went for Seymour. While Grant swept the electoral college by 214 to 80, his popular majority was only 307,000 out of a total of over 5.7 million votes. More than 500,000 black voters accounted for Grant's margin of victory.

EARLY APPOINTMENTS   Grant had proven himself a great leader in the war, but in the White House he seemed blind to the political forces and influence peddlers around him. He was awestruck by men of wealth and unaccountably loyal to some who betrayed his trust. The historian Henry Adams, who lived in Washington at the time, noted that to his friends "Grant appeared as intermittent energy, immensely powerful when awake, but passive and plastic in repose. . . . They could never measure his character or be sure when he would act. They could never follow a mental process in his thought. They were not sure that he did think." His conception of the presidency was "Whiggish." The chief executive carried out the laws; in the formulation of policy he passively followed the lead of Congress. This approach endeared him at first to party leaders, but it left him at last ineffective and others disillusioned with his leadership.

At the outset Grant consulted nobody on his cabinet appointments. Some of his choices indulged personal whims; others simply betrayed bad judgment. In some cases appointees learned of their nomination from the newspapers. As time went by Grant betrayed a fatal gift for losing men of talent and integrity from his cabinet. Secretary of State Hamilton Fish of New York turned out to be a happy exception; he guided foreign policy throughout the Grant presidency.

At first it looked as if Grant's free-wheeling style of choosing a cabinet signaled a sharp departure from the spoils system. But once Grant had taken care of his friends and relatives, he began to take care of party leaders. Cabinet members who balked at the procedure were soon eased out. This strengthened a nascent movement for a

President Ulysses S. Grant.

merit system in the civil service, modeled on systems recently adopted in Great Britain, Germany, and France. Grant finally approved a measure to set up a commission to look into the matter in 1872, a good gesture in a political year. The group duly brought in recommendations which in turn were duly shelved and forgotten once the election was over.

THE GOVERNMENT DEBT   Financial issues dominated the political agenda during Grant's presidency. After the war the Treasury had assumed that the $400 million worth of greenbacks issued during the conflict would be retired from circulation and that the nation would revert to a "hard-money" currency—gold coins. Many agrarian and debtor groups resisted this contraction of the money supply, believing that it would mean lower prices for their crops and would make it harder for them to pay long-term debts. They were joined by a large number of Radicals who thought a combination of high tariffs and inflation would generate more rapid economic growth. In 1868 congressional supporters of such a "soft-money" policy halted the retirement of greenbacks, leaving $356 million outstanding. There matters stood when Grant took office.

The "sound"- or hard-money advocates, mostly bankers and merchants, claimed that Grant's election was a mandate to save the country from the Democrats' "Ohio idea." Quite influential in Republican circles, they also had the benefit of a deeply ingrained popular assumption that hard money was morally preferable to paper currency. Grant agreed, and in his inaugural address he endorsed payment of the national debt in gold as a point of national honor. On March 18, 1869, the Public Credit Act endorsing that principle became the first act of Congress he signed. Under the Refunding Act of 1870 the Treasury was able to replace 6 percent Civil War bonds with a new issue promising 4–5 percent in gold.

SCANDAL AND REFORM   The complexities of the "money question" exasperated Grant, but that was the least of his worries, for his administration was soon adrift in a cesspool of scandal. The first hint of scandal touched Grant in the summer of 1869, when the crafty Jay Gould and the flamboyant Jim Fisk connived with the president's brother-in-law to corner the gold market. Gould concocted an argument that the government should refrain from selling gold on the market because the resulting rise in gold prices would raise temporarily depressed farm prices. Grant apparently smelled a rat from the start, but was seen in public with the speculators. As the rumor spread on Wall Street that the president had bought the argument, gold rose from $132 to $163 an ounce. When Grant finally persuaded his brother-in-law to pull out of the deal, Gould began quietly selling

The People's Handwriting on the Wall. *An 1872 engraving comments on the corruption engulfing Grant.*

out. Finally, on "Black Friday," September 24, 1869, Grant ordered the Treasury to sell a large quantity of gold and the bubble burst. Fisk got out by repudiating his agreements and hiring thugs to intimidate his creditors. "Nothing is lost save honor," he said.

The plot to corner the gold market was only the first of several scandals that rocked the Grant administration. During the campaign of 1872 the public first learned about the financial buccaneering of the Crédit Mobilier, a construction company which had milked the Union Pacific Railroad for exorbitant fees to line the pockets of insiders who controlled both firms. Rank-and-file Union Pacific shareholders were left holding the bag. One congressman had distributed Crédit Mobilier shares at bargain rates where, he said, "it will produce much good to us." This chicanery had transpired before Grant's election in 1868, but it touched a number of prominent Republicans. The beneficiaries had included Speaker Schuyler Colfax, later vice-president, and Representative James A. Garfield, later president. Of thirteen members of Congress involved, only two were censured by a Congress which, before it adjourned in March 1873, voted itself a pay raise from $5,000 to $7,500—retroactive, it decided, for two years. A public uproar forced repeal, leaving the raises voted the president ($25,000 to $50,000) and Supreme Court justices.

Even more odious disclosures soon followed, and some involved the president's cabinet. The secretary of war, it turned out, had accepted bribes from merchants at army posts in the West who traded with Indians. He was impeached, but resigned in time to elude trial by the Senate. Post-office contracts, it was revealed, went to carriers who offered the highest kickbacks. The secretary of the treasury had awarded a political friend a commission of 50 percent for the collection of overdue taxes. In St. Louis a "Whiskey Ring" bribed tax collectors to bilk the government of millions in revenue. Grant's private secretary was enmeshed in that scheme, taking large sums of money and other valuables in return for inside information. Before Grant's second term ended, the corruption crossed the Atlantic when the minister to London unloaded worthless stock in "Emma Mines" on gullible Britons. Only a plea of diplomatic immunity and a sudden exit spared him from British justice. There is no evidence that Grant himself was ever involved in, or that he personally profited from, any of the fraud, but his poor choice of associates earned him the public censure that was heaped upon his head.

Long before Grant's first term was out, a reaction against the Reconstruction measures, and against incompetence and corruption in the administration, had incited mutiny within the Republican ranks. Open revolt broke out first in Missouri where Carl Schurz, a German immigrant and war hero, led a group which elected a governor with Democratic help in 1870 and sent Schurz to the Senate. In 1872 the Liberal Republicans (as they called themselves) held a national convention at Cincinnati which produced a compromise platform condemning the party's southern policy and favoring civil service reform, but remained silent on the protective tariff. The meeting, moreover, was stampeded toward an anomalous presidential candidate: Horace Greeley, editor of the New York *Tribune*, a longtime champion of just about every reform of his times. His image as a visionary eccentric was complemented by his record of hostility to Democrats, whose support the Liberals needed. The Democrats nevertheless swallowed the pill and gave their nomination to Greeley as the only hope of beating Grant.

The result was a foregone conclusion. Republican regulars duly endorsed Radical Reconstruction and the protective tariff. Grant still had seven carpetbag states in his pocket, generous support from business and banking interests, and the stalwart support of the Radicals. Above all he still evoked the imperishable glory of Appomattox. Greeley, despite an exhausting tour of the country—still unusual for a presidential candidate—carried only six southern and border states and none in the North. Greeley's wife had died during the campaign, and worn out with grief and fatigue, he too was gone three weeks after the election.

PANIC AND REDEMPTION   Economic distress followed close upon the public scandal besetting the Grant administration. Contraction of the money supply brought about by the withdrawal of greenbacks and expansion of the railroads into sparsely settled areas had made investors cautious and helped precipitate a crisis. During 1873 the market for railroad bonds turned sour as some twenty-five roads defaulted on their interest payments before the end of August. The investment-banking firm of Jay Cooke and Company, unable to sell the bonds of the Northern Pacific Railroad, financed them with short-term deposits in hope that a European market would develop. But in 1873 the opposite happened when a financial panic in Vienna forced many financiers to unload American stocks and bonds. Caught short, Cooke and Company went bankrupt on September 18, 1873. The ensuing stampede forced the stock market to close for ten days. The Panic of 1873 set off a depression that lasted for six years, the longest and most severe that Americans had yet suffered, marked by widespread bankruptcies, unemployment, and a drastic slowdown in railroad building.

Hard times and scandals hurt Republicans in the midterm elections of 1874. The Democrats won control of the House of Representatives and gained in the Senate. The new Democratic House immediately launched inquiries into the scandals and unearthed further evidence of corruption in high places. The panic meanwhile focused attention once more on greenback currency.

Since greenbacks were valued less than gold, they had become the chief circulating medium. Most people spent greenbacks first and held their gold or used it to settle foreign accounts, which drained much gold out of the country. The postwar reduction of greenbacks in circulation from $432 million to $356 million had made for tight money. To relieve deflation and stimulate business, therefore, the Treasury reissued $26 million in greenbacks previously withdrawn.

For a time the advocates of paper money were riding high. But Grant vetoed in 1874 a bill to issue more greenbacks and in his annual message that December called for the gradual resumption of specie payments—that is, the redemption of greenbacks in gold. This would make greenbacks "good as gold" and raise their value to a par with the gold dollar. In January, before the Republicans gave up control of the House, Congress obliged by passing the Resumption Act of 1875. The payment in gold to people who turned in their paper money began on January 1, 1879, after the Treasury had built a gold reserve for the purpose and reduced the value of greenbacks in circulation. This act infuriated those promoting an inflationary monetary policy and provoked the formation of the National Greenback party, which elected fourteen congressmen in 1878. The much-debated "money question" was destined to remain one of the most divisive issues in American politics.

THE COMPROMISE OF 1877   Grant, despite the controversies swirling around him, was eager to run again in 1876, but the recent scandals discouraged any challenge to the two-term tradition. James G. Blaine of Maine, former Speaker of the House, emerged as the Republican front-runner, but he too bore the taint of scandal. Letters in the possession of James Mulligan of Boston linked Blaine to some dubious railroad dealings, and these "Mulligan letters" found their way into print.

The Republican convention in Cincinnati therefore eliminated Blaine and several other hopefuls in favor of Ohio's favorite son, Rutherford B. Hayes. Three times elected governor of Ohio, most recently as an advocate of hard money, Hayes had also made a name as a civil service reformer. But his chief virtue was that he offended neither Radicals nor reformers. As Henry Adams put it, he was "a third rate nonentity, whose only recommendation is that he is obnoxious to no one."

A Republican campaign piece from the 1876 election: "Yankee Doodle, that's the talk—/ We've found an honest dealer;/ And o'er the course we ride or walk,/ We'll go for Hayes and Wheeler."

The Democratic convention in St. Louis was abnormally harmonious from the start. The nomination went on the second ballot to Samuel J. Tilden, millionaire corporation lawyer and reform governor of New York who had directed a campaign to overthrow first the notorious Tweed Ring controlling New York City politics and then another ring in Albany which had bilked the state of millions.

The campaign generated no burning issues. Both candidates favored the trend toward conservative rule in the South. During one of the most corrupt elections ever, both candidates also favored civil service reform. In the absence of strong differences, Democrats waved the Republicans' dirty linen. In response, Republicans waved the bloody shirt, which is to say that they engaged in verbal assaults on former Confederates and the spirit of Rebellion, linking the Democratic party with Secession and with the outrages committed against the black and white Republicans in the South. As one Republican speaker insisted, "Every man that tried to destroy this nation was a Democrat. . . . The man that assassinated Abraham Lincoln was a Democrat. . . . Soldiers, every scar you have on your heroic bodies was given you by a Democrat!" The phrase "waving the bloody shirt" originated at the impeachment trial of President Johnson when Benjamin F. Butler, speaking for the prosecution, displayed the bloody shirt a Mississippi carpetbagger had been wearing when hauled out of bed and beaten by Ku Kluxers. Reporting such atrocities came to be known to Democrats as "grinding the outrage mills."

Early election returns pointed to a Tilden victory, but the Republican national chairman refused to concede. As it fell out, Tilden enjoyed a 300,000 edge in the popular vote and had 184 electoral votes, just one short of a majority, but Republicans claimed nineteen doubtful votes from Florida, Louisiana, and South Carolina, while Democrats laid a counterclaim to Oregon. But the Republicans had clearly carried Oregon. In the South the outcome was less certain, and given the fraud and intimidation perpetrated on both sides, nobody will ever know what might have happened if, to use a slogan of the day, "a free ballot and a fair count" had prevailed. As good a guess as any may be, as one writer suggested, that the Democrats stole the election first and the Republicans stole it back.

In all three of the disputed southern states rival canvassing boards sent in different returns. In Florida, Republicans conceded the state election, but in Louisiana and South Carolina rival state governments also appeared. The Constitution offered no guidance in this unprecedented situation. Even if Congress was empowered to sort things out, the Democratic House and the Republican Senate proved unable to reach an agreement.

Finally, on January 29, 1877, the two houses decided to set up a

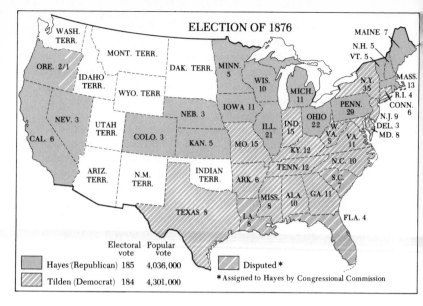

ELECTION OF 1876

	Electoral vote	Popular vote
Hayes (Republican)	185	4,036,000
Tilden (Democrat)	184	4,301,000

Disputed *

*Assigned to Hayes by Congressional Commission

special Electoral Commission which would investigate and report back its findings. It had fifteen members, five each from the House, the Senate, and the Supreme Court. Members were so chosen as to have seven from each major party with Justice David Davis of Illinois as the swing man. Davis, though appointed to the Court by Lincoln, was no party regular and was in fact thought to be leaning toward the Democrats. Republicans who voted for the commission, James A. Garfield said, were "fair-minded asses" who thought that "truth is always half way between God and the Devil." The panel appeared to be stacked in favor of Tilden.

But as it turned out, the panel got restacked the other way. Short-sighted Democrats in the Illinois legislature teamed up with minority Greenbackers to name Davis their senator. Davis accepted, no doubt with a sense of relief. From the remaining justices, all Republicans, the panel chose Joseph P. Bradley to fill the vacancy. The decision on each state went by a vote of 8 to 7, along party lines, in favor of Hayes. After much bluster and threat of filibuster by Democrats, the House voted on March 2 to accept the report and declare Hayes elected by an electoral vote of 185 to 184.

Critical to this outcome was the defection of southern Democrats who had made several informal agreements with the Republicans. On February 26, 1877, prominent Ohio Republicans and powerful southern Democrats struck a bargain at the Wormley House, a Washington hotel. The Republicans promised that, if elected, Hayes would withdraw the last federal troops from Louisiana and South Carolina, letting the Republican governments there collapse. In return the Democrats promised to withdraw their opposition to Hayes, to accept in good faith the Reconstruction amendments, and to refrain from partisan reprisals against Republicans in the South.

With this agreement in hand, southern Democrats could justify deserting Tilden because this so-called Compromise of 1877 brought a final "redemption" from the "Radicals" and a return to "home rule," which actually meant rule by white Democrats. Other, more informal promises, less noticed by the public, bolstered the Wormley House agreement. Hayes's friends pledged more support for Mississippi levees and other internal improvements, including federal subsidy for a transcontinental railroad along a southern route. Southerners extracted a further promise that Hayes would name a white southerner as postmaster-general, the cabinet position with the most patronage jobs at hand. In return, southerners would let Republicans make James A. Garfield Speaker of the new House.

THE END OF RECONSTRUCTION   After Hayes took office, most of these promises were either renounced or forgotten. They had served their purpose of breaking the crisis. In April 1877 Hayes withdrew federal troops from the state houses in Louisiana and South Carolina, and the Republican governments there collapsed—along with much of Hayes's claim to legitimacy. Hayes chose a Tennessean and former Confederate as postmaster-general. But after southern Democrats failed to permit the choice of Garfield as Speaker, Hayes expressed doubt about any further subsidy for railroad building, and none was voted.

As to southern promises regarding the civil rights of blacks, only a few Democratic leaders, such as the new governors of South Carolina and Louisiana, remembered them for long. Over the next three decades those rights crumbled under the pressure of white rule in the South and the force of Supreme Court decisions narrowing the application of the Reconstruction amendments. The Compromise of 1877, viewed in the light of its consequences, might justly bear the label that one historian gave it: "The betrayal of the Negro." But "betrayal" implies that a promise was made in the first place, and Reconstruction never offered more than an uncertain commitment to equality before the law. Yet it left an enduring legacy, the Thirteenth, Fourteenth, and Fifteenth Amendments—not dead but dormant, waiting to be warmed back into life.

FURTHER READING

Reconstruction has long been "a dark and bloody ground" of conflicting interpretations. The most recent reinterpretation is Eric Foner's *Reconstruction: America's Unfinished Revolution, 1863–1877* (1988). Other recent surveys are Michael Perman's *Emancipation and Reconstruction, 1862–1879* (1987) and James M. McPherson's *Ordeal by Fire: The Civil War and Reconstruction* (1982). John Hope Franklin's *Reconstruction after the Civil War* (1961) and Kenneth M. Stampp's *The Era of Reconstruction, 1865–1877* (1965) are also valuable.

More specialized works give closer scrutiny to the aims of the principal political figures. Peyton McCrary's *Abraham Lincoln and Reconstruction* (1978) deals with the Lincoln policies as they were carried out in Louisiana. For a study of Andrew Johnson, see Hans L. Trefousse's *Andrew Johnson: A Biography* (1989). Eric L. McKitrick's *Andrew Johnson and Reconstruction* (1960), LaWanda Cox and John H. Cox's *Politics, Principle, and Prejudice, 1865–1866* (1963), and William R. Brock's *An American Crisis* (1963) criticize Johnson's policies. Why Johnson was impeached is detailed in Michael Les Benedict's *The Impeachment and Trial of Andrew Johnson* (1973)° and Hans L. Trefousse's *Impeachment of a President* (1975).

Recent scholars have been fairly sympathetic to the aims and motives of the Radical Republicans. See, for instance, Herman Belz's *Reconstructing the Union* (1969). The ideology of these Radicals is explored in Michael Les Benedict's *A Compromise of Principle: Congressional Republicans and Reconstruction* (1974).

The intransigence of southern white attitudes is examined in Michael Perman's *Reunion without Compromise* (1973).° Allen W. Trelease's *White Terror* (1971)° covers the various organizations that practiced vigilante tactics, chiefly the Ku Klux Klan. The difficulties former planters had in adjusting to the new labor system are documented in James L. Roark's *Masters without Slaves* (1977).° Recent books on southern politics during Reconstruction include Michael Perman's *The Road to Redemption* (1984), Terry L. Seip's *The South Returns to Congress* (1983), Mark W. Summers's *Railroads, Reconstruction, and the Gospel of Prosperity* (1984), Dan T. Carter's *When the War Was Over* (1985), and George C. Rable's *But There Was No Peace* (1984).

Numerous works have appeared on the freedmen's experience in the South. Start with Leon F. Litwack's *Been in the Storm So Long* (1979),° which wonderfully covers the transition from slavery to freedom. Willie Lee Rose's *Rehearsal for Reconstruction* (1964) examines Union efforts to define the social role of former slaves during wartime emancipation. Joel Williamson's *After Slavery* (1965)° argues that South Carolina freedmen took an active role in pursuing their political and economic rights. Peter Kolchin's *First Freedom* (1972), a study of Alabama freedmen, is also useful. The role of the Freedman's Bureau is explored in William S. McFeely's *Yankee Stepfather: General O. O. Howard and the Freedmen* (1968).°

The land confiscation issue is discussed in Eric Foner's *Politics and Ideology in the Age of the Civil War* (1980)°; Beth Bethel's *Promiseland* (1981), on a South Carolina black community; and Janet S. Hermann's *The Pursuit of a Dream* (1981),° on the Davis Bend experiment.

The politics of corruption outside the South is depicted in Allan Nevin's

°These books are available in paperback editions.

Hamilton Fish: The Inner History of the Grant Administration (1936) and William S. McFeely's *Grant: A Biography* (1981).° The political maneuvers of the election of 1876 and the resultant crisis and compromise are explained in C. Vann Woodward's *Reunion and Reaction* (1951)° and William Gillette's *Retreat from Reconstruction, 1869–1879* (1979).°

19

NEW FRONTIERS:
SOUTH AND WEST

THE NEW SOUTH

A FRESH VISION   The major prophet of a New South emerged in an improbable setting—at New York's most elegant restaurant, Delmonico's—where on December 21, 1886, the New England Society of New York held its annual dinner to commemorate the first landing of the Pilgrims at Plymouth. The main speaker of the evening was Henry W. Grady, thirty-six-year-old editor of the Atlanta *Constitution*, who had gained notice with his vivid reports of the recent Charleston earthquake. Grady's topic was "The New South," and his eloquent words became the most celebrated statement of what came to be called the New South Creed, a classic speech that multitudes of schoolboy orators in the South would commit to memory.

In plain yet almost poetic language, Grady set forth the vision that inspired a generation of southerners: "The Old South rested everything on slavery and agriculture, unconscious that these could neither give nor maintain healthy growth. The New South presents a perfect democracy, the oligarchs leading in the popular movement—a social system compact and closely knitted, less splendid on the surface, but stronger at the core—a hundred farms for every plantation, fifty homes for every palace—and a diversified industry that meets the complex need of this complex age."

Many prophets had gone before Grady and still others stood with him as major spokesmen for the New South Creed. In the aftermath of the Civil War these men, and Yankee patrons like William D. "Pig Iron" Kelly of Pennsylvania, preached with evangelical fervor the gospel of industry. The Confederacy, they reasoned, had lost because it relied too much on King Cotton. In the future the South must follow the North's example and industrialize. From that central belief flowed certain corollaries: that a more diversified and efficient agriculture would be a foundation for economic growth, that more widespread education, especially vocational training, would promote material success, and that sectional peace and racial harmony would provide a stable environment for economic growth.

ECONOMIC GROWTH The first and chief fruit of the New South zealots was an expansion of the area's textile production that began in the 1880s and overtook the older New England industry by the 1920s. In the New South, as in New England and Old England, cotton textiles were the harbingers of the Industrial Revolution. Already in the 1870s new cotton mills dotted the landscape of the Carolina Piedmont, where their promotion generated an almost revivalistic fervor. From 1880 to 1900 the number of cotton mills in the South grew from 161 to 400, the number of mill workers (among whom women and children outnumbered the men) increased fivefold, and the consumption of cotton went up eightfold, from 182,000 bales to 1,479,000. This development was the product mainly of southern capital and southern labor at the outset, though later the decline of the textile industry in New England contributed labor and capital to the South.

Tobacco growth also increased significantly, entering a new era with the development of two varieties of the weed: burley, which first appeared in southern Ohio, and bright leaf, which was grown on otherwise infertile soils and cured by a charcoal process discovered by a slave in 1839. Knowledge of the bright-leaf type remained chiefly local until, in what seemed a misfortune, Union soldiers swarmed over central North Carolina in 1865.

One victim of their looting was John Ruffin Green, whose bright-leaf tobacco factory was ransacked by soldiers loitering around Durham Station. Within a few weeks orders began to pour in to Green's factory for the Best Flavored Spanish Smoking Tobacco "that did not bite." With this revival, Green adopted as his trademark a bull's head similar to that on Coleman's mustard, made in Durham, England. It did not take long for Green and his successors to make the image of Bull Durham ubiquitous, so much so that years later Mark Twain, who was not above embellishing a good story, claimed that when he visited Egypt he never got a clear view of the pyramids for the Bull Durham signs.

Even more important in the rise of tobacco and Durham was the Duke family, whose story started at a nearby farm. At the end of the

White Oak Cotton Mills, Greensboro, North Carolina. *These women are measuring, sewing, and finishing denim.*

Civil War, the story goes, old Washington Duke had a capital of fifty cents obtained from a Yankee soldier for a souvenir Confederate five-dollar bill. He took a barnful of tobacco and, with the help of his three sons, beat it out with hickory sticks, stuffed it in bags, hitched up two mules to his wagon, and set out across the state, selling tobacco as he went. From that start success followed quickly. By 1872 the Dukes had a factory producing 125,000 pounds of leaf annually, and Washington Duke prepared to settle down and enjoy success.

His son, Buck (James Buchanan Duke), however, had the same drive that animated the Carnegies and Rockefellers of that day. Buck Duke recognized early that the industry was "half smoke and half ballyhoo," and he poured large sums into advertising schemes. Duke also squeezed competitors by underselling them in their own markets, and by cornering the supply of ingredients. Eventually his competitors were ready to take the hint that they join forces, and in 1890 Duke brought most of them into the American Tobacco Company, which controlled nine-tenths of the nation's cigarette production and by 1904 about three-fourths of all tobacco production in the United States. In 1911 the Supreme Court found the company in violation of the Sherman Anti-Trust Act and ordered it broken up, but by then Duke had found new worlds to conquer in hydroelectric power and aluminum.

Systematic use of other natural resources brought into the New South that area along the Appalachian Mountain chain from West Virginia to Alabama. Coal production in the South (including West Virginia) grew from 4.6 million tons in 1875 to 49.3 million tons by

1900. At the southern end of the mountains, Birmingham, Alabama, sprang up during the 1870s in the shadow of Red Mountain, so named for its iron ore, and soon tagged itself the "Pittsburgh of the South." Birmingham's close proximity to coal, iron, and limestone gave it a strong advantage over Chattanooga, which had a meteoric career as an iron center after the war.

With economic growth came a need for housing, and after 1870 lumbering became a thriving industry in the South. Lumber camps and little "peckerwood" mills sprouted all across the mountains and flatlands. By the turn of the century their product, mainly southern pine, had outdistanced textiles in value. Tree cutting seemed to know no bounds. It went on and on, despite the ecological devastation it caused. In time the industry would be saved only by the warm climate, which fostered quick renewal, and the rise of scientific forestry, which had its beginnings on George Vanderbilt's Biltmore Estate near Asheville, North Carolina. Here the nation's first school of forestry opened in 1898.

The South still had far to go to achieve the "diversified industry" that Grady envisioned in the mid-1880s, but a profusion of other products poured from southern plants: phosphate fertilizers from coastal South Carolina and Florida; oysters, vegetables, and fruits from widespread canneries; ships, including battleships, from the Newport News Shipbuilding and Drydock Company; leather products; wagons and buggies; liquors and beverages; paper in small quantities; and clay, glass, and stone products.

At the turn of the century two great forces that would impel an even greater industrial revolution were already on the horizon: petroleum in the Southwest and hydroelectric power in the Southeast. The Corsicana field in Texas had been opened in 1895, and in 1901 the Spindletop gusher would bring a great bonanza. Local power plants dotted the map by the 1890s. Richmond, Virginia, had the nation's first electric streetcar system in 1888, and Columbia, South Carolina, had the first electrically powered cotton mill in 1894. The greatest advance would begin in 1905 when Buck Duke's Southern Power Company set out to develop entire river valleys in the Carolinas.

AGRICULTURE, OLD AND NEW   At the turn of the century, however, most of the South remained undeveloped, at least by northeastern standards. Despite the optimistic rhetoric of New South spokesmen, the typical southerner was less apt to be tending a loom or forge than, as the saying went, facing the eastern end of a westbound mule. King Cotton survived the Civil War and expanded into new acreage even as its export markets leveled off. The old tobacco belts of Virginia and Kentucky now reached across North Carolina and touched South Carolina. Louisiana cane sugar, probably the most war-devastated of all crops, flourished again by the 1890s.

In 1885 Seaman A. Knapp, an agriculturist from New York by way of Iowa, moved to Louisiana and developed a new rice belt on behalf of an English land company, using machinery imported from the wheatfields. In the process Knapp invented the demonstration method of agricultural education, which showed farmers the most productive practices on selected plots of land with the aim of teaching by example. Knapp later used the demonstration method to fight the boll weevil in Texas. His work led to the national system of county farm and home demonstration agents. In the old rice belt of coastal South Carolina and elsewhere truck farming sprang up with the advent of the railroads and refrigerator cars. Vegetables from the Sea Islands, strawberries from Louisiana, and citrus fruits from Florida combined with other produce to create a cash crop second only to cotton.

Sharecropping and tenancy became increasingly prevalent in the aftermath of emancipation, but they seldom produced the self-sufficiency that advocates envisioned. The sharecropper, who had nothing to offer the landowner but his labor, tilled the land in return for supplies and a share of the crop, generally about half. The tenant farmer, hardly better off, might have his own mule, plow, and line of credit with the country store, and therefore might claim a larger share, commonly three-fourths of the cash crop and two-thirds of the subsistence crop, which was mainly corn. There were, moreover, infinite variations that ranged from cash rental at best to outright

Black sharecroppers, ca. 1880–1890.

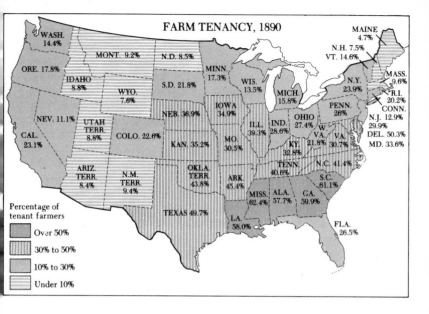

FARM TENANCY, 1890

WASH. 14.4%
ORE. 17.8%
MONT. 9.2%
IDAHO 8.8%
N.D. 8.5%
MINN. 17.3%
WIS. 13.5%
MICH. 15.8%
MAINE 4.7%
N.H. 7.5%
VT. 14.6%
NEV. 11.1%
WYO. 7.6%
S.D. 21.8%
IOWA 34.9%
NEB. 36.9%
ILL 39.3%
IND. 28.6%
OHIO 27.4%
PENN. 26%
N.Y. 23.9%
MASS. 9.6%
R.I. 20.2%
CONN. 29.9%
UTAH TERR. 8.8%
CAL. 23.1%
COLO. 22.6%
KAN. 35.2%
MO. 30.5%
KY. 32.8%
W. VA. 21.8%
VA. 30.7%
N.J. 12.9%
DEL. 50.3%
MD. 33.6%
ARIZ. TERR. 8.4%
N.M. TERR. 9.4%
OKLA. TERR. 43.8%
ARK. 45.4%
TENN. 40.6%
N.C. 41.4%
S.C. 61.1%
MISS. 62.4%
ALA. 57.7%
GA. 59.9%
TEXAS 49.7%
LA. 58.0%
FLA. 26.5%

Percentage of tenant farmers

Over 50%
30% to 50%
10% to 30%
Under 10%

peonage at worst. From the standpoint of efficiency the system approached the worst conceivable, for the tenant lacked incentive to care for the land and the owner had little chance to supervise the work. In addition the system bred a morbid suspicion on both sides, and the folklore of the rural South was replete with stories of tenants who remained stubbornly shiftless and improvident, and landlords who kept books with crooked pencils.

The crop lien system was equally flawed. At best, it supplied credit where cash was scarce. Country merchants furnished supplies in return for liens (or mortgages) on farmers' crops. To a few tenants and small farmers who seized the chance, credit offered a way out, but to most it offered only a hopeless cycle of perennial debt. The merchant, who assumed great risks, generally charged markups and interest which ranged, according to one publication, "from 24 percent to grand larceny." The merchant, like the planter (often the same man), demanded a cash crop that could be readily sold at harvest time. For all the wind and ink expended on preachments of diversification, the routines of tenancy and sharecropping yielded only with difficulty to other arrangements because the marketing, supply, and credit systems were still geared to a staple crop, usually cotton. The stagnation of rural life held millions, white and black, in bondage to privation and ignorance.

THE BOURBON REDEEMERS In politics, despite the South's formal democracy, habits of deference still prevailed. "Every community," one Union officer noted in postwar South Carolina, "had its great man, or its little great man, around whom his fellow citizens gather when they want information, and to whose monologues they listen with a respect akin to humility." After Reconstruction, southern politics was dominated by small coteries of such men, collectively known to history as Bourbons. Like the French Bourbons, the royal family which, Napoleon said, forgot nothing and learned nothing in the ordeal of revolution, the southern Bourbons were said to have forgotten nothing and learned nothing in the ordeal of Civil War. Yet the term, according to one historian, is one of "the most indefinable words ever used to describe Southern persons, places, and things, either solid or liquid."

The word functioned mainly as a hateful epithet, and few could glory in it. But their Republican, Independent, and Populist adversaries fixed the label so firmly in the vocabulary of the times that Bourbon came to signify the leaders of the Democratic party, whether they were real throwbacks or, more commonly, champions of an industrial New South who, if they had forgotten nothing, had at least learned something. They may have worshipped at the shrine of the old order, but they embraced a new order of economic development.

These Bourbons of the New South perfected a political alliance with eastern conservatives and an economic alliance with eastern capitalists. They generally pursued a policy of laissez-faire, except for the tax exemptions and other favors they offered to business. They avoided political initiatives, making the transition from Republican rule to Bourbon rule less abrupt than is often assumed. The Bourbons' favorable disposition toward the railroads was not unlike that of the Radicals. The Louisiana Lottery, a state lottery established during Reconstruction as a private monopoly, paid for "Redemption" from Republican rule in the state and was rewarded by Bourbons with a renewed tenure, written into the state constitution. And despite their reputation for honesty, Bourbon officeholders were occasionally caught with their fingers in the till.

Being basically antigovernment and haunted by the war, the Bourbons made a cardinal virtue of retrenchment. Their parsimony spelled austerity for public services, including the school systems started during Reconstruction. In 1871 the South Atlantic states were spending $10.27 per pupil; by 1880 the figure was down to $6.00 and in 1890 it stood at $7.63. One educational leader summarized conditions at the turn of the century: "In the Southern states, in schoolhouses costing an average of $276 each, under teachers receiving an average salary of $25 a month, we are giving children in actual attendance only 5 cents' worth of education a day for eighty-seven days only in the year." Illiteracy rates in the South at the time ran

The Effects of Radical and Bourbon Rule in the South. *This 1880 cartoon shows the South staggering under the oppressive weight of military Reconstruction* (left) *and flourishing under the "Let 'Em Alone Policy" of Hayes and the Bourbons* (right).

at about 12 percent of the native white population and 50 percent of the black population.

Private philanthropy, however, did help to keep southern schools afloat. In 1867 George Peabody, a London banker born in Massachusetts, established the Peabody Fund for Education, which was to spend some $3.6 million on public schools by 1914, when it was dissolved and most of its capital transferred to the George Peabody College for Teachers, established in 1875 in Nashville. Aid from the Peabody Fund was supplemented by the $1 million in the John F. Slater Fund, established in 1882 by a donor in Connecticut and earmarked for Negro schools. J. L. M. Curry, onetime soldier, preacher, teacher, and politician, became the general agent of both the Peabody and the Slater Funds. Curry pursued an extensive program of speaking and building support for education. He set up teachers' associations and started some of the first summer schools for teachers, and in general tried to foster exemplary schools.

The urge to economize created in the penal system one of the darkest blots on the Bourbon record: convict leasing. Necessity gave rise to the practice immediately after the Civil War; economy dictated its continuance. The destruction of prisons and the poverty of state treasuries combined with the demand for cheap labor on the railroads, in the mines, and in lumber and turpentine camps, to make the leasing of convict labor a way for southern states to avoid expenses and even bring in profits. The burden of detaining criminals grew after the war because freedmen, who as slaves had been subject to the discipline of masters, were now subject to the criminal law. Convict leasing, in the absence of state supervision, allowed inefficiency, neglect, and disregard for human life to proliferate.

The Bourbons scaled down not only expenditures but also the public debt, and by a simple means—they repudiated a vast amount of debt in all the former Confederate states except Florida and Mississippi. The corruption and extravagance of Radical rule were commonly advanced as justification for the process, but repudiation did not stop with Reconstruction debts. Altogether nine states repudiated more than half of what they owed, or nearly $130 million out of an estimated total of $248 million. The Bourbons, who respected the sanctity of property, were not of one mind about the process, however, and in Virginia their leaders honored the state debt so zealously, and at such cost to public services, that they were temporarily ousted by an Independent rebellion, the Readjuster party.

There are elements of diversity in the Bourbon record, however. Despite their devotion to economy, these frugal regimes, so ardently devoted to laissez-faire, did respond to the demand for commissions to regulate the rates charged by railroads for commercial transport. They established boards of agriculture, boards of public health, agricultural experiment stations, agricultural and mechanical colleges, teacher-training schools and women's colleges, and even state colleges for Negroes. Nor will any simplistic interpretation encompass the variety of Bourbon leaders. The Democratic party of the time was a mongrel coalition which threw Unionists, secessionists, businessmen, small farmers, hillbillies, planters, and even some Republicans together in alliance against the Reconstruction Radicals. Democrats therefore, even those who willy-nilly bore the Bourbon label, often marched to different drummers. And once they gained control, the conflicts inherent in any coalition began to assert themselves so that Bourbon regimes never achieved complete unity in philosophy or government.

Independent movements cropped up in all the southern states, endorsing a variety of proposals including debt repudiation, inflation, usury laws, and antimonopoly laws. Locally they fought Bourbon Democrats over fencing laws (poor farmers preferred to let their scrub stock forage for itself), patronage, and issues of corruption. On occasion they joined forces with third parties like the Greenbackers, and sometimes they elected local officials and congressmen. In Tennessee the division became so acute that the Republicans elected a governor in 1880. In Virginia, where the rebels sought reduction of the state debt, a Readjuster party captured the legislature in 1879, elected a governor in 1881, and sent their leader to the United States Senate.

For a brief time there emerged a wholesale collaboration between Republicans and Independents, which Chester A. Arthur, after he became president, promoted in the fall of 1881. The policy failed to make headway, however, because Republicans had little in common with the Independents except their opposition to the Democrats, and because the Republican machinery in the South had already been devastated by the overthrow of Reconstruction and by President Hayes's policy of reconciliation with the Bourbons immediately afterward. The Republicans maintained a secure foothold only in the Blue Ridge and Smoky Mountains, "the great spine of Republicanism which runs down the back of the South," where stubborn white Unionists passed the faith on to later generations.

Perhaps the ultimate paradox of the Bourbons' rule was that these paragons of white supremacy tolerated a lingering black voice in politics and showed no haste about raising the barriers of racial separation. A number of them harbored at least some element of patrician benevolence toward blacks. The old slaveowner, said a South Carolina editor, "has no desire to browbeat, maltreat, and spit upon the colored man"—clearly in part because the former slaveowner saw in freedmen no threat to his status. Blacks sat in the state legislatures of South Carolina until 1900 and of Georgia until 1908; some of these black representatives were Democrats. The South sent black congressmen to Washington in every election down to 1900 except one, though they always represented gerrymandered districts into which most of the state's black voters had been thrown. Under the Bourbons the disenfranchisement of black voters remained inconsistent, a local matter brought about mainly by fraud and intimidation, but it occurred enough to ensure white control of the southern states.

A like flexibility applied to other areas of race relations. The color line was drawn less strictly than it would be in the twentieth century. In some places, to be sure, racial segregation appeared before the end of Reconstruction, especially in schools, churches, hotels and rooming houses, and private social relations. In places of public accommodation such as trains, depots, theaters, and soda fountains, however, discrimination was more capricious. In 1885 a black journalist reported from his native state of South Carolina that he rode first-class cars on the railroads and in the streets, was served at saloons and soda fountains, saw Negroes dining with whites at train stations, and saw a black policeman arrest a white man on the streets of Columbia. Fifteen years later such scenes would be rare.

DISENFRANCHISING BLACKS   During the 1890s the attitudes that permitted such moderation eroded swiftly. One reason was that, despite signs of progress, many whites embraced a radical racism which held that blacks, loosed from the restraints of slavery, were "retrogressing" toward bestiality, especially the younger blacks who had not known slavery.

Another reason was political. The rise of the Populist party in the 1890s divided the white vote to such an extent that in some places the black vote became the balance of power. Populists courted black votes and brought blacks prominently into their councils. The Bourbons' response to all this was to revive the race issue, which they exploited with seasoned finesse, all the while controlling for their ticket a good part of the black vote in plantation areas. Nevertheless the Bourbons soon reversed themselves and began arguing that the black vote be eliminated completely from southern elections. It was imperative, said the governor of Louisiana in 1894, that "the mass of ignorance, vice and venality without any proprietary interest in the State" be denied the vote. Some leaders of the farmers hoped that disenfranchisement of Negroes would make it possible for whites to divide politically without raising the specter of "Negro domination."

But since the Fifteenth Amendment made it impossible to disenfranchise Negroes as such, the purpose was accomplished indirectly with devices such as poll taxes (or head taxes), and literacy tests. Some opposed such instruments of discrimination because they also trapped poor whites in the net. But this white opposition was neutralized by providing loopholes in the literacy tests through which illiterate whites could slip.

Mississippi led the way to near-total disenfranchisement of blacks. The state called a constitutional convention in 1890 for the express purpose of changing the suffrage provisions of the old Radical constitution of 1868. The Mississippi plan set the pattern that seven more states would follow over the next twenty years. First, a residence requirement—two years in the state, one year in the election district—struck at those tenant farmers who were in the habit of moving yearly in search of a better chance. Second, voters were disqualified if convicted of certain crimes. Third, all taxes, including a poll tax, had to be paid by February 1 of election year, which left plenty of time to lose the receipt before the fall vote. This proviso fell most heavily on the poor, most of whom were black. Fourth and finally, all voters had to be literate. The alternative, designed as a loophole for whites otherwise disqualified, was an "understanding" clause. The voter, if unable to read the Constitution, could qualify by being able to "understand" it—to the satisfaction of the registrar. Fraud was thus institutionalized rather than eliminated by "legal" disenfranchisement.

In other states, variations on the Mississippi plan added a few flourishes. In 1895 South Carolina tacked on the proviso that owning property assessed at $300 would qualify an illiterate voter. In 1898 Louisiana invented the "grandfather clause," which allowed illiterates to qualify if their fathers or grandfathers had been eligible to vote on January 1, 1867, when blacks were still excluded. Negro educator Booker T. Washington sent the convention a sarcastic telegram expressing hope that "no one clothed with state authority will be tempted to perjure and degrade himself by putting one interpretation upon it for the white man and another for the black man." By 1910 Georgia, North Carolina, Virginia, Alabama, and Oklahoma had all adopted the grandfather clause. The effectiveness of these measures can be seen in a few sample figures. Louisiana in 1896 had 130,000 black voters registered, and in 1900, 5,320. Alabama in 1900 had 121,159 literate Negro males over twenty-one, according to the census; only 3,742 were registered to vote.

More significant than the technical devices for disenfranchisement was the futility of attempting to overcome them. The literacy test in fact never had much to do with literacy. It was simply a device that could be used, fraudulently if need be, to exclude blacks. The fraud that had once prevailed at the ballot box was simply moved back one step to the registration process. Years later, when the Republican Calvin Coolidge got 1,000 votes in South Carolina, the state's senator remarked: "I do not know where he got them. I was astonished to know that they were cast and shocked to know that they were counted." Every southern state, moreover, adopted a statewide Democratic primary between 1896 and 1915, which became the only meaningful election outside isolated areas of Republican strength. With minor exceptions, the Democratic primaries excluded black voters altogether.

SEGREGATION SPREADS   "Jim Crow" segregation followed hard on disenfranchisement and in some states came first. The symbolic first target was the railway train. In the 1880s it was still common practice for American trains to have first- and second-class cars, which afforded a degree of racial segregation by the difference in ticket cost. In 1885, nevertheless, the novelist George Washington Cable noted that in South Carolina Negroes "ride in first class cars as a right" and "their presence excites no comment." From 1875 to 1883 in fact any racial segregation violated a federal Civil Rights Act, which forbade discrimination in places of public accommodation. But in 1883 the Supreme Court ruled on seven *Civil Rights Cases* involving discrimination against Negroes by corporations or individuals. The Court held, with only one dissent, that the force of federal law could not extend to individual action because the Four-

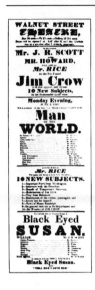

"Jim Crow," a stock character in the old minstrel shows, became a synonym for racial segregation in the twentieth century. Dan Rice developed the character in the 1830s.

teenth Amendment, which provided that "no State" could deny citizens the equal protection of the laws, stood as a prohibition only against *state* action.

This left as an open question the validity of state laws *requiring* separate facilities under the rubric of "separate but equal," a slogan popular with the New South prophets. In 1881 Tennessee had required railroads in the state to maintain separate first-class cars for blacks and whites. In 1888 Mississippi went a step further by requiring passengers, under penalty of law, to occupy the car set aside for their race. When Louisiana followed suit in 1890, the law was challenged in the case *Plessy v. Ferguson,* which the Supreme Court decided in 1896. The test case originated in New Orleans when Homer Plessy, an octoroon (a person having one-eighth Negro ancestry), refused to leave a white car when told to do so. He was convicted, and the case rose on appeal to the Supreme Court. The Court ruled that segregation laws "have been generally, if not universally recognized as within the competency of state legislatures in the exercise of their police power." The sole dissenter was John Marshall Harlan, a former slaveholder and Whig Unionist from Kentucky, who had written the only dissent in the *Civil Rights Cases.* "In my opinion," Harlan wrote, "the judgment this day rendered will, in time, prove to be quite as pernicious as the decision made by this tribunal in the Dred Scott Case." The Plessy ruling, he predicted, would "stimulate aggressions, more or less brutal, upon the admitted rights of colored citizens."

Very soon the principle of segregation by race extended into every area of southern life, including street railways, hotels, restaurants, hospitals, recreations, sports, and employment. If an activity was overlooked by the laws, it was not overlooked in custom and practice. The editor of the Richmond *Times* expressed the prevailing view: "It is necessary that this principle be applied in every relation of Southern life. God Almighty drew the color line and it cannot be obliterated. The negro must stay on his side of the line and the white man must stay on his side, and the sooner both races recognize this fact and accept it, the better it will be for both."

As for the "aggressions, more or less brutal," which Harlan foretold, they were already routine when he pronounced his dissent. From the days of slavery race relations had operated in a context of force and violence. The period of growing discrimination at the turn of the century was one of the worst. In the decade from 1890 to 1899 lynchings in the United States averaged 188 per year, 82 percent of which occurred in the South; from 1900 to 1909 they averaged 93 per year, 92 percent in the South. Whites constituted 32 percent of the victims during the first period, only 11 percent in the latter. A young Episcopal priest in Montgomery said that extremists had proceeded "from an undiscriminating attack upon the Negro's ballot to a like attack upon his schools, his labor, his life—from the contention that no Negro shall vote to the contention that no Negro shall learn, that no Negro shall labor, and (by implication) that no Negro shall live."

WASHINGTON AND DU BOIS   A few brave souls, black and white, spoke out against the new racist measures, but by and large blacks had to accommodate them as best they could. To be sure, the doctrine of "separate but equal" did open some doors, such as those to black schools, that had once been closed entirely. Some African-Americans even began to make a virtue of necessity. The chief spokesman for this philosophy was Booker T. Washington, the black prophet of the New South Creed. Born in Virginia of a slave mother and a white father, Washington had fought extreme adversity to get an education at Hampton Institute, one of thepostwar missionary schools, and then to build at Tuskegee, Alabama, a leading college for African-Americans.

Washington argued that American blacks should first establish an economic base for their advancement. They should focus "upon the everyday practical things of life, upon something that is needed to be done, and something which they will be permitted to do in the community in which they reside." In his famous speech at the Atlanta Cotton States and International Exposition in 1895, which propelled him to fame, Washington advised fellow blacks: "Cast down your bucket where you are—cast it down in making friends . . . of the people of all races by whom we are surrounded. Cast it down in agriculture, mechanics, in commerce, in domestic service, and in the professions." He conspicuously omitted politics and let fall an oblique endorsement of segregation: "In all things that are purely social we can be as separate as the five fingers, yet one as the hand in all things essential to mutual progress."

Some people bitterly criticized Washington then and since for making a bad bargain: the sacrifice of broad education and of civil rights for the dubious acceptance of white conservatives. W. E. B. Du Bois led blacks in this criticism of Washington. A native of Massachusetts, Du Bois once said defiantly that he was born "with a flood of Negro blood, a strain of French, a bit of Dutch, but thank God! no 'Anglo-Saxon.' " Du Bois first experienced southern racial practices as an undergraduate at Fisk University in Nashville, a missionary school which emphasized liberal education. Later he earned a Ph.D. in history from Harvard and briefly attended the University of Berlin. In addition to an active career in racial protest he left a distinguished record as a scholar and author. Trim and dapper in appearance, sporting a goatee, cane, and gloves, Du Bois possessed a combative spirit. Not long after he began his teaching career at Atlanta University in 1897, he began to assault Washington's accommodationist philosophy of black progress and put forward his own program of "ceaseless agitation."

Washington, Du Bois argued, preached "a gospel of Work and Money to such an extent as apparently almost completely to overshadow the higher aims of life." The education of Negroes, he maintained, should not be merely vocational but should nurture leaders

Booker T. Washington.

W. E. B. Du Bois.

willing to challenge segregation and discrimination through political action. He believed in work, "but work is not necessarily education. Education is the development of power and ideal." He demanded that disenfranchisement and legalized segregation cease and that the laws of the land be enforced. And he provided the formula for attaining such goals: "By voting where we may vote, by persistent, unceasing agitation, by hammering at the truth, by sacrifice and work." Du Bois minced no words in criticizing Washington's philosophy: "We refuse to surrender the leadership of this race to cowards and trucklers." He called Washington's 1895 speech "the Atlanta Compromise" and argued that it had made Washington the leader of his race only in the eyes of whites.

MYTH AND THE NEW SOUTH   Du Bois wanted to see a genuinely New South for blacks, one sharply different from the Old. But the connections between the New and Old South were strong. One of the strongest connections was symbolic. The champions of a New South used the romantic myth of an Old South to bolster their creed while still deploring the backwardness created by slavery and agrarianism. These New South spokesmen used the Old South myth because it salved the wounds of defeat, bolstered white self-esteem, gave a sense of regional identity, and blunted sectional enmity. By the end of the 1880s the image of the New South itself was moving into the realm of myth, as Southern boosters exaggerated the region's economic progress and ignored chronic social ills.

The ultimate achievement of the New South prophets and their allies, the Bourbons, was that like all lasting conservative movements they reconciled tradition with innovation. Their relative moderation in racial policy, at least before the 1890s, allowed them to accommodate just enough of the new to disarm adversaries and keep control. By accommodating themselves to the growth of industry, the Bourbons led the South into a new economic era, but without sacrificing what one historian called "the pageantry and rhetoric of the sentimental South." Bourbon rule left a permanent mark on the South, for as the historian C. Vann Woodward has noted, "it was not the Radicals nor the Confederates but the Redeemers who laid the lasting foundations in matters of race, politics, economics and institutions for the modern South."

THE NEW WEST

For vast reaches of western America the great epics of Civil War and Reconstruction were remote events hardly touching the lives of Indians, Mexicans, Asians, trappers, miners, and Mormons scattered through the plains and mountains. There the march of Manifest Destiny continued on its inexorable course, energized by a lust for land and a passion for profits. On one level, the settlement of the West beyond the Mississippi constitutes a colorful drama of determined pioneers overcoming all obstacles to secure their visions of freedom and opportunity amid the region's awesome vastness. This romantic vision of western history has long had a grip on the American imagination. But on another level the colonization of the Far West was a tragedy of short-sighted greed and irresponsible behavior, a story of reckless exploitation that nearly exterminated the culture of Native Americans, scarred the land, and decimated its wild animals. The history of the West seen from this perspective is not a grand success story but a tale of hardship, frustration, and failure. Both images of the process of western settlement are accurate in some respects, and it is now our task to strike the appropriate balance.

In the second tier of trans-Mississippi states—Iowa, Kansas, Nebraska—and in western Minnesota, the last frontier of farmers began pressing out onto the Great Plains after mid-century. From California the miners' frontier scattered enclaves east through the mountains at one new strike after another. From Texas the nomadic cowboys migrated northward into the plains and across the Rockies into the Great Basin. Now there were two frontiers of settlement, east and west, and even a third to the south; in another generation there would be none. After one final great rush the occupation of the continent would be complete, less than three centuries following the first English beachhead at Jamestown.

As settlement moved west, the environment gradually altered.

An American family on their way west.

The Great Plains were arid, swept by dry winds which had surrendered their moisture successively to the Pacific coastal ranges, the Sierra Nevadas and Cascades, and the Rockies. As Walter Prescott Webb wrote in *The Great Plains*, it was as if "east of the Mississippi civilization stood on three legs—land, water, and timber; west of the Mississippi not one but two of these legs were withdrawn—water and (for want of water) timber—and civilization was left on one leg—land." The scarcity of water and timber rendered useless or impossible the familiar trappings of the pioneer: the axe, the log cabin, the rail fence, and the accustomed methods of tilling the soil.

For a long time the region had been called the Great American Desert, a barrier to cross on the way to the Pacific, unfit for human habitation and therefore, to white Americans, the perfect refuge for Indians. But that pattern changed in the last half of the nineteenth century as a result of new finds of gold, silver, and other minerals, completion of transcontinental railroads, destruction of the buffalo, the collapse of Indian resistance, the rise of the range-cattle industry, and the dawning realization that the arid region need not be a sterile desert. With the use of what water was available, techniques of dry farming and irrigation could make the land fruitful after all.

MINING THE WEST   The miners' frontier was in fact not so much a frontier as a scattering of settlements in parts unsuitable for farming,

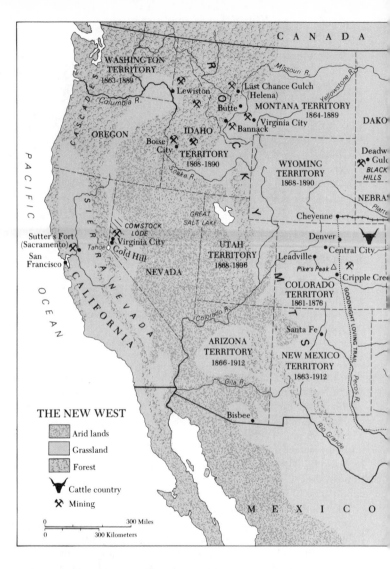

THE NEW WEST

Arid lands

Grassland

Forest

Cattle country

Mining

0   300 Miles

0   300 Kilometers

such as steep mountainsides, remote highlands, and barren desserts. The California miners of '49 set the typical pattern in which the sudden disorderly rush of prospectors to the new find was quickly followed by the arrival of the camp followers, a motley crew of peddlers, saloonkeepers, prostitutes, card sharps, hustlers, and assorted desperadoes, out to mine the miners. Then if the new field panned out, the forces of respectability and more subtle forms of exploitation slowly worked their way in. An era of lawlessness gave

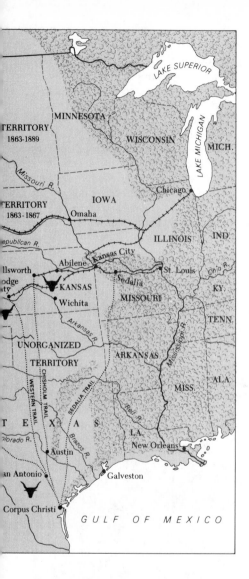

place to vigilante rule and, finally, to a stable community.

As mining became more dependent on capital, the day of the individual prospector began to wane. The Forty-niners first got at the gold by sifting off dirt and gravel through "placer" mining or "panning," or diverting a stream through a "sluice box" or "long tom." But once the rich diggings tailed off, efficient mining required shafts sunk into the ground or crushing mills built to extract the precious metal locked in quartz. The wild rush then gave way to

organized enterprise and the "sourdoughs" either moved on, settled
down to work for the bosses, or took up farming in the vicinity.

The drama of the 1849 gold rush was reenacted time and again in
the following three decades. Though the California fever had passed
by 1851, and no big strikes were made for seven years, new finds in
Colorado and Nevada revived hopes for riches. Along the South
Platte River, not far from Pike's Peak in Colorado, a prospecting
party found promise of gold in 1858, and stories of success there
brought perhaps 100,000 "Fifty-niners" into the country by June
1859, only to find that the rumors had been greatly exaggerated.
Wagons that headed west with the legend "Pike's Peak or Bust!" on
their sides were soon rumbling back with the sardonic message
"Busted, by gosh." Still, a few mines proved out, some new arrivals
took up farming to exploit high prices for farm goods in Denver and
other mining centers, and the census of 1860 showed 35,000 still in
the region. And new discoveries kept occurring: near Central City in
1859, at Leadville in the 1870s, and the last important strikes in the
West, again gold and silver, at Cripple Creek in 1891–1894. During
these years farming and grazing had given the economy a stable
base, and Colorado had become the "Centennial State" in July 1876.

While the early rushers were crowding around Pike's Peak, the
Comstock Lode was discovered more than a mile up the slopes of
Mount Davidson, near Gold Hill, Nevada. H. T. P. Comstock, "Old
Pancake," a Canadian-born fur trapper, had drifted to the Carson

Washing and panning for gold in the Dakota Territory.

River diggings opened in 1856. Possessed of a glib tongue, he talked his way into a share in a new discovery made by two other prospectors in 1859 and gave it his own name. The lode produced not only gold but a troublesome "blue earth" that turned out to contain silver. Close by, James Finney, known as "Old Virginia," located a lucrative new vein and gave his nickname to nearby Virginia City. Neither man had the foresight to develop his claim; both sold out for tiny sums what proved to be the two richest fields in the West. Within twenty years the Comstock Lode alone had yielded more than $300 million from shafts that reached hundreds of feet into the mountainside. In 1861 Nevada became a territory and in 1864 the state of Nevada was admitted in time to give its three electoral votes to Lincoln.

The Spaniards had found silver in New Mexico, but mining in Arizona began during the Civil War, when many in a company of California volunteers, going to meet a Confederate foray into New Mexico, deserted to the promising mining country near the Colorado River. In both Arizona and Montana the most important mineral proved to be neither gold nor silver, but copper. The richest copper mines included the Anaconda Mine in Butte, Montana, and the Phelps-Dodge Mine near Bisbee, Arizona.

The last great strike before the Cripple Creek (Colorado) find of the 1890s occurred in 1874–1875 in the Black Hills of South Dakota, which belonged by treaty to the Sioux Indians. Deadwood, the site of the strike, earned brief glory as the refuge of some of the West's most notorious desperadoes: "Calamity Jane," "Wild Bill Hickock," and a host of others. But in Deadwood, as elsewhere, when the gold and silver lodes ran out there was often little to support life in an arid, infertile terrain. The Virginia Citys, the Auroras, the Gold Hills, and others turned into ghost towns until the twentieth century, when shrewd promoters found a new bonanza in mining tourists of their vacation dollars.

The growing demand for orderly government in the West led to the hasty creation of new territories, and eventually the admission of a host of new states. After Colorado was admitted in 1876, however, there was a long hiatus because of the party divisions in Congress. Democrats were reluctant to create states out of territories that were heavily Republican. After the sweeping Republican victory of 1888, however, Congress admitted the Dakotas, Montana, and Washington in 1889, and Idaho and Wyoming in 1890, completing a tier of states from coast to coast. Utah entered in 1896 (after the Mormons abandoned the practice of polygamy), Oklahoma in 1907, and in 1912 Arizona and New Mexico finally rounded out the forty-eight contiguous states.

A railroad camp at Whitewood Canyon, South Dakota, 1890.

THE INDIAN WARS   As the frontier pressed in from east and west, the relentless greed and duplicity of whites pursued the Indians into what was supposed to be their last refuge. Mounted on horses which were a legacy of the Spaniards, perhaps 250,000 Indians in the Great Plains and mountain regions lived mainly off the herds of buffalo which provided food and, from their hides, clothing and shelter. No sooner was the Jacksonian removal policy complete than the onrush of migration in the 1840s began to crowd the Indians' land. Emigrants crossing to Oregon, California, Utah, and Santa Fe came into contact and sometimes into conflict with them. In 1851 the chiefs of the principal Plains tribes were gathered at Fort Laramie, where they agreed to accept more or less definite tribal borders and to leave the emigrants unmolested on their trails. It soon became easier to force one tribe to cede its lands without arousing the others, for the Indians could never realize the old dream of Tecumseh, a unified resistance.

From the early 1860s until the late 1870s the frontier was ablaze with Indian wars, and intermittent outbreaks continued through the 1880s. The first serious trouble developed in Minnesota, where a volunteer militia had taken the place of army garrisons fighting in the Civil War. Fighting started in 1862 when a band of Sioux, aroused by recent land cessions, killed five whites. Some of the Sioux fled farther west, but others remained and wrought havoc on the frontier, killing or capturing some 1,000 whites until the militia in overwhelming force drove them back and inflicted a devastating revenge. Out of 400 Indians captured, 300 were sentenced to death and eventually 38 were hanged in a mass execution the day after Christmas, 1862.

In Colorado, where chiefs of the Cheyennes and Arapahos accepted a treaty banishing them westward, protesting braves began sporadic raids on the trails and mining camps. In 1864 the territorial governor persuaded most of the warring Indians to gather at Fort Lyon on Sand Creek, where they were promised protection. Despite this promise, Colonel J. M. Chivington's militia fell upon an Indian camp flying the American flag and a white flag of truce, slaughtering 450 peaceful Indians—men, women, and children. General Nelson A. Miles called it the "foulest and most unjustifiable crime in the annals of America." Chivington, a former Methodist minister, later exhibited his personal collection of 100 scalps in Denver. In 1865 the survivors surrendered unconditionally and gave up their Sand Creek reservation for lands farther west.

With other scattered battles erupting, in 1865 a congressional committee began to gather evidence on the grisly Indian wars and massacres. Its 1867 *Report on the Condition of the Indian Tribes* led to an act to establish an Indian Peace Commission charged with ending the Sioux War and removing the causes of Indian wars in general. Congress decided this was best accomplished at the expense of the Indians, by persuading them to take up life on out-of-the-way reservations. This solution, in short, continued the persistent encroachment on Indian hunting grounds.

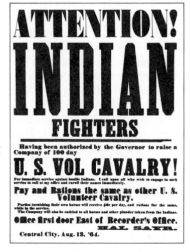

The Indian fighters who responded to this poster took part in the slaughter of 450 Indians at Sand Creek, Colorado, in 1864.

INDIAN WARS,
1864-1890

0   300 Miles
0   300 Kilometers

In October 1867 a conference at Medicine Creek Lodge, Kansas, ended with an agreement that the Kiowa, Comanche, Arapaho, and Cheyenne would accept lands in western Oklahoma. Smaller tribes from the southern Plains later were resettled on reservations in the same area. In the following spring a conference at Fort Laramie resulted in peace with the Sioux, who agreed to settle within the Black Hills reservation in Dakota Territory. But Indian resistance in the southern plains continued until the Red River War of 1874–1875. In a winter campaign of relentless pursuit, General Philip Sheridan scattered the Indians and finally brought them to terms in the spring of 1875.

But the trouble was brewing once again in the north. In 1874 General George A. Custer led an exploring expedition into the Black Hills, accompanied by gold seekers who began to find what they were after. Miners were soon filtering into the Sioux hunting grounds despite promises that the army would keep them out. The army had done little to protect the Indian lands, but when ordered to move against wandering bands of Sioux hunting on the range according to their treaty rights, the army moved vigorously. In 1876, after several indecisive encounters, General Custer found the main encampment of Sioux and their Cheyenne allies on the Little Big Horn River. Separated from the main body of his men Custer and a detachment of 200 were surrounded by a body of warriors numbering about 2,500 and completely annihilated.

But the Battle of the Little Big Horn was only one incident in this war. Instead of following up their victory, the Indians threw away their advantage in celebration and renewed hunting. When the army regained the offensive, the Indians began to melt away into the wilderness. Chief Sitting Bull escaped into Canada, only to return to the Sioux reservation several years later. Crazy Horse was captured and murdered by his guard. The remaining Sioux were forced to give up their hunting grounds and gold fields in return for payments. When a peace commission imposed this settlement, Chief Spotted Tail said: "Tell your people that since the Great Father promised that we should never be removed, we have been moved five times. . . . I think you had better put the Indians on wheels and you can run them about wherever you wish."

In the Rockies and westward the same story of hopeless resistance was repeated. The Blackfoot and Crow had to leave their homes in Montana. In a war along the California-Oregon boundary the Modocs held out for six months in 1871–1872 before they were overwhelmed. In 1879 the Utes were forced to give up their vast territories in western Colorado after a brief battle. In Idaho the peaceful Nez Perces finally refused to surrender lands along the Salmon River. Chief Joseph tried to avoid war, but when some

General George A. Custer (left), *and Chief Sitting Bull of the Sioux* (right).

unruly braves started a fight, he directed a masterful campaign against overwhelming odds, one of the most spectacular feats in the history of Indian warfare. After a retreat of 1,500 miles, through mountains and plains, across the Yellowstone region and through the Bitterroot Mountains of Montana, he was finally caught thirty miles short of the Canadian border, and exiled to Oklahoma.

In his character the heroic Joseph embodied the image of nobility. He maintained strict discipline among his followers, countenanced no scalpings or outrages against civilians, bought supplies which he could have confiscated, and kept his dignity to the end. His eloquent speech of surrender was an epitaph to the warrior's last stand against the march of empire: "I am tired of fighting. Our chiefs are killed. . . . The old men are all dead. . . . I want to have time to look for my children, and see how many of them I can find. . . . Hear me, my chiefs! I am tired. My heart is sick and sad. From where the sun now stands I will fight no more forever."

A generation of Indian wars virtually ended in 1886 with the capture of Geronimo, a chief of the Chiricahua Apaches, who had fought encroachments in the Southwest for fifteen years. But there would be one tragic epilogue. Late in 1888 Wovoka (or "Jack Wilson"), a Paiute in western Nevada, fell ill and in a delirium imagined he had visited the spirit world where he learned of a deliverer coming to rescue the Indians and restore their lands. To hasten the day, he said, they had to take up a ceremonial dance at each new moon. The Ghost Dance craze fed upon old legends of a coming Messiah and spread rapidly. In 1890 the Sioux took it up with such

Chief Joseph of the Nez Perce tribe.

Geronimo, a chief of the Chiricahua Apaches.

fervor that it alarmed white authorities. An effort to arrest Sitting Bull led to his death and shortly afterward, on December 29, 1890, a bloodbath at Wounded Knee, South Dakota. An accidental rifle discharge led nervous soldiers to fire into a group of Indians who had come to surrender. Nearly 200 Indians and 25 soldiers died in the "Battle of Wounded Knee." The Indian wars had ended with characteristic brutality.

Over the long run the collapse of Indian resistance resulted as much from the killing off of the buffalo herds on which they subsisted as from direct suppression. White hunters felled buffaloes for sport, sometimes firing from train windows for the joy of seeing them die. In the 1870s a systematic slaughter served the fashion of buffalo robes and overcoats in the East. By the mid-1880s the herds had reached the verge of extinction.

Most frontiersmen had little tolerance for moralizing on the Indian question. Easterners who were far removed from frontier dangers took a different view. The slaughter of the Indian wars was immensely unpopular. In his annual message of 1877 President Hayes echoed the protest: "Many, if not most, of our Indian wars have had their origin in broken promises and acts of injustice on our part." Statesmen and churchmen spoke out against mistreatment of Indians. In the 1880s Helen Hunt Jackson, a novelist and poet, focused attention on the Indian cause in *A Century of Dishonor* (1881), which struck a popular chord just as *Uncle Tom's Cabin* had done.

INDIAN POLICY   Indian policy gradually became more benevolent, but this did little to ease the plight of the Indians and actually helped to destroy the remnants of their cultures. The reservation policy inaugurated by the Peace Commission in 1867 did little more than extend a practice that dated from colonial Virginia. Partly humanitarian in motive, this policy also saved money: it cost less to house and feed Indians on reservations than it did to fight them. And one Indian commissioner wrote candidly: "That these reservations will cause any considerable annoyance to the whites we do not believe. They consist, for the most part, of ground unfitted for cultivation, but suited to the peculiar habits of the Indians." Mistakes would be made, of course. Too late it was discovered that the Utes and Osage and some other tribes were left sitting atop rich stores of oil and natural gas.

Well-intentioned reformers sought to "Americanize" the Indians by dealing with them as individuals rather than as tribes. The fruition of reform efforts came in the Dawes Severalty Act of 1887. Sponsored by Henry M. Dawes of Massachusetts, the act proposed to introduce the Indians to individual land ownership and agriculture. The Dawes Act permitted the president to divide the lands of any tribe and grant 160 acres to each head of family and lesser amounts to others. To protect the Indian in his property, the government held it in trust for twenty-five years, after which the owner won full title and became a citizen. Under the Burke Act of 1906 Indians who took up life apart from their tribes became citizens immediately. Members of the tribes granted land titles became subject to state and federal laws like all other persons. In 1901 citizenship was extended to the Five Civilized Tribes of Oklahoma, and in 1924 to all Indians.

But the more it changed, the more Indian policy remained the same. Despite the best of intentions, the Dawes Act struck a double blow at the Indians. It created the chance for more plundering of Indian land, and it disrupted what remained of the traditional cultures. Dawes himself had foreseen the result, but defended his bill as an effort to salvage something for the Indians. Few others had such foresight, except land grabbers and students of Indian "ethnology," the forerunners of the study of anthropology. One leading authority pronounced the Indian "entirely incapable" of dealing with the whites on an individual basis. The result would be "that in a very short time he would divest himself of every foot of land and fall into poverty." And so it happened. Those lands not distributed to Indian families were sold, while others were lost to land sharks because of the Indians' inexperience with private ownership, or simply their powerlessness in the face of fraud. Between 1887 and

1934 they lost an estimated 86 million of their 130 million acres. Most of what remained was unsuited to agriculture.

CATTLE AND COWBOYS   While the West was being taken from the Indians, cattle entered the grasslands where the buffalo had roamed, and the cowboy enjoyed his brief heyday, fading then into the folklore of the Wild West along with the sourdoughs (prospectors), the desperadoes, and the Plains Indians. From colonial times, especially in the South, cattle raising had been a common enterprise just beyond the fringe of settlement. In many cases the early slaves took care of the livestock. Later, in the West, African-American cowboys were still a common sight, although they were lost from view in the novels and "horse operas" which pictured a lily-white frontier. Much of the romance of the open-range cattle industry derived from its Mexican roots. The Texas longhorns and the cowboys' horses had in large part descended from stock brought over by the Spaniards, and many of the industry's trappings had been worked out in Mexico first: the cowboy's saddle, his chaps *(chaparejos)* to protect the legs, his spurs, and his lariat.

For many years wild cattle competed with the buffalo in the Spanish borderlands. Natural selection and contact with "Anglo" scrub cattle produced the Texas longhorns: lean and rangy, they were noted more for speed and endurance than for providing a choice steak. They had little value, moreover, because the largest markets for beef were too far away. Occasionally they were driven to market in Austin, Galveston, or New Orleans, and some even to the gold fields of California, Arizona, and Colorado. At the end of the Civil War, perhaps as many as 5 million roamed the grasslands of

Jesse Chisholm, a half Cherokee trader, who blazed the wagon road from San Antonio to Ellsworth and Abilene that became a main route of the cattle drives, the "Chisholm Trail."

Texas, still neglected—but not for long. In the upper Mississippi Valley, where herds had been depleted by the war, cattle prices ranged from $30 to $50 a head, while the Texas cattle could be had just for the effort of rounding them up.

So the cattle drives began anew after the Civil War, but on a scale far greater than before. In 1866 a large herd set out for Sedalia, Missouri, the western terminus of the Missouri-Pacific Railroad. But that route proved unsuitable because it was subject to raids by postwar bushwhackers, obstructed by woodlands, and opposed by Arkansas and Missouri farmers. New opportunities arose as railroads pushed farther west where cattle could be driven through relatively vacant lands.

Joseph G. McCoy, the youngest of three brothers already in the livestock business near Springfield, Illinois, recognized the possibilities for moving the cattle trade west. He turned Abilene into the first successful Kansas cowtown, while one brother took care of the farm in Illinois and the other looked after sales in New York. Located on the Kansas-Pacific Railroad at the northern end of a trail laid out through Indian Territory by the part-Cherokee Jesse Chisholm, Abilene was a "small, dead place, consisting of about one dozen log huts" when McCoy arrived in early 1867.

McCoy quickly began to develop the town. He bought up 250 acres for a stockyard, laid plans for a barn, an office building, livestock scales, a hotel, and a bank—and sent an agent into Indian Territory to cultivate owners of herds bound north. His first shipment went out in September. Over the next few years Abilene developed into a flourishing town. As the railroads moved west, however, so did the cowtowns and the trails: Ellsworth, Wichita, Caldwell, and Dodge City, all in Kansas, and farther north Ogallala, Nebraska, Cheyenne, Wyoming, and Miles City, Montana.

In their brief day, the cowtowns rivaled the mining camps for their raw lawlessness, as could be expected in societies with such shallow roots and so many people on the lookout for the main chance. Their penchant for violence, however, has since been exploited out of proportion for the sake of tourism and show business, or vivid writing.

During the twenty years after the Civil War some 40,000 cowboys roamed the Great Plains. They were young—the average age was twenty-four—and from diverse backgrounds. Thirty percent were either Mexican or African-American and hundreds were Indians. Many others were Civil War veterans from North and South who now rode side by side, and a number had come from Europe. The life of a cowboy, for the most part, was rarely as exciting as motion pictures and television shows have depicted. Being a ranchhand involved grueling, dirty, wage labor interspersed with drudgery and boredom.

The flush times of the cowtown soon passed, and many reverted to sleepy villages and occasional "boot hills" as reminders of the hell-roaring times. The long cattle drives played out too because they were economically unsound. The dangers of the trail, the wear and tear on men and cattle, the charges levied on drives across Indian Territory, and the advance of farms across the trails combined to persuade cattlemen that they could best function near the railroads. As railroads spread out into Texas and the Plains, the cattle business spread with them over the High Plains as far as Montana and on into Canada.

In the absence of laws governing the range, the cattlemen at first worked out a code of action largely dictated by circumstances. But in 1873 Joseph Glidden, an Illinois farmer, invented the first effective barbed wire, which ranchers used to fence off their claims at relatively low cost. More often than not these were parts of the public domain to which they had no valid title. In that same year an eastern promoter, John W. "Bet-a-Million" Gates, one of the early agents for Glidden, gave a persuasive demonstration of the barbed wire in San Antonio. Skeptical cattlemen discovered that their meanest longhorns shied away from the fence which, as Gates put it, was light as air, stronger than whiskey, and cheaper than dirt. Orders poured in, and Gates eventually put together a virtual monopoly in the Ameri-

Dodge City, Kansas, in 1879. *Dodge City was one of the most notorious of the western cowtowns.*

can Steel and Wire Company. The coming of barbed wire finally ended the open, free range.

The greatest boom in the range-cattle trade came in the early 1880s, when eastern and European investors began to pour money into the "Beef Bonanza." Cattle growing, like mining, entered a season of wild speculation, and then evolved from a romantic adventure into a prosaic business, often a corporate business. The cowboys settled into a more sedentary existence. Even in the heroic days a cowboy's life had been a lonely, wearisome affair, the romance of which lay mainly in the pages of books like Owen Wister's *The Virginian* (1902), in which the hero utters the famous line: "When you call me that, *smile!*" Within two short decades, 1866–1886, the glory was ended; it was always more in the eye of the beholder than anywhere else.

FARMERS AND THE LAND   Among the legendary figures of the West, the sodbusters projected an unromantic image in contrast to the sourdoughs and cowboys, the cavalry and the Indians. Farming has always been a risky and arduous endeavor, and it was made more so on the Great Plains by the unforgiving environment. After 1865, on paper at least, the land laws offered favorable terms to the farmer. Under the Homestead Act of 1862 a farmer could either realize the old dream of free land simply by staking out a claim and living on it for five years, or buy the land at $1.25 an acre after six months. But the land legislation of the Old Northwest was predicated upon an entirely different environment from that of the Plains, and the laws never completely adjusted to the fact that much of the land was suited only for cattle. Cattlemen were forced to garner land by gradual acquisition from homesteaders or land-grant railroads.

The unchangeable fact of aridity, rather than new land laws, shaped institutions in the New West. Where farming was impossible the cattlemen simply established dominance by control of the water, regardless of the laws. Belated legislative efforts to develop irrigable lands finally achieved a major success when the Newlands Reclamation Act (after the aptly named Senator Francis G. Newlands of Nevada) of 1901 set up the Bureau of Reclamation. The proceeds of public land sales in sixteen states became a fund for irrigation works, and the Reclamation Bureau set about building such major projects as Boulder (later Hoover) Dam on the Nevada-Arizona line, Roosevelt Dam in Arizona, and Elephant Butte Dam and Arrowrock Dam in New Mexico.

But the stubborn problem of water remained, rendering much of the West's land useless for field crops. The area in which rainfall averaged ten to twenty inches per year was marginal, but with the techniques of "dry farming" could support such crops as sorghum, kaffir corn, and Turkey wheat. Certain varieties of spring and winter wheat grew at the times of greatest rainfall. The eastern Plains from Minnesota and North Dakota down to Texas emerged as the wheat belt, the new breadbasket of the nation, and behind wheat the corn belt and corn-hog combination edged westward.

The lands of the New West, as on previous frontiers, passed to their ultimate owners more often from private hands than directly from the government. Much of the 274 million acres claimed under the Homestead Act passed quickly to cattlemen or speculators, and thence to settlers. The land-grant railroads got some 200 million acres of the public domain in the twenty years from 1851 to 1871, and sold much of this land to build population and traffic along the lines. The New West of cattlemen and farmers was in fact largely the product of the railroads.

For the first arrivals on the sodhouse frontier of the Great Plains, life was a grim struggle with danger, adversity, and monotony. If land was relatively cheap, horses, livestock, wagons, wells, fencing, seed, and fertilizer were not. Freight rates and interest rates on loans seemed criminally high. As in the South, indebtedness soon became a chronic condition that led strapped farmers to embrace virtually any plan to inflate the money supply. The virgin land itself, although fertile, resisted planting; the heavy sod broke many a plow and

The Shores family. *Black homesteaders near Westerville, Nebraska, in 1887.*

wearied many a back. Since wood was almost nonexistent on the prairies, pioneer families came to rely on dried dung (buffalo chips) for fuel. Farmers and their families also fought a constant battle with the elements: tornadoes, hailstorms, droughts, prairie fires, blizzards, and pests. Swarms of locusts would cloud the horizon, occasionally covering the ground six inches deep and consuming everything in their path. A Wichita newspaper reported in 1878 that the grasshoppers devoured "everything green, stripping the foliage off the bark and from the tender twigs of the fruit trees, destroying every plant that is good for food or pleasant to the eyes, that man has planted."

The grueling conditions wore down many farmers and their families. But the fight for survival on the Great Plains made men and women more equal partners than their eastern counterparts. Many women who lost their mates to the deadly toil of sodbusting thereafter assumed complete responsibility for their farms. Women on the prairie became more independent than those living domestic lives back east. One woman declared that she insisted on leaving out the phrasing about "obeying" her husband from their marriage vows. "I had served my time of tutelage to my parents as all children are supposed to. I was a woman now and capable of being the other half of the head of the family." Similar examples of feisty femininity abound. Explained one Kansas woman: "The outstanding fact is that the environment was such as to bring out and develop the dominant qualities of individual character. Kansas women of that day learned at an early age to depend on themselves—to do whatever work there was to be done, and to face danger when it must be faced, as calmly as they were able." Their goal, she added, was to carve out a new world, to "develop from wild prairie to comfortable homes."

As the railroads arrived bearing lumber from the wooded regions, farmers could leave their dugouts and homes of "Kansas brick" to build more familiar frame houses. New machinery helped open fresh opportunities for farmers. Back in 1838 John Deere of Illinois had developed the steel-faced plow and moldboard that conquered the clinging humus of the prairie. But its high cost encouraged further experiments, and in 1868 James Oliver of Indiana made a successful chilled-iron plow. With further improvements his "sodbuster" was soon ready for mass production, easing the task of breaking the shallow but tough grass roots of the Plains. Improvements and new inventions in threshing machines, hay mowers, planters, manure spreaders, cream separators, and other devices lightened the burden of labor but added to the capital outlay of the farmer.

In Minnesota, the Dakotas, and central California, the gigantic "bonanza farms" with machinery for mass production became the marvels of the age. On one farm in North Dakota, 13,000 acres of wheat made a single field. "You are in a sea of wheat," a bedazzled visitor wrote in 1880. "The railroad train rolls through an ocean of grain. . . . We encounter a squadron of war chariots . . . doing the work of human hands. . . . There are twenty-five of them in this one brigade of the grand army of 115, under the marshalship of this Dakota farmer." Another bonanza farm employed over a thousand migrant workers to tend 34,000 acres.

The small farmers who diversified their crops fared better at first than the "bonanza" farmers, especially in the eastern Plains. But even they, to make a go of it, had to make concessions to size. To get a start on a family homestead, one historian estimates, required a minimum capital investment of $1,000. And while the overall value of farm lands and farm products increased in the late nineteenth century, the small farmer did not keep up with the march of progress. His numbers grew, but decreased in proportion to the population at large. Wheat, like cotton in the antebellum period, provided the great export crop which evened America's balance of payments and spurred economic growth. But for a variety of reasons few small farmers prospered. Something was amiss, farmers began to reason, and by the decade of the 1890s they were in open revolt against the "system" of corrupt middlemen and avaricious bankers who they believed conspired against them.

"THE FRONTIER HAS GONE"   American life reached an important juncture in the postbellum years. After the 1890 population count, the superintendent of the census noted that he could no longer locate a continuous frontier line beyond which population thinned out to fewer than two per square mile. This fact inspired the historian Frederick Jackson Turner to develop his influential frontier thesis, first outlined in his paper "The Significance of the Frontier in American History," delivered to the American Historical Association in 1893. "The existence of an area of free land," Turner wrote, "its continuous recession, and the advance of American settlement westward, explain American development." The frontier had shaped the national character in fundamental ways. It was

> to the frontier [that] the American intellect owes its striking characteristics. That coarseness and strength combined with acuteness and acquisitiveness; that practical, inventive turn of mind, quick to find expedients; that masterful grasp of material things, lacking in the artistic but powerful to effect great ends; that restless, nervous energy; that dominant individualism, working for good and for evil, and withal that buoyancy and exuberance which comes with freedom—these are traits of the frontier, or traits called out elsewhere because of the existence of the frontier.

Oklahoma Territory, 1889. *The frenzy of activity on "Oklahoma Avenue" suggests Americans' "masterful grasp of material things" and "restless, nervous energy" which the historian Frederick Turner attributed to the frontier experience.*

In 1893 Turner concluded, "four centuries from the discovery of America, at the end of a hundred years under the Constitution, the frontier has gone and with its going has closed the first period of American history."

Turner's "frontier thesis" guided several generations of scholars and students in their understanding of the distinctive characteristics of American history. His view of the frontier as the westward-moving source of America's democratic politics, open society, unfettered economy, and rugged individualism, far removed from the corruptions of urban life, gripped the popular imagination as well. But it left much out of the story. The frontier experience Turner described exaggerated the homogenizing effect of the frontier environment and virtually ignored the role of women, blacks, Indians, Mormons, Hispanics, and Asians in shaping the diverse human geography of the western United States. Turner also implied that the West would be fundamentally different after 1890 because the frontier experience was essentially over. But in many respects that region has retained the qualities associated with the rush for land, gold, timber, and water rights during the post–Civil War decades. The mining frontier, as one historian has recently written, "set a mood that has never disappeared from the West: the attitude of extractive industry—get in, get rich, get out."

FURTHER READING

The concept of the "New South" is explored in Paul M. Gaston's *The New South Creed: A Study in Southern Mythmaking* (1970).° C. Vann Woodward's *Origins of the New South, 1877–1913* (1951)° is also useful, as are the relevant chapters in W. J. Cash's *The Mind of the South* (1941).° For Bourbon politics, see Jack P. Maddex's *The Virginia Conservatives, 1867–1879* (1970) and William J. Cooper's *The Conservative Regime: South Carolina, 1877–1890* (1968).° On the development of southern politics since Reconstruction, see Dewey W. Grantham's *The Life and Death of the Solid South: A Political History* (1988).

A good survey of industrialization in the South is James C. Cobb's *Industrialization and Southern Society, 1877–1984* (1984). Scholarship on the textile industry, which formed the heart of New South aspirations, includes Patrick J. Hearden's *Independence and Empire: The New South's Cotton Mill Campaigns, 1865–1901* (1982), David L. Carlton's *Mill and Town in South Carolina, 1880–1920* (1982),° and Jacqueline D. Hall et al.'s *Like a Family: The Making of a Southern Cotton Mill World* (1987). For developments in the tobacco industry, consult Robert F. Durden's *The Dukes of Durham, 1865–1929* (1975) and Nannie M. Tilley's *The R. J. Reynolds Tobacco Company* (1985). For the iron industry, see Carl V. Harris's *Political Power in Birmingham, 1871–1921* (1977). To see how industrialization affected the Appalachian South, see Ronald D Eller's *Miners, Millhands, and Mountaineers* (1982).°

C. Vann Woodward's *The Strange Career of Jim Crow* (3rd ed., 1974)° remains the standard on southern race relations. Some of Woodward's points are challenged in Howard N. Rabinowitz's *Race Relations in the Urban South, 1865–1890* (1978),° Joel Williamson's *The Crucible of Race* (1984; abridged as *A Rage for Order*, 1986°), and John W. Cell's *The Highest Stage of White Supremacy* (1982).° The attitudes of the two principal black leaders are described in Louis R. Harlan's two-volume biography *Booker T. Washington: The Making of a Black Leader, 1865–1901* (1983)° and Elliott M. Rudwick's *W. E. B. Du Bois: Propagandist of Negro Protest* (1960).° J. Morgan Kousser's *The Shaping of Southern Politics: Suffrage Restriction and Establishment of the One-Party South, 1880–1910* (1974)° handles disenfranchisement.

Several good books discuss developments in southern agriculture. Roger L. Ransom and Richard Sutch's *One Kind of Freedom: The Economic Consequences of Emancipation* (1977)° and Jonathan M. Wiener's *Social Origins of the New South: Alabama, 1860–1885* (1978)° examine the origins of

°These books are available in paperback editions.

sharecropping. Nate Shaw's *All God's Dangers* (1974) tells the story of one sharecropper.

The classic work on the "Great American Desert" is Walter Prescott Webb's *The Great Plains* (1931).° An overview of the transformation of the West is Rodman W. Paul's *The Far West and the Great Plains in Transition, 1859–1908* (1988). Other overviews include Frederick Merk's *History of the Western Movement* (1978) and more specifically Howard R. Lamar's *The Far Southwest, 1846–1912* (1966). The Turner thesis is best presented by Frederick Jackson Turner himself, in *The Frontier in American History* (1920).° A cultural history of the frontier is Henry Nash Smith's *Virgin Land: The American West as Symbol and Myth* (1950).° For a powerful reinterpretation of the frontier and the development of the West, see William Cronon, *Nature's Metropolis: Chicago and the Great West* (1991).

Much recent scholarship examines life among the western cowboys. Terry G. Jordan's *Trails to Texas: Southern Roots of Western Cattle Ranching* (1981) finds cowboy origins along the Atlantic seaboard, David Dary's *Cowboy Culture: A Saga of Five Centuries* (1981) traces the roots further back, and Richard W. Slatta's *Cowboys of the Americas* (1990) covers both North and South American cowboys.

The sodbusters also have their scholars. Gilbert C. Fite's *The Farmer's Frontier, 1865–1900* (1966) and Allan G. Bogue's *From Prairie to Corn Belt* (1963) detail the harsh Great Plains life. The views of important participants are analyzed in Joanna L. Stratton's *Pioneer Women: Voices from the Kansas Frontier* (1981)° and Annette Kolodny's *The Land Before Her* (1984).°

On the western miners, see Rodman W. Paul's *Mining Frontiers of the Far West, 1848–1880* (1963) and Duane A. Smith's *Rocky Mountain Mining Camps* (1967).° On the subject of women on the mining frontier, see Paula Petrik's *No Step Backward: Women and Family on the Rocky Mountain Mining Frontier, 1865–1900* (1987).

The best introduction to the history of the Plains Indians remains Wilcomb E. Washburn's *The Indian in America* (1975).° The Indian conflict with the encroaching white man is explored in Dee Brown's *Bury My Heart at Wounded Knee* (1971)° and two books by Robert M. Utley, *The Last Days of the Sioux Nation* (1963)° and *The Indian Frontier of the American West, 1846–1890* (1984).° See also Francis Paul Prucha's *American Indian Policy in Crisis: Christian Reformers and the Indians* (1976) and Robert F. Berkhofer's *The White Man's Indian: Images of the American Indian from Columbus to the Present* (1978).°

For a sense of the directions in which the "new western history" is heading, see *Under an Open Sky: Rethinking America's Western Past*, edited by William Cronon, George Miles, and Jay Gitlin (1992).

20 ✒

THE RISE OF BIG BUSINESS

THE POSTBELLUM ECONOMY

ECONOMIC EFFECTS OF THE CIVIL WAR   America's rise as an industrial giant in the late nineteenth century is a fact of towering visibility. It has led all too easily to the judgment that demands created by the Civil War powered a "takeoff" in economic growth and that the legislative program of the Republicans at the same time unleashed business, allowing it to guide and continue the process. The Civil War connection seemed to many so obvious as to exclude the need for detailed proof.

But the highly visible successes of wartime profiteers in arms and supplies, of speculators in various markets, and of such nabobs as investment banker Jay Cooke, who got rich selling Treasury bonds, have overshadowed the actual setbacks that marked the wartime economy. One historian's estimates of production for the nineteenth century have cast much doubt on the conventional story. According to these estimates, the decade of the 1860s was the only one in which, on a per-capita basis, output actually *decreased*, North and South, during the mid- to late nineteenth century.

Figures for specific goods tend to show the same effect in these years. The output of copper, railroad track, cotton, and woolen textiles all showed the lag. Most surprising of all, pig iron production, which grew 17 percent from 1855 to 1860 (despite a depression in 1857) and 100 percent from 1865 to 1870, grew only 1 percent during the war years. The Civil War, sometimes called the "first modern war," was in large part unmechanized. Rifles, bayonets, sabers, artillery, and ammunition consumed relatively little iron, and army railroads offset only partially the drop in civilian construction. Production declined largely because of unsettled wartime conditions and the loss of southern markets.

The postwar expansion, which started from a relatively high base and moved the economy to even higher levels, may have been fueled indirectly by the Civil War. Wartime inflation as usual enhanced the position of those owning property and making profits, while entrepreneurs forced to save by the war contributed to the immediate postwar period of speculation. It is not clear, though, that postwar Republican policies contributed uniquely to economic expansion. The National Banking Act created a sounder currency, but its effects on the economy were ambiguous. Government aid in building the great transcontinental and regional railroads simply continued the encouragement to railroads long offered by state and federal government. The postwar climate of favoritism to business was but slightly strengthened by the defeat of southern agrarianism. Postwar tariffs also had ambiguous effects, hampering foreign competitors but discouraging American exports. The emotional lift of victory provided an important, if indirect, spur to the northern economy. After the war Senator John Sherman of Ohio wrote to his brother, the famous general: "The truth is the close of the war with our resources unimpaired gives an elevation, a scope to the ideas of leading capitalists far higher than anything ever undertaken in this country. They talk of millions as confidently as before of thousands."

Within three generations after the Civil War, the nation was transformed from a predominantly rural society dependent upon household production and the rhythms of the seasons into the world's preeminent economic power, a highly structured urban-industrial society based on the imperatives of mass production, mass consumption, and time-clock efficiency. The industrial revolution "controls us all," recognized the Yale sociologist William Graham Sumner, "because we are all in it."

BUILDING THE TRANSCONTINENTAL RAILROADS   Whatever the explanation, the fact remains that between 1869 and 1899 the population nearly trebled, farm production more than doubled, and the value of manufactures grew sixfold (in constant prices). Basic to this economic growth was the expansion of railroads. They were the first big business, the first magnet for the great financial markets, and the first industry to develop a large-scale management bureaucracy. The railroads opened the West, connected raw materials to factories and markets, and in so doing created a national market. At the same time they were themselves gigantic markets for iron, steel, lumber, and other capital goods.

The renewal of railroad building after the Civil War increased the total mileage in roads from 30,600 in 1862 to 53,000 in 1870 and 94,000 by 1880. During the 1880s, the greatest decade of railroad building, mileage leaped to 167,000, and then to 199,000 by 1900. Most of this construction filled out the network east of the Mississippi, but the most spectacular exploits were the monumental transcontinental lines built across the desolate plains and rugged mountains. Running through sparsely settled lands the roads promised little quick return, but they served the national purpose of binding the country together and so received generous government support.

Until 1850 constitutional scruples had constrained federal aid, although many states had subsidized railroads within their borders, but in 1850 Stephen Douglas secured from Congress a grant of public lands to subsidize two north-south roads connecting Chicago and Mobile. Over the next twenty years federal land grants, mainly to transcontinentals, amounted to a net figure of some 129 million acres. In addition to land the railroads received financial aid from federal, state, and local governments. Altogether the roads received about $707 million in cash and $335 million in land.

Before the Civil War, sectional differences over routes held up the start of a transcontinental line. Secession finally permitted passage of the Pacific Railway Bill, which Lincoln signed into law in 1862. The

Workers of the Central Pacific Railroad laying track for the first transcontinental railroad.

act authorized a line along a north-central route, to be built by the Union Pacific Railroad westward from Omaha and the Central Pacific Railroad eastward from Sacramento. As amended in 1864, the act donated to these two corporations twenty sections of land per mile of track, in alternating blocs of railroad and government property, and loans of $16,000 to $48,000 per mile, depending on the difficulty of the terrain.

Both roads began construction during the war, but most of the work was done after 1865 as the companies raced to build most of the line and get most of the subsidy. The Union Pacific pushed across the plains at a rapid pace, avoiding the Rockies by going through Evans Pass in Wyoming. The work crews, with large numbers of ex-soldiers and Irish immigrants as laborers, had to cope with bad roads, water shortages, extreme weather, and Indian marauders. The movable encampments with their retinue of peddlers, gamblers, and prostitutes were aptly dubbed "Hell-on-wheels." Construction was hasty and much of it so flimsy that it had to be redone later, but the Union Pacific pushed on to its celebrated rendezvous with the Central Pacific.

The Central Pacific was organized and dominated by the Sacramento shopkeepers who made an indelible imprint on their state as the California "Big Four": Charles Crocker, Mark Hopkins, Collis P. Huntington, and Leland Stanford, who was elected governor in 1862. The Central Pacific crews were mainly Chinese recently arrived from the region around Canton on the southeast coast. Made destitute by the mid-century economic and political collapse in south

The celebration after the last spike was driven at Promontory, Utah, on May 10, 1869, completing the first transcontinental railroad.

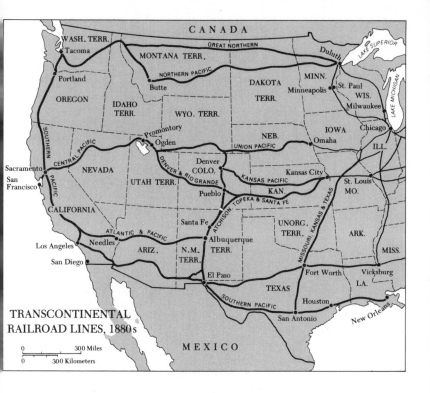

TRANSCONTINENTAL
RAILROAD LINES, 1880s

China, and lured first by the California gold rush and then by rail-road jobs, thousands of Chinese migrated to America, raising their numbers in the United States from 7,500 in 1850 to 105,000 in 1880. Most of these "coolie" laborers were single males intent upon ac-cumulating money and then returning to their homeland, where they could then afford to marry and buy a parcel of land. Their temporary status and dream of a good life back in China apparently made them more willing than American laborers to endure the dangerous work-ing conditions and low pay of railroad work. Many Chinese died on the job.

The grading and hauling were very dangerous, especially in the rugged mountains. Fifty-seven miles east of Sacramento, the con-struction crews encountered the towering Sierras, but they were eventually able to cut through to more level country in Nevada. The Union Pacific had built 1,086 miles to the Central Pacific's 689 when the race ended on the salt plains of Utah at Promontory. There, on May 10, 1869, Leland Stanford drove a gold spike which symbolized the road's completion as the telegraph lines signaled the taps of the hammer to a celebrating nation.

It was twelve years before the next transcontinental was completed, when the Atchison, Topeka and Santa Fe made contact with the Big Four's Southern Pacific at Needles in southern California. The Santa Fe built on to San Diego by 1884. Meanwhile the Southern Pacific, which had absorbed the Central Pacific, built on by way of Yuma to El Paso in 1882, where it made connections to St. Louis and New Orleans. To the north the Northern Pacific had connected Lake Superior with Portland by 1883, and ten years later the Great Northern, which had slowly and carefully been building westward from St. Paul, thrust its way to Tacoma—and without a land grant. Thus before the turn of the century five trunk lines existed, supplemented by connections which afforded other transcontinental routes.

FINANCING THE RAILROADS   The shady financial practices of the railroad men earned them the label of "robber barons," an epithet soon extended to the "captains of industry" as well. The building of both the Union Pacific and Central Pacific induced shameless profiteering through construction companies, controlled by insiders, which overcharged the railroad companies. The Crédit Mobilier Company, according to congressional investigators, bought congressmen like sacks of potatoes and charged the Union Pacific $94 million for construction that cost at most $44 million. The Credit and Finance Corporation, controlled by the California Big Four, did almost as well, taking the Central Pacific for $79 million, of which an estimated $36 million was profit. When the same men began building the Southern Pacific northward and southward, then eastward to El Paso, the Western Development Company looted the new road just as effectively. The vast economic and political power wielded by the California Big Four was lambasted by Frank Norris in *The Octopus*, but the novel could not alter the facts. Each of the Big Four at his death left an estate of $40 million or more.

In the long run, nevertheless, the federal government recovered much if not all of its investment in transcontinentals and accomplished the purpose of linking the country together. The roads increased incalculably the value of the alternate sections of land that remained in government hands, and until 1946 the government shipped freight and military personnel over land-grant roads at half fare.

Eastern lines, like those in the West, were subject to financial buccaneering, which centered first on the Erie Railroad, the favorite prey of manipulators. The prince of the railroad "robber barons" was Jay Gould, a secretive trickster who developed on a grand scale the fine art of buying up run-down railroads, making cosmetic im-

Jay Gould, prince of the railroad buccaneers.

provements, paying dividends out of capital, and selling out at a profit, meanwhile using corporate treasuries for personal speculation and judicious bribes. Ousted by a reform group after having looted the Erie, Gould moved on to richer spoils in western roads and a variety of other corporations, including Western Union. Nearly every enterprise he touched was either compromised or ruined, while Gould was building a fortune that amounted to $100 million upon his death at age fifty-six.

Few railroad fortunes were built in those free-wheeling times by methods of pristine purity, but compared to such as Gould, most railroads were giants of probity. They at least took some interest in the welfare of their companies, if not always in that of the public. Cornelius Vanderbilt, called "Commodore" by virtue of his early exploits in steamboating, stands out among the railroad barons. Already rich before the Civil War, he decided to give up the hazards of wartime shipping and move his capital into land transport. Under his direction the first of the major eastern consolidations took form.

Vanderbilt engineered the consolidation of separate trunk lines connecting Albany and Buffalo into a single powerful rail network led by the New York Central. This accomplished, he forged connections to New York City and then tried to corner the stock of his chief competitor, the Erie. But the directors of the line beat him there by the simple expedient of printing new Erie stock faster than he could buy it. In 1873, however, he bought the Lake Shore and Michigan Southern road, which gave his lines connections into the lucrative

"Commodore" Cornelius
Vanderbilt, who was seventy
years old when he entered the
railroad business, consolidated
control of the vast New York
Central Railroad in the 1860s.

Chicago market. After the Commodore's death in 1877, his son
William Henry extended the Vanderbilt railroads to include more
than 13,000 miles in the Northeast. The consolidation trend was
nationwide: about two-thirds of the nation's railroad mileage fell
under the control of only seven major groups by 1900.

ADVANCES IN MANUFACTURING   The story of manufacturing after the
Civil War shows much the same pattern of expansion and merger
in both old and new industries. The Patent Office, which had recorded only 276 inventions during its first decade of existence, the
1790s, registered 234,956 in the decade of the 1890s. And whether
or not necessity was the mother of invention, invention was the
mother of new industries—and new departures in old ones. New
processes in steelmaking and refining, for instance, were the foundation of the Carnegie and Rockefeller enterprises. The refrigerator car made it possible for the beef, mutton, and pork of the New
West to reach a national market, giving rise to the great packing-
house enterprises of Gustavus V. Swift in Chicago and Philip D.
Armour in Minneapolis. Corrugated rollers to crack the hard spicy
wheat of the Great Plains provided impetus to the flour milling
that centered in Minneapolis under the control of the Pillsburys
and others. Technological improvements in papermaking, which
occurred first in Europe, made it possible to satisfy the appetite of
continuous-action roller presses with cheap paper made from wood
pulps. Glassmaking came to be mechanized. In 1884 tobacco manufacturing moved into a new stage when the Duke interests employed a machine to roll cigarettes.

The list of innovations can be extended indefinitely: barbed wire, farm implements, George Westinghouse's air brake for trains (1868), steam turbines, gas distribution and electrical devices, Christopher Sholes's typewriter (1867), J. W. McGaffey's vacuum cleaner (1869), and countless others. Before the end of the century the internal-combustion engine and the motion picture, each the work of many hands, were laying foundations for new industries of the twentieth century.

These advances in technology altered the lives of ordinary people far more than did activities in the political and intellectual realms. In no field was this more true than in the applications of electricity to communications and power. Few if any inventions of the times could rival the importance of the telephone, which Alexander Graham Bell patented in 1876 and demonstrated at the Philadelphia Centennial Exposition the same year. To promote the new device the inventor and his supporters formed the Bell Telephone Association, out of which grew in 1879 the National Bell Telephone Company.

Almost from the first the Bell interests had to defend their patent against competitors. The most dangerous threat came from Western Union which, after turning down a chance to buy Bell's "toy," employed Thomas Edison to develop an improved version. Edison's telephone became the prototype of the modern instrument, with its separate transmitter and receiver. But Bell had a prior claim on the basic principle and Western Union, rather than risk a legal defeat, sold its rights and properties for a tidy sum, clearing the way for the creation of a monopoly. In 1885 the Bell interests organized the American Telephone and Telegraph Company. By 1899 it was a huge holding company in control of forty-nine licensed subsidiaries and itself an operating company for long-distance lines.

EDISON'S INVENTIONS   In the rise of electrical industries the name of Thomas Alva Edison stands above that of other inventors. He started his career at an early age as a railway news butcher, selling papers and candies on trains, soon learned telegraphy, and began making improvements in that and other areas. In 1876 Edison went full time into the "invention business." He invented the phonograph in 1877, the first successful incandescent light bulb in 1879, and altogether through his invention factories in New Jersey created or perfected hundreds of new devices and processes including the storage battery, dictaphone, mimeograph, dynamo, electric transmission, and the motion picture. In 1882, with the backing of J. P. Morgan, the Edison Electric Illuminating Company began to supply current to eighty-five customers in New York City, beginning the great electric utility industry. A number of companies making light bulbs merged into the Edison General Electric Company in 1888. Financially secure, Edison retired from business to devote himself full time once again to invention.

The use of direct current limited Edison's lighting system to a radius of about two miles. To get more distance required an alternating current, which could be transmitted at high voltage and then stepped down by transformers. George Westinghouse, inventor of the air brake, developed the first alternating-current system in 1886 and manufactured the equipment through the Westinghouse Electric Company. Edison resisted the new method as too risky, but just as Edison's instrument supplanted Bell's first telephone, the Westinghouse system won the "Battle of the Currents," and the Edison companies had to switch over. After the invention of the alternating-current motor by a Croatian immigrant, Westinghouse acquired and improved the motor and worked a revolution by enabling factories to scatter. They no longer had to cluster around waterfalls and coal supplies for their energy.

Edison and Westinghouse were rare examples of inventors with the luck and foresight to get rich from the industries they created. The great captains of industry were more often pure entrepreneurs, men skilled mainly in organizing and promoting industry. Three stand out both for their achievements and for their special contribu-

Thomas Edison in his laboratory.

tions: John D. Rockefeller, for his innovations in organizations; Andrew Carnegie, for his own achievements in organization and for contributions to the philosophical rationale for entrepreneurial activity; and J. Pierpont Morgan, for his development of investment banking.

ENTREPRENEURS

ROCKEFELLER AND THE OIL TRUST   Born in New York State, Rockefeller moved as a youth to Cleveland, where railroad and ship connections provided a strategic location for servicing the oil fields of western Pennsylvania, which were later found to extend into Ohio and West Virginia. Oil had long been known to exist in the region. One branch of the Allegheny River was called Oil Creek, from which farmers skimmed off the stuff to grease their wagon wheels. Medicine men bottled it and claimed it had miraculous curative powers. In the late 1850s Yale's Dr. Benjamin Silliman, Jr., at the behest of a local promoter, found that the oil could be refined into a good illuminant (kerosene) which served also for heating and cooking. The promoter, George Henry Bissell, set a friend to drilling on his lease near Titusville, Pennsylvania, where in 1859 the first well was struck, producing oil at a rate of twenty-five barrels a day. This proved the start of a great industry, based at first mainly on the sale of kerosene.

In economic importance the Pennsylvania oil rush of the 1860s far outweighed the California gold rush of just ten years before. If it duplicated many of the earlier scenes of disorder, it ended by yielding more wealth. Well before the end of the Civil War derricks checkered the area and refineries sprang up in Pittsburgh and Cleveland. Of the two cities, Cleveland had the edge in transportation, and John D. Rockefeller made the most of it. He started as a bookkeeper, but before age twenty-one was already a partner in a wholesale house. While other young men were going off to war, Rockefeller moved into the oil business. In 1860, sent out by business friends to look over the Pennsylvania fields, he advised against the risks of sinking wells, but saw that refining promised great profits at little risk. In 1862 he backed a refinery started by his friend Samuel Andrews. He then formed a partnership with Andrews, and in 1867 added H. M. Flagler to create the firm of Rockefeller, Flagler, and Andrews. In 1870 Rockefeller incorporated his various interests as the Standard Oil Company of Ohio, capitalized at $1 million.

Rockefeller was already the largest refiner, but as he put it, "the butcher, the baker, and the candlestick maker began to refine oil."

Drums of oil leaving Rouseville, Pennsylvania, by train. Rouseville was one of the centers of the Pennsylvania oil rush.

As a result, "the price went down and down until the trade was ruined." Rockefeller resolved to bring order out of chaos, which is to say he decided to weed out the competition, and he soon fastened upon an ingenious plan. In 1872 Rockefeller acquired the South Improvement Company, which he made the marketing agent for a large percentage of his oil shipments. By controlling this traffic, he gained clout with the railroads, which gave him large rebates (secret discounts) on the standard freight rates in order to keep his business. In some cases he forced them to provide information on competitors' shipments. Rockefeller then approached his Cleveland competitors and offered to buy them out at his own price. Most of them saw the wisdom of this course. As Rockefeller put it, "the conditions were so chaotic [that is, competitive] that most of the refiners were very desirous to get out of the business." By 1879 Standard Oil had come to control 90–95 percent of the oil refining in the country.

Much of Rockefeller's success was based on his determination to "pay nobody a profit." Instead of depending on the products or services of other firms, Standard undertook to make its own barrels, cans, staves, and whatever else it needed. In economic terms this is called *vertical integration*. The company also kept large amounts of cash reserves to make it independent of banks in case of a crisis. In line with this policy, Rockefeller set out also to control his transportation needs. With Standard owning most of the pipelines leading to railroads, plus the tank cars and the oil-storage facilities, it was able to dissuade the railroads from servicing eastern competitors. Those competitors who insisted on holding out then faced a giant marketing organization capable of driving them to the wall with price wars.

Eventually, in order to consolidate scattered business interests under a more efficient control, Rockefeller and his friends resorted to a new legal device: the trust. Long established in law to enable one or more people to manage property belonging to others, such as children or the mentally incompetent, the trust now was used for another purpose—centralized control of business. Since Standard Oil of Ohio was not permitted to hold property out of state, it began in 1872 to place properties or companies acquired elsewhere in trust, usually with the company secretary. This became impractical, however, since the death of the trustee would endanger the trust. To solve this problem, in 1882 all thirty-seven stockholders in various Standard Oil enterprises conveyed their stock to nine trustees, receiving "trust certificates" in return. The nine trustees were thus empowered to give central direction to all the Standard companies.

The original plan, never fully carried out, was to organize a Standard Oil Company in each state in which the trust did business. But the trust device, widely copied in the 1880s, proved legally vulnerable to prosecution under state laws against monopoly or restraint of

John D. Rockefeller, whose Standard Oil Company dominated the oil business.

trade. In 1892 the supreme court of Ohio ordered the Standard Oil Trust dissolved. For a while the company managed to unify control by the simple device of interlocking directorates, through which the board of directors of one company was made identical or nearly so to the boards of the others. Gradually, however, Rockefeller took to the idea of the holding company: a company which controlled other companies by holding all or at least a majority of their stock. In 1899 Rockefeller brought his empire under the direction of the Standard Oil Company of New Jersey, a holding company. Though less vulnerable to prosecution under state law, some holding companies proved vulnerable to the Sherman Anti-Trust Act of 1890. (This story will be told later, in Chapter 22.) Meanwhile the term "trust" had become so fixed in the public mind that it was used to describe large combinations under holding companies as well.

CARNEGIE'S GOSPEL OF WEALTH   Andrew Carnegie, like Rockefeller, experienced the untypical rise from poverty to riches that came to be known in those days as "the typical American success story." Born in Scotland, son of a hand weaver who fell upon hard times, he migrated in 1848 with his family to Allegheny, Pennsylvania. Then thirteen, he started out as a bobbin boy in a textile mill at wages of $1.20 per week. At fourteen he was earning $2.50 per week as a telegraph messenger and used his spare time learning to read messages by ear. Soon he was promoted to telegrapher and in 1853 became personal secretary and telegrapher to Thomas Scott, then district superintendent of the Pennsylvania Railroad and later its president. When Scott moved up, Carnegie took his place as superin-

Andrew Carnegie, apostle of "The Gospel of Wealth."

tendent. During the Civil War, when Scott became assistant secretary of war in charge of transportation, Carnegie went with him, developed a military telegraph system, and personally helped evacuate the wounded from Bull Run.

Carnegie kept on moving—from telegraphy to railroading to bridge building and then to iron- and steelmaking and investments. In 1865 Carnegie quit the railroad to devote full time to his own interests. These were mainly in iron and bridge building, but the versatile entrepreneur also made money in oil and sold railroad bonds in Europe. In 1872 he netted $150,000 on one trip, and on that trip met Sir Henry Bessemer, inventor of a new process of steelmaking. The next year Carnegie resolved to concentrate on steel, or as he put it, to put all his eggs in one basket and then watch that basket. He began first the J. Edgar Thompson Steel Works, which he shrewdly named after the head of the Pennsylvania Railroad. As competitors arose, Carnegie picked them off one by one. In 1882 when the Pittsburgh Bessemer Steel Company ran into labor troubles and slackening demand, Carnegie bought out their almost-new Homestead works approximately at cost. When the Duquesne Bessemer Steel Company ran afoul of a smear campaign describing their rails as unsafe, Carnegie bought them out at less than cost. By 1900 Carnegie Steel was paying dividends of $40 million.

Carnegie was never a technical expert on steel. He was a promoter, salesman, and organizer with a gift for finding and using men of expert ability. He always insisted on up-to-date machinery and equipment, and shrewdly used times of recession to expand more cheaply.

In much of this Carnegie was a typical businessman of the time, if abler and luckier than most. But he stands out from the lot especially as a thinker who fashioned and publicized a philosophy for big business, a conservative rationale that became deeply implanted in the conventional wisdom of Americans. Carnegie argued that however harsh their methods at times, captains of industry were on the whole public benefactors. At thirty-three he confided to his diary an ambition to retire early and devote his time to self-improvement, to being a "distributor" of wealth (he disliked the word "philanthropy"), and perhaps to public service. He did finally achieve that goal, but not until age sixty-five. Meanwhile, however, he found time to write magazine articles and to produce a modest shelf of books.

Carnegie's best-remembered piece was an essay, "The Gospel of Wealth," published in 1889. In this basic statement of his philosophy he drew upon the ideas of Charles Darwin and especially Darwin's English interpreter Herbert Spencer, who had invented the phrase "survival of the fittest." In the evolution of society, Carnegie argued, the contrast between the millionaire and the laborer measures the distance society has come. "Not evil, but good, has come to the race from the accumulation of wealth by those who have the ability and energy that produces it." The process had been costly in many ways, but the law of competition was "best for the trade, because it insures the survival of the fittest in every department."

Carnegie then delivered a sermon on the proper uses of wealth. Carnegie professed no religious faith, but surely had absorbed from his Presbyterian origins the Christian doctrine of stewardship. A rich man could leave his fortune to his children, Carnegie said, but experience suggested that this was not always wise or even kind. He might leave it at his death for public uses, but in his absence it would likely be misused. The best way to dispense a fortune was to administer it during one's lifetime for the public good. One should first set an example of humble living—in Carnegie's case this included ownership of Skibo Castle in Scotland—and provide for one's dependents, then consider the rest a trust fund for the public good. One should avoid alms-giving, for the pauper is a "social leper." Instead the wealthy should provide means for people to improve themselves by supporting universities, libraries, hospitals, parks, halls for meetings and concerts, swimming pools, and church buildings—in that order. To his credit, Carnegie meant it, devoting his wealth to many such benefactions and to the cause of world peace. Rockefeller, too, gave many gifts, mainly to education and medicine, but partly at least because he was persuaded it would make for good public relations.

Carnegie's gospel of wealth found widespread acceptance in the late nineteenth century's worship of success, an attitude of respect for the self-made man that owed perhaps more to the *Autobiography* of Benjamin Franklin and the sayings of Franklin's Poor Richard than to Charles Darwin and his interpreters. The popularity of such attitudes was shown by the market for inspirational literature touting the ancient verities of thrift, integrity, and hard work. Among the sages of that school none was better known than Horatio Alger, whose very name became a byword for success. A Unitarian minister in New York, he wrote novels for boys, mostly about poor boys who made good, with titles like *Ragged Dick* (1867), *Luck and Pluck* (1869), and *Tattered Tom* (1871). More often than not, however, Horatio Alger heroes made it, like Carnegie, by winning the favor of some well-placed man.

Popular biographies of self-made men such as Franklin, Lincoln, and Grant became the nonfiction counterparts to Alger's novels. On the lecture circuit the star was a Baptist minister who delivered his lecture, "Acres of Diamonds," more than 6,000 times. The message was that opportunity, acres of diamonds, was at everybody's door-step. "I say, get rich, get rich." It was a social and Christian duty.

J. P. MORGAN, THE FINANCIER   J. Pierpont Morgan, who was born to wealth and increased it enormously, was about as far from being a Horatio Alger hero as one could get. His father was a partner in a London banking house, which he later came to direct. Young Pierpont attended boarding school in Switzerland and university in Germany. After a brief apprenticeship, he was sent in 1857 to work in a New York firm which represented his father's London firm, and in 1860 set himself up as its New York agent under the name of J. Pierpont Morgan and Company. This firm, under various names, channeled much European capital into the country and grew into a financial power in its own right.

Morgan was an investment banker, which meant that he was engaged in a marketing operation. He would buy corporate shares and bonds wholesale and then sell them at a profit, much as other merchants would market, say, hardware, but on a larger scale. The growth of large corporations put Morgan's and other investment firms in an increasingly strategic position in the economy. The financial world began to take notice in 1869 when Morgan actually beat the wily entrepreneurial buccaneers Jay Gould and Jim Fisk in a fight to control a New York railroad.

Morgan early realized that railroads were the key to the times, and he acquired and reorganized one line after another. Since the

J. Pierpont Morgan. *This is the famous portrait by the photographer Edward Steichen, done in 1903.*

*A lavish dinner celebrated the merger of the Carnegie and Morgan
interests into U.S. Steel in 1901. These executives are seated at a table
shaped like a huge rail.*

investment business depended on the general good health of client
companies, investment bankers became involved in the operation of
their clients' firms, demanding places on boards of directors and
helping to shape their fiscal dealings. By these means bankers could
influence company policies, which, technicians often argued, resulted in heavy emphasis on fiscal matters to the detriment of technical innovation. Eventually people were speaking of the "money
trust," the greatest trust of all, with its hand in all kinds of other
enterprises.

To Morgan, however, the stability brought by his operations was
plain common sense. The railroad people and other businessmen, if
unrestrained, would act like anarchists. Morgan, one historian
wrote, "felt that the American economy should ideally be like a
company organizational chart, with each part in its proper place, and
the lines of authority clearly designated. He did not really believe in
the free-enterprise system, and like the most ardent socialists, he
hated the waste, duplication, and clutter of unrestrained competition."

Morgan's crowning triumph was consolidation of the steel industry, to which he was led by his interests in railroading. After a rapid
series of mergers in the iron and steel industry, Morgan bought out
Carnegie's huge steel and iron holdings in 1901. Carnegie set his own
price, which came to nearly $500 million, of which his personal share
was nearly $300 million. In rapid succession Morgan added other
steel interests and the Rockefeller holdings in both Minnesota's

Mesabi ore range and a Great Lakes ore fleet. The magnitude of such a fortune was enhanced by the absence of an income tax, a burden Americans would not face until 1914.

Altogether the new United States Steel Corporation, a holding company for these varied interests, was capitalized at $1.4 billion, a total that was heavily watered (valued well above the company's actual assets) but was soon made solid by large profits. The new giant was a marvel of the new century, the first billion-dollar corporation, the climactic event in that age of consolidation. By 1904 there were some 318 industrial trusts capitalized at over $7 billion.

Advances for Labor

THE DISTRIBUTION OF WEALTH   Accompanying the spread of such industrial combinations was a rising standard of living for most people. If the rich were still getting richer, a lot of other people were at least better off, and the pre–Civil War trend toward even higher concentrations of wealth slacked off. This, of course, is far from saying that disparities in the distribution of wealth had disappeared. One set of estimates reveals that in both 1860 and 1900 the richest 2 percent of American families owned more than a third of the nation's physical wealth, while the top 10 percent owned almost three-fourths, and all the nation's physical assets were in the hands of half its families. Studies of social mobility in towns across the country show, moreover, that while the rise from rags to riches was rare, "upward mobility both from blue-collar to white-collar callings and from low-ranked to high-ranked manual jobs was quite common."

The continuing demand for unskilled or semi-skilled workers meanwhile was filled by new groups entering the work force at the bottom: immigrants above all, but also growing numbers of women and children. Because of a long-term decline in prices and the cost of living, real wages and earnings in manufacturing went up about 50 percent between 1860 and 1890, and another 37 percent from 1890 to 1914. By latter-day standards, however, working conditions then were dreary indeed. At the turn of the century the average hourly wage in manufacturing was 21.6¢, and average annual earnings were $490. The average workweek was fifty-nine hours, or nearly six ten-hour days, but that was only an average. Most steelworkers put in a twelve-hour day, and as late as the 1920s a great many worked a seven-day or eighty-four-hour week.

A NEW SOCIAL WORLD   Rising wages in no way discount the high social costs of industrialization. In the crowded tenements that grew up in major cities the death rates ran substantially higher than in the countryside. Factories often maintained poor health and safety conditions. In 1913, for instance, there were some 25,000 factory fatalities and some 700,000 job-related injuries that required at least four weeks' disability. In this new bureaucratic world ever-larger numbers of people were dependent on the machinery and factories of owners whom they seldom if ever saw. In the simpler world of small shops, workers and employers could enter into close personal relationships; the larger corporation, on the other hand, was likely governed by a bureaucracy in which ownership was separate from management.

The coming of the railroads was basic to this development. The roads, the business historian Alfred Chandler wrote, "caused entrepreneurs to integrate and subdivide their business activities and to hire salaried managers to monitor and coordinate the flow of goods through their enlarged enterprises." What Chandler called the "visible hand" of management increasingly replaced the "invisible hand" which in Adam Smith's theory guided the marketplace through multitudes of individual decisions. As an old formulation had it, the corporation "has no soul to be damned and no body to be kicked." Much of the social history of the modern world in fact turns on the transition from a world of personal relationships to one of impersonal and contractual relationships.

The Illinois Central Railroad Station, Chicago, 1890. *The railroads were instrumental in transforming the social world in which Americans lived and worked.*

DISORGANIZED PROTEST   Under these circumstances it was far more difficult for workers to organize for mutual benefit than for a few captains of industry to organize for profit. Civic leaders respected property rights more than the rights of labor. Many businessmen held to the viewpoint that a "labor supply" was simply another commodity to be procured at the lowest possible price.

Among workers recently removed from an agrarian world the idea of durable unions was slow to take hold. Immigrant workers came from many cultures. They spoke many tongues and harbored ethnic animosities. Many if not most saw their jobs as transient, the first rung on the ladder to success. They hoped to move on to a homestead, or to return with their earnings to the old farms of their European homelands. With or without unions, though, workers often staged impromptu strikes in response to wage cuts and other grievances. But impromptu action often led to violence, and three violent incidents of the 1870s colored much of the public's view of labor unions thereafter.

The decade's early years saw a reign of terror in the eastern Pennsylvania coal fields, attributed to an Irish group called the Molly Maguires. Taking their name from an Irish patriot who had directed violent resistance against the British, the group aimed to right perceived wrongs against Irish workers by such methods as intimidation, beatings, and killings. Their actions excited high emotions which were reflected in later chronicles depicting them as either heroic defenders of the workingman in a genuine class war, or early practitioners of labor racketeering. The terrorism reached its peak in 1874–1875, and mine owners hired Pinkerton detectives to stop the movement. One of the agents who infiltrated the Mollies produced enough evidence to indict the leaders. At trials in 1876 twenty-four of the Molly Maguires were convicted; ten were hanged. The trials also resulted in a wage reduction in the mines and the final destruction of the Miners' National Association, a weak union the Mollies dominated. Later investigations have shown that agents of the mine operators themselves stirred up some of the trouble.

THE RAILROAD STRIKE OF 1877   Far more significant, because more widespread, was the Great Railroad Strike of 1877, the first major interstate strike. Wage cuts caused the Great Strike. After the Panic of 1873 and the ensuing depression, the major rail lines in the East had cut wages. In 1877 they made another 10 percent cut, which provoked most of the railroad workers at Martinsburg, West Virginia, to walk off the job and block the tracks. Without organized direction, however, their picketing degenerated into a mob that burned and plundered railroad property.

The Devastation Wrought by the Railroad Strike of 1877. *Railroad workers in Pittsburgh reacted violently to wage cuts.*

Walkouts and sympathy demonstrations spread spontaneously in the July heat from Cumberland, Maryland, to Chicago and San Francisco. The strike engulfed hundreds of cities and towns from New York to California, leaving in its wake over a hundred people killed and millions of dollars in property destroyed. Federal troops were mobilized to quell the violence. The greatest outbreak began at Pittsburgh on July 19, when the Pennsylvania Railroad put on "double-headers" (long trains pulled by two locomotives) in order to reduce crews. Public sympathy for the strikers was so great at first that local militiamen, called out to suppress them, instead joined the workers. Militiamen from Philadelphia managed to disperse one crowd at the cost of twenty-six lives, but then found themselves besieged in the railroad's roundhouse, where they disbanded and shot their way out.

Looting, rioting, and burning went on for another day until the frenzy wore itself out. A reporter described the scene as "the most horrible ever witnessed, except in the carnage of war. There were fifty miles of hot rails, ten tracks side by side, with as many miles of ties turned into glowing coals and tons on tons of iron car skeletons and wheels almost at white heat." Public opinion, sympathetic at first, tended to blame the workers for the looting and violence. Eventually the strikers, lacking organized bargaining power, had no choice but to drift back to work. Everywhere the strikes failed.

For many people, the strike raised the specter of a worker-based social revolution like the Paris Commune of 1871, in which disgruntled mobs chanted "Bread or Blood." As a Pittsburgh newspaper warned, "This may be the beginning of a great civil war in this country between labor and capital." Equally disturbing to those in positions of corporate and political power was the presence of many women among the protesters. A Baltimore journalist noted that the "singular part of the disturbances is the very active part taken by the women, who are the wives and mothers of the [railroad] firemen." From the point of view of organized labor, however, the Great Railroad Strike demonstrated potential strength and the need for tighter organization. As the labor leader Samuel Gompers later recalled, "The railroad strike of 1877, was the tocsin that sounded a ringing message of hope for us all."

THE "SAND LOT" INCIDENT In California the railroad strike indirectly gave rise to a political movement. At San Francisco's "Sand Lot" a meeting to express sympathy for the strikers ended with attacks on some passing Chinese. Within a few days sporadic anti-Chinese riots led to a mob attack on Chinatown. Depression had hit the West Coast especially hard, and the Chinese were a handy scapegoat for frustrations of the time.

Soon an Irish immigrant, Dennis Kearney, organized the "Workingmen's Party of California" mainly on a platform calling for the end of further Chinese immigration. A gifted agitator, himself only recently naturalized, he harangued the "sand lotters" about the "foreign peril" and assaulted the rich for exploiting the poor—sometimes at gatherings beside their mansions on Nob Hill. In 1878 his new party won a good number of seats in a state constitutional convention, but managed to incorporate in the state's basic law little more than ineffective attempts to regulate the railroads. The workingmen's movement peaked in 1879 when it elected many members of the new legislature and the mayor of San Francisco. Kearney lacked the gift for building a durable movement, but as his party went to pieces his anti-Chinese theme became a national issue, and in 1882 Congress voted to prohibit Chinese immigration for ten years.

TOWARD PERMANENT UNIONS Meanwhile efforts to build a permanent union movement had begun to bear fruit. Earlier efforts, in the

1830s and 1840s, had largely been dominated by reformers with schemes that ranged from free homesteads to utopian socialism. But the 1850s had seen the beginning of "job-conscious" unions in certain skilled trades. By 1860 there were about twenty such craft unions, and during the Civil War, because of the demand for labor, such unions grew in strength and numbers.

Until after the war, however, there was no overall federation of these groups. In August 1866 some seventy-seven delegates organized the National Labor Union at a convention in Baltimore and chose as their leader the head of the Iron Molders. Essentially the NLU comprised congresses of delegates from labor and reform groups more interested in political and social reform than in bargaining with employers. The groups espoused such ideas as the eight-hour day, workers' cooperatives, greenbackism, and equal rights for women and blacks. After the head of the union died suddenly, its support fell away quickly. The National Labor Union cannot be labeled a total failure, however. It was influential in persuading Congress to enact an eight-hour day for federal employees and to repeal the Contract Labor Law, which had been passed during the Civil War to encourage the importation of labor. The union, moreover, undertook to encourage the organization of black workers, but with little success.

THE KNIGHTS OF LABOR   Before the National Labor Union collapsed, another group of national standing was emerging: the Noble and Holy Order of the Knights of Labor. The name betokened a tendency to copy the forms of fraternal orders and to evoke the aura of medieval guilds. The founder of the Knights of Labor, Uriah S. Stephens, a Philadelphia tailor, was a habitual "joiner" involved with several secret orders, including the Masons. His early training for the Baptist ministry also affected his outlook. Secrecy, he felt, along with a semi-religious ritual, would protect members against retaliation and at the same time create a sense of solidarity.

In 1869, with Stephens as leader, nine Philadelphia tailors founded the order. At first it grew slowly, but in 1873 formed its first district assembly in the Philadelphia area. During the years of depression, as other unions collapsed, it spread more rapidly and in 1878 its first General Assembly established a national organization. Its preamble and platform endorsed the reforms advanced by previous workingmen's groups, including producers' and consumers' cooperatives, homesteads, bureaus of labor statistics, mechanics' lien laws (to ensure payment of salaries), elimination of convict-labor competition, the eight-hour day, and greenbacks. One plank in the platform, far ahead of the times, called for equal pay for equal work by both sexes.

Throughout its existence the Knights emphasized reform measures and preferred boycotts to strikes as a way to put pressure on employers. The constitution of the order allowed as members all who had ever worked for wages except lawyers, doctors, bankers, and those who sold liquor. Theoretically it was one big union of all workers regardless of race, color, creed, or sex, skilled and unskilled. Each local assembly was to be formed on such a basis, but in practice some local and district assemblies were organized on a craft basis, such as the telegraphers and cigarmakers. Above these stood the General Assembly, a General Executive Board, and at the head of the organization a Grand Master Workman.

Stephens was the first elected to this office, but in 1879 he gave way to Terence V. Powderly, the thirty-year-old mayor of Scranton, Pennsylvania. Born of Irish immigrant parents, Powderly had become a switchtender at sixteen but soon moved into the machine shop. In many ways he was unsuited to the new job. At once mayor, head of the Knights, county health officer, and part owner and manager of a grocery store, he had too many irons in the fire. He was physically frail, sensitive to criticism, and indecisive at critical moments. He was temperamentally opposed to strikes, and when they did occur, did not always back up the local groups involved. Yet the Knights owed their greatest growth to strikes that occurred under his leadership.

In the mid-1880s the union had a meteoric rise. In 1884 a successful strike against wage cuts in the Union Pacific shops at Denver led many railroad workers to form new assemblies. Then, in 1885, the

Terence V. Powderly in 1885. Powderly led the Knights of Labor at the height of the union's power.

Knights scored a startling victory over Jay Gould. Late the previous year and early in 1885 Gould had cut wages on the Missouri, Kansas, and Texas and Wabash roads. A spontaneous strike on these lines in February 1885 spread to Gould's Missouri-Pacific, and as organizers from the Knights of Labor moved in, Gould restored the wage cuts. In June another strike on the Wabash against the firing of union members brought another victory. These successes allowed the Knights to grow rapidly from about 100,000 members to more than 700,000 in 1886, a memorable year in the history of organized labor for several reasons.

One was that the Knights peaked and then went into rapid decline. Jay Gould, taken by surprise in 1885, set a trap for the Knights in 1886. He spoke favorably of unions and expressed his wish that all railroad workers were organized, but in February 1886 he provoked another strike by firing a foreman in the Texas-Pacific shops. When the Knights struck, Gould refused arbitration and hired Pinkerton agents to harass strikers and keep the trains running. On May 4 the Knights had to call off the strike. The organization was further damaged by an incident in Chicago's Haymarket Square that very night, with which the Knights had little to do but which provoked widespread revulsion against labor groups in general.

THE HAYMARKET AFFAIR   The Haymarket Affair grew indirectly out of agitation for the eight-hour day. This issue had first been championed by a little-known organization with an unwieldy name: the Federation of Organized Trades and Labor Unions of the United States and Canada, forerunner to the American Federation of Labor. In 1884 this group had set May 1, 1886, as the deadline for the eight-hour day in all trades. Powderly declined to join the federation in a call for strikes on that day, but some assemblies of the Knights did. Chicago became the center of the movement, and on May 3 the International Harvester plant became the site of an unfortunate clash between strikers and policemen in which one striker was killed.

Leaders of a minuscule anarchist movement in Chicago scheduled an open meeting the following night at Haymarket Square to protest the killing. After listening under a light drizzle to lengthy speeches promoting socialism and anarchism, the crowd was beginning to break up when a group of policemen arrived and called upon the meeting to disperse. At that point somebody threw a bomb at the police, killing one and wounding others. The police then fired into the crowd. In a trial marked by prejudice and hysteria, seven anarchist leaders were sentenced to death despite the lack of any evidence linking them to the bomb-thrower, whose identity was never

Attention Workingmen!

━━━━ GREAT ━━━━

MASS-MEETING

TO-NIGHT, at 7.30 o'clock,

━━━ AT THE ━━━

HAYMARKET, Randolph St., Bet. Desplaines and Halsted.

Good Speakers will be present to denounce the latest
atrocious act of the police, the shooting of our
fellow-workmen yesterday afternoon.

THE EXECUTIVE COMMITTEE.

Achtung, Arbeiter!

Große ⚑

Maſſen-Verſammlung

Heute Abend,½8 Uhr, auf dem

Heumarkt, Randolph-Straße, zwiſchen
Desplaines- u. Halſted-Str.

☞ Gute Redner werden den neueſten Schurkenſtreich der Polizei,
indem ſie geſtern Nachmittag unſere Brüder erſchoß, geißeln.

Das Exekutiv-Comite.

A handbill announcing (in English and German) the protest meeting to be held at Haymarket Square on the night of May 4, 1886.

established. Of these, two were reprieved and some years later pardoned, one committed suicide in prison, but four were hanged. All but one of the group were German-speaking, but that one held a membership card in the Knights of Labor.

Despite his best efforts, Powderly could never dissociate in the public mind the Knights from the anarchists. He clung to leadership until 1893, but after that the union evaporated and by the turn of the century it was but a memory. A number of problems accounted for the Knights' decline other than widespread fantasies of radicalism: a leadership devoted more to reform than to the nuts and bolts of organization, the failure of the Knights' cooperative enterprises, and a preoccupation with politics which led the Knights to sponsor labor candidates in hundreds of local elections. They won a surprising number of races in 1886, but their political efforts proved in the end to be a flash in the pan.

The Knights nevertheless attained some lasting achievements, among them the creation of the federal Bureau of Labor Statistics in 1884 as well as several state bureaus; the Foran Act of 1885 which, though weakly enforced, penalized employers who imported contract labor (an arrangement similar to the indentured servitude of colonial times in which workers were committed to a term of labor in exchange for transportation to America); and a national law enacted in 1880 for the arbitration of labor disputes. The Knights by example also spread the idea of unionism and initiated a new type of union organization: the industrial union, an industrywide union of the skilled and unskilled, begun in special assemblies of railway and telegraph workers. Industrial unions would have the power to match that of the organized concentrations of capital, but not for some time.

The craft unions opposed such industrial unionism. They organized workers who shared special skills, such as typographers or cigarmakers. In 1881 the Federation of Organized Trades and Labor Unions came into being as a group similar to the old National Labor Union; it was primarily an association of national craft unions but with representation of state and local assemblies as well. The craft unions were at first inclined to cooperate with the Knights, but the two groups were organized on different principles. Leaders of the crafts feared that joining with the unskilled would mean a loss of their separate craft identities and a loss of the bargaining power held by skilled workers.

GOMPERS AND THE AFL   As it turned out, however, the main threat to the Federation came from another direction when the Knights themselves organized a few special assemblies along craft lines. An effort by the Knights to organize a separate union in the New York cigar trade led the Cigarmakers International Union to call for stronger unity among the existing craft unions. In May 1886 delegates from twenty craft unions met in Philadelphia and called on the Knights to cease organizing in trades for which a national union already existed. When the Knights failed to heed the suggestion, a second conference met at Columbus, Ohio, and organized the American Federation of Labor (AFL). In structure it differed from the Knights in that it was a federation of national organizations, each of which retained a large degree of autonomy.

Samuel Gompers served as president of the AFL from its start until his death in 1924, with only one year's interruption. Born in London of Dutch-Jewish ancestry, Gompers came to the United States as a teenager, joined the Cigarmakers Union in 1864, and became president of his New York local in 1877. This background was significant. The Cigarmakers were the intellectuals of the labor movement; to relieve the tedium of their task, they hired young men to read aloud as they worked, and debated such weighty topics as socialism and Darwinism. But Gompers and other leaders of the union focused on concrete economic gains, avoiding involvement with utopian ideas or politics. "At no time in my life," Gompers once said, "have I ever worked out a definitely articulated economic theory." The head of the Cigarmakers put it more strongly: "We have no ultimate ends," he told a Senate hearing. "We are going on from day to day. We are fighting only for immediate objects—objects that can be realized in a few years."

Such job consciousness became the policy of the AFL under Gom-

*Samuel Gompers, head of the
American Federation of Labor.*

pers, whose lifetime concern was the effectiveness of the federation. He hired organizers to spread unionism, and worked as a diplomat to prevent overlapping unions and to settle jurisdictional disputes. The federation represented workers in matters of national legislation and acted as a sounding board for their cause. On occasion it exercised its power to request from members dues for the support of strikes. Gompers, it turned out, was temperamentally more fitted than Powderly for the rough-and-tumble world of unionism. He had a thick hide, liked to talk and drink with workers in the back room, and did not shy off from using the strike to achieve labor's objectives by trade agreements, including provisos for union recognition in the form of closed shops (which could hire only union members) or union-preference shops (which could hire others only if no union members were available).

One great objective which Gompers achieved at least in principle was making the eight-hour day standard. In 1889 the AFL voted to revive its May Day demonstrations for the eight-hour day, abandoned after the Haymarket Affair. But within a few years the demonstrations underwent a curious change. In July 1889 the founding congress of the Socialist International in Paris voted to sponsor demonstrations for the eight-hour day worldwide. Later, these evolved into demonstrations for general worker demands, labor solidarity, and socialism. Still later, Communists took up the May Day celebrations and paraded their armor through Moscow to observe a holiday which, its origins forgotten, began with an American demand for the eight-hour day.

The AFL at first grew slowly, but by 1890 it had surpassed the Knights of Labor in membership. By the turn of the century it claimed 500,000 members in affiliated unions; in 1914, on the eve of World War I, it had 2 million and in 1920 reached a peak of 4 million.

But even then it embraced less than 15 percent of the nonagricultural workers, and all unions, including the unaffiliated railroad brotherhoods, accounted for little more than 18 percent of these workers. Organized labor's strongholds were in transportation and the building trades. Most of the larger manufacturing industries, including steel, textiles, tobacco, and packinghouses, remained almost untouched. Gompers never frowned on industrial unions, and several became important affiliates of the AFL: the United Mine Workers, the International Ladies' Garment Workers, and the Amalgamated Clothing Workers. But the AFL had its greatest success in organizing skilled workers.

THE HOMESTEAD STRIKE   Two violent incidents in the 1890s nipped the emerging industrial union movement and set it back for forty years to come—the Homestead Steel Strike of 1892 and the Pullman Strike of 1894. The Amalgamated Association of Iron and Steel Workers, founded in 1876, had by 1891 a membership of more than 24,000 and was probably the largest craft union at that time. But it excluded the unskilled and had failed to organize the larger steel plants. The Homestead Works at Pittsburgh was an important exception. There the union had enjoyed friendly relations with the Carnegie company until H. C. Frick became its president in 1889. A showdown was delayed, however, until 1892 when the union contract came up for renewal. Andrew Carnegie, who had expressed sympathy for unions in the past, had gone to Scotland and left matters in the hands of Frick. Carnegie, however, knew what was afoot: a cost-cutting reduction in the number of workers through the use of labor-saving devices, and a deliberate attempt to smash the union.

As negotiations dragged on, the company announced it would treat workers as individuals unless an agreement was reached by June 29. A strike, or more properly a lockout of unionists, began on that date. Even before the negotiations ended, Frick had hired as plant guards 300 Pinkerton detectives whose specialty was union-busting. But on the morning of July 6, 1892, when the Pinkertons came up the Monongahela River on barges, unionists were waiting behind breastworks on shore. Who fired the first shot remains unknown, but a battle broke out in which six workers and three Pinkertons died. In the end the Pinkertons surrendered and were marched away, subjected to taunts from crowds in the street. Six days later the state militia appeared at the plant. The strike dragged on until November, but by then the union was dead at Homestead. Its cause was not helped when on July 23 an anarchist shot and wounded Frick.

THE PULLMAN STRIKE   The Pullman Strike of 1894 involved a dispute at the "model" town of Pullman, Illinois, which housed workers of the Pullman Palace Car Company. The town's idyllic appearance was deceptive. Employees were required to live there, pay rents and utility costs higher than in nearby towns, and buy goods from company stores. During the depression of 1893 George Pullman laid off 3,000 of 5,800 employees, and cut wages 25–40 percent, but not his rents and other charges. When Pullman fired three members of a grievance committee, a strike began on May 11, 1894.

During this tense period Pullman workers had been joining the American Railway Union, founded the previous year by Eugene V. Debs. The tall, gaunt Debs was a man of towering influence and charismatic appeal. A child of working-class Alsatian immigrants, he quit school in 1869 at age fourteen and began working for an Indiana railroad. There, he would later write, "I learned of the hardships of the rail in snow, sleet, and hail, of the ceaseless danger that lurks along the iron highway, the uncertainty of employment, scant wages and altogether trying lot of the workingman, so that from my very boyhood I was made to feel the wrongs of labor." He felt these wrongs so deeply that he eagerly accepted an invitation to start a local of the railroad brotherhood, a craft union of skilled workers.

Still, it was not until the Haymarket bombing that Debs came to see an inevitable conflict between labor and management. By the early 1890s he had become a tireless spokesman for labor radicalism, and he launched a crusade to organize *all* railway workers—skilled or unskilled—into the American Railway Union. Soon he was in charge of a powerful new labor organization, and he quickly turned his attention to the Pullman controversy.

After Pullman refused Debs's plea for arbitration, the union workers in June 1894 stopped handling Pullman cars and by the end of July had tied up most of the railroads in the Midwest. The roads then brought strikebreakers from Canada and elsewhere, instructing them to connect mail cars to Pullman cars so that interference with Pullman cars also meant interference with the mails. The U.S. attorney-general, a former railroad attorney himself, swore in 3,400 special deputies to keep the trains running, and when clashes occurred between these deputies and some of the strikers, lawless elements exploited the situation to repeat some of the scenes of the 1877 strike. Finally, on July 3, 1894, President Grover Cleveland answered an appeal from the railroads that he send federal troops into the Chicago area, where the strike was centered. Illinois governor John Peter Altgeld insisted that the state could keep order, but Cleveland claimed authority and a duty to ensure delivery of the mails. "If it takes every dollar in the Treasury and every soldier in

Eugene V. Debs, founder of the American Railway Union and later candidate for president as head of the Socialist Party of America.

the United States to deliver a postal card in Chicago," he vowed, "that postal card should be delivered."

Meanwhile the attorney-general won an injunction forbidding any interference with the mails or any combination to restrain interstate commerce; the principle was that a strike or boycott violated the Sherman Anti-Trust Act. On July 13 the union called off the strike and on the same day the district court cited Debs for violating the injunction and sentenced him to six months in jail. The Supreme Court upheld the decree in the case of *In re Debs* (1895) on broad grounds of national sovereignty: "The strong arm of the national government may be put forth to brush away all obstructions to the freedom of interstate commerce or the transportation of the mails." Debs served his term, during which time he read deeply in socialist literature, and he emerged to devote the rest of his life to that cause.

SOCIALISM AND THE UNIONS The major American unions, for the most part, never allied themselves with the socialists as many European labor movements did. But socialist ideas had been abroad in the country at least since the time Robert Owen visited America in the 1820s. Marxism, a strain of socialism, was imported mainly by German immigrants. Karl Marx's International Workingmen's Association, the First International, founded in 1864, inspired a few affiliates in the United States. In 1872, at Marx's urging, the headquarters was moved from London to New York. In 1876 the First

International expired, but the next year followers of Marx in America organized the Socialist Labor party, a group so filled with immigrants that German was its official language in the first years.

The movement gained little notice before the rise of Daniel DeLeon in the 1890s. As editor of its paper, *The People,* he became the dominant figure in the party. A native of the Dutch West Indies, DeLeon had studied law and lectured for some years at Columbia University. DeLeon proposed to organize industrial unions with a socialist purpose, and to build a political party which would abolish the state once it gained power, after which the unions of the Socialist Trade and Labor Alliance would become the units of control. His ideas seem to have influenced Lenin, leader of the Bolshevik Revolution of 1917, but DeLeon preached revolution at the ballot box, not by violence.

Debs was more successful at building a socialist movement in America. To many, DeLeon seemed doctrinaire and inflexible. Debs, however, built his new party by following a method now traditional in the United States: he formed a coalition, one which embraced viewpoints ranging from moderate reform to doctrinaire Marxism. In 1897 Debs organized the Social Democratic party from the remnants of the American Railway Union, and got over 4,000 votes as its candidate for president in 1900. In 1901 his followers joined a number of secessionists from DeLeon's party, led by Morris Hillquit of New York, to set up the Socialist Party of America. In 1904 Debs polled over 400,000 votes as the party's candidate for president and more than doubled that to almost 900,000 votes in 1912, or 6 percent of the popular vote. In 1910 the Socialists of Milwaukee elected Emil Seidel mayor and sent Victor Berger to Congress.

By 1912 the party seemed well on the way to becoming a permanent fixture in American politics. Thirty-three cities had Socialist mayors, including Berkeley, California; Butte, Montana; Flint and Jackson, Michigan; and Milwaukee, Wisconsin. The party sponsored five English daily newspapers, eight foreign-language dailies, and a number of weeklies and monthlies. Its support was not confined to urban workers and intellectuals. In the Southwest the party built a sizable grass-roots following among farmers and tenants. Oklahoma, for instance, in 1910 had more paid-up party members than any other state except New York, and in 1912 gave 16.5 percent of its popular vote to Debs, a greater proportion than any other state ever gave. But the party reached its peak in 1912. During World War I it was racked by disagreements over America's participation, and was split thereafter by desertions to the new Communist party. A brief revival during the Great Depression served only to interrupt, not halt, its decline.

THE WOBBLIES During the years of Socialist party growth there emerged a parallel effort to revive industrial unionism, led by the Industrial Workers of the World (IWW). The chief base for this group was the Western Federation of Miners, organized at Butte, Montana, in 1893. Over the next decade the Western Federation was the storm center of violent confrontation with unyielding bosses who mobilized private armies against it in Colorado, Idaho, and elsewhere. In June 1905 the founding convention of the IWW drew a variety of people who opposed the AFL's philosophy. Debs participated, although many of his comrades preferred to work within the AFL. DeLeon was of course happy at this chance to strike back at craft unionism. A radical manifesto issued from the meetings, arguing that the IWW "must be founded on the class struggle, and its general administration must be conducted in harmony with the recognition of the irrepressible conflict between the capitalist class and the working class."

But the IWW waged class war better than it articulated class ideology. Like the Knights of Labor, it was designed to be "One Big Union," including all workers, skilled or unskilled. Its roots were in the mining and lumber camps of the West, where unstable conditions of employment created a large number of nomadic workers, to whom neither the AFL's pragmatic approach nor the socialists' political appeal held much attraction. The revolutionary goal of the Wobblies, as they came to be called, was an idea labeled syndicalism by its French supporters: the ultimate destruction of the state and its replacement by one big Union. But just how it would govern remained vague.

Like other radical groups the IWW was split by sectarian disputes. Because of policy disagreements all the major founders withdrew, first the Western Federation of Miners, then Debs, then DeLeon. William D. "Big Bill" Haywood of the Western Federation remained, however, and as its leader held the group together. Although since embellished in myth, Haywood was in fact an imposing figure. Well over six feet tall, handsome, muscular, one-eyed, he commanded the attention and respect of his listeners. This hardrock miner, union organizer, and Socialist from Salt Lake City had nothing but disdain for the AFL and its conservative labor philosophy. He called Samuel Gompers "a squat specimen of humanity" with "small, snapping eyes, a hard cruel mouth," and "a personality vain, conceited, petulant, and vindictive." Instead of following Gompers's advice to organize only skilled workers, Haywood promoted the concept of one all-inclusive union whose credo would be the promotion of a socialism "with its working clothes on."

But Haywood and the Wobblies were reaching out to the fringe elements of least power and influence, chiefly the migratory workers of the West and the ethnic groups of the East. Always ambivalent about diluting their revolutionary principles, they scorned the usual labor agreements, even when they participated in them. Consequently they engaged in spectacular battles with capital but scored few victories, the largest of which was a textile strike at Lawrence, Massachusetts, in 1912, which ended with wage raises, overtime pay, and other benefits. But the next year a strike of silk workers at Paterson, New Jersey, ended in disaster, and the IWW entered a rapid decline.

The fading of the movement was accelerated by the hysterical opposition it provoked. The *Los Angeles Times,* for instance, declared that "I.W.W. stands for I won't work, and I want whiskey. . . . The average Wobbly, it must be remembered, is a sort of half wild animal." And many of the authorities treated them as such. Bragged one sheriff, "When a Wobbly comes to town, I just knock him over the head with a night stick and throw him in the river. When he comes up he beats it out of town."

William D. "Big Bill" Haywood (second from left), head of the Industrial Workers of the World, the "Wobblies."

Branded as anarchists, bums, and criminals, the Wobblies were effectively destroyed during World War I, when most of its leaders were jailed for conspiracy because of their militant opposition to the war. Big Bill Haywood fled to the Soviet Union, where he married a Russian woman, died in 1928, and was honored by burial in the Kremlin wall. But the IWW, decried as a conduit for alien ideas, was actually an American original, born of the rough-and-tumble world of western miners and migrants. The Wobblies left behind a rich folklore of nomadic working stiffs and a gallery of heroic agitators such as Elizabeth Gurley Flynn, a dark-haired Irish woman who at age eighteen chained herself to a lamppost to impede her arrest during a strike. The movement also bequeathed martyrs like the Swedish songster and labor organizer Joe Hill, framed (so the faithful assumed) for murder and executed by a Utah firing squad. His last words were written to Haywood: "Goodbye, Bill. I die like a true blue rebel. Don't waste any time mourning. Organize." The intensity of conviction and devotion to a cause shown by Hill, Flynn, and others ensured that the IWW's ideal of a classless society did not die.

FURTHER READING

For surveys of the Gilded Age, see Robert H. Wiebe's *The Search for Order, 1877–1920* (1966),° John A. Garraty's *The New Commonwealth, 1877–1890* (1968),° and Samuel P. Hays's *The Response to Industrialism, 1885–1914* (1957).° Of particular interest are Sidney Fine's *Laissez Faire and the General-Welfare State: A Study of Conflict in American Thought, 1865–1910* (1956),° which gauges public opinion on that topic, and Alfred D. Chandler's *The Visible Hand: The Managerial Revolution in American Business* (1977),° which details the strategies of the early corporate managers. Also useful are Douglass C. North's *Growth and Welfare in the American Past* (3rd ed., 1983),° Stuart Bruchey's *Growth of the Modern American Economy* (1975), and Robert L. Heilbroner's *The Economic Transformation of America* (1977).

Scholarship on the growth of railroads includes George R. Taylor and Irene D. Neu's *The American Railroad Network, 1861–1890* (1956) and Robert W. Fogel's *Railroads and American Economic Growth* (1964).° James H. Ducker's *Men of the Steel Rails* (1983) focuses on the life of the railroad workers. Gabriel Kolko's *Railroads and Regulation, 1877–1916* (1965)° argues that the entrepreneurs themselves sought regulation.

On entrepreneurship in the iron and steel sector, see Peter Temin's *Iron and Steel in Nineteenth Century America: An Economic Inquiry* (1964).

°These books are available in paperback editions.

Harold Livesay's *Andrew Carnegie and the Rise of Big Business* (1975)°
treats the titan of the steel mills. On J. P. Morgan, see Andrew Sinclair's
Corsair: The Life of J. Pierpont Morgan (1981); for Rockefeller see Allan
Nevins's *Study in Power: John D. Rockefeller* (1953). Maury Klein's *The Life
and Legend of Jay Gould* (1986) is sympathetic.

Nathan Rosenberg's *Technology and American Economic Growth* (1972)°
documents the growth of invention during the period. Robert V. Bruce's
Alexander Graham Bell and the Conquest of Solitude (1973) stresses the
social impact of technology.

A discussion of one justification for business growth is Richard Hofstadter's *Social Darwinism in American Thought* (rev. ed., 1955).° James
Weinstein's *The Corporate Ideal in the Liberal State, 1900–1918* (1968)°
critically analyzes laissez-faire capitalism.

Much of the recent scholarship on labor in the Gilded Age stresses the
traditional values and the culture of work which the work force brought to
the factory. Herbert G. Gutman's *Work, Culture, and Society in Industrializ-
ing America* (1976)° best introduces these themes. Also helpful is Daniel T.
Rodgers's *The Work Ethic in Industrial America, 1850–1920* (1978).° David
Montgomery, in *Beyond Equality: Labor and the Radical Republicans,
1862–1872* (1975)° and *Workers' Control in America: Studies in the History
of Work, Technology, and Labor Struggles* (1979), analyzes the evolution of
the work environment. In *The Fall of the House of Labor* (1987), Montgomery interprets labor-management conflicts over work organization.

As for the labor groups, Gerald N. Grob's *Workers and Utopias* (1961)
examines the difference in outlook between the Knights of Labor and the
American Federation of Labor. For the Knights, see Leon Fink's *Working-
men's Democracy* (1983).° Also useful is Susan Levine's *Labor's True
Woman* (1984), on the role of women in the Knights. A good work on the
leader of the AFL is Harold C. Livesay's *Samuel Gompers and Organized
Labor in America* (1978).° To trace the rise of socialism among organized
workers, see Nick Salvatore's *Eugene V. Debs: Citizen and Socialist* (1982).°
Gilded Age strikes are discussed in Daniel J. Walkowitz's *Worker City,
Company Town: Iron and Cotton Worker Protest in Troy and Cohoes, New
York, 1855–1884* (1978)° and Paul Avrich's *The Haymarket Tragedy* (1984).°

21

THE EMERGENCE OF
MODERN AMERICA

AMERICA'S MOVE TO TOWN

EXPLOSIVE URBAN GROWTH   The frontier was a safety valve, Frederick Jackson Turner said in his influential thesis on American development. Its cheap lands afforded a release for the population pressures mounting in the cities. If there was such a thing as a safety valve in his own time, however, he had it just backward. The flow of population toward the city was greater than toward the west, and "country come to town" epitomized the American people better than the occasional city "dude" who turned up in cow country.

Much of the westward movement in fact was itself an urban movement, spawning new towns near the mining digs or at the railheads, forming in the arid regions what a later historian would call an "oasis civilization." More often than not, western towns anticipated settlement. They supplied headquarters for the land boomers and services for the hinterlands. On the Pacific coast a greater portion of the population was urbanized than anywhere else; its major concentrations were around San Francisco Bay at first, and then in Los Angeles, which became a boom town after the arrival of the Southern Pacific and Santa Fe Railroads in the 1880s. Remarkably, its salubrious climate and clean air were among Los Angeles's chief selling points. Seattle grew quickly, first as the terminus of three transcontinental railroad lines, and by the end of the century as the staging area for the Yukon gold rush. Minneapolis, St. Paul, Omaha, Kansas City, and Denver were no longer the mere villages they had been in 1860. The South, too, produced new towns: Dur-

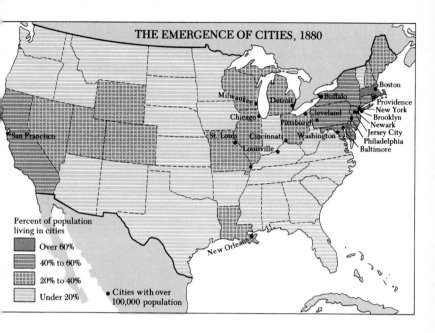

THE EMERGENCE OF CITIES, 1880

Milwaukee
Detroit
Buffalo
Boston
Providence
New York
Brooklyn
Newark
Jersey City
Philadelphia
Baltimore

Chicago
Cleveland
Pittsburgh

St. Louis
Cincinnati
Washington

Louisville

San Francisco

New Orleans

Percent of population
living in cities

Over 60%
40% to 60%
20% to 40%
Under 20%

● Cities with over
100,000 population

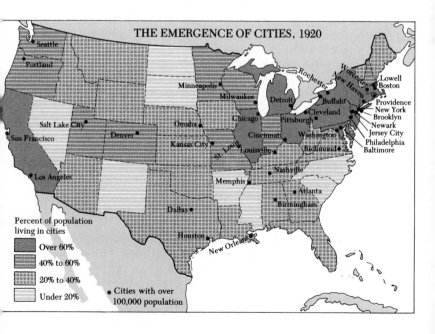

THE EMERGENCE OF CITIES, 1920

Seattle
Portland

Minneapolis
Milwaukee
Detroit
Rochester
Worcester
New Haven
Lowell
Boston

Salt Lake City
Denver
Omaha
Chicago
Buffalo
Cleveland
Pittsburgh
Providence
New York
Brooklyn
Newark
Jersey City
Philadelphia
Baltimore

San Francisco
Kansas City
St. Louis
Cincinnati
Louisville
Washington
Richmond

Los Angeles
Memphis
Nashville
Atlanta
Birmingham

Dallas

Houston
New Orleans

Percent of population
living in cities

Over 60%
40% to 60%
20% to 40%
Under 20%

● Cities with over
100,000 population

ham and Birmingham, which were centers of tobacco and iron manufactures, and Houston, which handled cotton and cattle, and soon oil.

Trade and transportation had been the city builders of the past. Eight of the nine cities that by 1860 had passed 100,000 in population were ports, and the ninth (Brooklyn) was a suburb to the largest port. By the late nineteenth century no city could hope to thrive without at least one railroad, and most could boast a cluster of railroads. But it was the explosive rise of industry that powered the growth of new cities during this period. Industry brought huge concentrations of labor, and both required the proliferation of services that became synonymous with city life.

The emergence of the major cities was completed during the years from 1860 to 1910. After that, new cities sprang up only in unusual circumstances: Miami was the product of tourism brought by the coastal railroad, while Tulsa sprung from an oil boom. In those fifty years, population in incorporated towns of 2,500 or more grew from 6 million to 45 million, or from 20 to 46 percent of the nation's total population. After 1920 more than half the nation's population would be urban.

While the Far West had the greatest proportion of urban population, the Northeast had far greater numbers of people in its teeming cities. There the situation that Jefferson had so dreaded was coming to pass: the people "piled high up on one another in the cities," and worse, these people increasingly were landless, tool-less, and homeless—an urban proletariat with nothing but their labor to sell. By 1900 more than 90 percent of the residents in New York's Manhattan lived in rented homes or tenements. In Boston, Fall River, Jersey City, and Memphis, four-fifths of the inhabitants were renters.

The cities expanded both vertically and horizontally to absorb their huge populations. In either case progress in the means of conveyance played an important role: the elevator, the streetcar, and, before the end of the century, the first automobiles. The first safety elevator, which would not fall if the rope or cable broke, was developed in 1852 by Elisha Graves Otis. In 1889 the Otis Elevator Company installed the first electric elevator, which made possible the erection of taller buildings. Before the 1860s few structures had gone higher than three or four stories.

Another support for the vertical city came from the engineers who developed cast-iron and steel-frame construction. Much of the impulse to new design centered in Chicago, which had to rebuild after the great fire of 1871. There William LeBaron Jenney built a metal skeleton for the ten-story Home Life Insurance Building, finished in 1885. Other architects added a sense of style to the new techniques. Louis Sullivan, whose motto was "Form Follows Function," pioneered a plain functional style in reaction against elaborate Victorian decoration.

Before the 1890s the chief sources of urban transport were either animals or steam. Horse- and mule-drawn streetcars had appeared in antebellum cities, but they were slow and cumbersome, and cleaning up after the animals added to the cost. Animal power, like the automobile later, contributed to severe pollution, but in its own way. In 1873 San Francisco became the first city to use cable cars which clamped onto a moving underground cable driven by a central power source. In the twentieth century it would become the last to use cable cars, after a few other cities tried and gave them up. Some cities used steam-powered trains on elevated tracks, but by the 1890s electric trolleys were replacing these.

Such systems spread rapidly, and in some places mass-transit companies began to dig underground passages for their cars. Around the turn of the century subway systems began operation in Boston, New York, and Philadelphia. Advances in bridge building through the use of steel and the perfection of the steel-cable suspension bridge also

Pedestrians, horse-drawn carts, trolleys, and electric trains all made their way between Brooklyn and Manhattan over the Brooklyn Bridge, completed in 1883.

enlarged the reach of commuters. The marvels of the age were James B. Eads's cantilevered steel bridge over the Mississippi at St. Louis (1874) and John A. and Washington Roebling's cable-supported Brooklyn Bridge (1883), which linked Brooklyn to Manhattan.

The spread of mass transit allowed large numbers of people to become commuters, and a growing middle class (working people often could not afford even the nickel fare) retreated to quieter tree-lined "streetcar suburbs" whence they could travel into the central city for business or entertainment. The pattern of urban growth often became a sprawl, however, since it took place usually without plan, in the interest of a fast buck, and without thought to the need for parks and public services. But some cities and developers had the wit to look ahead. New York in the early 1850s had set up a park commission which hired Frederick Law Olmsted as superintendent to plan Central Park. By 1870 as many as 100,000 people visited the park daily. Olmsted later planned parks and even new subdivisions in San Francisco, Brooklyn, Chicago, and other cities.

CITY PLANNING Chicago's World Fair, the Columbian Exposition of 1893–1894, inspired a "city beautiful" movement. The fair was of such size that a whole new city had to be built on Chicago's South Side lakefront and supplied with a complex of services. Olmsted helped with the choice of a site, and the planning brought together leading architects and engineers. One planning session was called "the greatest meeting of artists since the fifteenth century."

The success of what visitors took to calling the "White City" stirred a new interest in city planning. Among the early fruits of the enthusiasm was a project to commemorate Washington, D.C.'s centennial in 1900 by completing L'Enfant's plan for a mall from the Capitol to the Potomac. New civic centers sprang up in the big cities. Hartford created the first city-planning commission in 1907, and in 1916 the American City Planning Institute, a professional organization of planners, met for the first time.

CITY PROBLEMS AND POLITICS Although housing conditions in the mill villages of the New South could be bad indeed, one observer who saw laborers going to work through the pine woods of South Carolina noted the contrast to "the stuffy, crowded subways and the crowded elevated" of the metropolis. But workers in the big cities often had no choice other than crowded tenements, most of which were poorly designed. In 1900 Manhattan numbered 42,700 tenements which housed almost 1.6 million people, an average of 34 residents per building. Before the day of high-rise apartments this represented an extremely high density. Other cities were less

The Columbian Exposition of 1893–1894, held in Chicago, gave impetus to the city-planning movement.

densely populated, but the spread of slums with urban growth created immense problems of health and morale.

The sheer size of these cities helped create a new politics. Since individuals could hardly provide for themselves such necessary services as transit, paving, water, sewers, street lighting and cleaning, and fire and police protection, they came increasingly to rely on city government. Meanwhile, many city problems were handled by local political bosses who traded in patronage favors and graft. Big-city political machines were not altogether sinister in their effects: they provided food and money for the poor, fixed problems at city hall, and generally helped immigrants in their adjustment to a new life. One ward boss in Boston said: "There's got to be in every ward somebody that any bloke can come to—no matter what he's done—and get help. Help, you understand, none of your law and justice, but help."

In return the political professionals felt entitled to some reward for having done the grubby work of the local organization. George

The city tenements into which immigrants poured in the late nineteenth century were often overcrowded and unhealthy.

Washington Plunkitt, for instance, a power in Tammany Hall (New York City's Democratic organization) at the turn of the century, saw nothing wrong with a little honest graft. "Well, I'm tipped off, say, that they're going to lay out a new park at a certain place. . . . I go to that place and buy up all the land I can in the neighborhood. . . . Ain't it perfectly honest to charge a good price and make a profit on my investment and foresight?" Dishonest graft would consist of "robbin' the city treasury or levyin' blackmail on disorderly houses or workin' in with the gamblers and lawbreakers." For his own epitaph Plunkitt proposed: "He Seen His Opportunities, and He Took 'Em."

MOVING FROM COUNTRY TO CITY   But whatever the problems of the cities, the wonder of their glittering new arc and electric lights, their streetcars, telephones, amusements, newspapers and magazines, and a thousand other enticements exerted a magnetic lure on the youth of the farms. Hamlin Garland told in his autobiography, *A Son of the Middle Border*, of his mixed sense of dread and wonder at first visiting Chicago with his brother. The city first appeared from the train window enveloped in clouds of smoke, "the soaring banners of the great and gloomy inland metropolis, whose dens of vice and houses of greed had been so often reported to me." Later the two young men wandered the streets: "Everything interested us. The business section so sordid to others was grandly terrifying to us. . . . Nothing was commonplace, nothing was ugly to us."

The new cities threw into stark contrast the frustration of unending toil, the isolation and loneliness of country life. In times of rural depression thousands left for the cities in search of the opportunity that Horatio Alger and other writers of success literature dangled before their eyes. The exodus from the countryside was especially evident in the East, where the census documented the shift in population from country to city, and stories began to appear of entire regions where buildings were abandoned and going to ruin, where the wilderness was reclaiming farms that had been wrested from it during the previous 250 years.

THE NEW IMMIGRATION

AMERICA'S PULL   Newcomers to the cities arrived not only from the surrounding hinterland but from Europe and Asia as well. European immigrants also were often moving from country to city, and increasingly from the great agricultural areas of eastern and southern Europe directly to the foremost cities of America. They gathered in these cities in order to live with others of like language, customs, and religion, and also because they lacked the means to go west and take up farms. Though cities of the South and West (excepting the Far

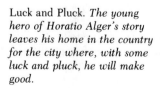

Luck and Pluck. *The young hero of Horatio Alger's story leaves his home in the country for the city where, with some luck and pluck, he will make good.*

West) drew their populations mainly from the native-born of their regions, American cities as a whole drew more residents from abroad. During the peak decade of immigration, 1900–1910, 41 percent of the urban newcomers arrived from abroad, while 30 percent were native Americans, 22 percent were the products of natural increase, and almost 8 percent lived in areas annexed to the cities.

Ethnic neighborhoods, sometimes populated by those from a single province or town, preserved familiar ways and shielded newcomers from the shocks of a strange culture. Such communities grew to be so large they soon overshadowed their Old World counterparts. In 1890 four out of five New Yorkers were foreign-born, a higher proportion than any other city in the world. New York had twice as many Irish as Dublin, as many Germans as Hamburg, and half as many Italians as Naples. "A map of the city, colored to designate nationalities," Jacob Riis (a native of Denmark) wrote in *How the Other Half Lives* (1890), "would show more stripes than . . . a zebra, and more colors than any rainbow." In 1893 Chicago claimed the largest Bohemian (Czech) community in the world, and by 1910 the size of its Polish population ranked behind only Warsaw and Lodz.

This nation of immigrants continued to draw new inhabitants for much the same reasons as always, and from much the same strata of society. Immigrants came in flight from famine or the grinding lack of opportunity in their native lands. They fled racial, religious, and political persecution, and compulsory military service. Yet one historian has suggested that "the desire to get cheap labor, to take in passenger fares, and to sell land have probably brought more immigrants than the hard conditions of Europe, Asia, and Africa have sent."

More immigrants probably were pulled by America's promise than were pushed out by conditions at home. American industries, seeking cheap labor, kept recruiting-agents on watch abroad and at American ports. Railroads, eager to sell land and build up the traffic on their lines, put out tempting propaganda in a medley of languages. Many of the western and southern states set up official bureaus and agents to attract immigrants. Under the Contract Labor Law of 1864, the federal government itself encouraged immigration by providing a lien on the immigrant's wages in order to pay for his or her passage. The law was repealed in 1868, but not until 1885 did the government forbid companies to import contract labor, which put immigrant workers under the control of their employers. Domestic service and some skilled occupations were exempted from the ban, and evasion was easy.

From 1820 (when by requirement of Congress official statistics on immigration began to be kept) to 1900 about 20 million immigrants

Steerage Deck of the S.S. *Pennland,* 1893. *These immigrants are about to arrive at New York's Ellis Island.*

entered American ports, more than half of them coming after the Civil War. The tide of immigration rose from just under 3 million in the 1870s to more than 5 million in the 1880s, then fell to a little over 3.5 million in the depression decade of the 1890s, and rose to its high-water mark of nearly 9 million in the first decade of the new century. The numbers declined to 6 million in the 1910s and 4 million in the 1920s, after which official restrictions cut the flow of immigration down to a negligible level.

A NEW WAVE During the 1880s the continuing search for cheap labor combined with renewed persecutions in eastern Europe to bring a noticeable change in the source of immigration, one fraught with meaning for American social history. Before 1880 immigrants were mainly of Teutonic and Celtic origin, hailing from northern and western Europe. But by the 1870s there were signs of a change. The proportion of Latin, Slavic, and Jewish peoples from southern and eastern Europe rose sharply. After 1890 these groups made up a majority of the newcomers, and by the first decade of the new century they formed 70 percent of the immigrants to this country. Among these new immigrants were Italians, Hungarians, Czechs, Slovaks, Poles, Serbs, Croats, Slovenes, Russians, Romanians, and

Greeks—all people of markedly different cultural and language stocks from those of western Europe, and most followers of different religions, including Judaism and Catholicism.

ELLIS ISLAND   As the number of immigrants passing through the Port of New York soared during the late nineteenth century, the state-run Castle Garden receiving center became rife with corruption. Money-changers cheated new arrivals, railroad agents overcharged them for tickets, and baggage handlers engaged in blackmail. With reports of these abuses filling the newspapers, Congress ordered an investigation of Castle Garden that resulted in the closure of the facility in 1890. Thereafter the federal government's new Bureau of Immigration took over the business of admitting newcomers to New York City.

To launch this effort, Congress funded the construction of a new reception center on a tiny island off the New Jersey coast, a mile south of Manhattan and some 1,300 feet from the Statue of Liberty. The statue, unveiled in 1886, was a centennial gift from the French government commemorating the Franco-American alliance during the Revolutionary War. But it soon came to be viewed as a symbol of hope for immigrants passing under "Lady Liberty." In the base of the statue, workers had chiseled the poet Emma Lazarus's tribute to the promise of new life in America:

> Give me your tired, your poor,
> Your huddled masses yearning to breathe free,
> The wretched refuse of your teeming shore.
> Send these, the homeless, tempest-tossed to me,
> I lift my lamp beside the golden door!

In 1892 Ellis Island (named after its late-eighteenth-century owner, Samuel Ellis) opened its doors to the "huddled masses" of the world, and before 1954, when it closed, some 12 million people first touched American soil there. Forty percent of Americans today have ancestors who passed through Ellis Island. In 1907, the center's busiest year, more than a million new arrivals filtered through the cavernous Great Hall, an average of about 5,000 per day; in one day alone immigration officials processed some 11,750 arrivals. These were the immigrants who arrived crammed into the steerage compartments deep in the ships' hulls. Those immigrants who could afford first- and second-class cabins did not have to visit Ellis Island; they were examined on board ship, and most of them simply walked down the gangway onto the docks in lower Manhattan.

The first Ellis Island Immigration Station—a 400-foot-long barn-

Immigrants, with identification papers, newly arrived at Ellis Island.

Immigrants waiting in the Registry Room for further inspections.

like structure made of Georgia pine—burned to the ground in 1897, and in its place rose a majestic structure, a 220,000-square-foot Main Building made of fireproof red brick and limestone. Four graceful copper-plated domes towered above the massive roof, giving the building the appearance of a European palace. The enormous dimensions of the Great Hall, with its arching two-story ceiling, must have awed the new arrivals as they sat on benches waiting to be processed. In the dining hall, thousands of people from different countries and with different tastes took their meals. As one administrator explained, "If I put pirogi and Mazovian noodles on the table, the Poles were happy and the rest discontented. Irish stew was no good for the English, and the English marmalade was gunpowder to the Irish. The Scotch distrusted both. The Welsh took what they could get."

The prevailing atmosphere at Ellis Island was not comforting. Its bureaucratic purpose was to process immigrants, not welcome them. An army of inspectors, doctors, nurses, and public officials questioned, examined, and documented the newcomers. Inspectors had a list of twenty-nine probing questions, including: Have you money, relatives, or a job in the United States? Are you a polygamist? An anarchist? Doctors and nurses poked and prodded, searching for any sign of debilitating handicap or infectious disease. All the while, the immigrant worried: "Will they let me in?" Although some who were sick or lame were detained for days or weeks, the vast majority of immigrants received stamps of approval and were on their way after three or four hours. "I was jostled and dragged and shoved and shouted at," recalled one immigrant. "I took it philosophically. I had been through the performance many times before—at the Hungarian border, at Vienna, in Germany, in Holland." Only 2 percent of the newcomers were denied entry altogether, usually because they were criminals, strikebreakers, anarchists, or carriers of some "loathsome or dangerous contagious disease," such as tuberculosis or trachoma, a contagious eye disease resulting in blindness. These luckless folk were then returned to their places of origin, with the steamship companies picking up the tab.

Between 1892 and 1954, 70 percent of all European immigrants circulated through Ellis Island (others landed at Boston, Philadelphia, Baltimore, New Orleans, and Galveston.) Among the arrivals at Ellis Island were many youngsters who would distinguish themselves in their new country: songwriter Irving Berlin (Russia), football legend Knute Rockne (Norway), Supreme Court justice Felix Frankfurter (Austria), singer Al Jolson (Lithuania), and comedian Bob Hope (England). But many others found America's opportunities harder to grasp. An old Italian saying expresses the disillusion-

An Italian immigrant family aboard a ferry from Ellis Island, 1905. The unfamiliar ways of immigrants from southern and eastern Europe reawakened nativist sentiment in America.

ment felt by many: "I came to America because I heard the streets were paved with gold. When I got here, I found out three things: First, the streets weren't paved with gold; second, they weren't paved at all; and third, I was expected to pave them."

MAKING THEIR WAY   Disembarking finally from the ferry onto American soil in Manhattan or New Jersey, the immigrants felt exhilaration, exhaustion, and usually a desperate need for work. Many were greeted by family and friends who had come over before; others by representatives of the many immigrant aid societies or by hiring agents offering jobs in mines, mills, and sweatshops. Since most knew little if any English and nothing about American employment practices, the immigrants were easy subjects for exploitation. In exchange for providing arrivals with a bit of whiskey and a job, obliging hiring agents claimed a healthy percentage of their wages. Among Italians and Greeks these agents were known as *padrones*, and they came to dominate the labor market in New York. Other contractors provided train tickets for immigrants to travel inland to jobs in cities such as Buffalo, Pittsburgh, Cleveland, Chicago, Milwaukee, Cincinnati, and St. Louis. Eager to retain a sense of community and to sustain skills they may have brought with them, the members of ethnic groups tended to cluster in particular vocations. Poles, Hungarians, Slovaks, Bohemians, and Italians used to the pick and shovel flocked to coal mines, just as the Irish, Cornish, and Welsh had done at mid-century; Slavs and Poles comfortable with muscle work gravitated to the steel mills; Greeks preferred working in textile mills; Russian and Polish Jews peopled the needle trades or pushcart markets of New York. A few determined peasants uprooted from their agricultural heritage made their way west and were able to find work on farms or even a parcel of land for themselves.

Most of the immigrants, however, settled in the teeming cities. Strangers in a new land, they naturally gravitated to neighborhoods populated by their own kind. These immigrant enclaves—nicknamed Little Italy, Little Hungary, Chinatown, and so on—served as crucial transitional communities between the newcomers' Old World past and their New World future. By 1920 Chicago had some seventeen separate Little Italy colonies scattered across the city representing various home provinces. In such kinship communities the immigrants could practice their religions and native customs, converse in their native tongue, and fill an aching loneliness. But they paid a price for such community solidarity. When the "new immigrants" moved into an area, older residents typically moved out, taking with them whatever social prestige and political influence they had achieved. The quality of living conditions quickly deteriorated as housing and sanitation codes went unenforced.

As the number of new arrivals mushroomed during the last quarter of the nineteenth century, cities grew so cramped and land so scarce that designers were forced to build upward. The result was the "dumbbell" tenement house. These structures, usually six to eight stories in height and jammed tightly against one another, came to line street after street. They derived their name from the fact that housing codes required a two-foot-wide air shaft between buildings, giving each structure the appearance of a dumbbell when viewed from overhead. Twenty-four to thirty-two families would cram into each building, meaning that some city blocks housed almost 4,000 people. The tiny air shaft provided little ventilation; instead it proved to be a fire hazard, fueling and conveying the flames from building to building. The early tenements were poorly heated, and had water closets outside in the yard or alley for communal use. By the end of the century they would feature two toilets on each floor, available to all comers. Shoehorned into such quarters, families had no privacy, free space, or sunshine; children had few places to play except in the city streets; infectious diseases and noxious odors were rampant. Not surprisingly, the mortality rate for urban immigrants was much higher than that of the general population. In one Chicago ethnic ghetto at the end of the century, three babies of every five died before their first birthday.

THE NATIVIST RESPONSE Not only did immigrants have to face difficult living conditions, they also confronted growing prejudice from native Americans. Many saw the new immigration as a direct threat to their settled way of life and their jobs. "Immigrants work for almost nothing," groused one American laborer, "and seem to be able to live on wind—something which I cannot do." Others saw in the tide of new immigrants a threat to traditional American culture and values. A Stanford University professor called them "Illiterate, docile, lacking in self-reliance and initiative, and not possessing the Anglo-Teutonic conceptions of law, order, and government." The undercurrent of nativism so often present in American culture now surfaced mainly in anti-Catholic, and secondarily anti-Semitic, sentiments. The Catholic church in America, long dominated by the English-speaking Irish, became a polyglot group all the more subject to misunderstanding and persecution. Similarly, Russian and Polish Jews came from a far different tradition than the Sephardic and German Jews who preceded them. Their unruly beards, long black coats, and distinctive language, Yiddish, made them seem strange and exotic.

More than religious prejudice underlay hostility toward the latest newcomers. Cultural differences confirmed in the minds of nativists the assumption that the Nordic peoples of the old immigration were superior to the Slavic and Latin peoples of the new immigration. Many of the new immigrants were illiterate, and more appeared so because they could not speak English. Some resorted to crime in order to survive in the new land, encouraging suspicions that criminals were being quietly helped out of Europe just as they had once been transported from England to the colonies. In the early 1890s vendettas among Italian gangs in New Orleans led to the murder of the police chief and the lynching of eleven Italian suspects, an incident which convinced many that the new immigrants were criminals.

The success of the Irish in city politics was emulated by the newer groups, who also thereby offended the sensibilities of well-born natives. Political and social radicals turned up among these immigrant groups in sufficient numbers to encourage nativists to blame labor disputes on alien elements. Such charges harbored a fine irony, however, because mainline labor organizations generally favored restricting immigration to keep down the competition for jobs. Em-

"G.W.: How They Have Changed!" *A cartoon expressing the suspicion and fear confronting the new wave of southern and eastern European immigrants to the United States.*

ployers sometimes used immigrants as strikebreakers; those who came from peasant origins, and were unfamiliar with strikes, were apt as not to think they were merely taking jobs that others had abandoned. Employers also learned quickly that a babel of tongues could confound unity of action among workers.

A resurgence of nativism in the 1880s was marked by the growth of groups devoted to saving the country from imaginary papal conspiracies. The most successful of these nativist groups, the American Protective Association, operated mainly in Protestant strongholds of the upper Mississippi Valley. Its organizer seemed addicted to paranoid fantasies of Catholic conspiracies, and was especially concerned to keep the public schools free from Jesuit control. The association grew slowly from its start in 1887 until 1893, when keen leaders took advantage of a severe depression to draw large numbers of the frustrated to its ranks. The APA soon vanished, swallowed up in the Populist and free-silver agitations, but while it lasted it promoted restricted immigration, more stringent naturalization requirements, refusal to employ aliens or Catholics, and the teaching of the "American" language in the schools.

IMMIGRATION RESTRICTION   The movement to restrict immigration had mixed success beyond the exclusion of certain individuals deemed undesirable. In 1875, for instance, a new law refused entry to prostitutes and to convicts whose sentences had been remitted in other countries on condition they leave. In 1882 a more general law added lunatics, idiots, and persons likely to become public charges, and over the years other specific undesirables joined the list. In 1891 Representative Henry Cabot Lodge of Massachusetts took up the cause of excluding illiterates—a measure that would have affected much of the new immigration even though the language did not have to be English. Bills embodying the restriction were vetoed by three presidents on the ground that they penalized people for lack of opportunity: Cleveland in 1897, Taft in 1913, and Wilson in 1915 and 1917. The last time, however, Congress overrode the veto.

Proponents of immigration restriction during the late nineteenth century did succeed in excluding the Chinese, who were victims of everything the European immigrants suffered, plus color prejudice as well. By 1880 there were some 75,000 Chinese in California, about one-ninth of the population. Their nemesis there was himself an immigrant (from Ireland), Dennis Kearney, leader of the Workingmen's party. Many white workers resented the Chinese for accepting lower wages, but their greatest sin, the editor of the New York *Nation* opined, was perpetuating "those disgusting habits of thrift, industry, and self-denial."

Exclusion of the Chinese was initially prevented by the Burlingame Treaty, which in 1868 gave China most-favored-nation status (the same as the best conceded to any other country) with respect to travel and immigration. But by 1880 the urgent need for railway labor had ebbed, and a new treaty with China permitted the United States to "regulate, limit, and suspend" Chinese immigration. In

The slogan of the Workingmen's party was "The Chinese Must Go!"

1882 President Chester A. Arthur vetoed a twenty-year suspension of immigration from China as actually a prohibition, but accepted a ten-year suspension, known as the Chinese Exclusion Act. This was periodically extended until it was made permanent in 1904.

The West Coast counterpart to Ellis Island was the Immigration Station on rugged Angel Island, six miles offshore from San Francisco. Opened in 1910, it served as a processing center for tens of thousands of Asian immigrants, most of them Chinese. Although the Chinese Exclusion Act had sharply reduced the flow of Chinese immigrants, it did not stop the influx completely. Those arrivals who could claim a Chinese-American parent were allowed to enter, as were certain officials, teachers, merchants, and students. The powerful prejudice the Chinese immigrants encountered helps explain why over 30 percent of the arrivals at Angel Island were denied entry. Those who appealed such denials were housed in prison-like barracks for weeks or months. One of the detainees scratched a poignant poem on a wall:

> This place is called an island of immortals,
> When, in fact, this mountainous wilderness is a prison.
> Once you see the open net, why throw yourself in?
> It is only because of empty pockets. I can do nothing else.

PUBLIC EDUCATION

THE SPREAD OF SCHOOLS   The spread of public education, spurred partly by the determination to "Americanize" immigrant children, helped quicken the emergence of a new America. "The spirit of American institutions is to be looked for in the public schools to a greater degree than anywhere else," wrote William T. Harris, the superintendent of St. Louis schools, philosopher, and proponent of graded schools and professional administration. By the time Harris wrote this in his annual report for 1871, America's commitment to public education was well nigh universal, though performance often fell short of the ideal.

The growing importance of public education is evident in statistics compiled by the national commissioner of education, whose office was created in 1867. In 1870 there were 6.8 million pupils in public schools; by 1920 the number had risen to 21.6 million. The percentage of school-age children in attendance went from 57 to 78 during these years. City schools quickly became schools of several rooms and separate grades with a teacher for each. In rural areas one-room schools lingered on into the twentieth century, when good roads

A public school in Valley Falls, Kansas.

made it possible to bus children to "consolidated schools." Despite these signs of progress, educational leaders all too often had to struggle against a pattern of political appointments, corruption, and incompetence in the public schools.

The spread of secondary schools accounted for a good bit of the increased enrollment in public schools. In antebellum America private academies prepared those who intended to enter college. At the beginning of the Civil War there were only about 100 public high schools in the whole country, but in the next decades their number grew rapidly to about 800 in 1880 and 6,000 at the turn of the century. Their curricula at first copied the academies' emphasis on higher mathematics and classical languages, but the public schools gradually accommodated their programs to those not going on to college, devising vocational training in such arts as bookkeeping, typing, drafting, and the use of tools.

VOCATIONAL TRAINING Vocational training was most intensely promoted after the Civil War by missionary schools for African-Americans such as Hampton Institute in Virginia, which trained Booker T. Washington, founder of Tuskegee Institute in Alabama. Another major prophet of the vocational training movement was Professor Calvin M. Woodward of St. Louis, who in setting up a school of engineering found his students woefully inept in the use of simple

History class at Tuskegee Institute, an early leader in vocational education for African-Americans.

tools. He called on the public schools to teach manual skills as well as more abstract knowledge. Prodded by the National Society for the Promotion of Industrial Education, high schools installed workshops for training in carpentry, printing, drafting, bricklaying, and machine work, and for home management, or "home economics," as well.

Congress had supported vocational training at the college level for many years. The Morrill Act of 1862 granted each state warrants for 30,000 acres per representative and senator, the income from which was to be applied to teaching agriculture and the mechanic arts in what came to be known as the "land-grant colleges." Among these new institutions were Clemson University, Pennsylvania State University, and Iowa State University. In 1890 a Second Morrill Act began the practice of making federal grants to these colleges. Their outreach, first attempted in Farmers' Institutes, greatly expanded with the rise of the demonstration technique perfected by Seaman A. Knapp, "schoolmaster to American agriculture." In 1903, about a decade after the Mexican boll weevil crossed the Rio Grande, Knapp set up a demonstration in Texas of the best techniques then known to fight the pest. From this beginning the demonstration technique spread rapidly as a means of getting knowledge into the field.

HIGHER EDUCATION   American colleges at this time, whether church schools or state "universities," sought to instill discipline, morality, and a curriculum heavy on mathematics and the classics (and in church schools, theology), along with ethics and rhetoric. History, modern languages and literature, and some science were tolerated, although laboratory work would likely be limited to a professor's demonstration to the class. The ill-assorted collection of books that passed for libraries drove faculties to take refuge in textbooks, which often represented the limits of their own knowledge. The college teacher was all too apt to be a young man seeking temporary refuge or a broken-down preacher seeking safe harbor. In 1871 a writer in *The Galaxy*, a literary monthly, called the typical professor "nondescript, a jack of all trades, equally ready to teach surveying and Latin eloquence, and thankful if his quarter's salary is not docked to whitewash the college fence."

Nevertheless the increasing demand for higher learning drove the college student population up from 52,000 in 1870 to 157,000 in 1890 and to 600,000 in 1920. During the same years the number of institutions rose from 563 to 998 and then to 1,041, and the number of faculty from 5,553 to 15,809 to 48,615. To accommodate the diverse needs of these growing numbers, colleges moved away from rigidly prescribed courses toward an elective system. In 1866 Washington College in Virginia, under its president, Robert E. Lee, adopted electives, and after 1869 Harvard College did so under its young president Charles W. Eliot. The new approach allowed students to favor their strong points and colleges to expand their scope. But as Henry Cabot Lodge complained, it also allowed students to "escape without learning anything at all by a judicious selection of unrelated subjects taken up only because they were easy or because the burden imposed by those who taught them was light."

Women's access to higher education improved markedly in the period. Before the Civil War a few male colleges had admitted women, and state universities in the West were commonly open to women from the start. But colleges in the South and East fell in line very slowly. Of the women's colleges, Vassar (1865) was the first to teach by the same standards as the best of the men's colleges, though it had to maintain a Preparatory Department for twenty-three years to upgrade poorly prepared entrants. In the 1870s two more excellent women's schools appeared in Massachusetts: Wellesley and Smith, the latter being the first to set the same admission requirements as men's colleges. The older women's colleges moved fast to upgrade their standards in the same way.

The dominant new trend in American higher education after the Civil War was the rise of the graduate school. The versatile professors of the old school had a knowledge more broad than deep. With some notable exceptions they engaged in little research, nor were they expected to advance the frontiers of knowledge. But gradually more and more Americans experienced a different system at the German universities, where training was more systematic and focused. After the Civil War the German system became the basis for the modern American university. Yale awarded its first Ph.D. in 1861, and Harvard its first in 1872.

The Johns Hopkins University, opened in Baltimore in 1876, set a new precedent by making graduate work its chief concern. The graduate students gathered in seminar rooms or laboratories, where under the guidance of an experienced scholar they learned a craft, much as journeymen had in the medieval guilds. The crowning achievement, signifying admission to full membership in the craft, was a masterpiece—in this case the Ph.D. dissertation, which it was expected would make an original contribution to knowledge. Clark University at Worcester, Massachusetts, founded in 1887, followed the model of Johns Hopkins.

In the early 1890s two more major universities were founded to

The Radcliffe College Class of 1884.

spread the gospel of Germanic education. The first, established by railroad magnate Leland Stanford (and named after his son), opened at Palo Alto, California, in 1891, and the following year the University of Chicago, endowed by oil baron John D. Rockefeller, began operation. Meanwhile other established institutions, including Harvard, Columbia, Cornell, Michigan, and Wisconsin, also set up graduate schools, and by 1900 American universities annually conferred hundreds of doctorates. The Ph.D. was fast becoming the ticket of admission to the guild of professors.

THE RISE OF PROFESSIONALISM

The Ph.D. revolution, moreover, was but one aspect of a growing emphasis on professionalism, with its imposition of standards, licensing of practitioners, and accreditation of professional schools. The number of professional schools grew rapidly in fields such as theology, law, medicine, dentistry, pharmacy, and veterinary medicine. While these fields accounted for 60 schools in 1850, there were 146 in 1875 and 283 in 1900. Growth in numbers brought pressures for higher standards. At Harvard in 1870 one could qualify for a medical degree by attending two lecture courses for four months, proving three years of medical experience, and passing a simple examination. Harvard president Charles Eliot then insisted on requiring three years of class attendance, together with laboratory and clinical work. In 1870 the Harvard Law School developed a rough equivalent to the laboratory by introducing the "case method," which required students to dig out the rules for themselves.

Along with advanced schooling went a movement for licensing practitioners in certain fields. The first state licensing law for dentistry, for instance, came in 1868, for pharmacy in 1874, for veterinary medicine in 1886, for accounting in 1896, and for architecture in 1897. By 1894 twenty-one states held standard examinations for doctors, and fourteen others recognized only graduates from accredited medical schools. Licensing benefited the public by certifying competence in a given field, but it also benefited members of the profession by limiting competition.

Learned and professional associations now began to proliferate. Earlier societies, such as the American Association for the Advancement of Science (1848), which had seemed specialized enough, made way for still more specialized groups such as the American Chemical Society (1876) and the National Statistical Association (1888). Modern-language scholars organized in 1883, American historians in

A Red Sox home game, 1897. Professional baseball became a major attraction in the late nineteenth century.

1884, economists in 1885, political scientists in 1889, folklorists in 1888, and all sponsored meetings and journals to keep members in touch with developments in the field. A host of commonplace and simple jobs entered the ranks of the "professions," including barbering, playing baseball, and planning vacations.

Athletic life in America felt the impact of professionalization after the Civil War. Before then sports and outdoor games tended to be informal activities centered on participation rather than entertainment for others. By 1900, however, many sports had developed uniform rules and regulations and had developed considerable spectator interest. Professional baseball teams appeared in the late 1860s, with umpires to call balls and strikes. In 1876 eight teams formed the National League, the "senior circuit," and the American League coalesced in 1901.

Other spectator sports such as horse racing and boxing also developed uniform rules and professional participants, and in the process they developed into huge commercial enterprises. Football was slower to turn professional, but it too became a mass spectator sport by the start of the twentieth century, with college games attracting upward of 50,000 fans. Early football games were brutal affairs. Without helmets or face masks and with little protective padding, players suffered frequent injuries (thirty players were killed and hundreds seriously injured in 1909 alone). Many college presidents complained that the football craze was eroding intellectual life on campus. When Dr. James Naismith nailed a peach basket to the gymnasium wall of the Springfield, Massachusetts, YMCA in 1891, America had a new sport—basketball—to play in between the fall football and spring baseball seasons.

THEORIES OF SOCIAL CHANGE

Every field of thought in the post–Civil War years felt the impact of Charles Darwin's *On the Origin of Species* (1859), which argued that existing species, including humanity itself, had evolved through a long process of "natural selection" from less complex forms of life. Those species that adapted to survival by reason of quickness, shrewdness, or other advantages reproduced their kind, while others fell by the wayside. The idea of species evolution shocked those of conventional religious views by contradicting a literal interpretation of the creation stories in Genesis. Heated arguments arose among scientists and clergymen. Some of the faithful rejected Darwin's doctrine, while others found their faith severely shaken not only by evolutionary theory but also by the urging of professional scholars to apply the critical standards of scholarship to the Bible itself, and by the study of comparative religion, which found parallels to biblical stories and doctrines in other faiths. Most of the faithful, however, came to reconcile science and religion. They viewed evolution as the Divine Will, as one of the secondary causes through which God worked.

SOCIAL DARWINISM   Though Darwin's theory applied only to biological phenomena, other thinkers drew broader inferences from it. The temptation to apply evolutionary theory to the social world proved irresistible. Darwin's fellow Englishman Herbert Spencer became the first major prophet of social Darwinism, and an important influence on American thought. Spencer, whose first works anticipated Darwin, brought forth in eight weighty tomes his *System of Synthetic Philosophy* (1862–1893), an effort to embrace all fields of knowledge within an overall system of Darwinian evolution. He argued that human society and institutions, like organisms, passed through the process of natural selection, which resulted, in Spencer's chilling phrase, in the "survival of the fittest." For Spencer, social evolution implied progress, ending "only in the establishment of the greatest perfection and the most complete happiness."

If, as Spencer believed, society naturally evolved for the better, then individual freedom was inviolable, and governmental interference with the process of social evolution was a serious mistake. This view amounted to a more ponderous version of Carnegie's "Gospel of Wealth"; it used biological laws to justify the workings of the free market. Social Darwinism implied a governmental policy of hands-off; it decried the regulation of business, the graduated income tax, sanitation and housing regulations, and even protection against medical quacks. Such interventions, Spencer charged, would only impede progress by contributing to the survival of the unfit. The only acceptable charity was voluntary, and even that was of dubious value. Spencer warned that "fostering the good-for-nothing at the expense of the good, is an extreme cruelty."

For Spencer and his many American supporters, accumulated wealth provided the best evidence of fitness. Successful businessmen and corporations were the engines of progress. If small businesses were crowded out by trusts and monopolies, that too was part of the process. As John D. Rockefeller told his Baptist Sunday school class: "The growth of a large business is merely a survival of the fittest. . . . The American Beauty rose can be produced in the splendor and fragrance which bring cheer to its beholder only by sacrificing the early buds which grow up around it. This is not an evil tendency in business. It is merely the working-out of a law of nature and a law of God."

The ideas of Darwin and Spencer spread quickly in America. *Popular Science Monthly,* founded in 1872, soon became the chief medium for popularizing Darwinism. That same year Darwin's chief

Charles Darwin.

Herbert Spencer, the first major prophet of social Darwinism.

academic disciple, William Graham Sumner, took up the new chair of political and social science at Yale. Trained for the ministry and formerly an Episcopal rector, he was given to preaching the gospel of natural selection under titles such as *What Social Classes Owe to Each Other* and "The Absurd Effort to Make the World Over."

Sumner's most lasting contribution, made in his book *Folkways* (1907), was to argue that social conditions were set by the working of tradition, or the customs of a community, and not by reason or natural laws. The implication here too was that it would be a mistake for government to interfere with established customs in the name of ideals of equality or natural rights. Democracy, according to Sumner, was a condition based not on reason but on customs arising from the availability of much free land in America. As available land diminished, customs would slowly change, showing democracy to be merely a temporary condition.

REFORM DARWINISM   The influence of Darwin and Spencer over the American mind did not go without challenge. Reform found its major philosopher in an obscure Washington civil servant, Lester Frank Ward, who had fought his way up from poverty and never lost his empathy for the underdog. Ward's book *Dynamic Sociology* (1883) singled out one product of evolution that previous pundits had neglected, the human brain. People, unlike animals, had minds that could shape social evolution. Far from being the helpless pawn of evolution, Ward argued, humanity could improve its situation by reflecting upon it and then acting. People thus had reached a stage at which they could control the process of evolution. The competition

Lester Frank Ward, proponent of reform Darwinism.

extolled by Sumner was in fact highly wasteful, and so was the natural competitive process: plant or cattle breeding, for instance, could actually improve on the results of natural selection.

Ward's reform Darwinism challenged Sumner's conservative social Darwinism, holding that cooperation, not competition, would better promote progress. Sumner's "irrational distrust of government" might have been justified in an earlier day of autocracy, but no longer under a representative system. Government could become the agency of progress by striving to reach two main goals: to ameliorate poverty, which impeded the development of the mind, and to promote the education of the masses. "Intelligence, far more than necessity," Ward wrote, "is the mother of invention," and "the influence of knowledge as a social factor, like that of wealth, is proportional to the extent of its distribution." Intellect, rightly informed by science, could plan successfully. In the benevolent "sociocracy" of the future, legislatures would function mainly to sanction decisions worked out in the sociological laboratory.

REALISM IN FACT AND FICTION

HISTORY AND THE SOCIAL SCIENCES   The pervasive effect of Darwinism in late-nineteenth-century America was comparable to the effect of romanticism in the first part of the century. Like the earlier reaction against the Enlightenment's praise of reason, the trend in social thought now was, as one scholar put it, the "revolt against formalism," that is, a turn against abstract logic and toward concrete reality. The revolt had two salient features: its emphasis on history, on looking to the past for explanations, and its interest in investigating reality broadly through a variety of the social sciences. Oliver Wendell Holmes, Jr., in *The Common Law* (1881), expressed the first feature succinctly. "The life of the law has not been logic; it has been experience," Holmes explained. And experience was history. "The law embodies the story of a nation's development through many centuries," Holmes wrote, "and it cannot be dealt with as if it contained only the axioms and corollaries of a book of mathematics."

In the milieu of Darwinism the study of history flourished. The historian, like the biologist, studied the process of development, but in the origins and the evolution of society. Under the influence of German scholarship, and the new emphasis on science, history aspired to become "scientific." This meant examining documents and manuscripts critically, using external and internal evidence to determine validity and relevancy. The ideal of the scientific historian was to reproduce history with perfect objectivity, as Leopold von Ranke suggested, as it actually was—a noble if unreachable goal. At the new Johns Hopkins University, Herbert Baxter Adams instilled into a whole generation of historians the "germ theory" of history, which held that the truth about things was to be found in their origins. For most American institutions the germ theory led to the forests of ancient Germany. Frederick Jackson Turner, a student of Adams, carried to his work on the American frontier his teacher's approach to history as an evolutionary process of adaptation.

Henry Adams of Harvard spent half a long lifetime in vain quest for the "laws" of history, and ended with the chilling thought that human history was a cycle marked by the accelerating capture and dissipation of energy, so that standards of living rose sharply, but with disruptive effects. "Power leaped from every atom," he wrote. "Man could no longer hold it off. . . . The railways alone approached the carnage of war; automobiles and fire-arms ravaged society, until an earthquake became almost a nervous relaxation."

Lester Frank Ward's achievements in *Dynamic Sociology* (1883) qualified him as the father of American sociology, but he, like many others, thought of the book as a broad synthesis of the social studies. It fell to Albion W. Small, head of the department at the University of Chicago, to define the field specifically. In his *General Sociology* (1905) Small confined it to the scientific analysis of social phenomena with emphasis on groups in human society. As founder (1895) and editor of the *American Journal of Sociology* Small wielded a strong influence in turning sociology from abstract speculation to the study of actual human relations. Theory, once all there was to sociology, gave way to a multitude of special interests: population, the family, ethnic groups, social class, public opinion, and social movements, to name but a few.

Economists made the same transition from abstract theory to the study of actual conditions. This transition was reflected in the statement of principles of the American Economics Association, founded in 1885. Economists looked "not so much to speculation as to historical and statistical study of actual conditions of economic life for the satisfactory accomplishment of [economic] study" and upheld the state "as an agency whose positive assistance is one of the indispensable conditions of human progress." One economist argued that the economic problem would soon no longer be scarcity, since modern technology would make possible a surplus of goods, but distribution: how best to distribute goods and services.

PRAGMATISM   Around the turn of the century the evolutionary idea found expression in a philosophical principle set forth in mature form by William James in his book *Pragmatism: A New Name for Some Old Ways of Thinking*. James, a professor of philosophy and psychology at Harvard, like Lester Frank Ward was concerned with the role of ideas in the process of evolution. Truth, to James, arose from the testing of new ideas, the value of which lay in their practical consequences. Similarly, scientists could test the validity of their ideas in the laboratory, and judge their import by their applications. James applied the principles of pragmatism even to religion in *Varieties of*

William James (left) *and John Dewey* (right).

Religious Experience (1902), where he noted that prayer in some cases seemed to raise the energy and potential of an individual, making prayer a true and valid experience for those people. Pragmatism reflected a quality often looked upon as genuinely American: the inventive, experimental spirit.

John Dewey, who would become the chief philosopher of pragmatism after James, preferred the term "instrumentalism," by which he meant that ideas were instruments, especially of social reform. Dewey, unlike James, threw himself into movements for the rights of labor and women, the promotion of peace, and the reform of education. Dewey believed that education was the process through which society would gradually progress toward the end of economic democracy. Dewey became the prophet of what was later labeled "progressive education." He emphasized the teaching of history, geography, and science in order to enlarge the child's personal experience. Dewey also pointed out that social conditions had so changed that schools had to find ways to inculcate values once derived from participation in family and community activities. Another important goal of the schools was to keep habits flexible to prepare children for a changing world. They needed not just knowledge but a critical intelligence to cope with a complex, modern world.

THE LOCAL COLORISTS   American literature responded in different ways to the changes in American life and thought. The local color movement, which emerged after the Civil War, reflected a reunited nation engrossed with the diversity of its peoples and cultures. This movement also expressed the nostalgia of a people moving from a rural to an urban culture, and longing for those places where the old folkways survived. In California, Bret Harte, the editor of the *Overland Monthly*, burst upon the national consciousness in the late 1860s with colorful stories of the gold country such as "The Outcasts of Poker Flat" and "The Luck of Roaring Camp." Hamlin Garland, in *Main-Traveled Roads* (1891), pictured the hardscrabble existence of farmers and their wives in his native country, the upper Midwest from Wisconsin to the Dakotas.

Sarah Orne Jewett depicted the down-easters of her native Maine, most enduringly in the stories and sketches collected in *The Country of the Pointed Firs* (1896), while Mary E. Wilkins Freeman wrote stories of village life in Vermont and Massachusetts gathered in *A Humble Romance* (1887) and other works. Jewett's creative glance was always backward-looking and affectionate. She looked upon her parents' "generation as the one to which I really belong—I who was brought up with grandfathers and granduncles and aunts for my best playmates." She told another writer that her head was always full of old women and old houses, and when the two came together the result was a richly textured fiction marked by the essential dignity of a bygone day.

Once the passions of war and Reconstruction were spent, the South became for many northern readers an inexhaustible gallery of quaint types. George Washington Cable exploited the local color of the Louisiana Creoles and Cajuns in *Old Creole Days* (1879), *The Grandissimes* (1880), and other books. Joel Chandler Harris, a newsman and columnist, wove authentic African-American folk tales into the unforgettable stories of Uncle Remus, gathered first in *Uncle Remus: His Songs and His Sayings* (1880). Few Americans, whether they have read the stories or not, can long remain ignorant of the wonderful tar-baby or the brier patch.

CLEMENS, HOWELLS, AND JAMES   The best of the local colorists could find universal truths in local life, but Samuel Langhorne Clemens (Mark Twain) transcended them all. A native of Missouri, Clemens was forced to work from the time he was twelve, becoming first a printer and then a Mississippi riverboat pilot. When the Civil War shut down the river traffic, he briefly joined a Confederate militia company, then left with his brother, Orion, for Nevada, where he wrote for the *Territorial Enterprise*. He moved on to California in 1864 and first gained widespread notice with his tall tale of the gold country, "The Celebrated Jumping Frog of Calaveras County"

Samuel Langhorne Clemens, or Mark Twain.

(1865). In 1867 the San Francisco *Alta Californian* staked him to a tour of the Mediterranean, and his humorous reports on the trip, revised and collected into *Innocents Abroad* (1869), established him as a funny man much in demand on the lecture circuit. With the success of *Roughing It* (1871), an account of his western years, he moved to Hartford, Connecticut, and was able to set up as a full-time author and hilarious lecturer.

Clemens was the first great American writer born and raised west of the Appalachians. His early writings accentuated his western background, but for his greatest books he drew heavily upon his boyhood in a border slave state and the tall-tale tradition of southwestern humor. In *The Adventures of Tom Sawyer* (1876) he evoked in fiction the prewar Hannibal, Missouri, where his own boyhood was cut so short. Its story of childhood adventures is firmly etched on the American memory. *Life on the Mississippi* (1883), based on articles written eight years before, drew upon what Clemens remembered as his happiest days as a young riverboat pilot before the war.

Clemens's masterpiece, *The Adventures of Huckleberry Finn* (1884), created unforgettable characters in Huck Finn, his shiftless father, the slave Jim, the Widow Douglas, the "King," and the "Duke." The product of an erratic upbringing, Huck Finn embodied the instinct of every red-blooded American boy to "light out for the territory" whenever polite society set out to civilize him. Huck's effort to help his friend Jim escape bondage expressed well the moral dilemmas imposed on everyone by slavery. Many years later another great American writer, Ernest Hemingway, would claim that "All modern American literature comes from one book by Mark Twain, called *Huckleberry Finn.*"

Clemens wrote other memorable books, but nothing to equal those three. Like many humorists he had a broad streak of pessimism. He preferred to laugh rather than gaze into the abyss, but eventually the laughter stopped. Speculative investments bankrupted him during the Panic of 1893 and sent him back to the lecture circuit. Then his oldest daughter died of meningitis and his wife went into a long decline. His later writings, many not published before his death, expressed despair about what Clemens took to calling "that damned human race," but he himself remained a revered national treasure. As his friend, William Dean Howells, observed, he was unique among his contemporaries: "Emerson, Longfellow, Lowell, Holmes—I knew them all and all the rest of our sages, poets, seers, critics, humorists; they were like one another and like other literary men; but Clemens was sole, incomparable, the Lincoln of our literature."

Howells himself was unique, for no other American writer ever so dominated the literary scene. Born in Ohio, he went to Boston in 1867 and soon became editor of the influential *Atlantic Monthly*. He left that post to devote himself to novel writing, but later served better than two decades as a columnist and critic for *Harper's Monthly*. Howells proclaimed the doctrine of realism, a sort of literary version of scientific history's effort to reproduce the past as it actually happened. He wrote that realism "was nothing more or less than the truthful treatment of . . . the motives, the impulses, the principles that shape the life of actual men and women." The realist commonly wrote of the middle class in a simple and direct language, taking a pragmatic point of view of people and events.

Howells wrote novels, plays, travel books, criticism, essays, biography, and autobiography. Amid the varied output of a long and productive life, *The Rise of Silas Lapham* (1885) stands out as his most famous novel. In it Howells sympathetically portrayed a *nouveau riche* paint manufacturer, one of the earliest fictional treatments of an American businessman. Soon after its publication, however, at the height of his career, Howells felt that "the bottom had dropped out" of his life. Converted to socialism by reading Tolstoy, horrified by the "civic murder" of the Haymarket anarchists, he entered a new phase. In *A Hazard of New Fortunes* (1890) he offered less sympathetic views of businessmen, included scenes of squalor and misery in the Bowery, and introduced a German-American socialist who lost his life in a police beating during a violent streetcar strike.

William Dean Howells (left) *and Henry James* (right).

The third major literary figure of the times, Henry James, moved in a world far different from those of Clemens or Howells. Brother of the pragmatist philosopher William James, Henry spent most of his adult life as a voluntary expatriate in London, where he produced elegant novels that explored the society of Americans in Europe. In novels such as *Daisy Miller* (1878), *Portrait of a Lady* (1881), *The Ambassadors* (1903), and *The Golden Bowl* (1904), James explored the tensions that developed between direct, innocent, and idealistic Americans (most often young women) and sophisticated, devious Europeans. James typically wrote of the upper classes, and his stories turned less on plot than on moral dilemmas. His intense exploration of the inner selves of his characters brought him the titles of "father of the psychological novel" and "biographer of fine consciences." He could also produce spine-tingling ghost stories such as "The Turn of the Screw" (1898) and "The Jolly Corner" (1907). In his later work he pioneered the technique of removing the author from the reader's awareness, becoming "invisible," as the poet T. S. Eliot said, a technique commonplace among later authors.

LITERARY NATURALISM During the 1890s the naturalists emerged as a new literary school, the heralds of twentieth-century modernism. The naturalists imported scientific determinism into literature, viewing man as part of the animal world, prey to natural forces and internal drives without control or full knowledge of them. From Darwin, their greatest inspiration, they drew biological determinism, from Newton a mechanistic determinism, and from Karl Marx a type of historical determinism. Frank Norris, who drew inspiration from the French novelist Émile Zola, pictured in *McTeague* (1899) the descent of a San Francisco dentist and his wife into madness, driven by greed, violence, and lust. Norris's *The Octopus* (1901), first of an unfinished trilogy on the lives of wheat farmers, presented the attempt of railroad owners to squeeze out the ranchers from the wheatfields of California.

Stephen Crane in *Maggie: A Girl of the Streets* (1893) and *The Red Badge of Courage* (1895) portrayed people caught up in situations beyond their control. *Maggie* depicted a girl driven to prostitution and death amid scenes so sordid that Crane had to finance publication himself. *The Red Badge of Courage*, his masterpiece, told the story of a young man going through his baptism of fire in the Civil War, and evoked nobility and courage amid the ungovernable carnage of war. Crane himself had had no experience of battle, which made his achievement the more remarkable.

Two of the naturalists achieved a degree of popular success: Jack London and Theodore Dreiser. Jack London of California was both a professed socialist and a believer in the German philosopher Friedrich Nietzsche's doctrine of the superman. In adventure stories like *The Call of the Wild* (1903) and *The Sea Wolf* (1904) London celebrated the triumph of brute force and the will to survive. He reinforced his point about animal force in *The Call of the Wild* by making his protagonist not a superman but a superdog which reverted to the wild in Alaska and ran with a wolf pack.

Theodore Dreiser shocked the genteel public probably more than the others with protagonists who sinned without remorse and without punishment. *Sister Carrie* (1900), a counterpoint to Crane's *Maggie*, departed from it in having Carrie Meeber survive illicit loves and go on to success on the stage. In *The Financier* (1912) and *The Titan* (1914) Dreiser's main character was a sexual athlete and a man of elemental force who rose to a dominant position in business and society. *An American Tragedy* (1925), generally regarded as Dreiser's masterpiece, pictured a less successful young man driven by the desire for sex and money to murder his pregnant mistress in order to marry wealth. He eventually was convicted and executed.

SOCIAL CRITICISM   Behind their dogma of determinism the naturalists harbored intense outrage at human misery. Other writers shared their indignation but addressed themselves more directly to protest and reform. Henry George, a California printer and journalist, was suddenly struck on a visit to New York by the contrast the city offered between wealth and poverty. "Once, in daylight, and in a city street, there came to me a thought, a vision, a call. . . . And there and then I made a vow." The vow was to seek out the cause of poverty in the midst of progress. Back in California, the spectacle of land boomers grabbing choice sites brought George a new insight. The basic problem, he reasoned, was the unearned increment in wealth that came to those who owned the land. The fruit of his thought, *Progress and Poverty* (1879), a thick and difficult book, started slowly but by 1905 had sold about 2 million copies in several languages.

George held that all people had as much right to the use of the land as to the air they breathed. Nobody had a right to the value that accrued from the land, since that was created by the community, not by its owner. Labor and capital, on the other hand, did have a just claim on the wealth they produced. One justifiable solution to the problem of unearned wealth was to socialize all property in land, but that would have been too disruptive. Better simply to tax the unearned increment in the value of the land, or the rent. George's "single-tax" idea was intended to free capital and labor from paying tribute for the land, and to put to use lands previously held out of production by speculators. George's idea was widely propagated and actually affected tax policy here and there, but his influence on the thinking of the day came less from his "single-tax" panacea than from the paradox he posed in his title, *Progress and Poverty*.

The journalist and free-lance writer Henry Demarest Lloyd addressed himself to what many found a more vital issue than Henry George's, not the monopoly in land but industrial monopoly. His best-known book, *Wealth Against Commonwealth* (1894), drew on more than a decade of studying the Standard Oil Company. Lloyd, like Lester Frank Ward, saw the key to progress in cooperation rather than competition. Economic activities in their cooperative aspects demonstrated a civilizing process; Lloyd argued that "the spectacle of the million or more employees of the railroads . . . dispatching trains, maintaining tracks, collecting fares and freights . . . is possible only where civilization has reached a high average of morals and culture." But those in charge of the machinery of industry were concerned only with wealth, not with promoting civilization. "Of gods, friends, learning, of the uncomprehended civilization they overrun, they ask but one question: How much? What is a good time to sell? What is a good time to buy?" To avoid destruction, civilization required changes. The cooperative principle should be applied "to all toils in which private sovereignty has become through monopoly a despotism over the public." Where monopoly had developed, it should be transferred to public operation in the public interest. In 1903, just before his death, Lloyd joined the Socialist party.

Thorstein Veblen brought to his social criticism a background of formal training in economics and a purpose of making economics more an evolutionary or historical science. By all accounts he taught miserably, even inaudibly, and seldom held a job for long, but he wrote brilliantly. In his best-known work, *The Theory of the Leisure Class* (1899), he examined the pecuniary values of the middle classes and introduced phrases that have since become almost clichés: "conspicuous consumption" and "conspicuous leisure." With the advent of industrial society, Veblen argued, property became the conventional basis of reputation. For the upper classes, moreover, it became necessary to consume time nonproductively as evidence of the ability to afford a life of leisure. In this and later works Veblen held that the division between industrial experts and business managers was widening to a dangerous point. The businessman's interest in profits combined with his ignorance of efficiency produced wasteful organization and a failure to realize the full potential of modern technology.

Edward Bellamy's *Looking Backward, 2000–1887* (1888) typified another genre of reform literature, the utopian novel. In Bellamy's futuristic story, a Bostonian who falls asleep in 1887 awakens in the year 2000 to find that the millennium has genuinely arrived. More than a hundred years in the future Julian West discovers a society transformed. The revolution which led to political equality has led on, by the democratic method, to a "Nationalist" society of economic equality under socialism. Everybody gets an equal share of the national product and labor is shared by the simple method of reducing the hours for distasteful jobs until someone is willing to do the work. All this is accomplished by public control under national planning. The book enjoyed a temporary vogue, became a best-seller, and led to the founding of Nationalist Clubs. The popularity of Bellamy's book gave rise to a spate of utopian novels, and some anti-utopian ones depicting model societies gone wrong.

THE SOCIAL GOSPEL

RISE OF THE INSTITUTIONAL CHURCH The churches responded slowly to the mounting social criticism, for American Protestantism had become one of the main props of the established order. The Reverend Henry Ward Beecher, pastor of the fashionable Plymouth Congregational Church in Brooklyn, preached success, social Darwinism, and the unworthiness of the poor. The English writer Rudyard Kipling in 1899 reported a visit to a church in Chicago where the minister pictured "a heaven along the lines of the Palmer House (but with all the gilding real gold, and all the plate-glass diamond). . . . One sentence . . . caught my delighted ear. It was apropos of some question of the Judgment, and ran: 'NO! I tell you God doesn't do business that way!' "

As the middle classes moved out to the streetcar suburbs, their churches followed. In the years 1868–1888, for instance, seventeen Protestant churches abandoned the areas below Fourteenth Street in Manhattan. In the center of Chicago 60,000 residents had no church, Protestant or Catholic. Where churches became prosperous they fell easily under the spell of respectability and do-nothing social Darwinism. Working-class people sometimes felt out of place in opulent edifices with stained-glass windows: "opera-singing churches," one revivalist called them.

Many churches responded to the human needs of the time by undertaking earthly functions in addition to saving souls. The institutional church devoted most of its resources to community service and care for the unfortunate. The Young Men's Christian Association had entered the United States from England in the 1850s and grew

A Salvation Army group in Flint, Michigan, 1894.

rapidly after 1870; the Salvation Army, founded in London in 1876, entered the United States four years later.

Churches in urban districts began to develop institutional features that were more social than strictly religious in function. Before the Civil War an Episcopal minister in New York organized St. Luke's Hospital and St. Johnland, a rural settlement in the Hudson Valley, as a refuge for slum dwellers. In the postbellum years this kind of work spread as church buildings acquired gymnasiums, libraries, lecture rooms, and other facilities for social programs. By 1894 there were enough such churches to form the Open and Institutional Church League. St. George's Episcopal Church exemplified the success of the institutional church: when it first offered institutional features in 1882 it had 75 members; by 1897 it had over 4,000 members. Russell Conwell's Baptist Temple in Philadelphia included, among other features, a night school for working people which grew into Temple University.

RELIGIOUS REFORMERS The involvement of Conwell, a leading spokesman for the gospel of success, signified that the institutional movement might be consistent with a conservative outlook. But other church leaders built upon the institutional movement by preaching what came to be called the social gospel. One of the earliest, Washington Gladden of Columbus, Ohio, managed to preach the social gospel from the pulpit of a middle-class Congregational church. The new gospel in fact expressed the social conscience of the middle class. Gladden accepted the new ideas of evolution and textual criticism of the Bible, which he said relieved him of defending the literal truth of the story of Jonah and the whale. In his many books Gladden set forth the idea that true Christianity lies not in rituals, dogmas, or even in the mystical experience of God, but in the principle that "Thou shalt love thy neighbor as thyself." Christian law should govern the operation of industry, with worker and employer united in serving each other's interest. He argued for labor's right to organize, and complained that the class distinctions of society had invaded and split congregations as well.

The acknowledged intellectual leader of the social gospel movement, however, was the Baptist Walter Rauschenbusch, professor at the Colgate-Rochester Theological Seminary—appropriately located in the unofficial capital of the old Burned-Over District. In *Christianity and the Social Crisis* (1907) and other works he developed a theological basis for the movement in the Kingdom of God. This kingdom existed in the churches themselves, but it embraced far more than these: "It is the Christian transfiguration of the social order. The church is one social institution alongside of the family, the industrial organization of society, and the State. The Kingdom of God is in all these, and realizes itself through them all." The church was indispensable to religion, but "the greatest future awaits religion in the public life of humanity."

THE CATHOLIC CHURCH   In the postbellum years Catholics remained inhibited from support of the new social movements by the *Syllabus of Errors* (1864), issued by Pope Pius IX, which declared erroneous such current ideas as progress, liberalism, rationalism, and socialism. James Cardinal Gibbons of Baltimore was instrumental, however, in moderating the effects of the *Syllabus*. In 1886 he forestalled an official condemnation of the Knights of Labor, which had abandoned secrecy and was headed by a Catholic, Terence Powderly. Gibbons also prevented the listing of *Progress and Poverty* on the *Index of Forbidden Books*.

The church's outlook altered drastically in 1891 when Pope Leo XIII issued his encyclical, *Rerum novarum* ("Of modern things"). This new expression of Catholic social doctrine upheld private property as a natural right but condemned capitalism where it had imposed poverty and degradation on workers. It upheld the right of Catholics to join labor unions and socialist movements insofar as these were not antireligious. But American Catholics for the most part remained isolated from reform movements until the twentieth century, though they themselves were among the victims of the slums.

EARLY EFFORTS AT URBAN REFORM

THE SETTLEMENT HOUSE MOVEMENT   While preachers of the social gospel dispensed inspiration, other dedicated reformers attacked the problems of the slums from residential and community centers called settlement houses. The movement sprang from the example of Toynbee Hall, founded in a London industrial district, where an English vicar invited students to join him in "settling" in a deprived section. By 1900 perhaps a hundred settlement houses existed in the United States, some of the best known being Jane Addams's and Ellen Starr's Hull House in Chicago (1889), Robert A. Woods's South End House in Boston (1891), and Lillian Wald's Henry Street Settlement (1895) in New York.

The settlement houses were populated mainly by idealistic middle-class young people, a majority of them college-trained women who had few other outlets for meaningful work outside the home. Settlement workers sought to broaden the horizons and improve the lives of slum dwellers in diverse ways. At Jane Addams's Hull House, for instance, workers sought to draw the neighborhood children into clubs and kindergartens, and a nursery served the infant children of working mothers. The program gradually expanded as Hull House sponsored health clinics, lectures, music and art studios, an employment bureau, men's clubs, training in skills such as bookbinding, a gymnasium, and a savings bank. The Hull House Players helped initiate the Little Theater movement.

Jane Addams and other settlement house leaders realized, however, that the spreading slums made their work as effective as bailing

Jane Addams.

out the ocean with a teaspoon. They therefore spoke out and organized political support for housing laws, public playgrounds, juvenile
courts, mothers' pensions, workmen's compensation laws, and legislation against child labor. Lillian Wald promoted the establishment
of the federal Children's Bureau in 1912 and Jane Addams, for her
work in the peace movement, received late in her life the Nobel
Peace Prize for 1931.

The settlement house movement was not all of one piece, however. Critics accused settlements of subtle and not-so-subtle forms of
social control, and of attempts to assimilate the ethnic poor to white,
middle-class Protestant standards. The cultural gap between middle-class social workers and slum dwellers could often lead to misunderstanding, and in the effort to "Americanize" immigrants, the
settlement houses and agencies of education sometimes lacked sensitivity to the values of other cultures. But on balance their contributions were more positive than negative. By the end of the century
both the Catholic church and Jewish agencies were taking up the
settlement house movement.

THE WOMEN'S SUFFRAGE MOVEMENT   Settlement house workers, insofar as they were paid, of course made up but a fraction of all
gainfully employed women. With the growth of population the number of employed women steadily increased, as did their percentage
of the labor force and of the total female population. The greatest
leaps forward came in the decades of the 1880s and the 1900s, both
of which were also peak decades of immigration, a correlation which
can be explained by the immigrant's need for income. The number
of employed women went from over 2.6 million in 1880 to 4 million
in 1890, then from 5.1 million in 1900 to 7.8 million in 1910. "Between 1880 and 1900 the employment of women in most parts of the
economy became an established fact," wrote one historian. "This
was surely the most significant event in the modern history of
women." Through all those years domestic work remained the largest category of employment for women; teaching and nursing also
remained among the leading fields. The main change was that clerical work (bookkeeping, stenographic work, and the like) and sales
jobs became increasingly available to women.

These changes in occupational status had little connection with
the women's rights movement, which increasingly focused on the
issue of suffrage. Immediately after the Civil War, Susan B. Anthony, a seasoned veteran of the movement though still in her for-
ties, demanded that the Fourteenth Amendment include a
guarantee of the vote for women as well as black males. She made
little impression on the defenders of masculine prerogative, how-

ever, who held resolutely to the notion that women belonged in the domestic sphere. "Their mission is at home, by their blandishments and their love to assuage the passions of men as they come in from the battle of life," said a New Jersey senator. "It will be a sorry day for this country when those vestal fires of love and piety are put out."

In 1869 the unity of the women's movement was broken in a manner reminiscent of the antislavery rift three decades before. The question once again was whether or not the movement should concentrate on one overriding issue. Anthony and Elizabeth Cady Stanton founded the National Woman Suffrage Association to promote a women's suffrage amendment to the constitution, but they looked upon suffrage as but one among many feminist causes to be promoted as well. Later that same year Lucy Stone, Julia Ward Howe, and other leaders formed the American Woman Suffrage Association, which focused single-mindedly on the suffrage as the first and basic reform.

It would be another half century before the battle could be won, and the long struggle for referenda and state legislation on the issue focused the women's cause ever more on the primary objective of the vote. In 1890, after three years of negotiation, the rival groups united as the National American Woman Suffrage Association, with Elizabeth Cady Stanton as president for two years, to be followed by Susan B. Anthony until 1900. The work thereafter was carried on by a new generation, led by Anna Howard Shaw and Carrie Chapman Catt. Over the years the movement slogged its way to some local and some partial victories, as a few states granted women suffrage in school board or municipal elections, or bond referenda. In 1869 the

Carrie Chapman Catt, a leader in the women's suffrage movement.

Territory of Wyoming granted full suffrage to women, and after 1890 retained women's suffrage as a state. Three other western states soon followed suit: Colorado in 1893, Utah and Idaho in 1896. But women's suffrage lost in a California referendum in 1896 by a dishearteningly narrow margin.

The movement remained in the doldrums thereafter until the cause won a Washington state referendum by a two-to-one margin in 1910, and then carried California by a close majority in 1911. The following year three more western states—Arizona, Kansas, and Oregon—joined in to make a total of nine western states with full suffrage. In 1913 Illinois granted women presidential and municipal suffrage. Not until New York acted in 1917 did a state east of the Mississippi adopt universal suffrage. In 1878 California's Senator A. A. Sargent introduced the "Anthony Amendment," which remained before Congress until 1896 and then vanished until 1913. It was word for word the women's suffrage amendment eventually ratified, but that triumph required another schism in the movement brought on by a new generation of militants who had been fired up by the direct action of the British suffragists (see Chapter 26).

Despite the focus on the vote, women did not confine their public work to that issue. In 1866 a Young Women's Christian Association, a parallel to the YMCA, appeared in Boston and spread elsewhere. The New England Women's Club, started in 1868 by Julia Ward Howe and others, was an early example of the women's clubs which then proliferated to the extent that a General Federation of Women's Clubs tied them together in 1890. Many women's clubs confined themselves to "literary" and social activities, but others became deeply involved in charities and reform. The New York Consumers League, formed in 1890, and the National Consumers League, formed nine years later, sought to make the buying public, chiefly women, aware of labor conditions. One of its devices was the "White List" of firms which met its minimum standards. The National Women's Trade Union League, founded in 1903, performed a similar function of bringing educated and middle-class women together with working women for the benefit of women unionists.

These and the many other women's groups of the time may have aroused the fear in opponents to women's suffrage that voting women would tilt toward reform. This was the fear of the brewing and liquor interests, large business interests generally, and political machine bosses. Others, mainly in the South, expressed opposition to women's suffrage on the ground that black women would be enfranchised, or because of states'-rights views.

A JUDICIAL HARBOR FOR LAISSEZ-FAIRE Even without the support of voting women in most places, the states groped toward rudimentary measures to regulate big business and labor conditions in the public interest. By the end of the century nearly every state had provided for the regulation of railroads, if not always effectively, and had moved to supervise banks and insurance companies. Between 1887 and 1897, by one count, the states and territories passed over 1,600 laws relating to conditions of work, which limited the hours of labor, provided special protection for women, limited or forbade child labor, required regular wage payments in cash, called for factory inspections, and outlawed blacklisting or the importation of "Pinkerton men." Nearly all states had boards or commissioners of labor, and some had boards of conciliation and arbitration. Still, the effect of the effort was limited by poor enforcement and a sizable body of contrary opinion which found a special lodgment in the courts, where conservative judges in this era were busily reading laissez-faire into the Constitution.

Their chief device was a revised interpretation of the Fourteenth Amendment clauses forbidding the states to "deprive any person of life, liberty or property without due process of law" or to deny any person "the equal protection of the laws." Two significant steps of legal reasoning turned the due-process clause into a bulwark of property. First, the judges reasoned that the word "person" in the clause included corporations, which in other connections were legally artificial persons with the right to own property, buy and sell, sue and be sued like natural persons—even though, in a common expression, they had neither tail to kick nor soul to be damned. Second, the courts moved away from the old view that "due process" referred only to correct procedures and toward a doctrine of "substantive due process" which allowed courts to review the substance of an action. Under this line of reasoning it was possible for legislatures by perfectly proper procedures to pass laws so extreme (in the view of the judges) as to deprive persons of property to an unreasonable degree, and thereby violate due process.

The Supreme Court first accepted the personality of the corporation in a tax case, *Santa Clara County v. Southern Pacific Railroad Company* (1886). That same year the Court in *Stone v. Farmers Loan and Trust Company* (1886) recognized the authority of Mississippi to regulate railroad rates, but declared that there might be cases in which the Court could review the rates: "Under pretense of regulating fares and freights, the State cannot require a railroad corporation to carry persons or property without reward." In *Chicago, Milwaukee and St. Paul Railway Company v. Minnesota* (1890) the justices declared unconstitutional a state law which forbade judicial review of rates set by a railroad commission. "The question of the reasonableness of a rate of charge . . . is eminently a question for judicial investigation," the Court ruled, "requiring due process of law for its determination." This was a direct reversal of the ruling in *Munn v. Illinois* (1877) that regulation was a legislative prerogative. It remained only for the Court to overturn rates set directly by a state legislature. That it did in *Smyth v. Ames* (1898), in which it struck down a Nebraska law for setting rates so low as to be, in the Court's view, unreasonable.

From the due-process clause the Court also derived a new doctrine of "liberty of contract," defined as being within the liberties protected by the due-process clause. Liberty, the Court ruled in 1897, involved "not only the right of the citizen to be free from the mere physical restraint of his person, . . . but the term is deemed to embrace the right of the citizen to be free in the enjoyment of all his faculties," and free "to enter into all contracts" proper to carrying out such purposes. When it came to labor laws, this translated into an employee's "liberty" to contract for work under the most oppressive conditions without interference from the state. The courts continued to apply such an interpretation well into the twentieth century.

Judges in some of the lower courts found no need to spin their theories so finely. In 1886 the Pennsylvania supreme court struck down an act to protect workers against payment in commodities instead of in cash, declaring it "an insulting attempt to put the

Bohemian Cigarmakers at Work in a Tenement. *Immigrant workers went unprotected by labor laws in the nineteenth century.*

laborer under a legislative tutelage, which is not only degrading to his manhood, but subversive of his rights as a citizen of the United States." The high court of West Virginia in 1889 condemned a similar law as an attempt to "foist upon the people a paternal government of the most objectionable character, because it assumes that the employer is a knave, and the laborer an imbecile." At least equally boggling in its blindness to reality was the opinion expressed by a New York judge in 1885, in which he ruled against a law forbidding cigarmaking in tenements. "It cannot be perceived," he said, "how the cigarmaker is to be improved in his health or his morals by forcing him from his home and its hallowed associations and beneficent influences, to ply his trade elsewhere."

As the turn of the century neared, opinion in the country stood poised between such conservative rigidities and a growing sense that new occasions teach new duties. "By the last two decades of the century," wrote one observer, "many thoughtful men had begun to march under various banners declaring that somewhere and somehow the promise of the American dream had been lost—they often said 'betrayed'—and that drastic changes needed to be made to recapture it."

The last two decades of the nineteenth century had already seen a slow erosion of laissez-faire values, which had found their most secure home in the courts. From the social philosophy of the reformers, Social Gospelers, and Populists there emerged a concept of the general-welfare state which, in the words of one historian, sought "to promote the general welfare not by rendering itself inconspicuous but by taking such positive action as is deemed necessary to improve the condition under which its citizens live and work." The reformers supplied no agreed-upon blueprint for a general-welfare utopia, but "simply assumed that government could promote the public interest by appropriate positive action . . . whenever the circumstances indicated that such action would further the common weal." The conflict between this notion and laissez-faire values went on into the new century, but by the mid-twentieth century, after the Progressive Movement, the New Deal, and the Fair Deal, the conflict would be "resolved in theory, in practice, and in public esteem in favor of the general-welfare state."

FURTHER READING

Recent surveys of urbanization include Eric H. Monkkonen's *America Becomes Urban* (1988) and Charles N. Glaab and A. Theodore Brown's *A History of Urban America* (3rd ed., 1983).° Case studies on the history of city life include Stephan Thernstrom's *The Other Bostonians: Poverty and Prog-*

ress in the American Metropolis, 1880–1970 (1973),° Howard P. Chudacoff's *Mobile Americans: Residential and Social Mobility in Omaha, 1880–1920* (1972), and James Borchert's *Alley Life in Washington: Family, Community, Religion, and Folk Life in That City, 1850–1970* (1980),° on black life in that city.

On city planning, see Stanley K. Schultz's *Constructing Urban Culture: American Cities and City Planning, 1800–1920* (1989). Urban politics is treated in John M. Allswang's *Bosses, Machines, and Urban Voters* (rev. ed., 1986).° Sam Bass Warner examines how space and distance changed urban configurations in *Streetcar Suburbs: The Process of Growth in Boston, 1870–1900* (2nd ed., 1978).° Martin V. Melosi's *Garbage in the Cities* (1981) takes a look at that problem. Eric H. Monkkonen's *Police in Urban America, 1860–1920* (1981) examines the changing nature of crime and law enforcement.

Immigration has an extensive scholarship. General surveys include Leonard Dinnerstein and David M. Reimers's *Ethnic Americans: A History of Immigration and Assimilation* (2nd ed., 1982)° and Alan M. Kraut's *The Huddled Masses* (1982).° John Higham's *Strangers in the Land: Patterns of American Nativism* (1955)° examines how old-stock residents reacted to the influx of new citizens.

More specific studies of ethnic groups include Rowland T. Berthoff's *British Immigrants in Industrial America, 1790–1950* (1953), John B. Duff's *The Irish in the United States* (1971), Josef F. Barton's *Peasants and Strangers: Italians, Rumanians, and Slovaks in an American City* (1975), Humbert S. Nelli's *Italians in Chicago, 1880–1930* (1970),° Stanford M. Lyman's *Chinese Americans* (1974), Irving Howe's *The World of Our Fathers: The Journey of the East European Jews to America and the Life They Made and Found* (1976),° and Yuji Ichioka's *The Issei: The World of the First Generation Japanese Immigrants, 1885–1924* (1988). See also Ronald Takaki's *Strangers From a Different Shore: A History of Asian Americans* (1989).°

Much of the recent work on education stresses how schools were designed to assimilate these new arrivals. This work includes David B. Tyack's *The One Best System: A History of American Urban Education* (1974).° For trends in higher education, consult Laurence Veysey's *The Emergence of the American University* (1965).° Burton J. Bledstein's *The Culture of Professionalism: The Middle Class and the Development of Higher Education in America* (1976)° is particularly insightful. Another aspect of higher education is examined in Ronald A. Smith's *Sports and Freedom: The Rise of Big-Time College Athletics* (1988).

Morton White and Lucia White's *The Intellectual versus the City* (1962)° surveys the insights of the Gilded Age's leading thinkers. Richard Hofstadter's *Social Darwinism in American Thought* (rev. ed., 1955)° and Cynthia E. Russett's *Darwin in America* (1976)° examine the impact of the theory of evolution. Bruce Curtis's *William Graham Sumner* (1981) discusses Darwin's leading disciple in America. To trace the contours of pragmatism,

---

° These books are available in paperback editions.

consult Bruce Kuklick's *The Rise of American Philosophy, Cambridge, Massachusetts, 1860–1930* (1977).°

Larzer's Ziff's *The American 1890s: The Lost Generation* (1966)° discusses the writers during that crucial decade. Specific studies include Justin Kaplan's *Mr. Clemens and Mark Twain* (1966)° and Kenneth S. Lynn's *William Dean Howells: An American Life* (1971).

John L. Thomas's *Alternative America: Henry George, Edward Bellamy, Henry Demarest Lloyd, and the Adversary Tradition* (1983) and Nick Salvatore's *Eugene V. Debs: Citizen and Socialist* (1982)° provide the best introductions to the social critics of the Gilded Age. Also helpful is James Weinstein's *The Decline of Socialism in America, 1912–1925* (1967).°

William L. O'Neill's *Everyone Was Brave: The Rise and Fall of Feminism in America* (1969) and Eleanor Flexner's *Century of Struggle: The Women's Rights Movement in the United States* (rev. ed., 1975)° present good introductions to the condition of women in the Gilded Age. More culturally oriented are Sheila M. Rothman's *Woman's Proper Place: A History of Changing Ideals and Practices, 1870 to the Present* (1978)° and Lois W. Banner's *American Beauty* (1983).° For the subject of working women, see Alice Kessler-Harris's *Out to Work* (1983),° Julie Matthaei's *An Economic History of Women in America* (1982),° and Susan E. Kennedy's *If All We Did Was to Weep at Home: A History of White Working-Class Women in America* (1979).° Peter Filene discusses changing sex roles in *Him/Her/Self* (2nd ed., 1986).° Elisabeth Briffith's *In Her Own Right* (1984)° is a biography of Elizabeth Cady Stanton.

An important profession is analyzed in Paul Starr's *The Social Transformation of American Medicine* (1982).° Gunther P. Barth discusses the emergence of a new urban culture in *City People: The Rise of Modern City Culture in Nineteenth Century America* (1980).° For the growth of urban leisure and sports, see Roy Rosenzweig's *Eight Hours for What We Will!* (1983) and Stephen A. Riess's *City Games: The Evolution of American Urban Society and the Rise of Sports* (1989). The rise of the consumer culture is traced in Daniel Horowitz's *The Morality of Spending* (1985).

22

GILDED AGE POLITICS
AND AGRARIAN REVOLT

Paradoxical Politics

In 1873 Mark Twain and Charles Dudley Warner created an enduring tag for their times when they collaborated on a novel entitled *The Gilded Age*. The most unforgettable character in the book was an engaging mountebank, Colonel Beriah Sellers, who always had afoot some slippery scheme to trade on political favors. Sellers had enough counterparts in the real politics of the day to enliven that story too, and their humbuggery reinforced the novelists' judgment that it was above all an age of jobbery, profiteering, and false glitter.

Perspectives on the times would eventually change, but generations of political scientists and historians have since reinforced the two novelists' judgment. As a young college graduate in 1879, Woodrow Wilson described the state of the American political system: "No leaders, no principles; no principles, no parties." His contemporary, the Harvard historian Henry Adams, shared this view. "The period," he complained, "was poor in purpose and barren in results." Indeed, the real movers and shakers of the Gilded Age were not the men who sat in the White House or the Congress but the captains of industry who flung railroads across the continent and decorated its cities with plumed smokestacks and gaudy mansions.

Lord James Bryce, the most acute foreign observer of America in the late nineteenth century, suggested in *The American Commonwealth* (1888) that the American system, unlike the parliamentary system, tended to bring mediocre men to the top. "Since the heroes of the Revolution died with Jefferson and Adams and Madison," he wrote, "no person except General Grant has reached the [presidential] chair whose name would have been remembered had he not been President, and no President except Abraham Lincoln has displayed rare or striking qualities in the chair."

On the national issues of the day the major parties pursued for the most part a policy of evasion. Only on the tariff were there clear-cut divisions between protectionist Republicans and low-tariff Democrats, but there were individual exceptions even on that. On questions of the currency, regulation of big business, farm problems, civil service reform, internal improvement, and immigration, one would be hard put to distinguish between the parties. Europeans, accustomed to more ideological parties, were repeatedly perplexed at the situation until, in Lord Bryce's words, the truth began to dawn that "neither party has any principles, any distinctive tenets. Both have traditions. Both claim to have tendencies. Both have certainly war cries, organizations, interests enlisted in their support. But those interests are in the main the interests of getting or keeping the patronage of government. Tenets and policies, points of political doctrine and points of political practice, have all but vanished. . . . All has been lost, except office or the hope of it."

Carnegie Furnaces, Braddock, Pennsylvania. *The real movers and shakers of American life in the late nineteenth century were not the men who sat in the White House but the captains of industry.*

What distinguished the American system was that the parties themselves comprised vast coalitions. In a country so large and diverse, James Madison had long ago argued in *The Federalist* Number 10, no one group, no one region, no one idea, no one interest could hope to constitute a majority. Such a situation protected liberty, he asserted. Any party with an expectation of governing had to include a variety of groups, interests, and ideas. The process was not unknown to European parliaments. There, splinter parties might form governing coalitions after elections. American parties simply moved the process forward one step, forming their coalitions at the party conventions in the course of choosing presidential candidates and writing platforms. The American system for electing presidents bent politics toward a two-party system.

Two factors, above all, accounted for the muddled politics of this period. Americans had before them the fearsome lesson of what had happened in 1860, when parties had taken clear-cut stands on a deeply felt moral issue, with bloody consequences. But the more compelling cause of political inertia was the even division between the parties. From 1869 to 1913, from Grant to Taft, Republicans occupied the White House except during the two nonconsecutive terms of Grover Cleveland, but Republican domination of national politics was more apparent than real. In the years between 1872 and 1896 no president won a majority of the popular vote. In 1888 Benjamin Harrison failed to muster even a plurality over Cleveland, but carried the election anyway because his popular vote was concentrated in the states with the larger electoral votes. And while Republicans usually controlled the Senate, Democrats usually controlled the House. Only during the years 1881–1883 and 1889–1891 did a Republican president have a Republican Congress; and only between 1893 and 1895 did a Democratic president have a Democratic Congress—the only time this occurred between the Civil War and 1913, and that during a severe depression.

No chief executive between Lincoln and Theodore Roosevelt could be described as a "strong" president. With the exception of Grant's, their administrations were reasonably effective and honest, but none seriously challenged the prevailing view that the formulation of policy belonged to Congress. The function of the chief executive, to these presidents, was simply to administer the government, just as the prewar Whigs had always insisted. At the same time, the almost equal strength of the parties in Congress worked against any vigorous new departures there, since most bills required bipartisan support to pass both houses. Congress thus was caught up in political maneuvers and could not come to grips with national issues.

Under such static conditions, the parties became machines for

The Bosses of the Senate. *This 1889 cartoon bitingly portrays the alliance between big business and politics in this period.*

seeking office and dispensing patronage in the form of government jobs and contracts. In the choice of candidates, more than ever, "availability" outweighed ability. The ideal presidential candidate displayed an affable personality, a willingness to cooperate with the bosses, and an ability to win votes from various factions, resided in a pivotal state, and boasted a good war record. He had no views that might alienate powerful voting blocs, and few or no political enemies. Vice-presidential candidates were chosen to balance the ticket, to placate a disappointed faction, or to improve the party's chances in a key state. This process placed a premium on candidates who were relatively obscure or at least removed from national party battles capable of arousing opposition.

An alliance of business and politics characterized the period and lent credence to the cynical maxim that the central institution of every government was the hog through. This alliance was not necessarily corrupt, since many a politician favored the interests of business out of conviction. Nor was the public as sensitive to conflicts of interest as it would be later. So James G. Blaine of Maine, and hosts of his supporters, saw nothing wrong in his accepting stock commissions from an Arkansas railroad after helping it win a land grant from Congress. It was, they thought, a reward after the event, not a bribe in advance. One Georgia senator freely accepted a retainer fee of $10,000 from the Southern Pacific Railroad, a sum larger than his salary, without losing his standing with his constituents. Railroad passes, free entertainment, and a host of other favors were freely given to and accepted by politicians, editors, and other leaders in positions to influence public opinion.

POLITICS AND THE VOTERS   But if many observers considered this a time of political futility in which the parties refused to face up to such "real issues" as the growth of an unregulated economy and its attendant social injustices, it is nonetheless clear that the voters of the time thought more was at stake. Voter turnout during the Gilded Age was commonly about 70–80 percent, even in the South, where the disenfranchisement of blacks was not yet complete. (By contrast, the turnout for the 1988 presidential election was barely over 50 percent.) How was it then that leaders who failed to face up to the real issues presided over the most highly organized and politically active electorate in American history?

The answer is partly that the politicians and the voters deeply believed that they *were* dealing with crucial issues, such as the tariff, monopolies, the currency, civil service reform, and immigration. They turned out in heavy numbers for political rallies and parades. Probably more than any other generation of Americans they had the patience to follow the intricacies of lengthy debates and heavy tomes on such matters. If the major parties then failed to resolve these issues, no later generation has resolved them either, and they remain live issues, still relevant to American life a century later.

A NEW VIEW OF POLITICAL HISTORY   But what most motivated party loyalties and voter turnout in these years were intense cultural conflicts among ethnic and religious groups. Recent practitioners of what has been called the "new political history" have come to this view by analyzing the political effects of local, ethnic, cultural, and religious divisions. These historians approach politics less as a simple contest among economic interests, as the "progressive" historians of the earlier twentieth century saw it, than as a complex interplay of motivations, a struggle in which voters follow not simply their pocketbooks but their ethnic prejudices, cultural heritage, and religious convictions as well. According to one of the new political historians: "It has become clear to us . . . that the energies shaping public life are emotional as well as rational, cultural as well as economic."

Far from being like two empty bottles that differed only in their labels, as Woodrow Wilson said of the parties before the turn of the century, each party contained a different mixture of ingredients picked up in the course of its history. The Republican party, legitimate heir to the Whig tradition, attracted political insiders and active reformers. Party members were mainly Protestants of British descent or established American stock. In their own eyes, and in the eyes of many immigrants, they were prototypical Americans. Their native seat was New England, and their other strongholds were New York and the upper Middle West, both of which they had seeded with Yankee stock. Legitimate heirs to the abolitionist tradition, Republicans drew to their ranks a host of reformers and moralists, spiritual descendants of the perfectionists who populated the revivals and the reform movements of the antebellum years. The party's heritage of anti-Catholic nativism, dating from the 1850s when the Republican party had become a haven for former Know-Nothings, would also make a comeback in the 1880s. The Republicans could also rely on the votes of blacks and Union veterans of the Civil War.

The Democrats, by contrast, tended to be outsiders. Since the days when Jefferson and Madison had linked up with New York's Tammany Hall, the Democrats had been a heterogeneous, often unruly coalition of unlikely allies. What they had in common was that in one way or another they differed from the Republicans. The Democratic party embraced southern whites, immigrants, Catholics of any origin, Jews, freethinkers, skeptics, and all those repelled by the "party of morality." As one Chicago Democrat explained, "A Republican is a man who wants you t' go t' church every Sunday. A Democrat says if a man wants to have a glass of beer on Sunday he can have it." The Democrats were the "party of personal liberty," a commitment which sometimes proved volatile. Democratic conventions tended to be more disorderly than Republican gatherings, and often the more interesting for it. There were exceptions to these broad generalizations, of course, including black Americans who, though outsiders for sure, clung to the party of Lincoln, and some Protestant immigrants drawn to the Republicans by the party's image of uprightness.

The new immigration of the postbellum years, coming largely from Catholic and Jewish strongholds in eastern and southern Europe, reinforced the Democratic ranks. One result was the rebirth of nativism. In 1887 a nativist group called the American Protective Association sprang up in Clinton, Iowa, and over the next few years spread like a prairie fire through the Middle West, which became its chief stronghold. In that region especially, Republicans pressed nativist causes, calling for tighter naturalization laws, restrictions on immigration and the employment of foreigners, and greater emphasis on the teaching of the "American" language in the schools. Nativists saw as a threat those parochial schools, usually but not always Catholic, which sought to preserve Old Country cultures. German Lutherans, for instance, often maintained their own schools, and while as Protestants they gravitated to the Republicans, as Germans they were driven toward the Democrats by Republican campaigns for cultural conformity.

Prohibitionism revived along with nativism in the 1880s. Among the immigrants who crowded into the growing cities were numbers of hard-drinking Irish, beer-drinking Germans, and wine-bibbing Italians. Democratic constituents in general were more bibulous than Yankees, who increasingly saw saloons as the central social evil around which all others revolved, including vice, crime, political corruption, and neglect of families. Republicans across New England and the Middle West took up the cause of prohibition and local option, and were joined after 1869 by a Prohibition party, after 1874 by the Women's Christian Temperance Union, and after 1893 by the Anti-Saloon League. Before the turn of the century these groups attracted few Democrats to their camp.

CORRUPTION AND REFORM

While grass-roots Republicans and Democrats differed over ethnic and cultural issues, their party leaders spent much of their time arguing over the so-called spoils of office. Each party had its share of corrupt officials willing to buy and sell government appointments or congressional votes, yet each also witnessed the emergence of factions promoting honesty in government. This struggle for clean government soon became one of the foremost issues of the day.

CIVIL SERVICE REFORM   In the aftermath of Reconstruction, Rutherford B. Hayes admirably embodied the "party of morality." Hayes brought to the White House in 1877 a new style of uprightness that contrasted with the graft and corruption of the Grant administration. The son of an Ohio farmer, Hayes entered politics as a Whig but became one of the early Republicans, was wounded four times in the Civil War, and was promoted to major-general. As a member of the House of Representatives for one term, from 1865 to 1867, he supported the congressional reconstruction program. Elected governor of Ohio in 1867, he served three terms, one nonconsecutive. Honest and respectable, competent and dignified, he lived in modest style with his wife, nicknamed "Lemonade Lucy" because of her refusal to serve strong drink on social occasions.

Yet Hayes's presidency was besmirched by the manner of his election. Snide references to him as the *"de facto* President" and "His Fraudulence" dogged his steps and denied him any chance at a second term, which he renounced from the beginning. Hayes's own party was split between so-called Stalwarts and Half-Breeds, led respectively by Senator Roscoe Conkling of New York and Senator James G. Blaine of Maine. The difference between these Re-

Rutherford B. Hayes.

publican factions was murkier than that between the parties. The Stalwarts generally supported Grant, a Radical southern policy, and the spoils system. The Half-Breeds took a contrary view on the first two and were even vaguely touched by the sentiment for civil service reform.

But for the most part the factions were loose alliances aimed at advancing the careers of Conkling and Blaine. The two men could not abide each other. Blaine once referred to Conkling as displaying a "majestic, supereminent, overpowering, turkey-gobbler strut." He was right. Conkling was distinctive for his good looks, fine clothes, and arrogant manner. He dressed and lived flamboyantly, sporting pastel bow ties, silk scarves, moon-colored vests, and patent-leather shoes. Yet underneath his glamorous facade, he was a ruthless power broker. Conkling viewed politics as a brute struggle for power. "Parties," he once declared, "are not built by deportment or by ladies' magazines, or gush." Politics "is a rotten business," he added. "Nothing counts except to win."

Hayes thought otherwise, and he aligned himself with the growing public discontent over the corruption that had prevailed under Grant. American leaders were just learning about the merit system long established in the bureaucracies of France and Germany, and the new British practice in which civil service jobs were filled by competitive examination. Prominent leaders such as James A. Garfield in the House and Carl Schurz in the Senate joined in the cause of civil service reform, and both Hayes and vice-presidential candidate Samuel J. Tilden raised the issue again during the campaign of 1876. Hayes repeated his support for reform in his inaugural address. While he failed to get legislation on the subject, he did take administrative measures for a change.

In letters to his cabinet members and in an Executive Order of June 1877, Hayes laid down his own rules for merit appointments: those already in office would be dismissed only for the good of the government and not for political reasons; party members would have no more influence in appointments than other equally respectable citizens; no assessments for political contributions would be permitted; and no officeholder could manage election campaigns or political organizations, although all could vote and express opinions.

The issue of honest and effective government came to a head in a dispute over the federal customs houses. They were notorious centers of corrupt politics, filled with political appointees with little or nothing to do but draw salaries and run political machines. Importers sometimes found that they might gain favor by cooperating with corrupt customs officials, and might be punished for making trouble. An inquiry into operations at the New York Customs House laid before Hayes evidence that both collector Chester A. Arthur and naval officer Alonzo Cornell were guilty of "laxity" and of using the customs house for political management on behalf of Senator Roscoe Conkling's organization. When hints went out that resignations would be welcomed, Conkling responded with an attack on reformers in a speech to the state Republican convention: "Their vocation . . . is to lament the sins of other people. Their stock in trade is rancid, canting self-righteousness. . . . When Dr. Johnson defined patriotism as the last refuge of a scoundrel, he was unconscious of the then undeveloped capabilities and uses of the word 'Reform!' "

On October 15, 1877, after removing Arthur and Cornell, Hayes named replacements, only to have the nominees rejected when Conkling appealed to the "courtesy of the Senate," an old custom whereby senators might control appointments in their own states. During a recess in the summer of 1878, however, Hayes appointed new replacements. When Congress reassembled, the administration put pressure on senators and, with Democratic support, carried the nominations. Even this, however, did not end the New York Customs House episode; it would flare up again under the next president.

For all his efforts to clean house, Hayes's vision of government's role remained limited. On the economic issues of the day he held to a conservative line which would guide his successors for the rest of the century. His solution to labor troubles, demonstrated in the Great Railroad Strike of 1877, was to send in troops and break the strike. His answer to demands for an expansion of the currency was to veto the Bland-Allison Act which, passed in 1878 over his veto, required only a limited expansion of silver currency through the government's purchase for coinage of $2 million to $4 million worth of silver per month.

GARFIELD AND ARTHUR   With Hayes unavailable for a second term, the Republicans were forced to look elsewhere in 1880. The Stalwarts, led by Conkling, brought Grant forward for a third time, still a strong contender despite the tarnish of his administration's scandals. For two days the Republican convention in Chicago was deadlocked, with Grant leading but strongly challenged by Blaine. On the thirty-fifth ballot Wisconsin suddenly switched sixteen votes to Senator-elect James A. Garfield, and on the thirty-sixth ballot the convention stampeded to the dark-horse candidate, carrying him to the nomination. The Stalwarts stubbornly stood by Grant and went down, 399 to 306, but as a sop to the losing faction the convention named Chester A. Arthur of New York Customs House fame for vice-president.

The Democrats selected Winfield Scott Hancock, a Union commander at Gettysburg, to counterbalance the Republicans' Major-General Garfield and thus ward off "bloody-shirt" attacks on their party as the vehicle of Rebellion. Old rebels, nevertheless, advised their constituents to "vote as you shot"—that is, against Republicans. In an election characterized by widespread bribery, Garfield eked out a plurality of only 39,000 votes with 48.5 percent of the vote, but with a comfortable margin of 214 to 155 in the electoral college.

A native of Ohio, Garfield had shown the foresight to be born in a log cabin and to have a brief career on a canal towpath. Both became political assets in his rise from canal boy to president, as Horatio Alger put it in a campaign biography. A graduate of Williams College, Garfield became president of Hiram College in Ohio, was admitted to the bar, and won election to the Ohio Senate as a Republican in 1859. During the Civil War he distinguished himself at Shiloh and Chickamauga and was mustered out as a major-general when he went to Congress in 1863. Noted for his oratory and parliamentary skills, he became one of the outstanding leaders in the House and eventually its Speaker.

On July 2, 1881, President Garfield started on a vacation in New England to get away from the siege of office seekers. As he passed through Baltimore and Potomac Station a deranged office seeker named Charles Guiteau shot him in the back. "I am a Stalwart," Guiteau explained to the arresting officers. "Arthur is now President of the United States," an announcement that would prove crippling to the Stalwarts. Garfield lingered near death for two long, hot months, his suffering eased by a contrived air conditioner—a blower rigged up by navy engineers to pass air over a vault of ice into the president's sickroom. Finally, on September 19, Garfield died of complications resulting from the shooting, having been president for a little over six months and able to transact business for fewer than four.

One of the chief henchmen of Stalwart leader Roscoe Conkling was now president. "Chet Arthur, President of the United States?" one of his friends exclaimed. "Good God!" Little in Arthur's past, save his record as an abolitionist lawyer who had helped secure the freedom of a fugitive slave, raised hopes that he would rise above customs-house politics. A native of Vermont, he had attended Union College, become a lawyer, and made a political career in appointive offices, most notably as New York quartermaster-general during the Civil War and collector of customs from 1871 to 1878. But Arthur demonstrated rare and striking qualities as president. He began by distancing himself from Conkling and the Stalwarts and establishing a genuine independence, almost a necessity after Guiteau's announcement.

As president he vigorously prosecuted the Star Route Frauds, a kickback scheme on contracts for postal routes which involved old political cronies of Arthur's. The president further surprised Washington in 1882 with the veto of an $18 million river and harbors bill, a "pork-barrel" measure that included something for most congressional districts. He also vetoed the Chinese Exclusion Act (1882) which in his view violated the Burlingame Treaty of 1868. Congress proceeded to override both vetoes.

Chester A. Arthur.

Most startling of all was Arthur's emergence as something of a civil service and tariff reformer. Stalwarts had every reason to expect him to oppose the merit system, but instead he allied himself with the reformers. While the assassin Guiteau had unwittingly added a certain urgency to the public support of reform, the defeat of a reform bill in 1882 sponsored by "Gentleman George" Pendleton, Democratic senator from Ohio, aroused public opinion further.

The Pendleton Civil Service Act passed in January 1883, setting up a three-member Civil Service Commission independent from the regular cabinet departments, the first such federal agency established on a permanent basis. About 14 percent of all government jobs came under the category of "classified services," in which new appointments had to be made on the basis of competitive examinations rather than political favoritism. What was more, the president could enlarge the classified services at his discretion. This had important consequences over the years because after each of the next four presidential elections the "outs" emerged as victors. Each new president thus had a motive to enlarge this category because it would shield his own appointees from political removal.

The high protective tariff, a heritage of the Civil War, had by the early 1880s raised revenues to the point that the government actually enjoyed an embarrassment of riches, a surplus which drew money into the Treasury and out of circulation. Some argued that lower tariff rates would reduce prices and the cost of living, and at the same time leave more money in circulation. In 1882 Arthur named a special commission to study the problem. The Tariff Commission recommended a 20–25 percent rate reduction, which gained Arthur's support, but Congress's effort to enact the proposal was marred by log-rolling to further local interests, resulting in the "Mongrel Tariff" of 1883, so called because of its diverse rates for different commodities. The tariff provided for a slight rate reduction, perhaps by 5 percent, but it actually hiked the duty on some articles.

SCURRILOUS CAMPAIGN When the 1884 election campaign began, Arthur's record might have commended him to the voters, but it did not set well with leaders of his party. So the Republicans dumped Arthur and turned to the glamorous Senator James G. Blaine of Maine, longtime leader of the Half-Breeds. A man with the personal magnetism a later generation would call "charisma," Blaine was the consummate politician. He never forgot a name or a face, he inspired the party faithful with his oratory, and at the same time he knew how to wheel and deal in the backrooms. He managed eloquence even when spouting the platitudes of party loyalty, waving the bloody shirt, and twisting the British lion's tail—the last of which held special appeal for the Irish, a group not normally drawn to Republicans.

Back in 1876 Blaine had been nominated for the presidency by Robert Ingersoll, who, in an eloquent flight of oratory of his own, had announced:

> The people called for the nomination of the man who has torn from the throat of treason the tongue of slander—for the man who has snatched the mask of Democracy from the hideous face of rebellion. . . . Like an armed warrior, like a plumed knight James G. Blaine marched down the halls of American Congress and threw his shining lance full and fair against the brazen forehead of the defamers of his country and maligners of his honor.

To his followers in 1884 Blaine was still the plumed knight, but in Democratic newspapers he became the plumed knave. The "defamers of his honor" were those who found in the "Mulligan letters" evidence that Blaine had sold his soul—and his votes—to the railroads.

During the campaign more letters surfaced with disclosures embarrassing to Blaine. For the reform element of the Republican party, this was too much, and one after another prominent leaders and supporters of the party bolted the ticket. Party regulars scorned them as "goo-goos"—the "good-government" crowd who ignored partisan realities—and the editor of the New York *Sun* jokingly called them Mugwumps, after an Algonquian word meaning a great chieftain. To regulars, in what soon became a stale joke, Mugwumps were unreliable Republicans who had their "mugs" on one side of the fence and their "wumps" on the other.

Senator James G. Blaine of Maine.

The rise of the Mugwumps, however, influenced the Democrats to nominate Stephen Grover Cleveland as a reform candidate. Cleveland had a rapid rise from obscurity to the White House. One of many children in the family of a small-town Presbyterian minister, he had been forced by his father's death to go to work at an early age. He won a job as clerk in a law office, read law, passed the bar examination, and became an assistant state attorney-general in New York in 1863 and later sheriff of Erie County. He first attracted national attention as mayor of Buffalo, elected in 1881, for battling graft and corruption. In 1882 the Democrats made him governor, and he continued to build a reform record by fighting New York's Tammany Hall organization. Cleveland saw the corruption of government by the rich and powerful as a constant danger. As mayor and as governor he repeatedly vetoed what he considered special-privilege bills serving sordid and selfish interests.

A stocky 250-pound man with a droopy mustache, Cleveland seemed the stolid opposite of Blaine. He possessed little charisma, but impressed the public with something that was more important that year, a stubborn integrity. One supporter called him an "Ugly-honest man," and another said that "We love him for the enemies he has made." Cleveland the reformer was a godsend to Democrats who at last sighted the Promised Land, the White House.

Then the Buffalo *Evening Telegraph* revealed some of bachelor Cleveland's earlier escapades with an attractive Buffalo widow, who had named Cleveland as the father of a child born to her in 1874, though there was no proof of paternity. Cleveland, it seemed, was only one of several likely fathers, but he took responsibility and provided for the child. When supporters asked Cleveland what to say, he answered "Tell the truth." Later he said: "The Republicans can have a monopoly of all the dirt in this campaign." Of course they did not, and the respective escapades of Blaine and Cleveland provided some of the most colorful battle cries in American political history. "Blaine, Blaine, James G. Blaine, the continental liar from the state of Maine," Democrats chanted. Republicans countered with "Ma, ma, where's my pa? Gone to the White House, ha, ha, ha!"

Near the end of the campaign Blaine and his supporters committed two fateful blunders. At New York's fashionable Delmonico's restaurant Blaine went to a private dinner with a clutch of millionaire bigwigs, including John Astor and Jay Gould, to discuss campaign finances. Cartoons and accounts of "Belshazzar's Feast" festooned the opposition press for days to come. And then one in a delegation of Protestant ministers visiting Republican headquarters in New York referred to the Democrats as the party of "rum, Romanism, and rebellion." The judgment had a certain validity, but the

Another Voice for Cleveland. *This 1884 cartoon attacks "Grover the Good" for fathering an illegitimate child.*

tone was insolent. Blaine, who was present, let pass and perhaps failed to catch the implied insult to Catholics—a fatal oversight, since he had always cultivated Irish-American support with his anti-British talk and public reminders that his mother was Catholic. Democrats spread word that he had let the insult pass, even that he had made it himself.

The incident may have tipped the election. The electoral vote in Cleveland's favor stood at 219 to 182, but the popular vote ran far closer; Cleveland's plurality was fewer than 30,000 votes.

CLEVELAND AND THE SPECIAL INTERESTS For all Cleveland's hostility to the spoils system and politics as usual, he represented no sharp break with the conservative policies of his predecessors, except in opposing governmental favors to business. "A public office is a public trust" was one of his favorite mottoes. He held to a strictly limited view of government's role in both economic and social matters, a rigid philosophy illustrated by his 1887 veto of the Texas Seed Bill, an effort to appropriate funds to meet the urgent need of drought victims for seed grain. Back to Congress it went with a lecture on the need to limit the powers and functions of government—"though the people support the government the government should not support the people," Cleveland asserted.

For a man who took such high ground philosophically, Cleveland had a mixed record on the civil service. He had good intentions, but he also had a hungry party with its first president since Buchanan in 1856. Before his inauguration Cleveland arranged to have the National Civil Service Reform League send him a letter warning that the spoils system would be a sensitive issue in the new administration. In response he repeated his support for the Pendleton Act and his intention to follow its spirit even where it did not apply; he would not remove able men on partisan grounds, he said. But he inserted one significant exception: those who had used federal jobs to forward the interests of the opposition party. In many cases, especially in the post offices, he thus had ample excuse to remove men who had practically made their offices into Republican headquarters.

Party pressures gradually forced Cleveland's hand. To a friend he remarked: "The damned everlasting clatter for office continues . . . and makes me feel like resigning and hell is to pay generally." When he left office about two-thirds of the federal officeholders were Democrats, including all internal revenue collectors and nearly all the heads of customs houses. But at the same time Cleveland had extended the classified civil service to cover about 27,000 employees, almost double the number that had been covered when he came in. The result was that he satisfied neither Mugwumps nor spoilsmen; indeed he managed to antagonize both.

On other matters Cleveland's stubborn courage and concern for the public treasury led him into conflicts with predatory interests, conflicts which eventually cost him the White House. One such dispute arose over misuse of the public domain in the West. Cleveland's secretary of the interior and the commissioner of the General Land Office uncovered one case after another of fraud and mismanagement: bogus surveys by government surveyors, public lands used fraudulently by lumbermen, mine operators, and cattlemen with the collusion of government officials, and at least 30 million acres of railroad land grants subject to forfeiture because the required lines were not built.

The administration brought suits against railroads to recover such lands, and against a subsidiary of the Northern Pacific Railroad for cutting trees on public forestlands. It nullified exploitive leases of Indian lands, such as that of one cattle company which had leased 6 million acres from the Cherokees for $100,000 and subleased the land for about five times as much. Cattle barons were ordered to remove fences enclosing waterholes and grasslands on the open range. In all, during Cleveland's first term about 81 million acres of public lands were restored to the federal government.

Cleveland incurred the wrath of Union veterans by his firm stand against their pension raids on the Treasury. Congress had passed the first general Civil War pension law in 1862 to provide for Union veterans disabled in service and for the widows, orphans, and dependents of veterans. By 1882 the Grand Army of the Republic, an organization of Union veterans and a powerful pressure group, was trying to get pensions paid for any disability, no matter how it was incurred. Meanwhile many veterans enjoyed such benefits by having private pension bills put through an obliging Congress. In Washington a large tribe of lawyers built careers on filing claims and pushing special laws for veterans.

Insofar as time permitted Cleveland examined such bills critically and vetoed those which seemed to him dubious. Although he signed more than any of his predecessors, running pension costs up from $56 million to $80 million, he also vetoed more. A climax came in January 1887 when Congress passed the Dependent Pension Bill, which provided funds for veterans dependent upon manual labor and unable to work for any reason, whether or not the reason was service connected. Cleveland sent it back with a ringing veto, declaring that the pension list would become a refuge for frauds rather than a "roll of honor."

About the middle of his term Cleveland set out after new special interests, leading in the adoption of an important new policy, railroad regulation. Since the late 1860s state after state had adopted regulatory laws, and from the early 1870s Congress had debated federal legislation to regulate the railroads. In 1886 a Supreme Court decision finally spurred action. In the case of *Wabash Railroad v. Illinois* the Court denied the state's power to regulate rates on interstate traffic. Cleveland urged in his annual message in December that since this "important field of control and regulation [has] thus been left entirely unoccupied," Congress should act.

It did, and in February 1887 Cleveland signed into law an act creating the Interstate Commerce Commission, the first such independent regulatory commission. The law empowered its five members to investigate carriers and prosecute violators. All rates had to be "reasonable and just." Railroads were forbidden to grant rebates, discriminate against persons, places, and commodities, or enter into pools (secret agreements to fix rates). The commission's actual powers, however, proved to be weak when first tested in the courts. If creating the ICC seemed to conflict with Cleveland's fear of big government, it accorded with his Jacksonian fear of big business. The Interstate Commerce Act, to his mind, was a legitimate exercise of sovereign power.

Cleveland's most dramatic challenge to special interests came in his efforts to force action on tariff reform. He had entered office as

Grover Cleveland made the issue of tariff reform central to the politics of the late 1880s.

the leader of the traditional low-tariff party, but his party was far from unified on the issue, and Cleveland himself confessed at first to little understanding of the tariff issue. Like most politicians of the time, he hesitated to plunge into that tangled thicket. But with greater exposure to the question and further study he decided that the rates were too high and included many inequities. Near the end of 1887 Cleveland decided on the deliberate step of dramatizing the issue by devoting his entire annual message to the subject. He did so in full knowledge that he was focusing attention on a political mine-field on the eve of an election year, against the warnings of his advisers. "What is the use of being elected if you don't stand for something?" he asked.

Cleveland's message was a classic summary and exposition of the current arguments against protection. He noted that tariff revenues had bolstered the surplus, making the Treasury "a hoarding place for money needlessly withdrawn from trade and the people's use." It pushed up prices for everybody, and while it was supposed to protect American labor against the competition of cheap foreign labor, the most recent census showed that of 17.4 million Americans gainfully employed only 2.6 million were in "such manufacturing industries as are claimed to be benefitted by a high tariff."

It was evident, moreover, that while business combinations could push prices up to the artificial level set by the prices of dutied foreign goods, prices often fell below that level when domestic producers were in competition, "proof that someone is willing to accept lower prices for such commodity and that such prices are remunerative." Congress, Cleveland argued, should study the more than 4,000 articles subject to duties with an eye to cutting the cost of necessities and of the raw materials used in manufacturing. "Our progress toward a wise conclusion will not be improved by dwelling upon the theories of protection and free trade. . . . It is a condition which confronts us, not a theory." The final sentence became an epigram so infectious that for the next few years public speakers worked it nearly to death.

That did not stop Blaine and other Republicans from denouncing the message as pure "free trade," a doctrine all the more suspect because it was also British policy. The House Ways and Means Committee soon reported a bill calling for modest reductions from an average level of about 47 percent of the value of imported goods to about 40 percent. House Democrats rallied to its support, some of them under assurances that it could not become law. Passed by the House, the bill stalled in the Republican Senate and finally died a lingering death in committee. If Cleveland's talk accomplished his purpose of drawing party lines more firmly, it also confirmed the fears of his advisers. The election of 1888 for the first time in years highlighted a difference between the major parties on an issue of substance.

Cleveland was inevitably the nominee of his party. The platform endorsed "the views expressed by the President in his last message to Congress." The Republicans passed up old warhorses like Blaine and Sherman and turned to the obscure Benjamin Harrison, who had all the attributes of availability. Grandson of a former president, a flourishing lawyer in Indiana, the diminutive Harrison resided in a pivotal state, and had a good war record and little in his political record to offend any voter. He had lost a race for governor and served one term in the Senate (1881–1887). The Republican platform picked up the gauntlet thrown down by Cleveland, accepted the protective tariff as the chief issue, and promised generous pensions to veterans.

The campaign thus became the first waged mainly on the tariff issue. Harrison's campaign chairman and Republican boss of Pennsylvania took the advice of a friend to "put the manufacturers of Pennsylvania under the fire and fry all the fat out of them." As insurance against tariff reduction, manufacturers obligingly larded the campaign fund, which was used to denounce Cleveland's un-American "free trade," and his pension vetoes. In Indiana party workers were told: "Divide the floaters into blocks of five and put a trusted man in charge . . . with the necessary funds, and make him responsible that none get away, and that all vote our ticket." Democratic poll watchers claimed that floaters received $15 to $20 each for their votes.

Personal attacks too were leveled against Cleveland. The old charges of immorality had played out. After Cleveland entered the White House he had married young Frances Folsom, who later presented him with a daughter whose name would be immortalized one day by the "Baby Ruth" candy bar. During the campaign, though, the rumor went abroad that a drunken Cleveland had taken to wife-beating. On the eve of the election Cleveland suffered a more devastating blow from the phony "Murchison letter." A California Republican had written British minister Sir Lionel Sackville-West over the false name "Charles F. Murchison." Posing as an English immigrant he asked advice on how to vote. Sackville-West, engaged at the time in sensitive negotiations over British and American access to Canadian fisheries, hinted that he should vote for Cleveland. Published on October 24, the letter aroused a storm of protest against foreign intervention and further linked Cleveland to British free-traders. Democratic explanations never caught up with the original sense of outrage.

The outcome was very close. Cleveland was vindicated in the popular vote by 5,538,000 to 5,447,000, but that was poor comfort. The distribution was such that Harrison, with the key states of Indiana and New York on his side, carried the electoral college by 233 to 168.

REPUBLICAN REFORM UNDER HARRISON   Harrison became a competent and earnest figurehead, overshadowed by his secretary of state, James G. Blaine. He proved something of a cold fish in personal relations. "Harrison can make a speech to ten thousand men and every man of them will go away his friend," said one observer. "Let him meet the same ten thousand in private and every one will go away his enemy." When his campaign manager came to call with the election returns, Harrison exclaimed fervently: "Providence has given us the victory." The cynical adviser later remarked that Harrison "ought to know that Providence hadn't a damn thing to do with it" and opined that the president "would never know how close a number of men were compelled to approach a penitentiary to make him president."

Harrison had aroused the hopes of civil service reformers. "In appointments of every grade and department," he said, "fitness and not party service should be the essential and discriminating test, and fidelity and efficiency the only sure tenure of office." Nevertheless he appointed a wealthy Philadelphia merchant as his postmaster-general, allegedly as a reward for a generous contribution. The first assistant postmaster-general announced less than a year later: "I have changed 31,000 out of 55,000 fourth-class postmasters and I expect to change 10,000 more before I finally quit." Harrison made a few feckless efforts to resist partisan pressures, but the party leaders had their way. His most significant gesture at reform was to

In an attack on Benjamin Harrison's spending policies, this cartoon shows Harrison pouring Cleveland's huge surplus down a hole.

name young Theodore Roosevelt to the Civil Service Commission.

Harrison owed a heavy debt to the old-soldier vote, which he discharged by naming an officer of the Grand army of the Republic (GAR) to the position of pension commissioner. "God help the surplus," the new commissioner reportedly exclaimed, and proceeded to approve pensions with such abandon that the secretary of the interior removed him six months and several million dollars later. In 1890 Congress passed, and Harrison signed, the Dependent Pension Act, substantially the same measure that Cleveland had vetoed. The pension rolls shot up from 490,000 in 1889 to 966,000 in 1893, and the program's costs from $89 million to $175 million.

During the first two years of Harrison's term the Republicans controlled the presidency and both houses of Congress for only the second time in the twenty years between 1875 and 1895. They were positioned to have pretty much their own way, and they made the year 1890 memorable for some of the most significant legislation enacted in the entire period. In addition to the Dependent Pension Act, Congress and the president approved the Sherman Anti-Trust Act, the Sherman Silver Purchase Act, the McKinley Tariff, and the admission of the last of the "omnibus states," Idaho and Wyoming, which followed the admission of the Dakotas, Montana, and Washington in 1889.

Both parties had pledged themselves to do something about the growing power of trusts and monopolies. The Sherman Anti-Trust Act, named for Senator John Sherman, chairman of the Senate Judiciary Committee that drafted it, sought to incorporate into federal law a long-standing principle against "restraint of trade." It forbade contracts, combinations, or conspiracies in restraint of trade or in the effort to establish monopolies in interstate or foreign commerce. A broad consensus put the law through, but its passage turned out to be largely symbolic. During the next decade successive administrations expended little effort on the act's enforcement. From 1890 to 1901 only eighteen suits were instituted, and four of those were against labor unions.

Congress meanwhile debated currency legislation against the backdrop of growing distress in the farm regions of the West and South. Hard-pressed farmers were now agitating to inflate the currency by an increased coinage of silver. Their purpose was to raise commodity prices, making it easier for farmers to earn the money with which to pay their debts. The silverite forces were also strengthened, especially in the Senate, by members from the new states that had silver-mining interests. Congress passed the new Sherman Silver Purchase Act in July 1890, replacing the Bland-Allison Act of 1878. It required the Treasury to purchase 4.5 million ounces of silver each month and to issue in payment Treasury notes redeemable in either gold or silver. The act failed to satisfy the demands of the silverites, however. Although it approximately doubled the amount of silver purchased, that was still too little to have an inflationary impact on the economy. Eastern business and financial groups, on the other hand, saw a threat to the gold reserve in the growth of paper currency which holders could redeem in gold at the Treasury. The stage was set for the currency issue to eclipse all others in a panic that swept the country three years later.

Republicans took their victory over Cleveland as a mandate not just to maintain the protective tariff but to raise it. But the mandate was less than clear, in view of Cleveland's popular-vote plurality, and passage of the new tariff remained doubtful until its backers struck their bargain with western silverites. Piloted through by William McKinley, House Ways and Means chairman, and Senator Nelson W. Aldrich, the McKinley Tariff of 1890 raised duties on manufactured goods to an average of about 49.5 percent, the highest to that time. And it included three interesting new departures. First, the protectionists reached out for farmers' votes with high duties on agricultural products. Second, they sought to lessen the tariff's impact on consumers by putting sugar, a universal necessity, on the free list—thus reducing its cost—and then compensating Louisiana and Kansas sugar growers with a bounty of 2¢ a pound out of the federal treasury. And third, the measure included a reciprocity section which empowered the president to hike duties on sugar, molasses, tea, coffee, and hides to pressure countries exporting those items into reducing unreasonably high duties on American goods.

The absence of a public consensus for higher tariffs became clearly visible in the 1890 midterm elections. By the time the November congressional election returns were in it seemed apparent, at least to Democrats, that the voters had repudiated the McKinley Tariff, which had become law in October, with a landslide of Democratic votes. In the new House Democrats outnumbered Republicans by almost three to one; in the Senate the Republican majority was reduced to eight. One of the election casualties was McKinley himself, the victim of a few tricks the Democrats used to reinforce the widespread revulsion against the increased duties. But there was more to the election than the tariff. Voters reacted also against the baldly partisan measures of the Harrison administration and its extravagant expenditures on pensions and other programs. Democrats raised a ruckus about the Republicans' "billion-dollar Congress," to which the Speaker of the House responded with the question: "Isn't this a billion dollar country?" But with expenditures rising and revenues dropping, largely because the tariff was so high as to discourage imports, the nation's surplus was shrinking at a rapid pace.

The large Democratic vote in 1890 may have also been a reaction to Republican efforts to legislate against alcohol and eliminate funding for state-supported Catholic schools. In the years from 1880 to 1890 sixteen out of twenty-one states outside the South held referenda on constitutional prohibition, and a number of state legislatures provided for votes on the issue of local option. In the referenda only six states voted for prohibition, however, and one of these, Rhode Island, reversed its dry vote three years later. With the politics of righteousness, then, Republicans were playing a losing game, arousing wets (antiprohibitionists) on the Democratic side. In 1889 Wisconsin Republicans compounded their party's problems by pushing through a law which struck at parochial schools. The law held that a school could be accredited only if it taught the basic subjects in the English language. That was the last straw: it turned large numbers of threatened and outraged immigrants into Democratic activists. In 1889 and 1890 the Democrats swept state after state.

The Problems of Farmers

The 1890 election results reflected something more than a reaction against the Republican tariff, spoils politics, extravagance, and moralizing. The returns revealed a deep-seated unrest in the farming communities of the South and West that was beginning to find voice in the new People's party, a grass-roots movement of considerable political and social significance.

ECONOMIC CONDITIONS   For some time farmers had been subject to worsening economic and social conditions. The source of their problem was a long-term decline in commodity prices from 1870 to 1898, the product of domestic overproduction and growing international competition for world markets. The vast new lands brought under cultivation in America poured an ever-increasing supply of farm products into the market, driving down prices. This effect was reinforced as innovations in transportation and communications brought American farmers ever more into competition with farmers around the world, further increasing the supply of farm commodities. Considerations of abstract economic forces, however, puzzled many farmers. They would never quite understand how want could be caused by plenty. They shared the puzzlement that Kansas's Populist governor professed at a friend's argument in the 1890s that "there were hungry people . . . because there was too much bread" and "so many . . . poorly clad . . . because there was too much cloth." How could one speak of overproduction when so many remained in need? Instead there must be a screw loose somewhere in the system.

The railroads and the middlemen who handled the farmers' products became the prime villains. Farmers felt victimized by the high railroad rates which prevailed in farm regions that had no alternative forms of transportation. Individual farmers could not get the rebates the Rockefellers could extract from railroads, and could not exert the political influence wielded by the railroad lobbies. In other ways farmers found themselves with little bargaining power as ei-

During the late nineteenth century farmers suffered from a long-term decline in the prices of farm commodities, including cotton. Domestic overproduction and international competition were among the causes.

ther buyers or sellers. When they went to sell wheat or cotton, the buyer set the price; when they went to buy a plow point, the seller set the price.

High tariffs operated to the farmers' disadvantage because they protected manufacturers against foreign competition, allowing them to raise the prices of factory goods on which farmers depended. Farmers, however, had to sell their wheat, cotton, and other staples in foreign markets, where competition lowered prices. Tariffs inflicted a double blow on farmers because insofar as they hampered imports, they indirectly hampered exports by making it harder for foreign buyers to get the necessary American currency or exchange to purchase American crops.

Debt, too, has been a perennial problem of agriculture. After the Civil War farmers became ever more enmeshed in debt—western farmers in mortgages to cover the costs of land and machinery, southern farmers in crop liens. As commodity prices dropped, the burden of debt grew because farmers had to cultivate more wheat or cotton to raise the same amount of money; and by growing more they furthered the vicious cycle of surpluses and price declines.

AN INADEQUATE CURRENCY   Currency deflation was yet another cause of declining prices. Ultimately, farm discontent focused on the currency issue, magnifying this grievance out of proportion to all others. The basic problem with the nation's currency in the late nineteenth century was that it lacked the flexibility to grow along with America's expanding economy. From 1865 to 1890 the amount of currency in circulation actually decreased from about $30.20 to $27.06 per capita. Three types of currency existed in those days: greenbacks, national bank notes, and hard money (gold and silver coins or certificates). The amount of greenback money in circulation had been set at $346 million in 1878, and had remained fixed at that amount, despite agitation for more paper money by debtors (largely farmers) and expansion-minded businessmen. National bank notes, based on government bonds, actually contracted in volume as the government paid off its bonds, which it was able to do rapidly with revenues from tariffs and land sales.

Metallic currency dated from the Mint Act of 1792, which authorized free and unlimited coinage of silver and gold at a ratio of 15:1.° The phrase "free and unlimited coinage" simply meant that owners of precious metals could have any quantity of their gold or silver

---

°The ratio meant that the amount of precious metal in a silver dollar weighed fifteen times as much as that in a gold dollar. This reflected the relative values of silver and gold at the time.

coined free, except for a nominal fee to cover costs. A fixed ratio of values, however, could not reflect fluctuations in the relative market value of the metals. When gold rose to a market value higher than that reflected in the official ratio, owners ceased to present it for coinage. The country was actually on a silver standard until 1837, when Congress changed the ratio to 16:1, which soon reversed the situation. Silver became more valuable in the market than in coinage, and the country drifted to a gold standard.

This state of affairs prevailed until 1873, when Congress passed a general revision of the coinage laws and, without fanfare, dropped the then-unused provision for the coinage of silver. The action came, however, just when silver production began to increase, reducing its market value through the growth in supply. Under the old laws this would have induced owners of silver to present it at the mint for coinage. Soon advocates of currency inflation began to denounce the "crime of '73," which they had scarcely noticed at the time. Gradually a suspicion, and in some cases a belief, grew that creditor interests had conspired in 1873 to ensure a scarcity of money. But the silverites had little more legislative success than the advocates of greenback inflation. The Bland-Allison Act of 1878 and the Sherman Silver Purchase Act of 1890 provided for some silver coinage, but too little in each case to offset the overall contraction of the currency.

AGRARIAN REVOLT

Frustrated by the unwillingness of Congress to ease their plight, disgruntled farmers began to organize after the Civil War. But the nascent farm organizations faced a complex array of obstacles to their growth. Unlike labor unions in their confrontations with management, the farmers had to deal with bankers, middlemen, and railroad and grain-elevator operators, as well as the fluctuating world market. Farm incomes also depended on the unpredictable forces of nature: droughts, blizzards, insects, erosion. Moreover, collective action by farmers was impeded by an ingrained tradition of rugged individualism and by their physical isolation. American farmers had long prided themselves on their hardy self-reliance, and many balked at sacrificing their independence. But for all the obstacles, farm activists persevered, and the results were dramatic, if not wholly successful.

THE GRANGER MOVEMENT   When the Department of Agriculture sent Oliver H. Kelley on a tour of the postbellum South in 1866, it was the farmers' isolation which most impressed him. Resolving to do something about it, Kelley and some government clerks in 1867 founded the Patrons of Husbandry, better known as the Grange (an old word for granary), as each chapter was called. In the next few years the Grange mushroomed, reaching a membership as high as 1.5 million by 1874. The Grange started as a social and educational response to the farmers' isolation, but as it grew it began to promote farmer-owned cooperatives for buying and selling and soon became indirectly involved in politics through independent third parties, especially in the Midwest, during the early 1870s.

The Grangers' chief political goal was to regulate the rates charged by railroads and warehouses. In five states they brought about the passage of "Granger Laws" which at first proved relatively ineffective, but laid a foundation for stronger legislation to follow. Owners subject to their regulation challenged these laws in cases which soon rose to the Supreme Court, where the plaintiffs in the "Granger Cases" claimed to have been deprived of property without due process of law. In a key case involving warehouse regulation, *Munn v. Illinois* (1877), the high court ruled that the state under its "police powers" had the right to regulate property in the interest of the public good where that property was clothed with a public interest. If regulatory power were abused, the ruling said, "the people must resort to the polls, not the courts." Later, however, the courts would severely restrict state regulatory powers.

The Granger movement gradually declined (but never vanished) as members' energies were drawn off into cooperatives, many of which failed, and into political action. Out of the independent political movements of the time there grew in 1875 a party calling itself the Independent National party, more commonly known as the Greenback party because of its emphasis on that issue. In the 1878 midterm elections it polled over 1 million votes and elected fifteen congressmen. But in 1880 the party's fortunes declined, and it disintegrated after 1884.

FARMERS' ALLIANCES   As the Granger waned, another farm organization grew in size and significance: the Farmers' Alliances. Farmers throughout the South and Midwest, where tenancy rates were highest, rushed to join the Alliance movement. They saw in collective action a way to seek relief from the hardships created by chronic indebtedness, declining prices, and devastating droughts. But a powerful attraction for many isolated, struggling farmers and their families was the sense of community provided by the Alliances. The Alliance gatherings resembled spiritual camp meetings. One observer described an Alliance meeting as "a religious revival . . . a

*After Reconstruction ended, many black families (called "Exodusters")
left the South to farm in Kansas. They laid the groundwork for later
organizations like the Colored Farmers' Alliance.*

pentecost . . . in which the tongue of flame sat upon every man, and
each spake as the spirit gave him utterance."

The Alliance movement was attractive to women and men alike.
Alliances welcomed rural white women and men over sixteen years
old who displayed a "good moral character," believed in God, and
demonstrated "industrious habits." One North Carolina woman in
1891 expressed her appreciation for the "grand opportunities" the
Alliance provided women to emerge from traditional domesticity.
"Drudgery, fashion and gossip," she declared, "are no longer the
bounds of woman's sphere." One of the Alliance publications made
the point explicitly: "The Alliance has come to redeem woman from
her enslaved condition, and place her in her proper sphere." Although not all Alliance groups embraced this agenda, overall the
number of women in the Alliance movement grew rapidly, and many
assumed key leadership roles.

By 1890 the Alliances had formed into two major groups: the
northwestern Alliance, organized in 1880, was never effective and by
the late 1880s was mostly a paper organization; the southern Alliance proved the more militant, effective, radical, and ultimately
more national of the two. The southern group, which started in 1877
in Texas, grew into the Grand State Alliance in 1879. In 1886 Dr.
Charles W. Macune became its leader and dazzled members with a
glittering vision of large-scale farm cooperatives, whereby farmers
would band together to handle the warehousing and marketing of

their crops, thus avoiding the much-despised middlemen. The cooperative ideal rapidly drew new converts to the organization. By
absorbing existing farm groups and organizing new locals, the Alliance movement swept the cotton belt and established strong positions in Kansas and the Dakotas. By 1890 it had members from New
York to California numbering about 1.5 million. A parallel Colored
Farmers' Alliance claimed over 1 million members.

The Alliance sponsored an ambitious social and educational program, and about 1,000 affiliated newspapers. But unlike the Grange,
the Alliance proposed from the start an elaborate economic program.
In 1890 Alliance agencies and exchanges in some eighteen states
claimed a business of $10 million, but they soon went the way of the
Granger cooperatives, victims of discrimination by wholesalers,
manufacturers, railroads, and bankers, but above all victims of inexperienced management and overextended credit. As the cooperatives struggled to survive, many southern Alliance members
supported Macune's subtreasury plan as the cure for their ills. Under
this plan, farmers would be able to store their crops in new government warehouses and secure government loans for up to 80 percent
of their crops' value at 1 percent interest. Besides providing immediate credit, the plan allowed the farmer the leeway to hold a crop for
a better price later, since he would not have to sell it immediately at
harvest time to pay off debts. The plan also promoted inflation
because these loans to farmers would be made in new legal-tender
notes. The subtreasury plan went before Congress in 1890, but was
never adopted. Its defeat as well as setbacks to other proposals
convinced many farm leaders that they needed political power to
secure railroad regulation, currency inflation, fertilizer inspections,
state departments of agriculture, antitrust laws, and farm credit.

In 1890 Alliance members plunged headlong into politics. In the
West, where hard times had descended after the blizzards of 1887,
farmers were ready for third-party action. In the South, however,
white Alliance members hesitated to bolt the Democratic party,
seeking instead to influence or control it. Both approaches gained
startling success. Independent parties under various names upset the
political balance in western states, electing a governor under the
banner of the People's party in Kansas, and taking control of one
house of the legislature there and both houses in Nebraska. In South
Dakota and Minnesota they gained a balance of power in the legislatures, while Kansas and Nebraska sent Populists to the Senate.

The farm movement produced colorful leaders, especially in Kansas, where the popular imagination was captured by Mary Elizabeth
Lease, who advised farmers "to raise less corn and more hell." Born
in Pennsylvania to parents who were political exiles from Ireland,

she grew up within a family traumatized by the Civil War. Her two brothers were killed in battle, and her father died in Georgia's notorious Andersonville Prison. Afterward she migrated to Kansas, taught school, raised a family, and finally failed at farming in the mid-1880s. She then studied law for a time, "pinning sheets of notes above her wash tub," and through strenuous effort became one of the state's first female lawyers. At the same time, she took up public speaking on behalf of various causes ranging from Irish nationalism to temperance to women's suffrage. By the end of the 1880s Lease had joined the Alliance as well as the Knights of Labor, and she soon applied her natural gifts as a fiery speaker to the cause of free silver. A tall, proud, and imposing woman, Lease drew excited and attentive audiences. "The people are at bay," she warned in 1894, "let the bloodhounds of money beware."

"Sockless Jerry" Simpson was an equally charismatic agrarian radical. Born in Canada, he had served as a seaman on Great Lakes steamships before buying a farm in northern Kansas. He, his wife, and young daughter made a go of the farm, but when he saw his child crushed to death in a sawmill accident, he and his wife relocated to the southern part of the state. There he raised cattle for several years before losing his herd in a blizzard.

Simpson was also a convert to the Alliance movement, and in 1890 he campaigned for Congress. A shrewd man with huge, calloused hands and pale blue eyes, Simpson effectively simplified the complex economic and political issues of the day. "Man must have access to the land," he maintained, "or he is a slave." Blaming their party's policies for so many farmers losing their lands, he warned Republicans: "You can't put this movement down by sneers or by ridicule, for its foundation was laid as far back as the foundation of the world. It is a struggle between the robbers and the robbed." Simpson dismissed his Republican opponent, a wealthy railroad lawyer, as an indulgent pawn of the corporations whose "soft white hands" and "silk hosiery" betrayed his true priorities. His outraged opponent thereupon shouted that it was better to have silk socks than none at all, providing Simpson with his folksy nickname.

"Sockless Jerry" won a seat in Congress, and so, too, did many other friends of "the people" in the Midwest. In the South, the Alliance won equal if not greater success by forcing the Democrats to nominate candidates pledged to their program. The southern states elected four pro-Alliance governors, seven pro-Alliance legislatures, forty-four pro-Alliance congressmen, and several senators. Among the most respected of the southern Alliancemen was Tom Watson of Georgia. The son of prosperous slaveholders who lost everything during and after the Civil War, he attended Mercer

University for two years before running out of funds, yet eventually became a successful lawyer and charismatic orator on behalf of the Alliance cause. He took the lead in appealing to black tenant farmers and sharecroppers to join with their white counterparts in ousting the Bourbon white political elite. "You are kept apart," he told black and white farmers, "that you may be separately fleeced of your earnings."

THE POPULIST PARTY   The success of the Alliances led many to consider the formation of a third political party. In May 1891 a conference in Cincinnati brought together delegates from farm, labor, and reform organizations to discuss strategy. The meeting endorsed a national third party and formed a national executive committee of the People's party. Few southerners were at Cincinnati, but many approved the third-party idea after their failure to move the Democratic party toward the subtreasury plan. In February 1892 a larger meeting at St. Louis called for a national convention of the People's party at Omaha on July 4 to adopt a platform and choose candidates. The stirring platform, written by Ignatius Donnelly of Minnesota, typified the apocalyptic, almost paranoid, style that increasingly characterized both the farmers' movement and its opponents:

> We meet in the midst of a nation brought to the verge of moral, political, and material ruin. Corruption dominates the ballot-box, the Legislatures, the Congress, and touches even the ermine of the bench. The newspapers are largely subsidized or muzzled, public opinion silenced, business prostrated, homes covered with mortgages, labor impoverished, and the land concentrating in the hands of the capitalists. . . . A vast conspiracy against mankind has been organized. . . . If not met and overthrown at once it forebodes terrible social convulsions . . . or the establishment of an absolute despotism.

The platform itself focused on issues of finance, transportation, and land. Its financial program demanded implementation of the subtreasury plan, free and unlimited coinage of silver at the 16:1 ratio, an increase in the amount of money in circulation to $50 per capita, a graduated income tax, and postal savings banks to protect depositors who otherwise risked disastrous losses in small-town banks vulnerable to farm depression. As to transportation, the time had come "when the railroad corporations will either own the people or the people must own the railroads." Let government therefore nationalize the railroads, and the telephone and telegraph systems as well. For land, "the heritage of the people," the Populist remedy was for the government to reclaim from railroads and other corporations lands "in excess of their actual needs," and to forbid land ownership by aliens. Finally, the platform endorsed the eight-hour day and restriction of immigration, and denounced the use of Pinkerton agents as strikebreakers. The party took these last positions to win support from the urban workers, whom Populists looked upon as fellow "producers."

The party's platform turned out to be more exciting than its candidate. The choice of Iowa's James B. Weaver was unfortunate, for Weaver, an able and prudent man, carried the stigma of his defeat on the Greenback ticket twelve years before. To balance Weaver, a Union general, the party named a former Confederate general for vice-president.

The Populist party was the startling new feature of the 1892 campaign, but for the major parties it was a repetition of 1888, with Grover Cleveland the Democratic candidate and Benjamin Harrison the Republican, and with the tariff the chief issue between them. The outcome, however, was different. Both major candidates polled over 5 million votes, but Cleveland carried a plurality of the popular votes and a majority of the electoral college. Weaver polled over 1 million votes, and carried Colorado, Kansas, Nevada, and Idaho, for a total of twenty-two electoral votes. Alabama was the banner Populist state of the South, with 36.6 percent of its vote for Weaver, even as reported by a Democratic returns board.

THE DEPRESSION OF 1893   Cleveland's second administration came to grief early. Before it ended, Cleveland had antagonized every major segment of the public: the farmers and silverites opposed his efforts to maintain the gold standard, business groups disliked his attempt to lower the tariff, and a large segment of labor was alienated when he put down the Pullman Strike. Worst of all, his second term coincided with one of the most devastating business panics in history, set off just before he took office by the failure of the Philadelphia and Reading Railroad and a panic on Wall Street.

By 1894 many people had reached bottom. That year some 750,000 workers went out on strike, including the Pullman workers; millions found themselves unemployed; railroad construction workers, laid off in the West, began tramping east and, to the dismay of alarmists who sniffed revolution in the air, talked of marching on Washington. Few of them made it to the capital. One group that did was the Army of the Commonweal of Christ, led by Jacob S. Coxey, a wealthy Ohio quarry owner turned Populist who demanded that the federal government provide unemployed people with jobs. Coxey, his wife, and their son, Legal Tender Coxey, rode in a carriage ahead of some 400 hardy protesters as they straggled into Washington. Coxey was arrested for walking on the grass, but his army as well as the growing political strength of Populism struck fear in many Americans. Critics portrayed Populist candidates as "hayseed socialists" whose election would endanger property rights.

In this climate of anxiety the 1894 midterm elections took place. The outcome disappointed the Populists, who had expected to profit from the discontent. North Carolina's was the only southern legislature lost by the Democrats, and that for only four years. Nationally, the elections amounted to a severe setback for Democrats, and the Republicans were the chief beneficiaries. The Populists emerged with six senators and seven representatives. They had polled 1.5 million votes for their congressional candidates and still expected the festering discontent to carry them to power in 1896.

SILVERITES VS. GOLDBUGS   The course of events, however, would dash that hope. In the mid-1890s events conspired to focus all agitations on the currency issue. One of the causes of the 1893 depression had been the failure of a British banking house, which led many British investors to unload their American investments in return for gold. Soon after Cleveland's inauguration the gold reserve fell below $100 million. To plug this drain on the Treasury the president sought repeal of the Sherman Silver Purchase Act in order to stop the issuance of silver notes redeemable in gold. Cleveland won the act's repeal in 1893, but at the cost of irreparable division in his own party. To further build the gold reserve, the administration struck a deal with J. P. Morgan in 1895. He and other financiers promised to supply half the gold needed to buy up a series of government bond issues, and to use their influence to stop demands on the Treasury. The deal worked, but it created the unfavorable image of Cleveland and the financial oligarchy working hand in glove.

Meanwhile the American Bimetallic League, heavily financed by silver miners, raised the agitation for silver coinage to a crescendo. Their greatest propaganda windfall came from the appearance in mid-1894 of William H. Harvey's book *Coin's Financial School*, which soon became a best-seller, the Uncle Tom's Cabin of the silver movement. In the book the youthful "Professor Coin" delivered lectures in which he resolutely confounded the "goldbugs" with his logic. The growing importance of the currency issue presented a dilemma for Populists: should the party promote the whole spectrum of reform it advocated, or should it try to ride the silver issue into power? The latter was the practical choice, so the Populist leaders decided, over the protest of more radical members, to hold their 1896 convention last, confident that the major parties would at best straddle the silver issue and that they would then reap a harvest of bolting silverite Republicans and Democrats.

THE ELECTION OF 1896 Contrary to these expectations the major parties took opposite positions on the currency issues. The Republicans, as expected, chose William McKinley on a gold-standard platform. McKinley, a former congressman and governor of Ohio, benefited from the political steamroller organized by his campaign manager, Marcus A. Hanna. On the Democratic side, early organizing paid off for the pro-silver forces, who captured the convention for their platform. William Jennings Bryan arranged to give the closing speech for the silver plank. The son of a judge who was a fervent Baptist moralist, Bryan was a two-term congressman from Nebraska who had been swept out in the Democratic losses of 1894; he had distinguished himself mainly with an exhausting three-hour speech against repeal of the Sherman Silver Purchase Act. In the months before the convention he had traveled the South and West, speaking for free silver. His rehearsed phrases swept the convention into a frenzy:

> I come to speak to you in defense of a cause as holy as the cause of liberty—the cause of humanity. . . . We have petitioned, and our petitions have been scorned. We have entreated, and our entreaties have been disregarded. We have begged, and they have mocked when our calamity came. We beg no longer, we entreat no more; we petition no more. We defy them!

William Jennings Bryan, whose "Cross of Gold" speech at the 1896 Democratic convention roused the delegates and secured him the party's presidential nomination.

By the time he reached his peroration there was little doubt that he would get the nomination: "You shall not press down upon the brow of labor this crown of thorns. You shall not crucify mankind upon a cross of gold!"

The next day Bryan was nominated on the fifth ballot, and in the process the Democratic party was fractured beyond repair. Groused one Cleveland supporter, "For the first time, I can understand the scenes of the French Revolution." Disappointed gold Democrats walked out of the convention and nominated their own candidate, Senator John M. Palmer of Illinois. "Fellow Democrats," he announced, "I will not consider it any great fault if you decide to cast your vote for William McKinley."

When the Populists met in St. Louis two weeks later they faced an impossible choice. They could name their own candidate and divide the silver vote or endorse Bryan and probably lose their identity. In the end they named Bryan, but chose their own vice-presidential candidate, former representative Thomas E. Watson of Georgia, and invited the Democrats to drop their vice-presidential nominee—an action which Bryan refused to countenance.

The thirty-six-year-old Bryan launched a whirlwind campaign. He crisscrossed the country, exploiting his spellbinding eloquence. McKinley, meanwhile, conducted a "front-porch campaign," receiving selected delegations of supporters at his home in Canton, Ohio, and giving only prepared responses. McKinley's campaign manager, Mark Hanna, shrewdly portrayed Bryan as a radical whose "communistic spirit" would ruin the capitalist system. Many observers agreed with the portrait. The New York *Tribune* denounced Bryan as a "wretched rattle-pated boy, posing in vapid vanity and mouthing resounding rottenness." Theodore Roosevelt had equally strong opinions. "The silver craze surpasses belief," he wrote a friend. "Bryan's election would be a great calamity."

By preying upon such fears, Hanna was able to raise a huge campaign chest and finance an army of Republican speakers who traveled the country in support of McKinley. At the battle's end the Democratic-Populist-Silverite candidates were overwhelmed by the well-organized and well-financed Republican campaign. McKinley won the popular vote by 7.1 million to 6.5 million and the electoral college by 271 to 176.

Bryan carried most of the West and the South below the border states, but the problem neither the Populists nor Bryan ever overcame was that of breaking into metropolitan centers east of the Mississippi and north of the Ohio and Potomac rivers. In the critical midwestern battleground, from Minnesota and Iowa eastward to Ohio, Bryan carried not a single state. Many Catholic voters, nor-

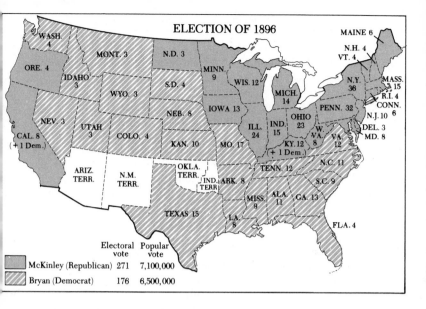

ELECTION OF 1896

	Electoral vote	Popular vote
McKinley (Republican)	271	7,100,000
Bryan (Democrat)	176	6,500,000

mally drawn to the Democrats, were no doubt repelled by Bryan's evangelical style. Farmers in the Northeast, moreover, were less attracted to agrarian radicalism than were farmers in the wheat and cotton belts, where there were higher rates of tenancy and a narrower range of crops. Among factory workers in the cities, Bryan found even less support. Despite efforts on his behalf by reformers and unionists in the Midwest and East, unorganized workers found it easier to identify with McKinley's "full dinner pail" than with Bryan's free silver. Some workers may have been intimidated by businessmen's threats to close shop if the "Demopop" heresies triumphed.

A NEW ERA   It had been a climactic political struggle, falling almost precisely in the middle of what one historian called the Grand Conjuncture between rural and metropolitan America, 1870–1920. And metropolitan America had won. Henry Adams, who lived through the 1890s, wrote in *The Education of Henry Adams*:

> For a hundred years . . . the American people had hesitated, vacillated, swayed forward and back, between two forces, one simply industrial [productive], the other capitalistic, centralizing and mechanical. . . . the majority at last declared itself, once and for all, in favor of the capitalistic system with all its necessary machinery. All one's friends, all one's best citizens, reformers, churches, colleges, educated classes, had joined the banks to force submission to capitalism.

Urban-industrial values had indeed taken firm hold of the political system. The first important act of the McKinley administration was to call a special session of Congress to raise the tariff again. The Dingley Tariff of 1897 became the highest to that time. By 1897 prosperity was returning, helped along by inflation of the currency, which bore out the arguments of greenbackers and silverites. But the inflation came, in one of history's many ironies, from neither green-backs nor silver, but from a new flood of gold into the market and into the mints. During the 1880s and 1890s new discoveries of gold in South Africa, in the Canadian Yukon, and in Alaska, aided by the development of a new cyanide process for extracting gold from its ore, led to spectacular new gold rushes. The Yukon alone, from 1897 to 1904, was estimated to have added some $100 million worth of gold to the world's store. In 1900 Congress passed a Gold Standard Act, which marked an end to the silver movement.

The old issues of tariffs and currency were now swallowed up by the Spanish-American War, which ushered in a new era. "The Spanish War finished us," said old Populist Tom Watson. "The blare of the bugle drowned the voice of the Reformer." And yet to compound the irony, most of the Populists' 1892 Omaha platform, which seemed so radical at the time, would be in effect within two decades.

Further Reading

Overviews of the Gilded Age cover politics in detail. See Robert H. Wiebe's *The Search for Order, 1877–1920* (1967),° John A. Garraty's *The New Commonwealth, 1877–1890* (1968),° and Morton Keller's *Affairs of State: Public Life in Nineteenth Century America* (1977).°

Some scholars approach politics through the party process. Leonard D. White's *The Republican Era, 1869–1901* (1958) concentrates on activities at the federal level. H. Wayne Morgan's *From Hayes to McKinley: National Party Politics, 1877–1896* (1969)° takes an organizational approach.

Much recent scholarship uses the ethnocultural approach to study Gilded Age politics. See the seminal works of Paul Kleppner, *The Cross of Culture: A Social Analysis of Midwestern Politics, 1850–1900* (1970) and *The Third Electoral System, 1853–1892* (1979), as well as Richard J. Jensen's *The Winning of the Midwest: Social and Political Conflicts, 1888–1896* (1971).

On the Gilded Age presidents, see William S. McFeely's *Grant: A Biography* (1981),° Allan Peskin's *Garfield: A Biography* (1978), Thomas C. Reeves's *Gentleman Boss: The Life of Chester Alan Arthur* (1975), and Lewis L. Gould's *The Presidency of William McKinley* (1980).

Scholars have also examined various Gilded Age issues and interest

°These books are available in paperback editions.

groups. John G. Sproat's *"The Best Man": Liberal Reformers in the Gilded Age* (1968)° and Gerald W. McFarland's *Mugwumps, Morals, and Politics, 1884–1920* (1975) examine the issue of government service. Tom E. Terrill's *The Tariff, Politics, and American Foreign Policy, 1874–1901* (1973) lends clarity to that complex issue. The finances of the Gilded Age are covered in Irwin Unger's *The Greenback Era: A Social and Political History of American Finance, 1865–1879* (1964) and Walter T. K. Nugent's *Money and American Society, 1865–1880* (1968).

One of the most controversial works on Populism is Lawrence Goodwyn's *Democratic Promise: The Populist Moment in America* (1976), also available in condensed form as *The Populist Moment* (1978).° Goodwyn's emphasis on the cooperative nature of agrarian protest contradicts the interpretations in John D. Hicks's *The Populist Revolt* (1931), which portrays agrarians as forerunners of liberal reform, and Richard Hofstadter's *The Age of Reform* (1955),° which focuses on their reactionary strain.

Biographies of leading agrarians include C. Vann Woodward's *Tom Watson, Agrarian Rebel* (1938),° Martin Ridge's *Ignatius Donnelly* (1962), and Louis W. Koenig's *Bryan: A Political Biography of William Jennings Bryan* (1971). For the role of the leading Populists in the election of 1896, consult Paul W. Glad's *McKinley, Bryan, and the People* (1964).

23

THE COURSE OF EMPIRE

TOWARD THE NEW IMPERIALISM

EXPANSION IN THE PACIFIC   Throughout most of the late nineteenth century, Americans displayed what one senator called "only a languid interest" in foreign affairs. Whereas most Americans were deeply affected by industrial development, western settlement, and domestic politics, foreign relations left the vast majority of Americans untouched. With the major diplomatic issues stemming from the Civil War having been quickly settled, an isolationist mood swept across the United States, which continued to enjoy what one historian has called "free security": wide oceans as buffers on either side, the British navy situated between America and the powers of Europe, and militarily weak neighbors in the Western Hemisphere.

Yet the spirit of Manifest Destiny remained alive, if muted, in the decades after Appomattox, and a few key figures sought to lead the United States out of its isolationist shell. For such expansionists, Asia offered an especially alluring temptation. Andrew Johnson's secretary of state, William H. Seward, was one who believed that the United States must inevitably exercise commercial domination "on the Pacific ocean, and its islands and continents." Eager for American manufacturers to capture Asian markets, Seward believed the United States first had to remove all foreign interests from the northern Pacific coast and gain access to that region's valuable ports. To that end he cast covetous eyes on the crown colony of British Columbia, sandwiched between Russian America (Alaska) and Washington Territory. Late in 1866, while encouraging annexation sentiment among the British Columbians, Seward learned of Russia's desire to sell Alaska, which for them had become an unprofitable possession. He leapt at the offer, and in March 1867 the United States bought Alaska for $7.2 million, thus removing the most recent colonial power from the New World. Critics scoffed at "Seward's folly" of buying the Alaskan "icebox," but it proved in time to be the biggest bargain for the United States since the Louisiana Purchase.

Seward obtained Alaska in part because he feared the British would buy it, and in part because he knew of the territory's rich mineral deposits and bountiful forests. He also hoped that its purchase by the United States would convince the British Columbians to request annexation. For a while that seemed a real possibility, but in 1870 British Columbia decided instead to join the new Confederation of Canada.

Seward articulated a vision of empire that "must continue to move on westward until the tides of the renewed and decaying civilizations of the world met on the shores of the Pacific Ocean." His successors at the State Department never completely lost sight of his expansionist vision, and the Pacific Ocean remained the major field of overseas activity through the rest of the nineteenth century. The urge to annex islands in the Pacific was first expressed in 1853–1854 by Commodore Perry, who had his eye on the Bonin Islands off the coast of Japan. He was overruled, but in the flush years of expansionism during the 1850s the United States laid claim to various small islands and coral atolls of the mid-Pacific, sometimes in conflict with the claims of other nations. Among those islands, two inhabited groups occupied especially strategic positions about twenty degrees from either side of the equator: Samoa on the south and Hawaii (the Sandwich Islands) on the north. Both had major harbors, Pago Pago and Pearl Harbor, respectively, with which Americans had made contact as early as the 1820s. In the

William H. Seward, secretary of state under Presidents Lincoln and Andrew Johnson, negotiated the purchase of Alaska from the Russians in 1867.

years after the Civil War American interest in these islands gradually deepened.

SAMOA   In 1872 a U.S. Navy commander negotiated a treaty with a Samoan chieftain giving the United States a naval station at Pago Pago, but the Senate took no action on the treaty. A special agent of President Grant then organized a government on his own initiative and installed himself as prime minister of Samoa, but was soon overthrown and deported on a British vessel. Finally, in 1878, a permanent American presence was established. The Samoans signed a treaty with the United States which granted a naval base at Pago Pago and extraterritoriality for Americans (meaning that in Samoa they remained subject only to American law), exchanged trade concessions, and called for the United States to extend its good offices in case of a dispute with another nation. The Senate ratified this accord and in the following year the German and British governments worked out similar arrangements on other islands of the Samoan group.

There matters rested until civil war broke out in 1887 when the Germans backed a pretender against the native Samoan king and finally installed him under a German protectorate. The sequel to this incident was a conference in Berlin (1889) which established a tripartite protectorate, with Germany, Great Britain, and the United States in an uneasy partnership.

HAWAII   In Hawaii the Americans had more nearly a clear field. The islands, a united kingdom since 1795, had a sizable settlement of American missionaries and planters and were strategically more important to the United States. Occupation by another major power might have posed a threat to American commercial interest and even to American defense. As early as 1842 Secretary of State Daniel Webster said that the United States would be "dissatisfied" to see any other power take possession.

In 1875 the kingdom entered a reciprocal trade agreement under which Hawaiian sugar entered the United States duty free. Hawaii also promised that none of its territory would be leased or granted to a third power. The agreement was renewed in 1887, when it was amended to grant the United States exclusive right to a fortified naval base at Pearl Harbor, near Honolulu. That same year the Americans on the islands forced the king to grant a constitutional government which they dominated. These agreements resulted in a boom in sugar growing, and American settlers in Hawaii soon farmed an economic elite. White planters built their fortunes on cheap immigrant labor, mainly Chinese, Japanese, and Portuguese. By the 1890s the native population had been reduced to a minority by smallpox and other foreign diseases, and Orientals quickly became the most numerous group in Hawaii.

In 1891 the king's sister, Queen Liliuokalani, ascended the throne and began efforts to reclaim a measure of power. Shortly before that the McKinley Tariff had destroyed Hawaii's favored position in the sugar trade by putting the sugar of all countries on the free list and granting growers in the United States a 2¢ bounty. The resultant discontent led Hawaii's white population to stage a revolt early in 1893. The American minister brought in marines from the cruiser *Boston* to support the coup. As he cheerfully reported to Washington, "The Hawaiian pear is now fully ripe, and this is the golden hour for the United States to pluck it." Within a month a committee of the new government turned up in Washington and in February signed a treaty of annexation.

The treaty, however, appeared just weeks before President Harrison left office, and Democratic senators blocked ratification. On March 9 President Cleveland withdrew the treaty and sent a special commissioner to investigate. He removed the American marines and reported that the American minister had acted improperly. Most Hawaiians opposed annexation, the commissioner found. He concluded that the revolution had been engineered mainly by sugar planters hoping to get the domestic sugar bounty by annexation. Cleveland therefore proposed to restore the queen in return for amnesty to the revolutionists. The provisional government refused and on July 4, 1894, proclaimed the Republic of Hawaii, which had in its constitution a standing provision for American annexation, presumably after Cleveland yielded to a president whose sensibilities were less easily offended.

Queen Liliuokalani.

STEPS TO WORLD POWER

The antebellum spirit of expansionism thus had neither died out with the 1850s nor gone completely dormant. It would return full blown in the 1890s with the addition of some new flourishes. European powers from about 1870 on set an example with a new surge of imperialism in Africa and Asia, where they seized colonies, protectorates, and economic privileges. All of Africa except Liberia and Ethiopia fell under outside dominion. Above all, the new imperialism was economic, a quest for markets and raw materials, and to more than one American the European example seemed relevant to the American experience. The closing of the frontier, brought forcefully to public attention by the census of 1890 and by Frederick Jackson Turner's classic essay on the significance of the frontier in 1893, might well signal the end of a constantly growing market and a need to seek markets overseas, many people reasoned. Turner himself had written: "He would be a rash prophet who would assert that the expansive character of American life has now entirely ceased. Movement has been its dominant fact, and, unless this training has no effect upon a people, the American energy will continually demand a wider field for its exercise."

Most Americans shared a concern with world markets as developments in transportation and communication quickened the pace of commerce and diplomacy. From the first, exports of farm products had been the basis of American economic growth. Now the conviction grew that American manufacturers had matured to the point that they could outsell foreign goods in the world market. The new conviction challenged an old Republican principle that industry must be protected against foreign competition in the domestic market. But should the expansion of markets lead to territorial expansion as well? Or to intervention in the internal affairs of other countries? On this point Americans disagreed, but a small, yet vocal group of public officials advocated overseas possessions; they were led by Senator Albert J. Beveridge of Indiana and Senator Henry Cabot Lodge of Massachusetts, Theodore Roosevelt, and not least of all, Captain Alfred Thayer Mahan.

NAVAL POWER   During the 1880s Captain Mahan became the leading proponent of sea power. A graduate of Annapolis, he served for years as president of the Naval War College at Newport, Rhode Island. A series of his lectures on naval history grew into a volume published in 1890, *The Influence of Sea Power upon History, 1660–1783*, in which he argued that national greatness and prosperity

The battleship Maine, *funded in 1886, shown here entering Havana Harbor in 1898.*

flowed from sea power, which had a fundamentally economic importance. To Mahan, economic development called for a big navy, a strong merchant marine, foreign commerce, colonies, and naval bases. The age of steam made coaling stations a new matter of strategic concern. Mahan expounded on America's destiny to control the Caribbean, build an isthmian canal, and spread Western civilization in the Pacific. His ideas were widely circulated in popular journals.

Even before Mahan's writings became influential a gradual expansion of the navy had begun, after a season of post–Civil War neglect led one journal to call the American fleet a "heterogeneous collection of naval trash." In 1880 the nation had fewer than a hundred seagoing vessels, many of them rusting or rotting at the docks. By the time Cleveland entered office four new steel vessels had been authorized, and Cleveland's navy secretary got funds for twenty more.

RACIAL THOUGHT   Meanwhile certain intellectual currents of the day worked to bolster the new spirit of Manifest Destiny. The Darwinian idea of natural selection afforded a handy argument for imperialism. If natural selection worked in the biological realm, would it not apply also in human society? Among nations, as among individuals, the fittest survive and prevail. "There is apparently much truth in the belief that the wonderful progress of the United States, as well as the character of the people, are the results of natural selection," Darwin wrote in *The Descent of Man* (1871), "the more energetic, restless and courageous men from all parts of Europe having emigrated during the last ten to twelve generations to that great country and having there succeeded best." Darwin himself, however, cannot fairly be tagged a champion of imperialism or of racial "purity."

John Fiske, the historian and popular lecturer on Darwinism, nevertheless developed racial corollaries from Darwin's idea. In *American Political Ideas* (1885) he stressed the superior character of "Anglo-Saxon" institutions and peoples. The English "race," he argued, was destined to dominate the globe: in the institutions, traditions, language, even in the blood of the world's peoples.

Josiah Strong, a Congregational minister, added the sanction of religion. In his book *Our Country: Its Possible Future and Its Present Crisis* (1885), Strong argued that "Anglo-Saxons" embodied two great ideas: civil liberty and "a pure spiritual Christianity." The Anglo-Saxon was "divinely commissioned to be, in a peculiar sense, his brother's keeper." Expansion to establish foreign missions found favor in both Protestant and Catholic churches, the chief opposition coming from minority groups like the Quakers and Unitarians.

LATIN AMERICA   By the 1890s events drew the United States more and more into the orbit of world affairs. One significant step came with the First International American Conference in Washington, which met from late 1889 through early 1890. Secretary of State James G. Blaine welcomed delegates from seventeen Latin American states. His ultimate hope was to initiate free trade among American nations. The Latin delegates, however, were afraid of damaging their ties with Europe for the benefit of manufacturers in the United States. They resolved therefore in favor of reciprocity agreements, and over the next few years Blaine secured tariff concessions from ten Latin countries by executive agreements under the provisions of the McKinley Tariff. Though it failed to set up machinery for the arbitration of disputes, the conference did establish a permanent agency as a clearinghouse for information: the Bureau of American Republics, later the Pan-American Union, which in 1948 became the Organization of American States.

CANADA AND SOUTH AMERICA   But not all was sweetness and light in the Western Hemisphere. In the 1880s and 1890s incidents in the Bering Sea, in Chile, and in Venezuela stirred the bumptious spirit of national pride that never lay far below the surface. At issue in the Bering Sea was the practice of pelagic (oceanic) sealing by foreign nationals, mostly Canadians, in offshore waters where the difficulty of distinguishing males and females resulted in the loss of many pups when their mothers were killed. This was an issue because a caprice of fashion had put sealskin coats and muffs much in demand. In 1886 American revenue cutters began seizing Canadian ships engaged in the practice, and in 1889 Congress declared the Bering a closed sea under United States dominion. In an exchange of notes in 1890, however, the British foreign minister refused to accept the legitimacy of Congress's claim. There was a flurry of bluster in the American press, but never much chance that the two countries would come to blows over what one newspaper called "a few greasy, ill-smelling sealskins." Eventually, under an arbitration treaty of 1892, it was decided that while the Bering was an open sea, by mutual agreement pelagic sealing was forbidden within sixty miles of the Pribilof Islands. Later, in 1911, by treaty with Britain, Russia, and Japan, pelagic sealing was prohibited throughout the North Pacific and Bering Sea.

Trouble in Chile flared intensely, but passed quickly. When civil war broke out in that country in 1891, American authorities briefly detained a rebel ship carrying arms from San Diego, then found that there had been no violation of neutrality laws. This left a lingering resentment among the rebels, who soon took over Chile's government. In October 1891, when the cruiser *Baltimore* called at Valparaiso, a mob attacked sailors returning from the True Blue Saloon. Two sailors were killed and seventeen hurt in the fracas, and some were thrown into jail. For a season tempers ran hot as the countries exchanged imprecations. By January 1892 Secretary Blaine was threatening to break off relations, and President Harrison waxed bellicose in a special message to Congress. Happily, tempers cooled in Valparaiso and Chile offered an apology and an indemnity of $75,000.

Far more serious was the Venezuelan boundary dispute with British Guiana, which had simmered since colonial days but took on new urgency when gold was found in the disputed area. When Venezuela suspended diplomatic relations with Britain in 1887, the American State Department suggested arbitration, but the matter was still unsettled in 1892 when Cleveland was reelected to the White House. In 1895 Congress passed a Republican- sponsored resolution for arbitration, and Cleveland was almost forced to "twist the lion's tail" or see his political opponents do it. He may even have found the occasion a welcome diversion from his domestic problems. His secretary of state, Richard L. Olney, drafted a note in which he invoked the Monroe Doctrine against British interference in the affairs of the New World. Cleveland claimed to have softened the "verbiage" a bit, but still dubbed it a "20 inch gun" note.

> Today [Olney wrote] the United States is practically sovereign on this continent, and its fiat is law upon the subjects to which it confines its interposition. Why? . . . It is because, in addition to all other grounds, its infinite resources combined with its isolated position render it master of the situation and practically invulnerable as against any or all other powers.

The note was calculated to provoke a quick reply, but the British minister let it lie for a maddening four months. The British government was preoccupied elsewhere and assumed the note was largely for domestic American consumption anyway. Britain finally rejected the demand for arbitration and noted that the Monroe Doctrine was not recognized international law, and in any case was irrelevant to a boundary dispute. Cleveland pronounced himself "mad clear through" at such a rebuff to the "friendly" suggestion of the United States. Congress, at Cleveland's request, unanimously voted for a boundary commission to run the line in spite of the British. Enthusiasm swept the country. Theodore Roosevelt vented his opinion that "this country needs a war." But cooler heads soon prevailed. The British faced more urgent problems in South Africa, and through the good offices of the United States finally came around to an arbitration treaty with Venezuela, signed in 1897. By the time an international commission handed in its findings in 1899, the focus of public attention was elsewhere. The settlement turned out to be about what the British had offered in the first place.

THE SPANISH-AMERICAN WAR

"CUBA LIBRE"   Until the 1890s a certain ambivalence about overseas possessions had checked America's drive to expand. Suddenly in 1898 and 1899 the inhibitions collapsed and American power thrust its way to the far reaches of the Pacific. The occasion for this explosion of imperialism lay neither in the Pacific nor in the quest for bases and trade, but to the south in Cuba. The chief motive was a sense of outrage at another country's imperialism.

Throughout the second half of the nineteenth century, Cubans had repeatedly revolted against Spanish rule, only to be ruthlessly suppressed. All the while, American investments in Cuba, mainly in sugar and mining, were steadily rising. The United States in fact traded more with Cuba than Spain did. On February 24, 1895, insurrection broke out again. Simmering discontent with Spanish rule had been aggravated by the Wilson-Gorman Tariff of 1894, which took sugar off the free list in the midst of a depression already damaging to the market for Cuban sugar. Raw sugar prices collapsed, putting Cubans out of work and thereby rekindling their interest in rebellion. Public feeling in the United States was with the rebels, and many Americans extended help to the Cuban Revolutionary party which organized the revolt from headquarters in New York. Its leader, José Martí, returned to the island soon after the outbreak and was killed in a skirmish with Spanish troops.

José Martí, leader of the Cuban revolt against Spanish rule.

The insurrectionists' strategy was to wage guerrilla warfare and to damage the economic life of the island, which in turn would excite the concern of American investors. The strategy dictated hit-and-run attacks on trains, railways, and plantations. The movement found one source of income by selling "protection" against attack. Such tactics forced people either into the insurgent forces or into garrisoned towns, which in turn might be cut off from food supplies. Revolutionary propaganda of course presented the effort in a different light, and Americans were more than ready to look upon the insurrection in the light of their own War of Independence. American attentions were distracted by the Venezuelan crisis and the election of 1896, but Spanish authorities insisted that only aid from the United States kept the revolt alive

The tactics needed to counter guerrilla warfare nearly always cast their practitioners in a bad light. In 1896 Spanish general Valeriano Weyler adopted a policy of gathering Cubans behind Spanish lines, often in detention (*reconcentrado*) centers so that no one could join the insurrections by night and appear peaceful by day. In some of the centers a combination of tropical climate, poor food, and unsanitary conditions soon brought a heavy toll of disease and death. The American press promptly christened the Spanish commander "Butcher" Weyler.

Events in Cuba supplied exciting copy for the popular press. Chance had it that William Randolph Hearst's New York *Journal* and Joseph Pulitzer's New York *World* were at the time locked in a monumental struggle for circulation. "It was a battle of gigantic proportions," one journalist later wrote, "in which the sufferings of Cuba merely chanced to furnish some of the most convenient ammunition." Another device of the circulation war was the newfangled comic strip, and one of the most popular was "The Yellow Kid," the cartoonist for which Hearst lured from Pulitzer with a high salary.

Hence, by association, the unbuttoned sensationalism at which the papers vied came to be called "yellow journalism." Hearst emerged as the undisputed champion. Frederick Remington, the artist best known for his cowboy pictures, supplied Hearst's *Journal* with an imaginary picture which left the impression that three Cuban women on a detained American ship had been forced to disrobe in the presence of male Spanish officers. Pulitzer was able to demonstrate the falsity of the report, but truth was a poor substitute for titillation. A Hearst reporter, by means of bribery and intrigue, spirited a Cuban woman out of a Spanish prison and away from Cuba, whereupon a member of Congress suggested hiring a thousand such reporters to liberate the whole island. The *Journal* excelled also at invective against "Weyler the brute, the devastator of haciendas, the destroyer of men."

At the outset the Cleveland administration tried to protect American rights but avoided involvement beyond an offer of mediation. Mounting public sympathy for the cause, however, manifested itself in Congress. By concurrent resolution on April 6, 1896, the two houses endorsed recognition of the Cuban belligerents and urged the president to seek a peace on the basis of Cuban independence. Cleveland, however, denied any designs against Spanish rule and offered to cooperate with Spain in bringing peace on the basis of home rule. The Spanish politely refused. Meanwhile America's revenue service and naval forces did their best to break up gun-running expeditions launched from the Atlantic and Gulf coasts.

PRESSURE FOR WAR   The posture of neutrality changed sharply when McKinley entered office. He had been elected on a platform that endorsed independence for Cuba, as well as American control of Hawaii and of an isthmian canal. In October 1897 a new Spanish commander set out to liberalize the reconcentration system and in November Spain's queen regent offered Cuba autonomy (self-government without formal independence) in return for peace. What the Cubans might once have welcomed, however, they now rejected, insurrectionists and Spanish loyalists alike. Spain was impaled on the horns of a dilemma, unable to end the war and unready to give up Cuba.

Early in 1898 events moved rapidly to arouse opinion against Spain. On January 12 a riotous demonstration of Spanish loyalists in Havana denounced Weyler's recall and the offer of autonomy. The American consul-general seized the occasion to request a warship to help assure the security of American citizens and property. The battleship *Maine* showed up on January 25, in Havana Harbor, ostensibly on a courtesy call. On February 9 Hearst's New York *Journal* released the text of a letter from Spanish minister Deputy de Lôme to a friend in Havana, stolen from the post office by a Cuban spy. In the letter de Lôme called President McKinley "weak and a bidder for the admiration of the crowd, besides being a would-be politician who tries to leave a door open behind himself while keeping on good terms with the jingoes of his party." This was hardly more extreme than what McKinley's assistant secretary of the navy Theodore Roosevelt had said about him: the "white-livered" president had "no more backbone than a chocolate eclair." But that comment had remained private. De Lôme resigned to prevent further embarrassment to his government.

Six days later, during the night of February 15, 1898, the American battleship *Maine* exploded in Havana Harbor and sank with a loss of 260 men, most of whom died in their hammocks. Those eager for a war with Spain now demanded an immediate declaration. Roosevelt called the sinking "an act of dirty treachery on the part of the Spaniards." A naval court of inquiry reported in March that an external mine had set off an explosion in the ship's magazine. Lack-

An American cartoon depicts the sinking of the Maine *in Havana Harbor. The uproar created by the incident and its coverage in the "yellow press" edged McKinley toward war.*

ing hard evidence, the court made no effort to fix the blame, but the yellow press had no need of evidence. The outcry against Spain reached a crescendo in the words "Remember the Maine!" Never mind that one cannot imagine any advantage Spain could derive from such an act. What actually happened, whether accidentally or on purpose, remains a mystery.

McKinley, under the mounting pressure of public excitement, tried to maintain a steady course. The president, a Civil War veteran, told an aide, "I have been through one war. I have seen the dead piled up, and I do not want to see another." But he was increasingly swayed by the weight of outraged public opinion and by the militants in his own party such as Roosevelt and Lodge. As one congressman remarked, McKinley "keeps his ear to the ground so close that he gets it full of grasshoppers much of the time." On March 9 the begrudgingly militant president coaxed from Congress a $50 million appropriation for defense. Still, McKinley sought to avoid war, as did most business spokesmen. Such caution infuriated Roosevelt. "We will have this war for the freedom of Cuba," he fumed on March 26, "in spite of the timidity of the commercial interests."

The Spanish government, sensing the growing militancy in the United States, announced a unilateral cease-fire in early April 1898. On April 10 the Spanish minister gave the State Department a message that amounted to a surrender: the United States should indicate the nature and duration of the armistice; Cuba would have an autonomous government; and the two countries would submit the question of the *Maine* to arbitration. The United States minister to Spain then cabled from Madrid: "I hope nothing will now be done to humiliate Spain, as I am satisfied that the present government is going, and is loyally ready to go, as fast and as far as it can." McKinley, he predicted, could win a settlement by August 1 on any terms: autonomy, independence, or cession of Cuba to the United States.

But the message came too late.

The following day McKinley sent Congress what amounted to a war message. He asked for power to use armed forces in Cuba to abate a nuisance off the United States' shores and to protect American property and trade. The Cuban situation, McKinley said, was a constant menace to the peace. Back to the president on April 20 came a joint resolution of Congress, which went beyond endorsing the use of the armed forces: it declared Cuba independent and demanded withdrawal of Spanish forces. The Teller Amendment, added on the Senate floor, disclaimed any American designs on Cuban territory. McKinley signed the resolution and a copy went off to the Spanish government, with notice that McKinley would execute it unless Spain gave a complete and satisfactory response by noon, April 23. Meanwhile, on April 22 the president announced a blockade of Cuba's northern coast and the port of Santiago. Under international law this was an act of war. Rather than give in to an ultimatum, the Spanish government declared war on April 24. Congress then, determined to be first, declared war on April 25, retroactive to April 21, 1898.

Why such a rush into war after the American minister had predicted that Spain would cave in before the summer was out? Chiefly because too much momentum and popular pressure had already built up for a confidential message to change the course of events. Also, leaders of the business community, which tolerates uncertainty poorly, were now demanding a quick resolution of the problem. Many lacked faith in the willingness or ability of the Spanish government to carry out a moderate policy in the face of a hostile public opinion. Still, it is fair to ask why McKinley did not take a stand for peace, knowing what he did. He might have defied Congress and public opinion, but in the end the political risk was too high. The Democrats were likely to adopt the popular cause of Cuba. The ultimate blame for war, if blame must be levied, belongs to the American people for letting themselves be whipped up into such a hostile frenzy.

DEWEY TAKES MANILA   The war itself was short, lasting four months, and for America, victorious. John Hay, soon to be secretary of state, called it "a splendid little war." The war's end was also the end of Spain's once great New World empire, which had begun with Columbus. It marked as well the emergence of the United States as a world power. If American participation saved many lives by ending the insurrection in Cuba, it also led to American involvement in another insurrection, in the Philippines, and created a host of problems that persisted into the twentieth century.

The war was barely under way before the navy produced a quick, spectacular victory in an unexpected quarter—Manila Bay. While public attention was fixed on Cuba, young Theodore Roosevelt was thinking of the Philippines. As assistant secretary of the navy, he had Commodore George Dewey appointed commander of the small Asiatic squadron, and had seen to it that ample supplies went out to the squadron at Hong Kong along with orders to engage Spain in the Philippines in case of war. President McKinley had approved those orders.

Arriving late on April 30 with four cruisers and two gunboats, Dewey destroyed or captured all the Spanish warships in Manila Bay. The Spanish force lost 381 men killed, while Dewey's squadron suffered only 8 wounded. Dewey, without an occupation force, was now in awkward possession of Manila Bay. Promised reinforce-

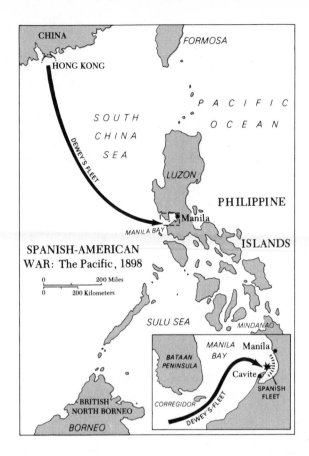

SPANISH-AMERICAN
WAR: The Pacific, 1898

ments, he stayed while foreign warships, including a German force equal if not superior to his own, hung about the scene like watchful vultures. Land reinforcements finally arrived, and with the help of Filipino insurrectionists under Emilio Aguinaldo, Dewey's forces entered Manila on August 13.

THE CUBAN CAMPAIGN While these events transpired halfway around the world, the war reached a quick climax closer to home, which was surprising because American preparation for this war was spotty. The navy was fit, but the army could muster only an ill-assorted guard of 28,000 regulars and about 100,000 militiamen. Altogether during the war about 200,000 more militiamen were recruited, chiefly as state volunteers. The armed forces suffered badly from both inexperience and maladministration, with the result that more died from disease than from enemy action. The United States' salvation was that Spanish forces were even worse off, their morale infinitely so.

A force of some 17,000 American troops hastily assembled at Tampa. One significant element of that force was the First Volunteer Cavalry, better known as the "Rough Riders" and best remembered because Lieutenant-Colonel Theodore Roosevelt was second in command. Eager to get "in on the fun," and "to act up to my preachings," Roosevelt had quit the Navy Department soon after war was declared, ordered a custom-fitted, fawn-colored uniform with yellow trim from Brooks Brothers, grabbed a dozen pairs of spectacles, and rushed to help organize a volunteer regiment of Ivy League athletes, leathery ex-convicts, Indians, and southwestern deadshots. Assessing this motley crew as they began training in Texas, Roosevelt wrote Lodge: "More than ever I fail to get the relations of this regiment and the universe straight." Their landing at the southeastern tip of Cuba was a mad scramble, as the horses were mistakenly sent elsewhere, leaving the "Rough Riders" to become the "Weary Walkers."

The major land action of the campaign occurred on July 1. About 7,000 Americans took the fortified village of El Caney from about 600 of the enemy garrison. While a much larger force attacked San Juan Hill, a smaller unit, including the dismounted Rough Riders, together with black soldiers from two cavalry units seized the enemy position atop nearby Kettle Hill. In the midst of the fray, Roosevelt felt the joy "when the wolf rises in the heart" and satisfied his bloodlust by seeing a Spaniard he shot double up "neatly

Lieutenant-Colonel Theodore Roosevelt posing with his "Rough Riders" after the battle of San Juan, 1898.

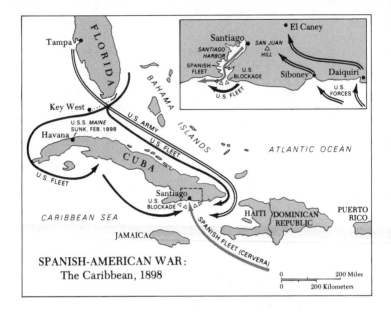

SPANISH-AMERICAN WAR:
The Caribbean, 1898

as a jackrabbit." He later claimed that he "would rather have led that charge than served three terms in the U.S. Senate." A friend wrote to Roosevelt's wife that her husband was "revelling in victory and gore." The two battles put American forces atop heights from which to the west and south they could bring Santiago and the Spanish fleet under seige. On July 3 the Spanish under Admiral Cervera made a gallant run for it, but their decrepit ships were little more than sitting ducks for the newer American fleet, which included five battleships and two cruisers. The casualties were as one-sided as at Manila: 474 Spanish were killed and wounded and 1,750 were taken prisoner, while only one American was killed and one wounded. The timely battle afforded Fourth of July orators the rarest opportunity they had had since the twin Union victories of Vicksburg and Gettysburg thirty-five years before. Santiago surrendered with a garrison of 24,000 on July 17. On July 25 an American force moved into Spanish-held Puerto Rico against minor resistance.

The next day the Spanish government sued for peace. After discussions lasting two weeks, an armistice was signed on August 12, less than four months after the war's start and the day before Americans entered Manila. The peace protocol specified that Spain should give up Cuba, and that the United States should annex Puerto Rico and occupy Manila pending disposition of the Philippines. Among more than 274,000 Americans who served during the war and the ensuing demobilization, 5,462 died, but only 379 in battle. Most succumbed to malaria, typhoid, dysentery, or yellow fever.

THE DEBATE OVER ANNEXATION   On October 1, a peace commission opened negotiations that led to the Treaty of Paris, signed on December 10. Most of the major points had been settled in the peace protocol, but two fundamental questions remained: the Cuban debt and the status of the Philippines. The United States simply refused to assume the Cuban government's debt of $400 million, incurred in the first place largely to subdue the insurrection. The Philippines posed a harder question, indeed one of the biggest decisions to face United States foreign policy to that time, and one that was sprung upon the country without preparation. McKinley, who claimed that at first he himself could not locate the islands within 2,000 miles, gave ambiguous signals to the peace commission. The commission itself was divided.

There had been no demand for annexation before the war, but Dewey's victory quickly kindled expansionist fever. Businessmen began thinking of the commercial possibilities not so much in the islands as in the nearby continent of Asia, such as oil for the lamps of China and textiles for its teeming millions. Missionary societies saw the chance to save the "little brown brother." The Philippines promised to provide a useful base for all such activities. It was neither the first nor the last time that Americans would get caught up in fantasies of saving Asia or getting rich there. McKinley pondered the alternatives and later explained his reasoning to a group of Methodists:

"*Well, I Hardly Know Which to Take First.*" *At the end of the nineteenth century it seemed that Uncle Sam had developed a considerable appetite for foreign territory.*

> And one night late it came to me this way—I don't know how it was, but
> it came: (1) that we could not give them back to Spain—that would be
> cowardly and dishonorable; (2) that we could not turn them over to
> France or Germany—our commercial rivals in the Orient—that would
> be bad business and discreditable; (3) that we could not leave them to
> themselves—they were unfit for self-government—and they would soon
> have anarchy and misrule over there worse than Spain's was; and (4)
> that there was nothing left for us to do but to take them all, and to
> educate the Filipinos, and uplift and civilize and Christianize them, and
> by God's grace do the very best we could by them, as our fellowmen for
> whom Christ also died. And then I went to bed, and went to sleep and
> slept soundly.

In one brief statement he had summarized the motivating ideas of
imperialism: (1) national honor, (2) commerce, (3) racial superiority,
and (4) altruism. So despite the fact that these candidates for conver-
sion were already largely Catholic, the word went forth to take the
Philippines. Spanish negotiators raised the delicate point that Ameri-
can forces had no claim by right of conquest, and had even taken
Manila after the armistice. American negotiators finally offered the
Spanish compensation of $20 million. The treaty thus added to
American territory Puerto Rico, Guam (a Spanish island in the
Pacific), and the Philippines.

Meanwhile Americans had taken other giant steps in the Pacific.
Hawaiian annexation, promised in McKinley's platform, failed to get
a two-thirds majority in the Senate, but the war demonstrated the
islands' strategic importance all the more. The administration therefore moved to annex Hawaii, like Texas, by joint resolution. The
resolution passed on July 7, 1898, in the midst of the war. Within a
year of the peace treaty, in 1899, after another outbreak of fighting
over the royal succession in Samoa, Germany and the United States
agreed to partition the Samoan Islands. The United States annexed
the easternmost islands; Germany took the rest, including the largest
island. Britain ceded its claims in Samoa in return for German
concessions in the Pacific and in Africa. Meanwhile, in 1898 the
United States had laid claim to Wake Island, located between Guam
and the Hawaiian islands, which would become a vital link in a
future trans-Pacific cable line.

The Treaty of Paris had yet to be ratified in the Senate, where
most Democrats and Populists, and some Republicans, opposed it.
Anti-imperialists argued that acquisition of the Philippines would
undermine American democracy. They appealed to traditional isolationism, American principles of self-government, the inconsistency
of liberating Cuba and annexing the Philippines, the involvement in
foreign entanglements that would undermine the logic of the

Monroe Doctrine, and the danger that the Philippines would become an Achilles heel, expensive if not impossible to defend. The prospect of incorporating so many alien peoples into American life was not the least of some people's worries. "Bananas and self-government cannot grow on the same piece of land," one senator claimed.

The opposition might have been strong enough to kill the treaty had not William Jennings Bryan influenced the vote for approval. Ending the war, he argued, would open the way for the future independence of Cuba and the Philippines. Finally, ratification came on February 6, 1899, by a vote of more than two to one. On February 14 the deciding vote of the vice-president defeated a resolution for Philippine independence. That same month in *McClure's* magazine Rudyard Kipling's poem "The White Man's Burden" called the American people to a new duty:

> Take up the White Man's burden—
> Send forth the best ye breed—
> Go, bind your sons to exile
> To serve your captive's need;
> To wait in heavy harness
> On fluttered folk and wild—
> Your new-caught sullen peoples,
> Half devil and half child.

By this time Americans had already clashed with Filipino insurrectionists near Manila. The Filipino leader, Emilio Aguinaldo, had been in exile until Commodore Dewey brought him back to Luzon to make trouble for the Spanish. Since Aguinaldo's forces were more or less in control of the islands outside of Manila, what followed was largely an American war of conquest which lasted more than two years. Organized Filipino resistance was broken by the end of 1899, but even after the capture of Aguinaldo in March 1901 sporadic guerrilla action lasted until mid-1902. It was a sordid little war, marked by massacre and torture on both sides.

Against the backdrop of this nasty guerrilla war the great debate over imperialism continued. The treaty debates inspired a number of anti-imperialist groups which united in October 1899 as the American Anti-Imperialist League. The league attracted members representing many shades of opinion; the main thing they had in common was that most belonged to an older generation. George S. Boutwell, the old Stalwart from Massachusetts, was president, but the group included as well Democrat "Pitchfork Ben" Tillman of South Carolina. Andrew Carnegie footed the bills, but on imperialism at least

Emilio Aguinaldo (seated third from right) and other leaders of the Filipino insurgents.

Samuel Gompers was in agreement with him. Presidents Charles Eliot of Harvard and David Starr Jordan of Stanford supported the group, along with social reformer Jane Addams and editor E. L. Godkin of the *Nation*. The drive for power, said the philosopher William James, had caused the nation to "puke up its ancient soul." Mark Twain suggested that, given current policies, the Philippine provincial flag should copy the American flag but should have "the white stripes painted black and the stars replaced by the skull and cross bones."

ORGANIZING THE NEW ACQUISITIONS Such criticism, however, did not faze the expansionists. Senator Beveridge boasted in 1900: "The Philippines are ours forever. And just beyond the Philippines are China's illimitable markets. We will not retreat from either. . . . The power that rules the Pacific is the power that rules the world. That power will forever be the American Republic."

In the Philippines McKinley had already moved toward setting up a civil government. In 1900 he dispatched a commission under Judge William Howard Taft with instructions to set up a system of government. Unlike some of the Americans on the scene, Taft seemed genuinely to like the Filipinos, encouraged them to participate, and eventually convinced them to sit on the commission itself.

On July 4, 1901, military government ended and under an act of Congress Taft became the civil governor with appointed provincial governors under his authority. The Philippine Government Act, passed by Congress in July 1902, made the Philippine Islands an "unorganized territory" and made the inhabitants citizens of the Philippines. In 1916 the Jones Act made both houses of the legislature elective and affirmed America's intention to grant the Philippines independence at an indefinite date. Finally, the Tydings-McDuffie Act of 1934 offered independence after a tutelary period of ten more years. A constitution was drafted and ratified, and on September 17, 1934, Manuel Quezon was elected the first president of the Philippines. Independence finally took effect on July 4, 1946.

Puerto Rico had been acquired in part to serve as an American outpost on the approaches to the Caribbean and any future isthmian canal. On April 12, 1900, the Foraker Act established a civil government on the island. The act passed two years later for the Philippines would resemble this one. The president appointed a governor and eleven members of an executive council, and an elected House of Delegates made up the lower house of the legislature. Residents of the island were citizens of Puerto Rico but not of the United States until 1917, when the Jones Act granted United States citizenship and made both houses of the legislature elective. In 1947 the governor also became elective, and in 1952 Puerto Rico became a commonwealth with its own constitution and elected officials, a unique status. Like a state, Puerto Rico is free to change its constitution insofar as it does not conflict with the United States Constitution.

The Foraker Act of 1900 also levied a temporary duty on imports from Puerto Rico. The tariff was challenged in the federal courts on the grounds that the island had become part of the United States, but the Supreme Court upheld the tariff. In this and other "Insular Cases" federal judges faced a question which went to the fundamental nature of the American Union, and to the civil and political rights of the people in America's new possessions: Does the Constitution follow the flag? The Court ruled in effect that it did not unless Congress extended it.

American authorities soon learned that "Cuba libre" posed problems at least as irksome as those in the new possessions. Having liberated the Cubans from Spanish rule, the Americans found themselves propping up a shaky new government. Cuba's insurgent government was weak and its economy in a state of collapse. Bad relations between American soldiers and Cubans set in almost immediately. When McKinley set up a military government for the island late in 1898, it was at odds with rebel leaders from the start.

Many Europeans expected annexation, and General Leonard Wood, who became Cuba's military governor in December 1899, thought this the best solution. But the United States finally did fulfill the promise of independence for Cuba after the military regime had restored order, gotten schools under way, and improved sanitary conditions. The problem of disease in Cuba provided a focus for the work of Dr. Walter Reed, who made an outstanding contribution to the health of people in tropical climates around the world. Named head of the Army Yellow Fever Commission in 1900, he directed experiments with volunteers which proved the theory of a Cuban physician that yellow fever was carried by stegomyia mosquitoes. This led the way to effective control of the disease.

In 1900, at President McKinley's order, General Wood called an election for a Cuban constitutional convention, which drafted a basic law modeled on that of the United States. The Platt Amendment to the Army Appropriations Bill passed by Congress in March 1901, however, sharply restricted the independence of the new government. The amendment required Cuba never to impair its independence by treaty with a third power, to maintain its debt within the government's power to repay out of ordinary revenues, and to acknowledge the right of the United States to intervene for the preservation of Cuban independence and the maintenance of "a government adequate for the protection of life, property, and individual liberty." Finally, Cuba was called upon to sell or lease to the United States lands to be used for coaling or naval stations—a proviso which eventuated in an American naval base at Guantanamo Bay.

Under pressure, in June 1901 the Cuban delegates added the Platt Amendment as an appendix to their own constitution. As early as August 1906 an insurrection arose against the new government, and President Theodore Roosevelt responded by sending Secretary of War William Howard Taft to "sit on the lid"—weighing in at more than 300 pounds, he was not a bad choice for the job. Backed up by American armed forces Taft assumed full governmental authority, as he had in the Philippines, and the American army stayed until 1909 when a new president was peacefully elected. Further interventions would follow for more than two decades: in 1912 under President Taft, in 1917 under Woodrow Wilson, and in 1933 when President Franklin D. Roosevelt dispatched warships to Cuba. In 1934, however, as part of his "Good Neighbor Policy," Roosevelt negotiated a new treaty which abrogated the Platt Amendment.

IMPERIAL RIVALRIES IN EAST ASIA

CHINA AND THE "OPEN DOOR" During the 1890s not only the United States but also Japan emerged as a world power. Commodore Perry's voyage of 1853–1854 had opened Japan to Western ways and the country began modernization in earnest after the 1860s. Flexing its new muscles, Japan engaged China's stagnant empire in the Sino-Japanese War (1894–1895) and as a result picked up the Pescadores Islands and the island of Taiwan (renamed Formosa). China's weakness, demonstrated in the war, brought the great powers into a scramble for "spheres of influence" on that remaining frontier of imperialist expansion. Russia secured the privilege of building a railroad across Manchuria and established itself in Port Arthur and the Liaotung Peninsula. The Germans moved into Shantung, the French into Kwangchow Bay, the British into Wei-Hai-Wei.

The bright prospect of American trade with China dimmed with the possibility that the great powers would throw up tariff barriers in their own spheres of influence. The British, ensconced at Hong Kong since 1840, had more to lose though, for they already had far and away the largest foreign trade with China. Just before the Spanish-American War, in March 1898, the British suggested joint action with the United States to preserve the integrity of China, and renewed the proposal early in 1899. Both times it was rejected by the Senate because it risked an entangling alliance.

U.S. INTERESTS IN THE PACIFIC
Dates indicate year of acquisition
or occupation by U.S.

In its origins and content, what soon came to be known as the Open Door Policy was reminiscent of the Monroe Doctrine. In both cases the United States proclaimed unilaterally a hands-off policy which the British had earlier proposed as a joint statement. The policy outlined in Secretary of State John Hay's Open Door Note, dispatched on September 6, 1899, to London, Berlin, and St. Petersburg, and a little later to Tokyo, Rome, and Paris, proposed to keep China open to trade with all countries on an equal basis. More specifically it called upon foreign powers, within their spheres of influence: (1) not to interfere with any treaty port (a port open to all by treaty) or any vested interest, (2) to permit Chinese authorities to collect tariffs on an equal basis, and (3) to show no favors to their own nationals in the matter of harbor dues or railroad charges. Hay's request that each of the powers accept these principles was, one diplomat later wrote, like asking everyone who believes in truth to stand: the liars would be the first on their feet. As it turned out, none except Britain accepted Hay's principles, but none rejected them either. The rest gave equivocal answers, usually conditioned on the action of the others. On March 20 Hay blandly announced that all powers had accepted the policy. None stood to deny it.

Soon after that a new crisis arose. In June 1900 a group of Chinese nationalists known to the Western world as Boxers ("Fists of Righteous Harmony") rose in rebellion against foreign encroachments on China, and laid siege to foreign embassies in Peking. An international expedition of British, German, Russian, Japanese, and Ameri-

The forces of the Western powers and Japan occupying the Forbidden City in Peking after putting down the Boxer Rebellion.

can forces was quickly mounted to relieve the embassy compound. Hay, fearful that the intervention might become an excuse to dismember China, took the opportunity to further refine the Open Door Policy. The United States, he said in a circular letter of July 3, 1900, sought a solution that would "preserve Chinese territorial and administrative integrity" as well as "equal and impartial trade with all parts of the Chinese Empire."

On August 14 the expedition reached Peking and broke the Boxer Rebellion. The occupying powers then agreed to settle for an indemnity from China of approximately $333 million. Of this total the United States got $25 million, of which nearly $11 million was refunded once all claims were paid. Most of this the Chinese government put into a fund to support Chinese students in American colleges.

The Open Door Policy, if rooted in the self-interest of American businessmen eager to exploit the markets of China, also tapped the deep-seated sympathies of those who opposed imperialism, especially as it endorsed China's territorial integrity. But it had little more legal standing than a pious affirmation. When the Japanese, concerned about Russian pressure in Manchuria, asked Hay how he intended to enforce the policy, Hay replied that the United States was "not prepared . . . to enforce these views on the east by any demonstration which could present a character of hostility to any other power." So it would remain for forty years, until continued Japanese expansion would bring America to war in 1941.

ROOSEVELT'S BIG STICK DIPLOMACY

More than any other American of his time, Theodore Roosevelt helped transform the role of the United States in world affairs. The country had emerged from the Spanish-American War a world power, and he insisted that this entailed major new responsibilities. To ensure that his country accepted such international obligations, Roosevelt was willing to stretch both the Constitution and executive power to the limit. In the process he pushed a reluctant nation onto the center stage of world affairs.

ROOSEVELT'S RISE   Born in 1858, the son of a wealthy New York merchant and a Georgia belle, "Teedie" Roosevelt grew up in Manhattan in cultured comfort, visited Europe as a child, spoke German fluently, and was graduated Phi Beta Kappa from Harvard in 1880. A sickly, scrawny boy with poor eyesight, he built himself up by sheer force of will into a physical and intellectual athlete who became a lifelong preacher and practitioner of the "strenuous life." Boxer, wrestler, mountain climber, dead-eyed hunter, and hardy outdoorsman, he was also an omnivorous reader, dedicated bird watcher, accomplished taxidermist, renowned historian and essayist, and outspoken moralist. His energy and fierce competitive spirit were both inexhaustible and infectious, and he was ever willing and able to express opinions on any and all subjects.

Within two years of graduating from Harvard, Roosevelt won election to the New York legislature and published *The Naval War of 1812*, the first of a number of historical, biographical, and other writings to flow from his pen. But with the world seemingly at his feet, disaster struck. In 1884 his beloved mother, only forty-eight years old, died. Eleven hours later, in the same house, his twenty-two-year-old wife died in his arms, soon after giving birth to their first child. That night Roosevelt drew a large cross over the entry in his diary: "The light has gone out of my life." The double funeral was so wrenching that the officiating minister wept throughout his prayer.

Roosevelt was devastated by this "strange and terrible fate." In an attempt to recover, he sold the family house and moved west to take up the cattle business on the Dakota frontier. There he played the part of a patrician cowboy, adorned in a custom-fit buckskin shirt, silver spurs, and alligator boots. He told a relative he was "having a glorious time here." The blue-blooded New Yorker came to relish hunting, leading roundups, capturing outlaws, fighting Indians—and reading Tolstoy by the campfire. When a drunken cowboy, a gun in each hand, tried to bully the tinhorn Roosevelt, teasing him about his glasses, the feisty Harvard dude laid him out with one punch. Although his western career was brief, he never quite got over being a cowboy.

Back in New York City, Roosevelt ran for mayor in 1886 and lost, and later served six years as civil service commissioner and two years as New York City's police commissioner. In the latter capacity he loved to don a black cloak and broad-brimmed hat and patrol the streets at midnight. When he came upon a sleeping policeman, Roosevelt would rap the man with his nightstick. In 1897, McKinley appointed the conscientious Roosevelt assistant secretary of the navy. After serving in Cuba and hastening into print his own account of the Rough Riders, Roosevelt easily won the governorship of New York, arousing audiences with his impassioned speeches and powerful personality.

In the 1900 presidential contest, the Democrats turned once again to Bryan, who sought to make imperialism the "paramount issue" of the campaign. The Democratic platform condemned the Philippine involvement as "an unnecessary war" which had "placed the United States, previously known and applauded throughout the world as the champion of freedom, in the false and un-American position of crushing with military force the efforts of our former allies to achieve liberty and self-government."

The Republicans welcomed the issue. They renominated McKinley, and named Roosevelt his running mate. After his role in both the Philippine and Cuban action, Roosevelt had virtually become "Mr. Imperialism." Now governor of New York, he profited from support in the West as well as the East, and perhaps as well from the eagerness of New York's Boss Platt to kick the independent Roosevelt upstairs into the harmless post of vice-president.

"Don't haul down the flag!" was a Republican slogan during the presidential campaign. But the trouble with Bryan's idea of a solemn referendum on imperialism was the near impossibility of making any presidential contest so simple. Bryan himself complicated things by insisting once again on free silver, and the tariff became an issue again too. The Republicans' biggest advantage was probably the return to prosperity, which they were fully ready to take credit for. So those who opposed imperialism but also opposed free silver or tariff reduction faced a bewildering choice. One voter was said to have reasoned finally: "It is a choice between evils, and I am going to shut my eyes, hold my nose, vote, go home and disinfect myself."

McKinley outpolled Bryan by 7.2 million to 6.4 million in the popular vote and by 292 to 155 in the electoral vote. But less than a year later, on September 6, 1901, while McKinley attended a reception at the Pan-American Exposition in Buffalo, a fanatical anarchist named Leon Czolgosz approached him with a gun concealed in a

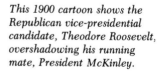

This 1900 cartoon shows the Republican vice-presidential candidate, Theodore Roosevelt, overshadowing his running mate, President McKinley.

bandaged hand and fired at point-blank range. McKinley died six days later and Theodore Roosevelt was suddenly elevated to the White House. "Now look," Mark Hanna, the Ohio businessman and politico, erupted, "that damned cowboy is President of the United States!"

Six weeks short of his forty-third birthday, Roosevelt was the youngest man ever to reach the office, but he brought to it more experience in public affairs than most and perhaps more vitality than any. One observer compared him to Niagara Falls: "both great wonders of nature." Teddy Roosevelt was an American original. His glittering spectacles, glistening teeth, and overflowing gusto were a godsend to the cartoonists, who added another trademark when he pronounced the adage: "Speak softly, and carry a big stick."

Along with Roosevelt's boundless energy went an unshakable righteousness and a tendency to cast every issue in moral and patriotic terms. He considered the presidency his "bully pulpit," and he delivered fist-smacking speeches on the virtues of righteousness, honesty, civic duty, and strenuosity. When asked by a friend how he knew so well the mood of the country, he replied: "I don't know the way the people *do* feel . . . I only know how they *ought* to feel." But appearances were deceiving. The boundless energy left a false impression of impulsiveness and the talk of morality cloaked a cautious pragmatism. Roosevelt could get carried away on occasion, but as he said of his foreign policy steps, this was likely to happen only when "I am assured that I shall be able eventually to carry out my will by force." Indeed, nowhere was President Roosevelt's forceful will more evident than in his conduct of foreign affairs.

BUILDING THE PANAMA CANAL   After the Spanish-American War the United States became more deeply involved in the Caribbean area. One issue overshadowed every other in the region: the Panama Canal. The narrow isthmus of Panama had excited dreams of an interoceanic canal ever since Balboa's crossing in 1513. Admiral Mahan regarded a canal as important to American commerce and naval power, a point dramatized in 1898 by the long voyage of the battleship *Oregon* around South America's Cape Horn to join the fleet off Cuba.

Transit across the isthmus had first become a strong concern of the United States in the 1840s when it became an important route to the California gold fields. Two treaties dating from that period loomed years later as obstacles to construction of a canal. The Bidlack Treaty (1848) with Colombia (then New Granada) guaranteed both Colombia's sovereignty over Panama and the neutrality of the isthmus, so that "free transit . . . not be embarrassed in any future time." In the Clayton-Bulwer Treaty (1850) the British agreed to acquire no more Central American territory, and the United States joined them in agreeing to build or fortify a canal only by mutual consent.

After the Spanish-American War, Secretary Hay commenced talks with the British ambassador to establish such consent. The outcome was the Hay-Pauncefote Treaty of February 1900, but the Senate rejected it on the grounds that it forbade fortification of the canal and required that the canal be neutral even in time of war. By then a bill was already pending in Congress for a Nicaraguan canal and the British apparently decided to accept the inevitable. In November 1901 the Senate ratified a second Hay-Pauncefote Treaty which simply omitted reference to the former limitations.

Other obstacles remained, however. From 1881 to 1887 a French company under Ferdinand de Lesseps, who had engineered the Suez Canal in 1877, had spent nearly $300 million and some 20,000 lives to dig less than a third of the canal through Panama, then under the control of Colombia. The company now wanted $109 million for its holdings. Consequently an Isthmian Canal Commission, appointed by McKinley, reported in 1901 that a Nicaraguan route would be cheaper. When the House of Representatives quickly passed an act for construction there, the French company lowered its price to $40 million and the Canal Commission switched to Panama.

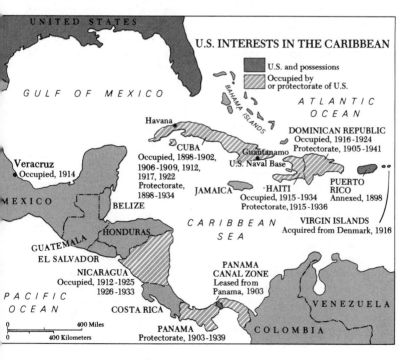

U.S. INTERESTS IN THE CARIBBEAN

- U.S. and possessions
- Occupied by or protectorate of U.S.

UNITED STATES

GULF OF MEXICO

ATLANTIC OCEAN

BAHAMA ISLANDS

Havana

CUBA
Occupied, 1898-1902, 1906-1909, 1912, 1917, 1922
Protectorate, 1898-1934

Guantanamo
U.S. Naval Base

DOMINICAN REPUBLIC
Occupied, 1916-1924
Protectorate, 1905-1941

Veracruz
Occupied, 1914

MEXICO

BELIZE

JAMAICA

HAITI
Occupied, 1915-1934
Protectorate, 1915-1936

PUERTO RICO
Annexed, 1898

GUATEMALA
EL SALVADOR

HONDURAS

CARIBBEAN SEA

VIRGIN ISLANDS
Acquired from Denmark, 1916

NICARAGUA
Occupied, 1912-1925
1926-1933

PANAMA CANAL ZONE
Leased from Panama, 1903

PACIFIC OCEAN

COSTA RICA

VENEZUELA

0   400 Miles
0   400 Kilometers

PANAMA
Protectorate, 1903-1939

COLOMBIA

Meanwhile Secretary Hay had opened negotiations with Ambassador Thomas Herrán of Colombia. In return for a Canal Zone six miles wide, the United States agreed to pay $10 million in cash and a rental fee of $250,000 a year. The United States Senate ratified the Hay-Herrán Treaty in 1903, but the Colombian Senate held out for $25 million in cash. At this action of those "foolish and homicidal corruptionists in Bogotá," Theodore Roosevelt, by then president, flew into a rage punctuated by references to "dagoes" and "contemptible little creatures." Meanwhile in Panama, an isolated province long at odds with the remote Colombian authorities in Bogotá, feeling was heightened by Colombia's rejection of the treaty. One Manuel Amador, an employee of the French canal company, then hatched a plot in close collusion with the company's representative Philippe Bunau-Varilla. Bunau-Varilla paid visits to Roosevelt and Hay and, apparently with inside information, informed the conspirators that the U.S.S. *Nashville* would call at Colón in Panama on November 2.

With an army of some 500, reinforced by Colón's fire department, Amador staged a revolt the next day. Colombian troops, who could scarcely penetrate the overland jungle, found American ships athwart the sea lanes. On November 13 the Roosevelt administration received its first ambassador from Panama, whose name happened to be Philippe Bunau-Varilla, and on November 18 signed a treaty which extended the Canal Zone from six to ten miles in width. For $10 million down and $250,000 a year the United States received "in perpetuity the use, occupation and control" of the zone. Just who grabbed the $40 million paid to the French canal company remains unknown. The U.S. attorney-general, asked to supply a legal opinion upholding Roosevelt's actions, responded wryly: "No, Mr. President, if I were you I would not have any taint of legality about it."

In 1904 Congress created a new Isthmian Canal Commission to direct construction. Despite sanitary problems, the biggest obstacle at first, Roosevelt instructed the commission to make the "dirt fly." He later explained: "If I had followed traditional, conservative methods I would have submitted a dignified State paper of probably 200 pages to Congress and the debates on it would have been going on yet; but I took the Canal Zone and let Congress debate; and while the debate goes on the Canal does also."

And so did a rankling resentment in Colombia. By needlessly offending Latin American sensibilities, Roosevelt had committed one of the greatest blunders in American foreign policy. Colombia eventually got its $25 million from the Harding administration, but only once America's interest in Colombian oil had lubricated the wheels of diplomacy. There was no apology, but the payment was made to

Roosevelt claimed to take the greatest pride in his role in the Panama imbroglio. Here he poses at the site of the canal under construction.

remove "all misunderstandings growing out of the political events in Panama, November, 1903." Meanwhile the canal had opened on August 15, 1914, less than two weeks after the outbreak of World War I in Europe.

THE ROOSEVELT COROLLARY Even without the canal, the United States would have been concerned with the stability of the Caribbean area, and particularly with the activities of any hostile power. A prime excuse for intervention in those days was to force the collection of debts owed to foreign nationals. In 1904 a crisis over the debts of the Dominican Republic gave Roosevelt an opportunity to formulate American policy in the Caribbean. In his annual address to Congress in 1904 he set forth what came to be known as the Roosevelt Corollary to the Monroe Doctrine: the principle, in short, was that since the Monroe Doctrine enjoined intervention in the region by Europeans, the United States was justified in intervening first to forestall the actions of outsiders.

In the president's words, the Roosevelt Corollary held that: "Chronic wrongdoing . . . may in America, as elsewhere, ultimately require intervention by some civilized nation, and in the Western Hemisphere the adherence of the United States to the Monroe Doc-

The World's Constable. *TR, shown here as the world's policeman, wields the "big stick" symbolizing his approach to diplomacy.*

trine may force the United States, however reluctantly, in flagrant cases of such wrongdoing or impotence, to the exercise of an international police power." As put into practice by mutual agreement with the Dominican Republic in 1905, the Roosevelt Corollary called for the United States to install and protect a collector of customs who would apply 55 percent of his revenues to debt payments.

THE RUSSO-JAPANESE WAR   In East Asia, meanwhile, the Open Door Policy received a serious challenge when rivalry between Russia and Japan flared into a fight over China and Korea. In 1896, Russia had forced China to sign a fifteen-year defensive treaty by which China conceded Russia the right to build a railway across Manchuria to the Pacific port of Vladivostok. Two years later Russia extracted from China a leasehold at Port Arthur on the Liaotung Peninsula. Its expansionist appetite whetted, Russia then cast its sights on Korea, which Japan also coveted.

By 1904 the Japanese had grown convinced that the Russians threatened both their own ambitions and their security. On February 8, Japan launched a surprise attack which devastated the Russian fleet at Port Arthur. They then occupied Korea and drove the Russians back into Manchuria. But neither side could score a knockout blow, and neither relished a prolonged war. Roosevelt sought to maintain a balance between the two powers and offered to mediate their conflict. When the Japanese signaled that they would welcome a negotiated settlement, Roosevelt agreed to sponsor a peace conference in Portsmouth, New Hampshire. In the Treaty of Portsmouth, signed on September 5, 1905, the concessions all went to the Japanese. Russia acknowledged Japan's "predominant political, military, and economic interests in Korea" (Japan would annex the kingdom in 1910), and both powers agreed to evacuate Manchuria.

AMERICA'S RELATIONS WITH JAPAN   Japan's show of strength in the war raised doubts among American leaders about the security of the Philippines. During the Portsmouth talks Roosevelt sent William Howard Taft to meet with the Japanese foreign minister in Tokyo and the two men arrived at the Taft-Katsura Agreement of July 29, 1905, in which the United States accepted Japanese control of Korea and Japan disavowed any designs on the Philippines. The understanding was reinforced by the Root-Takahira Agreement on November 30, 1908, negotiated by Secretary of State Elihu Root and the Japanese ambassador, in which both sides endorsed the status quo, promised to respect each other's possessions, and reinforced the Open Door Policy by supporting "the independence and integrity of China" and "the principle of equal opportunity for commerce and industry in China."

Behind the diplomatic facade of goodwill, however, lay mutual distrust. At Portsmouth the Japanese had hoped to get financial indemnities from Russia; they blamed their failure on the United States, and especially President Roosevelt, who had indeed opposed indemnities. For many Americans the Russian threat in East Asia now gave way to the "yellow peril" of Japan.° Racial animosities on the West Coast helped sour relations with Japan. In October 1906 the San Francisco school board ordered students of Chinese, Japanese, and Korean descent to attend a separate public school. The Japanese government sharply protested this show of prejudice, and President Roosevelt managed to talk the school board into changing its mind after making sure that Japanese authorities would not issue passports to "laborers" except former residents of the United States, the parents, wives, or children of residents, or those who already possessed an interest in an American farming enterprise. This "Gentlemen's Agreement" of 1907, the precise terms of which have never been revealed, halted the influx of Japanese immigrants and brought some respite in racial agitations in California.

THE UNITED STATES AND EUROPE   During the years of expansionism the United States was looking mainly westward and southward. Toward Europe's affairs the fixed policy was, as Admiral Mahan affirmed it should be, abstention. To Roosevelt, however, total ab-

°The term "yellow peril" was apparently coined by Kaiser Wilhelm II of Germany.

stention from European affairs was an improper stance for a newly arrived world power. While he was moving toward mediation of the Russo-Japanese War in 1905, another dangerous crisis began brewing in Morocco. There, on March 31, 1905, German kaiser Wilhelm II stepped ashore at Tangier and gave a saber-rattling speech defending the independence of the sultan. This was a deliberate response to growing French influence there, and particularly to the Franco-British Entente of 1904, under which Britain recognized French dominance in Morocco in return for French recognition of British dominance in Egypt. The kaiser's speech aroused a diplomatic storm of dangerous proportions. Roosevelt felt that the United States had something at stake in preventing the outbreak of a major war. At the kaiser's behest he talked the French and British into attending an international conference at Algeciras, Spain, with American delegates present. Roosevelt then maneuvered the Germans into accepting his lead.

The Act of Algeciras, signed on April 7, 1906, affirmed the independence of Morocco and guaranteed an open door for trade there, but provided for the training and control of Moroccan police by France and Spain. The United States Senate ratified the agreement, but only with the proviso that it was not to be construed as a departure from America's traditional policy of noninvolvement in European affairs. It was a departure, of course, and one that may well have prevented a general war, or at least postponed it until 1914. Roosevelt received the Nobel Peace Prize in 1906 for his work at Portsmouth and Algeciras. For all his bellicosity on other occasions, he had earned it.

Before Roosevelt left the White House he celebrated America's rise to world power with one great flourish. In December 1907 he sent the United States Navy, by then second only to the British, on a grand tour around the world, their commander announcing he was ready for "a feast, a frolic, or a fight." He got mostly the first two, and none of the last. At every port of call the "Great White Fleet" set off rousing celebrations, down the Atlantic coast of South America, up the west coast, out to Hawaii, and down under to New Zealand and Australia. It was the first such show of American naval might in the Pacific, and many feared the reaction of the Japanese, for whose benefit Roosevelt had in fact staged the show. They need not have worried, for in Japan the flotilla got the greatest welcome of all. Thousands of schoolchildren turned out waving tiny American flags and singing "The Star Spangled Banner" in English. The triumphal procession continued home by way of the Mediterranean, and steamed back into American waters in February 1909, just in time to close out Roosevelt's presidency on a note of success.

But it was a success that would have mixed consequences. As one close student of Roosevelt's role in America's rise to world power wrote: "One comes away from the study with admiration for Roosevelt's ability, his energy, and his devotion to his country's interests as he saw them but with a sense of tragedy that his abilities were turned toward imperialism and an urge for power, which were to have consequences so serious for the future." Roosevelt had influenced the United States "in a direction that . . . was to bring her face to face with grave dangers" before the mid-twentieth century.

Further Reading

A survey of Gilded Age diplomacy is Robert L. Beisner's *From the Old Diplomacy to the New, 1865–1900* (2nd ed., 1986).° William Appleman Williams's *The Tragedy of American Diplomacy* (2nd ed., 1972)° advances most clearly the economic interpretation. Robert Dallek's *The American Style of Foreign Policy* (1983) shows the relationship between foreign and domestic affairs. Emily S. Rosenberg's *Spreading the American Dream* (1982)° shows how foreign policy in the Gilded Age influenced policies through World War II.

For background to the events of the 1890s, see Walter LaFeber's *The New Empire: An Interpretation of American Expansion, 1860–1898* (1963).° Richard Hofstadter's *Social Darwinism in American Thought* (rev. ed., 1955)° details the intellectual justifications for expansion.

The dispute over American policy concerning Hawaii is covered in Thomas J. Osborne's *"Empire Can Wait": American Opposition to Hawaiian Annexation, 1893–1898* (1981).

David F. Trask's lenghty *The War with Spain in 1898* (1981) is the comprehensive volume on that conflict. See also H. Wayne Morgan's concise *America's Road to Empire: The War with Spain and Overseas Expansion* (1965).° Frank Freidel's *The Splendid Little War* (1958) shows what the war was like for those who fought it. Gerald F. Linderman's *The Mirror of War* (1974) discusses the war at home. For the war's aftermath in the Philippines, see Stuart C. Miller's *"Benevolent Assimilation": American Conquest of the Philippines, 1899–1903* (1982). Robert L. Beisner's *Twelve against Empire: The Anti-Imperialists, 1898–1900* (1968)° handles the debate over annexation.

A good introduction to American interest in China is Michael H. Hunt's *The Making of a Special Relationship* (1983).° Also useful is Marilyn B. Young's *The Rhetoric of Empire: America's China Policy, 1893–1901* (1968). For the immediate consequences of the Open Door Policy, see Warren I. Cohen's *America's Response to China* (2nd ed., 1980).° Kenton J. Clymer's

°These books are available in paperback editions.

John Hay: The Gentleman as Diplomat (1975) examines the role of this key secretary of state in forming policy.

Works that deal with the role of Theodore Roosevelt in foreign policy both before and during his time as president include Howard K. Beale's *Theodore Roosevelt and the Rise of America to World Power* (1956)° and Edmund Morris's *The Rise of Theodore Roosevelt* (1979).°

For American policy in the Caribbean and Central America, see Walter LaFeber's *Inevitable Revolutions* (1983)° and Bruce J. Calder's *The Impact of Intervention* (1984). David McCullough's *The Path between the Seas: The Creation of the Panama Canal, 1870–1914* (1977)° presents the fullest account of how the United States secured the Panama Canal.

24 ∕⸾⸾∕

PROGRESSIVISM: ROOSEVELT,
TAFT, AND WILSON

ELEMENTS OF REFORM

Theodore Roosevelt was an ambitious man whose eagerness to leave his mark moved easily from the world arena to his own country. But Roosevelt was more calculating in domestic politics than in foreign affairs and more inclined to follow the dictates of experience. He recognized that 1901 was no time for a "big stick" domestic policy.

The prudence Roosevelt displayed in making domestic policy, if uncharacteristic of the man, was a necessity of the time. Roosevelt's emergence as a national leader coincided roughly with the onset of progressivism, a movement so broad-gauged it almost defied definition.

The Progressives saw themselves as engaged in a democratic crusade against the abuses of urban political bosses and corporate robber barons. Their goals were greater democracy and social justice, honest government, more effective regulation of business, and a revived commitment to public service. What they shared was a common assumption that the complex social ills and tensions generated by the urban-industrial revolution required new responses, responses that frequently entailed expanding the scope of local, state, and federal government authority. Doing so, they hoped, would ensure the "progress" of American society. The "real heart of the movement," declared one self-described progressive reformer, was "to use the government as an agency of human welfare."

But the Kansas editor William Allen White hinted at a paradox in the movement when he called progressivism just populism that had "shaved its whiskers, washed its shirt, put on a derby, and moved up into the middle class." As White suggested, urban business and professional leaders brought to progressivism a certain respectability and political savvy that the Populists had lacked. They also brought a more businesslike, efficient approach to reform. While one strand in the varied fabric of progressivism retained the resonant appeal of agrarian democracy and its antitrust traditions, a new emphasis on efficiency soon gained ascendancy. Even farm groups abandoned the mass movement for more bureaucratic forms of organization. In so doing, they and other Progressives may have been trying to find identity, no longer derived from the local community, in business and professional groups.

Another paradox in the movement was that it contained an element of conservatism. In some cases the regulation of business turned out actually to be regulation *by* businessmen, who preferred regulated stability to the chaos and uncertainty of unrestrained competition. The progressive movement refers to the common spirit of an age rather than to an organized group or party. Much like the reform spirit of the 1830s and 1840s, once called Jacksonian Democracy, progressivism was diverse in both origins and tendencies. Few people adhered to all of the varied progressive causes.

ANTECEDENTS TO PROGRESSIVISM   Populism was indisputably one of the harbingers of progressivism. The Populist platform of 1892 outlined many reforms that would be accomplished in the progressive era. Many old Populists, in addition, believed that their movement achieved vindication in the progressive era. William Allen White wrote that populism "was the beginning of a movement that in another decade was to change the politics of the nation: indeed it was a symptom of a world wide drift to liberalism, which reached its peak . . . twenty-five years later."

After the collapse of the farmers' movement and the revival of the agricultural sector at the turn of the century, the focus of the reform spirit shifted to cities, where middle-class reformers had for years attacked the problems of political bossism and urban development. The Mugwumps, those gentlemen reformers who had fought the spoils system and promoted a civil service based on merit, supplied the Progressive movement with an important element of its thinking, the honest-government ideal. Over the years their ranks had been supplemented and the honest-government outlook broadened by leaders who confronted such new urban problems as crime, vice, and the efficient provision of gas, electricity, water, sewers, mass transit, and garbage collection.

Finally, another significant force in fostering the spirit of progressivism was the growing familiarity with socialist doctrines and their critiques of living and working conditions. The Socialist party of the time can be considered the left wing of progressivism. Still, most Progressives found socialist remedies unacceptable, and the Progressive reform impulse grew in part from a desire to counter the growing influence of socialist doctrines. More important in spurring Progressive reform, however, were those social critics who over the years had attacked the social evils of American life. Chief among these were thinkers such as Lester F. Ward, Henry George, Henry Demarest Lloyd, Jacob Riis, and Thorstein Veblen.

THE MUCKRAKERS Also important in stimulating reform activity were those social critics who publicized festering problems. The writers who thrived on exposing scandal got their name when Theodore Roosevelt compared them to a character in John Bunyan's *Pilgrim's Progress:* "A man that could look no way but downwards with a muckrake in his hands." The "muckrakers" (and TR was no mean muckraker himself) "are often indispensable to . . . society," Roosevelt said, "but only if they know when to stop raking the muck."

Henry Demarest Lloyd is sometimes cited as the first of the muckrakers for his critical examination of the Standard Oil Company and other monopolies, *Wealth against Commonwealth* (1894). Lloyd exposed the growth of corporate giants responsible to none but themselves, able to corrupt if not control governments. Another early muckraker was Jacob Riis, a Danish immigrant who, as an influential New York journalist, exposed slum conditions in *How the Other Half Lives* (1890). The chief outlets for these social critics were the inexpensive popular magazines which began to flourish in the 1890s, such as the *Arena* and *McClure's* magazine, founded in 1893 by Samuel S. McClure, an Irish immigrant who had begun the first newspaper syndicate in the country.

The golden age of muckraking is sometimes dated from October 1902 when *McClure's* began to run articles by the reporter Lincoln Steffens on municipal corruption, later collected into a book: *The Shame of the Cities* (1904). *McClure's* also ran Ida M. Tarbell's *History of the Standard Oil Company* (1904). McClure had set her to research on the project more than three years before. The result was a more detailed treatment than the earlier book by Lloyd, but all the more damaging in its detail. Other outstanding books which began as magazine articles exposed corruption in the stock market, the meat industry, the life insurance business, and the political world.

Lincoln Steffens, whose muckraking articles on municipal corruption were collected in the book The Shame of the Cities.

Without the muckrakers, progressivism surely would never have achieved the popular support it had. In feeding the public's appetite for facts about their new urban-industrial society, the muckrakers demonstrated one of the salient features of the Progressive movement, and one of its central failures. The Progressives were stronger on diagnosis than on remedy, thereby reflecting a naïve faith in the power of democracy. Let the people know, expose corruption, and bring government close to the people, went the rationale, and the correction of evils would follow automatically. The cure for the ills of democracy was more democracy.

THE FEATURES OF PROGRESSIVISM

DEMOCRACY The most important reform with which the Progressives tried to democratize government was the direct primary or the nomination of candidates by the vote of party members. Under the existing convention system, the reasoning went, only a small proportion of the voters attended the local caucuses or precinct meetings which sent delegates to county, and in turn to state and national, conventions. While the system allowed seasoned leaders to sift the candidates, it also lent itself to domination by political professionals who were able to come early and stay late. Direct primaries at the local level had been held sporadically since the 1870s, but after South Carolina adopted the first statewide primary in 1896 the movement spread within two decades to nearly every state.

The primary was but one expression of a broad movement for

direct democracy. In 1898 South Dakota became the first state to adopt the initiative and referendum, procedures which allowed voters to enact laws directly. If a designated number of voters petitioned to have a measure put on the ballot (the initiative), the electorate could then vote it up or down (the referendum). Oregon adopted a whole spectrum of reform measures including a voter registration law (1899); the initiative and referendum (1902); the direct primary (1904); a sweeping corrupt-practices act (1908); and the recall (1910), whereby public officials could be removed by petition and vote. Within a decade nearly twenty states had adopted the initiative and referendum and nearly a dozen the recall.

Most states came to use the party primary even in the choice of United States senators. Nevada was first, in 1899, to let voters express a choice which state legislators of their party were expected to follow in choosing senators. The popular election of senators required a constitutional amendment, and the House of Representatives, beginning in 1894, four times adopted such an amendment only to see it defeated in the Senate, which came under increasing attack as a "millionaire's club." By 1912 thirty states had provided preferential primaries. The Senate in that year finally accepted the inevitable and agreed to the Seventeenth Amendment, authorizing popular election of senators. The amendment was ratified in 1913.

EFFICIENCY   A second major theme of progressivism was the "gospel of efficiency." In the business world during those years Frederick W. Taylor, the original "efficiency expert," was developing the techniques he summed up in his book *The Principles of Scientific Management* (1911): efficient management of time and costs, the proper routing and scheduling of work, standardization of tools and equipment, and the like. In government, efficiency demanded the reorganization of agencies to prevent overlapping, to establish clear lines of authority, and to fix responsibility. One long-held theory had it that the greater the number of offices chosen by popular vote the greater the degree of democracy, but Progressives considered this inefficient. They believed that voters could make wiser choices if they had a shorter ballot and chose fewer officials in whom power and responsibility were clearly lodged. Many states and localities worked at rationalizing their finances by equalizing tax assessments, and during the first decades of the twentieth century by adopting budget systems. The federal government finally got around to a budget system with passage of the Budget and Accounting Act of 1921.

Two new ideas for making municipal government more efficient gained headway in the first decade of the new century. The commission system, first adopted by Galveston, Texas, in 1901, when local government there collapsed in the aftermath of a devastating hurricane and tidal wave, placed ultimate authority in a board composed of elected administrative heads of city departments—commissioners of sanitation, police, utilities, and so on. The more durable idea, however, was the city-manager plan, under which a professional administrator ran the government in accordance with policies set by the elected council and mayor. Staunton, Virginia, first adopted the plan in 1908. By 1914 the National Association of City Managers heralded the arrival of a new profession.

When America was a preindustrial society, Andrew Jackson's notion that any reasonably intelligent citizen could perform the duties of any public office may have been true. In the more complex age of the early twentieth century it was apparent that many functions of government and business had come to require expert specialists. This principle was promoted by progressive governor Robert M. La Follette of Wisconsin (1901–1906), who established a Legislative Reference Bureau to provide research, advice, and help in the drafting of legislation. The "Wisconsin Idea" of efficient government was widely publicized and copied. La Follette also worked for such reforms as the primary, stronger railroad regulation, the conservation of natural resources, and workmen's compensation. Born in a log cabin and educated at the University of Wisconsin, the short, muscular La Follette possessed an abiding faith in grass-roots democracy, in the power and judgment of the people. He was more enlightened about modern trends than William Jennings Bryan, and equally intense, sincere, and determined. He was also Bryan's equal as an orator; La Follette could talk for hours without taxing himself or his listeners.

Counterparts to La Follette appeared as progressive governors in other states. As counsel to a legislative committee in New York, Charles Evans Hughes became a national figure by uncovering spectacular insurance frauds and won the governorship in 1906. Voters in Georgia and Alabama that year elected governors who promised to regulate the railroads. Hiram Johnson of California, after getting in 1908 a conviction of the grafting boss of San Francisco, won the governorship in 1910 on the promise of reining in the Southern Pacific Railroad.

REGULATION Of all the problems facing American society at the turn of the century, one engaged a greater diversity of reformers, and elicited more—and more controversial—solutions than any other: the regulation of giant corporations, which became a third major theme of progressivism. Concern over the concentration of economic power had brought bipartisan support to the passage of the Sherman Anti-Trust Act in 1890, but the act had turned out to be more symbolic than effective.

The problem of economic power and its abuse offered a dilemma for Progressives. Four broad solutions were available, but of these, two were extremes which had limited support: letting business work out its own destiny under a policy of laissez-faire, or adopting a socialist program of public ownership. At the municipal level, however, the socialist alternative was rather widely adopted in public utilities and transportation—so-called gas and water socialism—but otherwise was not seriously considered as a general policy. The other choices were either to adopt a policy of trust-busting in the belief that restoring old-fashioned competition would best prevent economic abuses, or to accept big business in the belief that it brought economies of scale, but to regulate it to prevent abuses.

Efforts to restore the competition of small firms proved unworkable, partly because breaking up large combinations was complex and difficult. The trend over the years was toward regulation of big business. To some extent regulation and "stabilization" won acceptance among businessmen who, whatever respect they paid to competition in the abstract, preferred not to face it in person. In the long run, although it was not at first apparent, regulation posed the problem raised in an old maxim that would become relevant to American politics in the 1970s and 1980s: Who will guard the guards? Regulatory agencies often came under the influence or control of those they were supposed to regulate. Railroad men, for instance, generally had more intimate knowledge of the intricate details involved in their business, giving them the advantage over the outsiders who might be appointed to the Interstate Commerce Commission.

SOCIAL JUSTICE   A fourth important feature of the progressive spirit was the impulse toward social justice, which motivated diverse actions from private charities to campaigns against child labor and liquor. The settlement house movement of the late nineteenth century had spawned a corps of social workers and genteel reformers devoted to the uplift of slum dwellers. But with time it became apparent that social evils extended beyond the reach of private charities and demanded the power of the state. Progressives found that old codes of private ethics and accountability scarcely applied to a complex industrial order. One sociologist observed in 1907: "Unlike the old time villain, the latter-day malefactor does not wear a slouch hat and a comforter, breathe forth curses and an odor of gin, go about his nefarious work with clenched teeth and an evil scowl. . . . The modern high-powered dealer of woe wears immaculate

Addie Laird, 12 years old. Spinner in a Cotton Mill, Vermont, 1910. *Photograph by Lewis Hine.*

linen, carries a silk hat and a lighted cigar, sins with calm countenance and a serene soul, leagues or months from the evil he causes. Upon his gentlemanly presence the eventual blood and tears do not obtrude themselves."

Labor legislation was perhaps the most significant reform to emerge from the drive for social justice. The National Child Labor Committee, organized in 1904, led a movement for lawsbanning the still widespread employment of young children. Through publicity, the organization of state and local committees, and a telling documentation of the evils of child labor by the photographer Lewis W. Hine, the committee within ten years brought about legislation in most states banning the labor of underage children (the minimum age varied from twelve to sixteen) and limiting the working hours of older children. Closely linked with the child-labor reform movement was a concerted effort to regulate the hours of work for women. Spearheaded by Florence Kelley, the head of the National Consumers League, this progressive crusade promoted the passage of state laws to ameliorate the distinctive hardships that long working hours imposed on women who were wives and mothers. Many states also outlawed night work and labor in dangerous occupations for both women and children. But numerous exemptions and inadequate enforcement often virtually nullified the laws.

The Supreme Court pursued a curiously erratic course in ruling on state labor laws. It upheld a Utah law limiting the working day in mining and smelting to eight hours as a proper exercise of the state police power to protect the health and safety of workers. The Court even referred to the unequal bargaining power of workers and employers as a justification for state action. In *Lochner v. New York* (1905), however, the Court voided a ten-hour day because it violated workers' "liberty of contract" to accept any terms they chose. Justice Oliver Wendell Holmes, Jr., dissented sharply. "The 14th Amendment does not enact Mr. Herbert Spencer's *Social Statics,*" he said, meaning it did not enact Spencer's laissez-faire dogmas. Then in 1908 the high court upheld a ten-hour law for women largely on the basis of sociological data which Louis D. Brandeis presented regarding the effects of long hours on the health and morals of women. In *Bunting v. Oregon* (1917) the Court accepted a ten-hour day for both men and women, but held out for twenty more years against state minimum-wage laws.

Legislation to protect workers against accidents gained impetus from disasters like the 1911 fire at the Triangle Shirtwaist Company in New York in which 146 people, mostly women, died for want of adequate exits. They either were trapped on the three upper floors of a ten-story building or plunged to the street below. Stricter building codes and factory inspection acts followed. One of the most important advances along these lines was the series of workmen's compensation laws enacted after Maryland led the way in 1902. Accident insurance systems replaced the old common-law principle that an injured worker was entitled to compensation only if he could prove employer negligence, a costly and capricious procedure from which the worker was likely to win nothing or, as often happened, excessive awards from overly sympathetic juries.

For many activists the cause of prohibition absorbed reform energies. Opposition to strong drink was an ideal cause in which to merge the older private ethics and the new social ethics. Given the moral disrepute of saloons, prohibitionists could equate the "liquor traffic" with progressive suspicion of bossism and "special interests." When reform pressures mounted, prohibition offered an easy outlet, bypassing the complexities of corporate regulation.

The battle against booze dated far back into the nineteenth century. The Women's Christian Temperance Union had promoted the cause since 1874 and a Prohibition party had entered the field in 1876. But the most successful political action followed the formation in 1893 of the Anti-Saloon League, an organization which pioneered the strategy of the single-issue pressure group. By singleness of purpose it forced the prohibition issue into the forefront of state and

Triangle Shirtwaist Company Fire, New York City, 1911.

local elections. At its "Jubilee Convention" in 1913 the Anti-Saloon League endorsed a prohibition amendment to the Constitution, adopted by Congress that year. By the time it was ratified six years later, state and local action already had dried up areas occupied by nearly three-fourths of the nation's population.

ACTIVE GOVERNMENT   A fifth feature of progressivism, and perhaps the most significant of all in its long-term impact, was its emphasis on the public-service functions of government. Governments were now called upon to extend a broad range of direct services: schools, good roads (a movement propelled first by cyclists and then by automobilists), conservation, public health and welfare, care of the handicapped, farm loans, and farm demonstration agents.

ROOSEVELT'S PROGRESSIVISM

Theodore Roosevelt's version of Progressive reform was a cautious one. He cultivated party leaders in Congress, and steered away from such political meat-grinders as the tariff and banking issues.

And when he did approach the explosive issue of the trusts, he always took care to reassure the business community. For him, politics was the art of the possible. Unlike the more advanced progressives and the doctrinaire "lunatic fringe," as he called them, he would take half a loaf rather than none at all. Roosevelt acted in large part out of the conviction that reform was needed to keep things on an even keel. Control should rest in the hands of sensible Republicans, and not with irresponsible Democrats or, worse, the growing socialist movement.

EXECUTIVE ACTION   At the outset of his presidency in 1901 Roosevelt took up McKinley's policies and promised to sustain them. He touched base with McKinley's friend and manager Mark Hanna, and worked with Republican leaders in Congress, against whom the minority of new Progressives was as yet powerless. Republican Speaker Joe Cannon, who now wielded the dictatorial powers once held by "Czar" Thomas B. Reed, was able to announce on one occasion to a helpless House, "We will now perpetrate the following outrage."

Roosevelt, it turned out, would accomplish more by vigorous executive action than by passing legislation, and in the exercise of executive power he was not inhibited by points of legal detail. The president, he argued, might do anything not expressly forbidden by the Constitution. The Constitution, he said later, "must be interpreted, not as a straight jacket, not as laying the hand of death upon our development, but as an instrument designed for the life and healthy growth of the Nation." He was even credited with asking "What's the Constitution between friends?" but that query seems to have been apocryphal.

Caution suffused Roosevelt's first annual message, delivered in December 1901, but he felt impelled to take up the trust problem in the belief that it might be more risky to ignore it. The message carefully balanced arguments on both sides of the question. "The mechanism of modern business is so delicate," he warned, "that extreme care must be taken not to interfere with it in a spirit of rashness or ignorance." A widespread belief nevertheless held the great corporations "in certain of their features and tendencies hurtful to the general welfare." The president endorsed the "sincere conviction that combination and concentration should be, not prohibited, but supervised and within reasonable limits controlled." The first essential was "knowledge of the facts—publicity . . . the only sure remedy we can now invoke." Later would follow regulatory legislation, perhaps based on the experience of the Interstate Commerce Commission (ICC).

In August 1902 Roosevelt carried the trust issue to the people on a tour of New England and the Midwest. He endorsed a "square deal" for all, calling for enforcement of existing antitrust laws and stricter controls on big business. From the outset, however, Roosevelt believed that wholesale trust-busting was too much like trying to unscramble eggs. Effective regulation, he believed, was better than a futile effort to restore small business, which might be achieved only at a cost to the efficiencies of scale gained in larger operations. Roosevelt nevertheless soon acquired a reputation as a "trustbuster."

Because Congress boggled at regulatory legislation, Roosevelt sought to force the issue by a more vigorous prosecution of the Sherman Anti-Trust Act. He chose his target carefully. In the case against the sugar trust (*United States v. E. C. Knight and Company*, 1895) the Supreme Court had declared manufacturing a strictly intrastate activity. Railroads, however, were beyond question engaged in interstate commerce and thus subject to federal authority. In February 1902 Roosevelt ordered his attorney-general to move against the Northern Securities Company, a firm vulnerable to both the law and public opinion. That company, formed the previous year, had taken shape during a gigantic battle in the New York Stock Exchange between E. H. Harriman of the Union Pacific and James J. Hill and J. P. Morgan of the Great Northern and Northern Pacific. The stock battle raised the threat of a panic, and led to a settlement in which the chief contenders made peace. They formed Northern Securities as a holding company to control the Great Northern and Northern Pacific.

At about the time Roosevelt ordered suit against Northern Securities in 1902, he balanced his action with a speech at the South Carolina and West Indian Exposition in Charleston denouncing demagogues who raved "against the wealth which is simply the form of embodied thrift, foresight, and intelligence." But when J. P. Morgan invited Roosevelt to "send your man to my man and they can fix it up," the president refused. Hill complained: "It seems hard that we should be compelled to fight for our lives against the political adventurers who have never done anything but pose and draw a salary." Roosevelt pressed the case and in 1904 the Supreme Court ordered the combination dissolved.

THE COAL STRIKE Support for Roosevelt's use of the "big stick" against corporations was strengthened by the stubbornness of mine owners in the anthracite coal strike of 1902. On May 12 the United Mine Workers (UMW) walked off the job in Pennsylvania and West Virginia, demanding a 20 percent wage increase, a reduction in hours from ten to nine, and union recognition. The mine operators, having granted a 10 percent raise two years before, dug in their heels against further concessions, and shut down in preparation for a long struggle to starve out the miners. Their spokesman, George F. Baer, the president of the Reading Railroad, helped the union cause more than his own with an arrogant pronouncement: "The rights and interests of the laboring man will be protected and cared for," he said, "not by the labor agitators, but by the Christian men to whom God in his infinite wisdom has given control of the property interests of the country."

Facing the prospect of a coal shortage, Roosevelt called a conference at the White House. The mine owners, led by Baer, attended but refused even to speak to the UMW leaders. This outraged Roosevelt, who expressed his irritation at the "extraordinary stupidity and temper" of the "wooden-headed" owners. The president also confessed a temptation to grab Baer "by the seat of his breeches" and "chuck him out" a White House window. After the conference ended in an impasse, Roosevelt threatened to take over the mines and run them with the army. When a congressman questioned the constitutionality of such a move, an exasperated Roosevelt grabbed the man by the shoulders and roared: "To hell with the Constitution when the people want coal!" Such a comment and others like it over the years led Joe Cannon, the crusty House Speaker, to note: "Roosevelt's got no more respect for the Constitution than a tomcat has for a marriage license." Militarizing the mines would have been an act of dubious legality, but the owners feared that TR might actually do it and that public opinion would support him.

No Lack of Big Game. *A 1905 cartoon shows TR going after the trusts.*

The coal strike ended in October 1902 with an agreement to submit the issues to an arbitration commission named by the president. After a last-minute flurry over the operators' refusal to accept a union man on the panel, the president blithely reclassified the head of the railway conductors' union as an "eminent sociologist." The agreement enhanced the prestige of both Roosevelt and the union leader, although it produced only a partial victory for the miners. By the arbitrators' decision of March 21, 1903, the miners won a nine-hour day but only a 10 percent wage increase, and no union recognition.

TOWARD A SECOND TERM   Roosevelt continued to use his executive powers to enforce the Sherman Act, but he avoided conflict in Congress by drawing back from further antitrust legislation. Altogether his administration brought about twenty-five antitrust suits, the most notable victory coming in *Swift and Company v. United States* (1905), a decision against the "beef trust" through which most of the packers had avoided competitive bidding in the purchase of livestock. In this decision the Supreme Court put forth the "stream-of-commerce" doctrine which overturned its previous holding that manufacturing was strictly intrastate. Since both livestock and the meat products of the packers moved in the stream of interstate commerce, the Court reasoned, they were subject to federal regulation. This interpretation of the interstate commerce power would be broadened in later years until few enterprises would remain beyond the reach of federal regulation.

In 1903 Congress came around to legislation that somewhat strengthened both antitrust enforcement and governmental regulation. Within one week in February of that year, Congress approved three important measures: the Expedition Act, whereby circuit courts had to give priority to antitrust suits upon request of the attorney-general; an act creating the Department of Commerce and Labor, including the Bureau of Corporations; and the Elkins Act, which made it illegal to take as well as to give rebates.

The new Bureau of Corporations had no direct regulatory powers, but it did have a mandate to study and report on the activities of interstate corporations. The bureau followed a policy on concord rather than conflict. Its findings could lead to antitrust suits, but its purpose was rather to help corporations correct malpractices and avoid the need for lawsuits. Many companies, among them United States Steel and International Harvester, worked closely with the bureau, but others held back. When Standard Oil refused to turn over records, the government brought an antitrust suit which resulted in its breakup in 1911. The Supreme Court broke up the

American Tobacco Company at the same time. This approach fell short of the direct regulation which Roosevelt preferred, but without a congressional will to pass such laws, little more was possible. Trusts that cooperated were left alone; others had to run the gauntlet of antitrust suits.

Roosevelt's policies built a coalition of progressive- and conservative-minded voters which assured his election in his own right in 1904. He had skillfully used patronage, and his progressive policies, achieved mainly by executive action, had not challenged congressional conservatives. Nor did Roosevelt try to take on the Old Guard at the Chicago convention in June. He accepted a harmless platform which dwelt on past achievements, and the convention chose him by acclamation. The Democrats, having lost with Bryan twice, turned to Alton B. Parker who, as chief justice of New York, had upheld labor's right to the closed shop and the state's right to limit hours of work. Despite his liberal record party leaders presented him as a safe conservative, and his acceptance of the gold standard as "firmly and irrevocably established" bolstered such a view. The effort to present a candidate more conservative than Roosevelt proved a futile gesture for the party which had twice nominated Bryan. Despite Roosevelt's trust-busting proclivities, most businessmen, according to the New York *Sun,* preferred the "impulsive candidate of the party of conservatism to the conservative candidate of the party which the business interests regard as permanently and dangerously impulsive." Even J. P. Morgan and E. H. Harriman contributed handsomely to Roosevelt's campaign chest. Parker made little headway with his charge that businessmen expected favors in return.

An invincible popularity plus the sheer force of personality swept Roosevelt to an impressive victory by a popular margin of 7.6 million to 5.1 million. Parker carried only the Solid South of the former Confederacy and two border states: Kentucky and Maryland. It was a great personal triumph for Roosevelt. Amid the excitement of election night he announced that he would not run again, a statement he later had reason to regret.

LEGISLATIVE LEADERSHIP   Elected in his own right, Roosevelt approached his second term with heightened confidence and a stronger commitment to progressive reform. In December 1905 he devoted most of his annual message to the regulation and control of business. This understandably irked many of his corporate contributors. Said steel baron Henry Frick, "We bought the son of a bitch and then he did not stay put." The independent-minded Roosevelt took aim at the railroads first, and it was with reference to railroads that his demands most nearly approached success. The Elkins Act of 1903, finally outlawing rebates, had been a minor step. Railroad men themselves welcomed it as an escape from shippers clamoring for special favors. But the new Hepburn proposal was something else again, for it would both extend the authority of the ICC and give it effective control over rates for the first time.

Roosevelt had to mobilize all the pressure and influence at his disposal to push through the bill introduced by Representative Peter Hepburn of Iowa. Enacted on June 29, 1906, the Hepburn Act for the first time gave the ICC power to set maximum rates. The commission no longer had to go to court to enforce its decisions. While the carriers could challenge the rates in court, the burden of proof now rested on them rather than on the ICC. As part of the compromise required to pass the law, however, ICC rates under challenge by the carriers would be suspended pending decision of the courts. In other ways, too, the Hepburn Act enlarged the mandate of the ICC. Its reach now extended beyond railroads to pipelines, express companies, sleeping-car companies, bridges, and ferries, and it could prescribe a uniform system of bookkeeping to provide uniform statistics. In addition, the act forbade carriers to grant free passes except to their own employees, or to carry commodities they had produced themselves, such as coal or timber, except for their own use.

For more dedicated progressives like Senator La Follette, the Hepburn Act was but half a loaf. They would have preferred that

Elected in his own right in 1904, TR began his second term with a stronger commitment to progressive reform.

ICC rates continue in effect while appeals were pending, and to have the ICC estimate the overall value of the roads as a basis for rate-fixing. Before many years, though, they would get both of these.

Railroads took priority, but a growing movement for the regulation of meat-packers, food processors, and makers of drugs and patent medicines reached fruition, as it happened, on the very day after passage of the Hepburn Act. Discontent with abuses in these fields had grown rapidly as a result of the muckrackers' reports. They supplied evidence of harmful preservatives and adulterants in the preparation of "embalmed meat" and other food products. The *Ladies Home Journal* and *Colliers* published evidence of false claims and dangerous ingredients in patent medicines, what one report called "The Great American Fraud." One of the more notorious nostrums, Lydia Pinkham's Vegetable Compound, was advertised to work wonders in the relief of "female complaints"; it was no wonder, for the compound was 18 percent alcohol.

But perhaps the most telling blow against such abuses was struck by Upton Sinclair's novel *The Jungle* (1906). Sinclair meant the book to be a tract for socialism, but its main impact came from its portrayal of filthy conditions in Chicago's meatpacking industry: "It was too dark in these storage places to see well, but a man could run his hand over these piles of meat and sweep off handfuls of the dried dung of rats. These rats were nuisances, and the packers would put poisoned bread out for them, they would die, and then rats, bread, and meat would go into the hoppers together." Roosevelt, an omnivorous reader, read *The Jungle*—and reacted quickly. He sent two agents to Chicago and their report confirmed all that Sinclair had said: "We saw meat shovelled from filthy wooden floors, piled on tables rarely washed, pushed from room to room in rotten box carts, in all of which processes it was in the way of gathering dirt, splinters, floor filth, and the expectoration of tuberculous and other diseased workers."

The Meat Inspection Act of June 30, 1906, required federal inspection of meats destined for interstate commerce and empowered officials in the Agriculture Department to impose standards of sanitation. The Pure Food and Drug Act, enacted the same day, placed restrictions on the makers of prepared foods and patent medicines, and forbade the manufacture, sale, or transportation of adulterated, misbranded, or harmful foods, drugs, and liquors.

Thus during one week of February 1903, and during two days of June 1906, Theodore Roosevelt's campaign for regulatory legislation reached its chief goals: in 1903 the Expedition Act, the Elkins Act, and the establishment of the Department of Commerce and Labor with its Bureau of Corporations; in 1906 the Hepburn Act, the Meat Inspection Act, and the Pure Food and Drug Act. If in later years

Muckraking reports on fraudulent drugs and patent medicines, such as Lydia Pinkham's Vegetable Compound, prompted a growing movement for government regulation.

these would seem modest achievements for all of Roosevelt's bluster, they had moved the federal government a great distance from the laissez-faire policies which had prevailed before the turn of the century.

CONSERVATION   One of the most enduring legacies of the Roosevelt years was his energetic support for the conservation movement. Concern for protecting the environment grew with the rising awareness that the frontier was being exhausted by the end of the nineteenth century. A large section of Roosevelt's first annual message was devoted to the subject. As early as 1872 Yellowstone National Park had been set aside as a public reserve (the National Park Service would be created in 1916 after other parks had been added). In 1881 Congress had created a Division of Forestry in the Department of Agriculture, and Roosevelt's appointment of Gifford Pinchot, one of the country's first scientific foresters, as chief brought vigorous administration of forests on public lands. The president was determined to halt the unchecked destruction of the nation's natural resources and wonders by providing a barrier of federal regulation and protection. Roosevelt added fifty federal wildlife refuges, approved five new national parks, and initiated the system of designating national monuments such as the Grand Canyon. He also used the Forest Reserve Act (1891) to exclude from settlement or harvest some 172 million acres of timberland. Lumbermen were irate, but Roosevelt held firm. As he bristled, "I hate a man who would skin the land."

Forestry chief Pinchot worked vigorously, with TR's full support, to develop programs and public interest in conservation. Congressional resistance to their proposals led Pinchot and Roosevelt to publicize the cause through a White House Conference on Conservation in 1908, and later that year by setting up a National Conservation Commission which proposed a thorough survey of resources in minerals, water, forests, and soil. Within eighteen months some forty-one state conservation commissions sprang up, and a number of private groups took up the cause. The movement remained divided, however, between those who wanted to conserve resources for continuous human use and those who wanted to set aside wilderness areas. Pinchot, for instance, won the enmity of naturalist John Muir in 1906 when he endorsed a water reservoir in the wild Hetch Hetchy Valley of Yosemite National Park to supply the needs of San Francisco.

From Roosevelt to Taft

On the night of his election to the presidency in 1904, Roosevelt had vowed not to seek another term. Four years later he declared "I have had a great time as president" and prepared to turn over the mantle. Unlike most presidents, Roosevelt was strong

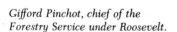
Gifford Pinchot, chief of the Forestry Service under Roosevelt.

enough to handpick a successor to carry out "the policies." He decided that the heir to the White House should be Secretary of War William Howard Taft, and the Republican convention ratified the choice on its first ballot in 1908. The Democrats, whose conservative strategy had backfired in 1904, decided to give William Jennings Bryan one more chance at the highest office. Still vigorous at forty-eight, Bryan retained a faithful following, but once again it was not enough. The Republican platform declared its support of Roosevelt's policies, including conservation and further strengthening of the ICC. On the tariff and the use of labor injunctions the platform made vague references to revision but without any specifics. The Democratic platform hardly differed on regulation, but endorsed a lower tariff and an AFL-supported plank opposing court injunctions against labor actions. Bryan himself went beyond support of regulation by calling for federal incorporation of interstate business and even government ownership of railroads, "not as an immediate issue, but as an ultimate solution." In the end the voters opted for Roosevelt's chosen successor: The popular vote showed Taft with 7,679,000, Bryan with 6,409,000, and Debs with 421,000. Taft swept the electoral college by 321 to 162. The real surprise of the election was the strong showing of the Socialist party candidate, labor hero Eugene V. Debs. His 421,000 votes revealed the depth of working-class resentment in the United States. The major political parties, Debs's supporters believed, were in collusion with large corporations.

Once out of office, still only fifty, Roosevelt left on a big-game hunt in Africa, prompting his old foe J. P. Morgan to mutter, "Let every lion do his duty." The new president he left behind was an entirely different kind of political animal, in fact hardly a political animal at all. Offspring of a family long prominent in Cincinnati—his father had been Grant's attorney-general—Taft had progressed through appointive offices, from judge in Ohio to solicitor in the Justice Department, federal judge, commissioner and governor-general in the Philippines, and secretary of war. The presidency was the only elective office he ever held. Later he would be chief justice (1921–1930), a job more suited to his temperament.

Weighing in at over 300 pounds, Taft had the dubious distinction of being the heaviest president in history. When he cabled a friend that he had just returned from a long horseback ride, the friend asked, "How is the horse?" The potbellied, bull-chested, short-legged Taft was a jovial slab of a man who loved eating and playing golf or poker, but he detested politics. "Politics, when I am in it," he admitted, "makes me sick." Taft never felt comfortable in the White House. He once observed that whenever someone said "Mr. Presi-

William Howard Taft.

dent," he looked around for Roosevelt. The political dynamo in the family was his wife, Nellie, who had wanted the White House more than he. One of the major tragedies of Taft's presidency was that Helen "Nellie" Taft suffered a debilitating stroke soon after they entered the White House, and for most of his term she remained unable to serve as his political adviser.

DOLLAR DIPLOMACY   In foreign affairs Taft practiced what critics labeled "dollar diplomacy." The policy so tagged had its origin in China in 1909, when President Taft personally cabled the Chinese government on behalf of American financiers interested in an international consortium to finance railroad lines in the Yangtze Valley. The secretary of state wrote that the government regarded such cooperation "as best calculated to maintain the Open Door and the integrity of China." In 1911 the Americans were let in on the deal with British, French, and German capitalists, and in 1912 entered an even larger scheme to make a gigantic loan to the new Chinese Republic. Both schemes were repudiated, however, when Woodrow Wilson became president in 1913, and the American investors, lacking support from the government, withdrew.

In Latin America "dollar diplomacy" worked differently and with somewhat more success. The idea was to encourage American bankers to help prop up the finances of shaky governments in the Caribbean region. In 1910 the administration got several lenders to invest in the national bank of Haiti. In 1911 it signed treaties with Nicaragua and Honduras providing them with private loans to bolster their treasuries and ensuring payment by installing American collectors of customs. The Senate refused to go along with the treaties, but the administration continued its private appeals for American bankers to assume debts in the region.

In 1912, however, when the Nicaraguan president asked for help in putting down disorders, American marines entered the country. An American collector of customs was then installed and the government placed on a monthly allowance doled out by a commission of two Americans and one Nicaraguan. American forces stayed until 1925, then returned in 1926 to stay until 1933. Similar forcible interventions occurred in Haiti in 1915 and the Dominican Republic in 1916.

TARIFF REFORM   Taft's domestic policies generated a storm of controversy within his own party. Contrary to Republican tradition he preferred a lower tariff, and he made this the first important issue of his presidency. Once a student of William Graham Sumner at Yale, Taft had absorbed the laissez-faire views of his mentor and had since differed with orthodox Republican protectionism. Early in the campaign, and against TR's advice, he had clarified the vague tariff plank in the platform by affirming that it meant revision downward. In keeping with the platform pledge for a special session, Taft called Congress to meet on March 15, 1909, eleven days after his inauguration. But if in pressing an issue that TR had skirted Taft seemed the bolder of the two, he proved the less adroit.

A tariff bill passed the House with surprising ease. It lowered rates less than Taft would have preferred but made some important reductions and enlarged the free list. But the chairman of the Senate Finance Committee, Nelson W. Aldrich, guided through a bill drastically revised by more than 800 changes. What finally came out of a conference committee was a measure close to the Senate version, although Taft did get some reductions on important items: hides, iron ore, coal, oil, cottons, boots, and shoes.

In response to the higher rates in Aldrich's bill, a group of midwestern Republicans took the Senate floor to fight what they considered a corrupt throwback to the days when the Republican party had served big business unquestioningly. In all, ten progressive Republicans joined the Democrats in an unsuccessful effort to defeat the bill. Taft at first agreed with them; then, fearful of a party split, he backed the majority and agreed to an imperfect bill. He lacked TR's love of a grand battle as well as his gift for working both sides of the street. Temperamentally conservative, inhibited by scruples about interfering too much with the legislative process, he drifted into the orbit of the Republican Old Guard and quickly alienated the progressive wing of his party, whom he tagged "assistant Democrats." Aware of rising discontent in the corn and wheat belts, Taft embarked in late summer on a speaking tour of the West only to make things worse when he pointedly ignored insurgent senators and pronounced the new bill the best tariff the Republican party had ever passed.

BALLINGER AND PINCHOT   In 1910 Taft's policies drove the wedge deeper between the Republican factions. What came to be called the Ballinger-Pinchot controversy made Taft appear to be a less reliable custodian of TR's conservation policies than he actually was. Taft's secretary of the interior, Richard A. Ballinger of Seattle, was well aware that many westerners opposed conservation programs on the ground that they held back full development of the region. The strongest conservation leaders were often easterners like TR and Gifford Pinchot of Pennsylvania. Ballinger threw open to use more than a million acres of waterpower sites which Roosevelt had withdrawn in the guise of ranger stations. Ballinger's reasoning was that the withdrawal had "gone far beyond legal limitations," and Taft agreed. At about the same time Ballinger turned over certain coal lands in Alaska to a group of Seattle men, some of whom he had represented as a lawyer. Apparently without Ballinger's knowledge, this group had already agreed to sell part of the lands to a Morgan-Guggenheim syndicate.

This was too much for one investigator with the General Land Office, who went to Chief of Forestry Pinchot with evidence of the collusion. Pinchot in turn called it to the attention of Taft, who then fired the investigator for his pains. When Pinchot went public with the controversy, he in turn was fired for insubordination early in 1910. A joint congressional investigation of Ballinger exonerated him from all charges of fraud or corruption, but progressive suspicions created such pressures that he resigned in 1911.

In firing Pinchot, Taft acted on the strictly legal view which his training had taught him to value, but circumstances tarnished his image in the public mind. "In the end," one historian has written, "the Ballinger-Pinchot affair had more impact on politics than it did on conservation." Taft had been elected to carry out the Roosevelt policies, his opponents said, and he was carrying them out—"on a stretcher."

Meanwhile, in the House of Representatives rebellion had broken out among the more progressive Republicans. When the regular session opened in March 1910 the insurgents joined Democrats in voting to investigate Ballinger. Flushed with that victory, they resolved to clip the wings of Speaker Joseph G. Cannon (R-Ill.), a conservative who held almost a stranglehold on procedures by his power to appoint all committees and their chairmen, and especially by his control of the Rules Committee, of which he was a member. A Democratic-insurgent coalition overrode a ruling from the Speaker and preceded to adopt new rules offered by George W. Norris (R-Neb.) which enlarged the Rules Committee from five to fifteen members, made them elective by the House, and excluded the Speaker as a member. About forty Republicans joined the Democratic minority in the move. In the next Congress the rules would be further changed to make all committees elective.

Events had conspired to cast Taft in a conservative role at a time when progressive sentiment was riding high in the countryside. The result was a severe rebuke to the president in the congressional elections of 1910, first by the widespread defeat of pro-Taft candidates in the Republican primaries, then by the election of a Democratic majority in the House and of enough Democrats in the Senate that insurgent Republicans could wield the balance of power.

TAFT AND ROOSEVELT   In June 1910 Roosevelt had returned from his travel abroad. He had been reading news accounts and letters about the Taft "betrayal," but unlike some of his supporters he refused to break with his successor. With rather severe politeness, however, Roosevelt refused an invitation to visit the White House. But, he wrote Taft: "I shall keep my mind open as I keep my mouth shut." Neither was easy for Roosevelt, who was beset by followers urging him to action. Soon he was rallying support for the Republican gubernatorial candidate in New York, and then he was off on a speaking tour of the West in advance of the congressional elections. At Osawatomie, Kansas, on August 31, 1910, he gave a catchy name to his latest principles, the "New Nationalism." Roosevelt issued a stirring call for an array of new federal regulatory laws and new measures of direct democracy, including the old Populist demands for the initiative, recall, and referendum. His purpose was not to revolutionize American life but to save it from the threat of revolution. "What I have advocated," he explained a few days later, "is not wild radicalism. It is the highest and wisest kind of conservatism."

Relations between Roosevelt and Taft remained tense, but it was another year before they came to an open break. It happened in the fall of 1911 when the Taft administration announced an antitrust suit against United States Steel, citing specifically as cause the company's acquisition of the Tennessee Coal and Iron Company in 1907, a move to which TR had given tacit approval in the belief that it would avert a panic. In mid-November Roosevelt published a sharp attack on Taft's "archaic" attempt to restore competition. The only sensible response to the problem, he argued, was to accept business combinations under modern circumstances but to enlarge the government's power to regulate them. His entry into the next presidential campaign was now only a matter of time.

Not all progressive Republicans wanted TR back in the White House. A sizable number proposed to back Senator La Follette in 1912, but some of La Follette's supporters were ready to switch if TR entered the race. An opening came on February 2, 1912, when La Follette betrayed signs of nervous exhaustion in a rambling speech in Philadelphia. As his following began to drop away, a group of seven Republican governors met in Chicago and called on Roosevelt to become a candidate. On February 24 Roosevelt threw his hat in the ring. "I hope that so far as possible the people may be given the chance, through direct primaries," Roosevelt wrote the governors, "to express their preference."

The rebuke implicit in Roosevelt's decision to run against Taft, his chosen successor, was in many ways undeserved. During Taft's first year in office one political tempest after another left his image irreparably damaged. The three years of solid achievement that followed came too late to restore its luster or to reunite his divided party. Taft had at least attempted tariff reform, which TR had never dared. He replaced Ballinger and Pinchot with men of impeccable credentials in conservation matters. He won from Congress the power to protect public lands for any reason, and was the first president to withdraw oil lands from use. Under the Appalachian Forest Reserve Act (1911) he enlarged the national forest by pur-

A skeptical view of TR, the Bull Moose candidate in 1912.

chase of lands in the East. In the end his administration withdrew more public lands in four years than TR's had in nearly eight, and brought more antitrust suits, by a score of eighty to twenty-five.

In 1910, with Taft's support, Congress passed the Mann-Elkins Act, which empowered the ICC for the first time to initiate rate changes, extended regulation to telephone and telegraph companies, and set up a Commerce Court to expedite appeals from the ICC rulings. Taft's reform record was further extended by passage of a postal-savings law (1910), the establishment of the Bureau of Mines and the Federal Children's Bureau (1912), and the provision of statehood for Arizona and New Mexico and territorial government for Alaska (1912). The Sixteenth Amendment (1913), authorizing a federal income tax, was ratified with Taft's support before he left office, and the Seventeenth Amendment (1913), providing for the popular election of senators, was ratified soon after he left office.

Despite this record, Roosevelt now hastened Taft's demise. In all but two of the thirteen states which held presidential primaries, Roosevelt won, even in Taft's Ohio. But the groundswell of popular support was no match for Taft's decisive position as president and party leader. In state conventions the party regulars held the line, so that Roosevelt entered the Republican national convention about 100 votes short of victory. The regulars' control of the convention machinery, operating under established rules, ensured their triumph and the Taft forces proceeded to nominate their man by the same "steamroller" tactics that had nominated Roosevelt in 1904. Outraged at such "naked theft," the Roosevelt delegates assembled in a rump convention. "If you wish me to make the fight I will make it," Roosevelt told the delegates, who then issued a call for a Progressive party convention, which assembled in Chicago on August 5. TR appeared, feeling "fit as a bull moose." He was "stripped to the buff and ready for the fight," he said. "We stand at Armageddon and we battle for the Lord." But few professional politicians turned up. Progressive Republicans decided to preserve their party credentials and fight another day. For the time being, with the disruption of the Republican party, the progressive torch was about to be passed on to the Democrats.

WILSON'S PROGRESSIVISM

WILSON'S RISE   The emergence of Thomas Woodrow Wilson as the Democratic nominee climaxed a political rise even more rapid than that of Cleveland. In 1910, before his nomination and election as governor of New Jersey, Wilson had been president of Princeton

University, but had never run for public office. Born in Staunton, Virginia, in 1856, the son of a "noble-saintly mother" and a stern Presbyterian minister, he had grown up in Georgia and the Carolinas during the Civil War and Reconstruction. Young Wilson, tall, slender, and a bit awkward, with a lean, long, sharply chiseled face, inherited his father's unquestioning piety, once declaring that "so far as religion is concerned, argument is adjourned." Wilson also developed a consuming ambition to "serve" humankind. Driven by a sense of destiny and duty, as well as by a certain moral fastidiousness, he once confessed: "I am too intense." Indeed, Wilson nurtured a righteous commitment to principle. Although he would prove to be an adept compromiser, his fits of stubborn inflexibility would prove to be his Achilles heel.

Wilson attended Davidson College in North Carolina for one year, finished his undergraduate career at Princeton in 1879, and after law school at the University of Virginia tried a brief, unfulfilling, and profitless legal practice in Atlanta. From there he went to the new Johns Hopkins University in Baltimore, where he found his calling in the study of history and political science.

Wilson's dissertation, *Congressional Government*, published in 1885, argued that the president, like the British prime minister, should be the leader of party government, as active in directing legislation as in the administration and enforcement of laws. In calling for a strong presidency he expressed views closer to those of Roosevelt than those of Taft. He also shared Roosevelt's concern that politicians should promote the general welfare rather than narrowly serve special interests. And, like Roosevelt, he was critical of big business, organized labor, socialists, and radical agrarianism. He later would express to a friend his desire to "do something, at once dignified and effective, to knock Mr. Bryan once and for all into a cocked hat."

After Johns Hopkins, Wilson taught at Bryn Mawr before moving to Princeton in 1890. There he quickly earned renown for his scintillating lectures, vigorous mind, and sharp debating skills. In 1902 he was unanimously elected president of the university. In that position he showed the first evidence of reform views. "We are not put into this world to sit still and know," he stressed in his inaugural address. "We are put into it to act." And act he did. At Princeton he modernized the curriculum, expanded and improved the faculty, introduced the tutorial system, raised admissions standards, and attacked the boisterous, snobbish eating clubs. But Wilson met defeat when he tried to integrate the new graduate school with the university. The dean opposed him and won the battle by gaining strong alumni backing. Thereafter Wilson faced a choice of giving up or leaving.

At this juncture the Democratic boss of New Jersey offered Wilson his support for the 1910 gubernatorial nomination, and Wilson accepted. The party leaders sought a respectable candidate to ward off progressive challengers, but they discovered too late that the supposedly innocent schoolmaster actually had an iron will of his own. Like Roosevelt, Wilson had come to shed some of his original conservatism and view progressive reform as a necessary expedient in order to stave off more radical social change. Elected as a reform candidate, Governor Wilson promoted progressive measures and pushed them through the legislature. He pressured lawmakers to enact a workmen's compensation law, a corrupt-practices law, measures to regulate public utilities, and ballot reforms. Such strong leadership in a state known as the "home of the trusts" for its lenient corporation laws brought Wilson to national attention.

THE ELECTION OF 1912   In the spring of 1911 a group of southern Democrats resident in New York opened a Wilson presidential campaign headquarters, and Wilson set forth on strenuous tours into all regions of the country, denouncing special privilege and political bossism. But by convention time, despite a fast start, the Wilson campaign seemed headed for defeat by Speaker Bennett Champ Clark of Missouri, who garnered supporters among Bryanites, the Hearst newspapers, and party hacks. Clark had enough for a majority in the early ballots, but the Wilson forces combined with supporters of Oscar Underwood of Alabama to prevent a two-thirds majority. On the fourteenth ballot Bryan came over to Wilson. When the Democratic boss of Illinois deserted Clark on the forty-second ballot and the Underwood delegates went over to Wilson on the forty-sixth, he swept to the nomination.

No sooner did the formal campaign open than Roosevelt's candidacy almost ended. On his way to deliver a speech in Milwaukee, he was shot while entering his car by a fanatic. The bullet went through Roosevelt's overcoat, spectacles case, and folded speech, then fractured a rib before lodging just below his right lung. "Stand back, don't hurt the man," he yelled at the crowd as it mobbed the attacker. Roosevelt then demanded that he be driven to the auditorium to deliver his speech. His dramatic sense unhampered, he showed the audience his bloodstained shirt and punctured text and vowed: "It takes more than this to kill a bull moose." He apologized for his halting delivery, but completed his speech before letting doctors remove the bullet.

As the race developed, it quickly became clear that in a three-man race Taft was out of the running. "There are so many people in the country who don't like me," he lamented. The campaign settled down to a running debate over the competing ideologies of the two front-runners: Roosevelt's "New Nationalism" and Wilson's "New Freedom." The inchoate ideas that Roosevelt fashioned into his New Nationalism had first been presented systematically in *The Promise of American Life* (1909) by Herbert Croly, a then-obscure New York journalist. Its central point was often summarized in a useful catch-phrase: Hamiltonian means to achieve Jeffersonian ends, meaning that Hamilton's program of governmental intervention, once identified with the business interests, should be used to achieve democratic and egalitarian Jeffersonian goals. The times required progressive to give up Jeffersonian prejudices against big government and use a strong central government to achieve democratic ends in the interest of the people.

The old nationalism had been used "by the sinister . . . special interests," TR said. His New Nationalism would enable government to achieve social justice, and more specifically to effect such reforms as graduated income and inheritance taxes, workmen's compensation, regulation of the labor of women and children, and a stronger Bureau of Corporations. These and more went into the platform of the Progressive party, which called for a federal trade commission with sweeping authority over business and a tariff commission to set rates on a "scientific basis." The Progressive platform, one historian has written, "provided the basis for the future development of the progressive movement in the United States after 1912, just as the

Democratic candidate Woodrow Wilson speaking from a train platform during the campaign of 1912.

Populist platform of 1892 had earlier provided a foundation for the first phase of American progressivism."

Before the end of his administration, Wilson would be swept into the current of New Nationalism too. But initially he adhered to the decentralizing antitrust traditions of his party. Before the start of the campaign Wilson conferred with Louis D. Brandeis, a progressive lawyer from Boston who focused Wilson's thought much as Croly had focused Roosevelt's. Brandeis's design for the New Freedom differed from Roosevelt's New Nationalism in its belief that the federal government should restore the competition among small economic units rather than regulate huge monopolies. This required a vigorous antitrust policy, lowering tariffs to allow competition with foreign goods, and breaking up the concentration of financial power in Wall Street. But Brandeis and Wilson saw the vigorous expansion of federal power as only a temporary necessity, not a permanent condition. Roosevelt, who was convinced that both corporate concentration as well as an expanding federal government were permanent developments, dismissed the New Freedom as mere fantasy.

The Republican schism opened the way for Woodrow Wilson to win by 435 electoral votes to 88 for Roosevelt and 8 for Taft. But in popular votes Wilson had only 42 percent of the total. Roosevelt received 27 percent, Taft 23 percent, and Debs 6 percent. It was the victory of a minority over a divided opposition. Taft took his loss with grace. When Yale University offered him the Kent Chair of Constitutional Law, the rotund ex-president accepted, noting, however, that a "Sofa of Law" might be more appropriate. In 1921 President Harding would appoint Taft to the Supreme Court, and he served with distinction as chief justice until his death in 1930.

The election of 1912 was significant in several ways. First, it was a high-water mark for progressivism. The election was the first to feature presidential primaries. The two leading candidates debated the basic issues of progressivism in a campaign unique for its focus on vital alternatives and for its high philosophical tone. Taft, too, despite his temperament and associations, showed his own progressive instincts. And the Socialist party, the left wing of progressivism, polled over 900,000 votes for Eugene V. Debs, its highest proportion ever.

Second, the election gave Democrats effective national power for the first time since the Civil War. For two years during the second Cleveland administration, 1893–1895, they had held the White House and majorities in both houses of Congress, but they quickly fell out of power during the most severe depression in American history to that time.

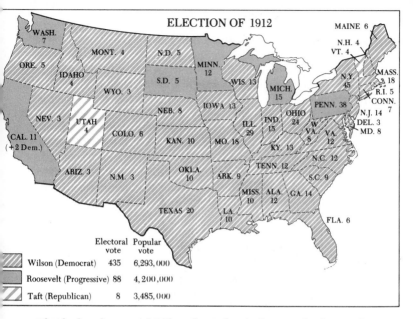

ELECTION OF 1912

	Electoral vote	Popular vote
Wilson (Democrat)	435	6,293,000
Roosevelt (Progressive)	88	4,200,000
Taft (Republican)	8	3,485,000

Third, the election of Wilson brought southerners back into the orbit of national and international affairs in a significant way for the first time since the Civil War. In Washington, one reporter said, "you feel it in the air . . . you listen to evidence of it in the mellow accent with which the South makes our English a musical tongue." Wilson himself once said that "the only place in the world where nothing has to be explained to me is the South." Five of his ten cabinet members were born in the South, three still resided there, and William Jennings Bryan, the secretary of state, was an idol of the southern masses. At the president's right hand, and one of the most influential members of the Wilson circle, at least until 1919, was Colonel Edward M. House of Texas. On Capitol Hill southerners, by virtue of their seniority, held the lion's share of committee chairmanships. As a result much of the progressive legislation of the Wilson era would bear the names of the southerners who guided it through Congress.

Fourth and finally, the election of 1912 had begun to alter the character of the Republican party. Even though most party professionals remained, the defection of the Bull Moose Progressives had weakened the party's progressive wing. The leader of the Republican party which would return to power in the 1920s would be more conservative in tone and temperament.

WILSONIAN REFORM   Wilson's inaugural address voiced in eloquent tones the ideals of social justice that animated many progressives.

"We have been proud of our industrial achievements," he said, "but we have not hitherto stopped thoughtfully enough to count the human cost . . . the fearful physical and spiritual cost to the men and women and children upon whom the dead weight and burden of it all has fallen pitilessly the years through." He promised specifically a lower tariff and a new banking system. "This is not a day of triumph; it is a day of dedication. Here muster, not the forces of party, but the forces of humanity."

Wilson offered his party its first chance since the Civil War to make a record of achievement. Democrats were bound to him by their need to disprove the slur voiced by a Republican congressman that they were "the organized incapacity of the country." They were bound even more by Wilson's determination to be their leader. If Roosevelt had been a strong president by force of personality, Wilson became a strong president by force of conviction. The president, he wrote in *Congressional Government,* "is . . . the political leader of the nation, or has it in his choice to be. The nation as a whole has chosen him, and is conscious that it has no other political spokesman. His is the only national voice in affairs."

Wilson courted popular support, but he also courted members of Congress through personal contacts, invitations to the White House, and visits to the Capitol. He used the patronage power to reward friends and punish enemies. He might have acted through a progressive coalition, but chose instead to rely on party loyalty. "I'd rather trust a machine Senator when he is committed to your program," he told his navy secretary, "than a talking Liberal who can never quite go along with others because of his admiration of his own patented plan of reform." Wilson therefore made use of the party caucus, in which disagreements among Democrats were settled, and often influenced caucus strategy.

THE TARIFF   Wilson's leadership faced its first big test on the issue of tariff reform. Wilson summoned Congress into special session on April 7, 1913, and the day after it convened he went before it in person—the first president to do so since John Adams. (Roosevelt was said to have asked, "Why didn't I think of that?") "The object of the tariff duties henceforth laid must be effective competition," Wilson said, "the whetting of American wits by contest with the wits of the rest of the world." Congress now acted vigorously on tariff reductions. In the House, where Oscar Underwood's Ways and Means Committee had been working since January, the outcome was never in doubt. Only four Democrats bolted the party line as the bill passed the House easily.

The crunch came in the Senate, the traditional graveyard of tariff reform. Swarms of lobbyists got so thick in Washington, Wilson said, that "a brick couldn't be thrown without hitting one of them." But Wilson turned the tables with a public statement that focused the spotlight on the "industrious and insidious" tariff lobby. "It is of serious interest to the country," he said, "that the people at large should have no lobby and be voiceless in these matters, while great bodies of astute men seek to create an artificial opinion and to overcome the interests of the public for their private profit." In the end the two "sugar senators" from Louisiana were the only Democrats to vote against the bill, which received the president's signature on October 3.

The Underwood-Simmons Tariff of 1913 reduced import duties on 958 items, raised them on only 86, and left 307 the same, with the effect of lowering the overall average duty from about 37 to about 29 percent. A free list of some 300 items, about 100 of them new to the list, included important consumer goods and raw materials: sugar, wool, iron ore, steel rails, agricultural implements, cement, coal, wood and wood pulp, and many farm products.

The act lowered tariffs but raised internal revenues with the first income tax levied under the newly ratified Sixteenth Amendment: 1 percent on incomes over $3,000 ($4,000 for married couples) and a surtax graduated from 1 percent on incomes of about $20,000 to 6 percent on incomes above $500,000. The highest total tax thus would be 7 percent. Opponents objected that the tax was class legislation and a sectional raid on eastern wealth, but Cordell Hull (D-Tenn.), who guided it through the House, disclaimed any purpose of sharing the wealth and justified the tax on the principle that eastern profits derived from all parts of the country.

THE FEDERAL RESERVE   Before the new tariff had cleared the Senate, the administration proposed the first major banking and currency reform since the Civil War. The need for a change had been acknowledged since the brief panic of 1907, which threatened to bring on widespread bank failures. The panic had occasioned the appointment of a National Monetary Commission which in 1912 recommended creation of a National Reserve Association with fifteen branches. The plan aimed to strengthen the banking system by pooling bank reserves and maintaining a flexible currency.

But to progressive Democrats it seemed a plan to revive the second Bank of the United States, which Jackson had destroyed, and to extend the Wall Street "Money Trust's" control of business and finance, which a House committee under A. P. Pujo (D-La.) began to expose in the fall of 1912. Dominant figures in framing the Democrats' counterproposal were Representative Carter Glass, a pugnacious redhead from Virginia, and the economist H. Parker Willis. Glass's chief contribution was a provision, which appealed to traditional Democratic fears of centralization, for regional reserve banks to be owned by member banks. Wilson, however, insisted on a central board of governors, comprising only a minority of bankers, as the capstone of the system.

A group of radical agrarians, with support from William Jennings Bryan, argued that the entire system, including the banks and the governing board, should be under governmental control. They won a compromise arrangement excluding bankers' representatives from the central board, making Federal Reserve Notes obligations of the federal government, and providing short-term, ninety-day farm loans as well as business loans. The Glass-Owen Federal Reserve Act, signed into law two days before Christmas 1913, created a new banking system along regional lines, with twelve Federal Reserve Banks, each owned by member banks in its district. All national banks became members; state banks and trust companies could join if they wished. Each member bank had to subscribe 6 percent of its capital to the Federal Reserve Bank and deposit a portion of its reserve there, the amount depending on the size of the community.

These "bankers' banks" dealt chiefly with their members and not at all with individuals. Along with other banking functions, the chief service to member banks was to rediscount their loans, that is, to take them over in exchange for Federal Reserve Notes, which member banks might then use to make further loans. The Federal Reserve Notes in turn were based 40 percent on government gold and

Reading the Death Warrant. *Wilson's plan for banking and currency reform spells the death of the "Money Trust," according to this cartoon.*

60 percent on commercial and agricultural paper (the promissory notes signed by borrowers). This arrangement made it possible to expand both the money supply and bank credit in times of high business activity, or as the level of borrowing increased. A Federal Reserve Board named three of the nine members on each Reserve Bank's board (member banks chose the remaining six) and exercised general supervision, including review of the rediscount rates. These rates might be raised to fight inflation by tightening credit or lowered to stimulate business by making credit more easily available.

This new system corrected three great defects in the previous arrangements. Now reserves could be pooled, affording greater security; both the currency and bank credit became more elastic; and the concentration of reserves in New York was lessened. The system represented a new departure in active governmental intervention and control in one of the most sensitive segments of the economy.

ANTITRUST LAWS   The next major issue confronting Wilson, after tariffs and banking, concerned the antitrust laws. In his campaign Wilson had made trust-busting the central focus of the New Freedom, and information gathered by the Pujo Committee showed that the concentration of economic power had continued to grow despite the Sherman Act and the Bureau of Corporations. Wilson's solution to the problem was revision of the Sherman Act to define more explicitly what counted as "restraint of trade."

During the summer of 1914, while Congress took up several bills, Wilson suddenly reversed himself and, influenced by Brandeis and others, decided to make a strong Federal Trade Commission the cornerstone of his antitrust program. Created by an act of September 1914, the five-member commission replaced Roosevelt's Bureau of Corporations and assumed new powers to define "unfair trade practices" and to issue "cease-and-desist" orders when it found evidence of unfair competition.

Having embraced the Brandeis principle of "controlled competition," Wilson seemed to lose interest in the antitrust bill drafted by Henry D. Clayton (D-Ala.) of the House Judiciary Committee, which followed the president's original idea of defining specific acts in restraint of trade. The Clayton Antitrust Act, passed in October 1914, outlawed such practices as price discrimination (charging different customers different prices for the same goods), "tying" agreements which limited the right of dealers to handle the products of competing manufacturers, interlocking directorates connecting corporations with a capital of more than $1 million (or banks with more than $5 million), and corporations' acquisition of stock in competing corporations. In every case, however, conservative forces in the

Senate qualified these provisions by tacking on the weakening phrase "where the effect may be to substantially lessen competition" or words of similar effect. In accordance with the president's recommendation, however, corporate officials were made individually responsible for any violations. Victims of price discrimination and tying agreements could sue for compensation three times the amount of damages suffered.

Agrarian radicals, in alliance with organized labor, won a stipulation which supposedly exempted farm labor organizations from the antitrust laws, but actually only declared them not to be, per se, unlawful combinations in restraint of trade. Injunctions in labor disputes, moreover, were not to be handed down by federal courts unless "necessary to prevent irreparable injury to property." Hailed by Samuel Gompers as labor's "Magna Carta," these provisions were little more than pious affirmations, as later court decisions would demonstrate. Wilson himself remarked that the act did little

Mr. Wilson Taking Charge of the School. *A cartoon depicting the professorial president taking on big business.*

more than affirm the right of unions to exist by forbidding their dissolution for being in restraint of trade.

Administration of the antitrust laws generally proved disappointing to the more vehement progressives under Wilson. In the wake of a business setback late in 1913 Wilson set out to reassure business that his purposes were friendly. As his secretary of commerce put it later, Wilson hoped to "create in the Federal Trade Commission a counsellor and friend to the business world." Its first chairman lacked forcefulness, and under its next head, a Chicago industrialist, the FTC practically abandoned its function of watchdog. The Justice Department meanwhile offered help and advice to businessmen interested in arranging matters so as to avoid antitrust prosecutions. The appointment of conservative men to the Interstate Commerce Commission and the Federal Reserve won plaudits from the business world and profoundly disappointed progressives.

SOCIAL JUSTICE   But Wilson had never been a strong progressive of the social-justice persuasion. He had carried out promises to lower the tariff, reorganize the banking system, and strengthen the antitrust laws. Swept along by the course of events, and the pressures of more far-reaching progressives, he was pushed further than he intended to go on some points. The New Freedom was now complete, he wrote Treasury Secretary William Gibbs McAdoo late in 1914; the future would be "a time of healing because a time of just dealing." Although Wilson endorsed state action for women's suffrage, he declined to support a suffrage amendment because his party platform had not. He had cultivated the support of black voters, but let members of his cabinet extend Jim Crow practices in the federal government and froze out all but a few black appointees. He withheld support from federal child-labor legislation because he regarded it a state matter. He opposed a bill for federal support of rural credits on the ground that it was "unwise and unjustifiable to extend the credit of the government to a single class of the community." Not until the second anniversary of his inauguration (March 4, 1915) did Wilson sign an important piece of social-justice legislation, the La Follette Seamen's Act. The product of stubborn agitation by the eloquent president of the Seamen's Union, the act strengthened safety requirements, reduced the power of captains, set minimum food standards, and required regular wage payments. Seamen who jumped ship before their contracts expired, moreover, were relieved of the charge of desertion.

PROGRESSIVE RESURGENCE   It was the need to weld a winning coalition in 1916 that pushed Wilson back on the road of reform. Progressive Democrats were restless, and after war broke out in Europe in

Louis D. Brandeis.

August 1914, further divisions arose over defense and foreign policy. At the same time the Republicans were repairing their own rift, as the Progressive party showed little staying power in the midterm elections and Roosevelt showed little will to preserve it. It was plain to most observers that Wilson could shape a majority only by courting progressives of all parties. In January 1916 Wilson scored points with them when he nominated Louis D. Brandeis to the Supreme Court. Conservatives waged a vigorous battle against Brandeis, but Senate progressives rallied to win confirmation of the social-justice champion, the first Jewish member of the Supreme Court.

Meanwhile Wilson began to embrace a broad program of farm and labor reforms. On farm credit, after having first opposed it he reversed himself abruptly, supporting early in 1916 a proposal to set up land banks to sponsor long-term farm loans. With this boost the Federal Farm Loan Act became law in July 1916. Under the control of a Federal Farm Loan Board, twelve Federal Land Banks, each with a minimum capital of $750,000, paralleled the Federal Reserve Banks and offered farmers loans of five to forty years' duration at low interest rates.

Thus the dream of cheap rural credits, sponsored by a generation of Alliance members and Populists, came to fruition. Democrats never embraced the Populist subtreasury plan, but made a small step in that direction with the Warehouse Act of 1916. This measure authorized federal licensing of private warehouses; federal backing made their receipts for stored produce more acceptable as collateral for short-term bank loans. Other concessions to farm demands came more readily in the Smith-Lever Act of 1914 and the Smith-Hughes Act of 1917, both of which passed with little controversy. The first provided federal grants-in-aid for farm demonstration agents under the supervision of land-grant colleges. The measure made permanent a program that had started a decade before in Texas and that had already spread to many localities. The second measure extended agricultural and mechanical education to high schools through grants-in-aid.

Farmers with automobiles had more than a passing interest as well in the Federal Highways Act of 1916, which provided dollar-matching contributions to states with highway departments that met certain federal standards. The measure authorized distribution of $75 million over five years, and marked a sharp departure from Jacksonian opposition to internal improvements at federal expense, just as the Federal Reserve System departed from Jacksonian banking principles. Although the argument that highways were one of the nation's defense needs weakened constitutional scruples against the act, it still restricted support to "post roads." A renewal act in 1921 would mark the beginning of a systematic network of numbered United States highways.

The progressive resurgence of 1916 broke the logjam on labor reforms as well. With newfound support from the administration, the Kern-McGillicuddy Bill, a workmen's compensation measure for federal employees, passed in August. Advocates of child-labor legislation persuaded Wilson that social-justice progressives would regard his stand on the issue as an important test of his humanitarian concerns, and Wilson overcame doubts of its constitutionality to support and sign the Keating-Owen Child Labor Act, which excluded from interstate commerce goods manufactured by children under fourteen. Both the Keating-Owen Act and a later act of 1919 to achieve the same purpose with a prohibitory tax were ruled unconstitutional by the Supreme Court on the ground that regulation of interstate commerce could not extend to the conditions of labor. Effective action against the social evil of child labor had to await the New Deal, although it seems likely that discussion of the issue contributed to the sharp reduction in the number of underage workers during the next few years.

Another important accomplishment was the eight-hour day for railroad workers, a measure that the Supreme Court upheld. The Adamson Act of 1916 was brought about by a threatened strike of railroad brotherhoods demanding the eight-hour day and other concessions. Wilson, who objected to some of the union demands, nevertheless went before Congress to request action on the hours limitation. The resulting Adamson Act required an eight-hour day, beginning January 1, 1917, with time and a half for overtime, and appointed a commission to study the problem of railroad labor.

In Wilson's first term progressivism reached its zenith. A creative time, the age of progressivism set at the beginning of the twentieth century a framework within which American politics and society would still function, by and large, near the end of the century. Progressivism had conquered the old dictum that the government is best which governs least, whatever political rhetoric might be heard to the contrary, and left the more extreme doctrines of limited government as dead as Herbert Spencer. Progressivism, an amalgam of agrarian, business, governmental, and social reform, amounted in the end to a movement for positive government. From two decades of ferment (three, if the Populist years be counted) the great fundamental contribution of progressive politics was the firm establishment and general acceptance of the public-service concept of the state.

The Limits of Progressivism

The Progressive period was an optimistic age in which reformers of various hues were persuaded, in Walter Lippmann's terms, that drift would give way to mastery over social ills and that no problem lay beyond solution. But like all great historic movements, progressivism displayed elements of paradox and irony. Despite its talk of democracy, it was the age of disenfranchisement for southern blacks—an action seen by many whites as progressive. The initiative and referendum, supposed democratic reforms, proved subject to manipulation by well-financed publicity campaigns. And much of the public policy of the time came to be formulated by experts and members of appointed boards, not by broad segments of the population. There is a fine irony indeed in the fact that the drive to increase the political role of ordinary people moved parallel with efforts to strengthen executive leadership and exalt expertise. This age of efficiency and bureaucracy, in business as well as government, brought into being a society in which more and more of the decisions affecting people's lives were made by faceless policy-makers.

Progressivism was largely a middle-class movement in which the poor and unorganized had little influence. The supreme irony was that a movement so dedicated to the rhetoric of democracy should experience so steady a decline in voter participation. In 1912, the year of the Bull Moose campaign, voting dropped off by between 6 and 7 percent. The new politics of issues and charismatic leaders proved to be less effective in turning out voters than party organizations and bosses had been. And by 1916 the optimism of an age that looked to infinite progress was already confronted by a vast slaughter. Europe had already stumbled into war, and America would soon be drawn in. The twentieth century, which dawned with such bright hopes, held in store episodes of unparalleled horror.

FURTHER READING

Good introductions to the topic of progressivism can be found in Arthur S. Link and Richard L. McCormick's *Progressivism* (1983)° and Lewis L. Gould's *Reform and Regulation: American Politics, 1900–1916* (2nd ed., 1986).° George E. Mowry's *The Era of Theodore Roosevelt, 1900–1912* (1958)° and Arthur S. Link's *Woodrow Wilson and the Progressive Era, 1910–1917* (1954)° remain useful.

Progressivism has been interpreted in many ways. Robert H. Weibe's *The Search for Order, 1877–1920* (1967)° presents the organizational model for reform. Richard Hofstadter's *The Age of Reform: From Bryan to FDR* (1955)° examines the consensus at the basis of reform. Gabriel Kolko sees reform as a means of social control in *The Triumph of Conservatism* (1963).° Dewey W. Grantham's *Southern Progressivism* (1983)° shows the distinctiveness of reform in that region. Other interpretive works include Samuel P. Hays's *The Response to Industrialism, 1885–1914* (1957),° David W. Noble's *The Progressive Mind* (rev. ed., 1981),° and Jean B. Quandt's *From the Small Town to the Great Community: The Social Thought of Progressive Intellectuals* (1970).

Biographers of the three progressive presidents elaborate on the complexity of reform. Edmund Morris's *The Rise of Theodore Roosevelt* (1979),° a favorable account, can be balanced with William H. Harbaugh's *Power and Responsibility: The Life and Times of Theodore Roosevelt* (1975).° Also helpful is John M. Blum's *The Republican Roosevelt* (2nd ed., 1977).° For the Taft years, see Paolo E. Coletta's *The Presidency of William Howard Taft* (1973). Arthur S. Link's multivolume biography *Wilson* (1947–1965)— particularly *The New Freedom* (1956)—is the place to start on that president. John Milton Cooper, Jr., compares Wilson and Roosevelt in *The Warrior and the Priest* (1983).°

The evolution of government policy toward business is examined in Martin J. Sklar's *The Corporate Reconstruction of American Capitalism, 1890–1916* (1988). On reform at the local level, see Richard M. Abram's *Conservatism in a Progressive Era: Massachusetts Politics, 1900–1912* (1964). Roy Lubove's *The Progressives and the Slums* (1962) and Jack M. Holl's *Juvenile Reform in the Progressive Era* (1971) examine the problem of urban decay. Steven A. Reiss's *Touching Base: Professional Baseball and American Culture in the Progressive Era* (1980) and Dominick Cavallo's

°These books are available in paperback editions.

Muscles and Morals: Organized Playgrounds and Urban Reform, 1880–1920 (1981) link athletics to new forms of organization and socialization. Other issues are covered in David M. Kennedy's *Birth Control in America: The Career of Margaret Sanger* (1970),° David J. Rothman's *Conscience and Convenience: The Asylum and Its Alternatives in Progressive America* (1980),° and John Ettling's *The Germ of Laziness: Rockefeller Philanthropy and Public Health in the New South* (1981).

On other aspects of the Progressive impulse, see James H. Timberlake's *Prohibition and the Progressive Movement, 1900–1920* (1963) and Ruth Rosen's *The Lost Sisterhood* (1982),° on prostitution. David I. Macleod's *Building Character in the American Boy* (1983) looks at the Boy Scouts and the YMCA in the context of Progressive reform. Samuel P. Hays's *Conservation and the Gospel of Efficiency: The Progressive Conservation Movement, 1890–1920* (1959)° and Harold T. Pinkett's *Gifford Pinchot: Private and Public Forester* (1970)° cover conservation and the Ballinger-Pinchot controversy. Frederick Turner's *Rediscovering America* (1985) looks at the role of conservationist John Muir. See also Fred Greenbaum's *Robert Marion La Follette* (1975).

Labor studies include Stephen Meyer III's *The Five Dollar Day: Labor Management and Social Control in the Ford Motor Company, 1908–1921* (1981)° and Tamara K. Hareven's *Family Time and Industrial Time: The Relationship between the Family and Work in a New England Industrial Community* (1982).° Patricia Cooper's *Once a Cigar Maker* (1986) details life and culture in the cigar factories.

Works by the muckrakers themselves remain available, and readers should consult the several that are listed in this chapter.

25 ∽

WILSON AND
THE GREAT WAR

WILSON AND FOREIGN AFFAIRS

When Woodrow Wilson was sworn in as president of the United States in March 1913 the former professor and college president brought to the office little background in the study of diplomacy and none at all in its practice. Wilson admitted as much when he remarked just before taking office, "It would be an irony of fate if my administration had to deal chiefly with foreign affairs." But events in Latin America and Europe were to make the irony all too real. From the summer of 1914, when the guns of August heralded a catastrophic World War, foreign relations increasingly overshadowed all else, including Wilson's domestic program, the New Freedom.

AN IDEALIST'S DIPLOMACY   Although lacking in international experience, Wilson did not lack ideas or convictions in this area. The product of a Calvinist past, he brought to diplomacy a version of progressivism more than a little touched with Calvinist righteousness. Both Wilson and his secretary of state, William Jennings Bryan, believed that America had been called to advance democracy and moral progress in the world. If they did not always follow principle at the expense of national self-interest, they did in many respects try to develop a diplomatic policy based on idealism.

The teetotaling Bryan, undismayed by ridicule of his "grape juice diplomacy," during 1913–1914 negotiated some thirty "cooling-off" treaties under which participating nations pledged themselves not to go to war over any disagreement for a period of twelve months pending discussion by an international panel. The treaties, however, were of little consequence, soon forgotten in the revolutionary sweep of world events that would make the twentieth century the bloodiest in recorded history.

One of the first applications of Wilsonian idealism to foreign policy came when the president renounced "dollar diplomacy." The government, he said, was not supporting any "special groups or interest." As good as his word, on March 18, 1913, he withdrew governmental support of the Six-Power Consortium then preparing to float a large loan to China. Such a monopolistic grant, he said, would compromise China's integrity and possibly involve the United States in a future intervention. Without governmental backing, American bankers withdrew.

INTERVENTION IN MEXICO   Closer to home Wilson found it harder to take such high ground. Nor did the logic of his "missionary diplomacy" always imply nonintervention. Mexico, which had been in the throes of revolution for nearly three years, presented a thorny problem. For most of the thirty-five years from 1876 to 1911 President Porfirio Díaz had dominated Mexico. As military dictator he had suppressed opposition and showered favors on his followers and on foreign investors, who piled up holdings in Mexican mines, petroleum, railroads, and agriculture. But eventually the dictator's hold slipped, and in 1910 popular resentment boiled over in revolt. In May 1911 revolutionary armies occupied Mexico City and Díaz fled.

The leader of the rebellion, Francisco I. Madero, proved unable to manage the tough customers drawn by the scramble for power. In February 1913 General Victoriano Huerta assumed power and Madero was murdered soon afterward. Confronted with this turn to rule by a military dictator, Wilson enunciated a new doctrine of nonrecognition: "We hold, as I am sure all thoughtful leaders of republican government everywhere hold, that just government rests upon the consent of the governed." Recognition, formerly extended routinely to governments which exercised *de facto* power, now might depend on judgments of their legality: an immoral government presumably would not pass muster.

Huerta's hold on power was still unsure, and for a while Wilson resisted the impulse to intervene. In October 1913 he sought to quiet fears of intervention with a statement that the United States "will never again seek one additional foot of territory by conquest." Nevertheless he obliquely expressed sympathy with the revolutionary movement and began to put diplomatic pressure on Huerta. "I am going to teach the South American republics to elect good men," he told a visiting British diplomat. Early in 1914 he removed an em-

General Victoriano Huerta, whose seizure of power in Mexico in 1913 aroused Wilson's opposition.

bargo on arms to Mexico in order to help the resurgent revolutionaries under Venustiano Carranza of the Constitutionalist party, and stationed warships off Veracruz to halt arms shipments to Huerta.

On April 9, 1914, several American sailors, gathering supplies in Tampico, strayed into a restricted area and were arrested. The local commander, a Huertista, quickly released them and sent an apology to the American naval commander. There the incident might have ended, but the naval commander demanded a salute to the American flag. Wilson backed him up and got from Congress authority to use force to bring Huerta to terms. Before the Tampico incident could be resolved, Wilson authorized a naval force to enter Veracruz and stop the imminent landing of an arms shipment. American marines and sailors went ashore on April 21, 1914, and occupied the town at a cost of 19 killed. The Mexicans lost at least 200 killed.

In Mexico the occupation aroused the opposition of all factions, and Huerta tried to rally support against foreign invasion. At this juncture Wilson accepted an offer of mediation by the ABC powers (Argentina, Brazil, and Chile), which in June proposed withdrawal of United States forces, the removal of Huerta, and installation of a provisional government sympathetic to reform. Huerta refused, but the moral effect of the proposal, his isolation abroad, and the growing strength of his foes forced him to leave office in July 1914. In August the Carranzistas entered Mexico City, and in November the Americans left Veracruz. Finally, in October 1915 the United States and several Latin American governments recognized Carranza as president of Mexico.

Still, the troubles south of the border continued. The disorders had

The Veracruz incident in April 1914 provoked this comment on Wilson's policy in Mexico.

spawned independent bands of freebooters, Pancho Villa's among the wildest. All through 1915 fighting between the forces of Villa and Carranza swayed back and forth. In January 1916 Villa seized a train and murdered sixteen American mining engineers in a deliberate attempt to provoke American intervention, discredit Carranza, and build himself up as an opponent of the "Gringos." That failing, he crossed the border on raids into Texas and New Mexico. On March 9 he entered Columbus, New Mexico, burned the town, and killed seventeen Americans.

Wilson then had to abandon his policy of "watchful waiting." With the reluctant consent of Carranza, he sent General John J. Pershing across the border with a force of 11,000 men and mobilized 150,000 National Guardsmen along the frontier. For nearly a year Pershing went on a wild-goose chase after Villa through northern Mexico and, missing his catch, was ordered home in January 1917. Carranza then pressed his own war against the bandits and put through a new liberal constitution in 1917. Mexico was by then well on the way to a more orderly government.

PROBLEMS IN THE CARIBBEAN   In the Caribbean, Wilson found it as hard to act on his ideals as in Mexico. The "dollar diplomacy" practiced by the Taft administration encouraged bankers in the United States to aid debt-plagued governments in Haiti, Guatemala, Honduras, and Nicaragua. Despite Wilson's public stand against using American force to back up American investments, he kept the marines in Nicaragua, where they had been sent by Taft in 1912, to prevent renewed civil war. Then in July 1915 he dispatched more marines to Haiti after two successive revolutions and subsequent disorders. "I suppose," Wilson told Secretary of State Bryan, "there is nothing to do but to take the bull by the horns and restore order." The American forces stayed in Haiti until 1934. Disorders in the Dominican Republic brought American marines to the country in 1916; they remained until 1924. The presence of these additional U.S. military forces in the region only exacerbated the Yankee phobia among many Latin Americans. And as the *New York Times* charged, Wilson's frequent interventions made Taft's dollar diplomacy look like "ten cent diplomacy."

THE GREAT WAR AND AMERICA

Such problems in Latin America and the Caribbean loomed larger in Wilson's thinking than the gathering storm in Europe. When the thunderbolt of war struck Europe in the summer of 1914 it came to most Americans, one North Carolinian wrote, "as lightning out of a clear sky." Whatever the troubles in Mexico, whatever disorders and interventions agitated other countries, it seemed unreal that civilized Europe could descend into such an orgy of destruction. Since the fall of Napoleon in 1815, Europe had known local wars but only as interruptions of a general peace that contributed to a century of unprecedented material progress.

But the assassination in Sarajevo of Austrian archduke Franz Ferdinand by a Serbian nationalist, Austria-Hungary's determination to punish Serbia, and Russia's mobilization in sympathy with its Slavic friends in Serbia suddenly triggered a European system of alliances: the Triple Alliance or Central Powers (Germany, Austria-Hungary, and Italy) and the Triple Entente or Allied Powers (France, Great Britain, and Russia). When Russia refused to stop its mobilization, Germany, which backed Austria-Hungary, declared war on Russia on August 1, 1914, and on Russia's ally France two days later. Germany then invaded Belgium to get at France, which brought Great Britain into the war on August 4. Japan, eager to seize German holdings in the Pacific, declared war on August 23 and Turkey entered on the side of the Central Powers in October. Italy stayed out, however, and struck a bargain under which it joined the Allied Powers in 1915.

AMERICA'S INITIAL REACTIONS   Shock in the United States was followed by gratitude that an ocean stood between America and the battlefields. "Our isolated position and freedom from entangling alliances," said the *Literary Digest*, "inspire our press with cheering assurance that we are in no peril of being drawn into the European quarrel." Beginning on August 4 President Wilson issued routine declarations of neutrality. He urged the American people to be "impartial in thought as well as action."

That was more easily said than done, not least for Wilson himself. Americans might want to stay out, but most of them cared which side won. In the 1910 population of 92 million, more than 32 million were "hyphenated Americans," first- or second-generation immigrants who retained ties to their old countries. Among the more than 13 million from the countries at war, by far the largest group was German-American, numbering 8 million. And 4 million Irish-Americans harbored a deep-rooted enmity to Britain, further heightened by British suppression of the Irish Easter Rebellion in 1916. These groups instinctively leaned toward the Central Powers.

But old-line Americans, largely of British origin, were sympathetic to the Allies. If, as has been said, Britain and the United States were divided by a common language, they were united by ties of culture and tradition. Americans identified also with France, which had contributed to American culture and ideas, and to independence

EUROPE AT WAR

- Central Powers (Triple Alliance)
- Allied Powers (Triple Entente)
- Neutral countries

Most Americans leaned toward the Allies, but all were shocked at the outbreak of the Great War. In this cartoon, the Samson-like War pulls down the temple of Civilization.

itself. Britain and France, if not their ally Russia, seemed the custodians of liberal democracy, while Germany more and more seemed the embodiment of autocracy and militarism. If not a direct threat to the United States, Germany would pose at least a potential threat if it destroyed the balance of power in Europe. High officers of the United States government were pro-British in thought from the outset. Robert Lansing, first counselor of the State Department, Walter Hines Page, ambassador to London, and colonel Edward House, Wilson's close adviser, saw in German militarism a potential danger to America.

Just what effects the propaganda of the warring powers had is unclear. The Germans and the British were most active, but German propaganda, which played on American dislike of Russian autocracy and Russian anti-Semitism, fell mainly upon barren ground. Only German- and Irish-Americans responded to a "hate England" theme. From the outset the British had one supreme advantage in this area. Once they had cut the direct cable from Germany early in the war, nearly all news from the battlefronts had to clear through London. Highly exaggerated reports of German atrocities were convincing to Americans, and there were real atrocities enough in the German occupation of Belgium to affront American feelings.

A STRAINED NEUTRALITY   At first the war bought a slump in American exports and the threat of a depression, but by the spring of 1915 the Allies' demand for supplies generated a wartime boom. The Allies at first financed their purchases by disposing of American securities, but ultimately they needed loans. Early in the war Secretary Bryan informed J. P. Morgan that loans to any warring nation were "inconsistent with the true spirit of neutrality." Money, he warned, "is the worst of all contrabands because it commands everything else." Still, by October 1914 Wilson quietly began approving short-term credits to sustain trade with the Allies. When in September 1915 it became apparent that the Allies could no longer carry on without long-term credit, the administration raised all restrictions and Morgan soon extended a loan of $500 million to England and France. American investors would advance over $2 billion to the Allies before the United States entered the war, and only $27 million to Germany.

The administration nevertheless clung to the fond hope of neutrality through two and a half years of warfare in Europe and tried to uphold the traditions of "freedom of the seas" which had guided American policy since the Napoleonic Wars. As the German drive through Belgium and toward Paris finally ground down into the stalemate of trench warfare, trade on the high seas assumed a new importance. In a war of attrition survival depended on access to supplies, and in such a war British naval power counted for a great deal. With the German fleet outnumbered and bottled up almost from the outset, the war in many ways assumed the pattern that had once led America into war with Britain in 1812. Indeed, as British Orders in Council (familiar from a century before) restricted trade with central Europe, they once again raised some of the old issues. Wilson remarked that only two Princeton men had been president, and that both he and Madison faced similar problems of "freedom of the seas."

On August 6, 1914, Secretary Bryan called upon the belligerents to accept the Declaration of London, drafted and signed in 1909 by leading powers but never ratified by the British. That document, the culmination of nineteenth-century liberal thought on the rules of warfare, reduced the list of contraband items and specified that a blockade was legal only when effective just outside enemy ports. The Central Powers promptly accepted. The British almost as promptly refused, lest they lose some of their advantage in sea power. Beginning with an Order in Council of August 20, 1914, Britain gradually extended the list of contraband goods to include all sorts of things formerly excluded, such as food, cotton, wood, and certain ores. Wilson protested, but Ambassador Page, personally pro-British, assured Foreign Secretary Sir Edward Grey that the two could find ways of getting around the problem. The British consequently gave little serious heed to further protests.

In November 1914 the British declared the whole North Sea a war zone, sowed it with mines, and ordered neutral ships to enter only by the Strait of Dover, where they could be easily searched. In

March 1915 they further announced that they would detain and carry into port ships carrying goods of presumed enemy destination, ownership, or origin. Previous rules had required search on the high seas and this, combined with Britain's new policy, caused extended delays, sometimes running into months. The same order also directed British ships to stop vessels carrying German goods via neutral ports. When the State Department protested, Grey reminded the Americans that this was the same doctrine of continuous voyage on which the United States had acted in the 1860s to keep British goods out of the Confederacy.

NEUTRAL RIGHTS AND SUBMARINES   British actions, including blacklisting of American companies that traded with the enemy and censorship of the mails, raised some old issues of neutral rights, but the German reaction introduced an entirely new question. With the German fleet bottled up by the British blockade, few surface vessels could venture out to harass the enemy. On February 4, 1915, in response to the "illegal" British blockade, the German government proclaimed a war zone around the British Isles. Enemy merchant ships in those waters were liable to sinking by submarines, the Germans declared, "although it may not always be possible to save crews and passengers." Since the British sometimes flew neutral flags as a ruse, neutral ships in the zone would also be in danger. U-boat *(Unterseeboot)* warfare violated the established procedure of stopping enemy vessels on the high seas and providing for the safety of passengers and crews, since the chief advantage was in surprise.

The United States pronounced the German policy "an indefensible violation of neutral rights" and warned that Germany would be held to "strict accountability" for any destruction of American lives and property. If the meaning of the phrase was unclear, the stern tone of the note was unmistakable. The administration asked the British to give up flying neutral flags and its blockade of foodstuffs in return for German renunciation of submarine warfare, but nothing came of the effort. On March 28, 1915, one American drowned when the Germans sank the British steamer *Falaba* in the Irish Sea. On May 1 the American tanker *Gulflight* went down with a loss of two lives. The administration was divided on the proper course of action. Bryan wanted to say that American citizens entered the war zone at their own risk; his counselor, Robert Lansing, and Colonel House wanted to imply a possible break in diplomatic relations with Germany. Then, as Wilson pondered the alternatives, the sinking of the British Cunard liner *Lusitania* provoked a crisis.

On May 7, 1915, the captain of the German U-20 sighted a four-stack liner moving slowly through the Irish Sea and fired a torpedo. It hit the mark, and the ship exploded and sank within a few minutes. Only as it tipped into the waves was he able to make out the name *Lusitania* on the stern. Before the ship left New York bound for Liverpool the German embassy had published warnings in the American press against travel to the war zone, but among the 1,198 persons lost were 128 Americans.

The American public was outraged. It was an act of piracy, Theodore Roosevelt declared. In an effort to quiet the uproar Wilson, speaking to newly naturalized citizens in Philadelphia, said: "There is such a thing as a man being too proud to fight. There is such a thing as a nation being so right that it does not need to convince others by force that it is right." Wilson's previous demand for "strict accountability," however, forced him to make a strong response. On May 13 Bryan reluctantly signed a note demanding that the Germans abandon unrestricted submarine warfare, disavow the sinking, and pay reparations. The Germans responded that the ship had been armed (which it was not) and carried a cargo of small arms and ammunition (which it did). A second note on June 9 repeated American demands in stronger terms. The United States, Wilson asserted, was "contending for nothing less high and sacred than the rights of humanity." Bryan, unwilling to risk war on the issue, resigned in protest

Americans were outraged when a German torpedo sank the Lusitania *on May 7, 1915.*

and joined the peace movement as a private citizen. His successor, Robert Lansing, signed the note.

In response to the uproar over the *Lusitania*, the German government had secretly ordered U-boat captains to avoid sinking large passenger vessels. When, despite the order, two American lives were lost in the sinking of the British liner *Arabic*, bound for New York, the Germans paid an indemnity and offered a public assurance on September 1, 1915: "Liners will not be sunk by our submarines without warning and without safety of the lives of non-combatants, provided that the liners do not try to escape or offer resistance." With this "Arabic pledge" Wilson's resolute stand seemed to have resulted in a victory for his policy.

During the fall of 1915 Wilson's trusted adviser Edward M. House proposed to renew a mediation effort he had explored on a visit to London, Paris, and Berlin the previous spring—before the *Lusitania* sinking. In January and February 1916 House visited those capitals again, but found neither side ready to begin serious negotiations. The French and British would soon be engaged in destructive battles, the French at Verdun and the British at the Somme, and both were determined to fight until they could bargain from strength.

Peace advocates in Congress now rose up to challenge the administration's policy on neutral rights. In February 1916 resolutions were introduced in the House and Senate warning Americans against traveling on armed belligerent vessels. Such surrender to the German threat, Wilson asserted, would be a "deliberate abdication of our hitherto proud position as spokesmen, even amidst the turmoil of war, for the law and the right." Once accept a single abatement of right and "the whole fine fabric of international law might crumble under our hands piece by piece." The administration worked desperately to bring Democratic congressmen in line, and with the help of some Republicans managed to defeat both resolutions by a solid margin. On March 24, 1916, a U-boat torpedoed the French steamer *Sussex* with injury to two Americans. When Wilson threatened to break off relations, Germany renewed its pledge that U-boats would not torpedo merchant and passenger ships.

THE DEBATE OVER PREPAREDNESS   The *Lusitania* incident, and more generally the quarrels over neutral commerce, contributed to a growing demand for a stronger army and navy. Even before the end of 1914 spokesmen for preparedness included Elihu Root, Lansing, Roosevelt, Senator Henry Cabot Lodge, and prominent journalists. On December 1, 1914, the champions of preparedness organized the National Security League to promote their cause.

After the *Lusitania* sinking the outcry from such people grew into a clamor. Although Wilson did not announce his intentions until November 4, 1915, war preparation plans were public knowledge the previous July, when Wilson asked the War and Navy Departments to draft proposals. In his annual message in December Wilson alerted Congress to forthcoming requests.

The response was far from unanimous. Progressives and pacifists, and a broad-based antiwar sentiment running through the rural South and West, awakened the traditional American suspicion of military establishments, especially standing armies, which dated back to the colonial period. The new Democratic leader in the House opposed "the big Navy and big Army program of the jingoes and war traffickers." In the East, leaders of the peace movement organized a League to Limit Armament. Jane Addams and suffragist Carrie Chapman Catt organized a Women's Peace party. Bryan, La Follette, and other leaders lent their voices to the peace movement.

The administration's plan to enlarge the regular army and create a national reserve force of 400,000 ran into stubborn opposition in the House Military Affairs Committee. Wilson was forced to accept a compromise between advocates of an expanded force under federal control and advocates of a traditional citizen army. The National Defense Act of June 3, 1916, expanded the regular army from 90,000 to 175,000 and permitted gradual enlargement to 223,000. It also expanded the National Guard to 440,000 made provision for their training, and gave federal funds for summer training camps for civilians.

The bill for an increased navy had less trouble because of the general feeling expressed by the navy secretary that there was "no danger of militarism from a relatively strong navy such as would come from a big standing army." The Naval Construction Act of August 15, 1916, authorized between $500 million and $600 million for a three-year program of enlargement, and another act on September 7 created the United States Shipping Board, empowered to spend up to $50 million for the building or purchase of merchant vessels suitable for use as naval auxiliaries.

Forced to relent on preparedness, progressive opponents of the action like Representative Claude Kitchen and Senator George Norris determined that the financial burden should rest on the wealthy people they held responsible for the effort. The income tax became their weapon. Supported by a groundswell of popular support, they wrote into the Revenue Act of 1916 changes which doubled the basic income tax from 1 to 2 percent, lifted the surtax to a maximum of 13 percent (for a total of 15 percent) on incomes over $2 million, added an estate tax graduated up to a maximum of 10 percent, levied a 12½ percent tax on gross receipts of munitions makers, and added a new tax on corporation capital, surplus, and excess profits. The new taxes on wealth amounted to the most clear-cut victory of radical progressives in the entire Wilson period, a victory further consolidated and advanced after America entered the war. It was the capstone to the edifice of progressive legislation which Wilson supported in preparation for the election of 1916.

THE ELECTION OF 1916   Republicans started that year hoping to regain their normal majority, and Roosevelt started out hoping to be their leader again. But he had committed the deadly sin of bolting his party in 1912 and, what was more, expressed a bellicosity on war issues that would scare off voters. Needing somebody who would draw Bull Moose Progressives back into the fold, the regulars turned to Justice Charles Evans Hughes, who had made a progressive record in New York where he was governor from 1907 to 1910. On the Supreme Court since then, he had neither taken a stand in 1912 nor spoken out on foreign policy. The remnants of the Progressive Party gathered in Chicago at the same time as the Republicans. Roosevelt had held out the vain hope of getting both nominations, but he now declined to lead a moribund party. Two weeks later the Progressive National Committee disbanded the party and endorsed Hughes; a minority, including their vice-presidential nominee, came out for Wilson.

The Democrats, as expected, chose Wilson once again, and in their platform endorsed a program of social legislation, neutrality, and reasonable preparedness. The party further commended women's suffrage to the states, denounced groups that placed the interests of other countries above those of the United States, and pledged support for a postwar League of Nations to enforce peace with collective security measures against aggressors. The Democrats found their most popular issue, however, when the keynote speaker, a former New York governor, got an unexpected response to his recital of historic cases in which the United States had refused under provocation to go to war. As he mentioned successive examples, the crowd chanted "What did we do? What did we do?" and the speaker responded: "We didn't go to war! We didn't go to war!" The peace theme, refined into the slogan "He kept us out of war," became the rallying cry of the campaign, one that had the merit of taking credit without making any promises for the future.

Rooseveltians found themselves drawn in large numbers to Wilson who, according to the journalist Walter Lippmann, "is temporarily at least creating, out of the reactionary, parochial fragments of the Democracy, the only party which at this moment is national in scope, liberal in purpose, and effective in action." The impression of Democratic purpose and effectiveness was heightened by Republican

Peace with Honor. *Wilson's neutral policies proved popular in the 1916 campaign.*

feuding and ineptitude. On foreign policy Hughes worked both sides of the street. While trying to keep the votes of German-Americans and other "hyphenates," Hughes refused to disavow Roosevelt, who was going about the country denouncing the kaiser. On social-reform issues Wilson was far ahead of Hughes, and Hughes found himself often the captive of old-line Republican bosses more eager to punish Bull Moose Progressives by excluding them than to win the election for Hughes.

In the end Wilson's twin rallying cries of peace and progressivism, a unique combination of issues forged in the legislative and diplomatic crucibles of 1916, brought victory. Early returns showed a Republican sweep in the East and Midwest, signaling a victory for Hughes, but the outcome remained in doubt until word came that Wilson had carried California by 3,772 votes, where one incident may have decided the outcome. While visiting California Hughes unintentionally snubbed the popular governor, Hiram Johnson, who, without Hughes's knowledge, was in the same hotel. The final vote showed a Democratic sweep of the Far West and South, enough for victory in the electoral college by 277 to 254, and in the popular vote by 9 million to 8.5 million.

LAST EFFORTS FOR PEACE   Late in the 1916 contest Wilson expressed a belief that this was the last world war the United States could avoid, although as a historian he should have known that America had been drawn into every general European war since colonization began. Relations with Britain in 1916 had become almost as troubled as relations with Germany. The British dragged their heels on Colonel House's mediation offer; they put down the Irish Easter Rebellion so severely that they offended American opinion in general; they stepped up their economic warfare, and blacklisted firms suspected of dealing with the Central Powers. Immediately after the election Wilson began to plan another peace move, but before he was ready the German government announced on December 12 its readiness to begin discussion of peace terms.

Six days later Wilson sent identical notes to the belligerent powers, asking each to state its war aims. The Germans responded promptly that they would state theirs only to a conference of the belligerents at a neutral site. In January 1917 the Allies made it plain that they intended to exact reparations, break up the Austro-Hungarian and Ottoman Empires, and destroy German power.

Wilson then decided to make one more appeal, in the hope that public opinion would force the hands of the warring governments. Speaking before the Senate on January 22, 1917, he asserted the right of the United States to a share in laying the foundations for a lasting peace, which would have to be a "peace without victory" for only a "peace among equals" could endure. The peace must be based on the principles of government by the consent of the governed, freedom of the seas, and disarmament, and must be enforced by an international league for peace established to make another such catastrophe impossible. "I would fain believe," the president ended, "that I am speaking for the silent mass of mankind everywhere who have as yet had no place or opportunity to speak their real hearts out concerning the death and ruin they see to have come already upon the persons and homes they hold most dear."

Although Wilson did not know it, he was already too late. Exactly two weeks before he spoke, German leaders had decided to wage unrestricted submarine warfare. They took the calculated risk of provoking American anger in the hope of scoring a quick knockout. On January 31 the new policy was announced, effective the next day. All vessels in the war zone, belligerent or neutral, would be sunk without warning. "Freedom of the seas," said the Brooklyn *Eagle,* "will now be enjoyed by icebergs and fish."

On February 3, 1917, Wilson told a joint session of Congress that the United States had broken diplomatic relations with the German government. Three weeks later Wilson asked for authority to arm American merchant ships and "to employ any other instrumentalities or methods that may be necessary and adequate to protect our ships and our people." There was little quarrel with arming merchantmen, but bitter opposition to Wilson's vague reference to "any other instrumentalities or methods." A group of eleven or twelve die-hard noninterventionists including Senators La Follette and Norris filibustered the measure until the regular session expired on March 4. Thus, in Wilson's words: "A little group of willful men, representing no opinion but their own, have rendered the great Government of the United States helpless and contemptible." On March 12 the State Department announced that a forgotten law of 1792 allowed the arming of merchant ships regardless of congressional inaction.

In the midst of the debate, on March 1, news of the Zimmermann Telegram broke in the American press. Word had reached Wilson four days earlier that the British had intercepted and decoded an important message from German foreign secretary Arthur Zimmermann to his minister in Mexico. The note instructed the envoy to offer an alliance and financial aid to Mexico in case of war between the United States and Germany. In return for diversionary action against the United States, Mexico would recover "the lost territory in Texas, New Mexico, and Arizona."

All this was contingent on war with the United States, but an electrified public read in it an aggressive intent. Wilson felt it betrayed a trust he had shown in permitting the Germans to use American wireless facilities to transmit the message. Then, later in March a revolution overthrew Russia's czarist government and established the provisional government of a Russian Republic. The fall of the czarist autocracy allowed Americans the illusion that all the major Allied powers were now fighting for constitutional democracy. Not until November 1917 was this illusion shattered when the Bolsheviks seized power in Russia.

AMERICA'S ENTRY

The overt acts Wilson awaited came in March when German submarines sank five American merchant vessels in the north Atlantic. On March 20 Wilson's cabinet unanimously endorsed a declaration of war and the following day the president called a special session of Congress. When it met on April 2, Wilson asked Congress to recognize the war that Imperial Germany was already waging against the United States, then turned to a discussion of the issues. The German government had revealed itself as a natural foe of liberty, and therefore "The world must be made safe for democracy.

Its peace must be planted upon the tested foundations of political liberty." The war resolution passed the Senate by a vote of 82 to 6 on April 4. The House concurred, 373 to 50, and Wilson signed the measure on April 6, 1917. It was Good Friday.

How had it come to this, less than three years after Wilson's proclamation of neutrality? Prominent among the various explanations of America's entrance into the war are the effects of British propaganda and America's deep involvement in trade with the Allies, which some observers then and later credited to the intrigues of war profiteers and munitions makers. Some Americans thought German domination of Europe would be a threat to American security, especially if it meant the destruction or capture of the British navy. But whatever the influence of such factors, they likely would not have been decisive without the issue of submarine warfare. Once Wilson had taken a stand for the traditional rights of neutrals and noncombatants, he was to some extent at the mercy of decisions by the German high command and was led step by step into a war over what to a later generation would seem a rather quaint, if noble, set of principles.

AMERICA'S EARLY ROLE   The scope of America's role in the European war remained unclear. Few on either side of the Atlantic expected more from the United States than a token military effort. Despite Congress's preparedness measures the army remained small and rudimentary. The navy also was largely undeveloped. This began to change, however, when Rear Admiral William S. Sims was given command of American ships in European waters. He then systematically built up the United States Navy, bringing the first contingent of six American destroyers to Queenstown, Ireland, in May 1917, and more later. The Americans, in addition, made two important contributions to Allied naval strategy. Previously, merchant ships had survived through speed and evasive action. Sims persuaded the Allies to adopt a convoy system of escorting merchant ships in groups, and the result was a decrease in Allied shipping losses from 881,000 tons in April 1917 to 289,000 in November of the same year. Later the United States Navy conceived and laid a gigantic minefield across the North Sea which threatened the U-boats' access to the North Atlantic.

Within a month of the declaration of war, British and French missions arrived in the United States. First they requested money with which to buy supplies, a request Congress had already anticipated in the Liberty Loan Act of April 24, which added $5 billion to the national debt in "Liberty Bonds." Of this amount, $3 billion could be loaned to the Allied powers. The United States was also willing to furnish naval support, credits, supplies, and munitions, but to raise and train a large army, equip it, and send it across a submarine-infested ocean seemed out of the question. Marshal Joseph Joffre, who came with the French mission, nevertheless insisted that the United States send a token force to bolster morale, and on June 26, 1917, the first contingent of Americans, about 14,500 men commanded by General John J. Pershing, began to disembark on the French coast. Pershing and his troops were able to reach Paris by July 4. On the scene, Pershing soon decided that the war-weary Allies would be unable to mount an offensive by themselves. He advised the War Department that plans should be made to send a million American troops by the following spring. It was done—through strenuous efforts.

When the United States entered the war the combined strength of the regular army and National Guard was only 379,000; at the end it would be 3.7 million. The need for such large numbers of troops converted Wilson to the idea of conscription. Under the Selective Service Act of May 18, 1917, all men aged twenty-one to thirty (later, from eighteen to forty-five) had to register for service. Registrants went into five classes, the first being able-bodied unmarried men

A Liberty Loan poster with an "honor roll" of ethnic Americans.

Fresh Recruits. *Some 2.8 million American men would be drafted to fight in the war.*

without dependents. From this group alone came all the 2.8 million ultimately drafted. All told, about 2 million Americans crossed the Atlantic and about 1.4 million saw some action. Training of the soldiers went on in thirty-two camps, half of them located in the South for reasons of climate. The example of the Spanish-American War was well learned: the camps were for the most part sanitary and equipped with modern plumbing, hospitals, and recreation centers.

MOBILIZING A NATION   Such a massive war required complete economic mobilization on the home front. "In the sense in which we have been wont to think of armies," Wilson said, "there are no armies in this struggle; there are entire nations armed." Germany especially had perfected this kind of mobilization under a system that came to be known as War Socialism. A group of War Companies fixed prices, allocated materials, set priorities, and dictated what should be produced throughout the economy. In the United States, war brought more regulation of industry than most progressives had dreamed of. Still, a lingering lack of coordination made wartime mobilization in the United States difficult. It was not the Wilson administration's finest hour.

The Army Appropriation Act of August 1916 had created a Council of National Defense, which in turn led to the creation of more new wartime agencies. The United States Shipping Board, organized in January 1917, operated the emergency Fleet Corporation, which by the fall of 1918 had more than forty steel and ninety wooden ships coming off the ways monthly. The Lever Food and Fuel Control Act of August 1917 created a Food Administration, headed by Herbert Hoover, a future president, and a Fuel Administration, under Harry A. Garfield, son of a former president. Hoover, a mining engineer and former head of the Commission for Relief in Belgium, had the responsibility of raising production while reducing civilian use of foodstuffs. "Food will win the war" was the slogan. Hoover had coercive authority, but preferred to use voluntary methods and directed a propaganda campaign which "Hooverized" the country with "Wheatless Mondays," "Meatless Tuesdays," "Porkless Thursdays," the planting of victory gardens, and the use of leftovers. Garfield's Fuel Administration introduced the country to daylight saving time and "heatless Mondays."

The War Industries Board (WIB), established in July 1917, soon became the most important of all the mobilization agencies. It was headed by Bernard Baruch, a brilliant Wall Street speculator, who exercised a virtual dictatorship over the economy. Under Baruch the purchasing bureaus of the United States and Allied governments submitted their needs to the board, which set priorities and planned production. The board could allocate raw materials, tell manufacturers what to produce, order construction of new plants, and with the approval of the president, fix prices. For the sake of greater efficiency the WIB standardized product styles and designs.

The National War Labor Board (WLB), set up in April 1918 under former president Taft and the labor lawyer Frank P. Walsh, encouraged conciliation and mediated labor disputes that could not be settled otherwise. Where settlement proved impossible the government resorted to coercion. When the Smith and Wesson Arms Company of Springfield, Massachusetts, rejected a WLB decision, the War Department took over the plant. Munitions workers who struck in defiance of the board were threatened with loss of their draft exemptions. AFL president Samuel Gompers built goodwill with a policy of limiting labor disputes. A separate War Labor Policies Board, under a young lawyer, Felix Frankfurter, standardized policies regarding wages, hours, and working conditions in the war industries.

With the high wartime demand for labor and the movement of many men from the labor force into the armed services, labor was in a position to score solid advances in employment and wages, despite the rise in prices. A newly created United States Employment Ser-

Women taking the place of male workers on the Great Northern Railway, Great Falls, Montana, 1918.

vice placed some 4 million workers in war-related jobs. Labor unions benefited from expanded employment, the increased demand for labor, government policies favorable to collective bargaining, and the goodwill built by Gompers. From 1913 to 1918 the AFL increased its membership by 37 percent.

The government sought to mobilize more than economic life: the progressive gospel of efficiency suggested mobilizing public opinion as well. On April 14, 1917, eight days after the declaration of war, an executive order established the Committee on Public Information, composed of the secretaries of state, war, and the navy. Its executive head, George Creel, a Denver newsman, sold Wilson on the idea that the best approach to influencing public opinion was "expression, not repression"—propaganda instead of censorship. Creel's purpose was to organize a propaganda machine that would carry word of the Allies' war aims to the people, and above all to the enemy, where it might encourage the forces of moderation.

To sell the war Creel gathered a remarkable group of journalists, photographers, artists, entertainers, and others useful to his purpose. Charles Dana Gibson, James Montgomery Flagg, and other artists contributed posters. Historians turned out little "Red, White, and

Blue Books" with such titles as *How the War Came to America* and *German War Practices*. A film division produced such pictures as *The Beast of Berlin,* starring, as the spike-helmeted embodiment of Prussian villainy, Erich von Stroheim. Hardly any public group escaped a harangue by one of the 75,000 Four-Minute Men, organized to give short speeches on Liberty Bonds, the need to conserve food and fuel, and other timely topics. Creel took special pains to get propaganda into Germany, where it was more likely to accentuate the size of the American war effort, Wilson's idealism, and offers of an easy peace if the German people would rebel against their government.

CIVIL LIBERTIES   The ultimate irony in Creel's "expression, not repression" was that the one led to the other. By arousing public opinion to such a frenzy, the war effort channeled the zeal of progressivism into grotesque campaigns of "Americanism" and witch-hunting. Wilson had foreseen such consequences. "Once lead this people into war," he said, according to the editor of the New York *World,* "and they'll forget there even was such a thing as tolerance." Popular prejudice equated anything German with disloyalty. Symphonies refused to perform Bach and Beethoven, schools dropped courses in the German language, violinist Fritz Kreisler was prevented from giving concerts, and patriots translated "sauerkraut" into "liberty cabbage," "German measles" into "liberty measles," and "dachshunds" into "liberty pups." In New Orleans, Berlin Street became General Pershing Street.

While mobs hunted spies and chased rumors, the federal government stalked bigger game, with results often as absurd. Under the Espionage and Sedition Acts, criticism of government leaders and war policies was in effect outlawed. The Espionage Act of June 15, 1917, set penalties of up to $10,000 and twenty years in prison for those who gave aid to the enemy, who tried to incite insubordination, disloyalty, or refusal of duty in the armed services, or who circulated false reports and statements with intent to interfere with the war effort. The postmaster-general could bar from the mails anything which violated the act or which advocated treason, insurrection, or forcible resistance to any United States law. The Sedition Act of May 16, 1918, extended the penalties to those who did or said anything to obstruct the sale of Liberty Bonds or advocate cutbacks in production, and—just in case something had been overlooked—for saying, writing, or printing anything "disloyal, profane, scurrilous, or abusive" about the American form of government, the Constitution, or the army and navy.

The penalties applied under these acts by the Democratic successors of Jefferson exceeded in both absurdity and severity anything done under the infamous Alien and Sedition acts of John Adams. Under Wilson's Espionage and Sedition Acts more than 1,500 prosecutions resulted in more than 1,000 convictions. According to one professor of law: "It became criminal to advocate heavier taxation instead of bond issues, to state that conscription was unconstitutional though the Supreme Court had not yet held it valid, to say that the sinking of merchant vessels was legal, to urge that a referendum should have preceded our declaration of war, to say that war was contrary to the teachings of Christ." One patriotic film producer drew a ten-year sentence for making a film on the American Revolution, *The Spirit of Seventy-six*, because it risked stirring sentiment against the British!

The impact of the acts fell with most severity upon Socialists and other radicals. Victor Berger, Socialist congressman from Milwaukee, received a twenty-year sentence for editorials in the Milwaukee *Leader* which called the war a capitalist conspiracy. Eugene V. Debs, who had polled over 900,000 votes for president in 1912, ardently opposed American intervention, declaring that "I am opposed to every war but one; I am for that war heart and soul, and that is the world-wide revolution." He repeatedly urged American men to refuse to serve in the military, even though he knew he could be prosecuted for such remarks under the Espionage Act. "I would a thousand times rather be a free soul in jail than a sycophant and a coward in the streets," he told a Socialist gathering on June 16, 1918. He received his wish. Two weeks later Debs was arrested and eventually given a twenty-year prison sentence for encouraging draft resistance. In 1920, still in jail, he polled nearly 1 million votes for president. In Chicago over 100 members of the Industrial Workers of the World went on trial for opposing the war effort. All were found guilty, and the IWW never fully recovered from the blow.

In two important decisions just after the war the Supreme Court upheld the Espionage and Sedition Acts. *Schenck v. United States* (1919) upheld the conviction of a man for circulating antidraft leaflets among members of the armed forces. In this case Justice Holmes said: "Free speech would not protect a man in falsely shouting fire in a theater, and causing a panic." The act applied where there was "a clear and present danger" that speech in wartime might create evils Congress had a right to prevent. in *Abrams v. United States* (1919) the Court upheld the conviction of a man who circulated pamphlets opposing intervention in Russia. Here Holmes and Brandeis dissented. The "surreptitious publishing of a silly leaflet by an unknown man," they argued, posed no danger to government policy.

"The Decisive Power"

American troops played little more than a token role in the fighting until early 1918. Before that they were parceled out in quiet sectors mainly for training purposes. All through 1917 the Allies remained on the defensive and late in the year their situation turned desperate. In October the Italian lines collapsed and were overrun by Austrian forces. With the help of Allied troops from France the Italians finally held their ground. In November the Bolshevik Revolution overthrew the infant Russian Republic, and the new Soviet government dropped out of the war. With the Central Powers now free to concentrate their forces on the Western Front, the American war effort became a "race for France" to restore the balance of strength. By March 1918 American troops had assumed responsibility for only 4.5 miles of the Western Front. Anticipating a major German offensive, French premier Georges Clemenceau appealed to the Americans to accelerate their mobilization: "A terrible blow is imminent," he predicted to an American journalist. "Tell your Americans to come quickly."

THE WESTERN FRONT   On March 21, 1918, Clemenceau's prediction came true when the Germans began the first of several offensives to end the war before the Americans arrived in force. On the Somme River they broke through at the juncture of British and French sectors and penetrated thirty-five miles, nearly to the rail and supply center at Amiens. Farther north, the Germans struck on April 9 in Flanders, where the Allies still held a corner of Belgium, broke

Fresh troops moving to an advanced position on the front, France.

A gun crew firing on entrenched German positions, 1918.

through at Lille, and pushed the British back along a front from Ypres to Armentières. At this critical point, on April 14 the Allies made French general Ferdinand Foch the supreme commander of all Allied forces.

On May 27 the Germans began their next drive along the Aisne River, took Soissons, and pushed on to the Marne River along a forty-mile front. By May 1918 there were 1 million fresh American troops in Europe, and for the first time they made a difference. In a counterattack American forces retook Cantigny on May 28 and held it. A week later, on June 2–3, a marine brigade blocked the Germans at Belleau Wood. Army troops took Vaux, and opposed the Germans at Château-Thierry. Though these actions had limited military significance, their effect on morale was immense. Each was a solid American success, and together they reinforced Pershing's demand for a separate American army.

Before that could come to pass, the turning point in the western campaign came on July 15, 1918, in the Second Battle of the Marne. On both sides of Reims, the eastern end of a great bulge toward Paris, the Germans commenced their push against the French lines. Within three days they had shot their bolt, and the Allies, mainly with American troops, went on the offensive.

Soon the British, French, and Americans began to roll the German

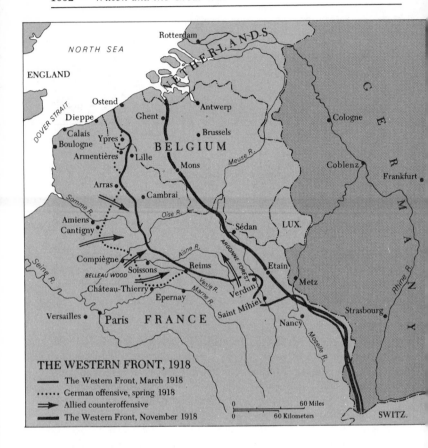

NORTH SEA

ENGLAND

THE WESTERN FRONT, 1918

— The Western Front, March 1918
••••• German offensive, spring 1918
⇒ Allied counteroffensive
━ The Western Front, November 1918

0   60 Miles
0   60 Kilometers

front back toward and into Belgium. Then on August 10 the first U.S. Army was organized with the consent of General Foch and assigned the task of liquidating the Germans at St. Mihiel, southeast of Verdun. There, on September 12, an army of more than 500,000 staged the first strictly American offensive of the war. Within three days the Germans had pulled back. The great Meuse-Argonne offensive, begun on September 26, then employed American divisions in a drive toward Sédan and its railroad, which supplied the entire German front. The largest American action of the war, it involved 1.2 million American troops and cost 117,000 American casualties, including 26,000 dead. Through October and early November the battle raged. By the first week of November the Americans were at the outskirts of Sédan and had brought the railroad under artillery fire. All along the front from Sédan to Flanders the Germans were in retreat. "America," wrote German general Erich Ludendorff, "thus became the decisive power in the war."

THE FOURTEEN POINTS   The approaching end of the war brought to the point of decision the question of war aims. Neither the Allies nor the Central Powers, despite Wilson's prodding, had stated openly what they hoped to gain. Wilson repeated that the Americans had no selfish ends. "We desire no conquest, no dominion," he stressed in his war message of 1917. "We seek no indemnities for ourselves, no material compensation for the sacrifices we shall freely make. We are but one of the champions of the rights of mankind." Unfortunately for his purpose, after the Bolsheviks seized power in November 1917 they published copies of secret treaties in which the Allies had promised territorial gains in order to win Italy, Romania, and Greece to their side. When an Interallied Conference in Paris late in 1917 failed to agree on a statement of aims, Colonel House advised Wilson to formulate his own.

During 1917 House had been drawing together an informal panel of American experts called "the Inquiry" to formulate plans for

Salvation Army worker writing a letter home for a wounded soldier.

Members of the U.S. 369th Infantry Regiment, which was awarded the Croix de Guerre for bravery at the battle of Meuse-Argonne.

peace. With advice from these experts, Wilson himself drew up a statement which would become the famous Fourteen Points. These he delivered to a joint session of Congress on January 8, 1918, "as the only possible program" for peace. The first five points in general terms called for open diplomacy, freedom of the seas, removal of trade barriers, reduction of armaments, and an impartial adjustment of colonial claims based on the interests of the populations involved. Most of the remainder called on the Central Powers to evacuate occupied lands and endorsed self-determination for various nationalities. Point 13 proposed an independent Poland with access to the sea. Point 14, the capstone in Wilson's thinking, championed a general association of nations to secure guarantees of independence and territorial integrity to all countries, great and small.

The Fourteen Points set forth a commitment in which Wilson persisted, but they also served the purposes of psychological warfare. One of their aims was to keep Russia in the war by a more liberal statement of purposes—a vain hope, as it turned out. Another was to reassure the Allied peoples that they were involved in a noble cause. A third was to drive a wedge between the governments of the Central Powers and their peoples by the offer of a reasonable peace.

Wilson's promise of "autonomous development" for the subject nationalities of Austria-Hungary (Point 10) might have weakened the polyglot Hapsburg Empire, though it was no part of his purpose to break up the empire. But the chaos into which central Europe descended in 1918, and the national aspirations of the empire's peoples, took matters out of his hands.

On September 29, 1918, German general Ludendorff advised his government to seek the best peace terms possible. On October 3, a new chancellor made the first German overtures for peace on the basis of the Fourteen Points. A month of diplomatic fencing followed between Colonel House and Allied representatives. Finally, a threat by House to pursue separate negotiations convinced the Allies to accept the Fourteen Points as a basis of peace, but with two significant reservations: they reserved the right to discuss freedom of the seas, and they demanded reparations for war damages.

Meanwhile the German home front was being torn apart by a loss of morale, culminating in a naval mutiny at Kiel. Germany's allies dropped out of the war: Bulgaria on September 29, 1918, Turkey on October 30, and Austria-Hungary on November 3. On November 9 the kaiser abdicated and a German Republic was proclaimed. On November 11, at 5 A.M., an armistice was signed. Six hours later, at

Celebration of the Armistice ending World War I, New York City, November 1918.

the eleventh hour of the eleventh day of the eleventh month, the guns fell silent. Under the Armistice the Germans had to evacuate occupied territories, pull back behind the Rhine, and surrender their naval fleet, railroad equipment, and other materials. The naval blockade would continue until a final peace settlement was reached, and the Germans were assured that the Fourteen Points would be the basis for the peace conference.

INTERVENTION IN RUSSIA   When the war broke out in 1914, Russia was one of the Allied powers. Over the next three years the Russians suffered some 5.5 million casualties. By 1917 there were shortages of ammunition for Russian troops and food for the Russian people. The czarist government was in disarray, and after the czar's abdication, first gave way to a provisional republican government which in turn succumbed in November 1917 to a revolution led by Vladimir Lenin and his Bolshevik party, who promised war-weary Russians "Peace, Land, and Bread."

Once in control of the government, the Bolsheviks unilaterally stopped fighting. With German troops deep in Russian territory, and with armies of "White" Russians organizing resistance to their power, on March 3, 1918, the Bolsheviks concluded a separate peace with Germany in the Treaty of Brest-Litovsk. In an effort to protect Allied supplies and to encourage anti-Bolshevik forces (the "Whites") in the developing Russian civil war, fourteen Allied nations sent forces into Russia's Arctic ports. On August 2, 1918, some 8,000 American troops landed there and two weeks later in eastern Siberia, where they remained until April 1920.

The Allied intervention in Russia failed. The Bolsheviks were able to consolidate their power, Russia took no further part in World War I, and did not participate in the peace settlement. The intervention also generated among Soviets long-lasting suspicion of the West.

The Fight for the Peace

WILSON'S ROLE   Wilson made a fateful decision to attend in person the peace conference which convened in Paris on January 18, 1919. It shattered precedent for a president to leave the country for so long a time, but it dramatized all the more Wilson's desire to ensure his goal of a lasting peace. From one viewpoint it was a shrewd move, for his prestige and determination made a difference in Paris. But he lost touch with developments at home. His progressive coalition was already unraveling under the pressures of wartime discontent. Western farmers complained about the government's control of wheat prices while southern cotton rode the wartime inflation. Eastern businessmen chafed at revenue policies designed, according to the New York *Sun*, "to pay for the war out of taxes raised north of the Mason and Dixon Line." Labor, despite manifest gains, was unhappy with inflation and the problems of reconversion to a peacetime economy.

In the midterm elections of 1918, Wilson made matters worse with a partisan appeal for a Democratic Congress to ensure support of his foreign policies. Republicans, who for the most part had supported war measures, took affront. In elections held on November 5, a week before the Armistice, the Democrats lost control of both houses of Congress. Wilson thus lost face at home just as he prepared to go abroad. With an opposition majority in the new Congress, he further weakened his standing by failure to involve a single prominent Republican in the peace negotiations. Humorist Will Rogers joked that Wilson was telling the Republicans, "I tell you what, we will split 50-50. I will go and you fellows can stay." Former president Taft groused that Wilson's real intention in going to Paris was "to hog the whole show."

When Wilson reached Europe in December 1918, enthusiastic demonstrations greeted him in Paris. The cheering millions had found in the American idealist a symbol of hope and a spokesman for

On his way to the Paris peace conference, Wilson was welcomed as a hero in Europe. Here he reviews a line of troops at Calais.

humanity. Their heartfelt support no doubt strengthened his hand at the conference, but Wilson had to deal with some tough-minded statesmen. The Paris conference comprised a body of delegates from all countries that had declared war or broken diplomatic relations with Germany. It was dominated at first by the Council of Ten (two each from Japan, Britain, France, Italy, and the United States), but ended with major decisions controlled by the Big Four: the prime ministers of Britain, France, and Italy, and the president of the United States. Japan restricted its interests to Asia and the Pacific. French premier Georges Clemenceau was a stern realist. He had little patience with Wilson's utopianism. "God gave us the Ten Commandments and we broke them," Clemenceau sneered. "Wilson gave us the Fourteen Points—we shall see." As the English economist John Maynard Keynes put it, Clemenceau had but one illusion—France. He insisted on harsh measures to weaken Germany and ensure French security. David Lloyd George of England was a gifted politician fresh from electoral victory on the slogan "Hang the Kaiser." Vittorio Orlando of Italy was there to pick up the spoils promised in the secret Treaty of London (1915) and, if possible, the Adriatic port of Fiume.

THE LEAGUE OF NATIONS   Wilson carried the point that his cherished League of Nations must come first, in the conference and in the treaty. Whatever compromises he might have to make, whatever

Wilson conferring with French prime minister Clemenceau at the Versailles conference.

mistakes might result, Wilson believed that a permanent agency of collective security would assure international stability. Wilson presided over the commission set up to work out a charter for the League.

Article X of the covenant, which Wilson called "the heart of the League," pledged members to consult on military and economic sanctions against aggressors. The use of arms would be a last (and an improvised) resort. The League, it was assumed, would exercise enormous moral influence, but when push came to shove it would have little force at its disposal. The League structure allowed each member an equal voice in the Assembly; the Big Five (Britain, France, Italy, Japan, and the United States) and four other nations would make up the Council; the administrative staff in Geneva would make up the Secretariat; and finally, a Permanent Court of International Justice (set up in 1921 and usually called the World Court) could "hear and determine any dispute of an international character." All treaties had to be registered with the Secretariat to be valid.

On February 14, 1919, Wilson reported the finished draft of the League covenant to the plenary session of the conference and departed the next day for a month-long visit home to see after routine business. Already he faced rumblings of opposition, and shortly before his return to Paris, Senator Henry Cabot Lodge announced that the covenant was unacceptable "in the form now proposed." His statement bore the signatures of thirty-nine Republican senators or senators-elect, more than enough to block ratification. That evening Wilson confidently retorted: "When the treaty comes back, gentlemen on this side will find the covenant not only in it, but so many threads of the treaty tied to the covenant that you cannot dissect the covenant from the treaty without destroying the whole vital structure."

TERRITORY AND REPARATIONS Yet, back in Paris, Wilson found it politic to seek amendments to meet the objections at home. These provided that any member nation could withdraw from the League on two years' notice, that none could be required to take a mandate to administer former enemy possessions now under League supervision, that domestic affairs remained outside League jurisdiction, and that regional understandings like the Monroe Doctrine would remain undisturbed. All these went pretty much without saying, but the French exploited Wilson's discomfort to press for harsh measures: territorial concessions and reparations from Germany to keep it weak for years to come. Wilson clashed sharply with Clemenceau, and after the president threatened to leave the conference they settled on a demilitarized Rhineland (up to 50 kilometers [31 miles] beyond the river), Allied occupation of this zone for fifteen years, and League administration of the Saar Basin. France could use Saar coal mines for fifteen years, after which a plebiscite would determine the region's status.

In other territorial matters Wilson had to compromise his principle of national self-determination. There was in fact no way to make boundaries correspond to ethnic divisions. The folk wanderings of centuries had left mixed populations scattered through central Europe. In some areas, moreover, national self-determination yielded to other interests: the Polish Corridor, for instance, gave Poland its much-needed outlet to the sea through German territory, and the South Tyrol, home for some 200,000 German-speaking Austrians, gave Italy a more defensible frontier at the Brenner Pass. One part of the Austro-Hungarian Empire became Czechoslovakia, which included the German-speaking Sudetenland, an area favored with good defenses. Another part of the empire united with Serbia to create the kingdom of Yugoslavia. Still other substantial parts passed to Poland (Galicia), Romania (Transylvania), and Italy (Trentino and Trieste).

Where political decisions did not override considerations of nationality the Big Four could more easily follow recommendations from the committees of experts who made exhaustive studies of history, geography, and populations. In a few cases issues in doubt were decided by plebiscites of the people themselves. All in all, despite aberrations, the new boundaries more nearly followed the ethnic divisions of Europe than the prewar lines.

The discussion of reparations (payments by the vanquished to the victors) began after the French felt they had already given up a great deal in territorial matters. Britain and France both sought reparations, and the French wanted enough to cripple Germany. Discussions of the issue were among the longest and most bitter at the conference. Despite a pre-Armistice agreement that Germany would be liable only for civilian damages, Clemenceau and Lloyd George proposed reparations for the entire cost of the war, including pensions. On this point Wilson made perhaps his most fateful concessions. He accepted in the treaty a clause by which Germany confessed responsibility for the war and thus for its entire costs. The "war guilt" clause was an offense to all Germans and a source of persistent bitterness. A down payment was to be extracted from Germany immediately; in 1921 a Reparations Commission estimated that Germany owed $33 billion in all.

On May 7, 1919, the victorious powers presented the treaty to the German delegates, who returned three weeks later with 443 pages

EUROPE AFTER
VERSAILLES
.... 1914 boundaries
▓ New nations
▨ Plebiscite areas
▦ Occupied area

of criticism protesting that the terms violated the Fourteen Points. A few changes were made, but when the Germans still refused to sign Marshal Foch prepared to move his army across the Rhine. On June 28 the Germans gave in and signed the treaty in the Hall of Mirrors at Versailles. Treaties with the lesser powers followed the arrangements already made.

WILSON'S LOSS AT HOME Wilson returned home with the Versailles Treaty on July 8, 1919. Two days later he called on the Senate to accept "this great duty." The force of Wilson's idealism struck deep, and he returned amid a great clamor of popular support. A third of the state legislatures had endorsed the League, as had thirty-three of forty-eight governors. Senator Henry Cabot Lodge, chairman of the Senate Foreign Relations Committee, later said: "What I may call the vocal classes of the community . . . were friendly to the League as it stood and were advocating it."

But Lodge himself harbored doubts. He did not wish the United States to withdraw from world affairs, but felt that the outcome at Versailles exhibited the weakness in "the beautiful scheme of making mankind virtuous by a statute or a written constitution." Americans, thought Lodge, were too prone to promise more than they could deliver when great principles entailed great sacrifices. Foreign policy would have to be built up from what the public would sustain rather than be imposed from above. A staunch Republican with an intense dislike for Wilson, Lodge sharpened his partisan knives. He knew the undercurrents already stirring up opposition to the treaty: the resentment of German, Italian, and Irish groups in the United States, the disappointment of liberals at Wilson's compromises on reparations and territories, the distractions of demobilization and the resulting domestic problems, and the revival of isolationism. Lodge's close friend, Theodore Roosevelt, still a popular figure, lambasted the League, noting that he keenly distrusted a "man who cares for other nations as much as his own."

Others agreed. In the Senate a group of "irreconcilables," fourteen Republicans and two Democrats, were unwilling to allow America entrance to the League on any terms. They were mainly western or midwestern progressives who stood on principle. The irreconcilables would be useful to Lodge's purpose, but he belonged to a larger group of "reservationists" who were ready to go partway with Wilson, but insisted on limiting American participation in the League and its actions. Wilson of course said that he had already amended the covenant to these ends, pointing out that with a veto in the League Council the United States could not be obligated to do anything against its will.

Lodge resorted to delays. First he arranged a reading of the entire treaty to a nearly empty committee room—the 264 pages consumed two weeks—then held lengthy hearings in which every critic could get in his licks. Lodge, who set more store by the old balance of power than by the new idea of collective security, brought forward a set of amendments, or reservations. Wilson responded by agreeing to interpretive reservations, but to nothing that would reopen the

Senator Henry Cabot Lodge, leader of the opposition to the League.

negotiations. He especially opposed weakening Article X, which provided for collective action against aggression.

By September, with momentum for the treaty slackening, Wilson decided to go to the people and, as he put it, "purify the wells of public opinion." Bold appeals to public opinion had helped get the New Freedom through Congress—why not the treaty? Against the advice of doctors and friends he set forth on a swing through the Midwest to the West Coast, pounding out speeches on his typewriter between stops. In all he traveled 8,000 miles in twenty-two days, gave thirty-two major addresses and eight informal ones, refuted his opponents, and voiced warnings. "Everywhere we go, the train when it stops is surrounded with little children," he said in Tacoma, Washington. "These glad youngsters with flags in their hands—I pray God that they may never have to carry that flag upon the battlefield!"

For a while he seemed to be regaining the initiative, but then his body rebelled. Six years as president, during which he wrestled with major issues of war and peace, had depleted his resources. After a speech at Pueblo, Colorado, on September 25, the signs of exhaustion were so clear that his doctor canceled the tour and hurried the president's train back to Washington. On October 2, 1919, Wilson suffered a severe stroke and paralysis on his left side, leaving him an invalid for the rest of his life. For more than seven months he did not meet the cabinet, and was kept isolated from all but the most essential business by a protective wife. The illness intensified his traits of stubbornness and hostility. He might have done better to stay in the White House and secure the best compromise possible, but now he refused to yield anything. As he scoffed to an aide, "Let Lodge compromise." Wilson ended up committing what one historian called the supreme infanticide, the destruction of his own brainchild.

Between November 7 and 19 the Senate adopted fourteen of Lodge's reservations, most having to do with the League. Wilson especially opposed the reservation to Article X which, he said, "does not provide for ratification but, rather, for the nullification of the treaty." As a result the Wilsonians found themselves thrown into an unlikely combination with irreconcilables who opposed the treaty under any circumstances. The Senate vote was 39 for and 55 against. On the question of taking the treaty without reservations, irreconcilables and reservationists combined to defeat ratification again, with 38 for and 53 against.

The American public, however, would not permit the treaty to be laid aside because senators professing support could not reach agreement on a few reservations. In the face of public reaction the Senate voted to reconsider. But the stricken Wilson remained adamant:

Three Senators Refuse the Lady a Seat. *Americans reacted against the Senate's defeat of the Versailles peace treaty.*

"Either we should enter the league fearlessly, accepting with responsibility and not fearing the role of leadership which we now enjoy, contributing our efforts toward establishing a just and permanent peace, or we should retire as gracefully as possible from the great concert of powers by which the world was saved." On March 19, 1920, twenty-one Democrats deserted Wilson and joined the reservationists, but the treaty once again fell short of a two-thirds majority by a vote of 49 yeas and 35 nays. The real winner was the smallest of the three groups in the Senate, neither the Wilsonians nor the reservationists but the irreconcilables.

Wilson still nourished the hope that he could make the next presidential election a "solemn referendum" on the League of Nations. He deluded himself, as Bryan had in 1900, for presidential elections are touched by many issues. When Congress declared the war at an end by joint resolution on May 20, 1920, Wilson vetoed the action; it was not until July 2, 1921, after he left office, that a joint resolution ended the state of war with Germany and Austria-Hungary. Peace treaties with Germany, Austria, and Hungary were ratified on October 18, 1921, but by then Warren Gamaliel Harding was president of the United States.

LURCHING FROM WAR TO PEACE

The Versailles Treaty, for all the time it took in the Senate, was but one issue clamoring for public attention in the turbulent period after the war. On the domestic scene Wilson's leadership was missing. He had been preoccupied by the war and the League, and once broken by his illness, became strangely grim and peevish. His administration floundered through its last two years.

Demobilization proceeded without plan, indeed without much sense that a plan was needed once the war was over. The War Industries Board closed shop on January 1, 1919, and vanished so quickly that Bernard Baruch paid out of his pocket travel expenses home for some of his aides. The sudden cancellation of war contracts left workers and businessmen to cope with reconversion on their own. By April 1919 the armed forces were discharging about 4,000 men daily, and within a year the process was nearly complete.

THE SPANISH FLU Amid the confusion of postwar life many Americans confronted a virulent menace that produced far more casualties than the war itself. It became known as the Spanish flu and its contagion spread across the globe. Erupting in the spring of 1918 and lasting a year, the pandemic killed more than 22 million people, twice as many as the number who died in World War I. In the United States alone the flu accounted for more than 500,000 deaths, five times the number of combat deaths in France. "Never before," a writer in *Science* magazine observed in 1919, had there been "a catastrophe at once so sudden, so devastating and so universal."

The origins of the epidemic remain a mystery. A severe outbreak occurred in China and was supposedly carried to Europe when 200,000 Chinese laborers were shipped to France in 1917 to help with the war effort. The disease spread rapidly from army to army and soon rolled across the Alps and Pyrenees into Italy and Spain. As many as 8 million Spaniards contracted the virus in May and June of 1918.

American servicemen returning from France brought the flu with them, and it raced through the congested army camps and naval bases. At Fort Riley, Kansas, 522 soldiers contracted the virus and were hospitalized during one week in March 1918. Still, no one seemed alarmed, for the flu remained a common if severe ailment. But then the hospitalized men started dying by the dozens, and it became obvious that this was no ordinary flu virus. In addition to the usual symptoms—coughing, chills, fever, body aches—the afflicted suffered from vomiting, dizziness, labored breathing, nosebleeds, and profuse sweating. Many contracted pneumonia as well, and a startling number of patients died. Most surprising was the fact that this flu epidemic exacted an unusually high toll among young adults rather than among children and the elderly. In fact, 43,000 American servicemen died of influenza in 1918.

By September 1918 the epidemic had spread into the civilian

population. In that month alone 10,000 Americans died from the disease. It was a baffling development. "Nobody seemed to know what the disease was, where it came from or how to stop it," observed the editors of *Science* magazine in 1919. Evangelist Billy Sunday blamed the plague on the Germans, charging that they had brought it across the Atlantic on submarines: "There's nothing short of hell they haven't stooped to do since the war began. Darn their hides!" Municipal health officers began fining people for spitting on the sidewalks or for sneezing without a handkerchief. Millions of people began wearing surgical masks to work. Phone booths were locked up, as were other public facilities such as dance halls, pool rooms, and theaters. Even churches and saloons in many communities were declared off-limits. Still, the death toll rose. In October another 196,000 succumbed. In Philadelphia 528 people were buried in a single day. From September 1918 to June 1919 some 675,000 Americans died of flu and pneumonia and a quarter of the population had contracted the illness. Life insurance companies nearly went bankrupt, hospitals were besieged, and cemeteries soon ran out of burial space.

Yet by the spring of 1919 the pandemic had run its course. It ended as suddenly—and as inexplicably—as it had begun. Although another outbreak occurred in the winter of 1920, the population had grown more resistant to its assaults. No disease, plague, war, famine, or natural catastrophe in world history killed so many people in such a short time. The most remarkable aspect of the flu pandemic was that people for the most part took it in stride. "Perhaps the most notable peculiarity of the influenza epidemic," wrote a *New York Times* editor in November 1918, "is the fact that it has been attended by no traces of panic or even of excitement." People seemed resigned to biological forces beyond their control while issues of war and peace in Europe and the home-front economy continued to dominate the headlines.

THE ECONOMIC TRANSITION   Events once again bore out the adage, attributed to Bismarck, that there seems to be a special providence for fools, drunkards, and the United States of America. An unforeseen postwar boom eased the country over the difficult economic transition from war to peace. The boom fed on markets renewed by pent-up demand and wartime savings, and on overseas trade left open because German and British shippers had been weakened by wartime damage. Both farmers and businessmen benefited. The $2 billion cotton crop, which resulted from a happy mix of high prices and high production in 1919, was the most valuable ever. Reports from the southern countryside marveled at the unaccustomed wealth to be found among tenants and sharecroppers, but this was soon ended by a drop in farm prices in 1920 and a general business slump in 1921.

Government quickly extricated itself from "War Socialism" in communications and transport. Telegraph, telephone, cable, and radio facilities were back in private hands by August 1919. On Christmas Eve 1919 Wilson announced that the railroads would go back to their owners on March 1, and Congress responded quickly with a law that undertook to retain some of the advantages of unified operation. Unlike previous railroad laws, it gave up the pretense of enforcing competition and instead encouraged consolidation. The ICC was authorized to work out plans to eliminate wasteful competition. It acquired in addition powers over the issuance of railroad securities, the construction or abandonment of track, and the fixing of minimum as well as maximum rates.

The problems of postwar readjustment were worsened by general labor unrest. Prices continued to rise after the war, and discontented workers, released from wartime constraints, were more willing to strike for their demands. In 1919, more than 4 million workers went out in thousands of disputes. Some workers in the East won their

"Shoeless Joe" Jackson. *The anxieties and illegalities Americans suffered in 1919 touched the national pastime as well, when the World Series was tainted by a scandal involving the Chicago White Sox and their star center fielder, "Shoeless Joe."*

demands early in the year, but after a general strike in Seattle public opinion began to turn hostile. The Seattle mayor denounced the walkout of 60,000 workers as evidence of Bolshevik influence. The strike lasted only five days, but public alarm at the affair damaged the cause of unions across the country.

An AFL campaign to organize steelworkers suffered from charges of radicalism against its leader, William Z. Foster, a former Bryanite who had joined the Socialists in 1900 and later emerged as a Communist. Attention to Foster's radicalism obscured the squalid conditions which had marked the steel industry since the Homestead Strike of 1892. The twelve-hour day, often combined with a seven-day week, was common for steelworkers. On September 22, 1919, after U.S. Steel refused to talk, about 340,000 men walked out. But the union succumbed to a back-to-work movement and gave up the strike four months later. When information about conditions became widely known, public opinion turned in favor of the steelworkers, but too late: the strike was over. Steelworkers remained unorganized until the 1930s.

The most celebrated postwar labor dispute was the Boston Police Strike. If less significant than the steel strike in the numbers involved, it inadvertently launched a presidential career. When a local society of police, the Boston Social Club, applied to the AFL for a union charter, the Boston police commissioner dismissed eight members. A citizens' committee named by the mayor to investigate the dismissals suggested arbitration and reinstatement of the fired officers, but the commissioner responded by firing nineteen more. On September 9, 1919, most of Boston's police force went out on strike. Governor Calvin Coolidge mobilized the National Guard to keep order, and after four days the strikers were ready to return, but the commissioner refused to take them. When Samuel Gompers appealed that they be reinstated, Coolidge responded in words that suddenly turned him into a national figure: "There is no right to strike against the public safety by anybody, anywhere, any time."

RACIAL FRICTION   The summer of 1919 also brought a season of race riots, North and South. What black leader James Weldon Johnson called "the Red Summer" ("Red" here signified blood) began in July, when whites invaded the black section of Longview, Texas, in search of a teacher who had allegedly accused a white woman of a liaison with a black man. They burned shops and houses and ran several blacks out of town. A week later in Washington reports of attacks on white women aroused white mobs and for four days gangs of white and black rioters waged race war in the streets until soldiers

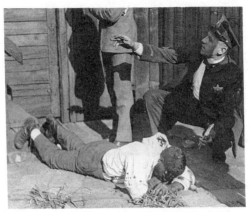

A victim of racial rioting in Chicago, July 1919.

and driving rains ended the fighting. These were but preliminaries to the Chicago riot of late July in which 38 people were killed and 537 injured. The climactic disorders of the summer occurred in the rural area around Elaine, Arkansas, where black tenant farmers tried to organize a union. According to official reports 5 whites and 25 blacks died, but whites told one reporter in the area that more than 100 blacks died. Altogether twenty-five race riots took place in 1919, and more threatened.

THE RED SCARE   Public reaction to the wave of strikes and riots was influenced by the impact of the Bolshevik Revolution. A minority of radicals thought America's domestic turbulence, like that in Russia, was the first scene in a drama of world revolution. A much larger public was persuaded that they might be right. After all, a tiny faction in Russia had exploited confusion to impose its will. In 1919 the Socialist party, already depleted by wartime persecution, suffered the further defection of radicals inspired by the Russian example. Left-wing members formed the Communist and the short-lived Communist Labor parties. Wartime hysteria against all things German was readily transformed into a postwar Red Scare.

Fears of revolution might have remained latent except for the actions of a lunatic fringe. In April 1919 the post office intercepted nearly forty bombs addressed to various prominent citizens. One slipped through and blew off the hands of a Georgia senator's maid. In June another destroyed the front of Attorney-General A. Mitchell

Palmer's house in Washington. Assistant Navy Secretary Franklin D. Roosevelt, who had just entered the house across the street, telephoned the police. The random violence of these criminals formed no part of Bolshevik tactics, but many Americans saw Red on all sides and condoned attacks on all kinds of minorities in retaliation.

Soon the government itself was promoting witch-hunts. Attorney-General Palmer, a Pennsylvania Quaker and once a progressive congressman with pro-labor leanings, harbored an entrenched distrust of aliens and a strong desire for the presidency. In June 1919 the Justice Department decided to deport radical aliens, and Palmer set up as the head of the new General Intelligence Division the young J. Edgar Hoover, who began to collect an index file on radicals. Raids began on November 7, 1919, when agents swooped down on the Union of Russian Workers in twelve cities. On December 22 the transport ship *Buford*, dubbed the "Soviet Ark," left New York for Finland with 249 people, including assorted anarchists, criminals, and public charges. All were deported to Russia without benefit of a court hearing. On January 2, 1920, a series of raids by police in dozens of cities swept up some 5,000 suspects, many taken from their houses without arrest warrants, of whom more than half were kept in custody. That same month the New York legislature expelled five duly elected Socialist members.

Basking in popular approval, Palmer continued to warn of the Red menace, but like other fads and alarms, the mood passed. Widespread disruptions predicted for May 1 never took place. By the summer of 1920 the Red Scare had begun to evaporate. Communist revolutions in Europe died out, leaving Bolshevism isolated in Russia; bombings tapered off; the strike wave and race riots

Whose Country Is This, Anyhow?
A 1920 cartoon reflects popular alarm at the "red menace" in America.

receded. Congress refused to pass peacetime sedition bills, although thirty-two states enacted criminal laws which made it illegal to join groups that called for the overthrow of the government by force. The attorney-general and his mimics began to seem more threatening to civil liberties than a handful of radicals. By September 1920, when a bomb explosion at the corner of Broad and Wall streets in New York killed thirty-eight people, Americans were ready to take it for what it was, the work of a crazed mind and not the start of a revolution. The Red Scare nevertheless left a lasting mark on American life. Part of its legacy was the continuing crusade for "100 percent Americanism" and restrictions on immigration. It left a stigma on labor unions and contributed to the anti-union open-shop campaign—the "American Plan," its sponsors called it. But for many Americans the chief residue of the Great War and its disordered aftermath was the profound disillusionment which pervaded American thought in the postwar decades.

FURTHER READING

Frederick S. Calhoun's *Power and Principle: Armed Intervention in Wilsonian Foreign Policy* (1986) surveys one aspect of Wilsonian diplomacy. For the Mexican intervention, consult P. Edward Haley's *Revolution and Intervention: The Diplomacy of Taft and Wilson with Mexico, 1910–1917* (1970) and Robert E. Quirk's *An Affair of Honor: Woodrow Wilson and the Occupation of Vera Cruz* (1962).°
A recent overview of events covered in this chapter is Robert H. Ferrell's *Woodrow Wilson and World War I, 1917–1921* (1985).° Different interpretations of why the United States entered the First World War appear in George F. Kennan's *American Diplomacy, 1900–1950* (1951)° and William Appleman Williams's *The Tragedy of American Diplomacy* (rev. ed., 1972).° Otis L. Graham, Jr.'s *The Great Campaigns: Reform and War in America, 1900–1928* (1971)° shows the link between progressive reform and the impulse for war.
A number of scholars concentrate on the neutrality issue. Arthur S. Link, Wilson's biographer, is sympathetic to the ideals of the president in *Woodrow Wilson: Revolution, War, and Peace* (1979).° For a more critical view, see Ross Gregory's *The Origins of American Intervention in the First World War* (1971).°
Edward M. Coffman's *The War to End All Wars: The American Military Experience in World War I* (1968)° is a detailed presentation of America's military involvement. David M. Kennedy's *Over Here: The First World War and American Society* (1980)° and Daniel M. Smith's *The Great Departure: The United States in World War I, 1914–1920* (1965)° survey the impact of

°These books are available in paperback editions.

the war on the home front. Maurine Weiner Greenwald's *Women, War, and Work: The Impact of World War I on Women Workers in the United States* (1980)° and Barbara Steinson's *American Women's Activism in World War I* (1982) discuss the role of women. Richard Polenberg's *Fighting Faiths: The Abrams Case, the Supreme Court, and Free Speech* (1987) examines the prosecution of a case under the 1918 Sedition Act.

The tensions of the immediate postwar years are chronicled in Robert K. Murray's *Red Scare: A Study of National Hysteria, 1919–1920* (1955)° and William Tuttle, Jr.'s *Race Riot: Chicago and the Red Summer of 1919* (1970).° Labor tensions are examined in David E. Brody's *Labor in Crisis: The Steel Strike of 1919* (1965) and Francis Russell's *A City in Terror: 1919, the Boston Police Strike* (1975). On the Spanish flu, see Alfred W. Crosby's *America's Forgotten Pandemic: The Influenza of 1918* (1990).

How American diplomacy fared in the making of peace has received considerable attention. In addition to the Link book on Wilson, the role of the president is treated in Arno J. Mayer's *Politics and Diplomacy in Peacemaking: Containment and Counterrevolution at Versailles, 1918–1919* (1967) and N. Gordon Levin, Jr.'s *Woodrow Wilson and World Politics: America's Response to War and Revolution* (1968).° The treaty controversy is handled in Thomas A. Bailey's *Woodrow Wilson and the Great Betrayal* (1945).

26

THE MODERN TEMPER

Reaction in the Twenties

On August 5, 1914, the day after Britain entered the Great War, the American novelist Henry James, living in London, wrote to a friend: "The plunge of civilization into this abyss of blood and darkness . . . so gives away the whole long age during which we have supposed the world to be . . . gradually bettering, that to have to take it all now for what the treacherous years were all the while really making for and *meaning* is too tragic for any words." The war, as James foresaw, dealt a shattering blow to what another author called "the prevailing . . . myth" that civilization was progressing, moving forward, a myth which had dominated the public consciousness for a century and which had been so powerful a stimulant to progressivism. The fighting imprinted on modern memory scenes of carnage worse than those once consigned to a barbaric past. The postwar disillusionment hastened a growing challenge to all the old values. Ernest Hemingway wrote in his war novel *A Farewell to Arms* (1929) that "abstract words such as glory, honor, courage or hallow were obscene beside the concrete names of villages, the number of roads, the names of rivers, the numbers of regiments and dates." Young men had simply gone off to die for a European civilization that was, in the words of the poet Ezra Pound, "an old bitch gone in the teeth, . . . a botched civilization."

To many others, watching the postwar wave of strikes, bombings, red scares, and race riots, it seemed that America had entered a frightening new terrain of diversity and change in which there lurked a thousand threats to the older truths. And those threats centered in the polyglot cities teeming with immigrants and foreign ideas. The defensive mood of the 1920s fed on a growing tendency to connect American nationalism with nativism, Anglo-Saxon racism, and militant Protestantism.

NATIVISM   The foreign connections of so many radicals strengthened the sense that sedition was chiefly foreign-made. That it went hand in hand with crime seemed confirmed by the most celebrated case of the times, which involved two Italian-born anarchists, Nicola Sacco and Bartolomeo Vanzetti. Arrested on May 5, 1920, for a payroll robbery and murder in South Braintree, Massachusetts, they were brought for trial before a judge who privately referred to the defendants as "those anarchist bastards." In the courtroom, wrote Felix Frankfurter of the Harvard Law School, the judge allowed the prosecutor to exploit the Communist hysteria and "thus to divert and pervert the jury's mind." The question of the two men's guilt remains in doubt, though not the bias of the court, and the belief persists that they were sentenced for their beliefs and their ethnic origins rather than for any crime they had committed. The case became a great radical and liberal cause célèbre of the 1920s, but despite pleas for mercy and public demonstrations around the world on behalf of the two men, they went to the electric chair on August 23, 1927, their last appeals denied.

The surging postwar nativism generated new efforts to restrict immigration. This campaign was reinforced by a pseudo-scientific

Sacco and Vanzetti. *From a series of paintings by Ben Shahn, 1931–1932.*

racism which found expression in a widely read book: Madison Grant's *The Passing of the Great Race* (1916)—the great race being the Nordics of northern Europe, threatened by the Slavic and Latin people of eastern and southern Europe. The flow of immigrants, slowed by the war, rose again at its end. From June 1920 to June 1921 more than 800,000 persons entered the country, 65 percent of them from southern and eastern Europe; and more were on the way.

An alarmed Congress passed the Emergency Immigration Act of 1921, which restricted new arrivals each year to 3 percent of the foreign-born of any nationality as shown in the 1910 census. A new quota law in 1924 reduced the number to 2 percent based on the 1890 census, which included fewer of the "new" immigrants. This law set a permanent limitation, which became effective in 1929, of slightly over 150,000 per year based on the "national origins" of the American people as of 1920. Since national origins could not be determined with precision, officials were called upon to use available statistics on migration, natural increase, and "such other data as may be found reliable." However inexact the quotas, the purpose clearly was to tilt the balance in favor of the old immigration from northern and western Europe, which was assigned about 85 percent of the total. The law completely excluded people from East Asia—a gratuitous insult to the Japanese, who were already kept out by their "Gentlemen's Agreement" with Theodore Roosevelt.

On the other hand the law left the gate open to new arrivals from Western Hemisphere countries, so that an ironic consequence was a great increase in the United States' Hispanic Catholic population. The legal arrivals from Mexico peaked at 89,000 in 1924. Lower figures after that date merely reflect policies of the Mexican government to clamp down on the outflow of labor and stronger American enforcement of old regulations like the 1882 exclusion of those immigrants likely to become public charges. Uncounted illegal immigrants continued to come, however, in response to southwestern agriculture's demand for "stoop" labor. People of Latin American descent (chiefly Mexicans, Puerto Ricans, and Cubans) became the fastest-growing ethnic minority in the country.

THE KLAN   During the postwar years the nativist tradition took on a new form, a revived Ku Klux Klan modeled on the group founded during Reconstruction, but, in a striking departure from its predecessor, devoted to "100 percent Americanism" and restricted in membership to native-born white Protestants. The new Klan was determined to protect its warped notion of the American way of life not only from African-Americans, but also from Roman Catholics, Jews, and other immigrants. America was no melting pot, the Klan's founder William J. Simmons warned: "It is a garbage can! . . . When the hordes of aliens walk to the ballot box and their votes outnumber yours, then that alien horde has got you by the throat." A habitual joiner and promoter of fraternal orders, Simmons had gathered a hooded group atop Stone Mountain near Atlanta on Thanksgiving night, 1915. There, "bathed in the sacred glow of the fiery cross, the invisible empire was called from its slumber of half a century to take up a new task." It was a "living memorial" to the earlier Klan, but also something of a fraternal order with an elaborate ceremonial and secret passwords.

In going nativist, the Klan had gone national and was no longer restricted to the South. Its appeal reached areas as widely scattered as Oregon and Maine. It flourished mainly among the uprooted and insecure newcomers to the cities and towns. The robes, the flaming crosses, the eerie processionals, the kneeling recruits, the occult liturgies—all tapped a deep American urge toward mystery and brought drama in to the dreary routine of a thousand communities.

At the same time the Klan was paradoxically a reflex against the strange and exotic, against shifting moral standards, the declining influence of churches, the broadmindedness of cities and colleges. It represented a degradation of the hopes aroused by progressivism and the war. In the Southwest it became more than anything else a moral crusade. "It is going to drive the bootleggers forever out of this land," declared a Texan. "It is going to bring clean moving pictures . . . clean literature . . . break up roadside parking . . . enforce the laws . . . protect homes." All these things it set out to achieve by nightriding and floggings. Enemies of the Klan, said a Kentucky Klansman, were uncertain who its members were, or how many. "It is the invisible something that gets their goat."

Simmons, always something of a dreamer, betrayed a fatal inability to control the tough customers attracted to the Klan by the scramble for power and booty. In 1922 a revolt toppled Simmons who, threatened with violence, abdicated to a new Imperial Wizard, Hiram Wesley Evans, a dentist from Dallas. The hooded order became a political power in thousands of communities. Officeholders either cultivated the Klan or were struck dumb on the subject. But the Klan never achieved much politically beyond securing the dismissal of a Catholic here and there or afflicting officials with blindness to floggings. Diligent research has uncovered only one Klan-inspired law, an Oregon act requiring Catholic children to attend public schools—and it was found unconstitutional. The order had neither a political program nor a dynamic leadership. Unlike kindred movements in postwar Europe, it conjured up no Mussolini, no Hitler.

In 1925 the Ku Klux Klan staged a 40,000-man parade down Pennsylvania Avenue in Washington, D.C.

Estimates of its peak membership, probably inflated, range from 3 million to 8 million, but the Klan's influence decayed as quickly as its numbers grew. For one thing, the Klan suffered from a decline in nativist excitement after passage of the 1924 immigration law. For another, it suffered recurrent factional quarrels and schisms. And its moral pretensions were tarnished by the violence it perpetrated, and above all by a sordid scandal involving the Indiana Klan leader. Grand Dragon David C. Stevenson organized a political machine which for a while dominated the state through control of the Republican party, but the whole thing collapsed in 1925 after he forced a State House secretary aboard a train and fatally assaulted her. Convicted of second-degree murder, Stevenson received a life sentence. When the governor (elected as his stooge) refused to pardon him, Stevenson drew from a "little black box" the evidence that sent a congressman and several other officials to jail. The governor barely escaped a bribery charge. The "best people" of many towns had joined what they thought was an agency of reform, but drifted away as the Klan became a cloak for immorality and corruption; in that respect, at least, the organization repeated the history of its ancestor.

FUNDAMENTALISM   While the Klan saw a threat mainly in the alien menace, many adherents of the old-time religion saw threats from modernism in the churches: new ideas that the Bible should be studied in the light of modern scholarship (the "higher criticism") or that it could be reconciled with evolution. Fearing that such notions had infected schools and even pulpits, orthodox Christians took on a new militancy in fundamentalism. The movement had acquired a name and definition from a series of pamphlets, *The Fundamentals* (1910), published in Los Angeles. Armed with the "Five Points" fundamental to the faith—an inerrant Bible, the Virgin Birth, the Vicarious Atonement, the Resurrection, and the Second Coming of Christ—the fundamentalists were distinguished less by their belief in a faith which many others shared than by their posture of hostility toward any other belief.

Among rural fundamentalist leaders only William Jennings Bryan had the following, prestige, and eloquence to make the movement a popular crusade. Although advancing age had cost Bryan his commanding physical presence, he remained as optimistic, pious, and silvery-tongued as ever. In 1921 Bryan sparked a drive for laws to prohibit the teaching of evolution. He denounced Darwin with the same zeal he had once directed against McKinley. Many old-time admirers thought he had gone over to the forces of reaction, but to Bryan's mind the old reformer still spoke through the new fundamentalist. "Evolution," he said, "by denying the need or possibility of spiritual regeneration, discourages all reforms, for reform is always based upon the regeneration of the individual." Anti-evolution bills began to turn up in the hoppers of legislatures in the Midwest and South, but the only victories came in the South—and there were few of those. Some officials took direct action without legislation. Governor Miriam "Ma" Ferguson of Texas ordered elimination from state schools of textbooks upholding Darwinism. "I am a Christian mother," she declared, "and I am not going to let that kind of rot go into Texas schoolbooks."

The climax came in Tennessee, where in 1925 the legislature passed a bill outlawing the teaching of evolution in public schools and colleges. The governor, unwilling to endanger a pending school program, signed the bill with the hope that it would probably never be applied. He was wrong. In Dayton, Tennessee, citizens convinced a young high school teacher, John T. Scopes, to accept an offer from the American Civil Liberties Union to defend a test case—chiefly to put their town on the map. They succeeded beyond their wildest hopes: the publicity was worldwide, and enduring. Before the opening day of the "monkey trial" on July 13, 1925, the streets of Dayton swarmed with sundry oddments of humanity drawn to the carnival:

publicity hounds, curiosity-seekers, professional evangelists and professional atheists, a blind mountaineer who proclaimed himself the world's greatest authority on the Bible, hot-dog and soda-pop hucksters, and a miscellany of reporters.

The two stars of the show—Bryan, who had offered his services to the prosecution, and Clarence Darrow, renowned trial lawyer of Chicago and confessed agnostic—united at least in their determination to make the trial an exercise in public education. When the judge ruled out scientific testimony, however, the defense called Bryan as an expert witness on biblical interpretation. In his dialogue with Darrow, he repeatedly entrapped himself in literal-minded interpretations and indeed his ignorance of biblical history and scholarship. He insisted that a "great fish" actually swallowed Jonah, that Joshua literally made the sun stand still, that the world was created in 4004 B.C.—all, according to Darrow, "fool ideas that no intelligent Christian on earth believes." It was a bitter scene. At one point the two men, their patience exhausted in the broiling summer heat, lunged at each other, shaking their fists, prompting the judge to adjourn court.

The next day testimony ended. The only issue before the court, the judge ruled, was whether or not Scopes had taught evolution, and no one denied that he had. He was found guilty, but the Tennessee supreme court, while upholding the act, overruled the $100 fine on a legal technicality. The chief prosecutor accepted the higher

Clarence Darrow (right) *shaking hands with John Scopes at the start of the notorious "monkey trial" in Dayton, Tennessee, 1925.*

court's advice against "prolonging the life of this bizarre case" and dropped the issue. With more prescience than he knew, Bryan had described the trial as a "duel to the death." A few days after it closed he died suddenly of a heart condition aggravated by heat and fatigue.

After Dayton the rest was anticlimactic. No other leader could assume Bryan's mantle, but in Mississippi the Bible Crusaders, led by the Reverend T. T. Martin, author of *Hell and the High Schools*, descended on the state legislature and got another anti-evolution law in 1926. One final fundamentalist victory came in Arkansas by the use of two progressive reforms, the initiative and the referendum, in 1928. With that, the fundamentalists had spent their fury. Their very victories were self-defeating, for they served to publicize evolution, the doctrine they opposed as heresy. The states that went through the fiercest controversies became prime markets for books on evolution, and the movement roused a liberal defense of academic freedom. Fundamentalists, usually defeated, suffered the complacent scorn of those people the sociologist Howard Odum called the "learned ignoranti," whose contempt for the beliefs of plain folk mirrored the intolerance of fundamentalists and whose own faith in science mirrored the fundamentalists' belief in the "Five Points."

PROHIBITION   Prohibition offered another example of reforming zeal channeled into a drive for moral righteousness and social conformity. Around the turn of the century the leading temperance organizations, the Women's Christian Temperance Union and the Anti-Saloon League, had converted from efforts to change individuals to a campaign for legal prohibition. Building upon the general moral disrepute of saloons, they were able to equate the "liquor traffic" with the trusts and "special interests." For the churches, prohibition could easily become, as one historian put it, "a surrogate for the Social Gospel." At the same time, contrary to certain old-time folk beliefs that alcohol was beneficial, medical and scientific opinion now showed that it did more harm than good. By the 1910s the Anti-Saloon League had become one of the most effective pressure groups in American history, mobilizing Protestant churches behind its single-minded battle to elect "dry" candidates.

At its "Jubilee Convention" in November 1913 the league endorsed a national prohibition amendment to the Constitution. That December some 4,000 White Ribboners marched on the Capitol to present resolutions for a constitutional amendment. The 1916 elections finally produced two-thirds majorities for prohibition in both houses of Congress. Soon the wartime spirit of sacrifice, the need to use grain for food, and wartime hostility to German-American brew-

Federal Agents Dumping Beer into Lake Michigan, 1919. *The Eighteenth Amendment, which sanctioned prohibition, was ratified in 1919 and took effect in January 1920.*

ers transformed the cause virtually into a test of patriotism. On December 18, 1917, Congress passed and sent to the states the Eighteenth Amendment which, one year after ratification on January 16, 1919, banned the manufacture, sale, or transport of intoxicating liquors.

By then, however, about three-fourths of the American people already lived in states and counties that were legally dry. The wartime Lever Food and Fuel Control Act, moreover, had banned the use of grain for distilling and brewing. In 1919 the Volstead Act extended the ban and defined as "intoxicating" all beverages containing more than 0.5 percent alcohol, which became illegal once the Eighteenth Amendment went into effect on January 16, 1920. On that date the corpse of John Barleycorn, alcoholic beverages personified, arrived in Norfolk, Virginia, on a special train. While his Satanic Majesty trailed along in deep mourning and anguish, twenty pallbearers carried an enormous coffin to a tabernacle where evangelist Billy Sunday preached the funeral oration to more than 10,000 people.

But John Barleycorn, like the labor hero Joe Hill, never died. The

Eighteenth Amendment had been in effect fewer than eight months when authorities found a still with a daily capacity of 130 gallons near Austin, Texas, on a farm belonging to Morris Shepard, the "Father of National Prohibition." Congress never supplied adequate enforcement, if such was indeed possible given the public thirst, the spotty support of local officials, and the profits to be made in bootlegging. In Detroit, the liquor industry was second in size only to automobiles. From Vancouver Island in the Northwest ships left with booze consigned to Mexico and returned empty within twenty-four hours—most likely not having gotten much beyond Seattle!

Imported liquors tended to be the real thing, but a lucrative trade developed in denatured grain alcohol, which could be redistilled or "cooked" to make it potable and then treated with flavoring and artificial coloring to impress desperate palates as facsimiles of bourbon, rye, or gin. But as "forbidden fruit," even fake liquor was all the more enticing and arrests for public drunkenness went up sharply. Speakeasies, hip flasks, and cocktail parties were among the social innovations of the prohibition era, along with increased drinking by women.

It would be too much to say that prohibition gave rise to organized crime, for organized vice, gambling, and extortion had long been practiced, and often tied in with the saloons. But prohibition supplied criminals an enormous new source of income, while the automobile and the submachine gun provided greater mobility and firepower. Gangland leaders showed remarkable gifts for exploiting loopholes in the law, when they did not simply buy up policemen and politicians. One crime boss who operated in the Midwest bought a chain of drugstores so he could order medicinal liquors and then hijack his own trucks as they transported the goods.

But the most celebrated gangster and racketeer (a word coined in the 1920s) was "Scarface" Al Capone, who moved from New York to Chicago in 1920 and within a few years became the city's leading bootlegger, and gambling and vice lord. In 1927 his bootlegging, prostitution, and gambling empire brought him an income of $60 million, which he flaunted in expensive suits and silk pajamas, a custom-upholstered and bulletproof Cadillac, an entourage of bodyguards, and lavish support for city charities. Capone always insisted that he was merely providing the public with goods and services it demanded: "What's Al Capone done, then? He's supplied a legitimate demand. Some call it bootlegging. Some call it racketeering. I call it business. They say I violate the prohibition law. Who doesn't?" He neglected to say that he himself had also bludgeoned to death several conspiring police lieutenants and ordered the execution of dozens of his rival criminals. Law-enforcement officials led by FBI

Al Capone in 1929.

agent Eliot Ness began to smash his bootlegging operations in 1929, but were unable to pin anything on Capone until a Treasury agent infiltrated his gang and uncovered evidence to nail him for tax evasion. Tried in 1931, Capone was sentenced to eleven years in prison, most of which he served at Alcatraz.

In light of the illegal activities of Capone and other organized-crime members, it came as no great surprise in 1931 when a commission under former attorney-general George W. Wickersham reported evidence that enforcement of prohibition had broken down. Of the commission's eleven members only five approved continued efforts to enforce prohibition without change, four favored modifications, and two personally favored repeal. Still, the commission as a whole voted for further trial, and President Hoover chose to stand by what he called the "experiment, noble in motive and far-reaching in purpose."

THE ROARING TWENTIES

In many ways the defensive temper of the 1920s and the repressive movements it spawned seem the dominant trends of the times, but they arose in part as reactions to a social and intellectual revolution that seemed about to sweep America away from its old moorings. In various labels given to the times, it was an era of excess, the era of wonderful nonsense, the jazz age, the roaring twenties, the ballyhoo years, the aspirin age. During those years a new cosmopolitan, urban America confronted an old insular, rural America, and cultural conflict reached new levels of tension.

The smart set of the sophisticated metropolis developed an active disdain for the old-fashioned rural/small-town values of the hinterlands. Sinclair Lewis's novel *Main Street* (1920) portrayed the stifling, mean, cramped life of the prairie town, depicting a "savorless people, gulping tasteless food, and sitting afterward, coatless and thoughtless, in rocking chairs prickly with inane decorations, listening to mechanical music, saying mechanical things about the excellence of Ford automobiles, and viewing themselves as the greatest race in the world." The banality of small-town life became a pervasive theme in much of the literature of the time. In *Look Homeword, Angel* (1929), Thomas Wolfe scandalized his native Asheville, North Carolina, with his unrelenting drive to escape the encircling hills for the "billion-footed city." Writing for the *Smart Set* and *American Mercury,* the Baltimore journalist H. L. Mencken was the most merciless in his attacks on the American "booboisie." The daily panorama of America, he wrote, had become "so inordinately gross and preposterous . . . that only a man who was born with a petrified diaphragm can fail to laugh himself to sleep every night, and to awake every morning with all the eager, unflagging expectation of a Sunday-school superintendent touring the Paris peep-shows." The hinterlands responded with counterimages of alien cities infested with vice, crime, corruption, and foreigners.

THE NEW MORALITY   Much of the shock to old-timers came from the revolution in manners and morals, evidenced first among young people, and especially on the college campuses, where H. L. Mencken had become a hero. In *This Side of Paradise* (1920), a novel of student life at Princeton, F. Scott Fitzgerald wrote of "the great current American phenomenon, the 'petting party.' " None of the Victorian mothers, he said, "had any idea how casually their daughters were accustomed to be kissed." One of the old muckrakers, Samuel Hopkins Adams, published a novel called *Flaming Youth* (1923), which gave an enduring tag to the phenomenon. From such novels and from magazine pieces the heartland learned about the wild parties, bathtub gin, promiscuity, the new uses to which automobiles were put on secluded lovers' lanes, speakeasies, roadhouses, and "shimmy dancers."

Whatever people did, however few flappers went "all the way," sex came to be discussed with a frankness once unheard of. One father said his daughter "would talk about anything; in fact, she hardly ever talked about anything else." Much of the talk derived from a spreading awareness of Dr. Sigmund Freud, the Viennese father of psychoanalysis. When in 1909 Freud visited Clark University in Massachusetts, he was surprised to find himself so well known "even in prudish America." The following year appeared the first English translation of his *Three Contributions to a Theory of Sex*. By the 1920s and 1930s his ideas had begun to percolate into the popular awareness, and the talk spread in society and literature about libido, inhibitions, Oedipus complexes, transference, sublimation, and repression.

An obsession with sex permeated much of the literature and popular media of the day. James Branch Cabell, who became famous when his novel *Jurgen* (1919) was banned in Boston, exploited his "phallic candour" in a string of novels, while Eugene O'Neill used Freudian themes onstage in *Desire under the Elms* (1924), *Mourning Becomes Electra* (1931), and other plays. Sex became the stock-in-trade of a prosperous tabloid press, and a new form of literature, the confession magazine, featured lurid stories about women who had gone wrong. In motion pictures "America's Sweetheart," the maidenly Mary Pickford, yielded stardom to the "vamp," Theda Bara, and the "It" girl, Clara Bow, followed in the 1930s by Jean Harlow, the movies' first "platinum blonde." A rising protest over such movie fare as *Up in Mable's Room*, *Sinners in Silk*, and *Her Purchase Price* impelled the movie industry to adopt stringent regulations about the content and language in films.

Radio singers during the 1920s belted out songs with titles like "Hot Lips," "I Need Lovin'," and "Burning Kisses." The new jazz music percolating in New Orleans and Chicago blended African and European musical traditions into a distinctive brew characterized by improvisation, "blue notes," and polyrhythms. Its leading performers included King Oliver, Jelly Roll Morton, and the great Louis Armstrong. The syncopated rhythms of jazz were immensely popular among young blacks and whites and helped spawn carefree dance steps such as the Charleston and Black Bottom that shocked custodians of morality.

Fashion also displayed signs of dramatic change. In 1919 women's skirts were typically six inches above the ground; by 1927 they were at the knees, and the "flapper"—with her bobbed hair, rolled stockings, cigarettes, lipstick, and sensuous dancing—was providing a shocking model of the new feminism. The name derived from the way fashionable women allowed their galoshes to "flap" about their ankles. Conservative moralists saw the flappers as just another sign of a degenerating society. Others saw in the "new women" an expression of rugged American individualism. "By sheer force of violence," explained the *New York Times* in 1929, the flapper has "established the feminine right to equal representation in such hitherto masculine fields of endeavor as smoking and drinking, swearing, petting, and upsetting the community peace."

By 1930 the thrill of rebellion was waning; the revolution against Victorian codes had run its course. Its extreme expressions in time aroused doubts that the indulgence of lust equaled liberation. Still, some new folkways had come to stay. In "Middletown" (Muncie, Indiana), the subject of Robert and Helen Lynd's classic community study in the mid-1920s, a young man told them on their return in 1935 that young people had "been getting more and more knowing and bold. The fellows regard necking as a taken-for-granted part of a date." In the late 1930s a survey disclosed that among college women almost one-half (47 percent) had yielded their virginity before marriage, but of these three-quarters had had sexual relations only with their future spouses.

The most pervasive change brought by the new moral code was in its views of marriage. The old code had made the husband head and master of the family, responsible for its support, while limiting the wife's "sphere" to the care of the home and the children, and the nurturing and gentling of the male animal. By the 1930s a code exalting romantic love and companionship as the basis for marriage

Margaret Sanger (left) *founded the American Birth Control League and in 1916 opened the first public clinic for counseling on contraception.*

had gained ascendancy. One sociologist announced in 1934 that the "breaking of the former taboo on sex has made possible for younger men and women a healthier attitude toward marital relationship" and a greater chance for mutual happiness. More important than breaking taboos may have been the social and economic evolution of a century which had taken away functions the family once had and delivered them to the factory, the school, and other institutions. Much alarm was expressed in the 1920s at the rising divorce rate. The rate declined briefly with the onset of the Great Depression in 1929, but picked up again during the later 1930s and 1940s. The divorce rate reflected perhaps less an increase in unsatisfactory marriages than a greater willingness and ability to abandon an intolerable situation.

THE WOMEN'S MOVEMENT Equal suffrage for women arrived in 1920. It had been an unconscionably long time in coming. A span of seventy-two years separated the Seneca Falls Declaration of 1848, which marked the start of the political movement for women's rights, from ratification of the Nineteenth Amendment, which secured women the vote. The suffrage movement, which had been in the doldrums since 1896, sprang back to life in the second decade of the new century.

In 1912 Alice Paul, a Quaker and social worker, returned from an apprenticeship with the militant suffragists of England, and became head of the National American Woman Suffrage Association's Congressional Committee. The day before Wilson's inauguration in 1913, when Washington was full of visitors, she organized a march to promote the suffrage amendment. When unruly crowds nearly broke up the parade, the resultant publicity revitalized the suffrage campaign. Paul's militant tactics and single-minded focus on the federal amendment, however, increasingly drove a wedge between her and the larger national group. The Congressional Union, formed by her committee in 1913, became a separate organization in 1915 and changed its name to the Woman's party in 1916. This group copied the British suffragists in holding the party in power responsible for failure to act, a reasonable stance under a parliamentary system but one which led them to oppose every Democrat, which the mainline suffragists found self-defeating in America. Alice Paul nevertheless knew how to get publicity for the cause. By 1917 she and her followers were engaged in picketing the White House and deliberately provoking arrests, after which they went on hunger strikes in prison. The authorities obligingly cooperated in making martyrs by the hundreds.

Meanwhile, Carrie Chapman Catt became head of the National

Alice Paul organized this march for women's suffrage in 1913. Held in Washington, D.C., the march preceded Wilson's inauguration by one day.

Suffrage Association once again in 1915 and revived it through her gift for organization. She brought with her a legacy of about $1 million from Mrs. Frank Leslie, publisher of *Leslie's Weekly*, dedicated "to the furtherance of the cause of woman suffrage." The money became available in 1917 and contributed to organizing the final campaigns for voting rights. For several years President Wilson evaded the issue of an amendment, but he voted for suffrage in a New Jersey referendum and supported a plank in the 1916 Democratic platform endorsing state action for women's suffrage. He also addressed the National Suffrage Organization that year, and thereafter worked closely with its leaders.

Finally, in 1918, after the House had passed the "Anthony Amendment," Wilson went before the Senate on September 30 to plead for its passage there. The Senate fell short of the two-thirds majority by two votes, but the attention centered on the issue helped defeat two antisuffrage senators. On June 4, 1919, the Senate finally adopted the amendment by a bare two-thirds majority. Ratification of the Nineteenth Amendment took another agonizing fourteen months. The Tennessee legislature had the distinction of completing the ratification, on August 21, 1920. It was one of the climactic achievements of the progressive era.

Even before ratification the suffrage organization began transforming itself into the League of Women Voters, founded in 1919, and women thereafter entered politics in growing numbers. But, it was often noted, this did not usher in a political millennium or any sudden release of women from all the trammels of custom and law. What was more, the suffrage victory left the broader feminist movement prey to a letdown that lasted for a generation. A few years after the triumph Carrie Chapman Catt wrote that suffragists were disappointed "because they miss the exaltation, the thrill of expectancy, the vision which stimulated them in the suffrage campaign. They find none of these appeals to their aspiration in the party of their choice."

One group, however, wanted to advance equality yet further. Alice Paul and the Woman's party set a new feminist goal, first introduced in Congress in 1923: an Equal Rights Amendment which would eliminate any remaining legal distinctions between the sexes—including the special legislation for the protection of working women put on the books in the previous fifty or so years. Feminists who had been caught up in the social-justice movement considered this a sacrifice of gains painfully accomplished. It would be another fifty years before Alice Paul would see Congress adopt her amendment in 1972; she did not live, however, to see it fall short of ratification.

The sharp increase in the number of women in the work force

Women workers in ship construction, Puget Sound, Washington, 1919.

during World War I proved ephemeral, but in the longer view a steady increase in the numbers of employed women occurred in the 1920s and, surprisingly, continued through the depression decade of the 1930s. Still, this phenomenon represented more evolution than revolution. The greatest breakthroughs had come in the nineteenth century, and by 1900 women had at least a token foothold in most of the gainful occupations. By 1910 they made up almost a quarter of all nonagricultural workers, and in 1920 were found in all but 35 of the 572 job categories listed by the census. The continued entry of women into the work force brought their numbers up from 8.2 million in the 1920 census to 10.4 million in 1930, and 13 million in 1940. Still these women remained concentrated in traditional occupations: domestics, office workers, teachers, clerks, salespeople, dressmakers, milliners, and seamstresses. In manufacturing they were found mainly in related work, such as textiles or garment making. On the eve of World War II women's work was little more diversified than it had been at the turn of the century, but by 1940 it was on the verge of a great transformation.

THE "NEW NEGRO"   The discriminations that have befallen African-Americans and women have many parallels, and the loosening of restraints for both have often coincided. The most significant development in black life during these years was the Great Migration. The movement of blacks northward began in 1915–1916 when war industries were depleting the ranks of common labor at a time when the war prevented replacement by foreign immigrants; legal restrictions on immigration continued the movement in the 1920s. Altogether, between 1910 and 1920 the Southeast lost some 323,000 blacks, or 5 percent of the native black population, and by 1930 had lost another 615,000, or 8 percent of the native black population in 1920. With the migration a slow but steady growth in black political influence set in, for not only were blacks freer to speak and act in a northern setting, they gained political leverage by concentrating in large cities located in states with many electoral votes.

Along with political activity came a bristling spirit of protest among blacks, a spirit which received cultural expression in a literary and artistic movement tagged the "Harlem Renaissance." Claude McKay, a Jamaican immigrant, was the first significant writer of the movement, which was a rediscovery of black folk culture and an emancipation from the genteel tradition. Poems collected in McKay's *Harlem Shadows* (1922) expressed defiance in such titles as "If We Must Die" and "To the White Fiends." Other emergent writers included the versatile and prolific Langston Hughes, poet, novelist, and columnist; Zora Neal Hurston, folklorist and novelist;

"A Negro Family Just Arrived in Chicago from the Rural South," 1922. *Between 1910 and 1930 almost 1 million blacks left the South in the Great Migration north.*

Countée Cullen, poet and novelist; and James Weldon Johnson, who pictured the Negro mecca in *Black Manhattan.* Perhaps the greatest single creation of the time was Jean Toomer's novel *Cane,* which pictured the lives of simple blacks in Georgia's black belt and the sophisticated inhabitants of Washington's brown belt. White writers like Eugene O'Neill, DuBose Heyward, Julia Peterkin, and Sherwood Anderson also took up the theme of what one observer in 1925 called the "New Negro," but more often than not they merely abandoned the old stereotype of the "darkie" for a new stereotype of the exotic primitive, a caricature the more fully alive for its want of inhibitions.

In its extreme expression the spirit of the New Negro found outlet in what came to be called "Negro nationalism," which exalted blackness, black cultural expression, and black exclusiveness. The leading spokesman for such views was the flamboyant Marcus Garvey, who in 1916 brought to New York the United Negro Improvement Association, which he had started in his native Jamaica two years before. His organization grew rapidly under the strains of the postwar years. Racial bias, he said, was so ingrained in whites that it was futile to appeal to their sense of justice. The only hope for blacks was to flee America and build a Negro republic in Africa. Garvey quickly enlisted half a million members and claimed as many as 6 million by 1923. At that point he was charged with fraudulent use of the mails in raising funds for his ancillary steamship line. Found guilty, he went to the Atlanta penitentiary in 1925, where he remained until President Coolidge pardoned and deported him to Jamaica in 1927. Garvey, one biographer concluded, had suffered from a lack of business experience rather than from an intent to defraud. He died in obscurity in London in 1940, but the memory of his movement kept alive an undercurrent of Negro nationalism which would reemerge later under the slogan of "black power."

The year in which the Great Migration began, 1915, marked another milestone with the passing of Booker T. Washington. His position of race leadership was taken up not by a single spokesman but more and more by an organization, the National Association for the Advancement of Colored People (NAACP). It had started with one writer's call for a revival of the abolitionist spirit in response to a 1908 race riot in Springfield, Illinois, Lincoln's hometown. Plans laid at a meeting in 1909 led to a formal organization in 1910. Two participants supplied a direct link to the abolitionists: Oswald Garrison Villard, who was the grandson of William Lloyd Garrison, wrote the call for the 1909 meeting, and Moorefield Storey, in his youth the secretary to the abolitionist Charles Sumner, became the organiza-

Marcus Garvey, founder of the United Negro Improvement Association and a leading spokesman for "Negro nationalism" in the 1920s.

tion's first president. Black participants came mainly from a group associated with W.E.B. Du Bois called the Niagara Movement, which had met each year since 1905 at a place associated with antislavery (Niagara Falls, Oberlin, Boston, Harper's Ferry) and issued a defiant statement against discrimination. Du Bois became the NAACP's director of publicity and research, and editor of its journal, *The Crisis*.

Although most progressives were not in harmony with the NAACP, the new group took seriously the progressive idea that the solution to social problems began with informing the people, and it planned an active press bureau to accomplish this. Its main strategy, however, came over the years to be legal action aimed at warming the Fourteenth and Fifteenth Amendments back to life. One early victory came with *Guinn v. United States* (1915), in which, after the NAACP submitted a friend-of-the-court brief, the Supreme Court struck down Oklahoma's grandfather clause, used in the state to deprive blacks of the vote. In *Buchanan v. Worley* (1917) the Court invalidated a residential segregation ordinance in Louisville.

Meanwhile, in 1919 the NAACP launched a campaign against lynching with a statistical survey of the practice and a conference. An anti-lynching bill to make mob murder a federal offense passed the House in 1922, but lost to a filibuster by southern senators. The bill stayed before the House until 1925, and NAACP field secretary James Weldon Johnson believed the continued agitation of the issue did more than the bill's passage would have to reduce lynchings, which fell off to a third of what they had been in the previous decade.

The emergent black political renaissance found expression in two events: Oscar DePriest's election from a Chicago district in 1928 as the first black congressman since 1901, the first ever from the North; and the fight against the confirmation of Judge John J. Parker for the Supreme Court in 1930. When President Hoover submitted Parker's name, the NAACP found that as the 1920 Republican candidate for governor of North Carolina Parker had pronounced Negro suffrage "a source of evil and danger." The NAACP conducted its campaign, Du Bois said, "with a snap, determination, and intelligence never surpassed in colored America." Parker lost by the close vote of 41 to 39; his defeat represented the first instance of significant black impact on Congress since Reconstruction.

In 1930 the NAACP began laying plans for a legal assault on segregation in American life. The administration of Franklin D. Roosevelt saw the political influence of blacks grow further after 1933. Like Wilson, Roosevelt did not give a high priority to Negro affairs, but he tolerated people in his administration who did. By 1936 there was a "Black Cabinet" of some thirty to forty advisers in government departments and agencies, and black voters were fast transferring their political loyalty from Republicans to Democrats.

During the 1930s the NAACP's legal campaign gathered momentum. A major setback occurred in *Grovey v. Townsend* (1935), which upheld the Texas Democrats' white primary as the practice of a voluntary association and thus not state action. But the *Grovey* decision held up for only nine years and marked the end of major decisions that for half a century had narrowed application of the Reconstruction Amendments. A trend in the other direction had already set in. Two important precedents arose from the celebrated Scottsboro case in 1931, in which nine black youths were convicted of raping two white women while riding a freight train in Alabama. The first verdict failed, the high court ruled in *Powell v. Alabama* (1932), for want of due process because the judge's appointing "all of the members of the bar" to defend the accused imposed "no substantial or definite obligation upon anyone." Another verdict fell to a judgment in *Norris v. Alabama* (1935) that the systematic exclusion of Negroes from Alabama juries had denied the defendants equal protection of the law—a principle that had significant and widespread impact on state courts.

The Culture of Modernism

SCIENCE AND SOCIAL THOUGHT   As the twentieth century advanced, the easy faith in progress and reform expressed by Social Gospelers and other liberals fell victim to a series of frustrations and disasters: the Great War, the failure of the League of Nations, the failure of prohibition, the Great Depression, the rise of Communist and fascist dictators, and continuing world crises. New currents in science and social thought also brought shocks to the easy faith in a rational or melioristic universe. Darwin's biology portrayed humans as more akin to apes than to angels. Darwin's contemporary Karl Marx influenced even people who rejected his Communist doctrine but saw relevance in his emphasis on the material, economic basis of society. In capitalist society, Marx argued, freedom was an illusion: people were actually driven by impersonal economic forces. In Freud's psychology people were also driven, but by needs arising from the depths of the unconscious. If Darwin, Marx, and Freud suggested that rational humans were not the controllers of their fate, startling new findings in physics further shook the verities underlying American life and thought in the progressive period.

The new findings in physics altered the image of the cosmos in ways that seemed almost a calculated assault on common sense. The conventional wisdom since Sir Isaac Newton held the universe to be governed by laws which the scientific method could ultimately uncover. The world was a machine, a scientific writer of the early twentieth century said. "In its motions there is no uncertainty, no mystery." A world of such certain order bolstered hopes of infinite progress in human knowledge, and good Victorians of the nineteenth century could readily accommodate even Darwinism to their optimistic outlook.

This world of order and certainty came apart when Albert Einstein, a young German physicist working in the Swiss patent office, puzzled over recent experiments and reasoned that space, time, and mass were not absolutes but relative to the location and motion of the observer. In 1905 he published a paper, "On the Electrodynamics of Moving Bodies," which became known as the special theory of relativity. Ten years later he elaborated his general theory of relativity, which challenged the Newtonian cosmos. Newton's mechanics, according to Einstein, worked well enough at relatively slow speeds, but the more nearly one approached the velocity of light (about 186,000 miles per second) the more all measuring devices would change accordingly, so that yardsticks would become shorter, clocks and heartbeats would slow down. An observer on another planet moving at a different speed would see a quite different universe from the one we see. Even more incredibly, a person traveling on a spaceship at immense velocity, and unaware that for him time had

Albert Einstein at his home in Berlin.

slowed relative to earth time, might return to find that centuries had passed in his absence.

Certainty dissolved the farther one reached out into the universe. The same thing happened the farther one reached down into the minute world of the atom. The discovery of radioactivity in the 1890s showed that atoms were not irreducible units of matter but that some of them emitted particles of energy. What this meant, Einstein noted, was that mass and energy were not separate phenomena but interchangeable. In 1907 Einstein quantified this relationship in the famous and deceptively simple formula $E = mc^2$, energy equals mass times the speed of light squared. Meanwhile the researches of Max Planck in Berlin had led Planck to find that electromagnetic emissions of energy, whether as electricity or light, came in little bundles which he called quanta. The development of the quantum theory suggested that atoms were far more complex than once believed and, as the German physicist Werner Heisenberg stated in his principle of uncertainty in 1927, ultimately indescribable. One could never know both the position and the velocity of an electron, Heisenberg concluded, because the very process of observation would inevitably affect the behavior of the particle, altering its position and velocity.

Heisenberg's thesis meant that beyond a certain point things could not possibly be measured, so that human knowledge had limits. "The physicist thus finds himself in a world from which the bottom has dropped clean out," a Harvard mathematician wrote in 1929. He had to "give up his most cherished convictions and faith. The world is not a world of reason, understandable by the intellect of man, but as we penetrate ever deeper, the very law of cause and effect, which we had thought to be a formula to which we could force God Himself to subscribe, ceases to have any meaning." Hard for the public to grasp, such findings proved too much even for Einstein, who spent much of the rest of his life in quest of an explanation through a unified field theory which would combine electromagnetism and gravitation in one system and unify the relativity and quantum theories. "I shall never believe that God plays dice with the world," Einstein said.

Though few people understood it, Einstein's theory especially captured the imagination of a public whose common experience told them that observers differently placed got a different view of things. Just as Enlightenment thinkers drew on Newton's laws of gravitation two centuries before to formulate their views on the laws governing society, the ideas of relativity and uncertainty in the twentieth century carried over into denials of absolute values in any sphere of society, and thus undermined the concepts of personal responsibility and absolute standards. Anthropologists aided the process by transforming the word "culture," which had before meant refinement, into a term for the whole system of ideas, folkways, and institutions within which any group lived. Even the most primitive groups had cultures and, all things being relative, one culture had no place imposing its value judgments on another. Two students of Columbia University anthropologist Franz Boas, Ruth Benedict and Margaret Mead, were especially effective in spreading this viewpoint. Benedict's *Patterns of Culture* (1934), a steady seller, introduced millions to the different values of unusual cultures from the North American Indians to the Melanesians, and Mead's *Coming of Age in Samoa* (1928) celebrated the healthfulness of the uninhibited sex she observed there. The uncertainty principle got an ironic twist in Mead's case, however, when over fifty years later another anthropologist insisted that Mead was the victim of a gigantic put-on by Samoans who told her what they thought she wanted to hear.

MODERNIST LITERATURE   The cluster of scientific ideas associated with Darwin and Einstein inspired a revolution in the minds of intellectuals and creative artists which they expressed in a new modernism. Some observers now count this new intellectual current as ranking with the Enlightenment, romanticism, or Victorianism in its sweep and significance. The historian Daniel J. Singal has identified certain major features of the modernist movement. First, it undertook "to plumb the nether regions of the psyche," to explore the irrational as an essential part of human nature. Second, it viewed the universe as turbulent and unpredictable, and presented uncertainty as a desirable condition. Third, it displaced the Victorian ideals of "bliss" and "peace" with a positive view of conflict. Finally, the modernist displayed "a critical temperament uninhibited by considerations of formal manners," for rules of gentility had to yield to "reality," no matter how distasteful.

In the various arts related technical features appeared: abstract painting which represented an inner mood rather than an image of an object, atonal music, free verse in poetry, stream-of-consciousness narrative, and interior monologues in stories and novels. Writers dramatized our separation from the past. They showed an intense concern with new forms in language in an effort to avoid outmoded forms and structures and to violate expectations and shock their audiences.

The search for the new centered in America's first major artistic bohemias: Chicago, where cheap housing built for visitors to the Columbian Exposition offered a haven on the South Side; and New York, where the area in lower Manhattan soon known as Greenwich Village offered a lure for aspiring artists and radicals—and their camp followers. In the words of the radical writer John Reed, the

Frankie "Half Pint" Jackson and His Band at the Sunset Cafe, Chicago, 1920s. *Jazz emerged during this period as an especially American expression of the modernist spirit. Black artists bent musical conventions to give fuller reign to improvisation.*

Village featured "inglorious Miltons by the score, and Rodins, one to every floor." As early as 1909 the photographer Alfred Stieglitz hung Matisse paintings in his Photo-Secession gallery on Fifth Avenue. At Mabel Dodge's Fifth Avenue salon intellectuals rubbed shoulders with IWW leader Big Bill Haywood and discussed the new ideas. In 1913 the Armory Show in New York, which went then to Chicago, Philadelphia, and Boston, shocked traditionalists with its display of the latest in experimental and nonrepresentational art: post-impressionists, Fauvists, expressionists, primitives, and cubists. Pablo Picasso's work made its American debut there. Mabel Dodge thought the show the most important event in America since 1776. It aroused a portion of shocked indignation and not a little good-natured ridicule, but it was a huge success. Audiences flocked to the show and buyers afterward snapped up the pieces for sale.

Suddenly in the teens everything was new: the "New Freedom," the "New Nationalism," the new poetry, the new art, the new ethics, the new marriage. In 1913 James Harvey Robinson of Columbia announced in *The New History* a purpose of making history a pragmatic science oriented toward explaining the present, and in the same year his colleague Charles A. Beard sent out shock waves with *An Economic Interpretation of the Constitution.* Late in 1912

Max Eastman had taken over the socialistic *Masses* and turned it into a lively magazine; in 1914 Herbert Croly established the less radical *New Republic*. Literary magazines mushroomed: the *Seven Arts, Dial*, the *Little Review*, the *Bohemian*, the *Criterion*, and many others.

"The fiddles are tuning as it were all over America," the Irish painter John Butler Yeats wrote. In Chicago, Harriet Monroe provided a sounding board in *Poetry: A Magazine of Verse*. A poet of some local renown, author of the official ode for the Columbian Exposition, and already past fifty when she started *Poetry* in 1912, she found her vocation as patron to a renaissance. Within a few years she had brought to light a dozen and more major figures: Carl Sandburg, celebrator of Chicago, "Stormy, husky, brawling, City of the Big Shoulders"; Vachel Lindsay, vagabond poet who sought to restore the "primitive singing voice" in poems like "General Booth Enters Heaven" and "The Congo"; Robinson Jeffers, poet of tragic despair; the imagists Amy Lowell, Conrad Aiken, and William Carlos Williams. To her eternal regret Harriet Monroe "missed" Edgar Lee Masters, a lawyer resident in Chicago and author of *Spoon River Anthology* (1915), his poetic epitaphs for midwestern types. She also missed Sherwood Anderson, whose stories of midwestern characters in *Winesburg, Ohio* (1919), offered a prose parallel to *Spoon River*.

The chief American prophets of modernism were in neither Chicago nor New York, but émigrés in Europe: Ezra Pound and T. S. Eliot in London, and Gertrude Stein in Paris, all deeply concerned with creating new and often difficult styles of expression. Pound, as foreign editor for *Poetry*, became the conduit through which many American poets achieved publication in America and Britain. At the same time he became the leader of the imagist movement, a revolt against the ornamental verbosity of Victorian poetry in favor of the concrete image, exclusion of "superfluous words," and the rhythm of the "musical phrase" rather than the "sequence of a metronome." In the course of a long life, Pound was to embrace political causes, continue his expatriation in Paris and Italy, encourage new writers, seek new poetic techniques, and compose as his lifetime project an endless series of difficult and obscure *Cantos*.

Pound's supreme protégé was T. S. Eliot, who in 1915 contributed to *Poetry* his first major poem, "The Love Song of J. Alfred Prufrock," the musings of an ineffectual man who "after tea and cakes and ices" could never find "the strength to force the moment to its crisis." Eliot's *The Waste Land* (1922) made few concessions to readers in its arcane allusions, its juxtaposition of unexpected metaphors, its deep sense of postwar disillusionment and melancholy, and its suggestion of a burnt-out civilization; but it became for a generation almost the touchstone of the modern temper along with the

Irishman James Joyce's stream-of-consciousness novel *Ulysses,* published the same year. As poet and critic in the *Criterion,* which he founded in 1922, Eliot became the arbiter of modernist taste in Anglo-American literature.

Gertrude Stein, in voluntary exile since 1903, was with her brother, Leo, an early champion of modern art and a collector of early Cézannes, Matisses, and Picassos. Long regarded as no more than the literary eccentric who wrote "Rose is a rose is a rose" and "Pigeons on the grass alas," she came later to be recognized as one of the chief originators and propagators of modernist style, beginning with *Three Lives* (1906). Included in this work is the classic "Melanctha," perhaps the first story by a white author to treat a black character as something other than a stereotype. Having studied psychology under William James, Stein sought to develop in writing the equivalent of nonrepresentational painting; her work captured interior moods in such books as *The Making of Americans* (1911, published 1925) and *Tender Buttons* (1914).

But she was long known chiefly through her influence on such 1920s expatriates as Sherwood Anderson and Ernest Hemingway, whom she told: "All of you young people who served in the war, you are the lost generation." The earliest chronicler of that generation, F. Scott Fitzgerald, blazed up brilliantly and then quickly flickered out, like all the tinseled, blithesome, sad young people of his novels.

Pablo Picasso's portrait of Gertrude Stein, 1906.

The Fitzgeralds Celebrate Christmas. *F. Scott Fitzgerald and his wife, Zelda, lived in and wrote about the "greatest, gaudiest spree in history."*

Successful and famous at age twenty-four with *This Side of Paradise* (1920), along with his wife, Zelda, he lived in and wrote up the "greatest, gaudiest spree in history," and then both had their crackup in the Great Depression. What gave depth to the best of his work was what a character in *The Great Gatsby* (1925), his finest novel, called "a sense of the fundamental decencies" amid all the surface gaiety—and almost always a sense of impending doom.

Hemingway's first novel, *The Sun Also Rises* (1926), pictures an even more desperate search for life by the expatriate crowd, chasing about frantically from the bistros of Paris to the bullrings of Spain. Young Jake Barnes, emasculated by a war wound, cannot marry his love, Lady Brett Ashley. "Oh, Jake," she says in the poignant ending, "we could have had such a damned good time together." "Yes," he replied. "Isn't it pretty to think so?" Hemingway's second novel, *A Farewell to Arms* (1929), is another tale of lost love. Based on Hemingway's experience in the ambulance corps in northern Italy, it pursues the love affair of a driver and a nurse who abandon the war for Switzerland, where the young woman dies in childbirth.

Already in these novels are found the lively, even frenetic action, and the cult of athletic masculinity (epitomized by the bullfighter), which became the stuff of the public image Hemingway cultivated for himself and the hallmark of such novels as *Death in the Afternoon* (1932), *To Have and Have Not* (1937), *For Whom the Bell Tolls* (1940), and *The Old Man and the Sea* (1952). Hundreds of writers tried to imitate Hemingway's terse style, but few had his gift, which lay less in what he had to say than in the way he said it. The critic Alfred Kazin passed judgment in one short sentence: "He brought a major art to a minor vision of life."

Culture in the Thirties

THE RETURN OF SOCIAL SIGNIFICANCE   In view of the studied alienation of writers caught in the materialistic world of the 1920s, one might have expected the onset of the Great Depression in 1929 to deepen the despair. Instead it brought a renewed sense of commitment and affirmation, as if people could no longer afford the art-for-art's-sake affectations of the 1920s. The surprisingly popular musical show *Pins and Needles* (1936), put on by members of the International Ladies' Garment Workers Union, caught the new feeling of dedication in one of its numbers: "Sing Me a Song with Social Significance."

In the early 1930s the commitment sometimes took the form of allegiance to revolution. For a time leftist politics and rhetoric made significant inroads in literary circles. By the summer of 1932 even the "golden boy" of the lost generation, F. Scott Fitzgerald, was saying that "to bring on the revolution, it may be necessary to work within the Communist party." In September 1932 fifty-three artists and intellectuals signed an open letter endorsing the Communist party candidate for president, and many writers flocked into the party's John Reed clubs, named for the American journalist who had observed and written about the Bolshevik Revolution.

Until 1935, following the line laid down by the Soviet dictator Joseph Stalin, the Communist party refused to collaborate with other groups. In 1935 the party line switched to endorse a broad "popular front" with democratic and socialistic groups opposed to fascism. In 1935 the John Reed clubs gave way to the more broadly based League of American Writers, which held an annual American Writers' Congress for several years. It paralleled other popular-front groups like the American Youth Congress, the American Negro Congress, and the American League for Peace and Democracy. It drew into its activities, among others, Hemingway, Erskine Caldwell, Waldo Frank, Archibald MacLeish, Richard Wright, John Dos Passos, Theodore Dreiser, John Steinbeck, and Langston Hughes.

John Reed, the American journalist whose Ten Days That Shook the World *is an eyewitness account of the Bolshevik Revolution.*

But few remained for long. Writers being a notoriously independent lot, they rebelled at demands to hew to a shifting line. Over the years a series of shocks persuaded most of them that Joseph Stalin practiced a tyranny and terror more efficient and more bloody than anything under the czars. The climactic events were the staged treason trials of Stalin's former comrades in 1936 and Stalin's Non-Aggression Pact with Hitler in 1939, which opened the way for World War II in Europe.

In the heyday of the "Red Decade" there was much talk of a proletarian literature, but the only product of lasting significance to come out of the leftist cultural movement was the *Partisan Review*, founded in 1934 as the organ of New York's John Reed Club and, after a brief hiatus in 1936–1937, revived as an anti-Stalinist literary journal. Among the writers who sang songs with social significance at least three novelists deserve special notice: John Dos Passos, John Steinbeck, and Richard Wright.

After Harvard and a stint as an ambulance driver in France and Italy during the Great War, Dos Passos first got wide notice with *Three Soldiers* (1921), an exposé of the sordid and brutal nature of war. *Manhattan Transfer* (1925) presented a similar picture of modern urban society and began to use the kaleidoscopic techniques of his great trilogy *U.S.A.* (collected 1938), which undertook no less than a panorama of American society from 1900 to 1936. In its three parts—*The 42nd Parallel* (1930), *1919,* (1932) and *The Big Money* (1936)—the sprawling story line served mainly as a device to place its eleven major characters at crucial junctures of the national experience. Three structural devices lent a special flavor to the book. One, the "Newsreel," presented a collage of newspaper stories and headlines, popular songs, and quotations from public figures to evoke a feeling of the times. The second, the "Camera Eye," gave brief impressionistic sketches of responses to the issues and scenes of the times. Third was the series of biographies of public figures such as Isadora Duncan, Robert La Follette, Thomas A. Edison, and many others.

The trilogy ends by contrasting a hungry, dirty hitchhiker by a roadside with a wealthy, well-fed executive passing overhead on a transcontinental plane. The scene underscored the radical vision of the trilogy that America had become divided into "two nations." Dos Passos's lengthy flirtation with Communist causes in the 1920s and early 1930s ended in disillusionment at the Communists' use of violence against Socialist opponents who preferred democratic methods. After the mid-1930s his viewpoint moved away from Marxism and ever more toward affirmations of patriotism, but his creative powers never again equaled those which produced *U.S.A.*

The single piece of fiction that best captured the ordeal of the depression, John Steinbeck's *The Grapes of Wrath* (1939), was also the most memorable "proletarian" novel of the times because it escaped political formula to treat workers as people. Steinbeck had taken the trouble to travel with displaced "Okies" driven from the Oklahoma Dust Bowl by foreclosures and farm combines to pursue the illusion of jobs in the fields of California's Central Valley. The story focused on the Joad family as they made their painful journey from Oklahoma west along U.S. 66, enticed by job ads aimed really

A migrant family on their way west to California.

at producing a labor surplus and depressed wages. Met chiefly with contempt and rejection, caught up in labor agitations, Ma Joad strove to keep hope alive and at the end, even as the family was breaking up under the pressure, she grasped at a broader loyalty: "Use'ta be the fambly was fust. It ain't so now. It's anybody. Worse off we get, the more we got to do." The novel was more than a period piece about the depression. As one critic observed: "It is an allegory that is applicable wherever prejudice and a sense of self-importance inhibit co-operation."

Steinbeck produced a bountiful harvest of writing, most successfully when he dealt with his native California, as in "The Red Pony" (1937, with additional material 1945), the story of a boy's maturing through experience of the tragic nature of life, or *Tortilla Flat* (1935) and *Cannery Row* (1935), which celebrated the vagabond lives of the mixed-blood *paisanos* and dockside bums of Monterey. Fame arrived for Steinbeck with *In Dubious Battle* (1936), about a strike of fruit pickers exploited both by the bosses for profit and by their Communist leader for the sake of power, and with *Of Mice and Men* (1937), about the tragedy of two ranchhands. He continued writing into the 1960s, but *The Grapes of Wrath* remains his masterpiece.

Among black novelists the supreme genius was Richard Wright. Born on a plantation near Natchez, Mississippi, the son of a matriarch whose husband deserted the family, Wright grew up in the course of moving from town to town, ended his formal schooling with the ninth grade (as valedictorian of his class), worked in Memphis, and greedily devoured books he borrowed on a white friend's library card, all the while saving up to go north. In Chicago, where he arrived on the eve of the depression, the Federal Writers' Project gave him a chance to perfect his talent, and his period as a Communist from 1934 to 1944 gave him an intellectual framework, Marxism, which did not, however, overpower his fierce independence. His first book, *Uncle Tom's Children* (1938), a collection of four novellas, and his autobiographical *Black Boy* (1945) revealed in their very rebellion against racial injustice his ties to the South, for, he wrote, "there had been slowly instilled into my personality and consciousness, black though I was, the culture of the South."

Native Son (1940), Wright's masterpiece, is set in the Chicago he had come to know before moving on to New York. It tells the story of Bigger Thomas, a product of the black ghetto, a man hemmed in and finally impelled to murder by forces beyond his control. "They wouldn't let me live and I killed," he said unrepentantly at the end. Somehow Wright managed to sublimate into literary power his bitterness and rage at what he called "The Ethics of Living Jim Crow," an art he never quite mastered. In the black experience, he wrote, America had "a past tragic enough to appease the spiritual hunger

Richard Wright, author of
Native Son *and* Black Boy.

of even a James; and . . . in the oppression of the Negro a shadow
athwart our national life dense and heavy enough to satisfy even the
gloomy broodings of a Hawthorne."

THE SOUTHERN RENAISSANCE   In different ways southern whites had
shared that tragic past. Out of the memory and the consciousness of
change the writers among them nurtured a renaissance that bur-
geoned into one of the most notable literary growths since the flow-
ering of New England a century before. There was little reason to
expect it in 1920 when H. L. Mencken published his essay "The
Sahara of the Bozart," which described the southern cultural landscape as a barren wasteland: "One thinks of the interstellar spaces,
of the colossal reaches of the now mythical ether. . . . It would be
impossible in all history to match so complete a drying-up of civilization." Among the writers Mencken missed was Ellen Glasgow, of
Richmond, Virginia, who in the Victorian twilight at the turn of the
century had begun a lonely revolt against the "twin conventions of
prudery and platitude" in her "Novels of the Commonwealth," a
realistic social history of Virginia from the Civil War. *Barren Ground*
(1925), about a heroic female figure of endurance, brought her recognition that was long overdue, and in 1941 she received a Pulitzer
Prize for *In This Our Life*.

What Mencken's essay had also missed was that the South had
reached a historical watershed, that it stood between two worlds:
the dying world of tradition and the modern, commercial world
struggling to be born. The resultant conflict of values, felt more
intensely in the South than in the North, aroused the Ku Klux Klan

and fundamentalist furies, but had quite another effect on the South's young writers. Allen Tate, a talented young poet, novelist, and critic, saw in the South the "curious burst of intelligence that you get at a crossing of the ways, not unlike, on an infinitesimal scale, the outburst of poetic genius at the end of the sixteenth century when commercial England began to crush feudal England."

That Mencken had touched a sensitive nerve was apparent from the frequent references to him in the literary groups and little magazines that sprang to life in his Sahara. The Poetry Society of South Carolina noted in its first *Year Book* (1921) that the desert had already sprouted oases where the fig trees were not entirely barren. In New Orleans *The Double Dealer* (1921–1926) became the focus of a literary bohemia which for a time included Sherwood Anderson and William Faulkner. In Nashville *The Fugitive: A Journal of Poetry* (1922–1925) announced the arrival of the most influential group in American letters since the New England transcendentalists.

The Fugitive poets began as a group of student intellectuals at Vanderbilt University who first gathered for discussions in 1915, then regrouped after the war with young Professor John Crowe Ransom as their dean and mentor. Four of the group eventually stood out in their commitment to literature as a profession: Ransom, Donald Davidson, Allen Tate, and Robert Penn Warren. The Fugitives admired T. S. Eliot and were committed to the new doctrines of modernism in literature. They cultivated a style distinguished by attention to from and language, by complexity and allusion that yielded only to the closest study. They began in revolt against the twin images of southern sentimentalists and commercial boosters. *"The Fugitive,"* Ransom wrote, "flees from nothing faster than from the high-caste Brahmins of the Old South."

It dawned on them that they had protested too much, however, when reporters drawn to the Scopes trial vied with Mencken in mocking the Bible Belt and the Benighted South. In reaction the Fugitives began to seek a usable past in the southern agrarian tradition. They brought others into the project, and their manifesto, *I'll Take My Stand* (1930), by twelve southerners, appeared fortuitously just when industrial capitalism seemed on the verge of collapse. In reaction agianst images of the New South and the Benighted South, the Vanderbilt agrarians championed, in Donald Davidson's words, a "traditional society . . . that is stable, religious, more rural than urban, and politically conservative," a society in which human needs were supplied by "Family, bloodkinship, clanship, folkways, custom, community. . . ." In the end their agrarianism proved less important as a social-economic force than as a context for creative literature. Yet their image of the agrarian South, as one critic later wrote, provided "a rich, complex metaphor through which they presented a critique of the modern world." Their critique of the frenzy of modernism "has since been echoed by commentator after commentator."

While agrarianism quickened a generation of southern writers with its vision of southern tradition beset by change, southern regionalism quickened a generation of social scientists with its vision of the "Problem South." The school of southern regionalism, based in the University of North Carolina at Chapel Hill, was led chiefly by the sociologists Howard W. Odum and Rupert B. Vance. They inspired no single manifesto but their most important works were Vance's *Human Geography of the South* (1932) and Odum's *Southern Regions of the United States* (1936). Odum proposed to overcome the divisiveness of traditional sectionalism by presenting regional diversity as a national strength. He explored the social problems plaguing the South, and argued that rational planning would aid the "Problem South" and develop its rich potential.

With remarkable speed after 1920 Mencken's cultural Sahara turned into a forest populated with nests of singing birds. "One may reasonably argue," wrote a critic in 1930, "that the South is the literary land of promise today." Just the previous year two vital figures had emerged: Thomas Wolfe, with *Look Homeward, Angel*, and William Faulkner, with *Sartoris* and *The Sound and the Fury*. Fame rushed in first on Wolfe and his native Asheville, North Carolina, which became in the last golden October of the 1920s a classic example of the scandalized community. "Against the Victorian morality and the Bourbon aristocracy of the South," Wolfe had "turned in all his fury," newspaper editor Jonathan Daniels, a former classmate, wrote. The reaction was not an uncommon response to the works of the southern renaissance, created by authors who had outgrown their hometowns and looked back from new perspectives acquired in travel and education.

For all his gargantuan lust for experience and knowledge, his demonic drive to escape the encircling hills for the "fabled" world outside, his agonized search for some "lost lane-end into heaven," Wolfe never completely severed his roots in the South. *Look Homeward, Angel*, his first novel, remained his most successful; it was the lyrical and searching biography of Eugene Gant's (actually Wolfe's) youth in Altamont (Asheville) and his college days in Pulpit Hill (Chapel Hill). It established him as "the giant among American writers of sensitive youth fiction." Three later books, two edited posthumously from a mountain of manuscript after his untimely death at age thirty-seven, traced his further wanderings as Eugene Gant in *Of Time and the River* (1935) and as George

Webber in *The Web and the Rock* (1939) and *You Can't Go Home Again* (1940).

William Faulkner himself ranked Wolfe first among contemporary novelists because he "made the best failure. . . . My admiration for Wolfe is that he tried to get it all said; he was willing to throw away style, coherence, all the rules of preciseness, to try to put all the experience of the human heart on the head of a pin, as it were." Faulkner's own achievement, more than Wolfe's, was rooted in the world that produced him. Born near Oxford, Lafayette County, Mississippi, he grew up there and transmuted his hometown into Jefferson, Yoknapatawpha County, in his fiction. After a brief stint with the Royal Canadian Air Force he passed the postwar decade in what seemed to fellow townspeople an aimless drifting. He briefly attended classes at the University of Mississippi, worked at odd jobs, and went to New Orleans where he wrote *Soldiers' Pay* (1926), a novel of postwar disillusionment, and *Mosquitoes* (1927), a caricature of the New Orleans bohemians yachting on Lake Pontchartrain. Between books he shipped out briefly for Europe, and after knocking around the Gulf Coast, returned to Oxford.

There, in writing *Sartoris* (1929), he began to discover that his "own little postage stamp of native soil was worth writing about" and that he "would never live long enough to exhaust it." In this book a postwar wasteland stood out the more starkly against a legend of past glory in the Sartoris family. Young Bayard Sartoris, denied the romantic end that befell his twin brother, who had been shot down over France, pursued a kind of gallant death wish by automobile and airplane until he found release in a plane crash. With *Sartoris* and the creation of his mythical land of Yoknapataw-

William Faulkner.

pha, Faulkner kindled a blaze of creative energy. Next, as he put it, he wrote his gut into *The Sound and the Fury* (1929), again the story of a demoralized family. It was one of the triumphs of the modernist style, but early readers, taking their cue from the title instead of the critics, found it signified nothing.

Faulkner's creative frenzy continued through the writing of *As I Lay Dying* (1930) and *Light in August* (1932). He began to fill in the early history of Yoknapatawpha with *Absalom! Absalom!* (1936), a story which unfolded slowly as Quentin Compson, in midnight conversations with his Canadian roommate at Harvard, attempted to reconstruct the story of Sutpen's Hundred, the main character's 100-acre estate, from bits and pieces of information he had picked up. The process, familiar to historians, was disconcerting to readers looking for the completed narrative. Faulkner rounded out further the history of Yoknapatawpha and the conflict between tradition and the modern world. *The Hamlet* (1940), *The Town* (1957), and *The Mansion* (1960) followed the rise of Flem Snopes and his myriad relatives, who lacked an ethical code and aimed to displace the old families who still clung to shopworn tradition.

Most critics at first missed what Faulkner was attempting. Some viewed him as an exemplar of what Ellen Glasgow called "Southern Gothic," the leader in a "cult of cruelty." Others found disturbing his obscurity, the slow unfolding of meaning, convoluted syntax, and runaway rhetoric of his novels. *Absalom! Absalom!*, one critic complained, used the "non-Stop or Life Sentence," a method of "Anti-Narrative, a set of complex devices used to keep the story from getting told." But that, of course, was Faulkner's point—to vary the usual strategies of rhetoric so that new insights overtook the reader by surprise. Not until the mid-twentieth century did critics generally begin to grasp that Faulkner, in composing his mythical history of Yoknapatawpha, had become also—certainly among Americans— the most skillful creator of modernist styles in the novel during the first half of the twentieth century.

DOCUMENTARY EXPRESSION IN THE THIRTIES Somewhere between belles lettres and academic treatise fell a literature of social exploration and descriptive journalism that formed the expression of what Alfred Kazin called the "now innocent, now calculating, now purely rhetorical, but always significant experience in national self-discovery that occurred in the 1930s." The New Deal, through the Works Progress Administration's Federal Writers' Project, among other things contributed to the collection of a "vast granary of facts" in fifty-one state and territorial guidebooks, catalogs of archives, collections of folklore and folk songs, and even records of tombstone

Sunday, Little Rock, Arkansas, October 1935. *The decade of the 1930s was a period of national self-discovery, as Ben Shahn's documentary photograph suggests.*

inscriptions. The Writers' Project pioneered in the oral history of the "inarticulate." In *These Are Our Lives* (1939), the Writers' Project in North Carolina, Tennessee, and Georgia gathered case histories of workers, sharecroppers, and Negroes in a form that the historian Charles A. Beard called "literature more powerful than anything I have read in fiction." *Lay My Burden Down* (1944) presented the life stories of former slaves as recorded by Writers' Project inter-viewers.

A new genre of documentary literature teamed social reporters with photographers: Erskine Caldwell and Margaret Bourke-White, *You Have Seen Their Faces* (1937) and *Say, Is This the USA?* (1941); Paul S. Taylor and Dorthea Lange, *An American Exodus* (1939); and James Agee and Walker Evans, *Let Us Now Praise Famous Men* (1941). The last of these, a sensitive and effective evocation of tenant life in Alabama, got little notice at the time but gradually came to be recognized as a unique masterpiece of documentation and art. Under the direction of Roy Stryker the Farm Security Administration built up an enormous photographic documentation of everyday life in America, making familiar in the credits such names as Dorothea Lange and Ben Shahn. Pare Lorenz pioneered the motion-picture documentary in *The Plow That Broke the Plains* (1936) and *The River* (1937).

In the 1930s America experienced what *Fortune* magazine called "a sort of cultural revolution," largely through the WPA projects in writing, arts, music, theater, and historical research. Americans learned that, like it or not, they had a culture and had had one all along—it had simply been overlooked. Now Americans tried to make up for lost time by tracking the culture down, recording, restoring, and celebrating it. They became intrigued with American art of all kinds, and particularly that least influenced by Europe: primitive, folk, or, as it was called most often, "popular" art. American "regionalist" artists, such as Grant Wood and Thomas Hart Benton, turned their attention to their homeland.

America's "cultural nationalism" in the 1930s would have been "thin and elitist" without the WPA, one historian wrote, but the "cultural revolution would have happened without the WPA arts projects or indeed any governmental impetus. Its causes—the depression, America's isolation in a menacing world, the Russian and German examples—were more compelling than any Washington could legislate." And so the two decades of the 1920s and 1930s, times of unusually creative vitality, ended with Americans engaged in the rediscovery of America.

FURTHER READING

For a standard survey of the interwar period, start with William E. Leuchtenburg's *The Perils of Prosperity, 1914–1932* (1958).° Still appealing is Frederick Lewis Allen's *Only Yesterday* (1931).° Allen covers cultural developments of the 1930s in his *Since Yesterday* (1940).° The best single introduction to the culture of the 1920s is Loren Baritz's *The Culture of the Twenties* (1970).° A good supplement is Richard H. Pell's *Radical Visions and American Dreams: Culture and Social Thought in the Depression Years* (1973).° Paula S. Fass's *The Damned and the Beautiful: American Youth in the 1920s* (1977)° describes the social attitudes of youth in general.

John Higham's *Strangers in the Land: Patterns of American Nativism, 1860–1925* (1955)° details the story of immigration restriction. For analysis of the more extreme nativist measures, see David M. Chalmers's *Hooded Americanism: The History of the Ku Klux Klan* (1965). Lawrence W. Levine's study of William Jennings Bryan, *Defender of the Faith: William Jennings Bryan, the Last Decade, 1915–1925* (1965), and Ray Ginger's *Six Days or Forever? Tennessee v. John Scopes* (1958)° cover the anti-evolution fight in Tennessee. Two contrasting views of prohibition are Andrew Sin-

°These books are available in paperback editions.

clair's *Prohibition: The Era of Excess* (1962) and Norman H. Clark's *Deliver Us From Evil* (1976).° Humbert S. Nelli's *The Business of Crime* (1976)° examines those who profited from bootlegging, including Al Capone. Francis Russell's *Sacco and Vanzetti* (1986) discusses the case against those accused radicals.

Other social groups also receive scholarly treatment. See Charles F. Kellogg's *NAACP* (1967)° for his analysis of the pioneering court cases against racial discrimination. Gilbert Osofsky's *Harlem: The Making of a Ghetto, 1890–1930* (2nd ed., 1971),° Nathan I. Huggins's *Harlem Renaissance* (1971),° and Jervis Anderson's *This Was Harlem: A Cultural Portrait, 1900–1950* (1982)° cover the cultural impact of the Great Migration in New York. For the political implications, see Theodore G. Vincent's *Black Power and the Garvey Movement* (1971). On the migration to Chicago, see James R. Grossman's *Land of Hope: Chicago, Black Southerners, and the Great Migration* (1989). Nicholas Lemann's *The Promised Land* (1991) is a fine exposition of the changes brought about by the Great Migration in both the South and North.

Women's suffrage is treated extensively in J. Stanley Lemon's *The Woman Citizen: Social Feminism in the 1920s* (1973) and Eleanor Flexner's *Century of Struggle: The Women's Rights Movement in the United States* (rev. ed., 1975).° Susan D. Becker's *The Origins of the Equal Rights Amendment: American Feminism between the Wars* (1981) is valuable. Christine A. Lunardini's *From Equal Suffrage to Equal Rights* (1986) is a study of Alice Paul. Changing attitudes toward women are traced in Lois W. banner's *American Beauty* (1983).°

Much of the theoretical basis for the chapter's discussion of "modernism" comes from Daniel J. Singal's *The War Within: From Victorian to Modernist Thought in the South, 1919–1945* (1982).° Also valuable is Morton G. White's *Social Thought in America: The Revolt against Formalism* (1949).° Nathan G. Hale, Jr.'s *Freud and the Americans* (1971) examines the impact of psychoanalysis.

Alfred Kazin's *On Native Grounds* (1942)° is an excellent introduction to the literature of the period. Studies on individual authors include Henry D. Piper's *F. Scott Fitzgerald: A Critical Portrait* (1965), Carlos H. Baker's *Ernest Hemingway* (1980),° Cleanth Brooks's *William Faulkner: The Yoknapatawpha Country* (1963),° and David Herbert Donald's *Look Homeward: A Life of Thomas Wolfe* (1987).

For the influence of H. L. Mencken, see Fred C. Hobson's *Serpent in Eden: H. L. Mencken and the South* (1974).° Louis D. Rubin, Jr., examines the Fugitives of Vanderbilt in *The Wary Fugitives* (1978).° The transformation of the traditional South into the modern, commercial South is described in Jack Temple Kirby's *Rural Worlds Lost: The American South, 1920–1960* (1987) and Pete Daniel's *Standing at the Crossroads: Southern Life in the Twentieth Century* (1986).

On developments in physics, see Stanley Goldberg's *Understanding Relativity: Origin and Impact of a Scientific Revolution* (1984).

27

REPUBLICAN RESURGENCE
AND DECLINE

The progressive coalition that reelected Woodrow Wilson in 1916 proved to be quite fragile, and by 1920 it had fragmented. It came apart because radicals and other opponents of the war grew disaffected with America's entrance into the conflict and the war's aftermath, because organized labor resented the administration's unsympathetic attitude toward the strikes of 1919–1920, and because farmers of the Great Plains and West thought that wartime price controls had discriminated against them. Intellectuals and elements of the middle class also drifted away from their former support of progressivism. The intellectuals became disillusioned with democracy because of popular support for prohibition and the anti-evolution movements. The larger middle class became preoccupied with building a new business civilization "based not upon monopoly and restriction," in the words of one historian, "but upon a whole new set of business values—mass production and consumption, short hours and high wages, full employment, welfare capitalism." Progressivism's final triumphs at the national level were already pretty much foregone conclusions before the war's end: the Eighteenth Amendment, ratified in 1919, which imposed national prohibition, and the Nineteenth Amendment, ratified in 1920, which extended women's suffrage to the entire country.

Progressivism, however, did not disappear in the 1920s. Progressives dominated Congress during much of the decade even while the White House was in conservative hands. The progressive impulse for "good government" and public services remained strong, especially at the state and local levels, where movements for good roads, education, public health, and social welfare all gained momentum during the decade. The progressive impulse for reform, however, was transformed into the drive for moral righteousness and conformity animating the Ku Klux Klan and the fundamentalist movement. Prohibition, at first a direct outgrowth of the reform spirit, came to be increasingly associated with the narrow intolerance of the times.

"Normalcy"

HARDING'S ELECTION   Amid the postwar confusion another presidential season approached. Wilson's physical collapse during 1919 symbolized his political deterioration as well. Most Americans now seemed weary of idealistic crusades and were suspicious of leaders sounding the trumpet of reform. In speaking of Wilson's fall from favor, one observer explained: "The moralist unquestionably secures wide popular support—but he also wearies his audience." Wilson himself recognized this fact. "It is only once in a generation," he remarked, "that a people can be lifted above material things. That is why conservative government is in the saddle two-thirds of the time."

When the Republicans met in Chicago in June 1920 the Old Guard was ready to reclaim its conservative heritage. The regulars found their man in Ohio senator Warren Gamaliel Harding, who had set the tone of his campaign when he told a Boston audience: "America's present need is not heroics, but healing; not nostrums, but normalcy; not revolution, but restoration; not agitation, but adjustment; not surgery, but serenity; not the dramatic, but the dispassionate; not experiment, but equipoise; not submergence in internationality, but sustainment in triumphant nationality." His speeches, said Wilson's treasury secretary, William G. McAdoo, were "an army of pompous phrases moving over the landscape in search of an idea."

Still, even though his rhetoric was clumsy, Harding caught the mood of the times, a longing for "normalcy" rather than government activism and experimentalism. The Republican convention, as Harding's campaign manager had predicted, reached a deadlock which was broken when a group of tired men sat down in a "smoke-filled room" and chose its candidate. Harding fit the bill because, though he might not set the pulses pounding, nobody was mad at him. He had all the classic attributes of availability. The vice-presidential choice fell on Calvin Coolidge, who had caught the public fancy with his pronouncement opposing the Boston Police Strike.

The Democrats met at San Francisco later in June in the first convention west of the Rockies. Their choice lay among three leading candidates: A. Mitchell Palmer, whose Red Scare had peaked too soon; William Gibbs McAdoo, Wilson's son-in-law, who was hobbled by Wilson's stubborn hope that the Democrats would again turn to him; and James Cox, former newsman and former governor of Ohio, who won the nomination on the forty-fourth ballot. For vice-president the convention named Franklin D. Roosevelt, who as assistant secretary of the navy occupied the same position his Republican cousin had held before him. Wilsonians tried to make the vote the "solemn referendum" their leader wanted, but the platform, while broadly endorsing the New Freedom, did not fully endorse the League of Nations. Cox waged an active campaign while the Republicans kept Harding home to conduct a front-porch campaign in the McKinley style—they even redid Harding's porch to look like McKinley's. The Republican platform was a masterpiece of evasion on the League of Nations. It pledged the party to "agreement among the nations to preserve the peace of the world" but "without the compromise of national independence." The phrasing satisfied both reservationists and irreconcilables. Harding himself scaled the clouded heights of obfuscation on the issue, denouncing Wilson's covenant but talking vaguely about a real "association of nations."

The issue was too foggy for a "solemn referendum." Besides, the Democrats' fate was sealed by the breakup of the Wilsonian coalition. In the words of William Allen White, Americans in 1920 were "tired of issues, sick at heart of ideals, and weary of being noble." Wilson therefore became the Republicans' target rather than Cox, who remained a nonentity, and the country voted overwhelmingly for a "return to normalcy." Harding got 16 million votes, about 60 percent of the total, to 9 million for Cox. Harding's electoral margin was 404 to 127. Cox carried no state outside the Solid South, even there losing Tennessee. In the minority again, the Democrats had returned to normalcy too.

EARLY APPOINTMENTS AND POLICY Harding in office had much in common with Ulysses Grant. His cabinet, like Grant's, mixed some of the "best minds" in the party, whom he had promised to seek out, with some of the worst, cronies who sought him out. Charles Evans Hughes, like Grant's Hamilton Fish, became a distinguished secretary of state. Herbert Hoover in the Commerce Department, Andrew W. Mellon in Treasury, and Henry C. Wallace in Agriculture

Warren Harding "bloviating" on the stump.

were men who functioned efficiently and made policy on their own. Of the others, the secretary of the interior landed in prison and the attorney-general narrowly escaped serving time. Many lesser offices went to members of the soon notorious "Ohio Gang," a group with which Harding met in a "Little House on H Street" to get away from the pressures of the White House.

Until he became president, Harding had loved politics. He was the party hack par excellence, "bloviating" (a verb of his own making, which meant speaking with gaseous eloquence) on the stump, jollying it up in the clubhouse and cloakroom, hobnobbing with the great and near-great in Washington. As president, however, Harding was simply in over his head, and self-doubt overwhelmed him. "I don't think I'm big enough for the Presidency," he confided to a friend. Woodrow Wilson had said once that it seemed impossible to get an explanation to lodge in Senator Harding's head, and President Harding later confessed as much to his secretary: "I don't know what to do or where to turn in this taxation matter. Somewhere there must be a book that tells all about it. . . . There must be a man in the country somewhere who could weigh both sides and know the truth. . . . But I don't know where to find him. . . . My God, this is a hell of a place for a man like me to be." How much better to get away with the "Ohio Gang," who shared his taste for whiskey, poker, and women. Alice Roosevelt Longworth, Theodore Roosevelt's oldest daughter, witnessed one poker session in the president's study. "Harding wasn't a bad man," she said later. "He was just a slob."

Harding and his friends set about dismantling or neutralizing as many of the social and economic components of progressivism as they could. To that end Harding took advantage of four Supreme Court vacancies by appointing conservatives to all, including Chief Justice William Howard Taft, who announced that he had been "appointed to reverse a few decisions." During the 1920s the Taft Court struck down a federal child-labor law and a minimum-wage law for women, issued numerous injunctions against striking unions, and passed rulings limiting the powers of federal regulatory agencies.

Moreover, Harding established a pro-business tone reminiscent of the McKinley White House. Big business, whipping-boy of the progressives, had won respectability and acceptance by expanding production during the war and by building a "New Era" of prosperity after the postwar slump in 1921. To sustain economic growth Secretary of the Treasury Mellon pushed vigorously a Republican policy of economy and tax reduction. To get a better handle on expenditures he persuaded a lukewarm Congress to pass the Budget and Accounting Act of 1921, which created a new Bureau of the Budget, headed by a Chicago banker, to prepare a unified budget, and a General Accounting Office to audit the accounts. General tax reductions from the wartime level seemed called for, but Mellon insisted that they should go mainly to the rich, on the Hamiltonian principle that wealth in the hands of the few would augment the general welfare through increased capital investment. Mellon's admirers tagged him "the greatest Secretary of the Treasury since Alexander Hamilton."

In Congress a group of western Republicans and southern Democrats fought a dogged battle to preserve the progressive principle built into wartime taxes, but Mellon, in office through the 1920s, eventually won out. At his behest Congress in 1921 repealed the wartime excess-profits tax and lowered the maximum rate on personal income from 65 to 50 percent. Subsequent revenue acts lowered the maximum rate to 40 percent in 1924 and 20 percent in 1926. The Revenue Act of 1926 extended further benefits to high-income groups by lowering estate taxes and repealing the gift tax. Unfortunately, much of the money released to wealthy people by these acts seems to have augmented the speculative excess of the late 1920s as much as it augmented gainful enterprise. Mellon, however, did balance the federal budget for a time. Governmental expenditures fell from $6.4 billion in 1920 to $3.4 billion in 1922, and to a low of $3 billion in 1927. The national debt went down from $25.5 billion in 1919 to $16.9 billion in 1929.

In addition to tax cuts, Mellon favored the time-honored Republican policy of high tariffs, and innovations in the chemical and metal industries revived the argument for protection of infant industries from foreign competition. The Fordney-McCumber Tariff of 1922 increased rates severely on chemical and metal products as a safeguard against the revival of German industries which had previously commanded the field. To please the farmers, who historically benefited little from tariffs, the new act further extended the duties on farm products.

Higher tariffs, however, had ramifications which had never prevailed before and which were not quickly perceived. During the war the United States had been transformed from a debtor to a creditor nation. In former years foreign capital had flowed into the United States, playing an important role in the economic expansion of the nineteenth century. But the private and public credits given the Allies during the war had reversed the pattern. Mellon insisted that the European powers must repay all that they had borrowed. But the tariff walls erected around the country made it all the harder for other nations to sell in the United States and thus acquire the dollars or credits with which to repay their war debts. For nearly a decade further extensions of American loans and investments sent more dollars abroad, postponing the reckoning.

Rounding out the Republican economic program during the 1920s was a more lenient attitude toward government oversight of corporations. Neither Harding nor his successor, Coolidge, could dissolve the regulatory agencies, but by naming commissioners who were less than sympathetic to regulation they rendered these agencies ineffective. Harding named conservative advocates of big business to the Interstate Commerce Commission, the Federal Reserve Board, and the Federal Trade Commission. In 1925 Coolidge's appointee as chairman of the FTC said the commission would not be used "as a publicity bureau to spread socialistic propaganda." He and his colleagues, in a departure from Wilson's principle of "pitiless publicity," decided to withhold publicity on all cases until they were settled. Senator George Norris characterized the new appointments as "the nullification of federal law by a process of boring from within." Senator Henry Cabot Lodge agreed, boasting that "we have torn up Wilsonism by the roots."

A CORRUPT ADMINISTRATION   Republican conservatives such as Lodge and Mellon were at least operating out of conviction. The "Ohio Gang," however, used White House connections to line their own pockets. In 1923 Harding learned that an official of the Veterans Bureau was systematically looting medical and hospital supplies. Found out, the official fled to Europe and resigned. Harding's general counsel then committed suicide in Harding's old house in Washington. Not long afterward, a close buddy of the attorney-general also shot himself. The corrupt crony held no appointment, but had set up an office in the Justice Department from which he peddled influence for a fee. The attorney-general himself was implicated in the fraudulent handling of German assets seized after the war. When this was discovered, he refused to testify on the ground that he might incriminate himself. Twice brought to court, he was never indicted for want of evidence, possibly because he had destroyed pertinent records. These were but the most visible among many scandals that touched the Justice Department, the Prohibition Bureau, and other agencies under Harding.

But one major scandal rose above all these petty peculations. Teapot Dome, like the Watergate Apartments fifty years later, became the catchword for an epoch of corruption. An oil deposit under the sandstone Teapot Rock in Wyoming, Teapot Dome had been set aside as a naval reserve administered by the Interior Department under Albert B. Fall. The move seemed at the time a sensible attempt to unify control over public reserves. But once Fall had control, he signed contracts letting private interests exploit the deposits: Harry Sinclair's Mammoth Oil Company at Teapot Dome and Edward L. Doheny's Pan-American Petroleum and Transport Company at Elk Hills. Fall argued that these contracts were in the government's interest. It was harder for Fall to explain, however, why he acted in secret, without allowing competitive bids.

Suspicion grew when Fall's standard of living suddenly rose. It turned out that he had taken loans of about $400,000 (which came

Bargain Day in Washington. *The Harding administration, according to this cartoon, put the government up for sale.*

in "a little black bag") from Sinclair and $300,000 from Doheny. As the scandal unraveled, Fall emerged as a figure of tragic weakness. Once wealthy, he had lost extensive mine holdings in the Mexican Revolution, which left him with little more than an expensive dream ranch in New Mexico. Desperate for money, he took loans extended by two old friends—he and Doheny and Sinclair had once worked together in the mines. For the rest of his life Fall insisted that the loans were unrelated to the leases, and that he had contrived a good deal for the government, but at best the circumstances revealed a fatal blindness to his impropriety.

The question of bribery aside, his actions activated the hostility of conservationists. Fall, like Ballinger before him, had regarded conservation as the doctrine of easterners indifferent to jobs and development in the West. After Senator La Follette demanded a senatorial investigation, a committee laid out the whole mess during 1924 to the accompaniment of public outrage.

Harding himself was spared the humiliation of public disgrace. How much he knew is unclear, but he knew enough to become visibly troubled. "My God, this is a hell of a job!" he confided to the editor William Allen White. "I have no trouble with my enemies, I can take care of my enemies all right. But my damn friends, my God-damn friends, White, they're the ones that keep me walking the floor nights!" In June 1923 Harding left on what would be his last journey, a western speaking tour and a trip to the Alaska Territory. Sailing to Alaska, he fell into conversation with Commerce Secretary Herbert Hoover: "If you knew of a great scandal in our administration," he asked, "would you for the good of the country and the party expose it publicly or would you bury it?" Hoover replied quickly: "Publish it, and at least get credit for integrity on your side." But little time was left to Harding. Back in Seattle he fell ill with what was diagnosed first as ptomaine poisoning, but was apparently a heart attack. He recovered briefly, then died in a San Francisco hotel of either coronary or cerebral thrombosis.

Not since the death of Lincoln had there been such an outpouring of grief for a "beloved President," for the kindly, ordinary man with the face of a Roman senator, the man who found it in his heart (as Wilson had not) to pardon Eugene Debs and receive him at the White House, and to pressure the steel magnates into giving up their barbarous seven-day week. As the black-streamered funeral train moved toward Washington, then back to Ohio, millions stood by the tracks to honor their lost leader. Eventually, however, grief yielded to scorn and contempt. For nearly a decade the revelations of scandal were paraded before committees and then courts. Harding's long affair with Nan Britton came to light, first the birth of their illegitimate child and later their pathetic couplings in a White House closet. Shortly before the centennial of his birth, Harding's love letters to another man's wife surfaced. As a result of his amorous detours and corrupt associates, Harding's foreshortened administration came to be widely viewed as one of the worst in American history.

Recent assessments of Harding's presidency, however, suggest that the scandals obscured some real accomplishments. Some historians credit Harding for leading the nation out of the turmoil of the postwar years and creating the foundation for the decade's remarkable economic boom. Revisionists also stress that he was a hardworking president who played a far more forceful role than previously assumed in shaping his administration's economic and foreign policies and in shepherding legislation through Congress. But even Harding's foremost scholarly defender admits that he lacked good judgment and "probably should never have been president."

"SILENT CAL"   Some kind of charmed existence seemed to put Calvin Coolidge in the right place at the right time. The news of Harding's death came when he was visiting his father in the mountain village of Plymouth, Vermont, his birthplace. There at 2:47 on the morning of August 3, 1923, by the light of a kerosene lamp, Colonel John Coolidge administered the oath of office to his son. The rustic simplicity of Plymouth, the very name itself, evoked just the image of roots and solid integrity that the country would long for amid the coming disclosures of corruption. The new first lady, Grace Coolidge, was as unpretentious as her husband, and Alice Roosevelt Longworth found the new atmosphere of the White House "as different as a New England front parlor is from the back room in a speakeasy."

Calvin Coolidge dresses up for the photographers.

Coolidge brought to the White House a clear conviction that the presidency should revert to its Gilded Age stance of passive deference to Congress. "Four-fifths of our troubles," Coolidge predicted, "would disappear if we would sit down and keep still." He abided by this rule, insisting on twelve hours of sleep and an afternoon nap. H. L. Mencken asserted that Coolidge's notable talent was that "he slept more than any other president, whether by day or by night. Nero fiddled, but Coolidge only snored."

But Americans took to their hearts the unflappability of "Silent Cal," his inactivity, and the pictures of him fishing, pitching hay, and wearing Indian bonnets while primly clad in business suit and necktie. His taciturn nature became the subject of affectionate humor, often no doubt apocryphal, as in the story of a dinner guest who bet Coolidge that she could make him say three words. "You lose," he replied.

The image of "Silent Cal," however, distorts as much as it illuminates his character. Although a man of few words, he was not as bland or as dry as critics claimed. Yet he was conservative. Herbert Hoover, the secretary of commerce, once stressed that Coolidge was a "real conservative, probably the equal of Benjamin Harrison. He was a fundamentalist in religion, in the economic and social order, and in fishing, too." (He used live worms for bait.) Even more than Harding, Coolidge embraced the orthodox creed of business. "The chief business of the American people is business," he intoned. "The man who builds a factory builds a temple. The man who works there worships there." Where Harding had sought to balance the interests of labor, agriculture, and industry, Coolidge focused on industrial development at the expense of the other two areas. He sought to unleash the free-enterprise system and, even more than Harding, he strove to end government regulation of business and industry. His pro-business stance led the *Wall Street Journal* to exult: "Never before, here or anywhere else, has a government been so completely fused with business."

THE 1924 ELECTION Coolidge was also married to politics, and proved better at it than Harding. He distanced himself from the Harding scandals, and put in charge of the prosecutions two lawyers of undoubted integrity. Yet Coolidge kept on Harding's attorney-general until growing evidence of his complicity led to his removal in March 1924. Coolidge quietly took control of the Republican party machinery and seized the initiative in the campaign for nomination, which he won with only token opposition.

The Coolidge luck held as the Democrats fell victim to internal dissensions. The source of the party's trouble was its uneasy alliance of incongruous elements which lent much truth to Will Rogers's classic statement: "I am a member of no organized political party. I am a Democrat." The party's divisions illustrated the deep alienation growing up between the metropolis of the Roaring Twenties and the more traditional hinterland, a gap that the Democrats could not bridge. After much factional fighting, it took the Democrats 103 ballots to bestow the tarnished nomination on John W. Davis, a Wall Street lawyer from West Virginia who could hardly outdo Coolidge in conservatism.

Meanwhile a growing farmer-labor coalition was mobilizing a third-party effort. In Minnesota during 1922 and 1923, a new Farmer-Labor party elected two United States senators, a congressman, and some lesser officeholders. In 1922 the railroad unions, smarting from administration opposition, sponsored a Conference for Progressive Political Action which got the support of many farmers who were suffering from price declines at the time. Meeting in Cleveland on July 4, 1924, the conference reorganized as the Progressive party and nominated Robert M. La Follette for president. The Wisconsin reformer also won the support of Minnesota's Farmer-Labor party, the Socialist party, and the American Federation of Labor.

In the campaign Coolidge chose to focus on La Follette, whom he called a dangerous radical who would turn America into a "communistic and socialistic state." The country preferred to "keep cool with Coolidge," who swept both the popular and electoral votes by decisive majorities. Davis took only the Solid South, and La Follette carried only his native Wisconsin. The popular vote went 15.7 million for Coolidge, 8.4 million for Davis, and 4.8 million for La Follette—the largest popular vote ever polled by a third-party candidate. The electoral result was 382 to 136 to 13.

THE NEW ERA

Businessmen interpreted the Coolidge victory as a vindication of their leadership, and Coolidge saw in the surging prosperity of the time a confirmation of his philosophy. In fact the prosperity and technological achievements of the time had much to do with Coolidge's victory over the Democrats and Progressives. Those in the large middle class who before had formed an important part of the Progressive coalition were now absorbed instead in the new world created by advances in communications, transportation, and business organization.

The gross national product had reached a peak of $88.9 billion in 1920; after a slump to $74 billion in 1921 and 1922, the GNP grew steadily to $104.4 billion in 1929. Per-capita income went from $672 in 1922 to $857 in 1929. A larger public than ever before had the money and leisure to taste of the affluent society, and a growing advertising industry fueled its appetites. By the mid-1920s advertising had become both a major enterprise, with a volume of $3.5 billion, and a major institution of social control. Old-time values of thrift and saving gave way to a new economic ethic that made spending a virtue. The innovation of installment buying made increased consumption feasible for many. A newspaper editorial insisted that the American's "first importance to his country is no longer that of citizen but that of consumer. Consumption is a new necessity."

MOVIES, RADIO, AND THE ECONOMY Consumer-goods industries fueled much of the boom from 1922 to 1929. Moderately priced creature comforts, including such items as hand cameras, wristwatches, cigarette lighters, vacuum cleaners, washing machines, and linoleum, became increasingly available. Inventions in communications and transportation, such as motion pictures, radio, telephones, and automobiles, not only fueled the boom but brought transformations in society.

In the 1890s a quick sequence of inventions had made it possible for a New York audience to see the first picture show in 1896. The first story depicted in a movie was *The Great Train Robbery* in 1903. By 1905 the first movie house opened in Philadelphia, and within

Charlie Chaplin in The Gold Rush *(1925)*.

A *farm family gathered around the radio, Hood River County, Oregon,*
1925.

three years there were nearly 10,000. By the teens Hollywood had
become the center of movie production, grinding out serials, features, Westerns, and the timeless two-reel comedies of Mack Sennett's Keystone Studios, where a raft of slapstick comedians, most
notably Charlie Chaplin, perfected their art into a form of social
criticism. The twelve-reel *Birth of a Nation,* directed in 1915 by D.
W. Griffith, became a triumph of cinematic art which marked the
arrival of the modern motion picture and at the same time per-
petuated a grossly distorted image of Reconstruction. Based on
Thomas Dixon's novel *The Clansman,* the movie was replete with
stereotypes of villainous Radicals, sinister mulattoes, blameless
white southerners, and faithful "darkies." The film grossed $18 mil-
lion and revealed the industry's enormous potential. By the mid-
1930s every large American city and most small towns had theaters,
and movies replaced oratory as the chief mass entertainment of
Americans. A further advancement in technology came with the
"talkies." The first movie with sound accompaniment was Warner
Brothers' *Don Juan* (1926), but the success of talking pictures was
established by Warners' *The Jazz Singer* (1927), starring Al Jolson.

Radio broadcasting had an even more spectacular growth. Except
for experimental broadcasts, radio served only for communication
until 1920. In August of that year WWJ in Detroit began transmitting
news bulletins from the Detroit *Daily News,* and in November
KDKA in Pittsburgh, owned by the Westinghouse Company, began

regular programs. The first radio commercial was aired by WEAF in New York, in 1922. By the end of that year there were 508 stations and some 3 million receivers in action. In 1926 the National Broadcasting Company, a subsidiary of RCA, began linking stations into a network; the Columbia Broadcasting System entered the field the next year. In 1927 a Federal Radio Commission was established to regulate the industry; in 1934 it became the Federal Communications Commission, with authority over other forms of communication as well.

AIRPLANES, AUTOMOBILES, AND THE ECONOMY   Advances in transportation were equally startling. Wilbur and Orville Wright of Dayton, Ohio, built and flew the first airplane at Kitty Hawk, North Carolina, on December 17, 1903, but the use of planes advanced slowly until the outbreak of war in 1914, after which the Europeans rapidly developed the plane as a military weapon. When the United States entered the war it still had no combat planes—American pilots did battle in craft of British or French make. An American aircraft industry developed during the war but foundered in the postwar demobilization. Under the Kelly Act of 1925, however, the government began to subsidize the industry through airmail contracts. This encouragement was greatly strengthened by the Air Commerce Act of 1926, which started a program of federal aid to air transport and navigation, including aid in establishing airports.

A psychological boost to aviation came in May 1927 with the solo flight of Charles A. Lindbergh, Jr., from New York to Paris in thirty-

Orville Wright pilots the first flight of a power-driven airplane, while his brother, Wilbur, runs alongside.

three hours and thirty minutes. The drama of the deed, which won him a prize of $25,000, was heightened by the fact that he was flying blind through a fog for part of the way and at times dropped to within ten feet of the water before sighting the Irish coast and regaining his bearings. The parade down Broadway in his honor surpassed even the celebration of the Armistice.

By 1930 the industry had forty-three airlines which carried 385,000 passengers over routes of 30,000 miles. Another great impetus came after 1936 when the slow Ford trimotor plane was displaced by the more efficient twin-engine Douglas DC-3 as the chief carrier. In 1940, nineteen airlines carried 2.8 million passengers over routes of 43,000 miles.

By far the most significant economic and social development of the time was the automobile. The first motor car had been manufactured for sale in 1895, but in 1900 the census did not even give the industry a separate listing. The founding of the Ford Motor Company in 1903 revolutionized the industry. Ford's reliable Model T (the celebrated "tin lizzie") came out in 1908 at a price of $850 (in 1924 it would sell for $290). Ford stated his objective: "I am going to democratize the automobile. When I'm through everybody will be able to afford one, and about everyone will have one." He was right. In 1916 for the first time the total number of cars manufactured passed 1 million; by 1920 more than 8 million were registered, and in 1929 more than 23 million. The production of automobiles consumed large parts of the nation's steel, rubber, glass, and textile output, among other materials. It gave rise to a gigantic market for oil products just as the Spindletop gusher (1901) in Texas heralded the opening of vast southwestern oil fields. It quickened the movement for good roads, financed in large part from a gasoline tax, speeded transportation, encouraged the sprawl of suburbs, and sparked real-estate booms in California and Florida.

The good-roads movement became the automobile-age equivalent of the nineteenth-century railroad movement. Through it the automobile industry received indirect subsidies greater than all government aid to railroads, which had now begun their decline. Road building ranked first or second in state budgets by the end of the 1920s, and the legislative lobbies of road builders and truckers supplanted those of the railroads in influence.

By virtue of its size and importance the automobile industry became the salient example of mass production. When Ford brought out the Model T in 1908, demand ran far ahead of production. Ford then hired a factory expert who, by rearranging the plant and installing new equipment, met his production goal of 10,000 cars in twelve months. The next year Ford's new Highland Park plant was planned

Ford Motor Company's Highland Park Plant, 1913. *Gravity slides and chain conveyors aided the mass production of automobiles.*

with job analysis in mind. In 1910 gravity slides were installed to move parts from one workbench to the next, and by the end of 1913 the system was complete, with endless chain conveyors pulling the parts along feeder lines and the chassis down the final-assembly line.

With mass production placing a greater premium on efficiency, American industry began to apply principles of scientific management to its operations. This involved detailed "time-motion" studies using stopwatches to determine the most efficient way to perform every task in a factory or business. The original "efficiency expert" was Frederick W. Taylor (1856–1915). In the 1880s, working as a foreman for the Midvale Steel Company, Taylor decided that the prevailing practice of having foremen pressure workers for greater output merely resulted in conflict: "Throughout American industry, management's concept of a proper day's work was what the foreman could drive workers to do and the workers' conception was how little they could do and hold their jobs." By the 1890s Taylor's ideas had drawn attention and he had set up shop as a consulting engineer in Philadelphia. In 1895 he outlined his ideas in a paper, "A Piece Rate System," read to the American Society of Mechanical Engineers. The basic principle was to use the carrot instead of the stick, to determine the maximum speed at which work could be done and then offer the incentive of higher piece rates to workers who could attain larger output. His book *The Principles of Scientific Management* (1911) summed up his ideas, which stressed proper organization, time-motion studies to improve factory arrangement, the use of standardized tools and equipment, proper routing and scheduling of work, and the development of planning departments. "Taylorization" caught on widely in the business world and efficiency experts became a normal part of the business scene. Labor tended to view them with skepticism, and in some cases careless or deliberate planning resulted only in ruthless speedups and more of the conflict that Taylor himself deplored. In the 1920s southern textile workers took to calling such bogus efficiency programs the "stretchout."

STABILIZING THE ECONOMY   The drive for efficiency, which had been a prominent feature of the progressive impulse, was now powering the wheels of mass production and consumption, and had become a cardinal belief of Republican leaders. Herbert Hoover, who served as secretary of commerce through the Harding-Coolidge years, was himself an engineer who had made a fortune in far-flung mining operations in Australia, China, Russia, and elsewhere. Out of his experiences in business and his management of Belgian relief, the Food Administration, and other wartime activities, Hoover had developed a philosophy which he set forth in his book *American Individualism* (1922). The idea might best be called "cooperative individualism," or in one of his favorite terms, "associationalism." The principle also owed something to his Quaker upbringing, which taught him the Friends' combination of the work ethic and mutual help. When he applied it to the relations of government and business, Hoover prescribed a kind of middle way between the regulatory and trust-busting traditions, a way of voluntary cooperation.

As secretary of commerce, Hoover was a human dynamo who made the trifling Commerce Department into the most dynamic agency of two listless administrations. During a period of governmental retrenchment he was engaged in expansion. Through an enlarged Bureau of Foreign and Domestic Commerce he sought out new opportunities and markets for business. A Division of Simplified Practice in the Bureau of Standards sponsored more than a thousand conferences on design, production, and distribution, carried forward the wartime move toward standardization of everything from automobile tires and paving bricks to bedsprings and toilet paper, and reduced in number the different kinds of bolts, nuts, and screws. "When I go to ride in an automobile," Hoover told the author Sherwood Anderson, "it does not matter to me that there are a million automobiles on the road just like mine. I am going somewhere and I want to get there in what comfort I can and at the lowest cost." In 1926 Hoover created a Bureau of Aviation and the next year set out to bring order into the new field of radio with the Federal Radio Commission.

Through conferences and organized public relations, techniques that he had used as food administrator, Hoover promoted his ideas. Most of all he endorsed the burgeoning trade-association movement. The organization of trade associations in business became his favorite instrument for "stabilization" to avoid the waste inherent in competition. Through such associations businessmen in a given field would gather and disseminate information on everything: sales, purchases, shipments, productions, and prices. This information allowed them to lay plans with more confidence, the advantages of which included predictable costs, prices, and markets, as well as more stable employment and wages. Sometimes abuses crept in as trade associations skirted the edge of legality by price-fixing and other monopoly practices, but the Supreme Court in 1925 held the practice of sharing information as such to be within the law.

As to the great business combinations themselves, the Supreme Court held to the "rule of reason" it had pronounced in dissolving the Standard Oil Company in 1911. In 1920 the Court found the United States Steel Company an acceptable combination under that rule. After that, wrote two constitutional historians, "almost any monopoly could put up a plausible argument for its social responsibility and thus claim to be a 'reasonable' combination."

THE BUSINESS OF FARMING   During the 1920s agriculture remained a weak point in the economy, in many ways as weak as its position in the 1890s when cities flourished and agriculture languished. Briefly after the war the farmers' hopes soared on wings of prosperity. The wartime boom lasted into 1920, and then prices collapsed. Wheat went in eighteen months from $2.50 a bushel to less than $1; cotton from 35¢ per pound to 13¢. Low prices persisted into 1923, especially in the wheat and corn belts, and after that improvement was spotty. A bumper cotton crop in 1926 resulted only in a price collapse and an early taste of depression in much of the South, where foreclosures and bankruptcies spread.

Yet in many ways farmers shared the entrepreneurial outlook of the New Era. Farms, like corporations, were getting larger, more efficient, and more mechanized. By 1930 about 13 percent of all farmers had tractors, and the proportion was even higher on the western plains. After 1925 the introduction of the smaller Farm-all tractor encouraged greater use of the machine on the smaller farms and hilly lands of the Southeast. Better plows, drills, cultivators, planters, and other machines were part of the mechanization process which accompanied improved crops, fertilizers, and animal breeding.

Farm organizations of the mid to late 1920s moved away from the alliance with urban labor that marked the Populist era and toward

While industry boomed, agriculture remained weak in the 1920s.

a new view of farmers as businessmen. During the postwar farm depression the idea of marketing cooperatives became the farmer's equivalent of the businessman's trade-association movement. Farm groups formed regional commodity-marketing associations which pushed for ironclad contracts with producers ("horse-high, bull-strong, and pig-tight") to deliver their crops over a period of years. They also promoted "orderly marketing," which required standards and grades, efficient handling of commodities and advertising, and a businesslike setup with professional technicians and executives.

Among the various farm groups, one did carry into the twentieth century the old-time gospel of Populism. The Farmers' Union, founded in Texas in 1902, had a mercurial growth in the Southeast much like the Farmers' Alliances, but emerged in the 1920s mainly as a western wheat-belt group. It was soon overshadowed by the American Farm Bureau Federation, a new group representing the "businesslike" attitude of commercial agriculture in the New Era. Founded in 1920 at a meeting in Chicago, the Farm Bureau was an unexpected outgrowth of the farm demonstration movement. Its philosophy stemmed in part from business leaders who supported the county farm bureaus, but more directly from the larger commercial farmers in its membership. Farm Bureau strength in the Midwest and South represented what by the 1920s was being called a "marriage of cotton and corn."

But if concern with marketing co-ops and other businesslike approaches drew farmers even further away from Populism, it was still inevitable that farm problems should invite political solutions. The most effective political response to the crisis of the early 1920s was the formation of the farm bloc, a coalition of western Republicans and southern Democrats that put through an impressive, if fairly moderate, program of legislation from 1921 to 1923. The farm bloc pushed legislation to prevent collusion designed to keep farm prices down. It won an act to exempt farm cooperatives from antitrust laws, and another which set up twelve intermediate credit banks on the model of the Federal Land Banks. The new banks filled the gap of six months to three years between the provisions of short-term loans under the Federal Reserve System and long-term loans by the Land Banks, and could lend to cooperative producing and marketing associations.

Meanwhile a new panacea appeared on the horizon. In the spring of 1924 Senator Charles L. McNary of Oregon and Representative Gilbert N. Haugen of Iowa introduced the first McNary-Haugen Bill. The bill embodied a plan worked out by two executives of the Moline Plow Company to secure "equality for agriculture in the benefits of the protective tariff." Complex as it would have been in operation, it was simple in conception: in short, a plan to dump American farm surpluses on the world market in order to raise prices in the home market. The goal was to achieve "parity"—that is, to raise domestic farm prices to a point where they would have the same purchasing power relative to other prices they had had between 1909 and 1914, a time viewed in retrospect as a golden age of American agriculture.

A McNary-Haugen Bill passed both houses of Congress in 1927, only to be vetoed by President Coolidge. The process was repeated in 1928. Coolidge pronounced the measure an unsound effort at price-fixing, and un-American and unconstitutional to boot. In a broader sense, however, McNary-Haugenism did not fail. The debates made the farm problem into an issue of national policy and defined it as a problem of surpluses. The evolution of the McNary-Haugen plan, moreover, revived the idea of an alliance between the South and West, a coalition which in the next decade became a dominant influence on national farm policy. That policy would follow a different procedure, but its chief focus would be on surpluses, its goal would be "parity," and George N. Peek, one of the Moline Plow Company executives, would preside over its management.

SETBACKS FOR UNIONS Urban workers shared more than farmers in the affluence of the times. "A workman is far better paid in America than anywhere else in the world," a French visitor wrote in 1927, "and his standard of living is enormously higher." Annual per-capita earnings for non-farm workers rose between 1921 and 1928 from an average of $1,171 to $1,408. Without a matching rise in living cost, this meant a gain of about 20 percent in real wages. Farm income rose only 10 percent. The benefits of this rise, however, were distributed unevenly. Miners and textile workers suffered a decline in real wages. In these and other trades technological unemployment followed the introduction of new methods and machines, because technology destroyed as well as created jobs.

Organized labor, however, did no better than organized agriculture in the 1920s. In fact unions suffered a setback after the growth years of the war. The Red Scare and strikes of 1919 left the uneasy impression that unions and subversion were linked, an idea which the enemies of unions promoted. The brief postwar depression of 1921 further weakened the unions, and they felt the severe impact of open-shop associations which proliferated across the country after the war, led by chambers of commerce and other business groups. In January 1921 local business groups came together at a meeting in Chicago where the open shop was officially designated the "American Plan" of employment. While the open shop in theory implied only the employer's right to hire anyone, in practice it meant discrimination against unionists and refusal to recognize unions even in shops where most of the workers belonged to one.

Nor were employers always above the use of strong-arm methods, such as requiring "yellow-dog" contracts that forced workers to agree to stay out of unions, using labor spies, exchanging blacklists, and resorting to intimidation and coercion. Some employers tried to kill the unions with kindness. They introduced programs of "industrial democracy" guided by company unions or various schemes of "welfare capitalism" such as profit-sharing, bonuses, pensions, health programs, recreational activities, and the like. The benefits of such programs were often considerable.

The mood of the times generally impelled governments as well as business into hostility toward unions. When in 1914 the Clayton Anti-Trust Act pronounced labor not an item of commerce, it was hailed as "Labor's Magna Carta." But this turned out to make little difference in the courts' willingness to issue labor injunctions. During the 1920s the high court ruled that the act might limit injunctions against the individual workers, but not against certain union activities. In a 1921 case the Court upheld an injunction against a secondary boycott (a boycott of one company's product by workers at another company). A more telling blow was struck by an injunction against the railway shopmen's strike of 1922. The Railway Labor Board in 1920 had approved a postwar wage cut of 12 percent; when it approved another such cut two years later, the shopmen walked out. On September 1, 1922, the attorney-general secured a sweeping injunction against picketing, strike meetings, statements to the public, expenditure of union funds for strike purposes, or the use of any means of communication by union leaders. "So long as I can speak for the government of the United States," he said, "I will use the power of the government . . . to prevent the labor unions of the country from destroying the open shop." The strike collapsed under the impact of the injunction, and while the union got contracts from friendly railroads for about 225,000 workers, some 175,000 were forced into company unions.

The combined result of prosperity, propaganda, welfare capitalism, and active hostility was a decline in union membership from about 5 million in 1920 to 3.5 million in 1929. In 1924 Samuel Gompers, founder and longtime president of the AFL, died; William Green of the mine workers, who took his place, embodied the conservative, even timid, attitude of unions during the period. The outstanding exception to the anti-union policies of the decade was passage of the Railway Labor Act in 1926, which abolished the Railway Labor Board and substituted a new Board of Mediation. The act also provided for the formation of railway unions "without interference, influence, or coercion," a statement of policy not extended to other workers until the 1930s.

PRESIDENT HOOVER, THE ENGINEER

HOOVER VS. SMITH   On August 2, 1927, while on vacation in the Black Hills of South Dakota, President Coolidge passed out slips of paper to reporters with the statement: "I do not choose to run for President in 1928." Exactly what he meant puzzled observers then and since. Apparently he at least half hoped for a convention draft, but his statement cleared the way for Herbert Hoover to mount an active campaign. Well before the June 1928 Republican convention in Kansas City, Hoover was too far in the lead to be stopped. The platform took credit for prosperity, economy ("raised to a principle of government"), debt and tax reduction, and the protective tariff ("as vital to American agriculture as it is to manufacturing"). It rejected the McNary-Haugen program, but promised a farm board to promote orderly marketing as a way to manage surpluses.

The Democratic nomination was quickly decided in Houston later in June. Governor Alfred E. Smith of New York faced no effective opposition. The party's farm plank, while not endorsing McNary-Haugen, did pledge "economic equality of agriculture with other industries." Like the Republicans, the Democrats pledged enforcement of the Volstead Prohibition Act and, aside from calling for stricter regulation of waterpower resources, promised nothing that departed from the conservative position of the Republicans.

The Democratic party had had its fill of factionalism in 1924, and all remained fairly harmonious until Smith gave the occasion, if not the cause, for revolt by stating in his acceptance speech a personal desire to liberalize the Volstead Act, and then by selecting for national party chairman a man who was Catholic, wet, a General Motors executive, and at least until recently a Republican. Hoover by contrast had pronounced prohibition "a great social and economic experiment, noble in motive and far-reaching in purpose," and called for a study of its enforcement.

The two candidates projected sharply different images which obscured the essential likeness of their programs. Hoover was the Quaker son of middle America, the successful engineer and businessman, the architect of Republican prosperity, while Smith was the prototype of those things rural/small-town America distrusted: the son of Irish immigrants, Catholic, wet, and a Tammanyite whose East Side twang as he spoke on the "raddio" offended the ears of the hinterland. Outside the large cities all those things were handicaps he could scarcely surmount for all his affability and wit.

In the election Hoover won in the third consecutive Republican landslide, with 21 million popular votes to Smith's 15 million, and an even more top-heavy electoral majority of 444 to 87. Hoover even cracked the Solid South, leaving Smith only a hard core of six Deep South states plus Massachusetts and Rhode Island. The election was above all a vindication of Republican prosperity. But the shattering defect of the Democrats concealed a portentous realignment in the making. Smith had nearly doubled the vote for Davis, the Democratic candidate of four years before. Smith's image, though a handicap in the hinterlands, swung big cities back into the Democratic column. In the farm states of the West there were signs that some disgruntled farmers had switched over to the Democrats. A coalition of urban workers and unhappy farmers was in the making.

HOOVER IN CONTROL The milestone year 1929 dawned with high hopes. Business seemed good, incomes were rising, and the chief architect of Republican prosperity was about to enter the White House. "I have no fears for the future of our country," Hoover told the audience at his inauguration. "It is bright with hope." For Hoover the presidency crowned a career of steady ascent, first in mining, then in public service. Hoover's image combined the benevolence fitting a director of wartime relief and the efficiency of a businessman and administrator. More than most presidents, he had articulated a philosophy of public affairs, to which in his last speech of the 1928 campaign he gave the misleading tag of "rugged individualism." But since he found initiative and enterprise best served by "orderly liberty" and by cooperation, his notion of individualism was less rugged than the slogan suggested.

Hoover approached his new duties much as he might have set about reshaping a mining venture during his days as a consulting engineer. He assigned specific duties to each member of the staff. He promoted voluntary cooperation through "publicity conferences," much as he had done at the Commerce Department. His passion for facts and figures resulted in several major studies of American life at the time: by the Wickersham Commission on Crime and Law Enforcement, and by the Committees on Recent Social Trends, on Recent Economic Change, and on Child Health and Protection—the last a lifetime concern of a man who had himself been orphaned.

Forgotten in the rush of later events would be Hoover's credentials as progressive and humanitarian. Over the objection of Treasury Secretary Mellon, he announced a plan for tax reductions in the low-income brackets. He took action against corrupt patronage practices, and refused to countenance "Red hunts" or interference with peaceful picketing of the White House. He defended his wife's right to entertain the wife of Oscar DePriest, the first black congressman

"I have no fears for the future of our country," Herbert Hoover told his audience at his inauguration in 1929.

since 1901 and the first ever from the North, sought more money for all-black Howard University, and proposed that the new federal parole board reflect the number of blacks and women in prison. He went along, however, with his party's "lily-white" strategy of ignoring or excluding African-Americans in most southern states.

His program to stabilize business carried over into his program for agriculture, the most visibly weak sector of the economy. To treat the malady of glutted markets he had two main remedies: federal help for cooperative marketing and higher tariffs on farm products. He pushed through a special session of Congress in June 1929 the Agricultural Marketing Act, which gave support to farm cooperatives by setting up a Federal Farm Board with a revolving loan fund of $500 million to help cooperatives market the major commodities. The act provided also, at the demand of the farm bloc, a program in which the Farm Board could set up "stabilization corporations" empowered to buy surpluses off the market. Unluckily for any chance of success the plan might have had, it got under way almost simultaneously with the onset of the depression that fall.

Farmers gained even less from tariff revision. What Hoover won after fourteen months of struggle with competing local interest was in fact a general upward revision on manufactures as well as farm goods. The Hawley-Smoot Tariff of June 1930 carried duties to an all-time high. Rates went up on some 70 farm products and more than 900 manufactured items. More than 1,000 economists petitioned Hoover to veto the bill because, they said, it would raise prices to consumers, damage the export trade, and thus hurt farmers, promote inefficiency, and provoke foreign reprisals. Events proved them right, but Hoover felt that he had to go along with his party in an election year.

THE ECONOMY OUT OF CONTROL   The tariff did nothing to check a deepening crisis of confidence in the economy. After the slump of 1921 the idea grew that with recovery business had entered a New Era of permanent growth. But real growth propelled an expansive ballyhoo, and a growing contagion of get-rich-quick schemes. Speculative mania fueled the Florida real-estate boom which began when the combination of Coolidge prosperity and Ford's "tin lizzies" gave people extra money and made Florida an accessible playground. By 1925 Miami had become a scene of frantic excitement. In the fun-fair of fast turnover the reckless speculator was, if anything, more likely to gain than the prudent investor, and the "binder boys" perfected to a fine art the practice of making money at little or no risk. The principle was to pay a small "binder" fee for an option to buy on promise of a later down payment, then reap a profit by selling

Miami Beach, 1925. *A real-estate boom transformed southern Florida in the early 1920s, but the bubble burst in mid-1926.*

binders which might pass through a dozen hands and might or might not convey title. It was the latest in a series of speculative bubbles that had been bursting on the American scene since the British South Sea Bubble of the eighteenth century. By mid-1926, when there were no more "bigger fools" left to whom one could "pass the baby," the Florida bubble burst.

For the losers it was a sobering lesson, but it proved to be but an audition for the Great Bull Market in stocks. Until 1927 stock values had gone up with profits, but then they began to soar on wings of pure speculation. Mellon's tax reductions had released money which, with the help of aggressive brokerage houses, found its way to Wall Street. Instead of trading binders on real estate, one could buy stock on margin—that is, make a small down payment (the "margin") and borrow the rest from a broker who held the stock as security against a down market. If the stock declined and the buyer failed to meet a margin call for more money, the broker could sell the stock to cover his loan. Brokers' loans more than doubled from June 1927 to September 1929.

Gamblers in the market ignored warning signs. By 1927 residential construction and automobile sales were catching up to demand, business inventories rose, and the rate of consumer spending slowed. By mid-1929 production, employment, and other measures of economic activity were declining. Still the market rose. Radio Corporation of America, for example, rose from under 100 in March 1928 to over 500 on September 3, 1929, which was when the market peaked.

By 1929 the market had entered a fantasy world. Conservative financiers and brokers who counseled caution were ignored. The president worried too, and urged stock exchange and Federal Reserve officers to discourage speculation. In August the Federal Reserve Board raised the rate on loans to member banks (the rediscount rate) to 6 percent, but with no effect. On September 4 stock prices wavered, and the day after that they dropped, opening a season of fluctuations. The Great Bull Market staggered on into October, trending downward but with enough good days to keep hope alive. On October 22 the president of the National City Bank, returning from Europe, told reporters: "I know of nothing fundamentally wrong with the stock market or with the underlying business and credit structure."

THE CRASH AND ITS CAUSES The next day prices crumbled, and the day after that a wild scramble to unload stocks lasted until word arrived that leading bankers had formed a pool to stabilize prices. Prices steadied for the rest of the week, but after a weekend to think the situation over, stockholders began to unload on Monday. The *New York Times* index of industrials went down 49 points. On Tuesday, October 29, the most devastating single day in the market's history, the index dropped another 43 points. The market reported sales of 16.4 million shares (at the time 3 million shares traded was a busy day) and some issues went begging for buyers. The plunge in prices fed on itself as brokers sold the shares they held for buyers who failed to meet their margin calls. During October stocks on the New York Exchange fell in value by 37 percent.

The first impulse of business and government leaders was to express hope. According to President Hoover, "the fundamental business of the country" was sound. John D. Rockefeller issued his first public statement in decades: "my son and I have for some days been purchasing sound common stocks." A well-known comedian retorted: "Sure, who else has any money left?" Some speculators who got out of the market went back in for bargains but found themselves caught in a slow, tedious erosion of values. By March 1, 1933, the value of stocks on the New York Exchange was less than a fifth of the value at the market's peak. The *New York Times* stock average, which stood at 452 on September 3, 1929, bottomed at 52 in July 1932.

Caution became the watchword for consumers and businessmen. Buyers held out for lower prices, orders fell off, wages fell or ceased

Apprehensive crowds gathered on the steps of the Subtreasury Building, across from the New York Stock Exchange, as news of a stock collapse spread, October 29, 1929.

altogether, and the decline in purchasing power brought further cutbacks in business. From 1929 to 1932 Americans' personal incomes declined by more than half, from $82 million to $40 million. Unemployment continued to rise. Farmers, already in trouble, faced catastrophe. More than 9,000 banks closed during the period, hundreds of factories and mines shut down, and thousands of farms were foreclosed for debt and sold at auction.

The crash had revealed the fundamental business of the country to be unsound. Most harmful was the ability of business to maintain prices and take profits while holding down wages and the cost of raw materials, with the result that about one-third of the personal income went to only 5 percent of the population. By plowing most profits back into expansion rather than wage increases, business brought on a growing imbalance between rising productivity and declining purchasing power. As the demand for goods declined, the rate of investment in the new plants began to decline. For a time the softness of purchasing power was concealed by greater use of installment buying, and the deflationary effects of high tariffs were concealed by the volume of loans and investments abroad which supported foreign demand for American goods. But the flow of American capital abroad began to dry up when the stock market began to look more attractive. Swollen profits and dividends, together with the Mellon tax policies, enticed the rich into market speculation. When trouble came, the bloated corporate structure collapsed.

Governmental policies also contributed to the debacle. Mellon's tax reductions brought oversaving, which helped diminish demand. The growing money supply fed the fever of speculation. Hostility toward labor unions discouraged collective bargaining and may have worsened the prevalent imbalances in income. High tariffs discouraged foreign trade. Lax enforcement of antitrust laws encouraged concentration, monopoly, and high prices.

HOOVER'S EFFORTS AT RECOVERY   Not only did the policies of public officials help bring on economic collapse, but few public leaders acknowledged the crisis: all that was needed, they thought, was a slight correction of the market. Those who held to the dogma of laissez-faire thought the economy would cure itself. The best policy, Secretary Mellon advised, would be to "liquidate labor, liquidate stocks, liquidate the farmers, liquidate real estate." Hoover himself had little patience with speculators, but he was unwilling now to sit by and let events take their course. Hoover in fact did more than any president had ever done before in such dire economic circumstances. Still, his own philosophy, now hardened into dogma, set limits to governmental action, and he was unready to set it aside even to meet an emergency.

As food administrator and promoter of voluntary associations Hoover had insisted on strong public relations departments. He believed also that the nation's fundamental business structure was sound and that the country's main need was confidence. In speech after speech Hoover exhorted the public to keep up hope, and he summoned business and labor leaders for talks at the White House. Hoover asked owners to keep the mills and shops open, maintain wage rates, and spread the work to avoid layoffs—in short to let the first shock fall on corporate profits rather than on purchasing power. In return union leaders, who had little choice, agreed to refrain from wage demands and strikes. As it happened, however, words were not enough, and the prediction that good times were just around the corner (actually made by the vice-president though attributed to Hoover) eventually became a sardonic joke.

Hoover did more than try to reassure the American public. He hurried the building of public works in order to provide jobs, but state and local cutbacks more than offset federal spending. At

There Is a Santa Claus! *An incredulous citizen watches as Hoover fills the Christmas stocking with business confidence. It proved cold comfort.*

Hoover's demand the Federal Reserve returned to an easier credit policy, and Congress passed a modest tax reduction to put more purchasing power in people's pockets. The Federal Farm Board stepped up its loans and its purchases of farm surpluses only to face bumper crops in 1930 despite droughts in the Midwest and Southwest. The high Hawley-Smoot Tariff, proposed at first to help farmers, brought reprisals abroad, devastating foreign trade.

As always, depression hurt the party in power. Democrats exploited Hoover's predicament for all it was worth, and more. But their role in building the depression image of Hoover has been overblown. In 1930 the floundering president was easy game. During the war, "to Hooverize" had signified patriotic sacrifice; now the president's name signified distress. Near the city dumps, along the railroad tracks, the dispossessed huddled in shacks of tarpaper and galvanized iron, old packing boxes, and abandoned cars. These squalid settlements became "Hoovervilles." A "Hoover blanket" was a newspaper; a "Hoover flag," an empty pocket turned inside out; "Hoover wagons" were cars pulled by mules; "Hoover hogs" were jackrabbits. In November 1930 the Democrats gained their first national victory since 1916, winning a majority in the House and enough gains in the Senate to control it in coalition with western agrarians.

One irony of the time was that the great humanitarian of wartime relief was recast as the stubborn opponent of depression relief. But Hoover was still doing business at the same old stand: his answer

"Hoovervilles" of tarpaper shacks sprang up around the country as the depression set in.

remained voluntarism. When the head of the Emergency Committee for Employment strongly recommended a governmental program of $840 million for road building and other public works, the president turned it down. His annual message to Congress in December 1930 demanded that each community and state undertake the relief of distress "with that sturdiness and independence which built a great Nation." One literary critic found it "a reassuring thought, in the cold weather, that the emaciated men in the bread lines, the men and women beggars in the streets, and the children dependent on them, are all having their fibre hardened."

In the first half of 1931 economic indicators rose, renewing hope for an upswing. Then, as recovery beckoned, another shock fell. In May 1931 the failure of Austria's largest bank triggered panic in central Europe. On June 20, to halt the domino effect of spreading defaults, President Hoover proposed a one-year moratorium on both reparations and war-debt payments. The moratorium, as it happened, became permanent simply by process of default. In July the major European nations accepted the moratorium and later also a temporary "standstill" on settlement of private obligations between banks. The general shortage of exchange drove Europeans to with-draw their gold from American banks and dump their American securities. One European country after another abandoned the gold standard and devalued its currency. In September even the Bank of England went off the gold standard. The United States meanwhile slid into the third bitter winter of depression.

CONGRESSIONAL INITIATIVES With a new Congress in session, de-mands for federal action impelled Hoover to stretch his individualis-tic philosophy to its limits. He was ready now to use governmental resources at least to shore up the financial institutions of the country. The former head of the War Finance Corporation prompted Hoover to bring back the agency for a new purpose. In January 1932 the new Congress set up the Reconstruction Finance Corporation (RFC) with $500 million (and authority to borrow $2 billion more) for emergency loans to banks, life insurance companies, building and loan societies, farm mortgage associations, and railroads. Under former vice-presi-dent Charles G. Dawes, it authorized $1.2 billion in loans within six months. The RFC staved off bankruptcies, but Hoover's critics found in it favoritism to business, the most damaging instance of which was a $90 million loan to Dawes's Chicago bank, made soon after he left the RFC in June 1932. The RFC nevertheless remained a key agency through the New Deal and World War II.

Further help to the financial structure came with the Glass-Stea-gall Act of February 1932, which broadened the definition of com-mercial loans that the Federal Reserve would support. The new arrangement also released about $750 million in gold formerly used to back Federal Reserve Notes, countering the effect of foreign withdrawals and domestic hoarding of gold at the same time that it enlarged the supply of credit. For homeowners the Federal Home Loan Bank Act of July 1932 created with Hoover's blessing a series of discount banks for home mortgages. They provided for savings and loan and other mortgage agencies a service much like that the Federal Reserve System provided to commercial banks.

All these measures reflected a dubious "trickle-down" theory, Hoover's critics said. If government could help banks and railroads, asked New York senator Robert G. Wagner, "is there any reason why we should not likewise extend a helping hand to that forlorn American, in every village and every city of the United States, who has been without wages since 1929?" By 1932 members of Congress were filling the hoppers with bills for federal relief. At that point Hoover might have pleaded "dire necessity" and, backed by his reputation in the field, taken the leadership of the relief movement and salvaged his political fortunes.

Instead he held back and only grudgingly edged toward federal relief. House Speaker John Nance Garner of Texas, with his own eye cocked to the White House, proposed a $1 billion bond issue for federal public works, another $1 billion for RFC loans to state and local public works, and $100 million for distribution to the needy. Senator Wagner proposed even more, but a compromise bill that came out of conference committee met a presidential veto. Then on July 21, 1932, Hoover signed the Emergency Relief and Construction Act, which avoided a direct federal dole but gave the RFC $300 million for relief loans to the states, authorized loans of up to $1.5 billion for state and local public works, and appropriated $322 million for federal public works.

Relief for farmers had long since been abandoned. In mid-1931 the government quit buying surpluses and helplessly watched prices slide. In 1919 wheat had fetched $2.16 a bushel; by 1932 it had sunk to 38¢. Cotton brought 17¢ a pound in 1929; before the 1932 harvest it went to 5¢. Other farm prices declined comparably. Net cash income for farmers dropped more than 55 percent from 1929 to 1932. Between 1930 and 1934 nearly a million farms passed from their owners to the mortgage holders.

Wisconsin farmers dumping milk in protest against low prices.

Unemployed veterans, members of the "Bonus Expeditionary Force," clash with Washington, D.C., police at Anacostia Flats, July 1932.

FARMERS AND VETERANS IN PROTEST   Faced with the loss of everything, some desperate farmers began to defy the law. Angry mobs stopped foreclosures and threatened to lynch the judges sanctioning them. In Nebraska farmers burned corn to keep warm. In Iowa, the former head of the state's Farmers' Union formed the militant Farmers' Holiday Association, which called a farmers' strike and forcibly blocked deliveries of produce. Dairymen dumped milk into roadside ditches. On the whole, like voluntary efforts to reduce acreage, the strikes failed, but they vividly dramatized the farmer's surly mood.

In the midst of the crisis there was desperate if nebulous talk of revolution. "Folks are restless," Mississippi's governor Theodore Bilbo told reporters in 1931. "Communism is gaining a foothold. . . . In fact, I'm getting a little pink myself." Bilbo was doing his usual put-on, but across the country the once-obscure Communist party began to draw crowds to its rallies and willing collaborators into its "hunger marches." In Alabama it formed a Share Croppers Union and reaped a propaganda windfall when the party went to the defense of the Scottsboro Boys, nine black itinerants accused on flimsy evidence of raping two white girls on a freight train in northern Alabama. Around Harlan, Kentucky, desperate coal miners embraced the Communist-run National Mine Workers' Union, which fell victim to guns and whips and ultimately to the rock-ribbed faith of miners who heard leaders "denounce our government and our flag and our religion." For all the sound and fury, few were converted to the Communist view. Party membership never rose much above 100,000.

Fears of mass disorder arose when unemployed veterans converged on Washington in the spring of 1932. The "Bonus Expeditionary Force" sent its first contingent of 330 late in May, and after that the number grew quickly to more than 15,000. Their purpose was to get immediate payment of the bonus to world-war veterans which Congress had voted in 1924. It took the form of endowment life insurance payable in 1945—or earlier to the heirs of veterans who died before that date. In 1931, over Hoover's veto, Congress had authorized loans of up to 50 percent of the value of each insurance certificate, but the veterans now wanted everything in cash. The House approved a bonus bill introduced by Wright Patman of Texas, but when the Senate voted it down in June most of the veterans went home. The rest, having no place to go, camped in vacant government buildings and in a shantytown at Anacostia Flats, within sight of the Capitol.

The chief of the Washington police, once the youngest brigadier-general of the American Expeditionary Force (the name given to American forces in Europe during the war), gave the squatters a friendly welcome and won their trust. But a fearful White House fretted. Eager to disperse them, Hoover convinced Congress to pay for their tickets home. More left, but others stayed even after Congress adjourned, hoping at least to meet with the president. Late in July the administration ordered the government buildings cleared. In the ensuing melee, one policeman panicked, fired into the crowd, and killed two veterans. The president then acceded to a request from his secretary of war to move in about 700 soldiers under General Douglas MacArthur, aided by junior officers Dwight D. Eisenhower and George S. Patton, Jr. The soldiers drove out the unarmed veterans and their families, injuring dozens, and burned the shacks. Among the evicted was a New Jersey man who had received the Distinguished Service Cross for a wartime exploit that saved the life of George Patton. The one fatality—from tear gas—was an eleven-week-old boy born at Anacostia.

General MacArthur said the "mob," animated by "the essence of revolution," was about to seize control of the government. The administration insisted that the Bonus Army consisted mainly of Communists and criminals, but neither a grand jury nor the Veterans Administration could find evidence to support the charge. One observer wrote before the incident: "There is about the lot of them an atmosphere of hopelessness, of utter despair, though not of desperation. . . . they have no enthusiasm whatever and no stomach for fighting."

Their mood, and the mood of the country, was much like that of Hoover himself. He worked hard, but took no joy from his labors. "I am so tired," he sometimes said, "that every bone in my body aches." He was, as William Allen White reported, "constitutionally gloomy, a congenital pessimist who always saw the doleful side of any situation." A private meeting with Hoover, his secretary of state said, was "like sitting in a bath of ink." News conferences became more strained and less frequent. When friends urged him to seize the reins of leadership he said, "I can't be a Theodore Roosevelt," or "I have no Wilsonian qualities." The gloom, the sense of futility, communicated itself to the country. In a mood more despairing than rebellious, people waited to see what another presidential campaign would produce.

FURTHER READING

The most recent synthesis of events immediately following the First World War is Ellis W. Hawley's *The Great War and the Search for a Modern Order: A History of the American People and Their Institutions, 1917–1933* (1979).° For a short introduction to the period, see William E. Leuchtenburg's *The Perils of Prosperity, 1914–1932* (1985).°

For an introduction to Harding, see Francis Russell's *The Shadow of Blooming Grove: Warren G. Harding in His Times* (1968). Robert K. Murray's *The Harding Era: Warren G. Harding and His Administration* (1969) is more favorable to Harding. On Coolidge, see Donald R. McCoy's *Calvin Coolidge: The Silent President* (1967). Studies on Hoover include Joan Hoff Wilson's *Herbert Hoover: Forgotten Progressive* (1975)° and George Nash's multivolume *The Life of Herbert Hoover* (1983–   ).

Studies of other prominent 1920s figures include Oscar Handlin's *Al Smith and His America* (1958) and William Harbaugh's *Lawyer's Lawyer: The Life of John W. Davis* (1973). Other works on politics include Burl Noggle's *Teapot Dome: Oil and Politics in the 1920s* (1962)° and David Burner's *The Politics of Provincialism: The Democratic Party in Transition, 1918–1932* (1968).° William H. Chafe's *The American Woman: Her Changing Social, Economic, and Political Roles* (1972)° is a good introduction to the achievement of suffrage.

The impact of transportation is gauged in Reynold M. Wik's *Henry Ford and Grassroots America* (1972).° Stuart Ewen looks at the effect of mass advertising in *Captains of Consciousness* (1976). Roland Marchand's *Adver-*

°These books are available in paperback editions.

tising the American Dream (1985) covers the development of national advertising in the 1920s. Susan J. Douglas's *Inventing American Broadcasting, 1899–1922* (1989) is a cultural history of the formative years of radio. Motion pictures are the subject of Robert Sklar's *Movie-Made America* (1975) and Lary May's *Screening out the Past* (1980).°

Overviews of the depression are found in C. P. Kindleberger's *The World in Depression* (rev. ed., 1986)° and Peter Fearon's *War, Prosperity and Depression: The U.S. Economy, 1917–1945* (1987). A review of the economics of the 1920s is given in John Kenneth Galbraith's *Money: Whence It Came, Where It Went* (1975). Galbraith details the fall of the stock market in *The Great Crash, 1929* (1955).° Another interpretation is given in Peter Temin's *Did Monetary Forces Cause the Great Depression?* (1976).°

John A. Garraty's *The Great Depression* (1986) describes how people survived the depression. Garraty's *Unemployment in History: Economic Thought and Public Policy* (1978) explores what the nation thought about its plight. Firsthand accounts of the Great Depression can be found in Tom E. Terrill and Jerrold Hirsch's *Such As Us* (1978),° Studs Terkel's *Hard Times* (1970),° Robert S. McElvaine's *Down and Out in the Great Depression* (1983),° and *"Slaves of the Depression": Workers' Letters about Life on the Job* (1989) edited by Gerald Markowitz and David Rosner.

28

FRANKLIN D. ROOSEVELT
AND THE NEW DEAL

From Hooverism to the New Deal

FDR'S ELECTION   On June 14, 1932, while the Bonus Army was still encamped in Washington, Republicans gathered in Chicago to renominate Hoover. The apathetic and dreary proceedings were enlivened only by debate over a prohibition plank, the final version of which straddled the issue. The delegates went through the motions in a mood of defeat.

The Democrats, in contrast, converged on Chicago late in June confident that they would nominate the next president. New York governor Franklin D. Roosevelt was already the front-runner with most of the delegates lined up, but he still faced an uphill battle for a two-thirds majority. Al Smith, long a favorite of the party machine, felt entitled to one more chance at the White House. But Smith's time had passed; he could not control even his own state's delegation. Among the favorite sons only House Speaker John Nance Garner of Texas had any serious chance. After a Garner delegation won the California primary, the Texan was in a position to deadlock the convention, but the memory of the 1924 deadlock remained strong. When Representative Sam Rayburn described the lineup on the telephone, Garner replied: "All right, release my delegates. . . . Hell, I'll do anything to see the Democrats win one more national election." Thus Roosevelt went over the top on the fourth ballot; Garner's reward was the vice-presidency, an office he later pronounced "not worth a pitcher of warm spit."

In a bold gesture, Roosevelt flew to Chicago and appeared before the convention in person to accept the nomination instead of awaiting formal notification. "Let it . . . be symbolic that . . . I broke traditions," he told the delegates. "Republican leaders not only have failed in material things, they have failed in national vision, because in disaster they have held out no hope. . . . I pledge you, I pledge myself to a new deal for the American people." What the New Deal would be Roosevelt himself had little idea as yet, but unlike Hoover, he was flexible and willing to experiment. What was more, his ebullient personality communicated joy and hope. His campaign song was "Happy Days Are Here Again."

Roosevelt was strengthened also by his background and experience. Born to a comfortable fortune in 1882, he had the advantage of a proper education at Groton School and Harvard, topped off by the Columbia Law School. Although raised a Democrat, he admired his distant cousin Theodore, and up to a point his career retraced the same path. Elected to the New York state legislature in 1910, he caught the public eye by opposing Tammany's candidate for the United States Senate. In 1912 he backed Wilson, and for both of Wilson's terms was his assistant secretary of the navy. Then in 1920, largely on the strength of his name, he became Cox's running mate. In defeat the parallel with Theodore ended, and the following year his career seemed cut short by an attack of poliomyelitis which left him permanently crippled, unable to stand or walk without braces. But the struggle for recovery transformed the once supercilious young aristocrat into one of the most outgoing political figures of the century. Justice Oliver Wendell Holmes, Jr., later summed up his qualities this way: "A second-class intellect—but a first-class temperament."

For seven years Roosevelt fought his way back to health and in 1928 emerged again on the national scene to nominate Al Smith for the presidency. At Smith's urging he ran for governor of New York to strengthen the ticket and won while Smith was losing the state. Reelected governor by a whopping majority of 700,000 in 1930, he became the front-runner for 1932.

Partly to dispel doubts about his health, Roosevelt set forth on a grueling campaign tour. He proposed to pin responsibility for the depression on Hoover and the Republicans, and to define the New Deal. Always deft at picking other men's brains, he relied mainly on a panel of advisers from Columbia University: Raymond Moley, G. Rexford Tugwell, and A. A. Berle, Jr. In turn this Brain Trust, as reporters quickly dubbed it, tapped other sources in preparing drafts for major speeches. Roosevelt of course tempered their ideas to political realities, often fuzzing them over to avoid offending any large bloc of voters, and usually hedged his bets by offering alternative courses of action.

Governor Franklin D. Roosevelt, the Democratic nominee, campaigning in Topeka, Kansas. Roosevelt's confidence inspired voters.

Like Hoover, Roosevelt made the requisite promise to balance the budget, but he left open the loophole that he would incur deficits to prevent starvation and dire want. On the tariff he was evasive. On farm policy he offered several options pleasing to farmers and ambiguous enough not to alarm city dwellers. He did call for strict regulation of utilities and for at least some development of public power, and he consistently stood by his party's pledge to repeal the prohibition amendment. At the Commonwealth Club in San Francisco the candidate gazed into a clouded crystal ball and announced that the era of freewheeling economic expansion, like Frederick Jackson Turner's frontier, had come to an end. Such opinions prevailed widely at the time. A mature economy would require national planning, Roosevelt said. "The country needs, and, unless I mistake its temper, the country demands bold, persistent experimentation. . . . Above all, try something."

What came across to voters, however, was less the content of his speeches than the confidence of the man. Hoover by contrast lacked assurance. He could turn a neat phrase, but many elegant passages suffered from the pedestrian manner of his delivery. Democrats, he argued, ignored the international causes of the depression. They

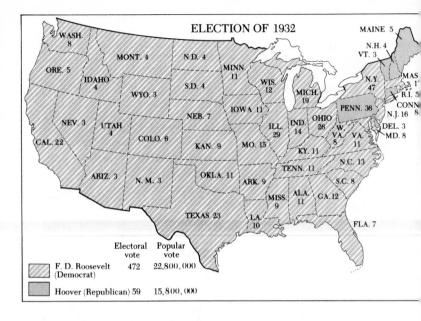

ELECTION OF 1932

	Electoral vote	Popular vote
F. D. Roosevelt (Democrat)	472	22,800,000
Hoover (Republican)	59	15,800,000

were taking a reckless course. Roosevelt's evasive stand on the tariff, he said, made the Democratic candidate look like a chameleon on plaid. Roosevelt's policies, he warned, "would destroy the very foundations of our American system." Pursue them, and "grass will grow in the streets of a hundred cities, a thousand towns." But few were listening. Amid the persistent depression the country wanted a new course, a new leadership, a new deal.

Many thoughtful observers took a dim view of both candidates. They agreed with Walter Lippmann's earlier judgment that Roosevelt was "a pleasant man, who, without any important qualifications for the office, would very much like to be President." Those who believed only a radical departure would suffice went over to Socialist Norman Thomas, who polled 882,000 votes, and some went on to the Communist party candidate, who got 103,000. The wonder is that a desperate people did not turn in greater numbers to radical candidates. Instead they swept Roosevelt into office by 22.8 million votes to Hoover's 15.8 million. Hoover carried only four states in New England plus Pennsylvania and Delaware, and lost in the electoral college by 472 to 59.

THE INAUGURATION For the last time the country waited four long months, until March 4, for a new president and Congress to take office. The Twentieth Amendment, ratified on February 6, 1933, provided that presidents would take office thereafter on January 20 and the newly elected Congress on January 3. Before the end of

November the president-elect visited the White House for an inconclusive conference. Hoover proposed a joint effort, but only on his own terms, so Roosevelt, like Lincoln, warily avoided commitment until power was his own. With policy abandoned to drift, the bleak winter of 1932–1933 became what one historian called "the interregnum of despair." Amid spreading destitution and misery, unemployment continued to rise and panic struck the banking system. Depositors played it safe by taking their cash out and squirreling it away. In Michigan, where automobile production stalled, the threat of runs on the banks impelled the governor to extend the Lincoln's Birthday closing indefinitely. As panic spread, governors of other states also found excuses for banking holidays. When the Hoover administration ended, four-fifths of the nation's banks were closed and the country was on the brink of economic paralysis.

The profound crisis of confidence that prevailed when Roosevelt took the oath of office on March 4, 1933, was tempered by a mood of expectancy. The new president exploited both with a spirit of assurance that conveyed a new sense of vigor and action. First, he asserted a "firm belief that the only thing we have to fear is fear itself—nameless, unreasoning, unjustified terror which paralyzes needed efforts to convert retreat into advance." Roosevelt promised to fill the vacuum of leadership: "The money changers have fled from their high seats in the temple of our civilization. We may now restore that temple to the ancient truths." He would not merely exhort, he promised: "This nation asks for action, and action now!" He warned that emergency measures might call for a temporary departure from the normal balance of executive and legislative authority. If need be, he said, "I shall not evade the clear course of duty. . . . I shall ask the Congress for the remaining instrument to meet the crisis—broad executive power to wage a war against the emergency as great as the power that would be given me if we were in fact invaded by a foreign foe." It was a measure of the country's mood that this call received the loudest applause.

Roosevelt was not the first to resort to what one historian has called "the analogue of war." Time and again the nation's mobilization for World War I was held up as a model for action in the new crisis. The Reconstruction Finance Corporation, started under Hoover but sometimes called the first New Deal agency, was but the War Finance Corporation reborn. Many of Roosevelt's appointees had been involved in the wartime mobilization. George Peek and Hugh S. Johnson, for instance, had once worked for the War Industries Board; soon they would head the New Deal farm and industrial recovery programs. Other cabinet officers drew upon backgrounds in social work. Frances Perkins, the secretary of labor, was the first female cabinet member. A graduate of Mount Holyoke, she worked with Jane Addams at Chicago's Hull House at the turn of the century. Later she was appointed executive secretary of the Consumers' League in New York and became an enormously effective advocate for labor reform.

It was Roosevelt's willingness to act decisively, to experiment with new programs and policies, that set his presidency apart. He was a pragmatist rather than an ideologue. As he once explained, "Take a method and try it. If it fails admit it frankly and try another." The new president compared himself to a football quarterback: he could not call the next play until he knew the results of the previous one. Roosevelt's "New Deal," therefore, would take the form of a series of trial-and-error actions.

STRENGTHENING THE MONETARY SYSTEM   The first order of business for the new administration was to unclog the channels of finance. On his second day in office, Roosevelt called Congress to meet in special session on March 9, and then declared a four-day banking holiday, invoking powers under the Trading with the Enemy Act of 1917. It took Congress only seven hours to pass the Emergency Banking Relief Act, which permitted sound banks to reopen under license from the Treasury and provided managers for those that remained in trouble. On March 12, in the first of his radio "fireside chats," the president told his audience it was safer to "keep your money in a reopened bank than under the mattress." The following day, deposits in reopened banks exceeded withdrawals, and by March 15 banks controlling nine-tenths of the nation's banking resources were once again open. The crisis had ended and the new administration was ready to get on with its broader program.

In rapid order Roosevelt undertook to meet two specific pledges in the Democratic platform. At his behest, on March 20 Congress passed an Economy Act granting the executive the power to cut salaries, reduce payments to veterans for non-service-connected disabilities, and reorganize agencies in the interest of economy. On March 22 the Beer-Wine Revenue Act amended the Volstead Act to permit sale of beverages with an alcoholic content of 3.2 percent. The Twenty-first Amendment, already submitted by Congress to the states on February 20, would be declared ratified on December 5, thus ending the "noble experiment" of prohibition.

The measures of March were but the beginning. During the session from March 9 to June 16, the so-called Hundred Days, Congress received and enacted fifteen major proposals from the president, with a dizzying speed unlike anything seen before in American history:

March 9	The Emergency Banking Relief Act
March 20	The Economy Act
March 31	Establishment of the Civilian Conservation Corps
April 19	Abandonment of the gold standard
May 12	The Federal Emergency Relief Act
May 12	The Agricultural Adjustment Act, including the Thomas Amendment which gave the president powers to expand the money supply
May 12	The Emergency Farm Mortgage Act, providing for the refinancing of farm mortgages
May 18	The Tennessee Valley Authority Act, providing for the unified development of the Tennessee Valley
May 27	The Federal Securities Act, requiring full disclosure in the issue of new securities
June 5	The Gold Repeal Joint Resolution, which abrogated the gold clause in public and private contracts
June 13	The Home Owners' Loan Act, setting up the Home Owners' Loan Corporation to refinance home mortgages
June 16	The National Industrial Recovery Act, providing for a system of industrial self-regulation under federal supervision and for a $3.3 billion public-works program
June 16	The Glass-Steagall Banking Act, separating commercial and investment banking and establishing the Federal Deposit Insurance Corporation
June 16	The Farm Credit Act, which reorganized the agricultural credit system

With the banking crisis over, there remained an acute debt problem for farmers and homeowners, and a lingering distrust of the banks which might yet be aroused again. On March 27, by executive decree, Roosevelt reorganized all farm credit agencies into the Farm Credit Administration (FCA). By the Emergency Farm Mortgage Act (May 12) and the Farm Credit Act (June 16) Congress confirmed that action and authorized extensive refinancing of farm mortgages at lower interest rates. Within seven months the FCA loaned farmers more than $100 million, nearly four times as much as all the land-bank loans made the previous year.

The Home Owners' Loan Act (June 13) provided a similar service to city dwellers through the new Home Owners' Loan Corporation (HOLC)—something which, incidentally, Hoover had vainly urged on Congress in 1931. The Glass-Steagall Banking Act (June 16) further shored up confidence in the banking system. It created the Federal Deposit Insurance Corporation (FDIC) to guarantee bank deposits of up to $5,000. To prevent speculative abuses, it separated investment and commercial banking corporations and extended the Federal Reserve's regulatory power over credit. The Federal Securities Act (May 27) required the full disclosure of information about new stock and bond issues, at first by registration with the Federal Trade Commission, later with the Securities and Exchange Commission (SEC), which was created on June 6, 1934, to regulate the stock and bond markets.

Throughout 1933 Roosevelt tinkered with devaluation of the currency as a way to raise prices and thus ease the debt burden. Having already put an embargo on the withdrawal of gold deposits at the outset of his administration, on April 5 he used powers granted by the Emergency Banking Act to order all gold turned in to the Federal Reserve Banks. On April 19 the government officially abandoned the gold standard: the consequent decline in the value of the dollar increased the prices of commodities and stocks at home. The Gold Repeal Joint Resolution (June 5) canceled the gold clause in federal and private obligations, made all contracts payable in legal tender, and thus completed the abandonment of the gold standard. The experiment ended when Congress passed the Gold Reserve Act of January 30, 1934, which authorized the president to impound all gold in the Federal Reserve Banks and reduce the theoretical gold value of the dollar. By executive order he set the price of an ounce of gold at $35, which in effect reduced the dollar's gold content. It was done, Roosevelt said, "to make possible the payment of . . . debts at more nearly the price level at which they had been incurred." Prices did rise, and the high price set on gold drew most of the world's supply to the United States, where it was buried in the vaults at Fort Knox, Kentucky.

RELIEF MEASURES   In 1933, relieving the widespread personal distress caused by the Great Depression was an urgent priority, as it would remain until World War II. As Roosevelt once remarked, the "test of our progress is not whether we add to the abundance of those who have much. It is whether we provide enough for those who have too little." A first step toward such relief came with the creation in March of the Civilian Conservation Corps (CCC), which was designed to give work relief to young men aged eighteen to twenty-five, and incidentally to remove them from the job market. Beginning on a cold, rainy day in April 1933 when a caravan of motor trucks set out from Washington to put up the first CCC camp in Virginia's George Washington National Forest, nearly 3 million young men took to the woods to work at a variety of jobs in forests, parks, recreational areas, and soil conservation projects at a nominal pay of $30 a month. Directed by army officers and foresters, they worked under a semi-military discipline and provided perhaps the most direct analogue of war in the whole New Deal.

FDR visits a Civilian Conservation Corps (CCC) camp in Virginia's Shenandoah Valley, 1933.

The Federal Emergency Relief Administration (FERA), created on May 12, 1933, with an authorization of $500 million, addressed the broader problems of human distress. Harry L. Hopkins, an indefatigable social worker who had directed Roosevelt's state relief program in New York, pushed the program with a seemingly boundless nervous energy, all the while giving off (in the words of one observer) "a suggestion of quick cigarettes, thinning hair, dandruff, brief sarcasm, fraying suits of clothes, and a wholly understandable preoccupation." The FERA continued and expanded the assistance that had begun under Hoover's RFC, but with a difference. Federal monies flowed to the states in grants rather than "loans." While FERA continued to channel aid through state agencies to relief clients mainly in direct payments, Hopkins enlarged its scope by gradually developing work programs for education, student aid, rural rehabilitation, and transient relief. He pushed an "immediate work instead of dole" approach on local officials, but they preferred the dole as an easier and quicker way to reach the needy.

The first large-scale experiment with work relief came with formation of the Civil Works Administration (CWA) during the winter of 1933–1934, when it had become apparent that even the largesse of the FERA would not prevent widespread privation. Created in November 1933, the CWA provided jobs and wages to those able to work. It was conceived and implemented in haste, and many of its projects were "make-work" jobs such as leaf-raking and ditch-digging; but it spent over $900 million (mostly in wages) for a variety of useful projects, from highway repairs to teaching jobs that helped keep the schools open. The CWA, unlike the FERA, was a federal operation from top to bottom. The CWA was abandoned in the spring of 1934, having served its purpose of helping people weather the winter; but Roosevelt and Hopkins continued to favor work relief over the dole, which they believed to have a debilitating effect psychologically on the unemployed.

Recovery through Regulation

Beyond rescuing the banks and providing relief lay the long-term goals of recovery for agriculture and business. Members of Roosevelt's Brain Trust and others who influenced policies during the Hundred Days were heirs largely to an earlier Roosevelt's New Nationalism, whether avowedly so or not. They held the trend toward economic concentration to be inevitable. They also believed that the mistakes of the 1920s showed that the only way to operate an integrated economy at capacity and in the public interest was through regulation and organized central planning, not through trust-busting. The success of centralized planning during World War I reinforced such ideas. New farm and recovery programs sprang from their beliefs.

AGRICULTURAL RECOVERY: THE AAA AND THE DUST BOWL   The Agricultural Adjustment Act, signed into law on May 12, 1933, contained nearly every major plan applicable to farm relief including authority to dump surpluses abroad, but only some of its provisions were implemented. The core of the act was a plan to compensate farmers for voluntary cutbacks in production. The goal was to restore farm prices to "parity," or the same level they had reached relative to other prices during the farmers' golden age of 1909–1914 (1919–1929 for tobacco). The act covered seven "basic commodities," a number later enlarged, and the money for benefit payments came from a processing tax levied on each—at the cotton gin, for example, or the flour mill.

By the time Congress acted, the growing season was already advanced. The most urgent problem was the prospect of another bumper cotton crop, and the AAA reluctantly resolved to sponsor a plow-under program. Using county demonstration agents the AAA signed up bewildered farmers. Trouble came sometimes from balky mules, trained to avoid trampling the crop, and occasionally from stubborn tenants who, like the old-time Populists, could not understand how prosperity could come from creating an artificial scarcity. To destroy a growing crop was a "shocking commentary on our civilization," Agriculture Secretary Henry A. Wallace lamented. "I could tolerate it only as a cleaning up of the wreckage from the old days of unbalanced production." Even more troubling was the spectacle of some 6 million little pink pigs slaughtered "before they could reach the full hogness of their hogdom." It could be justified, Wallace said, only as a means of helping farmers to do with pigs what steelmakers did with pig iron—cut production to fit the market.

It worked temporarily. Cotton farmers received about $112 million in benefit payments, and the crop was reduced by about 4 million bales below the estimate. Cotton prices rose above 11¢ per pound in July (parity was 12.7¢), but sagged again as the crop came in. In an effort to take up the slack, in October 1933 the president set up the Commodity Credit Corporation (another CCC!) which extended loans first on cotton and later on other crops kept in storage and off the market. In principle, if not in form, it was a revival of the old Farmers' Alliance–Populist subtreasury plan. With loans averaging 10¢ per pound on the 1933 crop and 12¢ per pound in 1934, it pegged the prices at those levels because no farmer had to sell for less. But the carryover surplus from the crops of previous years still weighed the market down. Another drastic step was taken on April 21, 1934, with passage of the Bankhead Cotton Control Act, which set marketing quotas; farmers who tried to sell more than their share of the quota would be stopped by a prohibitive tax. The Kerr-Smith Tobacco Control Act of 1934 applied similar quotas to tobacco.

For a while these farm measures worked. By the end of 1934 Wallace could report significant declines in wheat, cotton, and corn production and a simultaneous increase in commodity prices. Farm income increased by 58 percent between 1932 and 1935. The AAA, however, was only partially responsible for such gains. The devastating drought that settled over the Plains states between 1932 and 1935 played a major role in reducing production and creating the epic "Dust Bowl" migrations so poignantly evoked in John Steinbeck's *Grapes of Wrath*. Many of these migrant families had actually been driven off the land by AAA benefit programs that encouraged large farmers to take the lands worked by tenants and sharecroppers out of cultivation first. These displaced farmers joined a migratory stream rushing from the South and Midwest toward California, buoyed by currents of hope and desperation. One couple claimed

The Great Blow of 1934. *Severe drought and soil erosion created conditions for the dust storms that plagued the Middle West in the mid-1930s. This photograph is by Dorothea Lange.*

they had heard "how much money a man could make out there and we wanted to go."

Although frequently lumped together as "Okies," the Dust Bowl refugees were actually from cotton-belt communities in Arkansas, Texas, and Missouri as well as Oklahoma. During the 1930s and 1940s some 800,000 people left those four states and headed toward the West. Not all were farmers; many were professionals, white-collar workers, retailers, and farm implement salesmen whose jobs had been tied to the health of the agricultural sector. Ninety-five percent of the Dust Bowl migrants were white, and most were young adults in their twenties and thirties who relocated with spouses and children. Some traveled on trains or buses, others hopped a freight or hitched a ride; most rode in their own cars, the trip taking four to five days on average.

Most of the Dust Bowl migrants who had come from cities gravitated to urban areas—Los Angeles, San Diego, or San Francisco. Half of the newcomers, however, moved into the San Joaquin Valley, the agricultural heartland of the state. There they discovered that

California was no paradise. Only a few of the migrants could afford to buy land. Most (men and women) found themselves competing with local Hispanics and Asians for seasonal work as pickers in the cotton fields or orchards of large corporate farms. As a local health department report observed, the migrant workers "harvest cotton in the fall, go on relief until May, harvest the potatoes in the spring, work the vegetables and fruits in the summer and rest on relief until cotton harvest again." Living in tents or crude cabins and frequently on the move, they suffered from exposure and from poor sanitation. They also soon felt the sting of social prejudice. Native Californians scared by the influx of poor newcomers fastened upon cruel stereotypes to demean their presence. Steinbeck explained that "Okie us'ta mean you was from Oklahoma. Now it means you're a dirty son-of-a-bitch. Okie means you're scum. Don't mean nothing in itself, it's the way they say it." Such hostility led a third of the "Okies" to return to their native states. Most of the farm workers who stayed tended to fall back upon their old folkways rather than assimilate themselves into their new surroundings. These gritty "plain folk" brought with them their own prejudices against blacks and ethnic minorities as well as a potent tradition of evangelical Protestantism and a distinctive style of music variously labeled "country," "hillbilly," or "cowboy." This "Okie" subculture remains a vivid part of California society today.

Although it created unexpected problems, the AAA achieved real successes in boosting the overall farm economy. Then on January 6, 1936, in *United States v. Butler* the Supreme Court, by a vote of 6 to 3, held the AAA's processing tax unconstitutional because farm production was intrastate and thus beyond the reach of the power to regulate interstate commerce. In a sharp dissent, Justice Harlan Fiske Stone protested that "the present levy is held invalid, not for any want of power in Congress to lay such a tax" and argued that it came "within the specifically granted power to levy taxes to 'provide for the general welfare.'" But the decision stood. The administration hastily devised a new plan in the Soil Conservation and Domestic Allotment Act, which it pushed through Congress in six weeks. The new act, which became law on February 29, 1936, omitted processing taxes and acreage quotas, but provided benefit payments for soil conservation practices that took land out of soil-depleting staple crops—thus indirectly achieving crop reduction. Since the money came out of general funds and not from taxes, this approach was not vulnerable to suit. The act boosted a developing conservation movement directed by the Soil Conservation Service, which had been created in 1935.

The act was an almost unqualified success as an engineering and educational project because it went far to heal the scars of erosion and the plague of dust storms. But soil conservation nevertheless failed as a device for limiting production. With their worst lands taken out of production, farmers cultivated their fertile acres more intensively. In response, Congress passed the Second Agricultural Adjustment Act (February 16, 1938), which reestablished the earlier programs but left out the processing taxes. Benefit payments would come from general funds. By the time the second AAA reached a test in the Supreme Court, changes in the Court's personnel had changed its outlook. This time the law was upheld as a legitimate exercise of the interstate-commerce power. Agriculture, like manufacturing, was now held to be in the stream of commerce.

INDUSTRIAL RECOVERY: THE NRA   For industry, the New Deal's counterpart to the AAA was the National Industrial Recovery Act (NIRA), passed on June 16, 1933, the two major parts of which dealt with recovery and public works. The latter part, Title II, created the Public Works Administration (PWA) with $3.3 billion for public buildings, highway programs, flood control, and other improvements. The purpose was to "prime the pump" of business with new expenditures and provide jobs for the unemployed. Under the direction of Interior Secretary Harold L. Ickes, the PWA indirectly served the purpose of work relief, although Ickes directed it toward well-planned permanent improvements rather than the provision of hasty make-work, and he used private contractors rather than placing workers directly on the government payroll. PWA workers built Virginia's Skyline Drive, New York's Triborough Bridge, the Overseas Highway from Miami to Key West, and Chicago's subway system.

The more controversial and ambitious part of the NIRA created the National Recovery Administration (NRA), headed by General Hugh S. Johnson. Its purposes were twofold: first, to stabilize business with codes of "fair" competitive practice, and second, to generate more purchasing power by providing jobs, defining labor standards, and raising wages. Three related streams of thought merged in the creation of the NRA. One was Theodore Roosevelt's New Nationalism. The second was the idea that the New Deal was the analogue of war, that it could repeat the miracles wrought by the War Industries Board. Another source for the NRA was the trade-association movement, championed by Hoover in the 1920s and carried beyond his ideas of voluntary association now by force of law. The NRA also enlisted trade union hopes for protection of basic hour and wage standards and liberal hopes for comprehensive planning.

In each major industry, committees representing management,

labor, and government drew up the codes of fair practice. Hugh Johnson turned to existing trade associations for help in drafting them. A plan submitted by the Cotton Textile Institute, for instance, became the basis for Code No. 1, which imposed restraints on plant expansion, limited operations to eighty hours a week, and required reports on operations every four weeks. The labor standards featured in every code set a forty-hour week and minimum weekly wages of $13 ($12 in the South, where living costs were thought to be lower) which more than doubled earnings in some cases. Announcement of a proviso against child labor under the age of sixteen set off roars of applause in the hearing room. It did "in a few minutes what neither law nor constitutional amendment had been able to do in forty years," Johnson said.

As the drafting of other codes began to drag, Johnson proposed a "blanket code" pledging employers generally to observe the same labor standards as applied to cotton textiles. In mid-July he launched a crusade to whip up popular support for the NRA and its symbol of compliance, the "Blue Eagle," which had been modeled on an Indian thunderbird and embellished with the motto "We do our part." The eagle was displayed in show windows and stamped on products. It was a gamble, but the public responded. The climax to Johnson's effort came nearly in September when a Blue Eagle parade down New York's Fifth Avenue drew a quarter of a million marchers.

In this cartoon employer and employee agree to cooperate in the spirit of unity that inspired the NRA.

Some 2 million employers signed the pledge, and the impact of the campaign broke the logjam in code making.

For a time it worked, perhaps because a new air of confidence had overcome the depression blues and the downward spiral of wages and prices had ended. But as soon as recovery began, the honeymoon was over. The daily annoyances of code enforcement inspired growing hostility among businessmen. Charges mounted that the larger companies dominated the code authorities, that allocations froze the existing industrial structure and limited production, and that price-fixing robbed small producers of the chance to compete. In 1934 an investigating committee under Clarence Darrow, the noted lawyer, substantiated at least some of the charges. Limiting production, moreover, had discouraged investment. And because the NRA wage codes excluded agricultural workers and domestics, three out of every four employed blacks derived no direct benefit from the program. By 1935 the NRA had developed more critics than friends. When it died in May 1935, struck down by the Supreme Court as unconstitutional, few paused to mourn.

The NRA experiment was generally put down as a failure, but it left an enduring mark. With dramatic suddenness, the codes had set new standards, such as the forty-hour week and the end of child labor, from which it was hard to retreat. The NRA's endorsement of collective bargaining spurred the growth of unions. The codes, moreover, advanced trends toward stabilization and rationalization that were becoming the standard practice of business at large and that, despite misgivings about the concentration of power, would be further promoted by trade associations.

REGIONAL PLANNING: THE TVA   The philosophy of the New Deal embraced more than the restrictive approaches of the NRA. The creation of the Tennessee Valley Authority (TVA) was a truly bold venture. Among the measures of the Hundred Days, most of which were efforts to stem the wreckage of depression, TVA became a massive monument of growth, a living rebuttal to the idea that the economy had reached its full measure of mature development. It was the product neither of a single imagination nor of a single concept, but of an unfolding progression of purposes. In 1916, when the government started power and nitrate plants at Muscle Shoals, Alabama, strengthening national defense was the aim. New objectives unfolded in succession: nitrate fertilizers as well as nitrate explosives, general industrial development, and cheap public power to be used as a "yardstick" for private utility rates. Waterpower development pointed in turn to navigation, the control of stream flow for both power and flood control, and to conservation of soil and

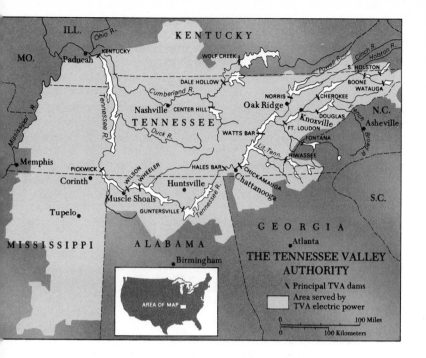

THE TENNESSEE VALLEY
AUTHORITY

\ Principal TVA dams

Area served by
TVA electric power

forests to prevent silting. The chain of connections led ultimately to
the concept of overall planning for an entire watershed, which included a total drainage area of 41,000 square miles overlapping
seven states, four-fifths the size of England.

Through the 1920s Nebraska senator George W. Norris had fought
off efforts to sell the Alabama project, but never won enough support
for his goal of public power. In 1932, however, he backed Roosevelt,
and then gained the new president's support for a vast enlargement
of the Muscle Shoals project.

Muscle Shoals, Roosevelt said, "gives us the opportunity . . . of
setting an example of planning, not just for ourselves but for generations to come, tying in industry and agriculture and forestry and
flood prevention . . . over a distance of a thousand miles." On May
18, 1933, Congress created the TVA as a multipurpose public corporation. Mobilizing local support under TVA director David E. Lilienthal's slogan of "grass-roots democracy," the TVA won almost
universal loyalty among the people of the region. By 1936 the TVA
board had six dams completed or under way, and a master plan to
build nine high dams on the main river, which would create the
"Great Lakes of the South," and other dams on the tributaries. The
agency, moreover, opened the rivers for navigation, fostered soil

Rural Electrification Cooperative Office, Lafayette, La., 1939.

conservation and forestry, experimented with fertilizers, drew new industry to the region, and sent cheap power pulsating through the valley. Cheap public power, Lilienthal's main passion, became more and more TVA's reason for being—a purpose that would become all the more important during World War II. TVA's success at generating greater power consumption and lower rates awakened private utilities to the mass consumer markets. Cheap power transported farmers of the valley from the age of kerosene to the age of electricity. "The women went around turning the switches on and off," said a Farm Bureau man who witnessed the transition. "The light and wonder in their eyes was brighter than that from the lamps." TVA's first rural cooperative, set up at Corinth, Mississippi, in 1934, pointed the way to the electrification of the nation's farms in the decade that followed. The Rural Electrification Administration (REA), formed as a relief agency by presidential order in 1935, achieved a permanent statutory basis in 1936. By 1940 it had extended loans of more than $321 million to rural electrical cooperatives.

LAUNCHING THE SECOND NEW DEAL

During Roosevelt's first year in office his programs and his personal charms aroused massive support. The president's travels and speeches, his twice-weekly press conferences, and his "fireside chats" over the radio generated vitality from a once-remote White House. In the congressional elections of 1934 the Democrats actually increased their strength in both House and Senate, an almost unprecedented midterm victory for the party in power. When it was over only seven Republican governors remained in office throughout the country.

Criticism of the New Deal was muted or reduced to helpless carping. But as the sense of crisis passed, the spirit of unity relaxed. In August 1934 a group of conservative businessmen and politicians, including Al Smith and John W. Davis, two previous Democratic presidential candidates, formed the American Liberty League to oppose New Deal measures and to "teach the necessity of respect for the rights of person and property."

THUNDER ON THE LEFT   But if there was any real threat to Roosevelt in those years, it came from the hucksters of social nostrums, old and new. The most flamboyant of the group, by far, was Louisiana's "Kingfish," Senator Huey P. Long, Jr. A short, strutting man with a round, rosy face and pug nose, Long sported pink suits and pastel-colored shirts, red ties, and two-toned shoes. He loved to make people think he was a country bumpkin, for underneath the carefully calculated image was a shrewd lawyer and consummate demagogue. First as governor, then as political boss of the state, he had delivered to its citizens tax favors, roads, schools, free textbooks, charity hospitals, and generally better public services, all at the cost of corruption and personal dictatorship.

Louisiana, however, became only the base from which Long ventured out to conquer other worlds. The vehicle was his Share Our Wealth program, first unveiled in 1932 and refined over the next three years. In one version Long proposed to liquidate large personal fortunes, guarantee every family an allowance of $5,000 and every worker an annual income of $2,500, grant pensions to the aged, reduce the hours of labor, pay veterans' bonuses, and assure a college education for every qualified student. His book *Every Man a King* (1933) held out the promise of economic security for all. Whether he had a workable plan or not, his scheme dramatized a fundamental issue in a society that had solved the problem of production but not that of distribution, an issue few politicians were so imprudent as to tackle directly. By early 1935 Huey Long was claiming 27,431 Share Our Wealth Clubs and a file of 7.5 million names.

Another popular scheme was hatched by a California doctor, Francis E. Townsend. Outraged by the sight of three haggard old women raking through garbage cans in Long Beach, Townsend proposed pensions for the aged. In January 1934 he and a real-estate promoter founded Old Age Revolving Pensions, Limited, to promote

The "Kingfish," Huey Long of Louisiana.

the Townsend Plan of paying $200 a month to every citizen over sixty who retired from employment and promised to spend the money within the month. The plan had the lure of providing both security for the aged and job openings for the young. As the Townsend Club grew, critics noted that the cost would be more than half the national income. "I'm not in the least interested in the cost of the plan," Townsend blandly told a House committee.

A third huckster of panaceas, Father Charles E. Coughlin, the "radio priest" of the Shrine of the Little Flower in Royal Oak, Michigan, founded the National Union for Social Justice in 1934. In broadcasts over the CBS radio network, he specialized in schemes for the coinage of silver and attacks on bankers which carried growing overtones of anti-Semitism.

Coughlin, Townsend, and Long drew support largely from a lower middle class squeezed by the depression. Of the three, Long had the widest following. A canvass by the Democratic National Committee showed that he could draw 5 million to 6 million votes as a third-party candidate for president, perhaps enough to undermine Roosevelt's chances of reelection.

A new militancy and new drives to organize labor added to the "thunder on the left." Beset by pressures from both ends of the political spectrum, Roosevelt drifted through months of hesitation before deciding to "steal the thunder" from the left with new programs of reform and social security. Political pressures impelled Roosevelt, but so did the growing influence of Justices Louis Brandeis and Felix Frankfurter. These men urged Roosevelt to be less cozy with big business and to push for restored competition and heavy taxes on large corporations.

LIGHTNING FROM THE COURT What finally galvanized the president into action was the behavior of the Supreme Court. Early in 1935 the Court for the first time struck down a piece of New Deal legislation, a provision of the National Industrial Recovery Act forbidding interstate shipment of "hot oil"—oil produced in excess of quotas set by the states. A few weeks later the gold resolution of 1933, which abandoned the gold standard, was barely upheld on a close vote of 5 to 4. Then on May 27, 1935, the Court in three decisions annulled a farm mortgage relief act, found that the president had wrongfully used his power to remove officeholders, and killed the National Industrial Recovery Act by unanimous vote.

In *Schechter Poultry Corporation v. United States* (1935), quickly tagged the "sick chicken" case, the defendants, who sold to kosher retailers, had been convicted of selling an "unfit chicken" and violating other code provisions as well. The high court ruled that Congress had delegated too much power to the executive when it granted the code-making authority and had exceeded its power under the commerce clause. Chief Justice Charles Evans Hughes's opinion held that the poultry in question had "come to permanent rest within the state," although it had been moved across state lines. In a press conference soon afterward, Roosevelt said: "We have been relegated to the horse-and-buggy definition of interstate commerce." The same line of reasoning, he warned, might endanger much of the New Deal program.

LEGISLATIVE ACHIEVEMENTS Roosevelt attempted to salvage his program in June by launching the so-called Second New Deal with demands for "must" legislation, most of which was already pending. The initiative broke the stalemate in Congress, which passed these measures with a rush:

July 5	The Wagner National Labor Relations Act, guaranteeing the right of labor to organize and bargain collectively
August 14	The Social Security Act, providing unemployment and old-age insurance and public-welfare programs
August 23	The Banking Act of 1935, strengthening the Federal Reserve System
August 28	The Wheeler-Rayburn Public Utility Holding Company Act, preventing the pyramiding of holding companies
August 30	The Revenue Act of 1935, the "Soak the Rich Tax"

The National Labor Relations Act, often called the Wagner Act, gave workers the right to bargain through unions of their own choice and prohibited employers from interfering with union activities. A National Labor Relations Board of five members could supervise

"Yes, You Remembered Me."
*The social legislation of the
Second New Deal prompted
this depiction of FDR as the
friend of "The Forgotten
Man."*

plant elections and certify unions as bargaining agents where a majority of the workers approved. The board could also investigate the actions of employers and issue "cease-and-desist" orders against specified unfair practices. Under the protection of the law, union activities quickly intensified.

The Wagner Act salvaged the labor guarantees of the National Industrial Recovery Act, while other measures revived other parts of the NIRA. The Public Contracts Act applied NRA wage and hour standards to work under government contracts.

The Social Security Act of 1935, Roosevelt announced, was the New Deal's "cornerstone" and "supreme achievement." Indeed, it has proven to be the most far-reaching of all the New Deal initiatives. The concept had its roots in the proposal of Progressives early in the 1900s for a federal system of social security for the aged, indigent, handicapped, and unemployed. Other nations had already enacted such programs, but the United States remained steadfast to its deeply rooted tradition of individual self-reliance. The Great Depression, however, revived the idea, and Roosevelt masterfully guided the legislation through Congress.

The Social Security Act included three major provisions. Its centerpiece was the creation of a pension fund for retired people over the age of sixty-five. In 1937, workers and employers began contributing payroll taxes to establish the fund, which three years later started to yield retirees average payments of $22 per month, a modest sum even for those depressed times. Roosevelt stressed that the pension program was not intended to guarantee a comfortable retirement; it was designed to supplement other sources of income and protect the elderly from some of the "hazards and vicissitudes of life." Only later did American voters and politicians come to perceive social security as the *primary* source of retirement income for most of the aged. By 1991 the average monthly payment was about $800.

The Social Security Act also set up a shared federal-state unemployment insurance program, financed by a payroll tax on employers. In addition, the new legislation committed the national government to a broad range of social-welfare activities based on the assumption that "unemployables"—people who were unable to work—would remain a state responsibility while the national government would provide work relief for the able-bodied. To that end the law inaugurated federal grants-in-aid for three state-administered public assistance programs—old-age assistance, aid for dependent children, aid for the blind—and further aid for maternal, child welfare, and public-health services.

Conservative critics charged that the social security system warred against traditions of American individualism. One New Jersey senator lamented that the new law would "take all the romance out of life. We might as well take the child from the nursery, give him a nurse, and protect him from every experience that life affords." But the new federal program was relatively conservative. It was the only government pension program in the world financed by taxes on the earnings of current workers. Most countries funded the program out of general tax revenues. Moreover, the social security payroll tax was regressive: based on a single fixed rate for all, regardless of income level, the tax hurt the poor more than the rich. It also weakened Roosevelt's efforts to revive the economy by reducing the disposable income of the employed. Another limit to the social security system was its initial exclusion of those classes of workers who needed financial security the most: farm workers, domestics, and the self-employed (these groups have since gained access to the program).

Roosevelt regretted these limitations, but he considered them compromises that would ensure congressional passage of the Social Security Act and enable it to withstand court challenges. As he replied to an aide who criticized funding the pension program through employee contributions, "I guess you're right on the economics, but those taxes were never a problem of economics. They are politics all the way through. We put those payroll contributions there so as to give the contributors a moral, legal, and political right to collect their pensions and their unemployment benefits. With those taxes in there, no damn politician can ever scrap my social security program."

Congress had already passed in April a $4.8 billion bill providing work relief for jobless workers. To manage these programs, the Works Progress Administration (WPA), headed by Harry L. Hopkins, replaced the Federal Emergency Relief Administration. The act did not provide a dole which, Roosevelt told Congress, had been "a narcotic, a subtle destroyer of the human spirit." Hopkins favored the lighter public works that would provide jobs quickly, with the consequence that some jobs appeared to be make-work or mere "leaning on shovels." But before the WPA died in World War II it left permanent monuments on the landscape in the form of buildings, bridges, hard-surfaced roads, airports, and schools. The WPA employed a wide range of talents, often saving them from atrophy, in the Federal Theater Project, the Federal Art Project, and the Federal Writers' Project. The National Youth Administration, under the WPA, gave part-time employment to students, set up technical training programs, and provided aid to jobless youth. Although the WPA took care of only about 3 million out of some 10 million jobless at any one time, in all it tided some 9 million clients over desperate times before it expired in 1943.

The Banking Act of 1935 strengthened the control of the Federal Reserve Board over rediscount rates and reserve requirements, and diminished the power of private bankers in the money market. It accomplished this by concentrating in the board's hands all open-market operations—that is, the buying or selling of government securities to increase (by buying) or decrease (by selling) the money supply. The act greatly strengthened the board's control of the whole monetary system.

The WPA sponsored public works and supported projects in the arts.

The Public Utility Holding Company Act struck at financial corruption in the public utility industry. Like railroads in the 1800s, utilities in their early stages of growth had spawned buccaneers interested more in manipulation than in good business. The act passed despite the high-pressure lobbying tactics of the utilities which, Representative Sam Rayburn said later, could "produce more noise and fewer votes than any crowd I ever saw." It limited the sphere of holding companies, and forbade the pyramiding of such companies.

The final measure endorsed by Roosevelt and the last of the major laws passed during this period was the Revenue Act of 1935, sometimes called the Wealth Tax Act, but popularly known as the "Soak the Rich Tax." In asking for the law, Roosevelt told Congress: "Our revenue laws have operated in many ways to the unfair advantage of the few, and they have done little to prevent an unjust concentration of wealth and economic power." The Revenue Act raised surtax rates on incomes above $50,000, and steeply graduated taxes to a maximum of 75 percent on incomes above $5 million. Estate and gift taxes went up, as did the corporate tax on all but small corporations—those with less than $50,000 income. Congress even added to Roosevelt's recommendations an "excess-profits" levy on corporate earnings above 10 percent.

By "soaking" the rich and enacting social security Roosevelt stole much of the thunder from the left, although the results fell short of the promise. The new tax law failed to increase revenue significantly, nor did it result in a redistribution of income: the wealthiest 1 percent of the nation in fact slightly increased its share of the wealth after the tax took effect. At the same time the hoopla over "soaking the rich" obscured the more significant impact of both the social security payroll tax—which fell more heavily on lower incomes—and the policy of returning indigents to the care of the states. Most states, insofar as they assumed this burden, raised the needed revenue with sales taxes, which were also regressive. Such taxes impeded recovery by reducing total purchasing power.

The viewpoint of the time was that Roosevelt had moved in a radical direction. But the extent of the new departure taken by the Second New Deal is easy to exaggerate. Such measures as work relief, social security, utility regulation, and progressive income taxes had long been in the works in Congress. The president himself had little use for theoretical speculation. He was still pursuing the bold experiments he promised before the election. "Roosevelt's program," one historian has written, "rested on the assumption that a just society could be secured by imposing a welfare state on a capitalist foundation."

THE ELECTION OF 1936   Whatever economic or philosophical judgment might be passed on the New Deal programs, Roosevelt's political instincts were acute. Businessmen fumed over his tax and spending policies. The wealthy resented their loss of status and the growing power of government and labor. They vented an intemperate rage against Roosevelt, whom they called "a traitor to his own class," and against all the works of the New Deal. So many landmarks of a once stable and secure world now seemed threatened, from the gold standard itself to one's right to run a business as one saw fit. Hoover called the New Deal an attack on "the whole philosophy of individual liberty." Visitors at the home of J. P. Morgan, Jr., were cautioned not to mention Roosevelt's name lest it raise his blood pressure. But the conservative coalition of business and wealth, by its incoherent rage, made a perfect foil for the confident president.

Another key to Roosevelt's unprecedented popularity as he approached the reelection campaign was his wife, Anna Eleanor Roosevelt, an enormous political asset to the president and one of the most influential women of her time. Theodore Roosevelt's favorite niece, she had lost both parents by age ten and was a shy, withdrawn youth. But Eleanor grew into a tall, willowy, outgoing woman, and in the White House she became more of a public figure than any previous First Lady. She had her own staff, held her own press conferences, enjoyed access to Democratic party leaders, and spoke

"Mother, Wilfred Wrote a Bad Word!" The so-called Soak the Rich Tax, and other measures in Roosevelt's New Deal, prompted affluent Americans to regard FDR as "a traitor to his own class."

Eleanor Roosevelt and Civil Rights Leader A. Philip Randolph. *The 1936 election marked the first time black voters cast a majority of their votes for a Democratic president.*

candidly to the president about appointing women to government posts and about his plans for various New Deal programs.

Her passion was social service. As a teen she had volunteered in a New York settlement house, and she remained thereafter ardently concerned about issues of human welfare and rights for women and blacks. She marched alongside a second army of "bonus marchers," leading them in singing "There's a long, long trail a-winding"; she convinced Congress to improve housing conditions for the poor in the District of Columbia; and she repeatedly reminded the president of pockets of injustice hidden from public scrutiny. As her secretary recalled, Eleanor Roosevelt "lived to be kind." She relished traveling around the country, representing FDR and the New Deal, defying local segregation ordinances by eating with blacks in segregated facilities, supporting women's causes, highlighting the plight of unemployed youth, and imploring Americans to live up to their egalitarian and humanitarian ideals. Eleanor Roosevelt became her husband's most visible and effective liaison with many liberal groups, brought labor leaders, women activists, and black spokesmen into the White House after hours, and deflected criticism of the president by taking progressive stands and running political risks he himself dared not. He was the politician, she once remarked, she the agitator. A Maine fisherman described her uniquely endearing qualities: "She ain't stuck up, she ain't dressed up, and she ain't afraid to talk."

The popularity of the Roosevelts and the New Deal impelled the Republican convention in 1936 to avoid candidates too closely identified with the "hate-Roosevelt" contingent. The party chose Governor Alfred M. Landon of Kansas, a former Bull Moose Progressive, who had fought the Ku Klux Klan, supported civil liberties, and favored regulation of business. While conservative in matters of finance, Landon had endorsed many programs of the New Deal. The most progressive Republican candidate in years, he was probably more liberal than most of his backers, and clearly more so than the party's platform, which accused the New Deal of usurping power.

Landon started the campaign on a moderate note, arguing that a Republican president could achieve the objectives of the New Deal more efficiently and thriftily. But as the campaign progressed, his statements became more and more conservative. Before the end, Republican party leaders even tried to make an issue of the social security program, which they denounced as dangerous "regimentation." The Social Security Act, said the vice-presidential candidate, "puts half the working people of America under federal control." The Republican party chairman warned that every worker would have to wear metal dogtags bearing his or her social security number.

Such appeals carried little weight. The chief hope of the Republicans was that the followers of Coughlin, Townsend, and other dissidents would combine to draw enough votes away from Roosevelt to throw the election to them. But that possibility faded when an assassin gunned down Huey Long. Coughlin, Townsend, and a remnant of the Long movement did support Representative William Lemke of North Dakota on a Union party ticket, but it was a forlorn and foredoomed effort that polled only 882,000 votes.

In 1936 Roosevelt was able to forge a new electoral coalition which would affect national politics for years to come. While holding the support of most traditional Democrats North and South, FDR made strong gains among beneficiaries of the farm program in the West. In the northern cities he held on to the strong support of ethnic groups gratified by New Deal welfare measures and by greater recognition in appointments. Middle-class voters, whose property had been saved by New Deal measures, flocked to Roosevelt's support, along with intellectuals stirred by the ferment of new ideas in government. The revived labor movement threw its support to Roosevelt, and Socialist voters deserted Norman Thomas for the New Deal coalition. In the most profound new departure of all,

African-American voters for the first time cast the majority of their ballots for a Democratic president. "My friends, go home and turn Lincoln's picture to the wall," a journalist told black Republicans. "That debt has been paid in full." In perhaps the most seismic and enduring change in the political landscape during the 1930s, a majority of politically active blacks moved away from their traditional adherence to the Republican party.

Roosevelt campaigned with tremendous buoyancy. In his acceptance speech to the Democratic convention in Philadelphia he dropped efforts to reassure businessmen. As the Americans of 1776 had sought freedom from political autocracy, he said, the Americans of 1936 sought freedom from the "economic royalists" who had created "a new despotism." "They complain that we seek to overthrow the institutions of America. What they really complain of is that we seek to take away their power." The campaign closed on an even more strident note, when Roosevelt spoke at Madison Square Garden in Manhattan: "I should like to have it said of my first Administration that in it the forces of selfishness and of lust for power met their match. I should like to have it said of my second administration that in it these forces met their master."

On November 3 the election went as the Democratic party chairman had predicted. Roosevelt carried every state except Maine and Vermont with a popular vote of 27.7 million to Landon's 16.7 million, and won what was the closest to a unanimous electoral vote since Monroe's victory in 1820, by 523 to 8. Democrats would dominate Republicans in the new Congress, by 77 to 19 in the Senate and 328 to 107 in the House. The editor William Allen White of Emporia, Kansas, wrote: "The water of liberalism has been dammed up for forty years by the two major parties. The dam is out. Landon went down the creek in a torrent." Roosevelt himself said he felt as if he had experienced "baptism by total immersion."

SECOND-TERM SETBACKS AND INITIATIVES

But as Jefferson and Jackson found (and Lyndon Johnson, Richard Nixon, and Ronald Reagan later discovered), some malevolent fate often seems to dog presidents who win such smashing victories, and Roosevelt found himself deluged in a sea of troubles over the next year. His second inaugural address, given on January 20, 1937, suggested that he was ready to move toward even further reform. The challenge of American democracy, he said, was that millions of citizens "at this very moment are denied the greater part of what the very lowest standards of today call the necessities of life. . . . I see one-third of a nation ill-housed, ill-clad, ill-nourished." The election of 1936 had been a mandate for extensive reform, he argued; and the overwhelming Democratic majorities in Congress ensured passage. But one major roadblock stood in the way: the Supreme Court.

THE COURT-PACKING PLAN   By the end of the 1936 term the Court had ruled against New Deal laws in seven of the nine major cases it reviewed. Having struck down both major accomplishments of the First New Deal, the AAA and the NRA, the Court moved on in 1936 to rule against the Guffey Coal Act. In the spring of 1936 it denied that states had the power to fix minimum wages. Since it had already ruled, in 1923, that the federal government had no such power, it had left, as Roosevelt protested, a " 'no-man's land,' where no Government—State or Federal" could act. Suits against the Social Security and Wagner Labor Relations Acts now pended. Given the established trend of rulings, often by margins of 5 to 4 or 6 to 3, the Second New Deal seemed in danger of being nullified like the first.

For that reason, Roosevelt and his attorney-general decided to change the Court by enlarging it, a move for which there was ample precedent and power. Congress, not the Constitution, determined the size of the Court, which at different times had numbered six, seven, nine, and ten justices, and in 1937 numbered nine. Roosevelt sent his plan to Congress without having consulted congressional leaders or more than a few within his administration. He wanted to create up to fifty new federal judges, including six new Supreme Court justices, and to diminish the power of judges who had served ten or more years or reached the age of seventy.

The "court-packing" maneuver, as opponents quickly tagged it, handed a viable issue to men who previously had shunned a fight with Roosevelt. The plan was a shade too contrived. In implying that some judges were impaired by senility, it affronted the elder statesmen of Congress, and especially Louis D. Brandeis, who was both the oldest and the most liberal of the justices. It also ran headlong into a deep-rooted veneration of the courts and aroused fears that another president might use the precedent for quite different purposes. One Virginia senator feared "the reversal of those decisions of the Court that saved the civilization of the South," by which he meant decisions upholding white supremacy. In the Senate the Republicans shrewdly stood aside while the Democrats plunged into a family squabble.

As it turned out, no direct vote ever tested senatorial convictions on the matter. Unforeseen events blunted Roosevelt's drive to change the Court. A sequence of Court decisions that spring reversed previous judgments in order to uphold a Washington State

ALL I SAID
WAS "GIMME
SIX MORE
JUSTICES!"

Roosevelt's "court-packing" scheme aroused strong opposition from fellow Democrats. The Democratic donkey here kicks up a storm.

minimum-wage law, the Wagner Act, and the Social Security Act. Chief Justice Charles Evans Hughes testified that the Court had kept up with its docket. Conservative justice Willis Van Devanter resigned, and Roosevelt named to the vacancy one of the most consistent New Dealers, Senator Hugo Black of Alabama.

Finally, in August, Vice-President Garner arranged a settlement providing reforms in court procedures and more generous retirement provisions, but adding no new judges. Roosevelt later claimed he had lost the battle but won the war. The Court had reversed itself on important New Deal legislation, and Roosevelt was able to appoint justices in harmony with the New Deal. But it was a Pyrrhic victory which sowed dissension in his party and blighted Roosevelt's own prestige. For the first time Democrats in large numbers deserted the "champ," and the opposition found an issue on which it could openly take the field. During the first eight months of 1937 the momentum of Roosevelt's great 1936 victory was lost.

A NEW DIRECTION FOR LABOR   Rebellions erupted on other fronts even while the Court bill pended. Under the impetus of the New Deal the moribund labor movement stirred anew. When Section 7a of the National Industrial Recovery Act demanded in every industry code a statement of the workers' right to organize, alert unionists quickly translated it to mean "The President wants you to join the union." John L. Lewis of the United Mine Workers was among the first to exploit the spirit of the Blue Eagle. Leading a union decimated by depression, he rebuilt it from 150,000 members to 500,000 within a year. Spurred by the mine workers' example, Sidney Hillman of the Amalgamated Clothing Workers and David Dubinsky of the International Ladies' Garment Workers joined Lewis in promoting a campaign to organize workers in the mass-production industries. As leaders of some of the few industrial unions in the AFL, they found the craft unions to be obstacles to organizing the basic industries.

In 1934 they persuaded the AFL and its president, William Green, to charter industrial unions in the unorganized industries. But Green and other craft unionists saw these "federal" unions as temporary pools from which to draw members into the crafts. Lewis and the industrial unionists saw them as a chance to organize on a massive scale. In 1935, with passage of the Wagner Act, action began in earnest. The industrial unionists formed a Committee for Industrial Organization (CIO) and craft unionists began to fear submergence by the mass unions. Jurisdictional disputes divided them, and in 1936 the AFL expelled the CIO unions, which then formed a permanent structure called after 1938 the Congress of Industrial Organizations. The rivalry spurred both groups to greater efforts.

The CIO's major organizing drives in automobiles and steel began in 1936, but until the Supreme Court upheld the Wagner Act in 1937 there was little compliance with unions on the part of industry. There was instead widespread use by industry of blacklisting, private detectives, labor spies, vigilante groups, and intimidation. Early in 1937 automobile workers spontaneously adopted a new technique, the "sit-down strike," in which workers refused to leave the shop until the employers granted collective bargaining. Many employers and much of the public saw in such revolutionary tactics a threat to property rights, an alarming gesture of contempt for authority, and further evidence of the New Deal's evil influence. Union leaders, fearing a backlash of public opinion, frowned on the tactic, but it brought the first union victory in a major industry. In February 1937 General Motors recognized the United Automobile Workers as bargaining agent for its employees. The following month, United States Steel capitulated to the Steel Workers Organizing Committee (later the United Steelworkers of America), granting it recognition, a 10 percent wage hike, and a forty-hour week.

Having captured two giants of heavy industry, the CIO went on in the next few years to organize much of industrial America: rubber, oil, electronics, and a good part of the textile industry, in which unionists had to fight protracted struggles to organize scattered plants. The laggard pace in textiles denied the CIO a major victory in the South comparable to its swift conquest of autos and steel, but even there a labor movement appeared that was at last something more than a vehicle for sporadic revolt. Some of the giants of heavy industry held out for yet a few years. The "Little Steel" companies, led by Republic Steel, and the Big Four meat-packers remained adamant, but all had capitulated by the end of 1941. Violence punc-

The Committee for Industrial Organization, formed in 1935, organized much of industrial America in the late 1930s and 1940s.

tuated these struggles, most vividly at the Republic Steel plant in Chicago where police killed ten strikers on Memorial Day in 1937. Company guards brutally beat up Walter Reuther and other organizers at Henry Ford's River Rouge plant in Detroit. In Harlan County, Kentucky, deputized company hoodlums conducted a reign of terror until the National Labor Relations Board forced operators to bargain with the United Mine Workers late in 1938.

Union organizing drives were helped by the sympathy or at least neutrality of public officials. The governor of Michigan, for instance, refused to use troops against sit-down strikers. The Wagner Act put the power of the federal government behind the principle of unionization. In the Congress, a Senate subcommittee under Robert M. La Follette, Jr., exposed practices of violence against unions, while President Roosevelt, though opposed to the tactic, refused to use force against sit-downers. The unions, he said, would soon learn that they could not continue to use a "damned unpopular" tactic. Roosevelt himself had come late to the support of unions and sometimes took exception to their behavior. In the fall of 1937 he became so irritated with the warfare between Lewis and Republic Steel that he pronounced "a plague on both your houses." The grandiloquent Lewis, who for a year had been trying to organize a union for steelworkers, responded: "It ill behooves one who has supped at labor's table and who has been sheltered in labor's house to curse with equal fervor and fine impartiality both labor and its adversaries when they become locked in a deadly embrace." In 1940 an angry Lewis would back the Republican presidential candidate, but he would be unable to carry labor with him. As workers became more organized, they more closely identified with the Democratic party.

A SLUMPING ECONOMY Beset by the divisive effects of the Court fight and the sit-down strikes, the Roosevelt administration in the fall of 1937 also faced a renewed depression. The years 1935 and 1936 had been marked by steady economic improvement. By the spring of 1937 output had moved above the 1929 level. Then in August the economy suddenly cracked, and in the following months it slid into a deep business slump, which the press called a "recession" to distinguish it from the "depression." Actually the collapse was sharper than that in 1929. The Dow-Jones stock averages fell some 40 percent between August and October. The *New York Times* business index in the same period went back to the level of 1935. By the end of the year 2 million people had been thrown out of work; scenes of the earlier depression reappeared.

The prosperity of early 1937 had been achieved largely through governmental spending. On top of relief and public-works outlays, Congress in 1936 had provided for cash payments of veterans' bonuses upon demand. But in June 1937 Roosevelt, worried about deficits and inflation, ordered sharp cuts in spending. At the same time the Treasury began to diminish disposable income by collecting $2 billion in social security taxes. Private spending could not fill the gap left by reductions in government spending, and business still lacked the faith to risk large investments. The result was the slump of 1937.

The recession brought to a head a fierce debate within the administration. One group, led by Treasury Secretary Henry Morgenthau, Jr., favored less spending and a balanced budget. The slow pace of recovery, Morgenthau thought, resulted from the reluctance of business to invest, and that resulted in turn from fear that federal spending would bring inflation and heavy taxes. The other group, which included Harry Hopkins and Harold Ickes, argued for renewed spending. The recession, they noted, had come just when the budget was brought into balance. "The Government," said another supporter of this view, "must be the compensatory agent in this economy; it must unbalance its budget during the deflation and create surpluses in periods of great business activity."

This view echoed that of the English economist John Maynard

In 1937, the "American Way" was out of reach for many.
Photograph by Margaret Bourke-White.

Keynes, who had given extended development to the idea in his book *The General Theory of Employment, Interest and Money* (1936). Keynesian economics offered a convenient theoretical justification for what New Dealers had already done in pragmatic response to existing conditions. Many, if not most, of the liberals attracted by Keynesian fiscal policies also subscribed to Brandeisian opposition to monopoly, which held that competition provided the best condition for a thriving economy. "Administered" prices, they argued, held back recovery. When demand slackened, large-scale industries could maintain their prices by cutting production and employment. This camp called for antitrust investigations and action. Their views marked a sharp break with the early New Deal's emphasis on regulation.

ECONOMIC POLICY AND LATE REFORMS   Roosevelt waited as the rival theorists sought his approval. "As I see it," Morgenthau remarked, "what you are doing now is treading water . . . to wait to see what happens this spring." Roosevelt responded: "Absolutely." When spring failed to bring recovery, Roosevelt endorsed the ideas of the spenders and antitrusters. On April 14, 1938, he asked Congress to adopt a large-scale spending program, and Congress voted $33 billion mainly for public works by the PWA and the WPA, with lesser amounts for other programs. In a short time the increase in spending reversed the economy's decline, but the recession and Roosevelt's reluctance to adopt the massive spending called for in Keynesian theory forestalled the achievement of full recovery by the end of the decade. Only during World War II would production and employment reach pre-1929 levels.

On April 29, two weeks after his spending message, Roosevelt asked Congress to look into the concentration of economic power. Congress responded by setting up the Temporary National Economic Committee, which drew half its members from Congress and half from federal agencies. It was the first major inquiry of the sort since the Pujo committee reported on the money trust in 1912. Over a period of three years the TNEC produced thirty-nine volumes of testimony and forty-three monographs, a treasure trove of information on the economy. Meanwhile Thurman Arnold, named chief of the Justice Department's Antitrust Division in 1938, swung into action. Within five years he filed almost as many antitrust suits as had been brought previously since passage of the Sherman Act in 1890, but neither he nor the TNEC was able to accomplish much of substance before national defense took precedence. Like earlier antitrust efforts, this one turned out to be largely ceremonial.

The Court fight, the sit-down strikes, and the recession in 1937 all undercut Roosevelt's prestige and dissipated the mandate of the 1936 elections. When the 1937 session ended, the only major new reforms enacted for the benefit of the "ill-housed, ill-clad, [and] ill-nourished" were the Wagner-Steagall National Housing Act and the Bankhead-Jones Farm Tenant Act. In 1938 came three more major reforms, the last of the New Deal era: the Second Agricultural Adjustment Act, the Food, Drug and Cosmetic Act, and the Fair Labor Standards Act.

The Housing Act set up the United States Housing Authority (USHA) in the Department of the Interior, which extended long-term loans to local agencies willing to assume part of the cost for slum clearance and public housing. The agency also subsidized low rents. Later, during World War II, it financed housing in connection with defense projects.

The Farm Tenant Act addressed the problem of rural poverty, which in some ways the New Deal's larger farm program had aggravated. Tenants were supposed to be kept on in spite of government-sponsored cutbacks in production, but landlords often made the most of cutbacks by evicting workers and withholding their shares of benefit payments. Social scientists and journalists called attention to the problem, and in northeastern Arkansas tenant farmers themselves found voice when they organized the Southern Tenant Farmers' Union (STFU) in 1934. The union, however, was never able to function effectively in collective bargaining with what one of its founders called "an industry that is disorganized, pauperized and kept alive only by government subsidy." But the union did focus public attention on the problem. Some programs offered loans and grants to keep farmers off the relief rolls, and several cooperative-farming communities grew up with New Deal support. These scattered efforts were regrouped into the Resettlement Administration (RA), created by executive order in 1935.

Then, on the recommendation of a President's Committee on Farm Tenancy, Congress in 1937 passed the Tenant Act, administered by a new agency, the Farm Security Administration (FSA). The program made available rehabilitation loans to shore up marginal farmers and prevent their sinking into tenancy. It also made loans to tenants for purchase of their own farms. But the idea of small homesteads by the late 1930s was, as the STFU warned, "an economic anachronism, doomed to failure." American mythology still exalted the family farm, but in reality the ever-larger agricultural unit predominated. In the end the FSA proved to be little more than another relief operation which tided a few farmers over difficult times. A more effective answer to the problem, sadly, awaited mobilization for war, which took many tenants off into the military ser-

The Farm Tenant Act (1937) and the Second Agricultural Adjustment Act (1938), among the last major reforms of the New Deal era, addressed the problem of rural poverty, which had worsened in the mid-1930s.

vices or defense industries, broadened their horizons, and taught them new skills.

The Agricultural Adjustment Act of 1938 was a response to renewed crop surpluses and price declines during the recession. It reenacted the basic devices of the earlier AAA, with some new twists. Before the government could apply marketing quotas to a given crop, for instance, it had to hold a plebiscite among the growers and win a two-thirds majority. The new Food, Drug and Cosmetic Act broadened the coverage of the 1906 Pure Food and Drug Act and forbade the use of false or misleading advertising. Enforcement of the advertising provision became the responsibility of the Federal Trade Commission. The Fair Labor Standards Act applied to enterprises that operated in or affected interstate commerce. It set a minimum wage of 40¢ an hour and a maximum workweek of forty hours, to be put into effect over several years. The act also prohibited child labor under the age of sixteen, and in hazardous occupations under eighteen.

The Legacy of the New Deal

SETBACKS FOR THE PRESIDENT   As the New Deal turned its focus from recovery to reform, an effective opposition emerged within the president's party, especially in the southern wing. Local power elites in the South felt that the New Deal jeopardized their position. They felt threatened, too, when in 1936 the Democratic convention eliminated the two-thirds rule for nominations, thereby removing the South's veto power, and seated African-American delegates. Southern Democrats were at best uneasy bedfellows with organized labor and northern blacks. Senator "Cotton" Ed Smith of South Carolina and several other southern delegates walked out of the convention, with Smith declaring that he would not support any party that views "the Negro as a political and social equal." Some disgruntled southern Democrats drifted toward coalition with conservative Republicans. By the end of 1937 a conservative bloc, if unorganized and mutable, had appeared.

In 1938 the conservative opposition stymied an executive reorganization bill amid cries that it would lead to dictatorship. They also secured drastic cuts in the undistributed-profits and capital-gains taxes to help restore business "confidence." The House also set up a Committee on Un-American Activities chaired by Martin Dies of Texas who took to the warpath against Communists. Soon he began to brand New Dealers as Red dupes. "Stalin baited his hook with a 'progressive' worm," Dies wrote in 1940, "and New Deal suckers swallowed bait, hook, line, and sinker."

As the political season of 1938 advanced Roosevelt unfolded a new idea as momentous as the Court plan—a proposal to reshape the Democratic party in the image of the New Deal. On June 24 he announced his purpose to intervene in Democratic primaries as the party leader, "charged with the responsibility of carrying out the definitely liberal declaration of principles set forth in the 1936 Democratic platform." The effort ended in a standoff, which broke the spell of presidential invincibility, or what was left of it. As in the Court fight, Roosevelt had risked his prestige while handing his adversaries persuasive issues. His opponents tagged his intervention in the primaries an attempted "purge"; the word evoked visions of Adolf Hitler and Joseph Stalin, tyrants who had purged their Nazi and Communist parties in blood.

The elections of November 1938 handed the administration another setback, a result partly of the friction among Democrats. Their majority in the House fell from 229 to 93, in the Senate from 56 to 42. The margins remained large, but the president headed a restive and divided party. In his State of the Union message in January 1939 Roosevelt for the first time proposed no new reforms, but spoke of the need "to invigorate the process of recovery, in order to *preserve* our reforms." In 1939 the administration won an extension of social security and finally put through its reorganization plan. Under the Administrative Reorganization Act the president could "reduce, co-ordinate, consolidate, and reorganize" the agencies of government. With that, Roosevelt's domestic initiatives feebly ended.

But the opposition was now able to cut relief expenditures, eliminate the Federal Theater Project, reject Roosevelt appointments, and abolish the undistributed-profits tax. The House set up an investigation of the National Labor Relations Board and attempted to narrow the scope of the wage-hour law. The conservative coalition and the administration had reached a standoff.

EMERGENCE OF THE BROKER STATE   The New Deal had lost momentum, but it had wrought some enduring changes. By the end of the 1930s the power of the national government was vastly enlarged over what it had been in 1932. Government had taken on the duty of ensuring the economic and social stability of the country. It had established minimum standards for labor conditions and public welfare. It had helped middle-class Americans hold on to their savings, their homes, and their farms. The protection afforded by deposit insurance, unemployment pay, and social security pensions would come to be universally accepted as a safeguard against such disasters as the depression.

Roosevelt had steered a course between the extremes of laissez-faire and socialism. The first New Deal had experimented for a time with a managed economy under the NRA, but had abandoned that experiment for a turn toward enforcing competition and priming the economy with government spending. The effect of heavy governmental expenditures, which finally lifted the economy out of the depression during World War II, seemed to confirm the arguments of Keynesians.

But the old progressive formulation of regulation versus trust-busting had finally been superseded by the rise of the "broker state," a government that mediated among major interest groups. Government's role was to act as an honest broker protecting a variety of interests, not just big business but workers, farmers, consumers, small business, and the unemployed.

Roosevelt himself, impatient with theory, was a pragmatist in developing policy: he kept what worked and discarded what did not. The result was, paradoxically, both profoundly revolutionary and profoundly conservative. The New Deal left America greatly changed in many ways, its economy more managed than before. At the same time it left the basic capitalistic structure of the economic system in place. "For a permanent correction of grave weaknesses in our economic system," Roosevelt said, "we have relied on new applications of old democratic processes."

FURTHER READING

A sound introduction to the decade of the New Deal is William E. Leuchtenburg's *Franklin D. Roosevelt and the New Deal, 1932–1940* (1963). Arthur M. Schlesinger, Jr., provides a more detailed account in *The Age of Roosevelt* (3 vols., 1957–1960). Paul Conkin's *The New Deal* (2nd ed., 1975)* is more critical.

Van L. Perkins's *Crisis in Agriculture* (1969) and Sidney Baldwin's *Poverty and Politics: The Rise and Decline of the Farm Security Administration* (1969) look at agricultural reforms. Michael E. Parrish's *Securities Regulation and the New Deal* (1970)* and Ellis W. Hawley's *The New Deal and the Problem of Monopoly* (1966)* analyze government attempts to forestall another market crash. Bernard Bellush's *The Failure of the NRA* (1977) studies government relations with business. William R. Brock's *Welfare,*

*These books are available in paperback editions.

Democracy, and the New Deal (1988) and Michael B. Katz's *In the Shadow of the Poorhouse: A Social History of Welfare in America* (1986) describe the development of welfare policy.

The New Deal can also be understood by studying its chief proponents. Frank Freidel's *Franklin D. Roosevelt* (4 vols., 1952–1973)° and Schlesinger's *The Age of Roosevelt* are multivolume, detailed works. James MacGregor Burns's *Roosevelt: The Lion and the Fox* (1956)° offers an astute political analysis. William E. Leuchtenburg's *In the Shadow of FDR* (rev. ed., 1985)° traces Roosevelt's influence on later presidents. The role of Eleanor Roosevelt may be studied in Lois Scharf's *Eleanor Roosevelt: First Lady of American Liberalism* (1987).

For scholarship about the various groups involved in the New Deal, consult Scharf's *To Work and to Wed* (1980), Susan Ware's *Beyond Suffrage* (1981), and Ware's *Partner and I: Molly Dewson, Feminism, and New Deal Politics* (1987), on women; Nancy J. Weiss's *Farewell to the Party of Lincoln* (1983)° and Harvard Sitkoff's *A New Deal for Blacks* (1978),° on blacks; and John M. Allswang's *A House of All Peoples: Ethnic Politics in Chicago, 1890–1936* (1971), on immigrants. Works on the critics of the New Deal include T. Harry Williams's *Huey Long* (1969)° and Alan Brinkley's *Voices of Protest: Huey Long, Father Coughlin, and the Great Depression* (1982).° For radical leftist reactions to reform, see Harvey Klehr's *The Heyday of American Communism* (1984) and David Shannon's *The Socialist Party of America* (1955).

One interest group that was both supportive and critical of New Deal policies was organized labor. See Sidney Fine's *Sit-down: The General Motors Strike of 1936–1937* (1969) and Jerold S. Auerbach's *Labor and Liberty: The La Follette Committee and the New Deal* (1966).°

The fullest introduction to the New Deal in the South remains the relevant chapters in George B. Tindall's *The Emergence of the New South, 1913–1945* (1967).° How Roosevelt dealt with the South is handled in Frank Freidel's *FDR and the South* (1965). How southern farmers fared is examined in David E. Conrad's *The Forgotten Farmers: The Story of the Sharecroppers in the New Deal* (1965) and Pete Daniel's *The Shadow of Slavery: Peonage in the South, 1901–1969* (1972). Dan T. Carter provides an insightful analysis of the influence of reform on race relations in the 1930s in his *Scottsboro: A Tragedy of the American South* (1969).°

For the cultural impact of the New Deal, consult Richard H. Pells's *Radical Visions and American Dreams: Cultural and Social Thought in the Depression Years* (1973)° and Richard D. McKinzie's *The New Deal for Artists* (1973).°

29

FROM ISOLATION TO GLOBAL WAR

Postwar Isolationism

THE LEAGUE AND THE UNITED STATES   In the late 1930s, as the winds of war swept Asia and Europe, the focus of American politics moved abruptly from domestic to foreign affairs. Another Democratic president had to shift attention from reform to preparedness and war. But between Woodrow Wilson and Franklin Roosevelt lay two decades of isolation from foreign connections. The postwar mood of 1920 set the pattern. The voters expressed their yearning for a restored isolationism, and President-elect Harding lost little time in indulging it by disposing of the League of Nations. "You just didn't want a surrender of the United States," he told the people in his victory speech. "That's why you didn't care for the League, which is now deceased." The spirit of isolation found other expressions as well: the higher tariff walls, the Red Scare, the rage for "100 percent Americanism," and tight immigration laws by which a nation of immigrants all but shut the door to any more newcomers.

The United States may have felt the urge to leave a wicked world to its own devices, but it could hardly stop the world and get off. American business, despite the tariff walls, now had worldwide connections. American investments and loans abroad put in circulation the dollars that purchased American exports. Overseas possessions, moreover, directly involved the country in world affairs, especially in the Pacific. Even the League of Nations was too great a fact to ignore, although messages from the League at first went unanswered by American diplomats. By the end of 1922, however, the United States had "unofficial observers" at the League, and after 1924 gradually entered into joint efforts on such matters as the international trade in drugs and arms, the criminal traffic in women and children, and a variety of economic, cultural, and technical conferences.

Americans had mixed feelings about adherence to the World Court. The Permanent Court of International Justice, established by the League at The Hague in 1922, was open to any country, whether a member of the League or not. The idea of bringing foreign disputes before a panel of jurists appealed to legal-minded Americans; the United States had in fact urged the idea in previous years. Still, it smacked too much of extranational authority for isolationists, even though its jurisdiction was always optional. Repeated efforts to join the World Court therefore met with rebuff from the Senate. Franklin D. Roosevelt pressed the issue in 1935, and the Senate voted 52 to 36 in favor, falling short of a two-thirds majority. American judges served on the Court panel, but the United States stayed out.

WAR DEBTS AND REPARATIONS Probably nothing did more to heighten American isolationism—or anti-American feeling in Europe—than the war-debt tangle. When in 1917 the Allies had begun to exhaust private credit in the United States, the government had advanced them funds first for the war effort and then for post-war reconstruction. A World War Foreign Debt Commission, created by Congress in 1922, renegotiated the Allied debt to America to a total of about $11.5 billion. Adding the interest payable over sixty-two years to this principal, the Allied debt came to something over $22 billion.

To Americans at large it all seemed a simple matter of obligation, but Europeans commonly had a different perception. In the first place, Americans who thought their loan money had flowed to Europe were wrong: most of it went toward purchases in the United States, which fueled the wartime boom. Then, too, the Allies held off the enemy at great cost of blood and treasure while the United States was raising an army. American states, the British noted, had been known to repudiate debts to British investors; and the French pointed out that they had never been repaid for help in the American Revolution. But most difficult were the practical problems of repayment. To get dollar exchange, European debtors had to sell their goods to the United States, but tariff walls went higher in 1921 and 1922, and again in 1930, making debt payment harder. Payment in gold would have undermined the European currencies. When the United States refused to relent, French newspapers rechristened Uncle Sam "l'Oncle Shylock."

The French and British insisted that they could pay America only as they collected reparations from Germany. Twice during the 1920s the resulting strain on Germany brought the structure of international payments to the verge of collapse, and both times the Reparations Commission called in private American bankers to work out rescue plans.

The whole structure finally did collapse during the Great Depression. In 1931 President Hoover negotiated a moratorium on both German reparations and Allied payment of war debts, thereby indirectly accepting the connection between the two. The purpose, among other things, was to shore up American private loans of several billion dollars in Germany, which for the time had kept the international credit structure intact. Once the United States had accepted the connection between reparations and war debt, the Allies virtually canceled German reparations. At the end of 1932, after Hoover's debt moratorium ended, most of the European countries defaulted on their war debts to the United States; by 1934 all but Finland had defaulted. In retaliation, Congress passed the Johnson Debt Default Act of 1934, which prohibited even private loans to any defaulting government.

ATTEMPTS AT DISARMAMENT   Yet, for all the isolationist sentiment of the time, Wilsonian idealism had struck a responsive chord in the American people. A lingering doubt, tinged with guilt, haunted many Americans about their rejection of the League. Before long Harding's advisers hit upon a happy substitute—disarmament. The conviction had grown after World War I that excessive armaments had been the war's cause, and that arms limitation would bring lasting peace. The United States had no intention of maintaining a large army, but under the building program begun in 1916 it constructed a navy second only to that of Britain. Neither the British nor the Americans had much stomach for the cost of a naval armaments race with the other, but both shared a common concern with the alarming growth of Japanese power.

During and after the war Japanese-American relations grew increasingly strained. The United States objected to continued Japanese encroachments in Asia. In 1902 Japan had made a defensive alliance with Great Britain, directed then at Russia but invoked in 1914 against Germany in order to pick up German concessions and territories in East Asia. The Japanese quickly took the Shantung Peninsula and the islands of Micronesia, which Germany had purchased not long before from Spain. The Paris Peace Conference reluctantly confirmed Japanese seizure of the Shantung Peninsula, to the outrage of the Chinese, and the League of Nations authorized a

Japanese mandate of Micronesia north of the equator. Occupation of Micronesia put the Japanese squarely athwart eastern approaches to the Philippines (see the map on page 1169).

During the war the Japanese had grabbed the chance for further moves against China. In 1915 the cabinet at Tokyo issued what came to be known as the Twenty-one Demands, which would have brought China virtually under Japanese control. The United States protested, and fortunately the Japanese decided not to force their most rigorous demands. In 1917, after the United States entered the war, Viscount Kikujiro Ishii visited Washington to secure American recognition of Japan's position in Asia, dropping hints that Germany had several times tried to get Japan to quit the war. To forestall such a result, Secretary of State Lansing entered an ambiguous agreement that recognized Japan's "special interests [translated by the Japanese as 'paramount interests'] in China." Americans were unhappy with the Lansing-Ishii Agreement, but it was feared that this was the only way to keep Japan in the war.

To deal with the growing strains, President Harding invited eight principal powers to a conference on arms and also on Pacific and East Asian affairs. The Washington Armaments Conference met on November 11, 1921, opening with a formal address from President Harding. Then American Secretary of State Charles Evans Hughes, in what was expected to be a perfunctory greeting, suddenly announced that "the way to disarm is to disarm." The only way out of an armaments race, he said, "is to end it now." He then offered concrete suggestions which ultimately became the basis of agreement. It was one of the most dramatic moments in American diplomatic history. In less than fifteen minutes, one electrified reporter said, Hughes had destroyed more tonnage "than all the admirals of the world have sunk in a cycle of centuries."

The upshot was that delegates from the United States, Britain, Japan, France, and Italy reached agreement on a Five-Power Naval Treaty incorporating Hughes's plan for tonnage limits and a naval holiday of ten years during which no capital ships (battleships and aircraft carriers) would be built. These powers also agreed to refrain from further fortification of their Pacific possessions. The result was to expose Hong Kong and the Philippines in the event of war, but Hong Kong was clearly indefensible and the Philippines only slightly less so given the Japanese presence in Micronesia. The agreement in effect partitioned the world: United States naval power became supreme in the Western Hemisphere, Japanese power in the western Pacific, British power from the North Sea to Singapore.

Two other major agreements came out of the Washington Conference. With the Four-Power Treaty, the United States, Britain,

The Washington Armaments Conference, 1921. *The Big Five at the conference were* (from left): *Prince Tekugawa (Japan), Arthur Balfour (Great Britain), Charles Evans Hughes (United States), M. Briand (France), and H. E. Carlo Sanchez (Italy).*

Japan, and France agreed to respect each other's possessions in the Pacific, and to refer any disputes or any outside threat to consultation. The Nine-Power Treaty for the first time formally pledged the signers to support the Open Door and the territorial integrity of China. The powers, in addition to those signing the Five-Power Treaty, were China, Belgium, Portugal, and the Netherlands.

With these agreements in hand, Harding could boast of a brilliant diplomatic stroke that relieved taxpayers of the need to pay for an enlarged navy, and warded off potential conflicts in the Pacific. A grateful Senate approved the naval treaty with one dissenting vote. The Four-Power Treaty aroused real opposition, but finally passed with the support of Democrats after the Senate tacked on a reservation that "there is no commitment to armed force, no alliance, no obligation to join in any defense."

There was the rub. Though the agreements tapped a deep urge toward peacemaking, they were uniformly without obligation and without teeth. The signers of the Four-Power Treaty agreed only to consult, not to help each other, a point that was clear even before the Senate tacked on its reservation. The formal endorsement of the Open Door in the Nine-Power Treaty was just as ineffective, and the American people remained unwilling to uphold the principle with anything but pious affirmation. The naval disarmament treaty set limits only on capital ships; the race to build cruisers, destroyers, submarines, and other smaller craft continued. Japan withdrew from the agreement in 1934. Thus twelve years after the Washington Conference the dream of naval disarmament died.

THE KELLOGG-BRIAND PACT During and after the "war to end war" the ideal of abolishing war caught the American imagination. Peace societies thrived and spawned innumerable programs, foremost among them the Carnegie Endowment for International Peace, founded in 1910. In 1921 a wealthy Chicagoan founded the American Committee for the Outlawry of War. "We can outlaw this war system just as we outlawed slavery and the saloon," said one of the more enthusiastic converts.

The glorious vision of abolishing war at the stroke of a pen culminated in the signing of the Kellogg-Briand Pact in 1928. This unique treaty started with an initiative from French Foreign Minister Aristide Briand, who had busied himself winning allies against a possible resurgence of German power. In 1927 Briand proposed to Secretary of State Frank B. Kellogg not an alliance but an agreement that the two countries would never go to war with each other. This innocent-seeming proposal was actually a clever ploy to draw the United States into the French security system by the back door. In any future war, for instance, such a pact would inhibit the United States from reprisals against any French intrusions on neutral rights. Kellogg gave the idea a cool reception, and was outraged to discover that Briand had urged leaders of the American peace movements to put pressure on the government to sign.

Finally Kellogg turned the tables on Briand. He countered with a scheme to have all nations brought into the pact, an idea all the more acceptable to the peace movements. Caught in a trap of his own making, the French foreign minister finally relented. The Pact of Paris (its official name), signed on August 27, 1928, solemnly declared that the signatories "condemn recourse to war . . . and renounce it as an instrument of national policy." Eventually sixty-two powers adhered to the pact, but all explicitly or tacitly reserved "self-defense" as an escape hatch. The United States Senate included a reservation declaring the Monroe Doctrine necessary to self-defense, and then ratified the agreement by a vote of 85 to 1. One senator who voted for "this worthless, but perfectly harmless peace treaty" wrote a friend later that he feared it would "confuse the minds of many good people who think that peace may be secured by polite professions of neighborly and brotherly love."

This judgment aptly described the euphoric assumptions of many

*Plans for international disarmament, popular in the 1920s,
proved impractical.*

Americans at the time. The treaty proved to be the grandest illusion
in an age of illusions. Its "only discernible influence," the historian
Robert H. Ferrell wrote, "was to inaugurate a fashion whereby wars
would be fought under justification of national defense and without
formal declaration of hostilities." Such a war broke out just a year
later in Manchuria, where Russian forces quickly put down a Chinese effort to regain control of the Chinese Eastern Railway. When
Hoover's secretary of state called the Soviet Union's attention to the
Pact of Paris, the Soviet foreign minister called attention to the fact
that the United States had not yet recognized the Soviet government,
and scorned the presumption of the secretary's communication.

THE "GOOD NEIGHBOR" POLICY   In Latin America the spirit of peace
and noninvolvement helped allay resentments against "Yankee imperialism," which had been freely practiced in the Caribbean during
the first two decades of the century. The Harding administration
agreed in 1921 to pay the republic of Colombia the $25 million it had
once demanded for canal rights. In 1924 American forces left the
Dominican Republic, occupied since 1916, although United States
officials continued to collect customs duties there for another twenty-
five years.

The marines left Nicaragua in 1925, but returned a year later with
the outbreak of disorders and civil war. There in 1927, the Coolidge
administration brought both parties into an agreement for Ameri-

can-supervised elections, but one rebel leader, César Augusto San-
dino, held out and the marines stayed until 1933. The unhappy
legacies of this intervention were enmity toward the United States
and a ruthless, corrupt Nicaraguan National Guard, created to keep
order after the marines left, but used in 1936 to set up the dictatorship of Anastasio Somoza. These legacies continue to have their
effects down to the present day.

The troubles in Nicaragua increased strains in relations with Mexico. Relations were already troubled by repeated Mexican threats to
expropriate American oil properties under the Constitution of 1917,
which nationalized all mineral and oil resources in the country. In
1928, however, the American ambassador so mollified the Mexicans
by his gestures of friendship that he was able to get an agreement
protecting American rights acquired before 1917. Expropriation did
in fact occur in 1938, but the Mexican government then agreed to
reimburse American owners.

In 1928, with problems apparently clearing in Mexico and Nicaragua, President Coolidge traveled to Havana to open the Pan-American Conference, sixth in a series that dated from 1889–1890. It was
an unusual gesture of friendship, and so was the choice of Charles
Evans Hughes, the former secretary of state, to head the American
delegation. Hughes announced United States' withdrawal from Nicaragua and Haiti as soon as possible, although he did block a resolution declaring that "no state has the right to intervene in the affairs
of another."

At the end of 1928 President-elect Hoover began a tour of ten
Latin American nations. Once in office he reversed Wilson's policy
of refusing to recognize "bad" regimes and reverted to the older
policy of recognizing governments in power. In 1930 he generated
more goodwill by permitting publication of a memorandum drawn
up in 1928 by Undersecretary of State J. Ruben Clark. The Clark
Memorandum denied that the Monroe Doctrine justified American
intervention in Latin America. It stopped short of repudiating intervention on any grounds, but that fine point hardly blunted the celebration in Latin America. Although Hoover never endorsed the
Clark Memorandum, he never intervened in the area. Before he left
office, steps had already been taken to withdraw American forces
from Nicaragua and Haiti.

Franklin D. Roosevelt likewise embraced "the policy of the good
neighbor" and soon advanced it in practice. In December 1933 at the
seventh Pan-American Conference the United States supported a
resolution saying "No state has the right to intervene in the international or external affairs of another." Under Roosevelt the marines
completed their withdrawals from Nicaragua and Haiti, and in 1934

the president negotiated with Cuba a treaty that abrogated the Platt Amendment and thus ended the last formal claim to a right of intervention in Latin America. Roosevelt reinforced hemispheric goodwill in 1936, when he opened the eighth Pan-American Conference with a speech declaring that outside aggressors "will find a Hemisphere wholly prepared to consult together for our mutual safety and our mutual good."

WAR CLOUDS

JAPANESE INCURSIONS IN CHINA   The lessening of irritants in the Western Hemisphere proved an exception in an otherwise dismal world scene, as war clouds thickened over Europe and Asia. Actual conflict came first in Asia, where unsettled conditions in China had invited foreign encroachments since before the turn of the century. The tottering Manchu dynasty had collapsed in 1911 and the series of governments that followed in Peking exercised only nominal authority over local warlords. Finally the Kuomintang (or National party) under Dr. Sun Yat-sen, and later Chiang Kai-shek, extended its power from a southern base around Canton to take Peking in 1928 and set up a new capital in Nanking. But when the new government tried to extend its power in Manchuria it ran into the vested interest of the Russians and Japanese there. Its effort to take over the Chinese Eastern Railway in 1929 led to a short undeclared war with Russia and humiliation for the Kuomintang. More important, Chinese nationalist aspirations convinced the Japanese that their own extensive rights in Manchuria, including the South Manchurian Railway, were in danger.

The Japanese army at the time had a nationalist movement of its own, led by a strong cadre of young officers devoted to ousting corrupt politicians and bringing about a moral regeneration for Japan. Economic pressures strengthened this nationalist movement, for Japan was suffering from the Great Depression and Chinese boycotts of Japanese goods. Manchuria offered both a tempting target and a promising market. Japanese occupation of Manchuria began with the Mukden Incident of September 18, 1931, an explosion which destroyed a section of track near that city. The Japanese "Kwantung Army," based in Manchuria to guard the railway, blamed the incident on the Chinese and used it as a pretext to begin its occupation, which it extended during the winter of 1931–1932 to all of Manchuria, including the Russian sphere of influence. In 1932 the Japanese converted Manchuria into the puppet empire of "Manchukuo" and resurrected the former boy emperor of China, deposed in 1911, to head the new state.

Japan's seizure of Manchuria in 1931 prompted this American condemnation.

The Manchuria Incident, as the Japanese called their undeclared war, was a flagrant breach of the Nine-Power Treaty, the Kellogg-Briand Pact, and Japan's pledges as a member of the League of Nations. But when China asked the League and the United States for help, neither was ready to take effective action. President Hoover was unwilling to invoke either military or economic sanctions. Secretary of State Stimson, who would have preferred to do more, issued a statement in January 1932 warning that the United States refused to recognize any treaty, agreement, or situation that violated American treaty rights, the Open Door, or the territorial integrity of China, or any situation brought about by violation of the Kellogg-Briand Pact. This statement, later known as the Stimson Doctrine, had no effect on Japanese action, for later in the same month the Japanese navy attacked and briefly occupied Shanghai, China's great port city.

Indiscriminate bombing of Shanghai's civilian population aroused indignation, but no further Western action. When the League of Nations condemned Japanese aggression in February 1933, Japan's response was to withdraw from the League and keep the islands of Micronesia, which until then had been under the administration of the League, as a souvenir. During the spring of 1933 hostilities in Manchuria gradually subsided and ended with a truce on May 31, 1933. Then an uneasy peace settled upon East Asia for four years, during which the leaders of Japan's military further extended their political sway.

ITALY AND GERMANY The rise of the Japanese militarists paralleled the rise of warlike dictators in Italy and Germany. In 1922 Benito Mussolini had seized power in Italy. A one-time Socialist leader, Mussolini had broken with the party over its antiwar stand, and after returning from World War I as a wounded veteran, had organized the Fascist movement, which was based on a composite faith in nationalism and socialism. The movement's name came from the ancient Roman *fasces,* a symbol of authority. The program, and above all Mussolini's promise to restore order in a country fragmented by dissension, enjoyed a wide appeal. Once in power, Mussolini largely abandoned the socialist part of his platform and gradually suppressed the opposition. By 1925 he wielded dictatorial power as Il Duce (the leader) in a one-party state.

To most Americans there was always something ludicrous about the strutting Mussolini, since Italy afforded but a limited power base in the total European picture. But Germany was another matter, and Americans were not amused, even at the beginning, by Il Duce's counterpart, Adolf Hitler, despite his Charlie Chaplin mustache. Hitler's National Socialist (Nazi) party duplicated the major features of Italian Fascism, including the ancient Roman salute. Hitler, having failed to duplicate Mussolini's success in a premature *Putsch* in 1923, did manage to win a foothold for his party in the German Reichstag (parliament). The impotence of Germany's democratic Weimar Republic in the face of world depression finally offered Hitler his opening. Made chancellor on January 30, 1933, he moved swiftly to intimidate the opposition, won dictatorial powers from a subservient Reichstag on March 24, and after the death of President Hindenburg in 1934 assumed the title of Reichsführer (national leader) with absolute powers. The Nazi police state cranked up the engines of tyranny, persecuting Jews, whom Hitler blamed for all Germany's troubles, and rearming in defiance of the Versailles Treaty. Hitler flouted international agreements, pulled

Mussolini and Hitler in Munich, Germany, June 1940.

Germany out of the League of Nations in October 1933, and frankly proclaimed that he meant to extend control over all German-speaking peoples. Despite one provocation after another the European democracies seemed to lack the will to resist his bold grab for power.

THE MOOD IN AMERICA   Americans, absorbed by the problems of the depression, chose to retreat all the more into isolationism during the early 1930s. In the campaign of 1932 Roosevelt had found it prudent to renounce his Wilsonian past and state that he now opposed joining the League of Nations. Once in office he rejected an early chance to deal with economic problems on an international basis. Hoover, convinced that the depression called for world action, had pledged the United States to participate in the London Economic Conference on reparations. The conference of sixty-four nations was to deal with the related issues of currency stabilization, world trade, and war debts. But when a group of gold-bloc nations (led by France) insisted on a return to the gold standard, Roosevelt demurred and the conference ended in futility. The president wanted to be free to experiment with currency manipulation as a device to fight the depression. Roosevelt's action dealt a severe blow to international cooperation. The epilogue was Europe's final default on the war debts, and further American drift toward isolation.

The chief exception to the administration's isolationism was Secretary of State Cordell Hull's grand scheme of reciprocal trade agreements. Hull, a former Tennessee judge and congressman, held to the firm conviction that to release the fetters on world trade would advance understanding and peace. In 1934 the administration threw its support behind Hull's pet project, and over the objections of business interests and Republicans Congress adopted the Trade Agreements Act, which authorized the president to lower tariff rates as much as 50 percent for countries that made similar concessions on American products. Agreements were made with fourteen countries by the end of 1935, reaching a total of twenty-nine by 1945. The economic results are hard to measure, since the following years were so troubled.

Another scheme for building foreign markets, diplomatic recognition of Soviet Russia, won more support in business quarters than had the reciprocity plan. The vast expanse of Russia stirred fantasies of a trade boom, much as China had at the turn of the century. By 1933 the reasons for American refusal to recognize the Bolshevik regime had grown stale. Japanese expansionism in Asia, moreover, gave Russia and the United States a common concern. Given an opening by the shift of opinion, Roosevelt invited Maxim Litvinov,

Soviet commissar for foreign affairs, to visit Washington. After nine days of talks, a formal exchange of notes on November 16, 1933, signaled the renewal of diplomatic relations. Litvinov promised that his country would abstain from propaganda in the United States, extend religious freedom to Americans in the USSR, and reopen the question of czarist debts.

THE EXPANDING AXIS   But a catastrophic chain of events in Asia and Europe sent the world hurtling toward disaster. In 1934 Japan renounced the Five-Power Naval Treaty. In 1935 Mussolini commenced an Italian conquest of Ethiopia. The same year a referendum in the Saar Basin, held in accordance with the Versailles Treaty, delivered that coal-rich region into the hands of Hitler. In 1936 Hitler reoccupied the Rhineland with armed forces, in violation of the Versailles Treaty but without any forceful response from the French. The year 1936 also brought the Spanish Civil

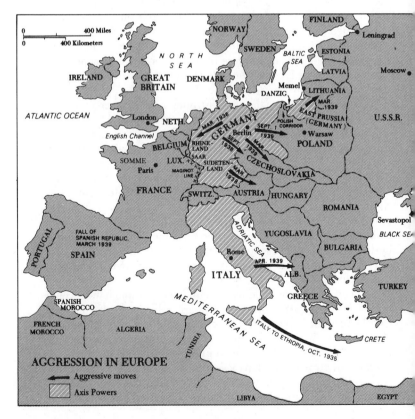

AGGRESSION IN EUROPE

The swastika, symbol of Nazi Germany, about to crush Poland.

War, which began with an uprising of the Spanish armed forces in Morocco, led by General Francisco Franco. In three years Franco had established a fascist dictatorship with help from Hitler and Mussolini while the democracies stood by and left the Spanish Republic to its fate. On July 7, 1937, Japanese and Chinese troops clashed at the Marco Polo Bridge near Peking. The incident quickly developed into a full-scale war which the Japanese persisted in calling the "China Incident." It was the beginning of World War II in Asia, two years before war came to Europe. That same year Japan joined Germany and Italy in the "Anti-Comintern Pact," allegedly directed at the Communist threat, thus establishing the Rome-Berlin-Tokyo "Axis."

By 1938 the peace of Europe trembled in the balance. Having rebuilt German military force, Hitler forced the *Anschluss* (union) of Austria with Germany in March 1938, and six months later took the Sudeten territory from Czechoslovakia after signing an agreement at Munich under which Britain and France abandoned a country that had probably the second-best army in central Europe. The mountainous Sudetenland, largely German in population, was vital to the defense of Czechoslovakia. Having promised that this was his last territorial demand, Hitler in March 1939 occupied the remainder of Czechoslovakia. In quick succession the Spanish Republic finally collapsed on March 28 and Mussolini seized the kingdom of Albania on April 7. Finally, during the summer Hitler heated up a "war of nerves" over control of the free city of Danzig and the Polish Corridor, and on September 1 launched his conquest of Poland. A few days before, he had reached a nonaggression pact with Russia. Having deserted Czechoslovakia, Britain and France now honored their commitment to go to war if Poland were invaded.

DEGREES OF NEUTRALITY During these years of deepening crisis, the Western democracies seemed paralyzed, hoping in vain that each concession would appease the appetites of fascist dictators. The American response was to retreat more deeply into isolation. The prevailing mood was reinforced by a Senate inquiry into the role of bankers and munitions makers in World War I. Under Senator Gerald P. Nye of North Dakota, a progressive Republican, the committee sat from 1934 to 1937, and concluded that bankers and munitions makers had made scandalous profits from the war. Although Nye never showed that greed for profit had actually impelled Wilson into war, millions of Americans became convinced that Uncle Sam had been duped by the "merchants of death."

Historians then rehashing the European origins of World War I challenged the idea of German war guilt; some condemned America's entry into the war. One of the most popular arguments of the time claimed that a combination of British propaganda, economic involvement with the Allies, and Wilson's uneven response to British and German violations of neutrality had sucked the United States into a war it should have avoided. In 1934 an influential article in the journal *Foreign Affairs* argued that modern warfare had rendered obsolete old notions of freedom of the seas. If the United States wanted to remain neutral in the current crisis, therefore, it would have to keep Americans out of war zones, keep belligerent vessels out of American ports, embargo arms shipments, and set quotas on the export of contraband. Such ideas became official policy as war enveloped Asia and Europe.

Like generals who are said to be always preparing for the last war, Congress occupied itself with keeping out of the last war. Neutrality laws of the 1930s moved the United States back toward Jefferson's embargo policies and complete isolation from the quarrels of Europe. Americans wanted to keep out of war, but their sympathies were more strongly than ever with the Western democracies, and the triumph of fascist aggression aroused growing fears for national security.

On August 31, 1935, President Roosevelt signed the first in a series of neutrality acts, one which anticipated Italy's invasion of Ethiopia. The Neutrality Act of 1935 forbade the sale of arms and munitions to all belligerents whenever the president proclaimed that a state of war existed. Americans who traveled on belligerent ships thereafter did so at their own risk. Roosevelt would have preferred discretionary authority to levy an embargo only against aggressors, but reluctantly accepted the act because it would be effective only six months, and for the time being "meets the need of the existing situation." That is, it would actually be enforced against Italy in its war with

Ethiopia. When he signed the act on August 31, Roosevelt nevertheless urged reconsideration of the arms embargo on all belligerents: "History is filled with situations that call for some flexibility of action. It is conceivable that situations may arise in which the wholly inflexible provisions . . . of this act . . . might drag us into war instead of keeping us out."

On October 3, 1935, Italy invaded Ethiopia and the president invoked the act. One shortcoming in its provisions became apparent right away: the key problem was neither arms traffic nor passenger travel, but trade in contraband not covered by the Neutrality Act. Secretary of State Hull warned, however, that anybody trading with the belligerents, meaning in effect Italy since there was little trade with Ethiopia, did so at his own risk. He asked, moreover, for a "moral embargo" on oil and other products. Sanctions imposed under the Neutrality Act had no deterrent effect on Mussolini or his suppliers. In the summer of 1936 Il Duce completed his conquest of Ethiopia.

When Congress reconvened in January 1936, it fell into a three-cornered debate among the advocates of mandatory embargoes, embargoes aimed only at aggressors, and traditional neutrality. After six weeks Congress simply extended the arms embargo and added a provision forbidding loans to belligerents. Then in July 1936, while Italian troops mopped up the last resistance in Ethiopia, the Spanish army led by Franco revolted in Morocco. Ironically, Roose-

The Debate over American Neutrality. *Critical of America's neutral policy, the cartoon at left depicts Hitler and Mussolini as grateful that the American ostrich has stuck its head in the sand. The cartoon at right approves of Uncle Sam's decision to sit out Europe's deathly dance.*

velt now became more isolationist than some of the isolationists. Although the Spanish Civil War involved a fascist uprising against a recognized, democratic government, Roosevelt accepted the French and British position that only nonintervention would localize the fight. There existed, moreover, a strong bloc of pro-Franco Catholics in America who worried that the Spanish Republic was a threat to the church. They feared Communist influence in the Spanish government; intrigues by Spanish Communists did prove divisive and the Soviet Union in fact did supply aid to the Republic, but nothing like the quantity of German and Italian aid to Franco.

Roosevelt asked for another "moral embargo" on the arms trade, and asked Congress to extend the neutrality laws to cover civil wars. Congress did so in January 1937 with only one dissenting vote— although many, including Senator Nye, had second thoughts later about leaving the Spanish Republic thus to its fate. The Western democracies then stood witness while German and Italian soldiers, planes, and armaments supported Franco's overthrow of Spanish democracy, which was completed in 1939.

In the spring of 1937 isolationist sentiment reached a peak. A Gallup poll found that 94 percent of its respondents preferred efforts to keep out of war over efforts to prevent war. That same spring Congress passed yet another neutrality law, which continued restraints on arms sales and loans, forbade Americans to travel on belligerent ships, and forbade the arming of American merchant ships trading with belligerents. The president also won discretionary authority to require that goods other than arms or munitions exported to belligerents be placed on a cash-and-carry basis. This was an ingenious scheme to preserve a profitable trade without running the risk of war.

The new law faced its first test on July 7, 1937, when Japanese and Chinese forces clashed at the Marco Polo Bridge west of Peking. Since neither side declared war, Roosevelt was able to use his discretion about invoking the neutrality law. He decided to wait, and in fact never invoked it. This was because its net effect would have favored the Japanese, since China had greater need of arms but few means to get supplies past the Japanese navy. A flourishing trade in munitions to China flowed around the world as ships carried arms across the Atlantic to England, where they were reloaded on British ships bound for Hong Kong. Roosevelt, by inaction, had challenged strict isolationism.

He soon ventured a step further. On October 5, 1937, Roosevelt delivered a forthright denunciation of the "reign of terror and international lawlessness" in which 10 percent of the world's population threatened the peace of the other 90 percent. "When an epidemic of

Japanese troops enter Peking after the clash at the Marco Polo Bridge, July 1937.

physical disease starts to spread, the community approves and joins in a quarantine of the patients in order to protect the health of the community. . . ." There should also be a quarantine against nations "creating a state of international anarchy and instability from which there is no escape through mere isolation or neutrality." On the whole, public reaction to the speech was mixed. The president quickly backed off from its implications and refused to spell out any specific program.

Then, on December 12, 1937, Japanese planes bombed and sank the American gunboat *Panay*, which had been lying at anchor in the Yangtze River and prominently flying the American flag, and then attacked three Standard Oil tankers. Two members of the *Panay* crew and an Italian journalist died; thirty more were injured. Though the Japanese government was quick to apologize and pay the reparations demanded—nearly $2¼ million—the incident reinforced American animosity toward Japan. The private boycott of Japanese goods spread, but isolationist sentiment continued strong, as was vividly demonstrated by support for the Ludlow Amendment in Congress. The proposed constitutional amendment would have required a referendum for a declaration of war except in case of attack on American territory. Only by the most severe pressure from the White House, and a vote of 209 to 188, was consideration of the measure tabled in January 1938.

Still, the continuing Japanese war against China brought public outrage and protests from Secretary Hull. On July 1, 1938, after nearly a year of war in China, the U.S. government notified domestic aircraft manufacturers and exporters that it opposed sales to those guilty of attacks on civilian populations. To have imposed an outright embargo would have violated a commercial treaty of 1911 with Japan, but after another year, on July 26, 1939, the United States gave six months' notice of the termination of the treaty—thus clearing the way for an embargo on war materials to Japan.

By then Hitler had brought Europe into war. After the German occupation of Czechoslovakia, Roosevelt no longer pretended impartiality in the impending struggle. He urged Congress to repeal the embargo and permit the United States to sell arms on a cash-and-carry basis to Britain and France, but to no avail. "You haven't got the votes," Vice-President Garner told him, "and that's all there is to it." When the German attack on Poland came on September 1, 1939, Roosevelt proclaimed neutrality, but in a radio talk said that he did not, like Wilson, ask Americans to remain neutral in thought because "even a neutral has a right to take account of the facts."

Congress, summoned into special session on September 21, was asked once again to amend the Neutrality Act. "I regret the Congress passed the Act," the president said. "I regret equally that I signed the Act." This time he got what he wanted by winning the support of conservative Democrats who had opposed his domestic policies. Under the Neutrality Act of 1939 the Allies could send their own freighters, buy for cash, and take away arms or anything else they wanted. American ships, on the other hand, were excluded from belligerent ports and from specified war zones. Roosevelt then designated as a war zone the Baltic Sea and the waters around Great Britain and Ireland from Norway south to the coast of Spain. One effect of this move was to relieve Hitler of any inhibitions against using unrestricted submarine warfare to blockade Britain.

American attitudes continued to vacillate. As the war crisis developed, an isolationist policy of hands-off prevailed. Once the great democracies of western Europe faced war, American public opinion, appalled at Hitler's tyranny, came to support measures short of war to help their cause. "What the majority of the American people want," an editor wrote in the *Nation*, "is to be as unneutral as possible without getting into war." On October 3, while Congress debated repeal of the arms embargo, the foreign ministers of the American republics adopted the Declaration of Panama, which created a "chastity belt" around the Americas, south of Canada, a zone

300 to 1,000 miles wide in which belligerents were warned not to pursue naval action. For a time it seemed possible that the Western Hemisphere could remain insulated from the war. After Hitler over-ran Poland in less than a month, the war settled into an unreal stalemate that began to be called the "Phony War." What lay ahead, it seemed, was a long war of attrition in which Britain and France would have the resources to outlast Hitler. The illusion lasted through the winter.

THE STORM IN EUROPE

BLITZKRIEG   In the spring of 1940 the winter's long *Sitzkrieg* sud-denly erupted into *Blitzkrieg*—lightning war. At dawn on April 9, without warning, Nazi troops entered Denmark and disembarked along the Norwegian coast. Denmark fell in a day, Norway within a few weeks. On May 10 Hitler released his dive bombers and panzer tank divisions on neutral Belgium and the Netherlands. On May 21 German forces moving down the valley of the Somme reached the English Channel, cutting off a British force sent to help the Belgians and French. A desperate evacuation from the beaches at Dunkirk enlisted every available boat from warship to tug. Some 338,000 men, about a third of them French, escaped to England.

Having outflanked the forts on France's eastern defense perime-ter, the Maginot Line, the German forces rushed ahead, cutting the French armies to pieces and spreading panic by strafing refugees in a deliberate policy of terror. On June 10 Mussolini entered the war. "I need only a few thousand dead to enable me to take my seat . . . at the peace table," Il Duce said. Speaking at the University of Virginia the same day, Roosevelt grimly ad-libbed: "The hand that held the dagger has plunged it into the back of France." On June 14 the swastika flew over Paris. On June 22 French delegates, in the presence of Hitler, submitted to his terms in the same railroad car at Compiègne in which German delegates had been forced to sign the Armistice of 1918.

AMERICA'S GROWING INVOLVEMENT   Britain stood alone, but in Par-liament Prime Minister Winston Churchill, who had replaced Cham-berlain amid the *Blitzkrieg*, breathed defiance. "We shall go on to the end," he said; "we shall never surrender." Even if the home islands should fall, the Empire "would carry on the struggle, until, in God's good time, the New World with all its power and might, steps forth to the rescue and liberation of the Old." Despite the grim resolution of the British, America seemed suddenly vulnerable as

St. Paul's Cathedral looms above the destruction wrought by German bombs during the Blitz. Churchill's response: "We shall never surrender."

Hitler turned his air force against Britain. President Roosevelt, who in his annual budget had requested $1.9 billion for defense, now asked for more, and called for the production of 50,000 combat planes a year. By October 1940 Congress had voted more than $17 billion for defense. In response to Churchill's appeal for military supplies, the War and Navy Departments began releasing stocks of arms, planes, and munitions to the British.

America continued to prepare its defense. On June 15, 1940, the president set up the National Defense Research Committee to coordinate military research, including a secret look into the possibility of developing an atomic bomb, suggested the previous fall by Albert Einstein and other scientists. To bolster national unity, on June 19 Roosevelt named two Republicans to the defense posts in his cabinet: Henry L. Stimson as secretary of war and Frank Knox as secretary of the navy. On July 20 Roosevelt signed a bill authorizing a two-ocean navy at a cost of $4 billion. In August the United States and Canada set up a Permanent Joint Board on Defense. At the end of the month units of the National Guard began to be inducted into federal service.

The summer of 1940 brought the desperate Battle of Britain, in which the Royal Air Force, with the benefit of the new technology of radar finding, outfought the numerically superior German Luftwaffe and finally forced the Germans to give up plans to invade. Submarine warfare meanwhile strained the resources of the battered Royal Navy. To relieve the pressure, Churchill urgently requested the transfer of American destroyers. Secret negotiations led to an executive agreement under which fifty "overaged" American destroyers went to the British in return for ninety-nine-year leases on naval and air bases in Newfoundland, Bermuda, the Bahamas, Jamaica, St. Lucia, Trinidad, Antigua, and British Guiana. It was, Roosevelt declared expansively, "the most important action in the reinforcement of our national defense that has been taken since the Louisiana Purchase." Two weeks later, on September 16, 1940, Congress adopted the first peacetime conscription in American history, requiring the registration of all men aged twenty-one to thirty-five for a year's military service within the United States.

The new state of affairs prompted vigorous debate between "internationalists" who believed national security demanded aid to Britain and isolationists who charged that Roosevelt was drawing the United States into a needless war. In May 1940 the nonpartisan Committee to Defend America by Aiding the Allies was organized. It drew its strongest support from the East and West Coasts and the South. In July 1940, on the other hand, isolationists formed the America First Committee, which included among its members Herbert Hoover and Charles A. Lindbergh. Before the end of 1941 the committee had about 450 chapters around the country, but probably two-thirds of its members lived within a 300-mile radius of Chicago. The isolationists argued that the war involved, in Senator William E. Borah's words, "nothing more than another chapter in the bloody volume of European power politics," and that a Nazi victory, while distasteful, would pose no threat to national security.

A THIRD TERM FOR FDR   In the midst of this turbulence the quadrennial presidential campaign came due. Isolationist sentiment was strongest in the Republican party and both the leading Republican candidates were noninterventionists, but neither loomed as a man of sufficient stature to challenge the "champ," assuming Roosevelt decided to run again. Senator Robert A. Taft of Ohio, son of the former president, lacked popular appeal, and New York district attorney Thomas E. Dewey, who had won fame as a "racket buster," at thirty-eight seemed young and unseasoned. This left an opening for an inspired group of political amateurs to promote the dark-horse candidacy of Wendell L. Willkie. Willkie seemed at first an unlikely choice: a former Democrat who had voted for Roosevelt in 1932, a utility president who had fought TVA, but in origins a Hoosier farm boy whose disheveled charm inspired strong loyalty. He was "a simple, barefoot Wall Street lawyer," in the devastating phrase of Interior Secretary Harold L. Ickes. Unlike the front-runners, he openly supported aid to the Allies, and the Nazi *Blitzkrieg* had brought many other Republicans to the same viewpoint. As late as April Willkie did not have a single delegate, but when the Republicans met at Philadelphia on June 28, six days after the French surrender, the convention was stampeded by the cry of "We Want Willkie" from the galleries.

The Nazi victory in France also ensured another nomination for Roosevelt. The president cultivated party unity behind his foreign policy and kept a sphinx-like silence about his intentions regarding the war. Amid the uncertainty no other hopefuls rose high enough to challenge him. The world crisis reconciled southern conservatives to the man whose foreign policy at least they supported. At the July convention in Chicago Roosevelt won nomination for a third term with only token opposition.

Through the summer Roosevelt assumed the role of a man above

GOP presidential nominee Wendell L. Willkie parading through Elwood, Indiana, 1940.

the political fray, busy rather with urgent matters of defense and diplomacy: Pan-American agreements for mutual defense, the destroyer-bases deal, and visits to defense facilities which took the place of campaign trips. Willkie inspired a more intense personal devotion than any Republican candidate since Theodore Roosevelt, but he had trouble positioning himself since there was little on which he disagreed with Roosevelt. The New Deal programs were too popular, in any case, to oppose head-on.

Like Landon, Willkie was reduced to attacks on New Deal red tape, and promises to run the programs better. A widespread reluctance to violate the tradition against a presidential third term strengthened his argument that new blood was needed in the White House. In the end, however, he switched to an attack on Roosevelt's conduct of foreign policy. In October he warned: "If you re-elect him you may expect war in April, 1941." To this Roosevelt responded, "I have said this before, but I shall say it again and again and again: Your boys are not going to be sent into any foreign wars." Three days before the election he declared in Buffalo: "Your President says this country is not going to war." Neither man distinguished himself with such hollow statements, since both knew the risks of all-out aid to Britain, which both supported.

Roosevelt won the election by a comfortable margin of 27 million votes to Willkie's 22 million, and a wider margin of 449 to 82 in the electoral college. Even so, the popular vote was closer than any presidential vote since 1916. Given the dangerous world situation a majority of the voters agreed with the Democrats' slogan: "Don't switch horses in the middle of the stream."

THE ARSENAL OF DEMOCRACY   Bolstered by the mandate for an unprecedented third term, Roosevelt moved quickly for greater measures of aid to Britain. Since the outbreak of war Roosevelt had corresponded with Winston Churchill, who soon after the election informed Roosevelt that British credit was fast running out. Since direct American loans would arouse memories of earlier war-debt defaults—the Johnson Act of 1934 forbade such loans anyway—the president created an ingenious device to bypass that issue and yet supply British needs, the "lend-lease" program.

In a fireside chat on December 29, 1940, Roosevelt told the nation that it must become "the great arsenal of democracy" because of the threat of Britain's fall. In his annual message to Congress on January 6, 1941, he warned that only the British navy stood between America and the peril of attack. Greater efforts to bolster British defenses were therefore imperative: "They do not need manpower. They do need billions of dollars worth of the weapons of defense." At the end of the speech he enunciated the Four Freedoms for which the democracies fought: freedom of speech, freedom of worship, freedom from want, and freedom from fear. The Lend-Lease Bill, introduced in Congress on January 10, authorized the president to sell, transfer, exchange, lend, lease, or otherwise dispose of arms and other equipment and supplies to "any country whose defense the President deems vital to the defense of the United States."

For two months a bitter debate over the bill raged in Congress and the country. Isolationists saw it as the point of no return. "The lend-lease-give program," said Senator Burton K. Wheeler, "is the New Deal's triple A foreign policy; it will plow under every fourth American boy." Roosevelt pronounced this "the rottenest thing that has been said in public life in my generation." Administration supporters denied that lend-lease would lead to war, but it did manifestly increase the risk. On March 11, 1941, lend-lease became law. The next day the president asked that the program be funded with an appropriation of $7 billion, the largest single appropriation in American history to that time. Congress complied, and Britain and China became the first beneficiaries.

While the nation debated, the war was spreading. In October 1940 when the presidential campaign approached its climax, Mussolini

Women picketing the White House to urge defeat of the lend-lease program. Like Senator Wheeler they feared that lend-lease would "plow under every fourth American boy."

launched attacks on Greece and, from Italian Libya, on the British in Egypt. But he had bitten off more than he could chew, and his forces had to fall back in both cases. In the spring of 1941 Hitler came to his aid. German forces under General Erwin Rommel joined the Italians in Libya, forcing the British, whose resources had been drained to help Greece, to withdraw into Egypt.

In April 1941 lightning attacks by Nazi panzer divisions overwhelmed Yugoslavia and Greece, and by the end of May airborne forces subdued the Greek island of Crete, putting Hitler in a position to menace the entire Middle East. With Hungary, Romania, and Bulgaria forced into the Axis fold, Hitler controlled nearly all of Europe. Then, on June 22, 1941, his forces suddenly fell upon Russia. Frustrated in the purpose of subduing Britain, Hitler thought to eliminate the potential threat on his rear with another lightning stroke. The Russian plains offered an ideal theater for *Blitzkrieg*, or so it seemed, and Russian resources were a seductive lure. With Romanian and Finnish allies, the Nazis moved on a 2,000-mile front from the Arctic to the Black Sea with seeming invincibility until, after four months, the Russian soldiers rallied in front of Leningrad, Moscow, and Sevastopol. During the winter of 1941–1942 Hitler began to learn the bitter lesson the Russians had taught Napoleon in 1812.

Winston Churchill had already decided to offer British support to Russia in case of such an attack. "If Hitler invaded Hell," he said, "I would make at least a favorable reference to the Devil in the House of Commons." Roosevelt adopted the same policy, offering American aid two days after the attack. Stalinist Russia, so long as it held out, ensured the survival of Britain. American aid was now indispensable to Europe's defense, and the logic of lend-lease led on to deeper American involvement. In order to deliver aid to Britain, goods had to be maneuvered through the U-boat "wolf packs" in the North Atlantic. So on April 11, 1941, Roosevelt informed Churchill that the United States Navy would extend its patrol areas in the North Atlantic nearly all the way to Iceland.

In August 1941 Roosevelt and Churchill held a secret rendezvous in Newfoundland, where they drew up a statement of principles that came to be known as the Atlantic Charter, issued as a press release on August 14. In effect the "common principles" upon which the parties based "their hopes for a better future for the world" amounted to a joint statement of war aims, its eight points a mixture of the idealistic goals of the New Deal and Wilson's Fourteen Points. It called for the self-determination of all peoples, equal access to raw materials, economic cooperation, freedom of the seas, and a new system of general security. In September it was announced that fifteen anti-Axis nations, including the Soviet Union, had endorsed the statement.

Thus Roosevelt had led the United States into a joint statement of war aims with the anti-Axis powers. It was not long before shooting incidents involved Americans in the North Atlantic. As early as May 21, 1941, in fact, a German U-boat had sunk an American freighter off the coast of Brazil, in retaliation for which Roosevelt froze all German and Italian assets in the United States, as well as those of Axis-controlled countries, and closed down German and Italian consulates. On September 4 came the first attack on an American warship, when a German submarine fired two torpedoes at the destroyer *Greer*. The president announced a week later orders to "shoot on sight" any German or Italian raiders ("rattlesnakes of the Atlantic") that ventured into American defensive waters. Five days later the United States Navy announced convoying all the way to Iceland. Then on October 17, while the destroyer *Kearny* was attacking German submarines, it sustained severe damage and loss of eleven lives from a German torpedo.

In his Navy Day speech of October 27 Roosevelt asserted that "America has been attacked" and that "the shooting has started." Three days later, on the night of October 30, 1941, a submarine torpedoed and sank the destroyer *Reuben James*, with a loss of ninety-six officers and men, while it was on convoy duty west of Iceland. This action hastened Congress into making changes in the neutrality act already requested by the president. On November 17 the legislation was in effect repealed when the bans on arming merchant vessels and allowing them to enter combat zones and belligerent ports were removed. Step by step the United States had given up neutrality and embarked on naval warfare against Germany. Still, the American people hoped to avoid taking the final step into all-out war. The decision for war, when it came, came in an unexpected quarter—the Pacific.

THE STORM IN THE PACIFIC

JAPANESE AGGRESSION   After the Nazi victories in the spring of 1940, relations with Japan also took a turn for the worse. Japanese militarists, bogged down in the vastness of China, now eyed new temptations: French Indochina, the Dutch East Indies, British Malaya, and Burma. Here they could cut off one of China's last links to the West, the Burma Road. What was more, they could incorporate into their "Greater East Asia Co-Prosperity Sphere" the oil, rubber, and other strategic materials which the crowded homeland lacked. As it was,

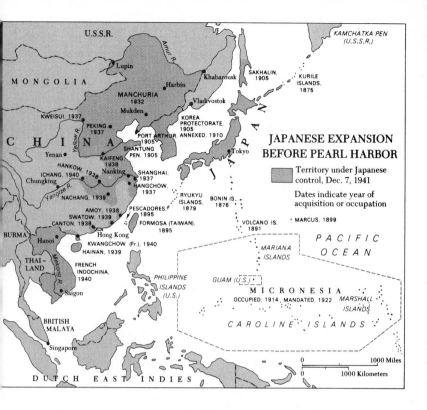

Within the map:

U.S.S.R.

KAMCHATKA PEN
(U.S.S.R.)

MONGOLIA

Lupin

Harbin

Khabarousk

SAKHALIN,
1905

KURILE
ISLANDS,
1875

MANCHURIA
1932

Mukden

Vladivostok

KWEISUI, 1937

PEKING, 1937

KOREA
PROTECTORATE,
1905
ANNEXED, 1910

CHINA

Yenan

Yellow R.

PORT ARTHUR, 1905
SHANTUNG
PEN. 1905

KAIFENG,
1938

HANKOW, 1938

ICHANG, 1940

Nanking

SHANGHAI,
1937

Tokyo

JAPAN

JAPANESE EXPANSION
BEFORE PEARL HARBOR

Territory under Japanese
control, Dec. 7, 1941

Dates indicate year of
acquisition or occupation

Chungking

Yangtze R.

NACHANG, 1939

HANGCHOW,
1937

AMOY, 1938
SWATOW, 1939

PESCADORES,
1895

RYUKYU
ISLANDS,
1879

BONIN IS.
1876

CANTON, 1938

FORMOSA (TAIWAN),
1895

VOLCANO IS.
1891

MARCUS, 1899

BURMA

Hanoi

Hong Kong

KWANGCHOW (Fr.), 1940

HAINAN, 1939

PACIFIC
OCEAN

MARIANA
ISLANDS

THAI-
LAND

Mekong R.

FRENCH
INDOCHINA,
1940

PHILIPPINE
ISLANDS
(U.S.)

GUAM (U.S.)

MICRONESIA
OCCUPIED, 1914, MANDATED, 1922

MARSHALL
ISLANDS

Saigon

BRITISH
MALAYA

CAROLINE   ISLANDS

Singapore

0   1000 Miles
0   1000 Kilometers

DUTCH   EAST   INDIES

they depended on the United States for important supplies, including 80 percent of their oil. During the summer of 1940 Japan forced the helpless French government at Vichy to permit the construction of Japanese airfields in French-controlled northern Indochina and to cut off the railroad into South China. The United States responded with a loan to China and the Export Control Act of July 2, 1940, which authorized the president to restrict the export of arms and other strategic materials to Japan. Gradually Roosevelt extended embargoes on aviation gas, scrap iron, and other supplies.

On September 27, 1940, the Tokyo government signed a Tripartite Pact with Germany and Italy, by which each pledged to declare war on any nation which attacked any of them. The pact could have been directed against either the United States or Russia. The Germans hoped to persuade Japan to enter Siberia when their forces entered Russia from the west. The Soviet presence in Siberia did inhibit the Japanese impulse to move southward, but on April 13, 1941, while the Nazis were sweeping through the Balkans, Japan signed a nonaggression pact with Russia and, once the Nazis invaded Russia in June, the Japanese were freed of any threat from the north.

Japan first moved southward on July 25, 1941, when it announced that it was assuming a protectorate over all of French Indochina. The next day Roosevelt took three steps in response: he froze all Japanese assets in the United States; he restricted exports of oil to Japan; and he took the armed forces of the Philippines into the Army of the United States and put their commander, General Douglas MacArthur, in charge of all United States forces in East Asia. By September the oil restrictions had tightened into an embargo. The commander of the Japanese navy estimated that their oil reserves would last two years at most, eighteen months in case of an expanded war. Forced by the embargo to secure other oil supplies, the Japanese army and navy began to perfect plans for attacks on the Dutch and British colonies to the south.

Actions by both sides put the United States and Japan on the way to a war which neither wanted. In his regular talks with the Japanese ambassador, Secretary of State Cordell Hull demanded that Japan withdraw from Indochina and China as the price of renewed trade. Though the United States was under no obligation to fuel the Japanese war machine, a more flexible position might have strengthened the moderates in Japan. The Japanese were not then pursuing a concerted plan of aggression comparable to Hitler's. The Japanese military had stumbled crazily from one aggression to another without approval from the government in Tokyo. Premier Fumimaro Konoye, however, while known as a man of liberal principles who preferred peace, caved in to pressures from the militants. Perhaps he had no choice.

The Japanese warlords, for their part, seriously misjudged the United States. The desperate wish of Americans to stay out of war might still have enabled the Japanese to conquer the British and Dutch colonies before an American decision to act. But the warlords decided that they dared not leave the American navy intact and the Philippines untouched on the flank of their new lifeline to the south.

TRAGEDY AT PEARL HARBOR   Thus a tragedy began to unfold with a fatal certainty mostly out of sight of the American people, whose attention was focused on the war in the Atlantic. Late in August 1941 Premier Konoye proposed a personal meeting with President Roosevelt. Hull smelled a rat, and he advised Roosevelt not to meet unless agreement on fundamentals could be reached in advance. Soon afterward, on September 6, an imperial conference approved preparations for an attack on Hawaii and gave Premier Konoye six more weeks to reach a settlement. The Japanese emperor's clear displeasure with the risks of an attack afforded the premier one last chance to pursue a compromise, but the stumbling block was still the presence of Japanese troops in China. In October Konoye urged War Minister Hideki Tojo to consider withdrawal while saving face by keeping some troops in North China. Tojo refused. Faced with this rebuff, and Tojo's threat to resign and bring down the cabinet, Konoye himself resigned on October 15; Tojo became premier the next day. The war party now assumed complete control.

On the very day that Tojo became premier a special Japanese envoy conferred with Hull and Roosevelt in Washington. His arrival was largely a cover for Japan's war plans, although neither he nor the Japanese ambassador knew that. On November 20 they presented Tojo's final proposal. Japan would occupy no more territory if the United States would cut off aid to China, restore trade, and help Japan get supplies from the Dutch Indies. In that case Japan would pull out of southern Indochina immediately and abandon the remainder once peace had been established with China—presumably on Japanese terms. Tojo expected the United States to refuse such demands. On November 26 Hull repeated the demand that Japan withdraw altogether from China. That same day a Japanese naval force began heading secretly across the North Pacific, through rough waters deserted by shipping in the late fall, toward Pearl Harbor.

Washington already knew that war was imminent. Reports of Japanese troop transports moving south from Formosa prompted Washington to send war warnings to American commanders in the Pacific, and to the British government. The massive movements southward clearly signaled attacks on the British and the Dutch possessions. American leaders had every reason to expect war in the southwest Pacific, but none expected that Japan would commit most of its carriers to another attack 5,000 miles away at Pearl Harbor.

In the early morning of December 7, 1941, American cryptanalysts decoded the last part of a fourteen-part Japanese message breaking off the negotiations. Japan's ambassador was instructed to deliver the message at 1 P.M. (7:30 A.M. in Honolulu), about a half hour before the Japanese attack, but delays held up delivery until more than an hour later than scheduled. The War Department sent out an alert at noon that something was about to happen, but the message, which went by commercial telegraph because radio contacts were broken, arrived in Hawaii eight and a half hours later. Even so, the decoded Japanese message had not mentioned Pearl Harbor, and everyone still assumed that any Japanese move would be in Southeast Asia.

It was still a sleepy Sunday morning when the first Japanese planes roared down the west coast and the central valley of Oahu to begin their assault. At 7:53 A.M. the flight commander, Mitsuo Fuchida, rounded Barber's Point and sounded the cry "Tora! Tora! Tora!" ("Tiger! Tiger! Tiger!"), the signal that the attackers had taken the American navy by surprise. For nearly two hours the Japanese planes kept up their attack on an unready Pacific fleet. Of the eight battleships in Pearl Harbor, three were sunk, one grounded, one capsized, and the others badly battered. Altogether nineteen ships were sunk or disabled. At the adjoining Hickam Field and other airfields on the island the Japanese found planes parked wing to wing, and destroyed in all about 150 of them. Few were able to get airborne, and Japanese losses numbered fewer than thirty planes. Before it was over the raid had killed more than 2,400 American servicemen and civilians, and wounded 1,178 more. The surprise attack fulfilled the dreams of its planners, but it fell short of total success in two ways. The Japanese ignored shore installations and oil tanks, without which the surviving ships might have been forced back to the West Coast, and they missed the American aircraft carriers which had fortuitously left a few days earlier. In the naval war to come, these carriers would prove decisive.

Later the same day (December 8 in the western Pacific) Japanese forces began assaults on the Philippines, Guam, and Midway, and on the British forces in Hong Kong and the Malay Peninsula. With one stroke the Japanese had silenced America's debate on neutrality, and a suddenly unified and vengeful nation prepared for the struggle. The next day President Roosevelt delivered his war message to Congress:

> Yesterday, December 7, 1941—a date which will live in infamy—the United States of America was suddenly and deliberately attacked by naval and air forces of the Empire of Japan. . . .
>
> The facts of yesterday speak for themselves. The people of the United States have already formed their opinions and well understand the implications to the very life and safety of our Nation. . . .

Congress voted for the war resolution unanimously, with the sole exception of Representative Jeanette Rankin, who was unable in conscience to vote for war in 1917 or 1941. For several days it was uncertain whether war with the other Axis powers would follow. The Tripartite Pact was ostensibly for defense only, and it carried no obligation for them to enter, but Hitler, impatient with continuing American aid to Britain, willingly joined his Asian allies. On December 11 Germany and Italy declared war on the United States. The separate wars in Asia and Europe had become one global war.

The Attack on Pearl Harbor. (Above) *The view from a Japanese fighter plane shows American battleships in vulnerable positions.* (Below) *The view from an American airfield shows the destruction and confusion brought on by the surprise attack.*

FURTHER READING

Robert Dallek's *Franklin D. Roosevelt and American Foreign Policy, 1932–1945* (1979)° covers the foreign policy of the 1930s. A number of revisionists stress the economic base of foreign policy; see William Appleman Williams's *The Tragedy of American Diplomacy* (rev. ed., 1972),° Walter LaFeber's *The American Age: United States Foreign Policy at Home and Abroad since 1750* (1989), and Joan Hoff-Wilson's *American Business and Foreign Policy, 1920–1933* (1971).

Other scholars have concentrated on diplomatic issues of the 1920s. Thomas H. Buckley's *The United States and the Washington Conference, 1921–1922* (1970) examines disarmament. Keith Nelson's *Victors Divided: America and the Allies in Germany, 1918–1923* (1975) deals with the reparations issue. For a study of the Kellogg-Briand Pact, see Robert H. Ferrell's *Peace in Their Time: The Origins of the Kellogg-Briand Pact* (1968).°

For American relations in East Asia during the period, see Akira Iriye's *After Imperialism: The Search for a New Order in the Far East, 1921–1933* (1965). More specific are Warren I. Cohen's *America's Response to China: An Interpretive History of Sino-American Relations* (2nd ed., 1981)° and Jonathan G. Utley's *Going to War with Japan, 1937–1941* (1985).

For relations with Latin America, see David Green's *The Containment of Latin America* (1971) and LaFeber's *Inevitable Revolutions* (1983).° The best general account of the onset of World War II is Donald Watt, *How War Came* (1990).°

A good study of America's entry into World War II is Waldo Heinrichs's *Threshold of War: Franklin D. Roosevelt and American Entry into World War II* (1988). Bruce M. Russett's *No Clear and Present Danger* (1972)° provides a critical account. Other interpretations of Roosevelt's diplomacy include Robert A. Divine's *The Reluctant Belligerent* (2nd ed., 1979)° and Patrick J. Hearden's *Roosevelt Confronts Hitler* (1986). Other scholars concentrate on American relations with Great Britain; see David Reynolds's *The Creation of the Anglo-American Alliance, 1937–1941* (1981) and Joseph P. Lash's *Roosevelt and Churchill, 1939–1941* (1976).

How some dissenting Americans reacted to the Roosevelt policies is traced by Wayne S. Cole in *Roosevelt and the Isolationists, 1932–1945* (1983). An unusual approach to the impact of foreign policy is found in David H. Culbert's *News for Everyman: Radio and Foreign Affairs in Thirties America* (1976). For lend-lease and domestic reaction, see Warren F. Kimball's *The Most Unsordid Act: Lend-Lease, 1939–1941* (1969).

On Pearl Harbor, see Gordon W. Prange's *At Dawn We Slept: The Untold Story of Pearl Harbor* (1981)° and John Toland's *Infamy* (1982).° The Japanese perspective is given in Robert J. C. Butow's *Tojo and the Coming of War* (1961).

°These books are available in paperback editions.

30

THE WORLD AT WAR

The Japanese attack on Pearl Harbor ended a period of tense neutrality for the United States, and launched America into an epochal event that would transform the nation's social and economic landscape as well as its position in international affairs. But in early December 1941, few Americans envisioned such seismic consequences. For the moment all attention was focused on halting the Japanese advance and mobilizing the whole nation for war.

America's Early Battles

SETBACKS IN THE PACIFIC   For months after Pearl Harbor the news from the Pacific was "all bad," as President Roosevelt frankly confessed. On the first day of the war American planes in the Philippines were caught lined up at Clark Field near Manila despite ten hours' notice of the attack on Pearl Harbor—an event that defies plausible explanation. That same day enemy planes sank the British battle cruiser *Repulse* and the battleship *Prince of Wales* near Singapore while Japanese land forces entered Malaya and Thailand. Thailand prudently surrendered, becoming a passive ally of the Japanese. In quick sequence these Allied outposts fell to the enemy before the end of December 1941: Guam, Wake Island, the Gilbert Islands, and Hong Kong. Rabaul in New Britain fell in January 1942, Singapore and Java in February. Admiral Thomas C. Hart's tiny Asiatic Fleet, with British and Dutch help, fought holding actions in the Dutch East Indies through January and February, all of them defeats climaxed by the disastrous Battle of the Java Sea (February 27 to March 1). The fall of Rangoon on March 9 cut off the Burma Road, the main supply route to Nationalist China.

In the Philippines, where General MacArthur abandoned Manila on December 27, the main American forces, outmanned and out-gunned, held out on Bataan Peninsula until April 9, and then on "The Rock," the fortified island of Corregidor. MacArthur slipped away in March, when he was ordered out to Australia to take command of Allied forces in the southwest Pacific. By May 6, 1942, when American forces surrendered Corregidor, Japan controlled a new empire that stretched from Burma eastward through the Dutch Indies and on out to Wake Island and the Gilberts.

If the Japanese had been willing to quit while they were ahead, they might have consolidated an almost impregnable empire with the resources they had seized. But the Japanese navy succumbed to what one of its admirals later called "victory disease." Though the Supreme Command decided to stop at the gates of India, behind the mountain barriers of Burma, it resolved to push on into the South Pacific, isolate Australia, and strike again at Hawaii. The aim was to draw out and destroy the American navy before the productive power of the United States could be brought to bear on the war effort.

A Japanese mistake and a stroke of American luck, however, enabled the United States Navy to frustrate the plan. Japan's failure to destroy the shore facilities at Pearl Harbor left the base relatively

American prisoners of war, captured by the Japanese on Bataan, 1942.

intact, and most of the ships damaged on December 7 lived to fight another day. The aircraft carriers at sea during the attack spent several months harassing Japanese outposts in the Gilberts and Marshalls. Their most spectacular exploit, an air raid on Tokyo itself launched on April 18, 1942, was delivered by B-25 bombers which took off from the carrier *Hornet* and, unable to land on its deck, proceeded to China. The raid caused only token damage, but did much to lift American morale amid a series of defeats elsewhere.

CORAL SEA AND MIDWAY   Japanese advances were finally halted in two decisive naval battles, the first of which started the day after Corregidor fell. The Battle of the Coral Sea (May 7–8, 1942) stopped a fleet convoying Japanese troop transports toward Port Moresby, on the southern coast of New Guinea. Planes from the *Lexington* and *Yorktown* sank one Japanese carrier, damaged another, and destroyed smaller ships. American losses were greater, and included the carrier *Lexington*, but the Japanese transports had to turn back. Port Moresby was secured, thwarting the Japanese advance on Australia.

Less than a month after the Coral Sea engagement the Japanese naval commander decided to force a showdown in the central Pacific. With nearly every capital ship under his personal command, he headed for Midway Island, from which he hoped to render Pearl Harbor helpless. This time it was the Japanese who were the victims of surprise. American cryptanalysts had by then broken their naval code, and Admiral Chester Nimitz, commander of the central Pacific, knew what was up. He reinforced Midway with planes and carriers.

The first Japanese foray against Midway, on June 4, severely damaged the island, but at the cost of about a third of the Japanese planes. Before another attack could be mounted, American torpedo planes and dive bombers had caught three of the four Japanese carriers in the process of servicing their planes. Most of the first wave of slow American torpedo bombers were shot down, but dive bombers disabled three Japanese carriers and left them to sink. The Japanese lost an additional carrier; the Americans, a carrier and a destroyer. The Japanese navy, having lost its four best aircraft carriers, all veterans of Pearl Harbor, was forced into retreat less than six months after the attack on Hawaii. The Japanese defeat was the turning point of the Pacific war, a loss they were never able to make up.

SETBACKS IN THE ATLANTIC   Early American setbacks in the Pacific were matched by setbacks in the Atlantic. Since the *Blitzkrieg* of 1940 German submarine "wolf packs" had issued out of bombproof pens on the French coast, wreaking havoc in the North Atlantic. In January 1942, after an ominous lull, German submarines suddenly appeared off American shores and began to sink coastal shipping, much of it tankers. Fourteen ships went down off the United States coast that month, and twelve in Canadian waters. By February, nineteen had been sunk in the Caribbean and Gulf of Mexico. Until April and May, when coastal cities were blacked out, passing freighters and tankers were like sitting ducks, silhouetted against the horizon. From January through June 1942 nearly 400 ships were lost in American waters before effective countermeasures brought the problem under control. The naval command hastened the building of small escort vessels, meanwhile pressing into patrol service all kinds of surface craft and planes, some of them civilian. During the second half of 1942 the losses diminished to a negligible number.

Mobilization at Home

The Pearl Harbor attack ended not only the long debate between isolation and intervention but also the long depression decade of the 1930s, and with the same finality with which the market crash of 1929 ended the prosperity decade of the 1920s. There was no doubt that the war effort would require all of America's huge productive capacity and full employment of the work force. Soon after Pearl Harbor, Winston Churchill recalled that, thirty years before, one observer had compared the United States to a gigantic boiler: "Once the fire is lighted under it, there is no limit to the power it can generate." Mobilization was in fact already further along than preparedness had been in 1916–1917. Selective services had been in effect for more than a year, and the army had grown to more than 1.4 million men by June 30, 1941. Altogether more than 15 million men and women served in the armed forces.

ECONOMIC CONVERSION   The economy, too, was already partially mobilized by lend-lease and defense efforts. The War Powers Act of December 18, 1941, gave the president a mandate to reshuffle government agencies, and a Second War Powers Act, of March 1942, empowered the government to allot materials and facilities as needed for defense, with penalties for those who failed to comply.

The War Production Board (WPB), created in January 1942 on the model of its counterpart during the First World War, directed industrial conversion to war production. Auto makers switched to producing tanks, makers of shirts switched to mosquito netting, model train plants to hardware, and the makers of refrigerators, stoves, and cash

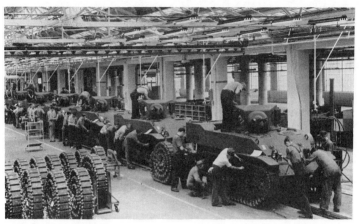

M5 tanks on the assembly line at a Cadillac plant in Detroit, 1942.

registers to munitions. The Reconstruction Finance Corporation, a depression agency, now financed war plants. For a year the War Production Board oversaw a wild scramble of manufacturers for available supplies. As War Secretary Stimson put it, it was "like . . . hungry dogs quarreling over a very inadequate bone" until the WPB instituted a plan to allocate scarce items to claimants according to its best judgment of need.

Some shortages called for more heroic efforts. "Use it up, wear it out, make do or do without," became the prevailing slogan. People collected scrap metal and grew their own food in backyard "victory gardens." The government named special administrators, or "czars," to promote production of rubber and oil. The president of Union Pacific Railroad, now the rubber "czar," pushed construction of synthetic rubber plants, which by 1944 produced 800,000 tons, or 87 percent of the country's requirements. Tire rationing began in December 1941, and gasoline rationing at the end of 1942. Since German sinkings of coastal tankers placed an unusual burden on railways in getting oil to the East Coast, Petroleum Administrator Harold Ickes hastened construction of the "Big Inch" pipeline, which was twenty-four inches in diameter and ran 1,250 miles from the Texas oilfields to the New York–Philadelphia region. Through the Office of Scientific Research and Development Dr. Vannevar Bush mobilized thousands of "scientists against time" to create and modify radar, sonar, the proximity fuse, the bazooka, means to isolate blood plasma, and myriads of other innovations.

The pressure of wartime needs and the stimulus of government spending sent the gross national product soaring from $100.6 billion in 1940 to $213.6 billion in 1945, a rise of 112 percent. Government expenditures during the war years rose from $20 billion in calendar year 1941 to $97.2 billion in 1944. From July 1, 1940, to June 30, 1946, expenditures totaled $337 billion, of which $304 billion went to the war effort. The figure for total expenditures was twice as great as the total of all previous federal spending in the history of the republic, and about 10 times what America spent in World War I, and 100 times the expenditures during the Civil War.

FINANCING THE WAR   To cover the war's huge cost the president preferred taxes to borrowing. "I would rather pay one hundred percent of taxes now than push the burden of this war onto the shoulders of my grandchildren," he said in December 1942. Taxes also had the merit of relieving upward pressures on prices. The wartime Congress, however, dominated by conservatives, feared taxes more than deficits and refused to go more than halfway with Roosevelt's fiscal prudence. The Revenue Act of 1942 provided for only about $7 billion in increased revenue, less than half that recommended by the Treasury. It also greatly broadened the tax structure. Whereas in 1939 only about 4 million people filed returns, the new act, in the words of a tax historian, "made the Federal income tax a genuine mass tax."

The result was that the government covered about 45 percent of its 1939–1946 costs with tax revenues. Roosevelt would have preferred to cover more, but the figure compared favorably with 30 percent for World War I and 23 percent for the Civil War. To cover the rest of its costs the government borrowed from the public. War-bond drives, including a Victory Drive in 1945, induced citizens to put aside more than $150 billion in bonds rather than use it to bid up prices. Financial institutions picked up most of the rest of the government's debt. In all, by the end of the war the national debt had grown to about $260 billion, about six times its size at the time of Pearl Harbor. One of its effects was to make converts to the Keynesian argument that government spending would end the depression.

The basic economic problem was no longer finding jobs but finding workers for the booming shipyards, aircraft factories, and gunpowder mills. Millions of people were brought fully into the economic system who before had lived on its margin, which leveled out somewhat the economic pyramid. Between 1939 and 1944 the share of the income going to the wealthiest 5 percent declined from 23.7 to 16.8 percent. Stubborn poverty did not disappear, but for most of those who stayed home the war spelled neither hardship nor suffering but a better life than ever before, despite shortages and rationing.

Mobilization for war deflected many New Deal programs.

ECONOMIC CONTROLS Increased incomes and spending during the war conjured up the specter of inflation. Some of the available money went into taxes and war bonds, but even so, more was sent chasing after civilian goods just as production was converting to war needs. Such consumer durables as cars, washing machines, and non-defense housing in fact ceased to be made at all. It was apparent that only strict restraints would keep prices from soaring out of sight. The administration, having set out in 1933 to raise prices, now reversed its ground and set out to hold them down. By July 1941 Roosevelt was seeking statutory price controls and finally, in January 1942, Congress authorized the Office of Price Administration (OPA) for the first time to set price ceilings. While some increases were deemed necessary as incentives to production, the General Maximum Price Regulation of April 1942 froze prices at the highest level they had reached the month before. With prices frozen, goods had to be allocated through rationing, which had begun with auto tires in December 1941 and was gradually extended to other goods in short supply, with coupons doled out for sugar, coffee, gasoline, and meats.

Wages and farm prices were not controlled, however, and this complicated things. War prosperity offered farmers a chance to redress the balance from two decades of distress, and farm-state congressmen fought successfully to raise both floors and ceilings on farm prices. Some farm prices rose to 150 percent of parity. Higher food prices reinforced worker demands for higher wages, and the War Labor Board tried to hold the line with a formula that permitted wage increases in line with the 15 percent increase in the cost of living since January 1941. The WLB, however, had jurisdiction only over wage increases resulting from labor disputes.

Both business and workers chafed at the wage and price controls. On occasion the government was forced to seize industries threatened by strike. The coal mines and railroads both came under government operation for a short time in 1943, and in 1944 the government briefly took over Montgomery-Ward Company. Soldiers had to carry its chairman bodily out of his office when he stubbornly defied orders of the War Labor Board. Despite these problems, the government effort to stabilize wages and prices was on the whole a success story. Roosevelt's "hold-the-line" order of April 8, 1943, freezing prices, wages, and salaries, finally brought the price level to a plateau for the rest of the war. By the end of the war consumer prices had risen about 31 percent, a far better record than the World War I rise of 62 percent.

SOCIAL EFFECTS: WOMEN   The war proved to be an important watershed in the changing status of women. The proportion of women working had barely altered from 1910 to 1940, but at a time when millions of men were going into military service the demand for labor shook up old prejudices about sex roles in the workplace—and in the military. Nearly 200,000 women served in the Women's Army Corps (WAC) and the navy's equivalent, Women Accepted for Volunteer Emergency Service (WAVES). Lesser numbers joined the Marine Corps, the Coast Guard, and the Army Air Force. Even more significant were the over 6 million women who entered the work force during the war, an increase of over 50 percent and in manufacturing alone of some 110 percent. Old barriers fell overnight as women entered employment of all sorts, becoming toolmakers, machinists, crane operators, lumberjacks, stevedores, blacksmiths, and railroad track workers. Such arduous occupations were no longer reserved for men.

By 1944 women made up 14 percent of all workers in shipbuilding and 40 percent in aircraft plants. The government, desperate for laborers in defense industries, launched an intense publicity campaign to draw women into traditional male jobs. "Do your part, free a man for service," one ad pleaded. "Rosie the Riveter," a beautiful

Women workers assembling the tail section of the B17F bomber (the Flying Fortress) at the Douglas Aircraft plant in Long Beach, California, 1942.

model dressed in overalls, became the cover girl for the campaign. One striking feature of the new scene was the larger proportion of older, married women in the work force. In 1940 about 15 percent of married women went into gainful employment; by 1945 it was 24 percent. In the work force as a whole, married women for the first time outnumbered single women. Attitudes sharply changed from those of the depression days, when over 80 percent of Americans opposed work by married women; by 1942 a poll showed 60 percent in favor of hiring married women in war industries. Defense jobs, however, were the ones most vulnerable to postwar cuts.

Still, there were many vocal opponents to this new trend. One disgruntled male legislator asked what would happen to traditional domestic tasks if women were in factories: "Who will do the cooking, the washing, the mending, the humble homey tasks to which every woman has devoted herself; who will rear and nurture the children?" Many women, however, were eager to get away from the grinding routine of domestic life. One woman welder remembered that her wartime job "was the first time I had a chance to get out of the kitchen and work in industry and make a few bucks. This was something I had never dreamed would happen." And it was something that many women did not want to relinquish after the war.

SOCIAL EFFECTS: BLACKS   The most inflammable issue ignited by the war was probably that of African-American participation in the defense effort. From the start black leaders demanded full recognition in the armed forces and defense industries. Eventually about a million African-Americans served in the armed forces, in every branch and every theater. But they served usually in segregated units that mirrored the society from which they came. Every army camp had its separate facilities and its periodic racial "incidents." The most important departure was a 1940 decision to give up segregation in officer candidate schools, except those for air force cadets. A separate flight school at Tuskegee, Alabama, trained about 600 black pilots, many of whom distinguished themselves in combat.

War industries were even less accessible to black influence and pressure, although government policy theoretically opposed discrimination. In February 1941 A. Philip Randolph, the tall, gentlemanly head of the Brotherhood of Sleeping Car Porters, organized a March on Washington Movement to demand an end to discrimination in defense industries. The administration, alarmed at the prospect of a mass descent on Washington, struck a bargain. The Randolph group called off its march in return for an executive order that forbade discrimination in defense work and training programs by requiring a nondiscrimination clause in defense contracts, and set up the Fair Employment Practices Commission (FEPC). The FEPC's authority

Members of the 99th Fighter Group of the U.S. Army Air Force, a unit of black pilots famous for their skill and bravery.

was chiefly moral, since it had no power to enforce directives. It nevertheless offered willing employers the chance to say they were following government policy in giving jobs to black citizens, and no doubt persuaded others to go along.

About 2 million blacks were working in war plants by the end of 1944. The demand for black labor revived migration out of the South, which had lagged during the depression, and large numbers of blacks now headed for the Far West as well as the North. States with the largest proportionate gains of black population in the 1940s were, in order, California, Michigan, Oregon, Washington, Utah, Colorado, Wisconsin, Illinois, and New York.

Blacks quickly broadened their drive for wartime participation into a more inclusive social and political front. Early in 1942 the Pittsburgh *Courier* endorsed the "Double V," which stood for victory at home and abroad. The slogan became immensely popular in black communities, and reflected a growing urge to rid the world not just of Hitler but of Hitlerism, as one editor put it. Blacks began to challenge more openly all kinds of discrimination, including racial segregation itself. "It was as if some universal message had come through to the great mass of Negroes," a sociologist wrote in 1943, "urging them to dream new dreams and to protest against the old order." A foundation was being laid for a great expansion of civil-rights efforts after the war. Membership in the NAACP grew during the war from 50,000 to 450,000. Blacks could look forward to greater political participation after the Supreme Court, in *Smith v. Allwright* (1944), struck down Texas's white primary on the ground that Democratic primaries were part of the election process and thus subject to the Fifteenth Amendment.

The growing militancy of blacks of course aroused antagonism from some whites. Racial violence this time did not approach the level of that in World War I, but growing tensions on a hot summer afternoon in Detroit sparked incidents on crowded Belle Isle, an offshore park in the Detroit River. Fighting raged through June 20–21, 1943, until federal troops arrived on the second evening to stop it. Twenty-five blacks and nine whites had been killed.

SOCIAL EFFECTS: JAPANESE-AMERICANS   The record on civil liberties during World War II was on the whole better than that during World War I, if only because there was virtually no opposition to the war effort after the attack on Pearl Harbor. Neither German-Americans nor Italian-Americans faced the harassments meted out to their counterparts in the previous war; few had much sympathy for Hitler or Mussolini. The shameful exception to an otherwise improved record was the treatment given to more than 100,000 Americans of

Young Japanese-Americans awaiting baggage inspection upon arrival at a "war relocation camp" in Turlock, California, 1942. Photograph by Dorothea Lange.

Japanese descent (Nisei) who were forcibly removed from homes and businesses on the West Coast to "War Relocation Camps" in the interior. Few, if any, were disloyal, but all were victims of fear and racial prejudice.

This was especially the case in the months following the attack on Pearl Harbor. A California barbershop offered "free shaves for Japs" but noted that it was "not responsible for accidents." Others were even blunter. Idaho's governor declared: "A good solution to the Jap problem would be to send them all back to Japan, then sink the island." As one Japanese-American poignantly complained, "What really hurts most is the constant reference to us evacuees as 'Japs.' 'Japs' are the guys we are fighting. We're on this side and we want to help. Why won't America let us?" Many did support the effort. Japanese-American Hawaiians and mainlanders made up two of the most celebrated infantry units in the war, fighting with distinction on the Italian front. Other thousands of Nisei served as interpreters and translators, the "eyes and ears" of the American armed forces in the Pacific. Not until 1983 did the government finally recognize the injustice of the internment policy. That year it authorized granting those Nisei still living $20,000 each in compensation.

DOMESTIC CONSERVATISM   In domestic politics the wartime period was marked by a growing conservatism. Discontent with price controls, labor shortages, rationing, and a hundred other petty vexations spread. In 1942 the congressional elections registered a national swing against the New Deal. Republicans gained forty-six seats in the House and nine in the Senate, chiefly in the farm areas of the middle states. Democratic losses outside the South strengthened the southern delegation's position within the party, and the delegation itself reflected conservative victories in southern primaries. A coalition of conservatives proceeded to eviscerate "nonessential" New Deal agencies. In 1943 Congress abolished the Works Progress Administration, the National Youth Administration, and the Civilian Conservation Corps, began to dismantle the Farm Security Administration, and liquidated the National Resources Planning Board by refusing it funds.

Organized labor, despite substantial gains during the war, was vulnerable to the conservative trend. In the spring of 1943, when John L. Lewis led the coal miners out on strike, widespread resentment led Congress to pass the Smith-Connally War Labor Disputes Act, which authorized the government to seize plants useful to the war, required pre-strike plebiscites, and forbade unions to make political contributions. The intended effect of the act was somewhat blunted by the tendency of unionists to vote routinely for strikes as a bargaining ploy. In 1943 a dozen states adopted laws variously restricting picketing and other union activities, and in 1944 Arkansas and Florida set in motion a wave of "right-to-work" legislation which outlawed the closed shop.

Congress generally cooperated with the administration's war effort. The Senate War Investigating Committee under Harry S. Truman of Missouri devoted itself to rooting out waste and inefficiency in the defense industries. Unity on foreign relations persisted through the war, and in 1943 both houses of Congress passed resolutions in favor of an international peacekeeping organization after the war.

THE ALLIED DRIVE TOWARD BERLIN

By mid-1942 the "home front" began to get news from the war fronts that some of the lines were holding at last. Japanese naval losses at the Coral Sea and Midway had secured Australia and Hawaii. By midyear a motley fleet of American air and sea subchasers was ending six months of happy hunting for U-boats off the Atlantic coast. This was all the more important because war plans called for the defeat of Germany first.

WAR AIMS AND STRATEGY   There were many reasons for the priority of defeating Hitler. Nazi forces in western Europe and the Atlantic posed a more direct threat to the Western Hemisphere; German war potential was greater and German science was more likely to come up with some devastating new weapon. Lose in the Atlantic, General George Marshall grimly predicted, and you lose everywhere. Hitler's attack on Russia in June 1941 strengthened the argument. Once defeat Germany, strongest of the Axis powers, and Japan would face overwhelming force. Despite the understanding, Japanese attacks involved Americans directly in the Pacific war from the start, and as a consequence, during the first year of fighting more Americans went to the Pacific than across the Atlantic.

The Pearl Harbor attack brought Prime Minister Churchill quickly to Washington for lengthy talks about a common war plan. Out of these exchanges emerged several major and numerous minor decisions, including the one, urged by General Marshall, to name a supreme commander in each major theater of war. Each commander would be subject to orders from the British-American Combined Chiefs of Staff. Other joint boards allotted munitions, raw materials, and shipping. American and British war plans thereafter proceeded in close concert, and often launched joint operations, especially against Germany. No such concert was ever effected with Russia, which fought its own war on the eastern front, separate except for the coordinated timing of some major offensives. In Washington on January 1, 1942, representatives of twenty-six governments then at war with the Axis signed the Declaration of the United Nations, affirming the principles of the Atlantic Charter, pledging their full resources to the war, and promising not to make separate peace with the common enemies. Finally, in the course of their talks the British and American leaders reaffirmed the priority of war against Germany.

Agreement on war aims, however, was not agreement on strategy. Roosevelt and Winston Churchill, meeting at the White House again in June 1942, could not agree on where to hit first. American military planners wanted to strike directly across the English Channel before the end of 1942, secure a beachhead, and move against Germany in 1943. The British preferred to keep the Germans off balance with hit-and-run raids and air attacks, while continuing to build up their forces. With vivid memories of the last war, the British feared a mass bloodletting in trench warfare if they struck prematurely. The Russians, bearing the brunt of the German attack in the east, insisted that the Western Allies must do something to relieve the pressure. Finally, the Americans accepted Churchill's proposal to invade French North Africa.

THE NORTH AFRICA CAMPAIGN   It was not only the Russians who needed a diversion, but British forces defending Egypt against invaders from Libya. If German general Erwin Rommel's Afrika Korps took Alexandria and Suez, little more than distance would stand between them and India, where they could link up with the Japanese. Late in October 1942 General Sir Bernard Montgomery began a counterattack on Rommel at El-Alamein. On November 8, 1942, Anglo-American forces under the command of General Dwight D. Eisenhower landed at Casablanca in Morocco and at Oran and Algiers in Algeria. Completely surprised, French forces under the Vichy government (which collaborated with the Germans) had little will to resist. Hitler therefore occupied the whole of France and sent German forces into French Tunisia. By chance Admiral Jean-François Darlan, second to Marshal Pétain in the collaborationist Vichy government, was visiting in Algiers and was persuaded by the Allies to order a cease-fire on November 11.

Since Darlan seemed the man the French forces would most likely obey, a deal was struck to make him the leader of the French in the North African colonies. A military expedient which probably saved thousands of Allied lives, this deal with a former Nazi collaborator was widely criticized in America and Britain until the assassination of Darlan on Christmas Eve relieved the Allies of the embarrassment. General Henri Giraud, who had escaped a Nazi prison, took

American soldiers catching a last smoke before combat.

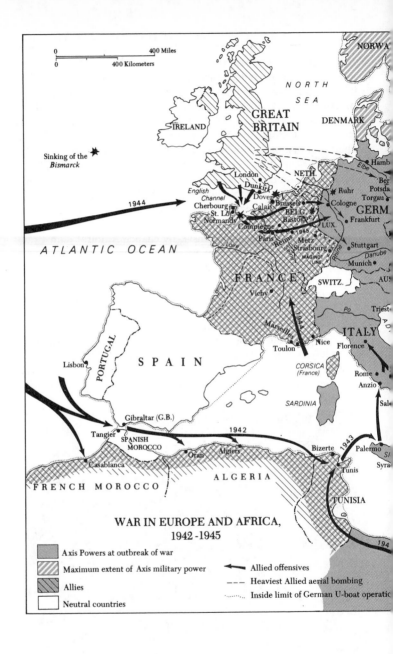

**WAR IN EUROPE AND AFRICA,
1942-1945**

Axis Powers at outbreak of war

Maximum extent of Axis military power

Allies

Neutral countries

Allied offensives

--- Heaviest Allied aerial bombing

.... Inside limit of German U-boat operation

FINLAND

Leningrad

ESTONIA

LATVIA

1944

LITHUANIA

Danzig

EAST
PRUSSIA

POLAND

1945

Warsaw

Vistula

HOSLOVAKIA

Budapest

HUNGARY

RUMANIA

1944

Belgrade

Bucharest

YUGOSLAVIA

Danube

BULGARIA

Sofia

ALBANIA

GREECE

AEGEAN
SEA

Athens

CRETE

MEDITERRANEAN SEA

Tobruk

LIBYA

EGYPT

Alexandria

El Alamein,
1942

Nile

Suez
Canal

PALESTINE

TRANS-
JORDAN

RED SEA

CYPRUS
(G.B.)

SYRIA

IRAQ

SAUDI

ARABIA

TURKEY

Ankara

BLACK SEA

Sevastopol

Yalta

SOVIET UNION

Moscow

Volga

1943

Dnieper

Don

1942

Stalingrad

SWEDEN

his place. Still, General Charles De Gaulle, leader of the "Free French" who had escaped to England, had little influence in North Africa. Not until October 1944 did the United States formally recognize him as leader of the French nation.

Farther east the tide had turned. General Montgomery's British forces were pushing the brilliant German tank commander, General Rommel, back across Libya, but green American forces were stalemated by seasoned Nazis pouring into Tunisia. Before spring, however, Montgomery had taken Libya and the Germans were caught in a gigantic pincers. By April Montgomery had linked up with American forces and one month later, on May 7, 1943, Bizerte fell to the Americans and Tunis to the British. The remaining Germans made a last stand on Cape Bon. Hammered from all sides, unable to retreat across the Mediterranean, an army of 275,000 surrendered on May 13, 1943, leaving all of North Africa in Allied hands.

While the battle of Tunisia was still shaping up, in January 1943 Roosevelt and Churchill and the Combined Chiefs of Staff met at Casablanca. Stalin declined to leave Russia for the meeting but continued to press for a second front in Europe. For the time, however, the decision was reached to postpone the cross-Channel invasion further, and to carry out Churchill's scheme to attack what he called the "soft underbelly of the Axis" by invading Sicily. Admiral Nimitz and General MacArthur were authorized meanwhile to start an offensive to dislodge the Japanese from the Pacific islands. Top priority, however, went to an antisubmarine campaign in the Atlantic.

Before leaving Casablanca, Roosevelt announced, with Churchill's endorsement, that the war would end only with the "unconditional surrender" of all enemies. An echo of Ulysses Grant's ultimatum to the Confederates, the formula was designed to reassure Stalin and to quiet suspicions aroused by the Darlan deal that the Western Allies might negotiate separately with the enemy. The announcement owed a good bit also to the determination that, as Roosevelt put it, "every person in Germany should realize that this time Germany is a defeated nation." This dictum was later criticized for having stiffened enemy resistance, but probably had little effect; in fact neither the Italian nor the Japanese surrender would be totally unconditional. But the decision did have one unexpected result: it opened an avenue for eventual Soviet control of Eastern Europe because it required Russian armies to pursue Hitler's forces all the way to Germany. And as they liberated the countries of eastern Europe, the Russians were determined to create new governments in their own image.

THE BATTLE OF THE ATLANTIC   While fighting raged in North Africa the more crucial Battle of the Atlantic reached its climax on the high seas. Several factors brought success to the Allied effort. Patrols by land-based planes covered much of the Atlantic from airfields in Britain and elsewhere, and in 1943 Portugal permitted American planes to operate from the Azores, thereby closing the last gap in coverage in the North Atlantic. Scientists perfected a variety of new detection devices: radar, which the British had already used to advantage in the Battle of Britain, bounced radio waves off objects above the surface and registered their positions on a screen; sonar gear detected sound waves from submerged U-boats, and sono-buoys, dropped from planes, radioed back their findings; advanced magnetic equipment enabled aircraft to detect objects under water. New escort carriers ("baby flat-tops") and improvements in depth charges added to the effectiveness of convoys.

By April 1943 there were in the western half of the North Atlantic at any time an average of 31 convoys with 145 escorts and 673 merchant ships, and a number of heavily escorted troopships. None of the troopships going to Britain or the Mediterranean was lost, although submarines sank three en route to Greenland and Iceland. The U-boats kept up the Battle of the Atlantic until the war's end; when Germany finally collapsed at least forty-nine were still at sea. But their commander later admitted that the Battle of the Atlantic was lost by the end of May 1943. He credited the difference largely to radar. What he did not know then was that the Allies had a secret weapon. By early 1943 their cryptanalysts were routinely decoding secret messages and telling their sub-hunters where to look for the German prey.

SICILY AND ITALY   The North African campaign won, the Allies prepared to attack Sicily. On July 10, 1943, about 250,000 British and American troops landed on Sicily, the largest single amphibious action in the war to that time, scoring a complete surprise. General George Patton's American Seventh Army landed on the southwest coast, and after a fierce battle at the beachhead, moved swiftly across the island to take Palermo twelve days later. Montgomery's British Eighth Army encountered more stubborn resistance near Syracuse, but the entire island was in Allied hands by August 17, although some 40,000 Germans escaped to the mainland.

Allied success in Sicily ended Mussolini's twenty years of Fascist rule. Italians never had much heart for the war into which he had dragged them. On July 25, 1943, Italy's King Victor Emmanuel III notified the dictator of his dismissal as premier. A new regime startled the Allies when it offered not only to surrender but to switch sides in the war. Unfortunately, mutual suspicions prolonged talks until September 3, while the Germans poured reinforcements into Italy and seized key points. In the confusion the Italian army disintegrated, although most of the navy escaped to Allied ports. A few army units later joined the Allied effort, and a good many of the soldiers joined bands of partisans who fought behind the German lines. Mussolini, plucked from imprisonment by a daring German airborne raid, became head of a shadowy puppet government in northern Italy.

Allied landings on the mainland therefore did not turn into a walkover. The main landing at Salerno on September 9 encountered heavy resistance, but American and British troops nevertheless secured beachheads within a week and by October 1 were in Naples. The Germans had reduced much of the city to rubble, but the bay and port facilities were soon cleared and back in operation. Before the end of September British forces had crossed the peninsula to Foggia, on the Adriatic. From there Allied fighters could cover the front and bombers could raid Nazi supply facilities in the Balkans.

Rome was the next objective, but mountainous country stood in the way. Fighting stalled in the Appenines where the Germans held the Allies through the winter of 1943–1944 in some of the most miserable, mud-soaked, and frostbitten fighting of the war. Cartoonist Bill Mauldin's Willie and Joe, in the GI newspaper *Yank*, slogged their way to fame in the Italian campaign as typical dogface infantry-

Major-General George S. Patton, commander of American invasion forces on Sicily.

"Joe, yestiddy ya saved my life an' I swore I'd pay ya back. Here's my last pair of dry socks." *Mauldin's Willie and Joe.*

men who distilled a saving humor out of their plight. On January 22, 1944, the Allies attempted an end-run by landing at Anzio, behind the German lines near Rome. This time they surprised the enemy, but failed to move quickly enough to the commanding Alban Heights. At Anzio they held on only by dogged determination until a series of savage attacks broke the German line in mid-May 1944 and lifted the siege. On June 4, 1944, the U.S. Fifth Army was in Rome, which fortunately had escaped the destruction visited on Naples. The capture of Rome provided only a brief moment of glory, for the long-awaited cross-Channel landing in France came two days later. Italy, always a secondary front, faded from the limelight of world attention.

STRATEGIC BOMBING OF EUROPE   Behind the long-postponed landings on the Normandy beaches lay months of preparation. While waiting, the United States Army Air Force (AAF) and the British Royal Air Force (RAF) carried the battle into the German-controlled areas of Europe. Late in January 1943 came the first American raid on Germany itself, on the port of Wilhelmshaven. By 1943 American strategic bombers were full-fledged partners of the RAF in the effort to pound Germany into submission. The RAF, to cut losses during the hard days after the fall of France, had confined itself mostly to night raids, and continued now to specialize in nocturnal attacks. The Americans believed that they could be more effective with high-level daylight precision bombing. Between them the AAF and RAF kept German defenders on watch day and night.

Yet despite the widespread damage it caused, the strategic air offensive ultimately failed to cut severely into German production or, some contend, to break civilian morale. German production in fact increased until the last few weeks of the war. Heavy Allied losses persisted through 1943. In six days of October, raids deep inside the continent resulted in the loss of 148 bombers, mainly from German fighters. By the end of 1943, however, jettisonable gas tanks permitted escort fighters to go as far as Berlin and back. In the "Big Week" of February 20–25, 1944, almost 4,000 American heavy bombers attacked aircraft plants in Germany. Badly damaged, the German aircraft industry continued to turn out planes to the end, but heavy losses of both planes and pilots forced the German Luftwaffe to conserve its strength and cease challenging every Allied mission.

Berlin, the air strategists assumed, was one target the German fighters would have to protect. But in March the capital became the object of repeated Allied raids, and the resultant losses left German fighters ever more reluctant to rise to the bait. The horror at enemy attacks on civilians earlier in the war proved no barrier to a response in kind. Germany, Churchill said, was reaping the whirlwind. With air supremacy assured, the Allies were free to concentrate on their primary urban and industrial targets, and when the time came, to provide cover for the Normandy landings. On April 14, 1944, General Eisenhower assumed control of the Strategic Air Forces for use in the Normandy landings, less than two months away. On D-Day he told the troops: "If you see fighting aircraft over you, they will be ours."

THE TEHERAN MEETING   By the summer of 1943 the growing American presence in Britain, combined with successes in the Battle of the Atlantic and the strategic bombing, brought Churchill around on the cross-Channel invasion. Late in the fall he and Roosevelt finally had their first joint meeting with Joseph Stalin, in Teheran, Iran. At a preliminary meeting of foreign ministers held in Moscow during late October 1943, one point went without agreement: the Russians refused to recognize the Polish government-in-exile in London. But when England and America gave assurance that a cross-Channel invasion was coming, the Russians in return promised to enter the war against Japan after Germany's defeat. The ministers also agreed to begin plans for an international organization, and set up a European Advisory Commission in London to lay plans for postwar Germany. It was this body that later fixed the zones of occupation.

On the way to the Teheran meeting with Stalin, Churchill and Roosevelt met in Cairo with China's General Chiang Kai-shek from November 22 to 26. The resultant Declaration of Cairo (December

1, 1943) affirmed that war against Japan would continue until Japan's unconditional surrender, that all Chinese territories taken by Japan would be restored to China, that Japan would lose the Pacific islands acquired after 1941, and that "in due course Korea shall become free and independent."

From November 28 to December 1 the Big Three leaders conferred in Teheran. Their chief subject was the planned invasion of France and a Russian offensive timed to coincide with it. Stalin repeated his promise to enter the war against Japan, and the three leaders reaffirmed the foreign ministers' decision in favor of planning an international organization. At further discussions in Cairo (December 4–6) Roosevelt and Churchill decided to put General Eisenhower in command of the cross-Channel invasion.

D-DAY AND AFTER   In January 1944 General Dwight D. Eisenhower arrived in London to take command at Supreme Headquarters, Allied Expeditionary Forces (SHAEF). Already battle-tested in North Africa and the Mediterranean, he now faced the supreme test of Operation "Overlord," the cross-Channel assault on Hitler's "Atlantic Wall." In April and May while the vast invasion forces made final preparations, the Allied air forces disrupted the transportation network of northern France, smashing railroads, bridges, and rolling stock. By early June all was ready, and after postponement for one day because of weather, D-Day fell on June 6, 1944.

The invasion force landed not across the narrow stretch from

General Dwight D. Eisenhower instructing paratroopers just before they board their airplanes to launch the D-Day assault.

Dover to Calais, where the Germans expected it, but along sixty miles of beach in Normandy. Airborne forces dropped behind the beaches during the night while planes and battleships pounded the coastal defenses. At dawn the invasion fleet of some 4,000 ships began to pour out their cargoes of troops and supplies on the shore. On Utah Beach the American invaders made it in against relatively light opposition, but farther east, on a four-mile segment designated Omaha Beach, bombardment had failed to take out German defenders and the Americans were caught by heavily mined water. They then had to make it across a fifty-yard beach exposed to crossfire from concrete pillboxes before they could huddle under a sea wall and begin to root out the defenders. Still farther east, British forces had less difficulty on Gold, Juno, and Sword beaches, but found themselves subjected to bitter counterattack by German forces determined to hold Caen.

Within two weeks the Allies had landed a million men and seized a beachhead sixty miles wide and five to fifteen miles deep. Before the end of June they had swept up the peninsula to the port of Cherbourg, only to find the harbor so completely blocked that it took two months to clear. But they continued to pour men and matériel onto the beaches, and contrived manmade harbors by scuttling old ships to create breakwaters. On into July the Allies edged inland through the Norman marshes and hedgerows. On July 19, 1944, General Omar Bradley's troops took St. Lô, a transportation hub for

The landing at Normandy, D-Day, June 6, 1944.

roads and railroads into the heart of France. Marshals Gerd von Rundstedt, the German commander, and Erwin Rommel advised withdrawal to defenses behind the Seine, but a stubborn Hitler removed both men and issued disastrous orders to contest every inch of land. Rommel, convinced that all was lost, began to intrigue for a separate peace. Other like-minded officers, convinced that the war was hopeless, tried to kill Hitler at his headquarters on July 20, 1944, but the Führer survived the bomb blast and hundreds of conspirators and suspects were tortured to death. Rommel was granted the option of suicide, which he took.

Meanwhile, the Führer's tactics brought calamity to the German forces in western France. On July 25 General Omar Bradley's First Army broke through west of St. Lô and, soon augmented by George Patton's Third Army, the American forces broke out westward into Brittany and eastward toward Paris. Patton moved east and north to link up with British forces coming south from Caen, and the two caught the German forces in a trap. Only remnants managed to escape before the pincers closed. Meanwhile on August 15 a joint American-French invasion force landed on the French Mediterranean coast, took Marseilles and Toulon in a walkover, and raced up the Rhône Valley. German resistance in France collapsed. A Free French division, aided by American forces, had the honor of liberating Paris on August 25. German forces retired pell-mell toward the German border, and in a rush by mid-September most of France and Belgium were cleared of enemy troops. By this time the Americans were in Aachen, the old seat of Charlemagne's empire, the first German town to fall.

SLOWING MOMENTUM   Events had moved so much faster than expected, in fact, that the Allies were running out of gas. Neither their plans nor their supply system could keep up with the movement. General Montgomery, whose British and Canadian forces had been the pivot of the Allied sweep, had moved forward into Belgium, where they took Antwerp on September 4. From there, he argued, a quick fatal thrust toward Berlin could end things. On the right flank, General Patton was just as sure he could take the American Third Army all the way. Eisenhower reasoned, however, that prudence demanded getting his supply lines in order first, which required clearing out stubborn German forces and opening a supply channel to Antwerp—a long, hard battle which lasted until the end of November. Before giving up his original plan, however, Montgomery tried one sharp thrust at Arnhem to make a bridgehead across the Rhine. His force proved inadequate, with the consequence that airborne troops dropped behind the German lines were cut off and decimated. Another winter of fighting would remain before the German collapse.

LEAPFROGGING TO TOKYO

Even in the Pacific, relegated to lower priority, Allied forces had brought the war within reach of the enemy homeland by the end of 1944. The war's first American offensive in fact had been in the southwest Pacific. There the Japanese, stopped at the Coral Sea and Midway, had thrust into the southern Solomons, and were building an airstrip on Guadalcanal from which they could attack transportation routes to Australia. On August 7, 1942, two months before the North Africa landings, the First Marine Division landed on Guadalcanal and seized the airstrip while other marines secured nearby Tulagi and its port.

These quick victories, however, provoked a savage Japanese response. Reinforcements poured in via the "Tokyo Express" down the central channel, the Solomons "Slot," and the opposing navies challenged each other in a confusing series of battles that battered both so badly the sailors named the Savo Island Sound "Iron Bottom Bay." But while the Americans had lost heavily, they delivered such punishment to Japanese carrier groups, already battered at Midway, that the Japanese navy remained on the defensive for the rest of the war. The marines, helped by reinforcements, finally cleared the steaming jungles of Japanese. By February 1943 only stragglers were left.

MACARTHUR IN NEW GUINEA   Meanwhile American and Australian forces under General MacArthur had begun to push the Japanese out of their advance positions on the north coast of New Guinea. These battles, fought through some of the hottest, most humid and mosquito-infested swamps in the world, bought advances at a heavy cost, but by the end of January 1943 the eastern tip of New Guinea was secured.

At this stage American strategists made a critical decision. MacArthur proposed to advance westward along the northern coast of New Guinea toward the Philippines and ultimately Tokyo. Admiral Nimitz, with headquarters at Pearl Harbor, argued for a sweep through the islands of the central Pacific ultimately toward Formosa and China. In March 1943 the Combined Chiefs of Staff, meeting in Washington, agreed to MacArthur's plan and allotted resources for the purpose. Soon afterward they agreed that Nimitz should undertake his sweep too, for the central Pacific island complex would expose MacArthur's northern flank to a constant threat if it were left in Japanese hands.

A new tactic expedited the movement. During the air Battle of the Bismarck Sea (March 2–3, 1943) American bombers sank eight Japanese troopships and ten warships bringing reinforcements. Thereafter the Japanese dared not risk sending transports to points under siege, making it possible to use the tactic of neutralizing Japanese strongholds with air and sea power, and moving on, leaving them to die on the vine. Some called it "leapfrogging," and Premier Tojo later acknowledged the strategy as a major cause of Allied victory. Meanwhile, in mid-April, before the offensive got under way, fighters from Guadalcanal shot down a plane which American code-breakers knew was carrying Admiral Yamamoto into Bougainville. The death of Japan's naval commander, the planner of the Pearl Harbor attack, was a shattering blow to Japanese morale.

The first strong point left stranded by the leapfrog strategy was Rabaul, New Britain, bastion of the "Bismarck Barrier" which threatened the flank of MacArthur's advance across New Guinea. The offensive got under way first with sharp amphibious and naval thrusts to secure the northern Solomons. After successful naval actions in the Solomons Slot (in one of which *PT 109*, Lieutenant John Fitzgerald Kennedy's torpedo boat, went down) American forces controlled the waters in the area. On November 1 an amphibious force landed on an undefended coast of Bougainville in the northern Solomons and carved out a beachhead from which fighters and bombers brought Rabaul under daily attack. A Japanese fleet that moved to challenge the operation was decisively beaten in the Battle of Empress Augusta Bay on November 2, 1943. In New Guinea, MacArthur's forces moved into command of the coast opposite Cape Gloucester, New Britain. Occupation of Arawe and Cape Gloucester in December secured the passageway to the north coast of New Guinea and the western Pacific. When the Admiralty Islands were taken in March 1944, the isolation of Rabaul was complete and nearly 100,000 Japanese were stranded. Thus by early 1944 the Bismarck Barrier was broken.

NIMITZ IN THE CENTRAL PACIFIC   Admiral Nimitz's parallel advance through the central Pacific had as its first target two tiny atolls in the Gilberts: Makin and Tarawa. After advance bombing raids, a fleet of 200 ships delivered infantry and marines ashore at dawn on November 20, 1943. Makin, where the Japanese had only a small force, was soon cleared; after three days an American general radioed the terse message, "Makin taken." Tarawa, with its concrete bunkers behind a long coral reef and beach obstructions of wire and logs, was

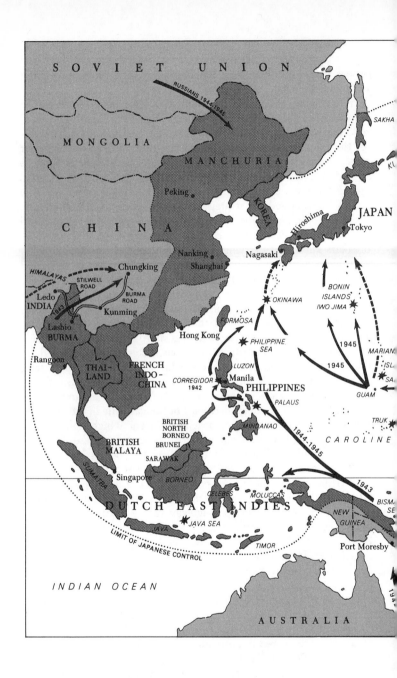

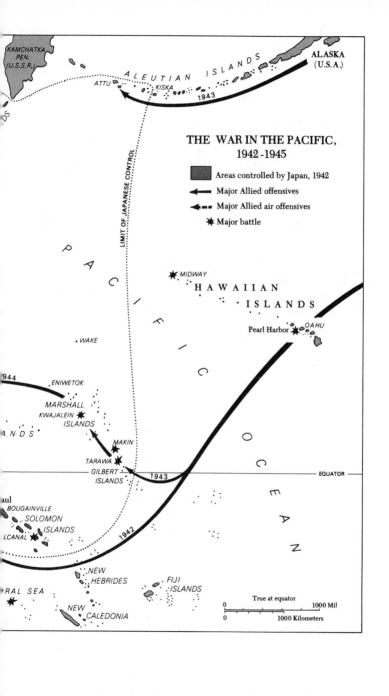

KAMCHATKA
PEN.
(U.S.S.R.)

ALASKA
(U.S.A.)

A L E U T I A N   I S L A N D S

ATTU   *KISKA*   1943

LIMIT OF JAPANESE CONTROL

THE WAR IN THE PACIFIC,
1942-1945

Areas controlled by Japan, 1942

Major Allied offensives

Major Allied air offensives

★ Major battle

P

★ *MIDWAY*

A C I

H A W A I I A N

I S L A N D S

F

OAHU

Pearl Harbor ★

• *WAKE*

I

944

• *ENIWETOK*

C

MARSHALL

KWAJALEIN ★

ISLANDS

O

A N D S

MAKIN

TARAWA ★

GILBERT   1943

ISLANDS

EQUATOR

C

aul

BOUGAINVILLE

SOLOMON

ISLANDS

E

LCANAL ★

1942

NEW

HEBRIDES

A

FIJI

ISLANDS

N

RAL SEA

★

True at equator

0   1000 Mil

NEW

CALEDONIA

0   1000 Kilometers

American troops attacking dug-in Japanese positions on Kwajalein Island, February 1944.

one of the most heavily protected islands in the Pacific. There nearly 1,000 American soldiers, sailors, and marines lost their lives rooting out a determined resistance by 4,000 Japanese who refused to surrender. The Gilberts provided costly lessons in amphibious operations, one of which was to confirm the value of bypassing strong points. The islands also provided airfields from which the Seventh Air Force began softening up strong points in the Marshall Islands. Japanese planes completely abandoned the region.

Invasion of the Marshalls, the next step "up the ladder" to Tokyo, began on January 31, 1944, at Kwajalein and Eniwetok, both of which were soon taken. During these operations a carrier raid wrought heavy destruction on enemy ships and aircraft at Truk, the Japanese "Pearl Harbor" in the Carolines. Then Truk, like Rabaul, was bypassed. The Americans took Saipan in the Marianas on June 15, which brought the new American B-29 bombers within striking distance of Japan itself. The Japanese navy therefore had to resist with all it had, which was not enough despite its crash program to build new carriers.

In the Battle of the Philippine Sea, the grand "Marianas Turkey Shoot" fought mostly in the air on June 19 and 20, 1944, the Japanese lost three more carriers, two submarines, and over 300 planes, at the cost of only 17 American planes. The battle secured the Marianas, and soon B-29s were winging their way to the first systematic bombings of the Japanese homeland. Defeat in the Marianas finally brought home to General Tojo the realization that the war was lost. On July 18, 1944, he and his entire cabinet resigned, and General Kunikai Koiso became the new premier.

THE BATTLE OF LEYTE GULF   With New Guinea and the Marianas all but conquered, President Roosevelt met with General MacArthur and Admiral Nimitz in Honolulu on July 27–28, 1944, to decide the next major step. Previous plans had marked China as the essential springboard for invading Japan, but a Japanese offensive in April 1944 had taken most of the south China airfields from which American air power had operated. This strengthened MacArthur's standing opinion that the Philippines would provide a safer staging area than Formosa. Sentimental and political considerations, as well as military, tipped the decision his way. After securing his flanks with the capture of Morotai in the Moluccas and Peleliu in the Palaus— the latter the scene of some of the bloodiest fighting of the war, ground out in heat up to 115°F—MacArthur made his move into the Philippines on October 20, landing first on the island of Leyte. Wading ashore behind the first landings, he issued an announcement: "People of the Philippines: I have returned. . . . Rally to me. . . . Let no heart be faint."

General Douglas MacArthur's landing at Leyte Gulf, the Philippines, October 1944.

The Japanese, knowing that loss of the Philippines would cut them off from the oil and other essential resources of the East Indies, brought in fleets from three directions. The three encounters that resulted on October 25, 1944, came to be known collectively as the Battle of Leyte Gulf. It proved to be the largest naval engagement in history. The Japanese lost most of their remaining sea power and the ability to protect the Philippines. The battle also brought the first of the suicide attacks by Japanese pilots who crash-dived into American carriers, sinking one and seriously damaging others. The "Kamikaze" units, named for the "Divine Wind" that centuries ago had saved Japan from Mongol invasion, were able to inflict severe damage on the American navy until the end of the war.

A NEW AGE IS BORN

ROOSEVELT'S FOURTH TERM   In 1944, war or no war, the calendar dictated another presidential election. This time the Republicans turned to the former crime-fighter and New York governor, Thomas E. Dewey, as their candidate. Once again no Democratic challenger rose high enough to contest Roosevelt, but a fight did develop over the second spot on the ticket. Vice-President Wallace had earned the enmity of both southern conservatives and northern city bosses who feared his ties with labor, but Roosevelt finally rejected the favorite of these groups. The outcome was the compromise choice of Missouri senator Harry S. Truman.

Dewey ran under the same handicap as Landon and Willkie before him. He did not propose to dismantle Roosevelt's programs, but argued that it was time for younger men to replace the tired old leaders of the New Deal. Roosevelt betrayed decided signs of illness and exhaustion, but nevertheless carried the battle to the enemy. His most memorable thrust was at a Teamsters Union dinner in Washington, where FDR responded in mock outrage to stories that he had sent a destroyer to the Aleutians to pick up his Scottie, Fala. The president did not resent the attacks, he said, but as for Fala, "his Scotch soul was furious. He has not been the same dog since." On November 7, 1944, Roosevelt was once again elected, this time by a popular margin of 25.6 million to 22 million and an electoral vote of 432 to 99.

CONVERGING FRONTS   After their quick sweep across France, the Allies lost momentum in the fall of 1944 and settled down to slugging at the frontiers of Germany. Along this line the armies fought it out all winter. While American forces took the Ruhr River dams, the

Lorraine fortress city of Metz, and Strasbourg in Alsace, the Germans sprang a surprise in the rugged Ardennes Forest, where the Allied line was thinnest. Hitting on December 16, 1944, under clouds that prevented air reconnaissance, they advanced along a fifty-mile bulge in Belgium and Luxembourg—hence the Battle of the Bulge. In ten days they penetrated nearly to the Meuse River on their way to Antwerp, but they stalled at Bastogne. Reinforced by the Allies just before it was surrounded, Bastogne held for six days against all the Germans could bring against it. On December 22 American general "Tony" McAuliffe gave his memorable answer to the demand for surrender: "Nuts." When a German major asked what the term meant, an American officer said, "It's the same as 'Go to Hell.' And I will tell you something else—if you continue to attack, we will kill every goddamn German that tries to break into this city." The American situation remained desperate until the next day when the clouds lifted, allowing Allied airpower to hit the Germans and drop in supplies. On December 26 American forces broke through to the relief of Bastogne, but it would be mid-January 1945 before the previous lines were restored.

Germany's sudden thrust upset Eisenhower's timetable, but the outcome shook German power and morale. Their effort had weakened the eastern front, and in January 1945 the Russians began their

An American infantry regiment marching through the ruins of Bensheim, Germany, March 1945.

final offensive. The western offensives started in February. Advancing all along the front, the Allies by early March had reached the banks of the Rhine nearly all the way from Holland to Switzerland. On March 6 they took Cologne, and the next day, by remarkable luck, the Allies seized the bridge at Remagen before the Germans could blow it up. Troops poured across the Rhine there and soon afterward at other points.

The Allies then encircled the Ruhr Valley, center of Germany's heavy industry. In quick sweeps the army closed the pincers on some 400,000 German soldiers in the region and pounded them into submission. By mid-April resistance there was over. Meanwhile the Russian offensive had also reached Germany itself, after taking Warsaw on January 17 and Vienna on April 13.

YALTA AND THE POSTWAR WORLD   As the final offensives got under way, the Yalta Conference (February 4–11, 1945) brought the Big Three leaders together again in a czar's palace at the Crimean resort. While the focus at Teheran in 1943 had been on wartime strategy, it was now on the shape of the postwar world. Two aims loomed large in Roosevelt's thinking. One was the need to ensure that the Soviet Union join the war against Japan. The other was based on the lessons he drew from the previous world war. Just as the Neutrality Acts of the 1930s were designed with lessons from the previous war in mind, thoughts about the future were now influenced by memories of the interwar years. Americans, one historian has written, visualized World War II as parallel to World War I. "They expected its aftermath to be in most respects the same. And they defined statesmanship as doing those things which might have been done to prevent World War II from occurring." Chief among the mistakes to be remedied this time were the failure of the United States to join the League of Nations and the failure of the Allies to maintain a united front against the German aggressors.

The Yalta meeting began by calling for a conference on world organization to be held in the United States, beginning on April 25, 1945. The Yalta conferees decided also that substantive decisions in the Security Council would require the acquiescence of its five permanent members: the United States, Britain, Russia, France, and China.

GERMANY AND EASTERN EUROPE   With Hitler's "Thousand-Year Reich" stumbling to its doom, arrangements for the postwar governance of Germany had to be made. The war map dictated the basic pattern of occupation zones: Russia would control the east and the Western Allies would control the rich industrial areas of the west. Berlin, isolated within the Russian zone, would be subject to joint occupation. At the behest of Churchill and Roosevelt, liberated France received an occupation zone along its border and also in Berlin. Similar arrangements were made for Austria, with Vienna like Berlin under joint occupation within the Russian zone. Russian demands for reparations of $20 billion, half of which would go to Russia, were referred to a Reparations Commission in Moscow. The commission never reached agreement, although the Russians made off with untold amounts of machinery and equipment from their occupation zone.

With respect to eastern Europe, where Russian forces were advancing on a broad front, there was little the Western Allies could do to influence events. Roosevelt was inhibited by his wish to win Russian cooperation in the fight against Japan and in the effort to build the proposed United Nations organization. Poland became the main focus of Western concern. Britain and France had gone to war in 1939 to defend Poland and now, six years later, the course of the war had left Poland's fate in the hands of the Russians.

Events had long foreshadowed the outcome. Controversy over the Katyn Forest massacre of 1940, in which the Russians had gunned down over 14,000 Polish officers, led the Russians in 1943 to break relations with the Polish government-in-exile in London. When Rus-

The Yalta Conference, February 1945. *Stalin* (right), *FDR* (center), *and Churchill* (left) *confer on the shape of the postwar world.*

sian forces reentered Poland in 1944, the Soviets placed civil administration under a Committee of National Liberation in Lublin, a
puppet regime representing few Poles. When Soviet troops reached
the gates of Warsaw, the underground resistance in the city rose
against the Nazi occupiers. The underground, however, held allegiance to the London government-in-exile. The Russians then
stopped their offensive for two months while the Nazis wiped out
thousands of Poles, potential rivals to the Lublin puppet government.

That optimism about postwar cooperation could survive such
events was a triumph of hope over experience. The attitude was
remotely reminiscent of 1919, when Wilson made concessions to win
approval of the League of Nations in the hope that the League could
later remedy any injustices which had crept into the peace settlement. But in any case the Western Allies at Yalta could do no more
than acquiesce or stall. On the Soviet proposal to expand the Lublin
Committee into a provisional government together with representatives of the London Poles, they acquiesced. On the issue of Poland's
boundaries, they stalled. The Russians proposed to keep eastern
Poland, offering land taken from Germany as compensation. Roosevelt and Churchill accepted the proposal, but considered the western
boundary at the Oder–Western Neisse rivers only provisional. But
the peace conference at which the western boundary of Poland was
to be settled never took place because of later disagreements. The
presence of the London Poles in the provisional government only
lent a tone of legitimacy to a regime dominated by the Communists,
who soon ousted their rivals.

At Yalta the Big Three promised to sponsor free elections, democratic governments, and constitutional safeguards of freedom
throughout the rest of Europe. The Yalta Declaration of Liberated
Europe reaffirmed faith in the principles of the Atlantic Charter and
the United Nations, but in the end it made little difference. It may
have postponed Communist takeovers in eastern Europe for a few
years, but before long Communist members of coalition governments had their hands on the levers of power and ousted the opposition. Aside from Czechoslovakia, though, the countries of eastern
Europe lacked strong democratic traditions in any case. And Russia,
twice invaded by Germany in the twentieth century, had reason for
wanting buffer states between it and the Germans.

YALTA'S LEGACY   The Yalta agreements were later attacked for giving eastern Europe over to Soviet domination. But the course of the
war shaped the actions at Yalta. By suppressing opposition, moreover, the Soviets were not acting under the Yalta accords, but in
violation of them.

Perhaps the most bitterly criticized of the Yalta understandings was a secret agreement on the Far East, not made public until after the war. As the Big Three met, fighting still raged in the Philippines and Burma. The Combined Chiefs of Staff still estimated that Japan could hold out for eighteen months after the defeat of Germany. Costly campaigns lay ahead and the atomic bomb was still an expensive gamble on the unknown. Roosevelt therefore accepted Stalin's demands on postwar arrangements in the Far East, subject technically to later agreement by Chiang Kai-shek. Stalin wanted continued Russian control of Outer Mongolia through its puppet People's Republic there, acquisition of the Kurile Islands from Japan, and recovery of rights and territory lost after the Russo-Japanese War in 1905. Stalin in return promised to enter the war against Japan two or three months after the German defeat, to recognize Chinese sovereignty over Manchuria, and to conclude a treaty of friendship and alliance with the Chinese Nationalists. Later Roosevelt's concessions would appear in a different light, but given their geographical advantages in Asia as in eastern Europe, the Soviets were in a position to get what they wanted in any case.

THE THIRD REICH COLLAPSES   The collapse of Nazi resistance was imminent, but President Roosevelt did not live to join the celebrations. All through 1944 his health had been declining, and photographs from early 1945 reveal a very sick man. Roosevelt had always before been able to recharge his batteries with brief rests, and in the spring of 1945 he went to his second home in Warm Springs, Georgia, to rest up for the Charter Conference of the United Nations at San Francisco. On April 12, 1945, while he was drafting a Jeffer-

A Russian soldier raises the Soviet flag over the Reichstag after the conquest of Berlin, May 1945.

son Day speech, a cerebral hemorrhage brought sudden death. The last words he wrote into the speech were: "The only limit to our realization of tomorrow will be our doubts of today. Let us move forward with strong and active faith."

The collapse of Hitler's Germany came less than a month later. The Allied armies rolled up almost unopposed to the Elbe River, where they met advance detachments of Russians on April 25. Three days later Italian partisans caught and killed Mussolini and his mistress as they tried to flee. In Berlin, which was under siege by the Russians, Hitler married his mistress, Eva Braun, in an underground bunker on the last day of April just before killing her and himself in a suicide pact. On May 2 Berlin fell to the Russians. That same day German forces in Italy surrendered. Hitler's designated successor desperately tried to surrender to the Western Allies, but Eisenhower declined to act except in concert with the Russians. Finally, on May 7 General Alfred Jodl signed an unconditional surrender in Allied headquarters at Reims. So ended the Thousand-Year Reich, little more than twelve years after its Führer came to power.

Massive celebrations of victory in Europe on V-E Day, May 8, 1945, were tempered by the tragedies that had engulfed the world: mourning for the lost president and the death and mutilation of untold millions. Most shocking was the discovery of the Holocaust, scarcely believable until the Allied armies came upon the death camps in which the Nazis had sought to apply their "final solution" to the Jewish "problem": the wholesale extermination of some 6 million Jews along with more than 1 million others who had suffered the Nazi contempt and displeasure.

During the war, testimony from underground and neutral relief agencies had piled up growing evidence of the Nazis' systematic genocide against the Jews of Europe. Reports appeared in major American newspapers as early as 1942, but were nearly always buried on inside pages. The falsehoods of World War I propaganda had conditioned too many people to doubt all atrocity stories, and rumors of such horror seemed beyond belief.

American government officials, even some Jewish leaders, dragged their feet for fear that relief for Jewish refugees might stir up latent anti-Semitism at home. Under pressure, Roosevelt set up a War Refugee Board early in 1944, but with few resources at its disposal. It nevertheless managed to rescue about 200,000 European Jews and some 20,000 others. More might have been done by broadcasts warning people in Europe that Nazi "labor camps" were really death traps. The Allies rejected bombing the rail lines into the largest death camp, Auschwitz in Poland, although American planes hit industries five miles away. And few refugees were accepted into the United States. The record was hardly one to inspire pride.

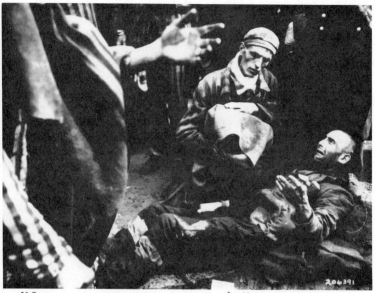

U.S. troops encounter surviving inmates at the Nazi concentration camp at Wobbelin, May 1945.

A GRINDING WAR The sobering thought that the defeat of Japan remained to be accomplished cast a further pall over the victory celebrations in Europe. American forces continued to penetrate and disrupt the Japanese Empire in the early months of 1945, but at heavy cost. Stubborn opposition by the Japanese slowed the reconquest of the Philippines. Japanese forces in Manila held out until March 4. In Luzon about 50,000 Japanese continued to fight until the end of the war. While fighting went on in the Philippines, on February 19, 1945, marine assault forces invaded Iowa Jima, a speck of volcanic rock 750 miles from Tokyo. It was needed to provide fighter escort for bombers over Japan and a landing strip for disabled B-29s. Nearly six weeks were required to secure an island five miles square from defenders hiding in an underground labyrinth. The cost was more than 20,000 American casualties and nearly 7,000 dead.

The fight for Okinawa, beginning on Easter Sunday, April 1, was even bloodier. The largest island in the Ryukyu chain, Okinawa was large enough to afford a staging area for invasion. It was the largest amphibious operation of the Pacific war, involving some 300,000 troops. From a beachhead on the northern coast the invaders fought their way sough through rugged terrain. Desperate Japanese counterattacks inflicted heavy losses on land, by air, and by sea. Kamikaze planes attacked by the hundreds. Finally, the battleship

Yamato, a survivor of Leyte Gulf, left Kyushu with nine other ships—the remnant of a once-great navy—with fuel only for a one-way trip, all that was available. American seaplanes intercepted the pathetic armada, sank the *Yamato* and two other warships, and badly damaged the rest. It was the end of the Japanese navy, but the fight for Okinawa raged until late June, when the bloody attrition destroyed any further Japanese ability to resist. The fighting brought nearly 50,000 American casualties; the dead included their commander, Lieutenant-General Simon Bolivar Buckner, Jr., the son and namesake of a Confederate general, and one of the GIs' favorite correspondents, Ernie Pyle. The Japanese lost an estimated 140,000 dead, but more than 10,000 surrendered. Casualties also included about 42,000 Okinawans.

The campaign was significant mainly for wearing down the remaining defenses of the Japanese. Now American ships could roam the coastline of Japan, shelling targets ashore. American planes bombed at will and mined the waters of the Inland Sea. Tokyo, Nagoya, and other major cities were devastated by firestorms from incendiary bombs, made all the worse by the prevalence of wooden structures in earthquake-prone Japan. Still, it seemed that ahead lay further beachheads and more bitter fighting against the same suicidal fury that had made Okinawa so costly a conquest. But as the irony of timing would have it, Okinawa was never needed as a staging area. When the Americans invaded Okinawa the emperor named a new premier, and when resistance on the island collapsed he instructed the new premier to seek peace terms. Washington had picked this up by decoding Japanese messages, which suggested either an effort to avoid unconditional surrender or perhaps just a stall.

THE ATOMIC BOMB   By this time, however, a new force had changed all strategic calculations: during the summer of 1945 President Truman learned of the first atomic explosion, the result of several years of intensive work. The strands of scientific development that led to the bomb ironically ran back to Germany. Except for the Nazi bigotry that drove scientists into exile, Germany might well have developed the atomic bomb first. Early in 1939 a German scientific journal revealed that the uranium atom had been split at the Kaiser Wilhelm Institute in Berlin; experiments in Denmark and the United States soon confirmed the finding. On October 11, 1939, President Roosevelt learned of the matter when an emissary delivered a letter from Albert Einstein and a memorandum explaining the potential of nuclear fission and warning that the Germans might steal the march. Roosevelt quickly set up a committee to coordinate information in the field, and in 1940 some army and navy funds were diverted into research which grew ultimately into the $2 billion top-secret Manhattan Project.

On August 13, 1942, the Army Engineers set up the Manhattan Engineering District to direct development and production of the bomb. On December 2, 1942, Dr. Enrico Fermi and other scientists achieved the first atomic chain reaction in a squash-court-turned-laboratory at the University of Chicago, removing any remaining doubts of the bomb's feasibility. Gigantic plants sprang up at Oak Ridge, Tennessee, and Hanford, Washington, to make plutonium, while a group of physicists under Dr. J. Robert Oppenheimer worked out the scientific and technical problems of bomb construction in a laboratory at Los Alamos, New Mexico.

On July 16, 1945, the first atomic fireball rose from the New Mexico desert. The awestruck Oppenheimer said later that in the observation bunker "A few people laughed, a few people cried, most people were silent. There floated through my mind a line from the Bhagavad-Gita in which Krishna is trying to persuade the prince that he should do his duty: 'I am become death, the shatterer of worlds.'" Colleagues crowded forward with their congratulations: "Oppie," said one, "now we're all sons of bitches."

The question of how to use this awful weapon had already come before a committee of military and political officials and scientists. Some of the scientists, awed at the ghastly prospect, favored a demonstration in a remote area, but the decision went for military use because only two bombs were available, and even those might misfire. More consideration was given to the choice of targets. Four cities had been reserved from conventional bombing as potential targets. After Secretary of War Stimson eliminated Kyoto, Japan's ancient capital and center of many national and religious treasures, and Kokura, priority went to Hiroshima, a major assembly point for Japanese naval convoys and a center of war industries, headquarters of the Second General Army, and command center for the homeland's defenses. This met Truman's guidelines. He had written that, even though "the Japs are savages, ruthless, merciless, and fanatic," only military personnel and installations rather than "women and children" should be targeted. Of course, he had no idea that the bomb would destroy virtually an entire city.

On July 25, 1945, President Truman, then at the Big Three Conference in Potsdam, Germany, ordered the bomb dropped if Japan did not surrender before August 3. The next day the heads of the American, British, and Russian governments issued the Potsdam Declaration demanding that Japan surrender or face "prompt and utter destruction." The deadline passed, and at 9:15 A.M. on August

6, 1945, a B-29 named the *Enola Gay*, with a crew commanded by Colonel Paul W. Tibbetts, dropped the bomb over Hiroshima.

A sudden flash wiped out four square miles of the city, wrecked the defense headquarters, wiped out most of the Second General Army, and killed in all more than 60,000 people. Dazed survivors wandered the streets, so painfully burned that their skin began to peel in large strips. In one of history's most pungent ironies, Captain Mitsuo Fuchida, flight commander of the Pearl Harbor attack, flew into Hiroshima Airport that morning and found himself facing "a procession of people who seemed to have come out of Hell." Even those who appeared unhurt began mysteriously to sicken and die, the first victims of a deadly radiation which blighted lives for years to come. In the United States, Americans greeted the first news with elation: it promised a quick end to the long nightmare of war. Only later would the awareness dawn that it marked the start of a more enduring nightmare, the atomic age.

Three days later an opportunistic Russia, eager to share in the spoils of victory, hastened to enter the war, and a few hours after that, about noon on August 9, the second bomb exploded over the

Nagasaki, Japan, one month after U.S. forces dropped an atomic bomb on the city.

port city of Nagasaki, a shipbuilding and torpedo-factory center, as well as the legendary home of Madame Butterfly and once the isolated kingdom's only window to the world, killing 36,000 more. That night the emperor urged his cabinet to accept the inevitable and surrender on the sole condition that he remain as sovereign. The next day the United States government, to facilitate surrender and an orderly transition, announced its willingness to let him keep the throne, but under the authority of an Allied supreme commander. Frantic exchanges ended with Japanese acceptance on August 14, 1945, when the emperor himself broke precedent to record a radio message announcing the surrender to his people. Even then a last-ditch palace revolt had to be squashed.

On September 2, 1945, General MacArthur and other Allied representatives accepted Japan's formal surrender on board the battleship *Missouri*. MacArthur then settled in at his headquarters in the Dai Ichi, "Building One," facing the Imperial Palace across the street, behind its moat. Just seventy-seven years after the Meiji Restoration had overthrown the last Tokugawa shogun, Japan had a new American shogun.

THE FINAL LEDGER Thus ended the most deadly conflict in human history. No effort to tabulate a ledger of death and destruction can ever take the full measure of the war's suffering, or hope to be more than an informed guess as to the numbers involved. One estimate has it that 70 million in all fought in the war, at a cost in human lives of 17 million military dead and more than 18 million civilian dead. Material costs were also enormous, perhaps $1 trillion in military expenditures and twice that in property losses. The Soviet Union suffered the greatest losses of all, over 6 million military deaths, over 10 million civilians dead, and at least 25 million left homeless. World War II was more costly for the United States than any other of the country's foreign wars: 294,000 battle deaths and 114,000 other deaths. But in proportion to population, the United States suffered a far smaller loss than any of the major Allies or enemies, and American territory escaped the devastation visited on so many other parts of the world.

The war's end opened a new era for the United States. It accelerated the growth of American power while devastating all other world powers, leaving the United States economically and militarily the strongest nation on earth. But Russia, despite its human and material losses, emerged from the war with much new territory and enhanced influence, making it the greatest power on the whole Eurasian land mass. Just a little over a century after Alexis de

Tocqueville predicted that western Europe would come to be overshadowed by the power of the United States and Russia, his prophecy had come to pass.

FURTHER READING

Russell F. Weigley's *The American Way of War: A History of United States Military Strategy and Policy* (1973)° provides a scholarly assessment of strategy and tactics. Roosevelt's wartime leadership is analyzed in Eric Larrabee's *Commander in Chief: Franklin Delano Roosevelt, His Lieutenants and Their War* (1987).

John Keegan's *The Second World War* (1990)° surveys the European conflict in its entirety, while Charles B. MacDonald's *The Mighty Endeavor: American Armed Forces in the European Theatre in World War II* (1969) concentrates on American involvement. Another perspective on the European conflict can be found in the memoirs of Dwight D. Eisenhower, *Crusade in Europe* (1948). On Eisenhower's generalship, see David Eisenhower's *Eisenhower: At War* (1986). Books on specific campaigns in Europe include Max Hasting's *Overlord* (1984)° and Cornelius Ryan's *The Longest Day* (1959),° on the D-Day operation; and John Toland's *The Last 100 Days* (1966),° on the last days of the Nazi resistance. Another view of the European conflict can be found in the memoirs of Omar M. Bradley, *A General's Life: An Autobiography* (1983).°

For the war in the Far East, see Toland's *The Rising Sun: The Decline and Fall of the Japanese Empire, 1936–1945* (1970),° Ronald H. Spector's *Eagle against the Sun* (1984),° Bill D. Ross's *Iwo Jima* (1985),° Gordon W. Prange's *Miracle at Midway* (1982),° and John Dower's award-winning *War Without Mercy: Race and Power in the Pacific War* (1986).°

Overviews of the war on the home front include Richard R. Lingeman's *Don't You Know There's a War On?* (1970) and John Morton Blum's *V Was for Victory: Politics and American Culture during World War II* (1976).° *"The Good War"* (1984),° edited by Studs Terkel, contains many fascinating reminiscences of the war years. Robert Dallek's *The American Style of Foreign Policy* (1983)° shows how war abroad shaped unity at home. The government's efforts to use movies to influence public opinion are described in Clayton R. Koppes and Gregory D. Black's *Hollywood Goes to War: How Politics, Profits and Propaganda Shaped World War II Movies* (1987).

Susan M. Hartmann's *The Home Front and Beyond* (1982) and Karen Anderson's *Wartime Women* (1981) treat the new working environment for women. Neil Wynn looks at the participation of blacks in *The Afro-American and the Second World War* (1976). The story of the oppression of Japanese-Americans is told in Peter Irons's *Justice at War* (1983) and is further illuminated in Thomas James's *Exile Within: The Schooling of Japanese Americans, 1942–1945* (1987).

°These books are available in paperback editions.

A sound introduction to American diplomacy during the conflict can be found in Gaddis Smith's *American Diplomacy during the Second World War, 1941–1945* (2nd ed., 1985). To understand the role played in policy-making, consult Raymond G. O'Connor's *Diplomacy for Victory: FDR and Unconditional Surrender* (1971)° and Robert A. Divine's *Roosevelt and World War II* (1969).° Diane Shaver Clemens is critical of Roosevelt in *Yalta* (1970).

Martin Gilbert's *Auschwitz and the Allies* (1981)° and David S. Wyman's *The Abandonment of the Jews* (1984)° discuss the Allies and the Holocaust.

An introduction to the issues and events that led to the deployment of atomic weapons is traced by Herbert Feis in *The Atomic Bomb and the End of World War II* (1966).° Also helpful are Gregg Herken's *The Winning Weapon* (1980),° Martin J. Sherwin's *A World Destroyed: The Atomic Bomb and the Grand Alliance* (1975),° Richard Rhodes's *The Making of the Atomic Bomb* (1988),° and Peter Wyden's *Day One: Before Hiroshima and After* (1984).° Gar Alperovitz's *Atomic Diplomacy: Hiroshima and Potsdam* (new ed., 1985)° details how the bomb helped shape American postwar policy. Paul S. Boyer's *By the Bomb's Early Light* (1985)° shows American cultural and intellectual responses to the bomb.

Robert A. Divine's *Second Chance: The Triumph of Internationalism in America during World War II* (1967)° chronicles America's emergence as a world leader.

31

THE FAIR DEAL
AND CONTAINMENT

DEMOBILIZATION UNDER TRUMAN

TRUMAN'S UNEASY START "Who the hell is Harry Truman?" Roosevelt's chief-of-staff asked the president in the summer of 1944. The question was on more lips when, after less than twelve weeks as vice-president, Harry Truman took the presidential oath on April 12, 1945. It may have recurred two days later, when he impulsively began his first speech to Congress and House Speaker Sam Rayburn interrupted in a whisper: "Just a minute. Let me present you, will you, Harry?" Clearly he was not Franklin Roosevelt, and that was one of the burdens he would bear. "With Roosevelt you'd have known he was President even if you hadn't been told," a journalist wrote years later. "He looked imperial, and he acted that way, and he talked that way. Harry Truman, for God's sake, looked and acted and talked like—well, like a failed haberdasher"—which he was.

In their origins Roosevelt and Truman came from different worlds. For Truman there had been no inherited wealth, no early contact with the great and near-great, no European travel, no Groton, no Harvard—indeed, no college at all. Born in 1884 in western Missouri, Truman had pioneer grandparents from Kentucky and a Southern Baptist background. He grew up in Independence, once the staging area for the Oregon and Santa Fe Trails, but by the time of his youth an unglamorous town near Kansas City. Too nearsighted to join in the activities of other boys, Truman became bookish and withdrawn. But after high school he moved to his grandmother's farm, spent a few years working in Kansas City banks, and grew into an outgoing young man.

During World War I Truman served in France as captain of an artillery battery. Afterward he and a partner went into the clothing business, but it failed in the recession of 1922, and Truman then became a professional politician under the tutelage of Kansas City's Democratic machine. Elected county judge in 1922, he was defeated in 1924 and elected once again in 1926. In 1934 Missouri sent him to the United States Senate, where he remained fairly obscure until he became chairman of the committee to investigate war mobilization.

Something about Harry Truman evoked the spirit of Andrew Jackson: his decisiveness, his feisty character, his family loyalty. But that was a side of the man that the American people came to know only as he settled into the job. On his first full day as president, he remained awestruck. "Boys, if you ever pray, pray for me now," he told a group of reporters. "I don't know whether you fellows ever had a load of hay fall on you, but when they told me yesterday what had happened, I felt like the moon, the stars and all the planets had fallen on me."

Truman's accession heartened the party bosses who had helped engineer his nomination. Six weeks after Roosevelt's death the Speaker of Mississippi's House of Representatives said Truman had "begun well and is making rapid progress towards returning this country to Fundamental Americanism." But as one observer put it, the men who put Truman in "knew what they wanted but did not know what they were getting." What they were getting was a man who favored much of the New Deal and was even prepared to extend it, but at the same time was uneasy with many New Dealers. "He was not of their clan and kidney," one newsman put it. Within ninety days he had replaced much of the Roosevelt cabinet with his own choices. These included fewer Missourians and "cronies" than his detractors claimed, but on the whole they were more conservative in outlook and included enough mediocrities to lend credence to the criticism. Truman suffered the further handicap of seeming to be a caretaker for the remainder of Roosevelt's time. Few, including Truman himself at first, expected him to run in 1948.

Truman gave one significant clue to his domestic policies on September 6, 1945, when he sent Congress a comprehensive peacetime program which in effect proposed to continue and enlarge the New Deal. Its twenty-one points included expansion of unemployment insurance, extension of the Employment Service, a higher minimum wage, a permanent Fair Employment Practices Commission, slum clearance and low-rent housing, regional development of the nation's river valleys, and a public-works program. "Not even President Roosevelt asked for so much at one sitting," said the House Republican leader. "It's just a plain case of out-dealing the New Deal." Beset by other problems, Truman was unable to set priorities on his demands, and his new domestic proposals were soon mired in disputes over the transition to a peacetime economy.

CONVERTING TO PEACE The raucous celebrations that greeted Japan's surrender signaled the habitual American response to victory: a rapid demobilization and a return to more congenial pursuits. The president and Congress were besieged by demands for bringing the boys home. By mid-1946 the wartime army and navy had been reduced from peaks of 8 million and 3.8 million, respectively, to 1.9 million and 1 million. By 1947 the total armed forces were down to 1.5 million and Congress had decreed further cuts. In his memoirs Truman termed this "the most remarkable demobilization in the history of the world, or 'disintegration' if you want to call it that." It was in fact the same pattern that had prevailed since the days of the colonial wars, and it went on for several years despite mounting international tensions. By early 1950 the army had fallen to 600,000 men, with only ten active divisions.

The veterans returned to schools, new jobs, wives, and babies. Population growth, which had dropped off sharply in the depression decade, now soared: the population increase of 9 million during the 1930s exploded to a growth of 19 million in the 1940s. The birth rate

The Eldridge General Store, Fayette County, Illinois. *Postwar America quickly demobilized, turning its attention to the pursuit of abundance.*

The Electronic Numerical Integrator and Computer (ENIAC), 1946. *Developed for the Army Ordnance Department by Dr. J. Presper Eckert, Jr., the ENIAC and its progeny would have profound consequences for the later twentieth-century world.*

per 1,000 of total population grew from 19.4 in 1940 to above 24 per annum by 1946, and did not begin to show a decline until the 1960s. Americans born during this postwar period composed what came to be known as the baby-boom generation, and that generation became a dominant force in the nation's social and cultural life.

The end of the war, with its sudden demobilization and reconversion to a peacetime economy, brought sharp dislocations but not the postwar depression that many feared. The economic impact of demobilization was cushioned by numerous shock-absorbers: unemployment pay and other social security benefits; the Servicemen's Readjustment Act of 1944, known as the "GI Bill of Rights," under which $13 billion was spent for veterans on education, vocational training, medical treatment, unemployment insurance, and loans for building houses or going into business; and most important, the pent-up demand for consumer goods that was fueled by wartime incomes. Instead of sinking into depression, businesses seized upon options to buy up properties from the Defense Plant Corporation and began a spurt of private investment in new plant and equipment. The gross national product first exceeded the 1929 level in 1940, when it reached $101 billion, but by annual increases (except in 1946) it had grown to $347 billion by 1952, Truman's last full year in office.

CONTROLLING INFLATION   The problem Truman faced was not depression but inflation, one problem which President Roosevelt had not encountered before the war. A historian summed up the political burden imposed by this difference: "Whereas the politics of depression generally allowed the Roosevelt administration, by bestowing benefits, to court interest groups and contribute to an economic upturn, the politics of inflation required a responsible government like Truman's to curb wages, prices, and profits and to deny the growing expectations of rival groups."

Released from wartime restraints, the demands of businessmen and workers alike combined to frustrate efforts at controlling rising prices. Truman endorsed demands for wage increases and argued that they were needed to cushion the shock of conversion and to sustain purchasing power. He felt that there was "room in the existing price structure" for business to grant such increases, a point management refused to concede. Within six weeks of war's end, corporations confronted a wave of union demands. In November 1945 Truman, like Wilson in 1919, called a labor-management conference to formulate a labor policy, but it had as little result as the one in 1919.

A series of strikes followed. The United Automobile Workers walked out on General Motors, with Walter Reuther, head of the union's General Motors division, arguing that the company could afford a 30 percent pay raise without raising car prices. (The company denied this claim.) A strike in the steel industry finally gave rise to a formula for settling most of the disputes. President Truman suggested a pay raise of 18½¢ per hour, which the Steel Workers accepted but United States Steel refused. To break the logjam the administration in February 1946 agreed to let the company increase its prices. That pattern then became the basis for settlements in other industries, and also set a dangerous precedent of price-wage spirals that would plague consumers in the postwar world.

Major disputes soon developed in the coal and railroad industries. John L. Lewis of the United Mine Workers wanted more than the 18½¢-per-hour wage increase. He also demanded improved safety regulations and a union health and welfare fund financed by a royalty on coal. Mine owners refused the demands, and a strike followed. The government responded by using wartime powers to seize the mines; Truman's interior secretary then accepted nearly all the union's demands.

In the rail dispute the unions and management reached an agreement, but two brotherhoods, the trainmen and locomotive engineers, held out for rule changes as well as higher wages. Truman seized the roads in May and won a five-day postponement of a strike.

But when the brotherhoods' leaders refused to budge further, the president went before Congress in a burst of fury against their "obstinate arrogance" and demanded authority to draft strikers into the armed forces. In the midst of the speech he was informed that the strike had been settled, but after telling a jubilant Congress, he went on with his message. The House passed a bill including the president's demands, but with the strike settled, it died in the Senate.

Into 1946 the wartime Office of Price Administration managed to maintain some restraint on price increases while gradually ending the rationing of most goods, and Truman asked for a one-year renewal of its powers. But during the late winter and spring of 1946 business people mounted a massive campaign against price controls and other restraints. Just a week before controls were to expire at the end of June, Congress passed a bill to continue the OPA, but with such cumbersome new procedures as to cripple the agency. Truman vetoed the bill, allowing controls to end. Congress finally extended controls in late July, but by then the cost of living had already gone up by 6 percent. When in August the OPA restored controls on meat prices, farmers responded by withholding beef from the market until they succeeded in forcing a reversal in October. After the congressional elections of 1946 Truman gave up the battle, ending all controls except on rents, sugar, and rice.

PARTISAN COOPERATION AND CONFLICT   But the legislative history of 1946 was not all deadlock and frustration. Amid the turmoil Congress and the administration worked out two signal new departures, the Employment Act of 1946 and the Atomic Energy Commission. A program of "full employment" had been a Democratic promise in the campaign of 1944, a pledge reaffirmed by Truman in 1945. The administration backed an employment bill which proposed that the government make an annual estimate of the investment and production necessary to ensure full employment, and key its spending to that estimate in order to raise production to full-employment level. Conservatives objected to what they denounced as carte blanche for deficit spending, and proposed a nonpartisan commission to advise the president on the economy. Compromise resulted in the Employment Act of February 1946, dropping the commitment to full employment and setting up a three-member Council of Economic Advisers to make appraisals of the economy and advise the president in an annual economic report. A new congressional Joint Committee on the Economic Report would propose legislation.

With regard to the new force that atomic scientists had released upon the world, there was little question that the public welfare required the control of atomic energy through a governmental monopoly. Disagreements over military versus civilian control were resolved when Congress, in August 1946, created the civilian Atomic Energy Commission. The president alone was given power to order the use of atomic weapons in warfare. Subject to "the paramount objective of assuring the common defense and security," the act declared a policy of peaceful development "so far as practicable . . . toward improving the public welfare, increasing the standard of living, strengthening free competition in private enterprise, and promoting world peace." Technical problems and high costs, however, would delay for two decades the construction of nuclear power plants, and even yet questions of feasibility, security, and public safety from radioactive pollution are unresolved.

As congressional elections approached in the fall of 1946, discontent ran high, most of it against the administration. Truman caught the blame for labor problems from both sides. A speaker at the CIO national convention tagged Truman "the No. 1 strikebreaker," while much of the public, angry at striking unions, laid the blame for strikes at the White House door. In September 1946 Truman fired Henry A. Wallace as secretary of commerce in a disagreement over foreign policy, thus offending the Democratic left. At the same time the administration was plagued by Republican charges that Communists had infiltrated the government. Republicans had a field day coining slogans. "To err is Truman" was credited to Martha Taft, wife of Senator Robert Taft. But most effective was the simple "Had enough?" attributed to a Boston ad agency: their message was that the Democrats had simply been in too long. Then in August came the

"To the Rescue!" *Labor is being pulled under by the Taft-Hartley law as Congress, which passed the bill over Truman's veto, makes sure there is no rescue.*

The CIO's Operation Dixie aimed to organize workers such as these in a North Carolina lumberyard.

cattlemen's embargo on meat. "This is going to be a damn *beefsteak* election," said one observer. Truman's removal of price controls on meat only worsened his image of vacillation. Republicans won majorities in both houses of Congress for the first time since 1928.

Given the head of steam built up against organized labor, the new Congress was sure to take up restrictive legislation, and seventeen such bills were indeed introduced on the first day of the new session. The feeling of many that labor "bosses" had grown too strong encouraged moves to restrict their actions, just as business abuses against labor were restricted under the Wagner Act of 1935.

The result was the Taft-Hartley Act of 1947, which banned any closed shop (in which nonunion workers could not be hired) but permitted a union shop (in which workers newly hired were required to join the union), unless banned by state law. It included provisions against "unfair" union practices such as secondary boycotts, jurisdictional strikes (by one union to exclude another from a given company or field), "featherbedding" (pay for work not done), refusal to bargain in good faith, and contributing to campaigns. Unions' political action committees were allowed to function, but on a voluntary basis only, and union leaders had to take oaths that they were not members of the Communist party. Employers were permitted to sue unions for breaking contracts, to petition the National Labor Relations Board (NLRB) for votes for or against the use of specific unions as collective-bargaining agents, and to speak freely during union campaigns. The act forbade strikes by federal employees, and imposed a "cooling-off" period of eighty days on any strike that the president found to be dangerous to the national health or safety.

Truman's veto of the bill, which unions called the "slave-labor act," restored his credit with labor, and many unionists who had gone over to the Republicans in 1946 returned to the Democrats. But the bill passed over Truman's veto, and as it turned out, had a less than ruinous effect on unions. Its most severe impact probably was on the CIO's "Operation Dixie," a drive to win for unions a more secure foothold in the South. By 1954 fifteen states, mainly in the South, had used the Taft-Hartley Act's authority to enact "right-to-work" laws forbidding the union shop and other union security devices.

Truman clashed with the Republicans on other domestic issues, including tax reduction passed by Congress but vetoed by Truman on the principle that in times of high production and employment the federal debt should be reduced. In 1948, however, Congress finally managed to override his veto of a $5 billion tax cut at a time when government debt still ran high. The controversy over the tax cut highlighted a soft point in Keynesian economics. In times of depression there was support for increasing governmental expenditures, but in prosperous times little support for the taxes needed to reduce the deficits. Truman paid a political price for this weakness in economic theory.

The conflicts between Truman and Congress, so visible in the 1948 campaign, obscured the high degree of bipartisan cooperation marking matters of governmental reorganization and foreign policy. After a postwar congressional investigation into the Pearl Harbor disaster made plain a fatal lack of coordination among the armed forces and intelligence services, a bipartisan majority in Congress set out to correct this problem by passing the National Security Act in July 1947. The act created a National Military Establishment, headed by a secretary of defense with subcabinet departments of army, navy, and air force, and a new National Security Council (NSC) which included the president, heads of the defense departments, and the secretary of state, among others. The act made permanent the Joint Chiefs of Staff, which had been a wartime innovation, and established the Central Intelligence Agency (CIA), descended from the wartime Office of Strategic Service (OSS), to coordinate intelligence. There was at the time no intention to have the CIA engage in covert actions as the OSS had done in the war, nor any purpose that it engage in domestic activities. But the act included two gigantic loopholes which would in time allow the CIA to engage in both: authority to perform "such other functions and duties related to intelligence" as the NSC might direct, and responsibility for "protecting intelligence sources and methods."

Congress also adopted President Truman's proposal for a change in the presidential succession. The existing law of 1886 put the secretary of state next in line after the vice-president, to be followed by other cabinet members according to rank, determined by the order in which their offices had been created. The Presidential Succession Act of 1947 inserted the Speaker of the House and the president pro tempore of the Senate ahead of the secretary of state, on the principle that the presidency should first go to elected rather than appointed officers. Congress itself took the initiative in adopting the Twenty-second Amendment, ratified in 1951, which limited presidents after Truman to two terms—a belated slap at Franklin Roosevelt.

The Cold War

BUILDING THE U.N. During World War II no one spouted slogans about making the world safe for democracy or that this was a war to end all wars. At the same time many came to reject isolationism and the disillusionment of an earlier time. As it turned out, however, the hope that the wartime concert of the United Nations would carry over into the postwar world proved but another great illusion. The pragmatic Roosevelt shared no such hope. To the contrary, one historian has argued: "His desire for a new world league . . . rested less on a faith in Wilsonian collective security than on the belief that it was a necessary vehicle for permanently involving the United States in world affairs." He expected that the Great Powers in the postwar world would have spheres of influence, but felt he had to obscure such *Realpolitik* with an organization "which would satisfy widespread demand in the United States for new idealistic or universalist arrangements for assuring the peace."

In the 1941 Atlantic Charter, Roosevelt and Churchill had looked forward to a "permanent system of general security." In the autumn of 1943 both houses of Congress passed a resolution introduced by Representative J. William Fulbright of Arkansas favoring "international machinery with power adequate to establish and to maintain a just and lasting peace." That same autumn the foreign ministers of the "Big Four" (the United States, Russia, Britain, and China) issued the Declaration of Moscow calling for an international organization, and in the 1944 elections the platforms of both major parties endorsed the principle.

On April 25, 1945, two weeks after Roosevelt's death and two weeks before the German surrender, delegates from fifty nations at war with the Axis met in San Francisco's Opera House to draw up the charter of the United Nations. These fifty were joined by Poland as charter members, with the provision that additional members could be admitted by a two-thirds vote of the General Assembly. This body, one of the two major agencies set up by the charter, included delegates from all member nations and was to meet annually in regular session to approve the budget, receive annual reports from U.N. agencies, and choose members of the Security Council and other bodies. The Security Council, the other major charter agency, would remain in permanent session and had "primary responsibility for the maintenance of international peace and security." Its eleven members included six elected for two-year terms and five permanent members: the United States, Russia, Britain, France, and China. Each permanent member had a veto on any question of substance, though not of procedure. The Security Council might investigate any dispute, recommend settlement or reference to the International Court, and take measures including a resort to military force.

Four other agencies rounded out the structure: an International Court of Justice at The Hague; a Secretariat to administer the U.N.; a Trusteeship Council to oversee administration of former Italian and Japanese colonies and the former mandates of the League of Nations; and an Economic and Social Council that might conduct studies, make recommendations, and draw agreements to bring into relationship with the U.N. existing international bodies such as the

The headquarters of the United Nations in New York City, 1953.

Food and Agricultural Organization, the United Nations Relief and Rehabilitation Administration (established in 1943), the International Monetary Fund, the International Bank for Reconstruction and Development (the World Bank), and the International Labor Office. All but the last of these had been created by negotiations during the war to provide relief and to ensure the stability of international finances after the war.

The United States Senate, in sharp contrast to the reception it gave the League of Nations, ratified the U.N. charter by a vote of 89 to 2 after only six days of discussion. The organization held its first meeting in London in 1946, and the next year moved to temporary quarters at Lake Success, New York, pending completion of its permanent home in New York City.

TRYING WAR CRIMINALS   There was also a consensus that those responsible for the atrocities of World War II should face trial and punishment. The Potsdam Conference, among other matters, gave final approval to the principle of war-crimes trials, for which a commission in London had been preparing since 1943. Both German and Japanese officials went on trial for crimes against peace, against humanity, and against the established rules of war. At Nuremberg, Germany, site of the annual Nazi party rallies, twenty-one major German offenders faced an International Military Tribunal. After a ten-month trial filled with massive documentation of Nazi atrocities, the court acquitted three, sentenced eleven to death, three to life imprisonment, and four to shorter terms. In Tokyo, a similar tribunal put twenty-five Japanese leaders on trial from May to November 1946, and pronounced death sentences on seven (including General Tojo), life imprisonment on sixteen, and committed two for lesser terms. Other international tribunals tried thousands of others, while many accused war criminals were remanded to the courts of the countries in which they had committed their crimes. Altogether well over 2,000 war-crimes trials are estimated to have taken place, not counting those in Russia and the East Bloc countries.

Critics argued that the trials set an unfortunate precedent of victors' taking revenge on the defeated. They argued as well that the convictions were condemnations *ex post facto*, for crimes against which no law existed at the time they were committed. Supporters responded by pointing to the Pact of Paris outlawing war, to the Geneva Convention for care of the sick and wounded prisoners, to the Hague declarations on the rules of war, and to the fact that crimes against humanity such as murder, rape, and pillage were already crimes under the laws of the countries where they occurred.

The Nuremberg Trials. *At far left sit the high-ranking Nazis on trial for war crimes. Among the defendants are Albert Speer (second row, third from right) and, in dark glasses, Hans Frank.*

DIFFERENCES WITH THE SOVIETS   There were signs of trouble in the Grand Alliance as early as the spring of 1945 as Russia moved to set up compliant governments in eastern Europe, violating the Yalta promises of democratic elections. On February 1 the Polish Committee of National Liberation, a puppet group already claiming the status of provisional government, moved from Lublin to Warsaw. In March the Soviets installed a puppet premier in Romania. Protests at such actions led to Russian counterprotests that the British and Americans were negotiating German surrender in Italy "behind the back of the Soviet Union" and that German forces were being concentrated against Russia. A few days before his death, Roosevelt responded to Stalin: "I cannot avoid a feeling of resentment toward your informers . . . for such vile misrepresentations."

Such was the atmosphere when Truman entered the White House. A few days before the San Francisco conference, Truman gave Soviet foreign minister Vyacheslav M. Molotov a dressing-down in Washington on the Polish situation. "I have never been talked to like that in my life," Molotov said. "Carry out your agreements," Truman snapped, "and you won't get talked to like that." On May 12, 1945, four days after victory in Europe, Winston Churchill sent a telegram to Truman: "What is to happen about Europe? An iron curtain is drawn down upon [the Russian] front. We do not know what is going on behind [it]. . . . Surely it is vital now to come to an understanding with Russia, or see where we are with her, before we weaken our armies mortally. . . ." Nevertheless, as a gesture of goodwill, and over Churchill's protest, the American forces withdrew from the occupation zone assigned to Russia at Yalta. Americans were still hopeful that the Yalta agreements would be carried out, at least after a fashion, and even more hopeful for Russian help against Japan.

Although the Russians admitted British and American observers to their sectors of eastern Europe, there was little the Western powers could do to prevent Russian control of the region even if they had not let their military forces dwindle. The presence of Soviet armed forces frustrated the efforts of non-Communists to gain political influence. Coalition governments appeared temporarily as an immediate postwar expedient, but the Communists followed a long-range strategy of ensconcing themselves in the interior ministries in order to control the police. Opposition political leaders found themselves under accusation, "confessions" were extorted, and the leaders of the opposition were either exiled, silenced, executed, or consigned to prison.

Secretary of State James F. Byrnes struggled on through 1946 with the problems of postwar settlements. As early as September 1945 the first meeting of the Council of Foreign Ministers broke up because of Byrnes's demand that the governments of Romania and Bulgaria be broadened. A series of almost interminable meetings of the Council of Foreign Ministers wrangled over border lines and reparations from Hitler's satellites, finally producing treaties for Italy, Hungary, Romania, Bulgaria, and Finland. The treaties, signed on February 10, 1947, in effect confirmed Russian control over eastern Europe, which in Russian eyes seemed but a parallel to American control in Japan and Western control over most of Germany and all of Italy. The Yalta guarantees of democracy in eastern Europe had turned out much like the Open Door Policy in China, little more than pious cant subordinate to the pressures of *Realpolitik*. Byrnes's impulse to pressure Russian diplomats by brandishing the atomic bomb only added to the irritations, intimidating no one.

The United States, together with Britain and Canada (partners in developing the atomic bomb), had exclusive possession of atomic weapons at the time, but in 1946 proposed to internationalize the control of atomic energy through a plan presented to the U.N. Atomic Energy Commission. Under the plan an International Atomic Development Authority would have a monopoly of atomic explosives and atomic energy. The Russians, fearing Western domination of the agency, proposed instead simply to outlaw the manufacture and use of atomic bombs, with enforcement vested in the Security Council and thus subject to a veto. Later they conceded the right of international inspection, but still refused to give up the veto, and the American government rejected the arrangement, which it considered a compromise of international control.

CONTAINMENT   By the beginning of 1947 relations with the Soviet Union had become more troubled. A year before, Stalin had already pronounced international peace impossible "under the present capitalist development of the world economy." His statement impelled George F. Kennan, counselor of the American embassy in Moscow, to send the secretary of state an 8,000-word dispatch in which he sketched the roots of Russian policy and warned that the Soviet Union was "committed fanatically to the belief that with the U.S. there can be no permanent *modus vivendi,* that it is desirable and necessary that the internal harmony of our society be disrupted, our traditional way of life be destroyed, the international authority of our state be broken, if Soviet power is to be secure."

More than a year later, by then back at the State Department in Washington, Kennan spelled out his ideas for a proper response to the Soviets in a July 1947 article published anonymously in *Foreign Affairs.* "It is clear," he wrote, "that the main element of any United States policy toward the Soviet Union must be that of a long-term, patient but firm and vigilant containment of Russian expansive tendencies. . . . such a policy has nothing to do with outward histrionics: with threats or blustering or superfluous gestures of outward 'toughness.' " Americans, he argued, could hope for a long-term moderation of Soviet ideology and policy, so that in time tensions with the West would lessen. There was a strong possibility "that Soviet power, like the capitalist world of its conception, bears within it the seeds of its own decay, and that the sprouting of those seeds is well advanced."

Kennan's containment strategy explained the new departure in American foreign policy which America's political leaders had already decided to take. Behind this shift lay a growing fear that

George F. Kennan, whose 1947 Foreign Affairs *article spelled out the doctrine of containment.*

Russian aims reached beyond eastern Europe, posing dangers in the eastern Mediterranean, the Middle East, and western Europe itself. The first major postwar crisis occurred in Iran, which borders the Soviet Union on the south and provided important trade routes to the USSR. Soviet troops had been stationed in northern Iran while British-American troops were in the south, and all were supposed to pull out six months after the war. But the Soviets remained beyond the deadline of March 2, 1946. The crisis finally blew over with a Russian withdrawal in early May.

Meanwhile the USSR was looking for a breakthrough into the Mediterranean, long important to Russia for purposes of trade and defense. After the war the USSR began to press Turkey for territorial concessions and the right to build naval bases on the Bosporus, an important gateway between the Black Sea and the Mediterranean. In August 1946 civil war broke out in Greece between a government backed by the British and a Communist-led faction which held the northern part of Greece and drew supplies from Yugoslavia, Bulgaria, and Albania. In February 1947 the British ambassador informed the American government that the British could no longer bear the economic and military burden of aiding Greece. When Truman conferred with congressional leaders on the situation, the chairman of the Senate Foreign Relations Committee recommended a strong appeal to the American people. On March 12, 1947, President Truman appeared before Congress to request $400 million for economic aid to both Greece and Turkey, and power to send American personnel to train their soldiers.

THE TRUMAN DOCTRINE AND THE MARSHALL PLAN   In his speech Truman stated what quickly came to be known as the Truman Doctrine, which justified aid to Greece and Turkey in terms more provocative than Kennan's idea of containment and more general than this specific case warranted. "I believe," Truman declared, "that it must be the policy of the United States to support free peoples who are resisting attempted subjugation by armed minorities or by outside pressures." In May 1947 Congress passed the Greek-Turkish aid bill, and by 1950 had spent $659 million on the program. Turkey achieved economic stability, and Greece defeated the Communist insurrection in October 1949, partly because President Tito of Yugoslavia had broken with the Russians in the summer of 1948 and ceased to aid the Greek Communists. But the principles embedded in the Truman Doctrine committed the United States to intervene throughout the world in order to "contain" the spread of communism, and this would produce tragic consequences as well as successes in the years to come.

The Truman Doctrine marked the beginning, or at least the open acknowledgment, of a contest which Bernard Baruch named in an April 1947 speech to the legislature of his native South Carolina: "Let us not be deceived—today we are in the midst of a cold war." Signs were growing that Greece and Turkey were but the front lines of an ideological struggle that would involve western Europe as well. There wartime damage and dislocation had devastated factory production, and severe drought in 1947, followed by a harsh winter, destroyed crops. Europe had become, in Winston Churchill's words, "a rubble heap, a charnel house, a breeding ground of pestilence and hate." Amid the chaos the Communist parties of France and Italy were flourishing, having gained credibility by working in the wartime resistance. Aid from the United Nations had staved off starvation, but had provided little basis for economic recovery.

In the spring of 1947 a State Department adviser reported to George C. Marshall, who had replaced Byrnes as secretary of state in January, that the United States had underestimated the extent of wartime damage in Europe. Only a program of massive aid could rescue western Europe from disaster. Late in May the Policy Planning Staff, under George Kennan, brought forth a plan which Secretary Marshall presented at the Harvard commencement on June 5. Taking Kennan's lead, Marshall avoided the ideological overtones of the Truman Doctrine. "Our policy," Marshall said, "is directed not against country or doctrine, but against hunger, poverty, despera-

George C. Marshall at the Harvard University commencement where he proposed the "Marshall Plan" for the reconstruction of Europe.

tion, and chaos." Marshall offered aid to all European countries, including Russia, and called upon them to take the lead in judging their own needs. On June 27 the foreign ministers of France, Britain, and Russia met in London to discuss Marshall's overture. Molotov arrived with eighty advisers, but during the talks he got word from Moscow to withdraw from this "imperialist" scheme. Two weeks later a meeting of delegates from western Europe formed a Committee of European Economic Cooperation (CEEC), which had a plan ready by September.

In December Truman submitted his proposal for the European Recovery Program to Congress. Two months later, a Communist coup d'état in Czechoslovakia ended the last remaining coalition government in eastern Europe. Coming less than ten years after Munich, the seizure of power in Prague assured congressional passage of the Marshall Plan. From 1948 until 1951 the Economic Cooperation Administration (ECA), which managed the Marshall Plan, poured $13 billion into European recovery through the CEEC.

DIVIDING GERMANY   The breakdown of the wartime alliance left the problem of postwar Germany unsettled. The German economy had stagnated, requiring the American army to carry a staggering burden of relief. Slowly, zones of occupation evolved into functioning governments. In February 1948 the British and Americans united their zones into what came to be called "Bizonia," which the French joined to create "Trizonia" in June. The West Germans were then invited to organize state governments and elect delegates to a federal constitutional convention.

Soviet reactions to the Marshall Plan and the unification of West Germany were sharp, and quickly focused on Berlin. In April 1948 the Russians began to restrict the flow of traffic into West Berlin; on June 23 they stopped all traffic. The blockade was designed to leave the Allies no choice but to give up either Berlin or the plan to unify West Germany. But the American commander in Germany proposed to stand firm. "When Berlin falls, Western Germany will be next," he told the Pentagon. "If we mean . . . to hold Europe against communism, we must not budge."

Truman agreed and, after considering the use of armed convoys to supply West Berlin, opted for a massive airlift. At the time this seemed an enormous and perhaps impossible task, requiring, according to one estimate, 4,500 tons of food and coal a day. But by quick work the Allied air forces brought in planes from around the world and by October 1948 were flying in nearly 5,000 tons of food and equipment a day. Altogether, from June 1948 to mid-May 1949 the Berlin Airlift carried in more than 1.5 million tons of supplies, or well over a half ton for each of the 2.2 million West Berliners. The

American commandant in Berlin meanwhile got in a few licks at his Soviet counterpart by cutting off a gas main that ran through the American sector to the Russian's house, forcing him to move. When Russian aides tried to truck their leader's furniture through the American zone, soldiers seized the furniture.

Finally, on May 12, 1949, after extended talks, the Russians lifted the blockade in return for a meeting of the Council of Foreign Ministers in Paris. This was purely a face-saving gesture, and the meeting resulted in no important decision on Germany. That same May, West Germany adopted a constitution, and before the end of the year the German Federal Republic had a government functioning under Chancellor Konrad Adenauer of the Christian Democratic party. At the end of May 1949 a German "Democratic" Republic arose in the eastern zone, formalizing the division of Germany. West Germany gradually acquired more authority, until the Western powers recognized its full sovereignty in 1955.

OCCUPATION OF GERMANY AND AUSTRIA

French zone   British zone   U.S. zone   Soviet zone

The Berlin Airlift. *An American airplane arrives in West Berlin with much-needed supplies, 1948.*

BUILDING NATO   As relations between the Soviets and western Europe chilled, transatlantic unity ripened into an outright military alliance. By March 1948, Britain, France, and the "Benelux" countries (Belgium, the Netherlands, and Luxembourg) had signed a fifty-year treaty of alliance and economic cooperation, the Brussels Pact. That June the Senate passed a resolution authorizing the administration to develop a collective defense pact under the U.N. charter. On April 4, 1949, the North Atlantic Treaty was signed at Washington by representatives of twelve nations: the five Brussels Pact countries plus the United States, Canada, Denmark, Iceland, Italy, Norway, and Portugal. Greece and Turkey joined the alliance in 1952, Germany in 1955, Spain in 1982.

The treaty pledged that an attack against any one of the signers would be considered an attack against all, and provided for a council of the North Atlantic Treaty Organization (NATO) which could establish other necessary agencies. In September 1950 the council decided to create an integrated defense force for western Europe and later named General Dwight Eisenhower to head the Supreme Headquarters of the Allied Powers in Europe (SHAPE). In 1955 the Warsaw Treaty Organization appeared as the eastern European counterpart to NATO. Senate ratification of the North Atlantic Treaty by a vote of 82 to 13 suggested that the isolationism of the prewar period no longer exerted a hold on the American people.

NATO, a hopeful sign for the West.

One other foreign policy decision with long-term consequences came during the eventful year 1948. Palestine, as the biblical Holy Land had come to be known, was under Turkish rule until the League of Nations made it a British mandate after World War I. Over the early years of the twentieth century many Zionists, who advocated a Jewish state in the region, had migrated there. More came after the British entered, and a greatly increased number came during the Nazi persecution in 1933 and after. Offered a promise by the British of a national homeland, the Jewish inhabitants demanded their own state.

Late in 1947 the U.N. General Assembly voted to partition Palestine into Jewish and Arab states, but this met fierce Arab opposition. Finally, the British mandate expired on May 14, 1948, and Jewish leaders proclaimed the independence of the state of Israel. President Truman, who had been in close touch with Jewish leaders, ordered recognition of the new state within minutes—the United States became the first nation so to act. The neighboring Arab states reacted by going to war against Israel, which, however, held its own. U.N. mediators gradually worked out truce agreements with Israel's Arab neighbors and an uneasy peace was restored by May 11, 1949, when Israel was admitted as a member of the United Nations. But the hard feelings and intermittent warfare between Israel and the Arab states have festered ever since, complicating American foreign policy, which has tried to maintain friendship with both sides.

HARRY GIVES 'EM HELL

SHAPING THE FAIR DEAL   The determination Truman projected in foreign affairs had not yet altered his image on the domestic front. By early 1948, after three years in the White House, Truman had yet to shake the impression that he was not up to the job. The columnists

Joseph and Stuart Alsop wrote before the Democratic convention that Truman would be running "the loneliest campaign in recent history." Rather than go with a loser, New Deal stalwarts and party regulars tried to draft General Eisenhower or Justice William O. Douglas, but in vain. The Democratic party seemed about to fragment: southern conservatives took umbrage at Truman's outspoken support of civil rights, while the left had flared up in 1946 over his firing of Secretary of Commerce Wallace after a speech critical of the administration's policy. "Getting tough," Wallace had argued, "never brought anything real and lasting—whether for schoolyard bullies or world powers. The tougher we get, the tougher the Russians will get." The left itself was splitting between the Progressive Citizens of America (PCA), formed in December 1946, which gave ear to Wallace, and the Americans for Democratic Action (ADA), formed in January 1947, which also criticized Truman but took a firm anti-Communist stance.

Unknown to all these groups, Truman had a game plan for 1948; it had been outlined in a long memorandum written by his aide, Clark Clifford, a young lawyer from St. Louis. Much of what later seemed desperate impulse actually followed Clifford's design, which urged an aggressive effort to shore up the New Deal coalition. Truman needed the midwestern and western farm belts, and happily had fairly strong support among farmers. In metropolitan areas the trick was to carry the labor and black vote, which Truman wooed by working closely with unions and liberals, and pressing the cause of civil rights. The Solid South, Clifford predicted, could be counted on to stay in the Democratic column. The Republicans would choose Thomas E. Dewey again, and Wallace, running on a third-party Progressive ticket, would be badly compromised by Communist support. With the South and West, Truman could afford to lose some New Deal strongholds in the East and still win. On nearly every point, Clifford called the turn. He erred chiefly in underrating the rebellion that took four Deep South states out of Truman's camp.

The grand new departure in Clifford's design was its forthright emphasis on civil rights—a politically advantageous issue now that so many blacks had migrated to northern cities in states with large electoral votes. Truman's motives in embracing the issue were complex. When in 1946 he appointed the President's Committee on Civil Rights, a panel of distinguished citizens, black and white, North and South, he acted not only in response to the pressures of black organizations, but out of outrage at several recent attacks on blacks. The committee's report, *To Secure These Rights* (1947), touched on virtually every category of racial discrimination and called for the "elimination of segregation based on race, color, creed, or national origin, from American life."

Like other presidents, Truman used his State of the Union message in January 1948 to set the agenda for an election year. The speech offered something to nearly every group the Democrats hoped to win over. The first goal, Truman said, was "to secure fully the essential human rights of our citizens" and he promised a special message later on civil rights. "To protect human resources," he asked for federal aid to education, increased and extended unemployment and retirement benefits, a comprehensive system of health insurance, more federal support for housing, and extension of rent controls. He continued to pile on the demands: for reclamation projects, more rural electrification, a higher minimum wage, laws to admit thousands of displaced persons to the United States, money for the Marshall Plan, and a "cost-of-living" tax credit. As one senator put it, the speech "raised all the ghosts of the old New Deal with new trappings that Tugwell and Harry Hopkins never thought of." On February 2 Congress received Truman's message on civil rights, which called for a broad range of actions, none of which he seriously hoped to get out of Congress. On July 26, 1948, however, he did ban racial discrimination in hiring federal employees, and four days later ordered an end to segregation in the armed forces.

THE 1948 ELECTION   The Republican Congress for the most part spurned the Truman program, an action it would later regret. Republican presidential hopefuls, scenting victory in November, entered a scramble for the nomination: Senator Taft, former Minnesota governor Harold E. Stassen, California governor Earl Warren, Governor Dewey, and an array of favorite sons. At the Philadelphia convention in June, Dewey won the nomination on the third ballot and designated Earl Warren as his running mate. The platform endorsed most of the New Deal reforms as accomplished fact and approved the administration's bipartisan foreign policy, but as Landon had in 1936 and Willkie had in 1940, promised to run things more efficiently.

In July a glum Democratic convention gathered in Philadelphia, expecting to do little more than go through the motions, only to find itself doubly surprised: first by the battle over the civil-rights plank, and then by Truman's acceptance speech. To keep from stirring southern hostility, the administration sought a platform plank that opposed discrimination only in general terms. ADA leaders, however, sponsored a plank that called on Congress for specific action and commended Truman "for his courageous stand on the issue of civil rights." Speaking last in favor of the change, Minneapolis mayor

The opening of the 1948 Democratic National Convention is marked by demonstrations against racial segregation, led by A. Philip Randolph (left).

Hubert H. Humphrey electrified the delegates and set off a ten-minute demonstration: "The time has arrived for the Democratic party to get out of the shadow of states' rights and walk forthrightly into the bright sunshine of human rights." Segregationist delegates from Alabama and Mississippi walked, instead, out of the convention.

After the convention had nominated Truman, and as his running mate Senator Alben Barkley, the president appeared on the rostrum during the wee hours of the morning to give his acceptance speech. It was a new Truman, showing a new fighting style in his speeches. To overcome Truman's tendency to read speeches in a flat drone, his staff encouraged him to talk off-the-cuff from an outline. "Senator Barkley and I will win this election and make the Republicans like it," he said, "don't you forget it!" Near the end he sprang a bombshell. On July 26, known in Missouri as "Turnip Day," he would call Congress back into session "to get the laws the people need," many of which the Republican platform had endorsed.

On July 17 a group of rebellious southern Democrats met in Birmingham and nominated South Carolina governor J. Storm Thurmond on a States' Rights Democratic ticket, quickly dubbed the "Dixiecrat" ticket. The Dixiecrats' dream was to draw enough elec-

The *"Dixiecrats"* nominate South Carolina governor J. Strom Thurmond to lead their ticket in the 1948 election.

toral votes to preclude a majority for either major party, throwing the election into the House where they might strike a sectional bargain like that of 1877. A few days later, on July 23, the left wing of the Democratic party gathered in Philadelphia to name Henry A. Wallace on a Progressive party ticket. These splits in the Democratic ranks seemed to spell the final blow to Truman. The special session of Congress petered out in futility.

But Truman, undaunted, set out on a 31,000-mile "whistle-stop" train tour during which he castigated the "do-nothing" Eightieth Congress to the accompaniment of cries from his audiences: "Pour it on, Harry!" and "Give 'em hell, Harry." And Harry would respond: "I don't give 'em hell. I just tell the truth and they think it's hell." Dewey, in contrast, ran a restrained campaign, designed to avoid rocking the boat. By so doing he may have snatched defeat from the jaws of victory. In trying to look "presidential," the dapper Dewey came across, in Alice Roosevelt Longworth's deadly simile, looking like the groom on the wedding cake. He deliberately studded his speeches with high-toned platitudes hailing the "creative genius" of a free people, damning the "prophets of gloom," and staying for the most part on what a reporter called "a high road of rich baritone homilies." In Phoenix he disclosed that "America's future—like yours in Arizona—is still ahead of us."

To the end the polls and the pundits predicted a sure win for Dewey, and most speculation centered on his cabinet choices. But on election day Truman chalked up the biggest upset in American history, taking 24.2 million votes (49.5 percent) to Dewey's 22 million (45.1 percent) and winning a thumping 303 to 189 margin in the electoral college. Thurmond and Wallace each got more than a million votes, but the revolt of right and left worked to Truman's advantage. The Dixiecrat rebellion reassured black voters who had questioned the Democrats' commitment to civil rights, while the Progressive movement made it hard to tag Truman as "soft on communism." Thurmond carried the four Deep South states in which his name was accompanied on the ballot by the Democratic party symbol (in Alabama one could not vote for Truman) and walked off with 39 electoral votes, including one from a Tennessee elector who repudiated his state's decision for Truman. Thurmond's success started a momentous disruption of the Democratic Solid South, which in a series of elections now divided its vote. But Truman's victory also carried Democratic majorities into Congress, where the new group of senators included Hubert Humphrey, Tennessee's Estes Kefauver, and by eighty-seven disputed votes, "Landslide Lyndon" B. Johnson of Texas.

The outcome seemed a vindication for the New Deal and a mandate for liberalism, and Truman so regarded it. "We have rejected the discredited theory that the fortunes of the nation should be in the hands of a privileged few," he said in January 1949. His State of the Union message repeated substantially the agenda he had set forth a year previously. "Every segment of our population and every individual," he said, "has a right to expect from his government a fair deal." Whether deliberately or not he had invented a tag, the "Fair Deal," to set off his program from the New Deal.

The president won some of his Fair Deal proposals, but they were mainly extensions or enlargements of New Deal programs already in place: a higher minimum wage, bringing more people under social

The Man Who "Done His Damndest." *Truman's victory in 1948 was a huge upset.*

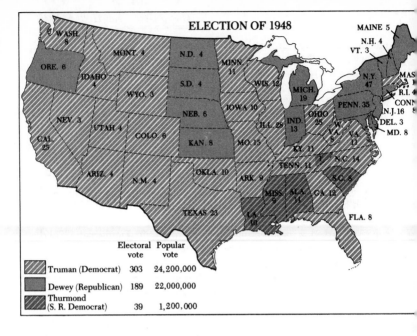

ELECTION OF 1948

	Electoral vote	Popular vote
Truman (Democrat)	303	24,200,000
Dewey (Republican)	189	22,000,000
Thurmond (S. R. Democrat)	39	1,200,000

security, extension of rent controls, farm price supports at 90 percent of parity, a sizable slum-clearance and public housing program, and more money for the Reclamation Bureau, the TVA, rural electrification, and farm housing. Despite Democratic majorities, however, the conservative coalition was able to resist any drastic new departures in domestic policy. Congress gave the cold shoulder to civil-rights bills, national health insurance, federal aid to education, and a plan to provide subsidies that would hold up farm incomes rather than farm prices. Congress also turned down Truman's demand for repeal of the Taft-Hartley Act.

THE COLD WAR HEATS UP

Global concerns, never far from center stage in the postwar world, plagued Truman's second term as they had his first. In his inaugural address Truman called for foreign policy to rest on four pillars: the United Nations, the Marshall Plan, NATO, and a "bold new plan" for technical assistance to underdeveloped parts of the world, a sort of global Marshall Plan which came to be known simply as "Point Four." This program to aid the postwar world began in 1950 with a modest outlay of $35 million. But it never accomplished its goals, in part because other international problems soon diverted Truman's attention.

"LOSING" CHINA AND THE BOMB   One of the most intractable problems, the China tangle, was fast coming unraveled in 1949. The Chinese Nationalists (Kuomintang) of Chiang Kai-shek had at first accepted the help of Communists, but expelled them from the ranks in 1927. When a new leader, Mao Tse-tung,° began to rebuild the Communist party by organizing the peasants instead of urban workers, the Nationalists drove him out of his stronghold in the south. After an arduous trek, which the Communists later celebrated as the "Long March" of 1934–1935, they entrenched themselves in northern China at Yenan. The outbreak of war with Japan in 1937 relieved them of pressure from the Nationalists, and at the same time enabled them to assume a patriotic stance by fighting the Japanese. During the war Roosevelt, and Stalin as well, believed that the Nationalists would organize China after the war.

The commanders of American forces in China during World War II concluded that Chiang's government was hopelessly corrupt, tyrannical, and inefficient. After the war, American forces nevertheless ferried Nationalist armies back into the eastern and northern provinces as the Japanese withdrew, and themselves temporarily occupied some of the major coastal cities in China. United States'

°The traditional (Wade-Giles) spelling is used here. In 1958 the Chinese government adopted the "pinyin" transliterations that became more widely used after Mao's death in 1976, so that, for example, Mao Tse-tung became Mao Zedong, and Peking became Beijing.

Mao Tse-tung on the march with Red Army troops in northern China, 1947.

policy during and immediately after the war was to promote peace between the factions in China, but sporadic civil war broke out late in 1945.

It soon became a losing fight for the Nationalists, as the Communists radicalized the land-hungry peasantry. By early 1949 the Communists were in Peking and headed southward. By the end of the year they had taken Canton, and the Nationalist government had fled to the island of Formosa, which it renamed Taiwan.

From 1945 through 1949 the United States had funneled some $2 billion in aid to the Nationalists, to no avail. Administration critics now asked bitterly: "Who lost China?" A State Department study blamed Chiang for his failure to hold the support of the Chinese people. In fact it is hard to imagine how the United States government could have prevented the outcome short of massive military intervention, which would have been very risky and unpopular. The United States continued to recognize the Nationalist government on Taiwan as the rightful government of China, delaying formal relations with Red China for thirty years. Seeking to shore up friendly regimes in Asia, in February 1950 the United States recognized the French-supported regime of Emperor Bao Dai in Vietnam and shortly afterward extended aid to the French in their battle against Ho Chi Minh's guerrillas there.

As the Communists gained control of China, American intelligence in September 1949 found an unusual radioactivity in the air, evidence that the Soviets had set off an atomic device. The American nuclear monopoly had lasted just four years, but under the umbrella of security that it seemed to offer, the wartime military establishment had been allowed to dwindle. In a crisis, this left American leaders the choice of doing nothing or cremating millions of people. The discovery of the Russian bomb provoked an intense reappraisal of the strategic balance in the world, causing Truman in 1950 to end a dispute among his scientific advisers by ordering the construction of a hydrogen bomb, a weapon far more frightful than those dropped on Japan, lest the Russians make one first. The discovery also led the National Security Council to produce a top-secret document that called for rebuilding conventional military forces to provide options other than nuclear war. This represented a major departure from America's time-honored aversion to keeping large standing armies in peacetime, and was an expensive proposition. But the American public was growing more receptive to the nation's world role, and an invasion of South Korea by Communist forces from the north clinched the issue for most.

WAR IN KOREA   The division of Korea at the end of World War II, like the division of Germany, began as a temporary expedient and

THE KOREAN WAR, 1950

CHINA
MANCHURIA
Vladivostok
U.S.S.R.
Yalu R.
Chosan
NORTH KOREA
SEA OF JAPAN
Pyongyang
NORTH KOREAN OFFENSIVE, JUNE-SEPT. 1950
38°
Inchon Seoul
SOUTH KOREA
YELLOW SEA
U.N. POSITION SEPT. 1950
Pusan
KOREA STRAIT
0   100 Miles
0   100 Kilometers

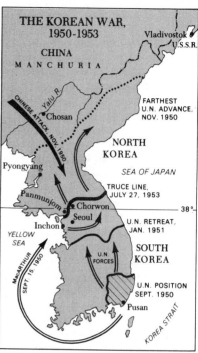

THE KOREAN WAR, 1950-1953

CHINA
MANCHURIA
Vladivostok
U.S.S.R.
CHINESE ATTACK NOV. 1950
Yalu R.
Chosan
FARTHEST U.N. ADVANCE, NOV. 1950
NORTH KOREA
SEA OF JAPAN
Pyongyang
Panmunjom
Chorwon
TRUCE LINE, JULY 27, 1953
38°
Inchon Seoul
YELLOW SEA
MacArthur SEPT. 15, 1950
U.N. RETREAT, JAN. 1951
U.N. FORCES
SOUTH KOREA
U.N. POSITION SEPT. 1950
Pusan
KOREA STRAIT

ended as a permanent fact. In the hectic days of August 1945 a State-War-Navy Coordinating Committee adopted a hasty proposal to divide Korea at the 38th parallel. The Soviets accepted, to the surprise of American officials involved. Since they bordered on Korea, the Russians could quickly have occupied the whole country. With the onset of the Cold War, it became clear that agreement on unification was no more likely in Korea than in Germany, and by the end of 1948 separate regimes had appeared in the two sectors and occupation forces had withdrawn. American leaders then inadvertently may have given false impressions to the Communists. General MacArthur during 1949 and Secretary of State Dean Acheson in January 1950 omitted both Korea and Formosa (Taiwan) from an American defense perimeter which included the Philippines, the Ryukyu Islands, and Japan. The weakened state of the American military contributed to the impression that South Korea was vulnerable.

For whatever reasons, North Korean forces crossed the boundary on June 25, 1950, and swept down the peninsula. President Truman responded decisively. Korea might have been outside America's defense perimeter, but its southern tip was dangerously close to Japan. Besides, American policy was still much subject to what might be called the "Munich syndrome," or what MacArthur called "history's clear lesson . . . that appeasement but begets new and bloodier war." Failure to act, Truman reasoned, would embolden Communist leaders "to override nations closer to our own shores."

An emergency meeting of the U.N. Security Council quickly censured the North Korean "breach of peace." The Soviet delegate, who held a veto power, was at the time boycotting the council because it would not seat Red China in place of Nationalist China. On June 27, its first resolution having been ignored, the Security Council called on U.N. members to "furnish such assistance to the Republic of Korea as may be necessary to repel the armed attack and to restore international peace and security in the area." Truman ordered American air, naval, and ground forces into action. In all, some fourteen other U.N. members sent in military units, the largest from Britain and Turkey, and five sent medical units. Later, when the U.N. voted a unified command, General MacArthur was designated to take charge. The war remained chiefly an American affair, and one that set a precedent of profound consequence: war by order of the president rather than by vote of Congress. It had the sanction of the U.N. Security Council, to be sure, and could technically be considered a "police action," not a war. And other presidents had ordered American troops into action without a declaration of war, but never on such a scale.

For three months the fighting went badly indeed for the Republic of Korea (ROK) and U.N. forces. By September they were barely hanging on to the Pusan perimeter in the southeast corner of Korea. Then, in a brilliant ploy, on September 15, 1950, MacArthur landed a new force to the North Korean rear at Inchon, port city of Seoul. Synchronized with a breakout from Pusan, the sudden blow stampeded the enemy back across the border. At this point, MacArthur convinced Truman to allow him to push on and seek to reunify Korea. The Russian delegate was back in the Security Council, wielding his veto, so on October 7 the United States won approval for this course from the U.N. General Assembly, where the veto did not apply. United States forces had already crossed the boundary by October 1, and now continued northward against minimal resistance. President Truman, concerned over broad hints of intervention by Red China, flew to Wake Island for a conference with General MacArthur on October 15. There the general discounted chances that the Red Army would act, but if it did, he predicted "there would be the greatest slaughter."

That same day Peking announced that China "cannot stand idly by." But by October 20 U.N. forces had entered Pyongyang, the North Korean capital, and on October 26 advance units had reached Chosan on the Yalu River border with China. MacArthur predicted

U.N. forces recapture Seoul from the North Koreans, September 1950.

total victory by Christmas. But on the night of November 25 Chinese "volunteers" counterattacked, and massive "human wave" attacks, with the support of tanks and planes, turned the tables on the U.N. forces, sending them into a desperate retreat just at the onset of winter. It had become "an entirely new war," MacArthur said. Soon he was putting out word that the fault for the war's continuance lay with the administration for requiring that he conduct a limited war. He proposed air raids on China's "privileged sanctuary" in Manchuria, a blockade of China, and an invasion of the mainland by the Taiwan Nationalists. MacArthur seemed to have forgotten altogether his one-time reluctance to bog the country down in a major war on the Asian mainland.

Truman stood against leading the United States into the "gigantic booby trap" of war with China, and the U.N. forces soon rallied. By January 1951 U.N. troops under General Matthew B. Ridgway finally secured their lines below Seoul, and then launched a counterattack that in some places carried them back across the 38th parallel in March. When Truman seized the chance and offered negotiations to restore the boundary, MacArthur undermined the move by issuing an ultimatum for China to make peace or be attacked. Truman decided then that MacArthur would have to go. On April 5, on the floor of the House, the Republican minority leader read a letter in which MacArthur criticized the president and said that "there is no substitute for victory." Such an act of open insubordination left the commander-in-chief no choice but to accept MacArthur's policy or fire him. Civilian control of the military was at stake, Truman later said, and he did not let it remain at stake very long. The Joint Chiefs of Staff all backed the decision, and on April 11, 1951, the president removed MacArthur from all his commands and replaced him with Ridgway.

Truman's action ignited an immediate uproar in the country, and a tumultuous reception greeted MacArthur upon his return home for the first time since 1937. MacArthur's speech to a joint session of Congress provided the climactic event. "Once war is forced upon us," he said, "there is no alternative than to apply every available means to bring it to a swift end. War's very object is victory.... Why, my soldiers asked of me, surrender military advantages to an enemy in the field? I could not answer them." MacArthur ended the speech in memorable fashion. He recalled a barracks ballad of his youth "which proclaimed most proudly that old soldiers never die, they just fade away." And like the old soldiers of that ballad, he said, "I now close my military career and just fade away, an old soldier who tried to do his duty as God gave him the light to see that duty." A Senate investigation brought out the administration's arguments, best sum-marized by General Omar Bradley, chairman of the Joint Chiefs of Staff. "Taking on Red China," he said, would lead only "to a larger deadlock at greater expense." The MacArthur strategy "would in-volve us in the wrong war at the wrong place at the wrong time and with the wrong enemy." Americans, nurtured on classic Western showdowns in which good always triumphed over evil, found the logic of limited war hard to take, but also found the logic of General Bradley persuasive.

On June 24, 1951, the Soviet representative at the United Nations proposed a cease-fire and armistice along the 38th parallel; Secre-

"The Heat Is On." *Truman's firing of MacArthur was unpopular with the American public.*

tary of State Acheson accepted in principle a few days later with the consent of the United Nations. China and North Korea responded favorably—at the time General Ridgway's "meat-grinder" offensive was inflicting severe losses—and truce talks started on July 10, 1951, at Panmunjom, only to drag out for another two years while the fighting continued. The chief snags were prisoner exchanges and the insistence of South Korean president Syngman Rhee on unification. By the time a truce was finally reached on July 27, 1953, Truman had relinquished the White House to Dwight D. Eisenhower. The truce line followed the front at that time, mostly a little north of the 38th parallel, with a demilitarized zone of 2½ miles separating the forces; repatriation of prisoners would be voluntary, supervised by a neutral commission. No final peace conference ever took place, and Korea, like Germany, remained divided. The war had cost the United States more than 33,000 battle deaths and 103,000 wounded and missing. South Korean casualties, all told, were about 1 million, and North Korean and Chinese casualties an estimated 1.5 million.

ANOTHER RED SCARE In calculating the costs of the Korean War one must add in the far-reaching consequences of the Second Red Scare, which had grown since 1945 as the domestic counterpart to the Cold War abroad and reached a crescendo during the Korean conflict. Since 1938, a House Committee on Un-American Activities had kept up a drumbeat of accusations about subversives in government. In 1945 government agents found that secret American documents had turned up in the offices of a Communist-sponsored magazine, and more dramatic revelations came from a Canadian royal commission which uncovered several spy rings in the Canadian bureaucracy. On March 21, 1947, just nine days after the president announced the Truman Doctrine, he signed an executive order setting up procedures for an employee loyalty program in the federal government. Every person entering civil employ would be subject to a background investigation. By early 1951 the Civil Service Commission had cleared over 3 million people, while over 2,000 had resigned and 212 had been dismissed for doubtful loyalty, but no espionage ring was uncovered. The program covered all government employees, not just those in sensitive positions.

The Truman program was designed partly if not mainly to protect the president's political flank, but it failed of that purpose, mainly because of disclosures of earlier Communist penetrations into government that were few in number but sensational in character. The loyalty review program may in fact have heightened the politically explosive hysteria over Communist infiltration.

Perhaps the single case most damaging to the administration involved Alger Hiss, president of the Carnegie Endowment for International Peace, who had served in several government departments, and while in the State Department had been secretary-general of the United Nations charter conference. Whittaker Chambers, a former Soviet agent and later an editor of *Time* magazine, told the House Un-American Activities Committee in 1948 that Hiss had given him secret documents ten years earlier, when Chambers worked for the Soviets. Hiss sued for libel, and Chambers produced microfilms of the State Department documents he said Hiss had passed on to him. Before a federal grand jury Hiss denied the accusation, whereupon he was indicted for perjury and, after one mistrial, convicted in January 1950. The charge was perjury, but he was convicted of lying about espionage—for which he could not be tried because the statute of limitations on the crime had expired.

Most damaging to the administration was the fact that President Truman, taking at face value the many testimonials to Hiss's integrity, called the charges against him a "red herring." Secretary of State Acheson compounded the damage when, meaning to express compassion, he said: "I do not intend to turn my back on Alger Hiss." The Hiss affair had another political consequence: it raised to national prominence a young California congressman, Richard M. Nixon, who doggedly insisted on pursuing the case and then exploited an anti-Communist stance to win election to the Senate in 1950.

More cases surfaced. In 1949 eleven top Communist party leaders were convicted under the Smith Act of 1940, which outlawed any conspiracy to advocate the overthrow of the government. The Supreme Court upheld the law under the doctrine of a "clear and present danger," which overrode the right to free speech. What was more, in 1950 the government unearthed the existence of a British-American spy network that had fed information about the development of the atomic bomb to Russia. These disclosures led to the arrest of, among others, Klaus Fuchs in Britain and Julius and Ethel Rosenberg in the United States. The Rosenbergs, convicted of espionage, were executed in 1953.

MCCARTHY'S WITCH-HUNT   Such revelations encouraged politicians to exploit public fears. If a man of such respectability as Hiss were guilty, many wondered, who then could be trusted? The United States, which bestrode the world like a colossus in 1945, had since "lost" eastern Europe and Asia, and "lost" its atomic secrets to Russia. (Physicists, however, insisted that there was nothing secret about the basic principles underlying the bomb.) Early in 1950 the hitherto obscure Republican senator Joseph R. McCarthy of Wisconsin suddenly surfaced as the shrewdest and most ruthless exploiter of such anxieties. Seeking a way to augment his chances of reelection in 1952, he took up the cause, or at least the pose, of anticommunism. He began with a speech at Wheeling, West Virginia, on February 9, 1950, in which he said that the State Department was infested with Communists and that he held in his hand a list of their names. Later there was confusion as to whether he had said 205, 81, 57, or "a lot" of names, and even whether the sheet of paper carried a list. But such confusion always pursued McCarthy's charges.

Challenged to provide names, he finally pointed to Owen Lattimore of the Johns Hopkins University, an Asia expert, as head of "the espionage ring in the State Department." A special committee under Senator Millard Tydings looked into the matter and pronounced McCarthy's charges "a fraud and a hoax." McCarthy then turned, in what became his common tactic, to other charges, other names. Whenever his charges were refuted, he loosed a scattershot of new charges. In his hit-and-run tactics, McCarthy displayed the instincts of Shakespeare's Iago, planting suspicions without proof and growing ever more impudent. "He lied with wild abandon," one commentator wrote; "he lied without evident fear; . . . he lied vividly and with bold imagination; he lied, often, with very little pretense of telling the truth."

Despite all of his outlandish claims, McCarthy never uncovered a single Communist agent in government. But with the United States at war with Korean Communists in mid-1950, he mobilized true believers. In the elections of 1950 he intervened in Maryland and helped defeat the conservative Tydings with trumped-up charges that Tydings was pro-Communist. Republicans encouraged him to keep up the game. By 1951 he was riding so high as to list General George C. Marshall among the disloyal. His smear campaign went unchallenged until the end of the Korean War.

Under the influence of anti-Communist hysteria the Congress in 1950 passed the McCarran Internal Security Act over President Truman's veto. The act made it unlawful "to combine, conspire, or agree with any other person to perform any act which would sub-

Senator Joseph McCarthy.

stantially contribute to . . . the establishment of a totalitarian dictatorship." Communist and Communist-front organizations had to register with the attorney-general. Aliens who had belonged to totalitarian parties were barred from admission to the United States, a provision that discouraged any temptation for Communists to defect to the United States.

The McCarran Act, Truman said in his veto message, would "put the Government into the business of thought control." He might in fact have said as much about the Smith Act of 1940, or even his own program of loyalty investigations. In the mid-1950s, looking back over the recent era of hysteria, a former adviser in the Hoover administration said, "in reality we have been establishing something like a new system of preventive law applicable to the field of ideas and essentially different from traditional American procedures."

During the late summer of 1951, while the off-and-on peace negotiations continued in Korea, the United States buttressed its defense perimeter through treaties with offshore allies which, just six years after the end of World War II, now included Japan. On September 8, 1951, in the San Francisco Opera House, the United States and forty-eight other nations—the USSR declined to participate—signed a peace treaty with Japan, which recognized restoration of Japan's sovereignty but stripped the empire of all claims to Korea, Formosa, the Pescadores, the Kuriles, Sakhalin, and the Pacific islands formerly held under League of Nations mandate. These, along with the Ryukyu and Bonin Islands, now passed to a U.N. trusteeship under the United States. By another treaty signed with Japan that same day, the United States was permitted to maintain armed forces in the defeated country. Just a week earlier, on September 1, as the delegates gathered for the peace conference, the United States, Australia, and New Zealand entered a Tripartite Security Treaty which provided for mutual defense. Two days before that, on August 30, the presidents of the United States and the Philippines signed a similar agreement in Washington.

ASSESSING THE COLD WAR   In retrospect the onset of the Cold War takes on an appearance of terrible inevitability. American and Soviet misunderstanding of each other's motives was virtually unavoidable. America's preference for international principles, such as self-determination and democracy, conflicted with Stalin's preference for international spheres of influence. Russia, after all, had been invaded by Germany twice in the first half of the twentieth century, and Soviet leaders wanted tame buffer states on their borders for protection. The people of eastern Europe, as usual, were caught in the middle. But the Communists themselves held to a universal principle: world revolution. And since the time of President Monroe,

Americans had bristled at the thought of foreign intervention in their own sphere of influence, the Western Hemisphere.

If international conditions set the stage for the Cold War, the actions of political leaders and thinkers set events in motion. President Truman may have erred in seeming to include all the world in his 1947 doctrine. The loyalty program, following on the heels of the Truman Doctrine, may have spurred on the anti-Communist hysteria of the times. Containment itself proved hard to contain, its author later confessed, in part because he failed at the outset to spell out its limits explicitly. "Repeatedly," George Kennan wrote in his *Memoirs*, "I expressed in talks and lectures the view that there were only five regions of the world—the United States, the United Kingdom, the Rhine Valley with adjacent industrial areas, the Soviet Union, and Japan—where the sinews of military strength could be produced in quantity; I pointed out that only one of these was under Communist control; and I defined the main task of containment, accordingly, as one of seeing to it that none of the remaining ones fell under its control."

The years after World War II were unlike any other postwar period in American history. Having taken on global burdens, the nation had become, if not a "garrison state," at least a country committed to a major and permanent National Military Establishment, along with the attendant National Security Council, Central Intelligence Agency, and by presidential directive in 1952, the enormous National Security Agency, entrusted with monitoring of media and communications for foreign intelligence. The policy initiatives of the Truman years had led the country to abandon its long-standing aversion to peacetime alliances not only in the NATO pact but in other agreements with Japan, the Philippines, and the other American states. It was a far cry from the world of 1796, when George Washington in his Farewell Address warned his countrymen against "those overgrown military establishments which . . . are inauspicious to liberty" and advised his country "to steer clear of permanent alliances with any portion of the foreign world." But, then, Washington had warned only against participation in the "ordinary" combinations and collisions of Europe, and surely the postwar years had seen extraordinary events.

FURTHER READING

The Cold War, like Reconstruction, is an area of American history still hotly debated by scholars. Traditional interpretations by Herbert Feis in *From Trust to Terror: The Onset of the Cold War, 1945–1950* (1970) and John L. Gaddis in *The United States and the Origins of the Cold War,*

1941–1947 (1972)° can be balanced with the revisionists Walter LaFeber in *America, Russia, and the Cold War, 1945–1980* (1981)° and Gabriel Kolko in *The Limits of Power: The World and United States Foreign Policy, 1945–1954* (1972).

Other scholars concentrate on more specific events in the buildup of international tensions. Lynn Etheridge Davis's *The Cold War Begins: Soviet-American Conflict over Eastern Europe* (1974) and Bruce Kuklick's *American Policy and the Division of Germany* (1972) deal with initial tensions at the close of the war. Feis's *Between War and Peace: The Potsdam Conference* (1960) examines Truman's attitude. For the Truman administration's reliance on the atomic bomb monopoly, see Michael Mandelbaum's *The Nuclear Question: The United States and Nuclear Weapons, 1946–1976* (1979) and Daniel Yergin's *Shattered Peace: The Origins of the Cold War and the National Security State* (1977).° On the proposer of the Marshall Plan, see Mark A. Stoler's *George C. Marshall: Soldier-Statesman of the American Century* (1989).

Two favorable biographies of Truman are Margaret Truman's *Harry S. Truman* (1973) and Merle Miller's *Plain Speaking: An Oral Biography of Harry S. Truman* (1974).° Other scholars view Truman through his activities as president; they include Robert J. Donovan's *Conflict and Crisis: The Presidency of Truman, 1945–1948* (1977)° and Alonzo L. Hamby's *Beyond the New Deal: Harry S. Truman and American Liberalism* (1973).

The domestic policies of the Fair Deal receive analysis in William C. Berman's *The Politics of Civil Rights in the Truman Administration* (1970), Richard M. Dalfiumes's *Desegregation of the United States Armed Forces* (1969), and Maeva Marcus's *Truman and the Steel Seizure* (1977).

For an introduction to the tensions in Asia, see Akira Iriye's *The Cold War in Asia* (1974). More specific to China are E. J. Kahn, Jr.'s *The China Hands: America's Foreign Service Officers and What Befell Them* (1975) and Kenneth E. Shewmaker's *Americans and the Chinese Communists, 1927–1945* (1971). For the Korean conflict, see Callum A. MacDonald's *Korea: The War before Vietnam* (1986). The high-command perspective is shown in Michael Schaller's *Douglas MacArthur: The Far Eastern General* (1989) and John W. Spanier's *The Truman-MacArthur Controversy* (1965).

The anti-Communist syndrome which helped produce McCarthy is surveyed in David Caute's *The Great Fear: The Anti-Communist Purge under Truman and Eisenhower* (1978).° Thomas C. Reeves's *The Life and Times of Joe McCarthy* (1982)° covers McCarthy himself. For the Rosenberg trial, consult Walter and Miriam Schneir's *Invitation to an Inquest* (1972). Allen Weinstein's *Perjury! The Hiss-Chambers Conflict* (1978)° covers that subject well.

°These books are available in paperback editions.

32

THROUGH THE PICTURE WINDOW: SOCIETY AND CULTURE, 1945–1960

The United States emerged from World War II elated, justifiably proud of its military strength and industrial might. As the editors of *Fortune* magazine proclaimed in 1946, "This is a dream era, this is what everyone was waiting through the blackouts for. The Great American Boom is on." So it was, from babies to Buicks to Admiral television sets. An American public that had known mostly deprivation and sacrifice for the last decade and a half began to enjoy unprecedented prosperity. The postwar era was one of tremendous economic growth and rising social contentment. Divorce and homicide rates fell, the birth rate soared, and the prevailing mood of the country was aggressively upbeat.

Yet in the midst of such rising affluence and comfortable domesticity, many social critics, writers, and artists expressed a growing sense of unease. Was postwar American society becoming too complacent, too conformist, too materialistic? That such questions were being asked reflected the perennial tension in American life between idealism and materialism, a tension that arrived with the first settlers and remains with us today. Americans have always struggled to accumulate goods and cultivate goodness. During the postwar era the nation again tried to do both. And for a while, at least, it appeared to succeed.

PEOPLE OF PLENTY

THE POSTWAR ECONOMY The dominant feature of post–World War II American society was its remarkable prosperity. After a surprisingly brief postwar recession, the economy soared to record heights.

1259

The gross national product (GNP) nearly doubled between 1945 and 1960, and the 1960s witnessed an even more spectacular expansion of the economy. The industrial sector was producing a feast of goods and services and the highest standard of living ever achieved by so many people in the history of the planet. By 1970 the gap between living standards in the United States and the rest of the world had become a chasm: with 6 percent of the world's population, America produced and consumed two-thirds of the world's goods.

During the 1950s government officials assured the citizenry that they should not fear another economic collapse. "Never again shall we allow a depression in the United States," President Eisenhower promised. This was not just political rhetoric. The leading economists of the postwar era likewise agreed that with the New Deal safeguards built into the economy there need be no more dramatic downturns. They and others led the public to believe that perpetual economic growth was possible, desirable, and, in fact, essential. The expectation of unending plenty became the reigning assumption of social thought in the postwar era.

Several factors contributed to this prolonged economic surge. The massive federal expenditures for military needs during World War II had catapulted the economy out of the Great Depression. They were renewed in the postwar era, thanks to the tensions generated by the Cold War and, in the early 1950s, the increase in defense spending provoked by the Korean conflict. Defense spending after 1945 represented the single most important stimulant to the postwar economic boom. Military-related research also helped spawn the new glamour industries of the postwar era: chemicals, electronics, and aviation.

Most of the other major industrial nations of the world—England, France, Germany, Japan, Russia—had been physically devastated during the war, which meant that American manufacturers enjoyed a virtual monopoly over international trade. In addition, technological innovations contributed to the "automation" of the workplace and thereby created spectacular increases in productivity. The widespread use of new and more efficient machinery and computers led to a 35 percent jump in worker productivity between 1945 and 1955. In 1945 it took 310 hours to make a car; in 1960, only 150.

The major catalyst in promoting economic expansion after 1945 was the unleashing of pent-up consumer demand. During the war Americans had postponed purchases of such major items as cars and houses and in the process had saved over $150 billion. Now they were eager to buy. Likewise, many young couples who had delayed having children were intent on making up for lost time. The United States after World War II thus experienced both a purchasing frenzy and a population explosion.

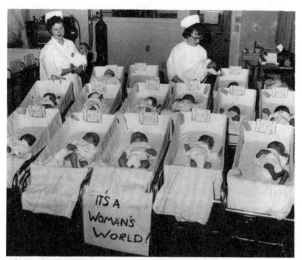

The Baby Boom. *Much of America's social history since the 1940s has been the story of the "baby-boom" generation.*

The return of some 15 million soldiers to private life helped generate a postwar "baby boom," which peaked in 1957. Between 1945 and 1960 America's total population grew by some 40 million, an increase of almost 30 percent. Large families were back in style. When asked why he wanted six children, a Harvard University senior replied that it was a "minimum production goal." Much of America's social history since the 1940s has been the story of the unusually large "baby-boom" generation and its progress through the stages of life. The initial effect of the baby-boom generation was to create a massive demand for diapers, baby food, toys, medicines, schools, books, teachers, and housing.

AN EXPANDING CONSUMER CULTURE American factories soon adjusted to new consumer demands. Native and foreign observers alike marveled at the widespread abundance generated by America's prolific industrial plant. In 1950 almost 37 percent of American homes were deemed substandard; in 1970 only 9 percent. The proportion of homeowners in the population increased by 50 percent between 1945 and 1960. And those new homes filled up with the latest appliances—refrigerators, washing machines, sewing machines, vacuum cleaners, freezers, electric mixers, carving knives, shoe polishers.

By far the most popular new household product was the television set. In 1946 there were only 7,000 primitive black-and-white television sets in the country; by 1960 there were 50 million high-quality sets. Nine out of ten homes had one, and by 1970, 38 percent owned one of the new color sets. *TV Guide* was the fastest-growing new periodical of the 1950s. In 1953 *Business Week* noted that city engineers across the country had been befuddled by erratic surges in water consumption during the evening hours, only to discover that Americans were using their bathrooms at the end of television shows and during commercials. And with the development of frozen "TV" dinners and "TV" trays, families no longer had to assemble around a common dinner table; they could eat while watching favorite shows. Television thus had a transforming effect on the patterns of daily living. Time previously devoted to reading, visiting, playing, or moviegoing was now spent in front of the "electronic hearth." Television, one social commentator recognized in 1950, "is even upsetting the established patterns of courtship and the marketing of beer." Said one housewife, "Until we got that TV set, I thought my husband had forgotten how to neck."

What differentiated the affluence of the post–World War II era from earlier periods of prosperity was its ever-widening dispersion. Although pockets of rural and urban poverty persisted, destined to explode in the 1960s, during the Eisenhower years few noticed such exceptions to the prevailing prosperity. "Pronged antennas, the

"I Love Lucy," starring Lucille Ball (right), *was one of the most popular television series in the 1950s.*

proud badge of TV ownership," observed one reporter, "sprout like antlers from all kinds of roofs." Weekly visits to beauty parlors and shopping centers became routine activities for working-class house-wives, and families with two cars were not uncommon. Many boasted a boat or camper as well. When George Meany was sworn in as head of the AFL-CIO in 1955, he proclaimed that "American labor never had it so good." Such widespread plenty was a source of great national pride, especially in the midst of the Cold War. *Life* magazine gleefully reported shoppers filling a "$5 million grocery store, picking from the thousands of items on the high-piled shelves until their carts became cornucopias filled with an abundance that no other country in the world had ever known."

To perpetuate the postwar prosperity, economists repeated the basic marketing strategy of the 1920s: the public must be taught to consume more and expect more. Experts knew that Americans had more money than ever before. The average consumer had twice as much *real* income in 1955 as in the rosy days of the late 1920s before the Crash. Still, many adults who had undergone the severities of the Great Depression and the rationing required for the war effort had to be weaned from a decade and a half of imposed frugality in order to nourish the consumer culture. A motivational researcher told a business group that the fundamental challenge facing the modern capitalist economy was to demonstrate to the consumer that "the hedonistic approach to life is a moral, not an immoral one."

Marketing specialists accelerated their efforts to engineer a revo-lution of rising expectations and self-gratification. As Vance Packard demonstrated in *The Waste Makers* (1960), packaging emerged as an ever-more seductive art form in the 1950s, and planned obsoles-cence became a guiding principle for many manufacturers. A promi-nent department store executive insisted that "basic utility cannot be the foundation of a prosperous apparel industry. We must accelerate obsolescence." He advised others in his industry that the primary purpose of their marketing efforts should be "to make women un-happy with what they have. . . . We must make these women so unhappy that their husbands can find no happiness or peace in their excessive savings."

Advertising became an even more crucial component of the con-sumer culture, and during the postwar era advertisers proved much more adept at exciting consumer desires and social envy. An adver-tisement for Ford automobiles assured customers that "you'll bask in the envious glances which Ford's Thunderbird styling draws." It then added, "Why not own two?" Manufacturers were quick to recognize the power of television, and TV advertising expenditures increased 1,000 percent during the 1950s. Such startling results led

Mink Coat for Father. *An advertisement for a Ford Thunderbird claims that "What a mink coat does to perk up a lady, a Thunderbird does for a male."*

the president of the National Broadcasting Company (NBC) to claim in 1956 that the primary reason for the postwar economic boom was that "advertising has created an American frame of mind that makes people want more things, better things, and newer things."

Paying for such "things" was no problem; the age of the credit card had arrived. Between 1945 and 1957, consumer credit soared 800 percent. Where families in other industrialized nations were typically saving 10–20 percent of their income, American families by the 1960s were saving only 5 percent. "Never before have so many owed so much to so many," *Newsweek* announced in 1953. "Time has swept away the Puritan conception of immorality in debt and godliness in thrift." President Eisenhower reflected this attitude when he advised the public during a slight business dip: "Buy anything."

This consumer revolution had far-reaching cultural effects. Shopping became a major recreational activity. In 1945 there were only 8 shopping centers in the entire country; by 1960 there were 3,840. Much as life in a medieval town revolved around the cathedral, life in postwar America seemed to center on the new giant shopping centers and malls. Playwright Arthur Miller addressed this phenomenon in *The Price:*

> Because you see the main thing today is—shopping. Years ago a person, if he was unhappy, didn't know what to do with himself—he'd go to

church, start a revolution—*something*. Today you're unhappy? Can't figure it out? What is the salvation? Go shopping.

Shopping became increasingly important for young Americans. By the late 1950s the "baby-boom" generation was entering its teens, and the disproportionate number of adolescents in the population generated a vast new specialized market for goods ranging from transistor radios, Hula Hoops, and "rock-and-roll" records to cameras, surfboards, *Seventeen* magazine, and Pat Boone movies. Most teenagers had far more discretionary income than previous generations. "Today," explained a corporate executive in 1957, "the teenager's income runs to $10 to $15 a week as opposed to $1 to $2 fifteen years ago. It is getting to the point where nearly every teenager has a radio or phonograph, and, in many cases, more than one." Teenagers in the postwar era knew nothing of economic depressions or wartime rationing; immersed in abundance from an early age, the children of prospering parents took the notion of carefree consumption for granted. As a fifteen-year-old Los Angeles girl described her use of a $65 monthly allowance, "I have to save $10, but the rest is mine to do what I want with. I spend about $40 on clothes and the rest on records and jewelry. All the teenagers are on that swing. We just find it neat to spend money."

Elvis Presley, 1956. *The teenage children of middle-class America made rock 'n' roll a thriving industry in the 1950s, and Elvis its first star.*

THE CRABGRASS FRONTIER   One reason there were so many new shopping centers was that the burgeoning population was creating new communities and requiring an array of new services. Almost the entire population increase of the 1950s and 1960s (97 percent) was an urban and suburban phenomenon. Dramatic new technological advances in agricultural production reduced the need for manual laborers and thereby accelerated the flight from the farm in the postwar years: 20 million Americans left the land for the city between 1940 and 1970.

Much of the urban population growth occurred in the South, the Southwest, and the West, in an arc that stretched from the Carolinas down through Texas and into California, diverse states that by the 1970s were being lumped together into the "Sunbelt." Air conditioning, developed by Willis Haviland Carrier in the first decade of the century, became a common household fixture in the 1950s and enhanced the appeal of warm climates. But the Northeast remained the most densely populated area; by the early 1960s, 20 percent of the national population lived in the corridor that stretched from Boston to Norfolk, Virginia.

While more concentrated in cities, Americans were simultaneously spreading out within metropolitan areas. In 1950 the Census Bureau redefined the term "urban" to include suburbs as well as central cities. During the 1950s suburbs grew six times faster than cities. By 1970 more Americans lived in suburbs (76 million) than in central cities (64 million). "Suburbia," proclaimed the *Christian Century* in 1955, "is now a dominant social group in American life." During the 1950s some 3,000 acres of grassland and forests were bulldozed each day to make room for new suburban developments.

William Levitt, a brassy New York developer, led the suburban revolution. Born in Brooklyn in 1907, he dropped out of New York University because "I got itchy. I wanted to make a lot of money. I wanted a big car and a lot of clothes." He got his wish. Levitt and his brother made a fortune during the depression by building houses. But the Levitts really struck it rich after the war, when the demand for new housing skyrocketed, and they developed an efficient system of mass production. In 1947, on 1,200 flat acres of Long Island farmland, they built 10,600 houses which were immediately sold and inhabited by more than 40,000 people—mostly young adults under thirty-five and their children. "Everyone is so young," one Levittowner noted, "that sometimes it's hard to remember how to get along with older people."

Within a few years there were similar Levittowns in Pennsylvania and New Jersey, and other developers soon followed suit in places such as Lakewood, near Long Beach, California, and Park Forest,

Moving Day, 1953. *A new subdivision opens its doors.*

thirty miles south of Chicago. The houses perched along the hillsides of Daly City, near San Francisco, inspired a popular song, "Little Boxes": "And they're all made out of ticky-tacky and they all look just the same." This suburban revolution was aggressively fostered by the federal government. "If it weren't for the government," one San Francisco developer explained, "the boom would end overnight." By insuring loans for up to 95 percent of the value of a house, the Federal Housing Administration made it easy for a builder to construct low-cost houses. In addition the government insured the buyer's mortgage, thus making the purchase of a house as affordable as renting. Veterans got added benefits. A veteran could buy a Levitt house with no down payment and monthly installments of $56.

Expanded automobile production and highway construction also facilitated the rush to the suburbs as more and more people were able to commute longer distances to work. Car production soared from 2 million in 1946 to 8 million in 1955, and a "car culture" soon emerged. As one commentator observed, the proliferation of automobiles "changed our dress, manners, social customs, vacation habits, the shape of our cities, consumer purchasing patterns, [and] common tastes." Widespread car ownership also necessitated an improved road network. Local and state governments built many new roads, but the guiding force was the federal government. In 1947 Congress authorized the construction of 37,000 miles of highways, and nine years later it funded over 42,000 additional miles in a new national system of expressways.

Cars and roads provided access to the suburbs, and Americans—mostly middle-class white Americans—rushed to take advantage of

Jackie Robinson, 1949. *Racial discrimination remained widespread through the postwar period. Jackie Robinson of the Brooklyn Dodgers in 1947 became the first black to play major-league baseball.*

the new living spaces. The motives for moving to the suburbs were numerous. The availability of more spacious homes as well as greater security and better educational opportunities for children all played a role. Racial considerations were also a factor. After World War II African-Americans migrated to the cities of the North and Midwest. And as they moved in, white residents moved out. Those engaged in "white flight" were usually eager to maintain residential segregation in their new suburban communities. Contracts for houses in Levittown, Long Island, for example, specifically excluded "members of other than the Caucasian race." Such discrimination, whether explicit or implicit, was widespread; the nation's suburban population in 1970 was 95 percent white.

A CONFORMING CULTURE

As evidenced in many of the new look-alike suburbs sprouting up across the land, much of middle-class American social life during the two decades after the end of World War II exhibited an increasingly homogenized character. Fears generated by the Cold War initially played a key role in encouraging orthodoxy. But McCarthyism was simply the most visible symbol of the many political and social forces promoting common standards of behavior. Suburban life itself encouraged uniformity. In new communities of strangers people quickly felt a need for companionship and a sense of belonging. "Nobody wants people around who criticize and sit off by themselves and don't take part," observed one resident. Changes in corporate life as well as the influence of the consumer culture also played an important socializing role. "Conformity," predicted an editor in 1954, "may very well become the central social problem of this age."

CORPORATE LIFE   The composition of the American work force and the very nature of work itself were dramatically changing during the postwar era. During these years more time became available for leisure, as the standard workweek shrank from five and a half days to five days. Fewer and fewer people were self-employed, and manual labor was rapidly giving way to mental labor. By the mid-1950s white-collar (salaried) workers outnumbered blue-collar (hourly-wage) workers for the first time in American history. By 1955, 60 percent of the population was said to be enjoying a "middle-class" standard of living (defined as annual family incomes of $3,000 to $10,000 in constant dollars). In 1929, before the stock market crash,

Office in a Small City. *Edward Hopper's 1953 painting suggests the alienation associated with "white-collar" work and a new corporate atmosphere in the 1950s.*

only 31 percent were so designated. Managers, teachers, professors, researchers, salespeople, government employees, and office workers now constituted the bulk of the work force, and they tended to work in larger and larger organizations.

During World War II big business grew bigger. The government relaxed antitrust activity, and huge defense contracts tended to promote corporate concentration and consolidation. In 1940, for example, 100 companies were responsible for 30 percent of all manufacturing output; three years later they were providing 70 percent. After the war a wave of mergers occurred, and dominant corporate giants appeared in every major industry, providing the primary source of new jobs. By 1960, 38 percent of the work force was employed by organizations with more than 500 employees. In such huge companies, as well as similarly large government agencies and universities, the working atmosphere began to take on a distinctive new cast. The traditional notion of the hard-working, strong-minded individual advancing by dint of competitive ability and creative initiative gave way to a new managerial personality and an ethic of corporate cooperation and achievement.

WOMAN'S PLACE Increasing conformity in the middle-class workplace was mirrored in the middle-class home. A special issue of *Life* magazine in 1956 featured the "ideal" middle-class woman, a thirty-two-year-old "pretty and popular" suburban housewife, mother of four, who had married at age sixteen. She was described as an excellent wife, mother, hostess, volunteer, and "home manager" who made her own clothes, hosted dozens of dinner parties each year, sang in the church choir, worked with the school PTA and Campfire Girls, and was devoted to her husband. "In her daily round," *Life* reported, "she attends club or charity meetings, drives the children to school, does the weekly grocery shopping, makes ceramics, and is planning to study French." She also exercised on a trampoline in order "to keep her size 12 figure."

Life's description of the American middle-class woman was symptomatic of a veritable cult of feminine domesticity that witnessed a dramatic revival in the postwar era. The soaring birth rate reinforced the deeply embedded notion that a woman's place was in the home as tender of the hearth and guardian of the children. "Of all the accomplishments of the American woman," the *Life* cover story proclaimed, "the one she brings off with the most spectacular success is having babies."

Thus, even though millions of women had responded to intense wartime appeals and joined "Rosie the Riveter" in the traditionally male work force, afterward they were encouraged—and even forced—to turn their jobs over to the returning male veterans and resume their full-time commitment to home and family. A 1945 article in *House Beautiful* entitled "Home Should Be Even More Wonderful Than He Remembers It" lectured women on their postwar responsibilities. The returning veteran was "head man again. . . . Your part in the remaking of this man is to fit his home to him, understanding why he wants it this way, forgetting your own preferences." Women were also to forget wartime-generated thoughts of their own career in the workplace. "Back to the kitchen" was the repeated refrain. "Women must boldly announce," a Barnard College trustee asserted in 1950, "that no job is more exacting, more necessary, or more rewarding than that of housewife and mother." She then pleaded: "God protect us all from the efficient, go-getter businesswoman whose feminine instincts have been completely sterilized."

Many, perhaps most, women agreed. A housewife who was married at the end of the war and had her first child in 1947 declared in the *Atlantic Monthly:* "We *like* this business of running a home after a few years of contemplating what life would be like without our

The Ideal Woman. *A 1956* Life *magazine cover story pronounced the ideal woman a "pretty and popular" suburban housewife who "attends club or charity meetings, drives the children to school, does the weekly grocery shopping, makes ceramics, and is planning to study French."*

husbands." When a woman writing in the same magazine called for government-supported nurseries so as to allow mothers more time for self-culture and careers outside the home, a female reader replied that such a proposal "invokes shades of Communism, and any plan which even *seems* related to Communism already has two strikes against it."

These were not isolated examples. Throughout the postwar era, educators, politicians, ministers, advertisers, and other commentators exalted the cult of domesticity and castigated the few feminists who were encouraging women to broaden their horizons beyond crib and kitchen. Two social psychologists, Marynia Farnham and Ferdinand Lundberg, published a best-selling book in 1947 entitled *Modern Woman: The Lost Sex,* in which they seemed to lend the authority of science to the view that women could achieve fulfillment *only* by accepting their natural functions as wives and mothers. Such notions sound far-fetched today, but they were widely embraced in the postwar era. Even such a liberal politician and self-styled progressive intellectual as Adlai Stevenson preached a similar doctrine. He reminded Smith College graduates in 1955 that their heroic purpose in life was to "influence man and boy" in the "humble role of housewife."

RELIGIOUS REVIVAL   Another illustration of the conformist tendencies of middle-class life during the Eisenhower years was the growth of membership in social organizations. Americans were on the move after World War II. Not only were they moving from the central cities to the suburbs, they were moving from suburb to suburb, farm to city, state to state. Some 20 percent of the population changed their place of residence each year. In Levittown an average of 3,000 homes per year turned over. A major cause of such mobility was the standard policy of the largest corporations to relocate their sales and managerial employees. IBM executives told friends that the company initials actually stood for "I've Been Moved." Such flux led people to search for a sense of community and rootedness. Hence middle-class Americans, even more than usual, tended to be joiners; they joined civic clubs, garden clubs, bridge clubs, car pools, and babysitting groups.

They also joined churches and synagogues in record numbers. "One comes early to get a seat in suburban churches," a writer observed in 1956; "they overflow, and new ones are being built every day." The postwar era witnessed a massive renewal of religious participation, and the Cold War was a strong impetus behind the awakening. "Since Communists are anti-God," FBI director J. Edgar Hoover urged, "encourage your child to be active in the church." Many American parents heeded his warning. In 1940 less than half the adult population belonged to institutionalized churches; by 1960 over 65 percent were official communicants. *Time* announced in 1954 that "the Christian faith is back in the center of things." Sales of Bibles soared during the postwar era, and books, movies, and songs with religious themes were stunning commercial successes. Hollywood glamour girl Jane Russell, hitherto noted more for her buxom bosom and sultry smile than her spiritual intensity, was one of many celebrities who promoted the religious revival. "I love God," she confessed. "And when you get to know him, he's a livin' doll."

President Eisenhower repeatedly promoted a patriotic crusade to bring Americans back to God. "Recognition of the Supreme Being," he declared, "is the first, the most basic, expression of Americanism. Without God, there could be no American form of government, nor an American way of life." The president had himself first joined a church in 1953, but he characterized himself as the "most intensely religious man I know." Not to be outdone, Congress in 1954 added the phrase "one nation under God" to the Pledge of Allegiance, and the following year made the statement "In God We Trust" mandatory on all American currency.

Another major reason for the increase in popular piety and church membership was that religious groups adopted the same marketing techniques successfully employed by American manufacturers. Billboards across the country urged viewers to "bring the whole family to church," and television commercials declared that the "family that prays together stays together." Catholic Bishop Fulton J. Sheen's weekly television show, "Life Is Worth Living," was a prime-time hit. At another point on the denominational spectrum, Baptist evangelical Billy Graham used both radio and television in promoting his huge crusades. Religious leaders even catered to the new car culture by performing services at "drive-in" theaters.

The prevailing tone of the popular religious revival during the 1950s was upbeat and soothing. Many ministers assumed that people were not interested in "fire-and-brimstone" harangues from the pulpit; they did not want their consciences overly burdened with a sense of personal sin or social guilt over such issues as racial segregation or inner-city poverty. Instead they wanted to be reassured that their own comfortable way of life was indeed God's will. As the Protestant Council of New York City explained to its corps of radio and television speakers, their addresses "should project love, joy, courage, hope, faith, trust in God, goodwill. Generally avoid condemnation, criticism, controversy. In a very real sense we are 'selling' religion, the good news of the Gospel."

By far the best salesman of this gospel of reassuring "good news" was the Reverend Norman Vincent Peale. Drawing on a long tradition of "positive thinking" in American social and religious thought, Peale became the impresario of feel-good theology. No speaker was more in demand during the 1950s, and no writer was more widely read. Peale's book *The Power of Positive Thinking* (1952) was a phenomenal best-seller throughout the decade—and for good reason. It offered a simple "how-to" course in personal happiness. "Flush out all depressing, negative, and tired thoughts," Peale advised. "Start thinking faith, enthusiasm, and joy." By following this simple formula for success, he pledged, the reader could become "a more popular, esteemed, and well-liked individual."

Peale's message of psychological security and material success was powerfully reassuring, and the psychological needs he addressed were indeed real. By 1957 tranquilizers were the fastest-growing new medication in the country, suggesting that anxiety was indeed accompanying America's much-trumpeted affluence. Many people, living uneasily amid the moral and social dilemmas of the postwar period, were profoundly anxious about the meaning of life in general and their lives in particular. Peale offered them peace of mind and soul, assuring them that everything was fine and for the best as long as they believed in God, the American Way, and themselves.

NEO-ORTHODOXY   "Stop worrying and start living" was Peale's simple credo. But was it too simplistic? The "peace of mind" and "positive thinking" psychology promoted by Peale and other feel-good ministers struck some members of the religious community as shallow and dangerously misleading. In *Protestant–Catholic–Jew* (1955), Will Herberg, professor of Judaic Studies at Drew University, described the popular spiritual revival as representing "religiousness without religion, a religiousness with almost any kind of content or none, a way of sociability or 'belonging,' rather than a way of reorienting life toward God." Such consoling religiosity, he felt, lacked genuine conviction and depth of commitment. Herberg and other theologians steadfastly resisted the dilution of traditional Judeo-Christian beliefs. These advocates of "neo-orthodoxy" especially criticized those who identified the United States as the only truly providential society and who used faith as a sanction for the social status quo.

The towering spokesman for such "neo-orthodoxy" was Reinhold Niebuhr (1892–1970). A brilliant, penetrating, ironic, and erratic preacher-professor at New York's Union Theological Seminary, Niebuhr repeatedly lashed out at the "undue complacency and conformity" which had settled over American life in the postwar era. Like Herberg he found the popular religion of self-assurance and psychology of material success woefully inadequate prescriptions for the ills of modern society. "They can not be taken seriously by responsible religious or secular people," he scowled in 1955, "because they do not come to terms with the basic collective problems of our atomic age, and because the peace which they seek to inculcate is rather too simple and neat." True peace, Niebuhr insisted, involves not the cheap comfort and sedating reassurance offered by Peale and other popular evangelists but the reality of pain, a pain "caused by love and responsibility" for the well-being of the entire human race, rather than concern only with one's tortured self. Self-love, he reminded smug Americans, was the very basis of sin.

CRACKS IN THE PICTURE WINDOW

Niebuhr was one of many impassioned disturbers of the peace who challenged the moral complacency and social conformity that he and others felt had come to characterize American social life during the 1950s and early 1960s. The 1950s, the novelist Herbert Gold maintained, had produced happy people with happy problems. To a degree, such self-satisfaction was deserved. After all, the economy was booming, and the average life expectancy lengthened from sixty-six years in 1945 to seventy-one in 1970.

But justified pride in tangible achievements often led to a blissful indifference toward festering social ills and a self-absorbed materialism. One of the most striking aspects of postwar American life was the sharp contrast between the buoyant public mood and the increasingly bitter criticism of American life coming from intellectuals, theologians, novelists, playwrights, poets, and artists. As the philosopher and editor Joseph Wood Krutch recognized in 1960, "the gap between those who find the spirit of the age congenial and those who do not seems to have grown wider and wider."

THE LONELY CROWD   The criticism of postwar American life and values began in the early 1950s and quickly gathered momentum. Scores of books and articles swollen with both mournful righteousness and unsettling truths lambasted virtually every area of the nation's social life. What unified such fulminations was a common fear: America in the age of Eisenhower was becalmed in a sea of conformity, content to succumb to the soul-denying demands of the corporate "rat race," and eager to wallow in the consumer culture. In *The Affluent Society* (1958), for example, the economist John Kenneth Galbraith attacked the prevailing notion that sustained economic growth would solve America's chronic social problems.

The public sector was starved for funds, Galbraith argued, and public enterprises were everywhere deteriorating. He reminded readers that for all of America's vaunted postwar prosperity, the nation had yet to eradicate poverty.

Another frequent target of postwar cultural criticism was the supposed serenity of middle-class corporate and suburban life. John Keats, in *The Crack in the Picture Window* (1956), launched the most savage assault on life in the huge suburban developments. He ridiculed Levittown and other such mass-produced communities as having been "conceived in error, nurtured in greed, corroding everything they touch." In these rows of "identical boxes spreading like gangrene," commuter fathers were always at work and "mothers were always delivering children, obstetrically once and by car forever after." Locked into a monotonous routine, hounded by financial insecurity, and engulfed by mass mediocrity, suburbanites, he concluded, were living in a "homogeneous, postwar Hell."

Mass-produced suburban developments did exhibit a startling sameness. Levittown, for example, encouraged and even enforced uniformity. The houses all sold for the same price—$7,990—and

Commuters on the 5:57, Park Forest, Illinois. *Postwar social critics commented on the overwhelming conformity of middle-class corporate and suburban life.*

featured the same floor plan and accessories. Each had a picture window, a living room, bath, kitchen, and two bedrooms. Kitchens were equipped with a refrigerator, stove, and Bendix washer, and the living room featured a built-in Admiral television set. A tree was planted every twenty-eight feet. Homeowners were required to cut their grass once a week, fences were prohibited, and laundry could not be hung out on weekends. Yet Levittown was in many ways distinctive rather than representative. There were thousands of suburbs by the mid-1950s, and few were as regimented or as unvarying as Keats and other critics implied. Keats also failed to recognize the benefits that the suburbs offered those who would have otherwise remained in crowded urban apartments.

Still, there was more than a grain of truth to the charge that postwar American life was becoming oppressively regimented, and the huge modern corporation was repeatedly cited by social critics as the primary villain. The most comprehensive and provocative analysis of the docile new corporate character was David Riesman's *The Lonely Crowd* (1950). Riesman and his research associates detected a fundamental shift in the dominant American personality from what they called the "inner-directed" to the "other-directed" type. Inner-directed people possessed a deeply internalized set of basic values implanted by strong-minded parents or other elders. This core set of fixed principles, analogous to the traditional Protestant ethic of piety, diligence, and thrift, acted, in his words, like an internal gyroscope. Once set in motion by parents and other authority figures, the inner-directed person was kept on a steady course by the built-in stabilizer of fixed values.

Such an assured, self-reliant personality, Riesman argued, had been dominant in American life throughout the nineteenth century. But during the mid twentieth century an other-directed personality had displaced it. As the emphasis of American industry shifted from manipulating machines to manipulating workers, the new corporate culture demanded employees who could win friends and influence people rather than rugged individualists indifferent to personal popularity. Other-directed people had few internalized convictions and standards; they did not follow their conscience so much as they sought to adapt to the prevailing standards of the moment. They were more concerned with being well liked than being independent. In the workplace they were always smiling, always glad-handing, always trying to please the boss. To illustrate the distinction, Riesman noted that in the popular nursery rhyme "This Little Pig Went to Market," each pig went his own way. "Today, however, all little pigs go to market; none stay home; all have roast beef, if any do; and all say 'we-we.'"

Dr. Benjamin Spock's The
Common Sense Book of
Baby and Child Care *was
enormously influential with
the parents of
baby-boomers.*

Riesman amassed considerable evidence to show that the other-directed personality was not just an aspect of the business world; its premises were widely dispersed throughout middle-class life. Dr. Benjamin Spock's advice on raising children, Riesman pointed out, had become immensely influential. Spock's popular manual, *The Common Sense Book of Baby and Child Care*, sold an average of 1 million copies a year between its first appearance in 1946 and 1960. Although Spock never endorsed the anarchic permissiveness attributed to him by later critics, he did insist that parents should foster in their children qualities and skills that would enhance their chances in what Riesman called the "popularity market." The middle-class mother thus becomes a "chauffeur and booking agent," determined to "cultivate all the currently essential talents, especially the gregarious ones. It is inconceivable to some that a child might prefer his own company or that of just another child." In fact, in 1952 a mother received the following report card assessment of her son: "He was doing fine in some respects but his social adjustment was not as good as it might be. He would pick one or two friends to play with—and sometimes he was happy to remain by himself."

By the mid-1950s social commentators were growing increasingly concerned that such a managerial personality was indeed becoming pervasive. In his influential study, *White Collar Society* (1956), the sociologist C. Wright Mills vigorously attacked the attributes and influence of modern corporate life. "When white collar people get jobs," Mills explained, "they sell not only their time and energy, but their personalities as well. They sell by the week or month their smiles and their kindly gestures, and they must practice the prompt repression of resentment and aggression." William A. Whyte, Jr., the editor of *Fortune*, presented a similar critique in his widely discussed book *The Organization Man* (1956). The new corporate culture, he charged, stressed "a belief in the group as the source of creativity; a belief in 'belongingness' as the ultimate need of the individual."

ALIENATION ON THE STAGE   Many of the best plays of the postwar period reinforced Riesman's image of modern American society as a "lonely crowd" of individuals, hollow at the core, groping for a sense of belonging and affection. Arthur Miller's play *Death of a Salesman* (1949), for example, was a powerful exploration of the theme. Willy Loman, an aging, confused salesman in decline, has centered his life and that of his family on the notion that material success is secured through personal popularity, only to be abruptly told by his boss that he is in fact a failure. Loman repeatedly insists that it is "not what you say, it's how you say it—because personality always wins the day." He had tried to raise his sons, Biff and Happy, in his own image, encouraging them to be athletic, outgoing, popular, and ambitious. As he instructs them: "Be liked and you will never want." Happy followed his father's advice but was anything but happy: "Sometimes I sit in my apartment—all alone. And I think of the rent I'm paying. And it's crazy. But then, it's what I always wanted. My own apartment, a car, and plenty of women. And still, goddammit,

In Arthur Miller's Death of a Salesman, *Willy Loman (center, played by Lee J. Cobb) destroys his life and family with the credo "Be liked and you will never want."*

I'm lonely." Such vacant loneliness is the play's recurring theme. Willy, for all his puffery about being well liked, admits in a fit of candor that he is "terribly lonely." He has no real friends; even his relations with his family are neither honest nor intimate. "He never knew who he was," Biff sighs. When Willy finally realizes that he has been leading a counterfeit existence, he is so haunted and dumbfounded that he decides he can endow his life with meaning only by ending it.

Death of a Salesman and many other postwar plays written by Arthur Miller, Edward Albee, and Tennessee Williams portray a central concern of American literature and art during the postwar era: the sense of alienation experienced by sensitive individuals in the midst of an oppressive mass culture. As the novelist Philip Roth, author of *Goodbye Columbus* (1959), observed in 1961: "The American writer in the middle of the twentieth century has his hands full in trying to understand, and then describe, and then make credible much of American reality. It stupefies, it sickens, it infuriates, and finally it is even a kind of embarrassment to one's own meager imagination." Such a gloomy assessment was typical of the revulsion felt by other writers and artists, and many of them were determined to lay bare the conceits and illusions of their times.

THE NOVEL "What's your idea of who runs things?" asks a character in Saul Bellow's *The Victim* (1947). The question illustrates the recurring theme of the best postwar fiction. The most enduring novels of the period display a shared preoccupation with the individual's struggle for survival amid the smothering and disorienting forces of mass society. While the millions were reading heartwarming religious epics such as *The Cardinal* (1950), *The Robe* (1953), and *Exodus* (1959), critics were praising the more unsettling and sobering writings of James Baldwin, Saul Bellow, John Cheever, Ralph Ellison, Joseph Heller, James Jones, Norman Mailer, Joyce Carol Oates, J. D. Salinger, William Styron, John Updike, and Eudora Welty.

Few happy endings here—and even fewer celebrations of contemporary American life. J. D. Salinger's *Catcher in the Rye* (1951) was an unsettling exploration of a young man's search for meaning and self in a smothering society. Holden Caulfield finally decides that rebellion against conformity is useless. "If you want to stay alive," he concludes, "you have to say that stuff, like 'Glad to meet you' to people you are not at all glad to meet." This brooding sense of resigned alienation animated the best literature in the two decades after 1945. The characters in novels such as Jones's *From Here to Eternity*, Ellison's *Invisible Man*, Bellow's *Dangling Man* and *Seize the Day*, Styron's *Lie Down in Darkness*, and Updike's

Rabbit, Run, among many others, tended to be like Willy Loman—restless, tormented, impotent individuals who are unable to fasten on a satisfying self-image and therefore can find neither contentment nor respect in an overpowering or uninterested world.

In *From Here to Eternity* (1951) the hero, Private Prewitt, can neither "stomach nor understand nor explain nor change" the world around him. African-American writer Ralph Ellison also explored the theme of the lonely individual imprisoned in privacy in his kaleidoscopic novel *Invisible Man* (1952). By using a black narrator struggling to find and liberate himself in the midst of an oppressive white society, Ellison forcefully accentuated the problem of alienation. The narrator opens by confessing: "All my life I had been looking for something, and everywhere I turned someone tried to tell me what it was. I accepted their answers too, though they were often in contradiction and even self-contradictory. I was naïve. I was looking for myself and asking everyone except myself questions which I, and only I, could answer."

Tommy Wilhelm in Bellow's *Seize the Day* (1956) is also looking for meaning and affection amid a frenetic and overpowering urban world. He is a perpetual loser. A failure at his chosen profession of acting, separated from his wife, dependent on his rich father who despises him, stripped of his best sales territory, and cast aside by his mistress, Wilhelm is utterly alone and adrift, unable to "seize the day" and achieve the success he so desperately desires. That someone should take a sincere interest in him "was what he craved, that someone should care about him, wish him well. Kindness, mercy, he wanted." But he received only indifference or an-

Ralph Ellison, author of Invisible Man.

tagonism. He, too, was invisible in the midst of the swirling crowds of modern life.

The bleak tone of *Invisible Man* and *Seize the Day* was symptomatic of most of the writers whom *Time* magazine dismissed as making up the "dread-despair-and-decay camp of American letters." But the writers insisted that such themes, as well as the innovative techniques they employed to explore them, were far more "real" than the confectionary approach of the more popular and consoling authors. As Ellison replied in response to a question about *Invisible Man*, "I didn't select the surrealism, the distortion, the intensity, as an experimental technique, but because reality is surreal." Joyce Carol Oates likewise explained that her literary objective was to "defantasize" American experience, to cut through the layers of boosterism and illusory optimism and reveal the poignant tragedy of spiritual yearnings suffocated by a pervasive materialism. The power of truly compelling writing, she asserted, "lies in its insistence upon the barrenness of life."

PAINTING   The artist Edward Hopper (1882–1967) adopted a similar outlook in his paintings. Since the start of his career in the early twentieth century, Hopper was preoccupied with the theme of desolate loneliness in urban-industrial American life. But his concern grew more acute in the postwar era. Virtually all of his paintings of the period depict isolated individuals, melancholy, anonymous, motionless. A woman undressing for bed, a diner in an all-night restaurant, a housewife in a doorway, a businessman at his desk (see page 1269), a lone passerby in the street—these are the characters in Hopper's world. The silence of his scenes is deafening, the monotony striking, the alienation absorbing.

A younger group of painters in New York City were convinced that postwar society was so violent and chaotic that it precluded any attempt at literal representation. As Jackson Pollock maintained, "the modern painter cannot express this age—the airplane, the atomic bomb, the radio—in the old form of the Renaissance or of any past culture. Each age finds its own technique." The technique Pollock adopted came to be called abstract expressionism, and during the late 1940s and 1950s it dominated not only the American art scene, but the international field as well. In addition to Pollock, its adherents included Robert Motherwell, William de Kooning, Arshile Gorky, Franz Kline, Clyfford Still, and Mark Rothko. "Abstract art," Motherwell explained, "is an effort to close the void that modern men feel."

In practice this meant that the *act* of painting was as important as the final result. If artists could not bridge the gap between themselves and their contemporary society, they could find meaning through the spontaneous expression of their subjective selves. To do so they adopted a technique called "action painting." Pollock, for example, would place his huge canvases flat on the floor, then walk around each side, pouring and dripping his paints, all in an effort to "literally be *in* the painting." As an approving art critic recognized, "What was to go on the canvas was not a picture but an event. . . . It is the artist's existence . . . he is living on the canvas." Such action paintings conveyed the whole spectrum of aesthetic qualities: they were vibrant, frenzied, meditative, disorienting, provocative. Needless to say, the general public found them simply provoking. As one wit observed: "I suspect any picture I think I could have made myself."

THE BEATS   In Saul Bellow's novel *Dangling Man* (1946), a character concludes that the dynamic of life is the "desire for pure freedom." The desire to liberate self-expression, to surmount organizational constraints and discard traditional conventions, was an abiding goal of the abstract expressionists. It was also the central concern of a small, but highly visible and controversial group of young writers, poets, painters, and musicians known as the Beats. These angry young men—Jack Kerouac, Allen Ginsberg, Gary Snyder, William Burroughs, and Gregory Corso, among others—were alienated by the regimented horrors of war and the mundane horrors of middle-class life. *Time* called the Beats "a pack of oddballs who celebrate booze, dope, sex, and despair." The Beats, however, were not lost in despair; they strenuously embraced life. But it was life on their own terms, and their terms were shocking to most observers.

The Beats grew out of the bohemian underground in New York's Greenwich Village. They were all unique personalities. Ginsberg, a skinny New Jersey boy with horn-rimmed glasses, an unstable mother, and an intense love for poetry and ideas, had declared at age fourteen that "I'll be a genius of some kind or another, probably in literature. Either I'm a genius, I'm eccentric, or I'm slightly schizophrenic. Probably the first two." Probably all three, some thought. Kerouac, his "romantic, moody, dark-eyed" friend, was a handsome, athletic, working-class kid from Lowell, Massachusetts, who went to Columbia University on a football scholarship. In 1943 he quit school to join the navy. But he soon tired of military discipline, and one day he simply lay down his gun at drill and went to the library. He was arrested and confined in the psychiatric ward, and later was discharged for "indifferent character." Ginsberg also studied at Columbia, where a dean directed him to undergo psychotherapy. Ginsberg chose Burroughs as his therapist.

It was an interesting choice, for Burroughs was indeed the most eccentric of the trio. A graduate of Harvard in 1936, he had studied medicine in Vienna, then worked as an advertising copywriter, detective, bartender, and pest exterminator. He had also cut off one of his fingers during a "Van Gogh kick." Later he would become a heroin addict, kill his wife while trying to shoot an apple off her head, and write the influential experimental novel *Naked Lunch* (1959).

This fervent threesome was joined by Neal Cassady, a twenty-year-old ex-convict who arrived in New York from Denver, hoping to enroll at Columbia. Cassady was pure physical and sensual energy. He could throw a football seventy yards and run a hundred yards in less than ten seconds. He claimed he had stolen over 500 cars and had had sex with almost as many people. Ginsberg, Kerouac, and Burroughs were enthralled by Cassady's frenzied sexuality and vital force. He was in their view a mythic cowboy turned "cool" hipster, utterly free and rootless because he defied both maturity and reason. Soon others joined this quartet in quest of *real* life, and the Beat culture was born. Ginsberg explained that the glue binding them together was their sense of estrangement from a hostile culture and their ability to confess to each other their innermost feelings. Equally binding was their absolute rejection of authority. "Control," Burroughs wrote in *Naked Lunch,* "can never be a means to any practical end. It can never be a means to anything but mere control."

In New York this group of self-described "Beats" began their quest for a visionary sensibility and spontaneous way of life. Essentially apolitical throughout the 1950s, they were more interested in transforming themselves than in reforming the world. They sought personal rather than social solutions to their anxieties. In this sense they resembled the Transcendentalists, whom Longfellow had described as constituting a "divine insanity of noble minds." Kerouac defined the Beat generation as "basically a religious generation. Beat means beatitude, not beat up. You *feel* this. You feel it in a beat, in jazz—real cool jazz or a good gutty rock number." As Kerouac insisted, they were not beat in the sense of beaten; they were "mad to live, mad to talk, mad to be saved." Their road to salvation lay in hallucinogenic drugs and alcohol, relentless sex, a penchant for jazz and the street life of urban ghettos, an affinity for Buddhism, and a restless, vagabond spirit that took them speeding back and forth across the country between San Francisco and New York during the 1950s.

This existential mania for intense experience and frantic motion provided the subject matter for the Beats' writings. Ginsberg's long prose-poem *Howl,* published in 1956, featured an explicit sensuality as well as an impressionistic attempt to catch the color, movement, and dynamism of modern life. In this it bore a marked resemblance to Walt Whitman's *Leaves of Grass.* But *Howl* lacked Whitman's celebratory tone; its mood was bitter and critical. Ginsberg howled at the "Robot apartments! invincible suburbs! skeleton treasuries! blind capitals! demonic industries!" Kerouac issued his autobiographical novel *On the Road* a year later. In frenzied prose and plotless ramblings it portrayed the Beats' life of "bursting ecstasies" and maniacal traveling. At one point Dean Moriarty (Neal Cassady) has the following exchange with Sal Paradise (Kerouac): "We gotta go and never stop going till we get there." "Where we going, man?" "I don't know, but we gotta go."

Howl and *On the Road* provoked sarcasm and anger from many reviewers, but the books enjoyed a brisk sale, especially among young people. *On the Road* made the best-seller list, and soon the term "Beat generation" or "beatnik" was being applied to almost any young rebel who openly dissented from the comfortable ethos of middle-class life. Defiant, unruly actors such as James Dean and Marlon Brando were added to the pantheon of Beat "anti-heroes." In *The Wild One* (1954) a waitress asks Brando what he is rebelling against. He replies: "Whattaya got?" Acid-tongued comedians Mort Sahl and Lennie Bruce displayed affinities with the Beats, and a young folksinger from Minnesota named Bob Dylan was directly inspired by *Howl* and *On the Road.* In this sense the anarchic gaiety of the Beats played an important role in preparing the way for the more widespread youth revolt of the 1960s.

Allen Ginsberg

A PARADOXICAL ERA

For all their color and vitality, the Beats had little impact on the larger patterns of postwar social and cultural life. Nor did most of the other critics who attacked the smug conformity and excessive materialism they saw pervading their society. The tone of the nation's social life was instead marked by a sense of tranquil fulfillment and bouncy optimism. The public had become understandably weary of larger concerns in the aftermath of the depression and the war, and they eagerly focused their efforts on personal and family goals and took great pride in their material achievements.

Yet those achievements, real as they were, eventually created a new set of problems. The benefits of abundance were by no means equally distributed, and millions of Americans still lived mired in poverty. For those more fortunate, unprecedented affluence and security fostered greater leisure and independence, which in turn provided opportunities for more diverse notions of what the good life entailed. Yet the conformist mentality of the Cold War era discouraged experimentation. By the mid-1960s, however, tensions between innovation and convention would erupt into open conflict. Ironically, the children of the postwar boom times would become the leaders of the 1960s rebellion against the corporate and consumer cultures. Even more ironically, the person who would warn Americans of the 1960s about the mounting dangers of the burgeoning "military-industrial complex" was the president who had long symbolized its growth—Dwight D. Eisenhower.

FURTHER READING

There are a number of excellent overviews of social and cultural trends in the postwar era. Among the best are William H. Chafe's *The Unfinished Journey* (1986),° William E. Leuchtenburg's *A Troubled Feast* (1982),° and Lawrence S. Wittner's *Cold War America* (1978).° For fascinating insights into the cultural life of the 1950s, see Douglas T. Miller and Marion Nowak's *The Fifties* (1977) and Jeffrey Hart's *When the Going Was Good: American Life in the Fifties* (1982). Paul Carter's *Another Look at the Fifties* (1983)° provides a succinct revisionist assessment of the decade.

The "baby-boom" generation and its impact are vividly described in Landon Jones's *Great Expectations: America and the Baby Boom Generation* (1980) and Paul Charles Light's *Baby Boomers* (1988). Readers interested in economic trends should consult Harold Vatter's *The U.S. Economy in the*

°These books are available in paperback editions.

1950s (1963) and Walt W. Rostow's *The Stages of Economic Growth* (1959).°
Information on various aspects of the consumer culture can be found in the
major periodicals of the era—*Time, Life, Look, Newsweek*, and *U.S. News
& World Report.* Interesting contemporary discussions of the cultural effects
of unprecedented prosperity include John K. Galbraith's *The Affluent Society* (1958)° and David Potter's *People of Plenty* (1954).° The emergence and
impact of the television industry are discussed in Erik Barnouw's *Tube of
Plenty* (1982).°

The literature on suburban America is abundant. An excellent comprehensive account of the process of suburban development is Kenneth Jackson's award-winning study *The Crabgrass Frontier* (1985).° Also see Robert
Fishman's *Bourgeois Utopias: The Rise and Fall of Suburbia* (1987) and John
R. Stilgoe's *Borderland: Origins of the American Suburb, 1820–1939* (1988).
Herbert Gans's *The Levittowners* (1957)° represented a pathbreaking sociological study of suburban life. The automobile's relationship to suburbaniza-
tion is addressed in John B. Rae's *The Road and the Car in American Life*
(1971). Michael Danielson examined racial discrimination in the suburbs in
The Politics of Exclusion (1976).°

The middle-class ideal of family life in the 1950s is examined in Elaine
Tyler May's *Homeward Bound: American Families in the Cold War Era*
(1988). In addition to Betty Friedan's *Feminine Mystique* (1963),° another
good source of information about the status of women during and after the
war years is Susan M. Hartmann's *The Homefront and Beyond: American
Women in the 1940s* (1982).°

For an overview of the resurgence of religion in the 1950s, see George
Marsden's *Religion and American Culture* (1990). Gibson Winter explored
the role of religion in suburbia in *The Suburban Captivity of the Churches*
(1960).

A lively discussion of movies of the 1950s can be found in Peter Biskind's
Seeing Is Believing (1983).° The origins and growth of rock-and-roll music
are surveyed in Carl Belz's *The Story of Rock* (1972).° The colorful Beats are
brought to life in John Tytell's *Naked Angels: The Lives and Literature of
the Beat Generation* (1976).° Thoughtful interpretive surveys of postwar
American literature include Josephine Hendin's *Vulnerable People* (1978),°
Marcus Klein's *After Alienation: The American Novel at Mid-Century*
(1978),° and Malcolm Bradbury's *The Modern American Novel* (1984).°
Developments in American art since World War II are assessed in *The New
American Art* (1965) edited by Richard Kostelanetz, and Serge Guibaut's
How New York Stole the Idea of Modern Art (1983).° Those interested in
learning more about Edward Hopper should begin with Gail Levin's *Edward
Hopper* (1980).°

33

CONFLICT AND DEADLOCK:
THE EISENHOWER YEARS

"TIME FOR A CHANGE"

By 1952 the Truman administration had piled up a heavy burden of political liabilities. Its bold stand in Korea had brought a bloody stalemate abroad, renewed wage and price controls at home, reckless charges of subversion and disloyalty, and the exposure of corrupt lobbyists and influence peddlers who rigged favors in Washington. The disclosure of corruption led Truman to fire nearly 250 employees of the Bureau of Internal Revenue and, among others, an assistant attorney-general in charge of the Justice Department's Tax Division. But doubts lingered that Truman, protégé of the Kansas City Pendergast machine, would ever finish the housecleaning. There were two Trumans, a newscaster had said: "The White House Truman does all the big things right, and the courthouse Truman does all the little things wrong." But by 1952 few things, big or little, seemed to be going right. The country had bogged down in "Plunder at home, blunder abroad."

EISENHOWER'S POLITICAL RISE   It was, Republicans claimed, "time for a change," and South Dakota Senator Karl Mundt favored a simple formula for Republican victory: $K_1 C_2$—Korea, communism, and corruption. The Republican field quickly narrowed to two men, Senator Robert A. Taft and General Dwight D. Eisenhower, with General MacArthur alert for a deadlock. The party wheelhorses turned instinctively to Taft, "Mr. Republican," long a faithful party worker. Taft had become the foremost spokesman for domestic conservatism and for a foreign policy that his enemies branded isolation-ist. A man of stubborn integrity, he did not usually trim his sails to the prevailing winds. He had openly opposed the war-crimes trials, for instance, arguing that they were *ex post facto* and a dangerous precedent. His conservatism left room for federal aid to education and public housing, and his foreign policy, a "unilateralist" one, favored an active American role in opposing communism but op-posed "entangling alliances" such as NATO. He joined the "Asia Firsters" in stressing the strategic importance of the Pacific area, but warned against the dangers of a land war on the Asian mainland. In Korea, he felt, the time had come to go all out for victory or to withdraw completely.

But Taft inspired little enthusiasm beyond the party regulars. He projected a lackluster image, and as a leader used to taking contro-versial stands, he had made enemies. The eastern, internationalist wing of the party turned instinctively to Eisenhower, then the NATO commander. As a war hero he had the glamour that Taft lacked, and his captivating and unpretentious manner inspired con-fidence. His leadership had been tested in the fires of war, but as a professional soldier he had escaped the scars of political combat. He stood, therefore, outside and above the vulgar arena of public life, although his political instincts and skills were sharpened during his successful army career.

Eisenhower nevertheless seemed genuinely immune to the presi-dential bug until Senator Henry Cabot Lodge, Jr., and others ap-pealed to his sense of duty: only he could stop Taft and the isolationists. In January 1952 the general affirmed that he was a Republican and in the following months permitted his name to be entered in party primaries. In June he left his NATO post and joined the battle in person. An outpouring of public enthusiasm began to overwhelm Republican party regulars. Bumper stickers across the land announced simply, "I like Ike." The closely divided convention resolved itself into a series of contests between rival delegations which the younger Taft could not control. Eisenhower won the nomi-nation on the first ballot. He balanced the ticket by choosing as his running mate a youthful Californian, the thirty-nine-year-old Sena-tor Richard M. Nixon, who had built a career on opposition to "subversives" and gained his greatest notoriety as the member of the House Un-American Activities Committee most eager in the pursuit of Alger Hiss.

THE 1952 ELECTION   The Twenty-second Amendment, ratified in 1951, forbade any president to seek a third term. The amendment exempted the incumbent, but weary of the war, harassed by charges

Dwight D. Eisenhower (right) *and Richard M. Nixon* (left), *the Republican standardbearers for 1952.*

of subversion and corruption in government, his popularity declining, Truman chose to withdraw and his exit threw the Democratic race wide open. Truman's choice as successor was Governor Adlai E. Stevenson of Illinois but, rebuffed by the governor's insistent refusal, the president threw his support to Vice-President Alben W. Barkley. Just before the convention, however, a group of "certain self-appointed political labor leaders" told Barkley he was too old (at seventy-five) and asked him to withdraw. When he did, Truman threw his support again to Governor Stevenson, who aroused the delegates with an eloquent speech welcoming them to Chicago. On the third ballot the convention drafted Stevenson, who then chose Senator John J. Sparkman of Alabama as his running mate.

The campaign matched two of the most magnetic personalities ever pitted in a presidential contest. Both men attracted new followings among people previously apathetic to politics, but the race was uneven from the start. Eisenhower, though a political novice, was a world figure who had been in the public eye for a decade. Stevenson, the politician, was hardly known outside of Illinois and was never able to escape the burden of Truman's liabilities. The genial general, who had led the crusade against Hitler, now opened a domestic crusade to clean up "the mess in Washington." To this he added a promise, late in the campaign, that as president-elect he would go to Korea to secure "an early and honorable" peace. The Democrats' charge that he was grandstanding had little impact in the face of his long military experience. Stevenson's forte was a lofty eloquence spiced with a quick wit, but his resolve to "talk sense" and "tell the truth to the American people" came across as just a bit too aloof, a shade too intellectual. The Republicans hastened to cast him in the role of an "egghead," an indecisive, latter-day Hamlet, in contrast to Eisenhower, the man of the people, the man of decision and action.

The war hero triumphed in a landslide of 34 million votes to Stevenson's 27 million, and 442 electoral votes to Stevenson's 89. The election marked a turning point in Republican fortunes in the South: for the first time since the heyday of the Whigs the South was moving toward a two-party system. Stevenson carried only eight southern states plus West Virginia: Eisenhower picked up five states in the outer South: Florida, Oklahoma, Tennessee, Texas, and Virginia. In the former Confederacy the Republican ticket garnered 49 percent of the votes. The "nonpolitical" Eisenhower had made it respectable, even fashionable, to vote Republican in the South. Elsewhere, too, the general made inroads in the New Deal coalition, attracting supporters among the ethnic and religious minorities in the major cities.

The voters, it turned out, liked Ike better than they liked his party. Democrats retained most of the governorships, lost control of the House by only eight votes, and broke even in the Senate, where only the vote of the vice-president ensured Republican control. The con-

Truman supported Governor Adlai E. Stevenson of Illinois for the Democratic presidential nomination in 1952.

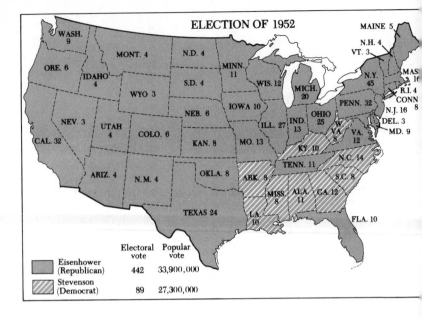

ELECTION OF 1952

WASH. 9
ORE. 6
IDAHO 4
MONT. 4
N.D. 4
MINN. 11
S.D. 4
WIS. 12
WYO 3
NEV. 3
UTAH 4
COLO. 6
NEB. 6
IOWA 10
CAL. 32
ARIZ. 4
N.M. 4
OKLA. 8
KAN. 8
MO. 13
TEXAS 24
ARK. 8
LA. 10
MISS. 8
ALA. 11
GA. 12
TENN. 11
KY. 10
ILL. 27
IND. 13
OHIO 25
MICH. 20
PENN. 32
W. VA. 8
VA. 12
N.C. 14
S.C. 8
FLA. 10
MAINE 5
N.H. 4
VT. 3
N.Y. 45
MASS. 16
R.I. 4
CONN 8
N.J. 16
DEL. 3
MD. 9

		Electoral vote	Popular vote
▓	Eisenhower (Republican)	442	33,900,000
▨	Stevenson (Democrat)	89	27,300,000

gressional elections two years later would weaken the Republican grip on Congress, and Eisenhower would have to work with a Democratic Congress until he left office.

IKE   Born in Dennison, Texas, on October 14, 1890, Dwight David Eisenhower grew up in Abilene, Kansas. After finishing West Point he went on to spend nearly his entire adult life in the military service. He spent World War I stateside as a tank instructor, and then worked his way through the ranks. He served as staff officer to General MacArthur in Washington and the Philippines. After Pearl Harbor, General George C. Marshall made Brigadier-General Eisenhower his chief of operations. Later, as a major-general, Eisenhower took command of American forces in the European theater and directed the invasion of North Africa in November 1942. Two years later he assumed the post of supreme commander of Allied forces in preparation for the invasion of the continent. After the war, by then a five-star general of the army, he became chief-of-staff and supreme commander of NATO forces, with a brief interlude in between as president of Columbia University.

Eisenhower's inauguration brought a change in style to the White House. The contrast in character between the feisty Truman and the avuncular Ike was reinforced by a contrast in philosophy and approach to the presidency. Eisenhower's military experience developed in him an instinct for methodical staff work. He met with the cabinet and the National Security Council nearly every week, and he relied heavily on them as consultative bodies. His chief assistant, former New Hampshire governor Sherman Adams, required that all paperwork sent to the Oval Office be compressed into single-page summaries. "I count the day lost," Adams said, "when I have not found some new way of lightening the President's load."

Such procedures, it seemed, tended to isolate the president from conflicting viewpoints and to reduce the policy choices available to him. The public image of Ike confirmed that view, but it endeared him all the more to the people as a man who rose above politics. He was unpretentious, an ardent golfer, a common man with a winning smile who read little but Western novels, uninformed on the currents of intellectual and artistic life, and given to copybook maxims: "Everybody ought to be happy every day. Play hard, have fun doing it, and despise wickedness." George Kennan said: "He was the nation's number one Boy Scout."

But those who were closer to Ike have presented another side to the man. When provoked he could release a fiery temper and scalding profanity. While Ike talked with genuine feeling about such traditional virtues as duty, honesty, and thrift, he was not above a calculated dissimulation. The scrambled syntax in which he answered reporters' questions was sometimes intentional evasion. Eisenhower deliberately toned down eloquent passages which speechwriters tried to smuggle into his public utterances. One student of Eisenhower's techniques has spoken of a "hidden-hand presidency" in which Ike deliberately cultivated an image of passivity to hide his active involvement in policy decisions.

"DYNAMIC CONSERVATISM" AT HOME   Like Ulysses Grant, however, Eisenhower betrayed a weakness for hobnobbing with rich men. His cabinet, a columnist in the *New Republic* quipped, consisted of "eight millionaires and a plumber." The plumber, Secretary of Labor Martin Durkin, resigned after eight months, charging that the administration had reneged on a promise to change the Taft-Hartley Act. The president of General Motors became secretary of defense, and two auto distributors became secretary of the interior and postmaster-general, respectively. The New Dealers, Adlai Stevenson wryly remarked, "have all left Washington to make way for the car dealers."

Unaccustomed to the glare of Washington publicity, several cabinet members succumbed to foot-in-mouth disease. It was perhaps innocent enough for the former GM president to say at his confirmation hearings, "I thought what was good for our country was good for General Motors, and vice versa," except that it was readily translated into: "What is good for General Motors is good for the country." The interior secretary put it more baldly: "We're here in the saddle as an Administration representing business and industry." The treasury secretary, former head of Mark Hanna's old coal and oil firm in Cleveland, put Andrew Mellon's picture on the wall, and replied when asked if he had read Hemingway's *The Old Man and the Sea*: "Why would anybody be interested in some old man who was a failure and never amounted to anything anyway?"

Eisenhower called his program "dynamic conservatism," which meant being "conservative when it comes to money and liberal when it comes to human beings." Stevenson conjectured: "I assume what it means is that you will strongly recommend the building of a great many schools to accommodate the needs of our children, but not provide the money." Budget cutting was a high priority for the new administration, which set out after both domestic programs and national defense. Eisenhower warned repeatedly against the dangers of "creeping socialism," "huge bureaucracies," and budget deficits.

Eisenhower began by abolishing the Reconstruction Finance Corporation, ending wage and price controls, and reducing farm price subsidies. Eisenhower also moved the government away from the Roosevelt-Truman commitment to public power. In fact, had Ike had his way the government would have sold the TVA. The Republican Congress rejected a proposal in 1953 to build a new TVA steam plant to supply the power needs of Memphis, Tennessee. Opposed to any further expansion of the TVA, the administration instead got behind a plan to build a private plant. Controversy over the proposal dragged out for two years until investigations revealed that the government consultant who recommended the private plant stood to benefit from the deal. The administration was rescued from further embarrassment when the city of Memphis offered to build its own power plant without federal assistance.

Another protracted struggle over public power ended differently when the Idaho Power Company won a license to build three small dams on the Snake River in place of a gigantic federal dam proposed for Hell's Canyon. Still another step away from public power came with the Atomic Energy Act of 1954, which opened the door for construction of private nuclear power plants under AEC license and safeguards. In 1974 a Nuclear Regulatory Commission (NRC) would replace the AEC.

In fiscal policy the administration found its passion for budget cutting encumbered by unyielding facts. Its first budget had already been prepared by Truman's men, providing for expenditures of $80 billion and a deficit of $9.9 billion, which Eisenhower's heroic efforts reduced by only $4.4 billion. In 1954 the administration formulated tax reductions that resembled Republican programs of the 1920s in providing benefits mainly to corporations and individuals in the upper brackets. The new budget slashed expenditures by $6.5 billion, nearly 10 percent, and the Federal Reserve Board reinforced administration policy by tightening credit and raising interest rates to avert inflation. But the business slump which followed reduced government revenues, making it harder to balance the budget. After that experience Eisenhower's fiscal and monetary policies became less doctrinaire and more flexible. The government accepted easier credit and deficits as necessary "countercyclical" methods. The Keynesian Age, if not yet acknowledged, endured.

Although Eisenhower chipped away at several New Deal programs, his presidency in the end served rather to legitimate the New Deal by keeping its basic structure and premises intact during an era of prosperity. In a letter to his brother in 1954, he observed: "Should any political party attempt to abolish social security and eliminate labor laws and farm programs, you would not hear of that party again in our political history." In some ways, the administration not only maintained the New Deal but extended its reach, especially after 1954 when it had the help of Democratic Congresses. Amendments to the Social Security Act in 1954 and 1956 brought coverage to millions in categories formerly excluded: professional people, domestic and clerical workers, farm workers, and members of the armed forces. In 1959 the program's benefits went up 7 percent. The federal minimum wage rose in 1955 from 75¢ to $1 an hour. Federal expenditures for public health rose steadily in the Eisenhower years and the president went so far as to endorse federal participation in health insurance, but Congress twice refused to act. Low-income housing continued to be built, although on a much-reduced scale.

Some farm-related aid programs were expanded during the Eisenhower years. The Rural Electrification Administration announced on its twenty-fifth birthday in 1960 that 97 percent of American farms had electricity. In 1954 the government undertook on a large scale to finance the export of surplus farm products in exchange for foreign currencies, an idea much like the McNary-Haugen scheme of the 1920s. Surpluses were exported also as gifts to needy nations and to provide milk for schoolchildren. In 1959 surpluses became available to the needy by issuing food stamps redeemable at grocery stores.

Despite Eisenhower's general disapproval of public power programs, he continued to support public works for which he saw a legitimate need. Indeed two such programs left major monuments to his presidency: the St. Lawrence Seaway and the interstate highways. The St. Lawrence Seaway, designed to open the Great Lakes to oceangoing ships by means of locks and dredging, had languished in Congress since the time of President Hoover because of opposition by eastern business and railroad interests afraid of the competition. In 1954 Eisenhower finally broke the opposition by pointing to Canadian determination to go ahead anyway and to the growing need of American steel producers for Canadian ore as domestic deposits gave out. Congress then approved joint participation with the Canadians, and five years later the seaway was open. In 1956 a new federal highway construction act authorized the federal government to put up 90 percent of the cost of building 42,500 miles of limited-access interstate highways to serve the needs of commerce and defense, as well as private convenience. The states put up the remaining 10 percent. It was only afterward that people realized that the huge national commitment to the automobile might have come at the expense of America's railroad system, already in a state of advanced decay.

CONCLUDING AN ARMISTICE   America's new responsibilities in the postwar world, however, continued to absorb Eisenhower's attention. The most pressing problem when he entered office was the continuing, painful deadlock in the Korean peace talks. The main stumbling block was the insistence of North Korea and Red China that all prisoners be returned regardless of their wishes. To break the deadlock, Eisenhower resolved upon a bold stand. In mid-May 1953 he stepped up aerial bombardment of North Korea, then had Secretary of State Dulles convey to Peking through the Indian government

In 1953 Eisenhower announced an uneasy armistice, which separated North and South Korea just above the 38th parallel.

a secret threat to remove all limits on weapons and targets. It was a thinly veiled warning of atomic warfare against Red forces, perhaps even against China itself. Whether for that reason or others, negotiations then moved quickly toward an armistice along the established battle line just above the 38th parallel, and toward a complicated arrangement for prisoner exchange which allowed captives to accept or refuse repatriation.

On July 26, 1953, President Eisenhower announced the conclusion of the armistice. But most of the Korean peninsula was devastated. Whether Eisenhower had pulled a masterful bluff in getting the armistice has never become clear; no one knows if he would have used atomic weapons. Perhaps the more decisive factors in bringing about a settlement were the size of Chinese Communist losses, which they increasingly found unacceptable, and the new spirit of uncertainty and caution felt by Russian Communists after the death of Joseph Stalin on March 5, 1953—six weeks after Ike's inauguration.

CONCLUDING A WITCH-HUNT The Korean armistice helped to end another dismal episode: the meteoric career of Senator Joseph R. McCarthy, which had flourished amid the anxieties of wartime. Convinced that the government was infested with Communists and spies, the Wisconsin senator launched a splenetic crusade to root them out. In the process he and his aides lied, falsified evidence, and bullied or blackmailed witnesses. During the summer of 1953 he sent two assistants, Roy M. Cohn and G. David Schine, on a junket to Europe to purge American government libraries of "subversive works" such as the writings of Emerson and Thoreau, Dreiser and Steinbeck. Eventually McCarthy's unscrupulous tactics led to his self-destruction, but not before he had left still more careers and reputations in ruins. The Republicans thought their victory in 1952 would curb his recklessness, but McCarthy actually grew more outlandish in his charges and his investigative methods. And many Americans caught up in the anti-Communist hysteria viewed him as a heroic knight doing battle against the forces of darkness.

McCarthy finally overreached himself when he tried to peddle the absurdity that the United States Army itself was "soft" on communism. The cases in point, it seemed, were a "pink" dentist at Fort Monmouth, New Jersey, since given an honorable discharge, and the army's refusal to give special treatment to a draftee, G. David Schine, McCarthy's former assistant. A confusing tangle of charges and countercharges led to hearings by McCarthy's subcommittee.

From April 22 to June 17, 1954, the Army-McCarthy hearings displayed McCarthy to a large television audience at his capricious

worst, bullying witnesses, dragging out lengthy irrelevancies, repeatedly calling "point of order." He became the perfect foil for the
army's gentle but unflappable counsel, Joseph Welch of Boston,
whose rapier wit repeatedly drew blood. When a witness used the
word "pixie," McCarthy demanded a definition and Welch sweetly
explained that a pixie was "a kind of fairy." But when McCarthy
tried to smear one of Welch's young associates, the counsel went into
a cold rage: "Until this moment, Senator, I think I never really
gauged your cruelty or your recklessness. . . . Have you no sense of
decency, sir, at long last?" When the audience burst into applause,
the confused, skulking senator was reduced to whispering, "What
did I do?"

Perhaps McCarthy never found out, but at that point the house he
had thrown together began to crash around his ears. He descended
into new depths of scurrility, now directed at his own colleagues,
calling one senator "senile" and another "a living miracle . . . the
only man who has lived so long with neither brains nor guts." On
December 2, 1954, the Senate voted 67 to 22 to "condemn"
McCarthy for contempt of the Senate. Samuel J. Ervin, Jr., of North
Carolina, a newly appointed senator, accused him of "disorderly
conduct by flyblowing . . . a strong Anglo-Saxon word, but a very
expressive one." McCarthy was finished, and increasingly took to
alcohol. Three years later, at the age of forty-eight, he was dead.

The Army-McCarthy Hearings, June 1954. *Joseph Welch (head in hand)
listens dejectedly after McCarthy's attempt to smear one of Welch's
associates.*

The witch-hunt was over. McCarthyism, Ike joked, had become McCarthywasm, though not for those whose reputations and careers had been wrecked. To the end Eisenhower kept his resolve not to "get down in the gutter with that guy" and sully the dignity of the presidency, but he did work resolutely against McCarthy behind the scenes. Eisenhower shared, nevertheless, the deeply held conviction of many citizens that espionage posed a real danger to national security. He denied clemency to Julius and Ethel Rosenberg, convicted of transmitting atomic secrets to the Russians, on the grounds that they "may have condemned to death tens of millions of innocent people." Although few (if any) scientists believed the principle of the bomb was a secret, the Rosenbergs went to the electric chair on June 19, 1953.

INTERNAL SECURITY   Even earlier, Eisenhower stiffened the government security program that Truman had set up six years before. In 1953 an executive order broadened the basis for firing government workers by replacing Truman's criterion of "disloyalty" with the new category of "security risk." Under the new edict federal workers lost their jobs because of dubious associations or personal habits that might make them careless or vulnerable to blackmail. In December 1953 the Atomic Energy Commission removed the security clearance of the physicist J. Robert Oppenheimer, the "father of the atomic bomb," on the grounds that he had expressed qualms about the hydrogen bomb in 1949–1950 and had associated with Communists or former Communists in the past. Lacking evidence of any disloyalty or betrayal, the AEC nevertheless branded him a "security risk" because of "fundamental defects in his character."

The Supreme Court, however, modified some of the more extreme expressions of the Red Scare. In September 1953 Eisenhower appointed former governor Earl Warren of California as chief justice, a decision the president later pronounced the "biggest damnfool mistake I ever made." Warren, who had seemed safely conservative while active in politics, proved to have a social conscience and a streak of libertarianism which another Eisenhower appointee, William I. Brennan, Jr., shared. The Warren Court (1953–1969), under the chief justice's influence, became an important agency of social and political change on through the 1960s.

In connection with security programs and loyalty requirements, the Court veered back in the direction of traditional individual rights. A 1957 opinion by Justice John Marshall Harlan narrowly construed the Smith Act of 1940, aimed at conspirators against the government, to apply only to those advocating revolutionary action. Merely teaching revolutionary doctrine in the abstract could not be construed as a crime under the act. This, plus other decisions setting rigid standards for evidence, rendered the Smith Act a dead letter.

DULLES AND FOREIGN POLICY   The Eisenhower administration promised new departures in foreign policy under the direction of Secretary of State John Foster Dulles. Grandson of one former secretary of state and nephew of another, Dulles had pursued a lifetime career as an international lawyer and sometime diplomat. In 1919 he had assisted the American delegates at the Versailles Conference. As counselor to the Truman State Department he had, among other things, negotiated the Japanese peace treaty. Son of a minister and himself an active Presbyterian layman, Dulles, in the words of the British ambassador, resembled those old zealots of the wars of religion who "saw the world as an arena in which the forces of good and evil were continuously at war." Tall, spare, and stooped, he gave the appearance of dour sternness and Calvinist righteousness. But he was also a man of immense energy, intelligence, and experience. As Eisenhower once said of Dulles, "There's only one man I know who has seen *more* of the world, and talked with more people and *knows* more than he does—and that's me."

The foreign policy planks of the 1952 Republican platform, which Dulles wrote, showed both the moralist and the tactician at work. The policy of containment was needlessly defensive, Dulles thought. This conviction meshed nicely with the conventional wisdom of the right wing that the Yalta agreements were perhaps a betrayal, at best a blunder. The 1952 platform, therefore, promised to "repudiate all commitments . . . such as those of Yalta which aid Communist enslavement" and to end "the negative, futile and immoral policy of 'containment' which abandons countless human beings to a despotism and godless terrorism." A new policy of liberation, the platform promised, "will inevitably set up strains and stresses within the captive world which will make the rulers impotent to continue in their monstrous ways and mark the beginning of the end."

The policy came perilously close to proclaiming a holy war, but Dulles took care to explain that he did not intend forcible liberation. Soon it became apparent that it was less a policy than a web of rhetoric to catch ethnic voters whose homelands had fallen captive. The Republican party's new Ethnic Origins Division made the most of it. Eisenhower in his inaugural address promised to "unleash" Chiang Kai-shek—that is, cancel the Seventh Fleet's orders to prevent his invading the Chinese mainland. The fleet's more realistic mission of protecting Taiwan continued, however.

When it came to repudiating Yalta, the administration drew back. Ike was conscious of his own vulnerability as the commander who

Secretary of State John
Foster Dulles.

had implemented the agreement and who had stopped American
forces short of Berlin and Prague. The administration's Captive Peoples Resolution merely rejected any misuse of the Yalta agreements,
"which have been perverted to bring about the subjugation of free
peoples." The real betrayal, in short, had been Russian violation of
the Yalta accords. Even that resolution died in congressional committee. That the liberation rhetoric rang false became more evident in
June 1953 when workers in East Germany rebelled against working
conditions and food shortages. When Russian tanks rolled over the
demonstrators, the administration did nothing except to deplore
the situation. For three years more Dulles was able to maintain the
belief that his rhetoric was undermining the Communist hold on
eastern Europe—until suppression of the 1956 uprising in Hungary
underscored the danger of stirring futile hopes among captive peoples.

COVERT ACTIONS Insofar as American interventions occurred
abroad, they were covert operations by the Central Intelligence
Agency in countries outside the Soviet sphere. Under Eisenhower,
Allen Dulles, brother of the secretary of state, rose from second in
command to chief of the CIA. A veteran of the wartime Office of
Strategic Services, he had already had a hand in beefing up the CIA's
capacity for cloak-and-dagger operations. In two cases early in the
Eisenhower years this capability was actually used to overthrow
governments believed hostile to American interests: in Iran (1953)
and in Guatemala (1954).

In Iran, Premier Mohammed Mossadegh, a seventy-year-old nationalist, whipped up popular feeling against British control of Iranian oil production and then took over the foreign properties. In challenging Western interests he had the support of the Tudeh, Iran's Communist party, and left the impression that he either had joined their side or would become their dupe. Under these circumstances, Allen Dulles sent a crack CIA agent along with an adviser to help the shah of Iran, Mohammed Reza Pahlavi, organize his secret police. Armed chiefly with about a million dollars, they stirred up street demonstrations against Mossadegh which, reinforced by soldiers loyal to the shah, toppled the premier, sent him to jail, and brought the young shah back from exile in Rome. A new premier made an arrangement under which the British and Americans each got 40 percent of Iran's exported oil production, the Dutch 14 percent, and the French 6 percent.

In Guatemala, Jacobo Arbenz Guzman had become president in an election in which he had Communist backing. While the administration lacked evidence that Arbenz was a Communist, the American ambassador said "he talked like a Communist, he thought like a Communist, and he acted like a Communist, and if he is not one, he will do until one comes along." Critics of the intervention contended that Arbenz's chief sin was that he had expropriated 225,000 acres of United Fruit Company land. He had also secured weapons from East Germany with which to arm a peasant militia.

With Eisenhower's consent the CIA chose a Guatemalan colonel to stage a coup from a base in Honduras. The operation, however, was mainly a war of nerves, with rumors spread by clandestine radio stations and token raids on Guatemala City run by surplus planes from World War II. Arbenz panicked, resigned, and fled the country. Defenders of the action agreed with the conclusion of a committee commissioned to investigate the CIA in 1955: "It is now clear that we are facing an implacable enemy whose avowed objective is world domination by whatever means and at whatever cost. There are no rules in such a game. Hitherto acceptable norms of conduct do not apply."

BRINKSMANSHIP   Actually, for all his bold talk of liberation, Dulles made no significant departure from the strategy of containment created under Acheson and Truman. Instead he institutionalized containment in the rigid mold of his Cold War rhetoric and extended it into the military strategy of deterrence. He betrayed a fatal affinity for colorful phrases which left him, according to one observer, "perpetually poised between a cliché and an indiscretion." To his lexicon of "liberation" and "roll back," Dulles added two major new contributions while in office: "massive retaliation" and "going to the brink."

"Massive retaliation" was actually a shorthand version of Dulles's phrase "massive retaliatory power," a description of the "New Look" in military strategy, an effort to get, in the slogan soon current, "more bang for the buck" or "more rubble for the ruble." Budgetary considerations lay at the root of military plans, for Eisenhower and his cabinet shared the fear that in the effort to build a superior war power the country could spend itself into bankruptcy. During 1953 members of the Joint Chiefs of Staff set to work on planning a new military posture. The heart of their so-called New Look was the assumption that nuclear weapons could be used in limited-war situations, allowing reductions in conventional forces and thus budgetary savings. Dulles, who announced the policy on January 12, 1954, explained that savings would come "by placing more reliance on deterrent power, and less dependence on local defensive power." No longer could an enemy "pick his time and place and method of warfare." American responses would be "by means and at places of our choosing." No longer would "the Communists nibble us to death all over the world in little wars," Vice-President Nixon explained in March 1954.

By this time both the United States and Russia had exploded hydrogen bombs. With the new policy of deterrence, what Winston Churchill called a "balance of terror" had replaced the old "balance of power." The threat of nuclear holocaust was terrifying, but the notion that the United States would risk such a disaster in response to local wars had little credibility.

Dulles's policy of "brinksmanship" depended for its strategic effect on those very fears of nuclear disaster. Dulles argued in 1956 that in following a tough policy of confrontation with communism, one sometimes had to "go to the brink" of war: "The ability to get to the verge without getting into war is the necessary art. If you

"Don't Be Afraid—I Can Always Pull You Back." *Secretary of State Dulles pushes a reluctant America to the brink of war.*

cannot master it, you inevitably get into war. . . . We walked to the brink and we looked it in the face. We took strong action." The first occasion on which a firm stand had halted further aggression had been America's threat in 1953 to break the Korean stalemate by removing restraints from the armed forces. The second had come in 1954, when aircraft carriers moved into the South China Sea "both to deter any Red Chinese attack against Indochina and to provide weapons for instant retaliation."

INDOCHINA: THE BACKGROUND TO WAR Dulles's reference to Indochina was an oversimplification: it neglected the complexity of the situation there, which presented a special if not unique case of the nationalism that swept the old colonial world of Asia and Africa after World War II, damaging both the power and prestige of the colonial powers. By the early 1950s most of British Asia was independent or on the way: India, Pakistan, Ceylon (later Sri Lanka), Burma, and the Malay States (later the Federation of Malaysia). The Dutch and French, however, were less ready than the British to give up their colonies and thus created a dilemma for American policy-makers. Americans sympathized with colonial nationalists who sometimes invoked the example of 1776, but Americans also wanted Dutch and French help against communism. The Truman administration felt obliged to answer their pleas for aid. Both the Dutch and the French were obliged to reconquer areas which had passed from Japanese occupation into the hands of local patriots. In the Dutch East Indies the Japanese had created a puppet Indonesian Republic which emerged from World War II virtually independent. The Dutch effort to regain control met resistance which exploded into open warfare.

Eventually, American pressure persuaded the Dutch to accept self-government under a Dutch-Indonesian Union in 1949, but that lasted only until 1954 when the Republic of Indonesia became independent. In April 1955 the Bandung Conference in Indonesia, attended by delegates from twenty-nine independent countries of Asia and Africa, signaled the emergence of a "Third World" of underdeveloped countries, unaligned with either the United States or the Soviet bloc. Among other actions the conference condemned "colonialism in all its manifestations," a statement which implicitly condemned both the USSR and the West.

French Indochina, created in the nineteenth century out of the old kingdoms of Cambodia, Laos, and Vietnam, offered a variation on Third World nationalism. During World War II Japanese control of the area had required their support of pro-Vichy French civil servants and opposition to the local nationalists. Chief among the latter were the Vietminh (Vietnamese League for Independence), who fell under the influence of Communists led by Ho Chi Minh. At the end of the war this group controlled part of northern Vietnam, and on September 2, 1945, Ho Chi Minh proclaimed a Democratic Republic of Vietnam, with its capital in Hanoi.

Ho's declaration borrowed from Thomas Jefferson, opening with the words "We hold these truths to be self-evident. That all men are created equal." American officers were on the reviewing stand in Hanoi and American planes flew over the celebration. Ho had received secret American help against the Japanese during the war, but bids for further aid after the war went unanswered. Vietnam took low priority in American diplomatic concerns at the time.

In March 1946 the French government, preoccupied with domestic politics, recognized Ho's new government as a "free state" within the French union. Before the year was out, however, Ho's forces came into conflict with French efforts to establish another regime in the southern provinces, and this clash soon expanded into the First Indochina War. In June 1949, having set up puppet rulers in Laos and Cambodia, the French reinstated Bao Dai as head of state in Vietnam. The victory of the Chinese Communists later in 1949 was followed by Red China's diplomatic recognition of the Vietminh government in Hanoi, and then the recognition of Bao Dai by the United States and Britain.

The Vietminh movement thereafter became more completely dominated by Ho Chi Minh and his Communist associates, and more dependent on Russia and Red China for help. In 1950, with the outbreak of fighting in Korea, the struggle in Vietnam took on more and more the appearance of a battleground in the Cold War. When

Ho Chi Minh.

the Korean War ended, American aid to the French in Vietnam, begun by the Truman administration, continued. By the end of 1953 the Eisenhower administration was paying about two-thirds of the cost of the French effort, or about $1 billion annually. By 1954 the United States found itself at the edge of the "brink" to which Dulles later referred. A major French force had been sent to Dien Bien Phu, near the Laos border, in the hope of luring Vietminh guerrillas into a set battle and grinding them up with superior firepower. The French instead found themselves trapped by a superior force which threatened to overrun their stronghold.

In March 1954 the French government requested an American air strike to relieve the pressure on Dien Bien Phu. Eisenhower himself seemed to endorse forceful action when he advanced his "domino theory" at a news conference on April 7, 1954: "You have a row of dominoes set up, you knock over the first one, and what will happen to the last one is the certainty that it will go over very quickly." He was nevertheless playing a cautious game. When congressional leaders expressed reservations, he took a stand against American intervention unless the British lent support. When they refused, he backed away from unilateral action in Vietnam.

THE GENEVA ACCORDS AND U.S. POLICY   On May 7, 1954, the massive attacks loosed by Vietminh general Vo Nguyen Giap finally overwhelmed the last French resistance at Dien Bien Phu. It was the very eve of the day an international conference at Geneva took up the question of Indochina. Six weeks later, as French forces continued to meet defeats in Vietnam, a new French government promised to get an early settlement. On July 20 representatives of France, Britain, Russia, the People's Republic of China, and the Vietminh reached agreement on the Geneva Accords, and the next day produced their Final Declaration which proposed to neutralize Laos and Cambodia and divided Vietnam at the 17th parallel. The Vietminh would take power in the north and the French would remain south of the line until elections in 1956 should reunify Vietnam. American and South Vietnamese representatives refused either to join in the accord or to sign the Final Declaration, with the result that Russia and China backed away from their earlier hints that they would guarantee the settlement. In the end, nobody at all signed the Declaration and participants confined themselves to unilateral statements in which they endorsed or dissociated themselves from particular parts of the Geneva Accords.

Dulles responded by organizing mutual defense arrangements for Southeast Asia. On September 8, 1954, at a meeting in Manila, the United States joined seven other countries in an agreement that Dulles wanted known as the Manila Defense Accord (MANDAC), but which the press quickly labeled as the Southeast Asia Treaty Organization (SEATO). The impression that it paralleled NATO was false, for the Manila Accord was neither a common defense organization like NATO nor was it primarily Asian. The signers agreed that in case of attack on one, the others would act according to their "constitutional practices," and in case of threats or subversion they would "consult immediately." The members included only three Asian countries—the Philippines, Thailand, and Pakistan—together with Britain, France, Australia, New Zealand, and the United States. India and Indonesia, the two most populous countries in the region, refused to join. A special protocol added to the treaty extended coverage to Indochina. The treaty reflected what Dulles's critics

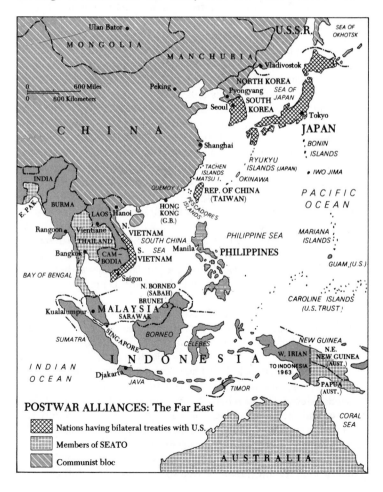

POSTWAR ALLIANCES: The Far East

- Nations having bilateral treaties with U.S.
- Members of SEATO
- Communist bloc

called "pactomania," which by the end of the Eisenhower administration contracted the United States to defend forty-three other
countries.

Eisenhower announced that though the United States "had not
itself been party to or bound by the decision taken at the [Geneva]
Conference," any renewal of Communist aggression "would be reviewed by us as a matter of grave concern." In Vietnam, when Ho
Chi Minh took over the north, those who wished to leave for South
Vietnam, mostly Catholics, did so with American aid. Power in the
south gravitated to a new premier imposed on Emperor Bao Dai by
the French at American urging: Ngo Dinh Diem, who had opposed
both the French and the Vietminh, took office during the Geneva
talks. Before that he had been in exile at a Catholic seminary in New
Jersey. In October 1954 Eisenhower offered to assist Diem "in developing and maintaining a strong, viable state, capable of resisting
attempted subversion or aggression through military means." In
return the United States expected "needed reforms." American aid
was forthcoming in the form of CIA and military cadres charged with
training Diem's armed forces and police.

Instead of instituting political and economic reforms, however,
Diem tightened his grip on the country, suppressing opposition on
both right and left, offering little or no land distribution, and permitting widespread corruption. In 1956 he refused to join in the elections to reunify Vietnam and, after French withdrawal from the
country, he ousted Bao Dai and installed himself as president. His
efforts to eliminate all opposition played into the hands of the Communists, who found recruits and fellow travelers among the discontented. By 1957 guerrilla forces known as the Vietcong had begun
attacks on the government, and in 1960 the resistance coalesced as
the National Liberation Front. As guerrilla warfare gradually disrupted the country, the Eisenhower administration was helpless to
do anything but "sink or swim with Ngo Dinh Diem."

QUEMOY AND MATSU   Having backed away from the "brink" in Vietnam, Eisenhower and Dulles soon found themselves approaching
another. Just before the Manila conference in September 1954, Red
Chinese artillery began shelling the South China Sea islands of
Quemoy and Matsu, held by Chiang Kai-shek's Nationalists. On his
way back from Manila Dulles stopped in Taipei and worked out a
mutual defense treaty which bound the United States to defend
Taiwan and the nearby Pescadores Islands, and which bound Taiwan to undertake offensive action only with American consent. The
treaty omitted mention of the offshore islands, and the mainland
Chinese continued their pressure, occupying one of the Tachens. In
January 1955 the president secured in Congress a resolution giving

him full power to go to the defense of Taiwan and the Pescadores, and also authorizing him to secure and protect "related positions of that area now in friendly hands" in order to defend Taiwan. Congress's endorsement was overwhelming—the resolution drew only three negative votes in each house—for so sweeping a grant of power.

The Red Chinese kept up their provocative activity nonetheless, and under pressure from the American government the Nationalists evacuated the Tachens as indefensible. But Quemoy and Matsu became symbols of the will to protect Taiwan, and were perhaps strategically useful too. In any case the American chief of naval operations "leaked" word to journalists that the administration was considering a plan "to destroy Red China's military potential and thus end its expansionist tendencies." Soon afterward the Chinese backed away from the brink. At the Bandung Conference in April, with diplomatic encouragement from other Asian nations, Premier Chou En-lai said Red China was ready to discuss the Formosa Strait issue directly with the United States. In May 1955 representatives of the two governments began meetings in Geneva, and the guns fell silent.

A THAW IN THE COLD WAR   The quiet in the Formosa Strait was but one signal of a "thaw" in the Cold War. Europe remained the chief focus of American foreign policy, and there friendly gestures came from the Soviet government and the Communist party secretary Nikita Khrushchev, who had come out on top in the post-Stalin power struggles. The Soviets agreed to the 1955 Austrian State Treaty, ending the four-power occupation of that little country and restoring its independence as a neutral but Western-oriented state. At Geneva, during July 18–23, 1955, President Eisenhower joined the British prime minister and the premiers of France and the Soviet Union in the first summit conference since the one at Potsdam ten years before, but unlike the Potsdam meeting this one was strictly a cosmetic affair. The leaders displayed cheerful grins and conveyed a mood of affability that had journalists writing about the amicable "spirit of Geneva." But they decided nothing of substance on any of the major issues they discussed.

The high point of the conference occurred on July 21, when Eisenhower set forth what came to be called his "Open Skies" proposal, a prelude to disarmament by which Russia and the United States would give each other "a complete blueprint of our military establishments from beginning to end," and would each open its skies to the other for aerial surveillance. Khrushchev, who was present at the meeting, told the president privately that it was "a very transparent espionage device." It would give Americans information they did not already have while providing the Russians little they did not already know. In consequence the conference did nothing except to lay the groundwork for cultural and diplomatic exchanges. The conference left behind a vague aura of peace, but it also made clear the arrival of a thermonuclear stalemate.

CIVIL RIGHTS IN THE FIFTIES

The warm afterglow of Geneva diminished the prospect of nuclear conflict. With the guns silent in Vietnam and the Formosa Strait, the world enjoyed its first season of peace in nearly two decades. But race relations in the United States threatened to explode the domestic tranquility masking years of injustice.

STIRRINGS IN CIVIL RIGHTS   If the Eisenhower presidency seems an interlude of relative harmony between two decades of domestic and foreign strife, it should be remembered that those years also saw the onset of a revolution in race relations that historians have come to call the Second Reconstruction. Eisenhower entered office committed to civil rights in principle, and pushed the issue in areas of federal authority. During his first three years, public services in Washington, D.C., were desegregated, as were navy yards and veterans hospitals. Beyond that, however, two aspects of the president's philosophy inhibited vigorous action: his preference for state or local action, and his doubt that law could be effective in such matters. "I don't believe you can change the hearts of men with laws or decisions," he said. For the time, then, leadership in the civil-rights field came from the judiciary more than from the executive or legislative branch of the government.

In the 1930s the NAACP had resolved to test the "separate but equal" doctrine which had upheld racial segregation since the *Plessy* decision in 1896. Charles H. Houston, dean of the Howard University Law School, laid the plans and his former student, Thurgood Marshall, served as chief NAACP lawyer. They decided to begin with the expensive field of postgraduate study. At the time no southern or border state provided such study for blacks, although some offered grants for them to go out of state. In the case of Lloyd L. Gaines (1938) the Supreme Court ruled that such a grant failed to provide the equal protection of the laws required under the Fourteenth Amendment. Missouri hastily improvised a separate law school, but before Gaines's lawyers could resolve the issue, he mysteriously vanished. In *Sweatt v. Painter* (1950) the Court ruled that a separate black law school in Texas failed to measure up because of

Segregation began to be tested in the courts by the NAACP in the late 1930s.

intangible factors, such as its isolation from most of the future lawyers with whom its graduates would interact.

THE *BROWN* DECISION   By that time challenges to segregation in the public schools were rising through the appellate courts. Five such cases, from Kansas, Delaware, South Carolina, Virginia, and the District of Columbia—usually cited by reference to the first, *Brown v. Board of Education of Topeka, Kansas*—came to the Supreme Court for joint argument in 1952. Chief Justice Earl Warren wrote the opinion, handed down on May 17, 1954, in which a unanimous Court declared that "in the field of public education the doctrine of 'separate but equal' has no place." In support of its opinion the Court cited current sociological and psychological findings presented by the eminent Kenneth Clark, a black psychologist. It might well have cited historical evidence that Jim Crow facilities had been seldom equal and often not available to blacks at all. A year later, after further argument, the Court directed "a prompt and reasonable start toward full compliance"; the process should move "with all deliberate speed."

The white South's first response was relatively calm, deceptively so as it happened. Eisenhower refused to take any part in leading white southerners toward compliance. Privately he remarked: "I am convinced that the Supreme Court decision *set back* progress in the South *at least fifteen years*. The fellow who tries to tell me you can do these things by *force* is just plain *nuts*." While token integration began as early as 1954 in the border states, hostility mounted in the Deep South and Virginia, led by the newly formed Citizens' Councils and similar groups. Before the end of 1955, moderate sentiment in the South gave way to surly reaction. Virginia senator Harry F. Byrd supplied a rallying cry: "Massive Resistance." State legislatures passed pupil assignment laws and adopted other dodges, all futile, to interpose their power between the courts and the schools. In March 1956, 101 southern members of Congress lent their names to a "Southern Manifesto" which denounced the Court's decision as "a clear abuse of judicial power." At the end of 1956, in six southern states, not a single black child attended school with whites. In several of the others the degree of desegregation was minuscule.

THE MONTGOMERY BUS BOYCOTT   At the end of 1955 the drive for civil rights took a new turn in Montgomery, Alabama, "the cradle of the Confederacy." There, on December 1, 1955, Mrs. Rosa Parks, a black seamstress tired after a day's work, was arrested for refusing to give up her seat on a city bus to a white man. As was the case in many southern communities, Montgomery had a local ordinance that required blacks to give up their bus or train seat to a white when asked. The next night black community leaders met in the Dexter Avenue Baptist Church to organize a massive bus boycott under the aegis of the the Montgomery Improvement Association.

In Dexter Avenue's twenty-six-year-old pastor, Martin Luther King, Jr., the movement found a charismatic leader who spoke eloquently in cadences familiar to the Bible Belt. Born in Atlanta, the grandson of a slave and the son of a minister, King was endowed with intelligence, courage, and charisma. After attending Morehouse College in Atlanta and then receiving a seminary degree, he earned a Ph.D. in philosophy from Boston University before accepting a call to preach in Montgomery. He brought the movement a message of nonviolent, passive resistance compounded from the Gospels, the writings of Thoreau, and the example of Mahatma Gandhi in India. "We must use the weapon of love," he told his people. "We must realize so many people are taught to hate us that they are not totally responsible for their hate." To his antagonists he said: "We will soon wear you down by our capacity to suffer, and in winning our freedom we will so appeal to your heart and conscience that we will win you in the process."

The bus boycott achieved a remarkable solidarity. For months blacks in Montgomery formed car pools, hitchhiked, or simply walked. But the white town fathers, who were not quickly worn down, held out against the boycott and against the pleas of a bus company tired of losing money. The boycotters finally won through the federal courts a case they had initiated against bus segregation, and on December 20, 1956, the Supreme Court let stand without review an opinion of a lower court that "the separate but equal doctrine can no longer be safely followed as a correct statement of the law." The next day King and other blacks boarded the buses, but they still had a long way to travel before Jim Crow could be laid finally to rest. Trying to keep alive the spirit of the bus boycott, King and a group of associates in 1957 organized the Southern Christian Leadership Conference (SCLC).

Despite Eisenhower's reluctance to take the lead in desegregating schools, he supported the right to vote. In 1956, hoping to exploit divisions between northern and southern Democrats and to reclaim some of the black vote for Republicans, Eisenhower proposed legislation which became the Civil Rights Act of 1957. The first civil-

Martin Luther King, Jr., here facing arrest for leading a civil-rights march, advocated nonviolent resistance to racial segregation.

rights law passed since Reconstruction, it finally got through the Senate, after a year's delay, with the help of Majority Leader Lyndon B. Johnson, who won southern acceptance by watering down the act. Still, it established for a period of two years the Civil Rights Commission, which was later extended indefinitely, and a new Civil Rights Division in the Justice Department, which could seek injunctions to prevent interference with the right to vote. The SCLC promptly announced a campaign to register 2 million black voters. The Civil Rights Act of 1960 provided for federal court referees to register blacks where a court found a "pattern and practice" of discrimination, and also made it a federal crime to interfere with any court order or to cross state lines to destroy any building.

LITTLE ROCK There had been sporadic violence in resistance to civil-rights efforts, but a few weeks after the 1957 act passed, the governor of a state for the first time openly defied the law. Arkansas governor Orval Faubus called out the National Guard to prevent nine black students from entering Little Rock's Central High School under federal court order. A conference between the president and the governor proved fruitless, but on court order Faubus withdrew the Guard. When the students tried to enter the school, a hysterical mob forced their removal for their own safety. At that point Eisenhower, who had said two months before that he could not "imagine any set of circumstances that would ever induce me to send federal troops," ordered a thousand paratroopers to Little Rock to protect the students, and placed the National Guard on federal service. The soldiers stayed through the school year.

The following year Faubus closed the high schools of Little Rock, and court proceedings dragged on into 1959 before the schools could be reopened. The year 1959 proved an important turning point, for in that year massive resistance in Virginia collapsed when both state and federal courts struck down state laws that had cut off funds from integrated schools. Thereafter, massive resistance for the most part was confined to the Deep South where five states, from South Carolina west through Louisiana, still held out against even token integration.

A LANDSLIDE FOR IKE When President Eisenhower suffered a "moderately severe" coronary seizure during a Colorado vacation in September 1955, some journalists felt that he could not have chosen a more opportune time: there was no immediate crisis on the horizon. He recovered quickly and was getting back in harness within a month. In February 1956, after his doctor pronounced him recovered, the president announced his decision to run again. In August the Republican convention renominated Eisenhower by acclamation and again named Nixon as the vice-presidential candidate. The party platform endorsed Eisenhower's "modern Republicanism."

The Democrats turned again to Stevenson, who had campaigned vigorously in the primaries against Senator Estes Kefauver. After Stevenson freed the convention to name its own candidate for vice-president, the delegates chose Kefauver by a narrow margin over young Massachusetts senator John F. Kennedy. The platform evaded the civil-rights issue and otherwise stuck to Democratic staples: less "favoritism" to big business, repeal of the Taft-Hartley Act, parity for farmers, tax relief for those in low-income brackets.

Neither candidate generated much excitement during the campaign. The Democrats did what they could with the issue of the president's health, but centered their fire on the heir apparent, Richard Nixon, a "man of many masks." Stevenson aroused little enthusiasm for two controversial proposals: to drop conscription and rely on an all-volunteer army, and to ban H-bomb tests by international agreement. Both involved military questions which put Stevenson at a disadvantage by pitting his judgment against that of a successful general.

During the last week of the campaign the season of world peace was broken by shooting wars along the Suez Canal and in the streets of Budapest. The two crises made it possible for Stevenson to declare the administration's foreign policy "bankrupt." Most voters, however, reasoned that the crises spelled a poor time to switch horses, and they handed Eisenhower a landslide victory. He lost one border state, Missouri, but in carrying Louisiana became the first Republican to win a Deep South state since Reconstruction; nationally, he carried all but seven states. The decision was unmistakably clear: he won more than 35 million popular votes to a little over 26 million for Stevenson, 457 electoral votes to the Democrat's 73.

A Season of Troubles

CRISIS IN THE MIDDLE EAST   The twin crises of 1956 in the Suez and Hungary were unrelated but occurred almost as if placed in malicious juxtaposition by some evil force. The attack on Egypt by Britain, France, and Israel disrupted the Western alliance and damaged any claim to moral outrage at Russian actions in Hungary. For the Soviets, the Suez War afforded both a smokescreen for the subjugation of Hungary and a chance to enlarge their influence in the Middle East, an increasingly important source of oil.

After 1953 the Eisenhower-Dulles policy in the region departed from the Truman-Acheson focus on Israel and distanced itself from

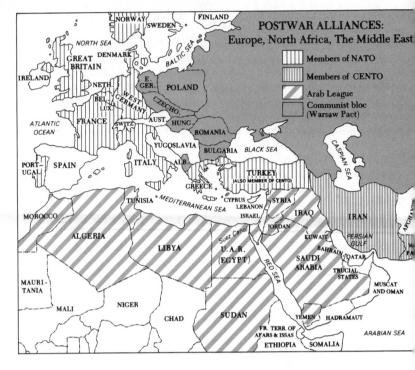

POSTWAR ALLIANCES:
Europe, North Africa, The Middle East

▨ Members of NATO

▨ Members of CENTO

▨ Arab League

▢ Communist bloc (Warsaw Pact)

British-French economic interests in order to cultivate Arab friendship. To forestall Russian penetration, Dulles in 1955 completed his line of alliances across the "northern tier" of the Middle East. Under American sponsorship Britain joined the Muslim states of Turkey, Iraq, Iran, and Pakistan in the Middle East Treaty Organization (METO), or Baghdad Pact, as the treaty was commonly called. By linking the easternmost NATO state (Turkey) to the westernmost SEATO state (Pakistan), METO had a certain superficial logic, but after Iraq, the only Arab member, withdrew in 1959 it became clear that the whole thing had been moribund from the start. Below the northern tier, moreover, the Arab states remained aloof from the organization. These were the states of the Arab League (Egypt, Jordan, Syria, Lebanon, and Saudi Arabia), which had warred on Israel in 1948–1949 and remained committed to its destruction.

The most fateful developments in the region turned on the rise of Egyptian general Gamal Abdel Nasser after the overthrow of King Farouk in 1952. The bone of contention was the Suez Canal, which had opened in 1869 as a joint French-Egyptian venture. But in 1875 the British government had acquired the largest block of stock and from 1882 on British forces were posted there to protect the British Empire's "lifeline" to India and other colonies. When Nasser's new regime pressed for the withdrawal of British forces from the canal zone, Eisenhower and Dulles supported its demand, and in 1954 an Anglo-Egyptian treaty provided for British withdrawal within twenty months. Nasser, like other leaders of the Third World, remained unaligned in the Cold War and sought to play both sides off against each other. The United States, meanwhile, courted Egyptian support by offering the prospect of American assistance in building a great hydroelectric plant at Aswan on the Nile River.

From the outset the administration's proposal was opposed by Jewish constituencies concerned with Egyptian threats to Israel, and by southern congressmen who feared the competition from Egyptian cotton. When Nasser then increased trade with the Soviet bloc and recognized Red China, Dulles abruptly canceled the loan offer in July 1956. The outcome was far from a triumph of American diplomacy. The chief victims, it turned out, were Anglo-French interests in the Suez. Unable to retaliate against the United States, Nasser nationalized the Suez Canal Company and earmarked its revenues for the Aswan project, thereby enhancing his prestige in the Arab world. The British and French, directly challenged and faced with loss of control of the crucial Suez Canal, reacted strongly. Fruitless negotiations dragged out through the summer, and finally, on October 29, 1956, Israeli forces invaded the Gaza Strip and the Sinai peninsula. The Israelis invaded ostensibly to root out Arab guerrillas, but actually to synchronize with the British and French, who began bombing Egyptian air bases and on November 3 occupied Port Said. Their actions, the British and French claimed, were meant to protect the canal against the opposing belligerents.

The Suez War put the United States in a quandary. Either the administration could support its Western allies and see the trouble-

The Twentieth-Century Dilemma. *The Suez crisis forced America into a difficult choice between support for its Western allies and support for an anticolonial, nationalist movement.*

some Nasser crushed, or it could stand on the United Nations charter and champion Arab nationalism against imperialistic aggression. The latter course was adopted, with the unusual result that Russia sided with the United States' position. Once the threat of American embargoes had forced Anglo-French-Israeli capitulation, the Russians capitalized on the situation by threatening to use missiles against the Western aggressors. This belated bravado won for Russia some of the credit in the Arab world for what the United States had done.

REPRESSION IN HUNGARY   All the while, Khrushchev was engaged in the subjugation of Hungary, a sharp reversal to the campaign of "de-Stalinization" he had launched in his "secret" speech on the crimes of the Stalin era, delivered at the Communist Party Congress in February 1956. Khrushchev joined this confession of Communist tyranny with hints of relaxed policies and suggestions that different countries might take "separate roads to socialism." In the satellite countries this put Stalinist leaders on the defensive and emboldened the more independent national leaders. In June riots in the Polish city of Poznan led to the rise of Wladyslaw Gomulka, a Polish nationalist, to leadership of the Polish Communist party. Gomulka managed to win a greater degree of independence by avoiding an open break with the Russians.

In Hungary, however, a similar movement got out of hand. On October 23 fighting broke out in Budapest, followed by the installation of Imre Nagy, a moderate Communist, as head of the government. Again the Russians seemed content to let "de-Stalinization" follow its course, and on October 28 they withdrew their forces from Budapest. But Nagy's announcement three days later that Hungary would withdraw from the Warsaw Pact brought Russian tanks back into Budapest. They installed a more compliant leader, Janos Kadar, and hauled Nagy off to Moscow, where a firing squad executed him in 1958. It was a tragic dénouement to a movement that, at the outset, promised the sort of moderation which might have vindicated Kennan's policy of "containment," if not Dulles's notion of "liberation."

LEGISLATIVE STUMBLING   In the euphoria of his landslide victory on November 6, Eisenhower declared on election night: "I think that modern Republicanism has now proved itself. And America has approved of modern Republicanism." He later defined this as "the political philosophy that recognizes clearly the responsibility of the Federal Government to take the lead in making certain that the productivity of our great economic machine is distributed so that no one will suffer disaster, privation, through no fault of his own."

Eisenhower Republicans, it seemed clear, had assimilated the New Deal as an accomplished fact. But as decisive as the vote for Eisenhower was, the winner's coattails failed to swing a congressional majority for his own party in either house, the first time this had happened since the election of Zachary Taylor in 1848.

New troubles followed Eisenhower's smashing victory. It began with the "great budget battle" of 1957. In January the president sent up to Capitol Hill a $72 billion budget for fiscal 1958, up $3 billion from the previous year, the biggest peacetime budget ever. The size of the budget, which increased foreign aid, military spending, and allocations for atomic energy, housing, public works, and education, startled and alarmed even the president, who had little time to cut it back. Eisenhower sent the bill to Congress, still hopeful that continued prosperity and high revenues would supply a surplus.

On the day the budget went to Congress the secretary of the treasury told reporters "there are a lot of places in this budget that can be cut," and suggested that if government could not reduce the "terrific" tax burden "you will have a depression that will curl your hair." Eisenhower claimed to share this desire to reduce the budget, but the spectacle of a treasury secretary challenging the budget on the day it went to Congress conveyed an impression of divided purpose and conflict in the administration. Both Democrats and Old Guard Republicans declared an open season on the administration's budget requests, and in the end they hacked out about $4 billion, including heavy cuts in foreign aid, the United States Information Agency, and the Defense Department. By the time the battle was over in August, an economic slump had set in and tax revenues dropped. In spite of the cuts, the administration projected a $500 million deficit.

SPUTNIK On October 4, 1957, came the Soviet launching of the first man-made satellite, called *sputnik*, an acronym for the Russian phrase "fellow traveler of earth." Sputnik I weighed 194 pounds, but less than a month later the Soviets launched a capsule of 1,120 pounds, and it carried a dog wired up for monitoring. Americans, until then complacent about their technical primacy, suddenly discovered an apparent "missile gap." If the Russians were so advanced in rocketry, then perhaps they could hit American cities. All along Eisenhower knew that the "gap" was more illusory than real, but could not reveal that high-altitude American U-2 spy planes were gathering this information. Even so, American missile development was in a state of disarray, with a tangle of agencies and committees engaged in waste and duplication. The launching of Explorer I, the first American satellite, on January 31, 1958, did not quiet the outcry.

By the Rocket's Red Glare. *The Soviet success in space shocked Americans.*

Russia's success with Sputnik launched efforts in America to enlarge defense spending, to offer NATO allies intermediate-range ballistic missiles (IRBMs) pending development of long-range intercontinental ballistic missiles (ICBMs), to set up a new agency to coordinate space efforts, and to establish a crash program in science education. The "sputnik syndrome," compounded by a sharp recession through the winter of 1957–1958, loosened the purse strings of economy-minded congressmen, who added to the new budget more than Eisenhower wanted for both defense and domestic programs. During 1958 Britain, Italy, and Turkey accepted American Thor and Jupiter missiles on their territory. In July 1958 Congress created the National Aeronautics and Space Administration (NASA) to coordinate research and development in the field. Before the end of the year NASA had a program to put a manned craft in orbit, but the first manned flight, by Commander Alan B. Shepard, Jr., did not take place until May 5, 1961. Finally, in September 1958 Congress enacted the National Defense Education Act, which authorized federal grants especially for training in mathematics, science, and modern languages, as well as for student loans and fellowships.

CORRUPT PRACTICES   During the first two years of Eisenhower's second term, public confidence in his performance, as registered by opinion polls, dropped sharply from 79 percent to 49 percent. Emotional issues such as civil rights and defense policy had compounded his troubles. The president's image was further tarnished when congressional investigations revealed that the administration, which had promised to clean up "the mess in Washington," was itself soiled by scandals, one of which involved Sherman Adams, the White House "chief-of-staff." Adams, it seemed, had done little more than open some doors at the Securities and Exchange Commission and the

Federal Trade Commission with introductions for a Boston industrialist, but he had taken in return gifts of a fur coat and an Oriental rug. In September 1958 the president reluctantly accepted Adams's resignation. Republicans also faced the growing opposition of farmers, angry with cuts in price supports, and of labor, angry because many Republicans had made "right-to-work" (or open-shop) laws a campaign issue in 1958. The Democrats came out of the midterm elections with nearly two-to-one majorities in Congress: 282 to 154 in the House, 64 to 34 in the Senate.

Eisenhower would be the first president to face three successive Congresses controlled by the opposition party. One consequence was that the president could manage few new departures in domestic policy. The most important legislation of the last two years in the Eisenhower presidency were the Landrum-Griffin Labor-Management Act of 1959, the Civil Rights Act of 1960, and the admission of the first states not contiguous to the continental forty-eight. Alaska became the forty-ninth state on January 3, 1959, and Hawaii the fiftieth on August 21, 1959.

The Landrum-Griffin Act, aimed at controlling union corruption, was actually a compromise between the views of its House sponsors and the somewhat less stringent views of Senator John F. Kennedy and some of his colleagues. It reflected, nevertheless, popular feeling against racketeering and monopolistic practices in unions, especially the Teamsters, which had been revealed by an extensive Senate probe. The act safeguarded democratic procedures, penalized the misuse of union funds and coercion of members, and excluded from office persons convicted of certain crimes. The act also strengthened restrictions on secondary boycotts and blackmail picketing. Most of its provisions were directed against unfair union practices, but the act also monitored employer payments to union officers or labor-management consultants.

FESTERING PROBLEMS ABROAD   Once the Suez and Hungary crises faded from the front pages, Eisenhower enjoyed eighteen months of smooth sailing in foreign affairs. A brief flurry occurred in May 1958 over hostile demonstrations in Peru and Venezuela against Vice-President Nixon, who was on a goodwill tour of eight Latin American countries. Then in July 1958 the Middle East flared up again. By this time the president had secured from Congress authority for what came to be called the Eisenhower Doctrine, which promised to extend economic and military aid to Middle East nations, and to use armed forces if necessary to assist any such nation against armed aggression from any Communist country.

President Nasser of Egypt meanwhile had emerged from the Suez crisis with heightened prestige, and in February 1958 created the United Arab Republic (UAR) by merger (a short-lived one) with Syria. Then on July 14 a leftist coup in Iraq, supposedly inspired by Nasser and the Russians, threw out the pro-Western government and killed King Faisal, the crown prince, and the premier. In Lebanon, already unsettled by internal conflict, the government appealed to the United States for support against a similar fate. Eisenhower immediately ordered 5,000 marines into Lebanon on July 15, where they limited themselves to the capital, Beirut, and its airfield. He proposed to go no farther because, he said later, if the government could not hold out with such protection, "I felt we were backing up a government with so little popular support that we probably should not be there." British forces meanwhile went into Jordan at the request of King Hussein. Once the situation stabilized, and the Lebanese factions reached a compromise, American forces (up to 15,000 at one point) withdrew in October.

East Asia heated up again when, on August 23, 1958, Red China renewed its shelling of the Nationalists on Quemoy and Matsu. In September the American Seventh Fleet began to escort Nationalist convoys, but stopped short of entering Chinese territorial waters. To abandon the islands, President Eisenhower said, would amount to a "Western Pacific 'Munich.'" But on October 1 he suggested that a cease-fire would provide "an opportunity to negotiate in good faith." Red China ordered such a cease-fire on October 6, and on October 25, which happened to be the day the last American forces left Lebanon, said that it would reserve the right to bombard the islands on alternate days. With that strange stipulation the worst of the crisis passed, but the problem continued to fester.

The problem of Berlin festered too: Premier Khrushchev called it a bone in his throat. West Berlin provided a "showplace" of Western democracy and prosperity, a listening post for Western intelligence, and a funnel through which news and propaganda from the West penetrated what Winston Churchill had called "the iron curtain." Although East Germany had sealed its western frontiers, refugees could still pass from East to West Berlin. On November 10, 1958, at a Soviet-Polish friendship rally in Moscow, Khrushchev threatened to transfer Soviet obligations in the occupation to East Germany. After the deadline he set, May 27, 1959, Western occupation authorities would have to deal with the East German government, in effect recognizing it, or face the possibility of another blockade.

But Eisenhower refused to budge from his position on Berlin. At the same time he refused to engage in saber-rattling or even to cancel existing plans to reduce the size of the army. As one Eisenhower biographer wrote: "He thought the greatest danger in the

Soviet premier Nikita Khrushchev speaking on the problem of Berlin, 1959.

Berlin crisis was that the Russians would frighten the United States into an arms race that would bankrupt the country." Khrushchev, it turned out, was no more eager for confrontation than Eisenhower. In talks with British Prime Minister Harold Macmillan, he suggested that the main thing was to begin discussions of the Berlin issue, and not the May 27 deadline. Macmillan in turn won Eisenhower's consent to a meeting of the Big Four foreign ministers.

There was little hope of resolving different views on Berlin and German reunification, but the talks distracted attention from Khrushchev's deadline of May 27: it passed almost unnoticed. In September, after the Big Four talks had adjourned, Premier Khrushchev paid a visit to the United States, going to New York, Washington, Los Angeles, San Francisco, and Iowa, and dropping in on Eisenhower at Camp David. In talks there Khrushchev endorsed "peaceful coexistence," and Eisenhower admitted that the Berlin situation was "abnormal." They agreed that the time was ripe for a summit meeting in the spring.

THE U-2 SUMMIT   The summit meeting, however, blew up in Eisenhower's face. On May 1, 1960, near Sverdlovsk, east of the Urals, a Soviet rocket brought down an American U-2 spy plane. Such planes had been flying missions over Russia for three and a half years. Khrushchev played up the news for domestic consumption to keep in good standing with Soviet "hard-liners." He set out to entrap Eisenhower and succeeded, by announcing first only that the plane had been shot down. When the State Department insisted that there had been no attempt to violate Soviet airspace, Khrushchev then announced that the Soviets had pilot Francis Gary Powers, "alive and kicking," and his pictures of Soviet military installations. On

May 11 Eisenhower finally took personal responsibility—an unprecedented action for a head of state—and justified the action on grounds of national security. "No one wants another Pearl Harbor," he said. In Paris, five days later, Khrushchev withdrew an invitation for Eisenhower to visit the USSR and called on the president to repudiate the U-2 flights and "pass severe judgment on those responsible." When Eisenhower refused, Khrushchev left the meeting. (Later, in 1962, Powers was exchanged for a Soviet spy.)

CASTRO'S CUBA   The greatest thorn in Eisenhower's side was the Cuban regime of Fidel Castro, which came to power on January 1, 1959, after three years of guerrilla warfare against the dictator Fulgencio Batista. In their struggle against Batista, Castro's forces had the support of many Americans who hoped for a new day of democratic government in Cuba. When American television picked up trials and executions conducted by the victorious Castro, however, such hopes were dashed. Staged like a Roman holiday before crowds of howling spectators, the trials vented anger against Batista's officials and police, but offered little in the way of legal procedure or proof. Castro, moreover, planned a social revolution and opposed the widespread foreign control of the Cuban economy. When he began programs of land reform and nationalization of foreign-owned property, relations worsened. Some observers believed, however, that by rejecting Castro's requests for loans and other help the American government lost a chance to influence the direction of the revolution, and by acting on the assumption that Communists already had the upper hand in his movement the administration may have ensured that fact.

Castro, on the other hand, showed little reluctance to accept the Communist embrace. In February 1960 he entered a trade agreement to swap Cuban sugar for Soviet oil and machinery. In July, after Cuba had seized three British-American oil refineries which refused to process Soviet oil, Eisenhower cut sharply the quota for Cuban sugar imports. Premier Khrushchev in response warned that any military intervention in Cuba would encounter Russian rockets. In October 1960 the United States suspended imports of Cuban sugar and embargoed most shipments to Cuba. One of Eisenhower's last acts as president was to suspend diplomatic relations with Cuba on January 3, 1961. In the hope of creating "some kind of nondictatorial 'third force,' neither Castroite nor Batistiano," as Eisenhower put it, the president authorized the CIA to begin training a force of Cuban refugees (some of them former Castro stalwarts) for a new revolution. But the final decision on its use would rest with the next president, John F. Kennedy.

Fidel Castro (center) *became Cuba's premier in 1959 after three years of guerrilla warfare against the Batista regime.*

Assessing the Eisenhower Years

The Eisenhower years have not drawn much acclaim from journalists and historians. One journalist called Ike's administration "the time of the great postponement," during which the president "lived off the accumulated wisdom, the accumulated prestige, and the accumulated military strength of his predecessors" and left domestic and foreign policies "about where he found them in 1953." Yet even these critics granted that Eisenhower had succeeded in ending the war in Korea and settling the dust raised by McCarthy. But if he had failed to end the Cold War and in fact had institutionalized it as a global confrontation, he sensed the limits of American power and kept its application to low-risk situations. If he took few initiatives in addressing the social problems that would erupt in the 1960s, he left the major innovations of the New Deal in place and thereby legitimized them. If he tolerated unemployment of as much as 7 percent at times, inflation remained at an average rate of 1.6 percent during his terms. His farewell address to the American people, delivered on radio and television three days before he left office, showed his remarkable foresight in his own area of special expertise, the military.

Like Washington, Eisenhower couched his wisdom largely in the form of warnings: that America's "leadership and prestige depend, not merely upon our unmatched material strength, but on how we use our power in the interests of world peace and human betterment"; that the temptation to find easy answers should take into account "the need to maintain balance in and among national problems"; and above all that Americans "must avoid the impulse to live only for today, plundering, for our own ease and convenience, the precious resources of tomorrow."

As a former soldier, Eisenhower highlighted perhaps better than anyone else could have the dangers of a military establishment in a time of peace. "This conjunction of an immense military establishment and a large arms industry is new in the American experience," he noted. "In the councils of government we must guard against the acquisition of unwarranted influence, whether sought or unsought, by the military-industrial complex. The potential for the disastrous rise of misplaced power exists and will persist." With the new importance of technology, "a government contract becomes virtually a substitute for intellectual curiosity" in directing university research. This new circumstance created the dual danger "of domination of the nation's scholars by Federal employment," and the shaping of policy by "a scientific-technological elite."

His great disappointment as he lay down his responsibilities, Eisenhower concluded, was his inability to affirm "that a lasting peace is in sight," only that "war has been avoided." But he prayed "that, in the goodness of time, all peoples will come to live together in a peace guaranteed by the binding force of mutual respect and love."

FURTHER READING

Scholarship on Eisenhower is extensive. The best overview of the period is Charles C. Alexander's *Holding the Line: The Eisenhower Era, 1951–1961* (1975). Other studies include Herbert S. Parmet's *Eisenhower and the American Crusade* (1972) and James L. Sundquist's *Politics and Policy: The Eisenhower, Kennedy, and Johnson Years* (1968). For the manner in which Eisenhower conducted foreign policy, see in particular Robert A. Divine's *Eisenhower and the Cold War* (1981). See also Stephen Ambrose's two-volume biography, *Eisenhower: Soldier, General of the Army, President-Elect* (1983) and *Eisenhower: The President* (1984).

The conservatism of the 1950s is documented best in studies of Congress and its members. A good start is James T. Patterson's *Mr. Republican: A Biography of Robert A. Taft* (1975). Also helpful is George H. Nash's *The Conservative Intellectual Movement in America: Since 1945* (1976).° On the relationship between business and government, see Louis Galambos and Joseph Pratt's *The Rise of the Corporate Commonwealth: United States Business and Public Policy in the 20th Century* (1988).

Among the numerous studies of the Cold War, several cover the Eisenhower years, including John L. Gaddis's *Strategies of Containment: A Critical Appraisal of Postwar American National Security Policy* (1982) and Norman A. Graebner's *The Age of Global Power: The United States since 1938* (1979).

For the buildup of American involvement in Indochina, consult Lloyd C. Gardner's *Approaching Vietnam: From World War II through Dienbienphu* (1988), James P. Harrison's *The Endless War: Fifty Years of Struggle in Vietnam* (1982), and George C. Herring's *America's Longest War: The United States and Vietnam, 1950–1975* (1979).° How the Eisenhower Doctrine came to be implemented is traced in Stephen Ambrose's *Rise to Globalism: American Foreign Policy, 1938–1980* (1981).°

Two introductions to the impact wrought by the Warren Supreme Court during the 1950s are Alexander Bickel's *The Supreme Court and the Idea of Progress* (1970)° and Paul Murphy's *The Constitution in Crisis Times* (1972).° Also helpful is Archibald Cox's *The Warren Court: Constitutional Decision as an Instrument of Reform* (1968).° Biographical studies of the chief justice include G. Edward White's *Earl Warren: A Public Life* (1982). A masterful study of the important Warren Court decision on school desegregation is Richard Kluger's *Simple Justice: The History of Brown v. Board of Education and Black America's Struggle for Equality* (1975).°

For the story of Montgomery, see David L. Lewis's *King: A Critical Biography* (1970)° and Stephen B. Oates's *Let the Trumpet Sound: The Life of Martin Luther King, Jr.* (1982).° William H. Chafe's *Civilities and Civil Rights: Greensboro, North Carolina, and the Black Struggle for Freedom* (1980)° examines how one community dragged its feet on the Brown implementation order. See the books listed at the end of Chapter 34 for more on King and the civil-rights movement.

°These books are available in paperback editions.

34

NEW FRONTIERS:
KENNEDY AND JOHNSON

Eisenhower's misgiving about the military-industrial complex sounded a warning that countered the complacency and buoyant optimism of the 1950s. By the end of that decade a chorus of voices was deploring the triumph of materialistic values. If we are so rich, social critics wondered, why do we feel so poor? "With the supermarket as our temple and the singing commercial as our litany," asked Adlai Stevenson, "are we likely to fire the world with an irresistible vision of America's exalted purposes and inspiring way of life?"

Eisenhower greeted these lamentations in the traditional way: he named a presidential commission to study the matter. *Goals for Americans: A Report of the President's Commission on National Goals* (1960) appeared just as Eisenhower was leaving office. The commission saw no need to worry. The gross national product had more than doubled since the end of the war and there was no reason to doubt its continued growth. If government investment in education kept pace with the economy, one could expect a new cadre of professionals—doctors, economists, social workers—to solve the problems that came with prosperity. The only real danger came from abroad, in the form of Communist aggression and subversion. The report contrasted the Communist ideal of the state with the American ideal of the individual. How a nation of 180 million individuals could achieve a sense of collective purpose while still pursuing their unbridled self-interest was, appropriately, a matter best left to the individuals themselves.

But the members of the commission were better historians than prophets. As the complacent 1950s yielded to another decade, few if any people foresaw the collapse of consensus, the hopes dashed, the ironic turns of fortune ahead. An alert prophet might have found a sign in an unlikely quarter—the Woolworth lunch counter in Greensboro, North Carolina, where just one month into the 1960s, on February 1, four black freshmen from a nearby college sat down and asked for coffee. It took them nearly six months to get service, but by then they had set in motion the completion of a Second Reconstruction and had introduced two salient styles of the 1960s: civil disobedience and the youth rebellion, two protean phenomena that would assume many different shapes before the decade ended.

THE NEW FRONTIER

KENNEDY VS. NIXON   In 1960, however, few sensed such dramatic change on the horizon. The presidential election of that year pitted two candidates—Richard M. Nixon and John F. Kennedy—who seemed to symbolize the unadventurous politics of the 1950s. Though better known than Kennedy because of his eight years as Eisenhower's vice-president, famous for his "kitchen debate" with Soviet premier Nikita Khrushchev in an exhibit of an American kitchen in Moscow, Nixon had also developed the reputation of a cunning chameleon, the "Tricky Dick" who concealed his duplicity behind a series of masks. "Nixon doesn't know who he is," Kennedy told an aide, "and so each time he makes a speech he has to decide which Nixon he is, and that will be very exhausting."

But Nixon could not be so easily dismissed. He possessed a shrewd intelligence and a compulsive love for politics, the more combative the better. His tragic flaw was a blind spot for the rules of political combat, a trait he displayed from his first campaign to his last. Born in suburban Los Angeles in 1913, he grew up amid a Quaker family struggling to make ends meet. Acquaintances remembered the young Richard Nixon as a quiet, introverted, diligent fellow. "He wasn't a little boy that you wanted to pick up and hug," recalled one family friend.

In 1946, having completed law school and a wartime stint in the navy, Richard Nixon jumped into the political arena as a Republican, and, with the help of a powerful group of conservative southern California businessmen, he unseated a popular congressman. Nixon arrived in Washington eager to reverse the tide of New Deal liberalism. "I was elected to smash the labor bosses," he explained. Four years later he won election to the Senate. In his campaigns, Nixon unleashed scurrilous personal attacks on his opponents, employing half-truths, lies, and rumors, and he shrewdly manipulated and fed the growing anti-Communist hysteria. Yet Nixon became both a respected and effective member of Congress, and by 1950 he was the most requested Republican speaker in the country. The reward for his rapid rise to political stardom was the vice-presidential nomination in 1952, which led to successive terms as the highly visible partner of the popular Eisenhower.

In comparison to his Republican opponent, Kennedy was inexperienced. Despite an abundance of assets, including a record of heroism in World War II, a glamorous young wife, a Harvard education, a rich and powerful family, a handsome face, charming manner, and robust outlook, the forty-three-year-old Kennedy had not distinguished himself in the House and Senate. Indeed, his political rise was owing not so much to his abilities or accomplishments, but to the effective public relations campaign on his behalf engineered by his ambitious father.

Joseph Kennedy was a self-made tycoon, the grandson of poor Irish-Catholic immigrants. Early on he developed a ferocious determination to achieve the American Dream and in the process assault prevailing stereotypes of the Irish. A ruthless opportunist, he made millions on Wall Street in the twenties, gained control of much of the Hollywood film industry in the thirties, and finessed from President Franklin Roosevelt an appointment as ambassador to Great Britain. Ambassador Kennedy soon developed a consuming ambition to see one of his sons elected president, and when the eldest boy, Joseph Jr., was killed in the war, the mantle of paternal expectation fell on John's shoulders. When John Kennedy decided to run for his first office, his father declared: "We're going to sell him like soap flakes."

Kennedy subsequently suffered from criticism that there was more image to him than substance. And there was some truth to the charge. Although he won a Pulitzer Prize for *Profiles in Courage* (1956), a book about past political leaders who had "made the tough decisions," Kennedy, claimed Washington critics, had shown more profile than courage during the McCarthy episode of the early 1950s, and had a weak record on civil rights. Eleanor Roosevelt declined to endorse Kennedy in 1960, noting that presidential authority should not be vested in "someone who understands what courage is and admires it, but has not quite the independence to have it."

During his campaign for the Democratic nomination, Kennedy had shown that he had the energy to match his grace and ambition. As the first Catholic to run for the presidency since Al Smith, he strove to dispel the impression that his religion was a major political liability. "If the nomination ever goes into a back room," he told a friend, "my name will never emerge." By the time of the convention in August 1960, he had traveled over 65,000 miles, visited 25 states, and made over 350 speeches. Kennedy knocked Hubert Humphrey, the buoyant liberal senator from Minnesota, out of the race in the West Virginia primary. In his acceptance speech, Kennedy found the stirring, muscular rhetoric that would stamp the rest of his campaign and his presidency: "We stand today on the edge of a New Frontier—the frontier of unknown opportunities and perils—a frontier of unfulfilled hopes and threats."

Three events shaped the campaign that fall. First, in a speech before the Houston Ministerial Association on September 12, 1960, Kennedy confronted the political implications of his Catholicism directly. In America, he told the Protestant clergy, "the separation of church and state is absolute" and "no Catholic prelate would tell the President—should he be a Catholic—how to act and no Protestant minister should tell his parishioners for whom to vote." The religious question thereafter drew little public attention; Kennedy's candor had neutralized it.

Second, Nixon violated one of the cardinal rules of politics when he agreed to debate his less prominent opponent on television. During the first of four debates, few significant policy differences surfaced, allowing viewers to shape their opinions more on matters of style. Some 70 million people watched this first-ever television debate, and they saw an obviously uncomfortable Nixon, still weak from a recent illness, perspiring heavily and sporting his perpetual

John F. Kennedy's poise and precision in the debates with Richard Nixon impressed viewers and voters.

five-o'clock shadow. He looked haggard, uneasy, and even sinister before the camera. Kennedy, on the other hand, projected a cool poise and offered crisp answers that made him seem equal, if not superior, in his fitness for the office. Kennedy's popularity immediately shot up in the polls. Reporters discovered that he had "charisma" and noted the giddy young people who now greeted his arrival at campaign stops. In the words of a bemused southern senator, Kennedy combined "the best qualities of Elvis Presley and Franklin D. Roosevelt."

Still, the momentum created by the first debate was not enough to ensure a Kennedy victory. The third key event in the campaign involved the civil-rights issue. Democratic strategists knew that in order to offset the loss of southern Democratic conservatives suspicious of Kennedy's Catholicism and civil-rights positions, they must woo black voters. To do so they set up a special committee to increase minority voter registration and attract the black vote. Their task was made easier when Nixon's running mate, Ambassador Henry Cabot Lodge, Jr., of Massachusetts, pledged that the Republicans, if elected, would appoint a black cabinet member, only to have Nixon reject such a commitment. Perhaps the most crucial incident of the campaign occurred on October 19 when Martin Luther King, Jr., and some fifty other demonstrators were arrested in Atlanta for "trespassing" in an all-white restaurant. Although the other demonstrators were soon released, King was sentenced to four months in prison, ostensibly because of an earlier traffic violation. Thereupon Robert Kennedy, the candidate's younger brother and campaign manager, called the judge handling King's case, who also happened to be a close friend of the Georgia governor, alerting him "that if he was a decent American, he would let King out of jail by sundown. I called him because it made me so damned angry to think of that bastard sentencing a citizen to four months of hard labor for a minor traffic offense and screwing up my brother's campaign and making our country look ridiculous before the world." The call had its intended effect. King was soon released on bail, and the Kennedy campaign seized full advantage of the outcome, distributing some 2 million pamphlets in black neighborhoods extolling Kennedy's efforts on behalf of Dr. King.

When the votes were counted, Kennedy and his running mate, Lyndon B. Johnson of Texas, had won the closest presidential election since 1888. The winning margin was only 118,574 votes out of 68 million cast. Kennedy's wide lead in the electoral vote, 303 to 219, belied the paper-thin margin in several key states, especially Illinois, where Chicago mayor Richard Daley's Democratic machine appeared to have lived up to its legendary campaign motto: "In Chi-

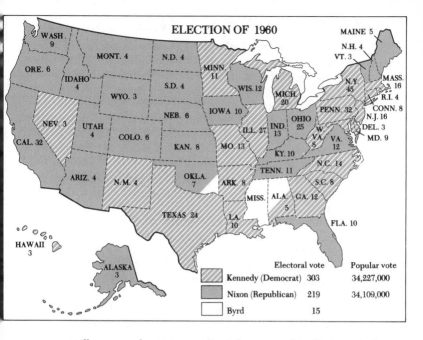

ELECTION OF 1960

MAINE 5
N.H. 4
VT. 3
WASH. 9
MONT. 4
N.D. 4
MINN. 11
WIS. 12
MICH. 20
N.Y 45
MASS. 16
R.I. 4
CONN. 8
N.J. 16
DEL. 3
MD. 9
ORE. 6
IDAHO 4
S.D. 4
IOWA 10
OHIO 25
PENN. 32
WYO. 3
NEB. 6
ILL. 27
IND. 13
W. VA. 8
VA. 12
NEV. 3
UTAH 4
COLO. 6
KAN. 8
MO. 13
KY. 10
CAL. 32
N.C. 14
ARIZ. 4
N.M. 4
OKLA. 7
ARK. 8
TENN. 11
S.C. 8
MISS. 8
ALA. 5
GA. 12
TEXAS 24
LA. 10
FLA. 10
HAWAII 3
ALASKA 3

	Electoral vote	Popular vote
Kennedy (Democrat)	303	34,227,000
Nixon (Republican)	219	34,109,000
Byrd	15	

cago we tell our people to vote early and to vote often." Nixon had in fact carried more states than Kennedy, sweeping most of the West, and holding four of the six southern states Eisenhower had carried in 1956. Kennedy's majority was built out of victories in southern New England, the populous Middle Atlantic states, and key states in the South where black voters provided the critical margin of victory. Yet ominous rumblings of discontent appeared in the once-solid Democratic South, as all eight of Mississippi's electors and six of Alabama's eleven defied the national ticket and voted for Virginia senator Harry Byrd, the arch-segregationist.

THE NEW ADMINISTRATION   Kennedy was the nation's youngest president, and his cabinet appointments put an accent on youth and "Eastern Establishment" figures. As a self-described "idealist without illusions," he was determined to attract the "best and the brightest" minds available, individuals who would inject a tough, pragmatic, and vigorous outlook into governmental affairs. Adlai Stevenson was favored by liberal Democrats for secretary of state, but Kennedy chose Dean Rusk, a career diplomat who then headed the Rockefeller Foundation. Stevenson received the relatively minor post of ambassador to the United Nations. Robert S. McNamara, one of the "whiz kids" who had reorganized the Ford Motor Company with his "systems-analysis" techniques, was asked to bring his managerial magic to bear on the Department of Defense. C. Douglas

Dillon, a banker and a Republican, was made secretary of the treasury in an effort to reassure conservative businessmen. When critics attacked the appointment of Kennedy's thirty-five-year-old brother, Robert, as attorney-general, the president quipped, "I don't see what's wrong with giving Bobby a little experience before he goes into law practice." McGeorge Bundy, whom Kennedy called "the second smartest man I know," was made special assistant for national security affairs, lending additional credence to the impression that foreign policy would remain under tight White House control. Speaking of Kennedy's advisers, House Speaker Rayburn expressed to Lyndon Johnson a wry wish that "just one of them had run for sheriff once."

The inaugural ceremonies of January 20, 1961, set the tone of elegance and youthful vigor that would come to be called the "Kennedy style." The bracing and glittering atmosphere of snow-clad Washington seemed to symbolize fresh promise. After Robert Frost paid tribute to the administration in verse, Kennedy dazzled listeners with uplifting rhetoric. "Let the word go forth from this time and place," he proclaimed, "Let every nation know, whether it wishes us well or ill, that we shall pay any price, bear any burden, meet any hardship, support any friend, oppose any foe, to assure the survival and success of liberty. And so, my fellow Americans: ask not what your country can do for you—ask what you can do for your country." Spines tingled at the time; Kennedy, one journalist wrote, was the first president to be a Prince Charming.

THE KENNEDY RECORD   But for all of his idealistic and energetic rhetoric, Kennedy had a difficult time launching his New Frontier domestic program. Elected by a razor-thin margin, he enjoyed no

Kennedy and his wife, Jacqueline, at the inauguration, January 20, 1961.

popular mandate. Moreover, the Congress, although overwhelmingly Democratic, remained in the grip of a conservative coalition that blocked Kennedy's efforts to increase federal aid to education, provide health insurance for the aged, and create a new Department of Urban Affairs. The Senate killed his initiatives on behalf of unemployed youth, migrant workers, and mass transit. When in January 1963 Kennedy finally came around to the advice of his Keynesian advisers and submitted a drastic tax cut of $13.6 billion, Congress blocked that as well.

Administration proposals, nevertheless, did win some notable victories in Congress. Those involving defense and foreign policy generally won favor; indeed defense appropriations exceeded administration requests. On foreign aid there were some cuts, but Congress readily approved broad "Alliance for Progress" programs to help Latin America, and the celebrated Peace Corps, created in March 1961 to supply volunteers for educational and technical services abroad. Kennedy's biggest legislative accomplishment may have been the Trade Expansion Act of 1962, which eventually led to tariff cuts averaging 35 percent between the United States and the European Common Market.

In the field of domestic social legislation the administration did score a few victories. They included a new Housing Act which earmarked nearly $5 billion for urban renewal over four years, a raise in the minimum wage from $1 to $1.25 and its extension to more than 3 million additional workers, the Area Redevelopment Act of May 1961 which provided nearly $400 million in loans and grants to "distressed areas," an increase in social security benefits, and additional funds for sewage treatment plants. Kennedy also won support for an accelerated program to reach the moon before the end of the decade.

CIVIL RIGHTS   The most important development in American domestic life during the Kennedy years occurred in the area of civil rights. Kennedy entered the White House reluctant to challenge conservative southern Democrats on the race issue. He was never as personally committed to the cause of civil rights as his brother Robert or Hubert Humphrey were. Despite a few dramatic gestures of support toward black leaders, John Kennedy only belatedly grasped the moral or emotional significance of the most widespread reform movement of the decade. Eventually, however, his conscience was pricked by the grass-roots civil-rights movement so ably led by Martin Luther King.

After the Montgomery bus boycott of 1955–1956, King's philosophy of "militant nonviolence" inspired others to challenge the deeply entrenched patterns of racial segregation in the South. At the same time, lawsuits to desegregate the schools got thousands of parents and young people involved. The momentum generated the first genuine mass movement in African-American history when four black college students sat down and demanded service at a "whites-only" Woolworth lunch counter in Greensboro, North Carolina, on February 1, 1960. Within a week the "sit-in" movement had spread to six more towns in the state, and within a month to cities in six more states.

In April 1960 the student participants, black and white, formed the Student Nonviolent Coordinating Committee (SNCC), which worked with King's Southern Christian Leadership Conference (SCLC) to broaden the movement. The "sit-ins" at restaurants became "kneel-ins" at churches and "wade-ins" at segregated public pools, and everywhere the protesters refused to retaliate, even when struck with clubs or poked with cattle prods. The conservative white editor of the *Richmond News Leader* conceded his admiration for their courage:

Sit-in at the Woolworth's Lunch Counter in Greensboro, North Carolinia, February 2, 1960. *The four protesters, students at North Carolina A&T College, were (from left) Joesph McNeil, Franklin McCain, Billy Smith, and Clarence Henderson.*

Here were the colored students, in coats, white shirts, ties, and one of them was reading Goethe, and one was taking notes from a biology text. And here, on the sidewalk, was a gang of white boys come to heckle, a ragtail rabble, slack-jawed, black-jacketed, grinning fit to kill, and some of them, God save the mark, were waving the proud and honored flag of the Southern States in the last war fought by gentlemen.

Several of the black demonstrators paid for such courage and commitment with their lives.

In May 1961 the Congress of Racial Equality (CORE) sent a group of black and white "freedom riders" on buses to test a federal court ruling that had banned segregation on buses and trains and in terminals. In Alabama mobs attacked the travelers, burned one of the buses, and assaulted Justice Department observers, but the demonstrators persisted and drew national attention, generating new respect and support for their cause.

Then in 1962 Governor Ross Barnett of Mississippi, who believed that God made the Negro "different to punish him," defied a court order and refused to allow James H. Meredith, a black student, to enroll at the University of Mississippi. Attorney-General Robert Kennedy thereupon dispatched federal marshals to enforce the law. When they were assaulted by a white mob, federal troops had to intervene, but only after two deaths and many injuries. Meredith was finally registered at "Ole Miss" a few days later.

Everywhere it seemed black activists and white supporters were challenging deeply entrenched patterns of segregation and prejudice. In April 1963 Martin Luther King launched a series of nonviolent demonstrations in Birmingham, Alabama, where Police Commissioner Eugene "Bull" Connor served as the perfect foil for King's tactic of nonviolent civil disobedience. Connor used attack dogs, tear gas, electric cattle prods, and fire hoses on the protesters while millions of outraged Americans watched the confrontation on television.

King, who was arrested and jailed during the demonstrations, took the opportunity to write his "Letter from Birmingham City Jail," a stirring defense of the nonviolent strategy that became a classic of the civil-rights movement. "One who breaks an unjust law," he stressed, "must do so openly, lovingly, and with a willingness to accept the penalty." He also signaled a shift in his strategy for social change. Heretofore, King had emphasized the need to educate southern whites about the injustice of segregation and other patterns of discrimination. Now he focused more on gaining federal enforcement and new legislation by provoking racists to display their violent hatreds in public. As King admitted in his "Letter," he sought through organized nonviolent protest to "create such a crisis and

Eugene "Bull" Connor's police unleash attack dogs on civil- rights demonstrators in Birmingham, Alabama, May 1963.

foster such a tension that a community which has constantly refused to negotiate is forced to confront the issue."

The sublime courage and resolve that King and many other protesters displayed in carrying out their program of nonviolent coercion proved instrumental in mobilizing national support for their integrationist objectives. (Indeed, in 1964 King would be awarded the Nobel Peace Prize.) Nudged by his brother Robert, President Kennedy finally decided that enforcement of existing statutes was not enough; new legislation was needed to deal with the race question. In June 1963 he told the nation that racial discrimination "has no place in American life or law," and he then endorsed an ambitious civil-rights bill intended to end discrimination in public facilities, desegregate the public schools, and protect black voters. But the bill was quickly blocked in Congress by southern conservatives.

Throughout the Deep South, traditionalists remained steadfast. In the fall of 1963, Governor George Wallace dramatically stood in the doorway of a building at the University of Alabama to block the enrollment of several black students, but he stepped aside in the face of insistent federal marshals. That night President Kennedy spoke eloquently of the moral issue facing the nation: "If an American, because his skin is black, cannot enjoy the full and free life which all of us want, then who among us would be content to have the color of his skin changed and stand in his place? Who among us would be content with the counsels of patience and delay?" Later the same night, NAACP official Medgar Evers was shot to death as he returned home in Jackson, Mississippi.

The high point of the integrationist phase of the civil-rights movement occurred on August 28, 1963, when over 200,000 blacks and whites marched down the Mall in Washington, D.C., toward the Lincoln Memorial singing "We Shall Overcome." The March on Washington was the largest civil-rights demonstration in American history. Standing in front of Lincoln's statue, King delivered one of the memorable public speeches of the century:

> I say to you today, my friends, that in spite of the difficulties and frustrations of the moment I still have a dream. It is a dream deeply rooted in the American dream.
>
> I have a dream that one day this nation will rise up and live out the true meaning of its creed: "We hold these truths to be self-evident; that all men are created equal."
>
> I have a dream that one day . . . the sons of former slaves and the sons of former slaveowners will be able to sit together at the table of brotherhood.

That the time for such racial harmony had not yet arrived, however, became clear a little over two weeks later when a bomb exploded in a Birmingham church, killing four black girls who had arrived early

Martin Luther King, Jr. (second from left), *and other civil-rights leaders at the head of the March on Washington for Jobs and Freedom, August 28, 1963.*

for Sunday school. Yet King's dream—shared and promoted by thousands of other activists—survived. The intransigence and violence that civil-rights workers encountered won converts to their cause all across the country.

THE WARREN COURT   Under Chief Justice Earl Warren, the Supreme Court continued to be a decisive influence on American domestic life during the 1960s. During the Kennedy-Johnson years, the Court's decisions on civil liberties proved as controversial as its earlier decisions on civil rights. In 1962 the Court had ruled that a school prayer adopted by the New York State Board of Regents violated the constitutional prohibition against an established religion. In *Gideon v. Wainwright* (1963) the Court required that every felony defendant be provided a lawyer regardless of the defendant's ability to pay. In 1964 the Court ruled in *Escobedo v. Illinois* that a person accused of a crime must also be allowed to consult a lawyer before being interrogated by police. Two years later, in *Miranda v. Arizona*, the Court issued perhaps its most bitterly criticized ruling when it ordered that an accused person in police custody must be informed of certain basic rights: the right to remain silent; the right to know that anything said can be used against the individual in court; and the right to have a defense attorney present during interrogation. In addition, the Court established rules for police to follow in informing suspects of their legal rights before questioning could begin.

FOREIGN FRONTIERS

EARLY SETBACKS   Kennedy's record in foreign relations, like that in domestic affairs, was mixed, though more spectacularly so. Although he had made the existence of a "missile gap" a major part of his campaign, he discovered upon taking office that there was no "missile gap"—the United States was far ahead of the Soviets in nuclear weaponry. Kennedy also discovered that there was in the works a CIA operation training 1,500 anti-Castro Cubans for an invasion of their homeland. The Joint Chiefs of Staff assured Kennedy that the plan was feasible; diplomatic advisers predicted that the invasion would inspire Cubans on the island to rebel against Castro. In retrospect, it is clear that the scheme, poorly planned and poorly executed, had about as much chance of succeeding as John Brown's raid on Harper's Ferry a little over a century earlier. When the invasion force landed at the Bay of Pigs in Cuba on April 19, 1961, it was brutally subdued in three days and 1,200 men were captured. A *New York Times* columnist lamented that the United States "looked like fools to our friends, rascals to our enemies, and incompetents to the rest." It was hardly an auspicious way for the new president to demonstrate his mastery of foreign policy. "Victory has a thousand fathers," Kennedy said sadly, "but defeat is an orphan."

Two months after the Bay of Pigs debacle Kennedy met Russian premier Khrushchev in Vienna, Austria. It was a tense confrontation during which Khrushchev browbeat the inexperienced Kennedy and threatened to limit Western access to Berlin, the divided city located deep within East Germany. Kennedy was shaken by the aggressive Soviet stand, but returned home determined to demonstrate American resolve. He called up reserve and National Guard units and asked Congress for another $3.2 billion in defense funds. The Soviets responded by throwing up the Berlin Wall, begun with barbed wire and eventually solidified into a cinder-block barrier which cut off movement between East and West Berlin. Although no shooting incident triggered an accidental war, the Berlin Wall plugged the most accessible escape hatch for East Germans, showed Soviet willingness to challenge American resolve in Europe, and became another intractable barrier to the opening of new frontiers.

THE MISSILE CRISIS   A year later Khrushchev posed another challenge, this time ninety miles off the coast of Florida. Kennedy's unwillingness to commit the forces necessary to overthrow Castro and his acquiescence in the Berlin Wall seemed to signify a failure of will, and the Russians apparently reasoned that they could install missiles in Cuba with relative impunity. American officials feared that such missiles would come from a direction not covered by radar systems and arrive too quickly for warning. More important to Kennedy was the psychological effect of American acquiescence to a Soviet presence on its doorstep. This might weaken the credibility of the American deterrent for Europeans and demoralize anti-Castro elements in Latin America. At the same time the installation of missiles served Khrushchev's purpose of demonstrating his toughness to both Chinese and Russian critics of his earlier advocacy of peaceful coexistence. But he misjudged the American response.

On October 14, 1962, American intelligence discovered from photographs made on high-altitude U-2 flights that Russian missile sites were under construction in Cuba. From the beginning the administration decided that they had to be removed; the only question was how. In a series of secret meetings the Executive Committee of the National Security Council narrowed the options down to a choice between a "surgical" air strike and a blockade of Cuba. They opted for a blockade, which was carefully disguised by the euphemism "quarantine," since a blockade was technically an act of

*Russian missiles under construction at San Cristobal, Cuba,
October 23, 1962.*

war. It offered the advantage of forcing the Soviets to shoot first, if
it came to that, and left open the further options of stronger action.
Monday, October 22, began one of the most anxious weeks in world
history. On that day the president announced to members of Congress and then to the public the discovery of the missile sites in
Cuba; he also announced the quarantine.

Tensions grew as Khrushchev blustered that Kennedy had pushed
humankind "to the abyss of a world missile-nuclear war." Soviet
ships, he declared, would ignore the quarantine. But on Wednesday,
October 24, five Soviet ships, presumably with missiles aboard,
stopped short of the quarantine line. Two days later an agent of the
Russian embassy privately approached an American television reporter with a proposal for an agreement: Russia would withdraw the
missiles in return for a public pledge by the United States not to
invade Cuba. The reporter was asked to relay the idea to the White
House. Secretary of State Rusk sent back word that the administration was interested, but told the newscaster: "Remember, when you
report this, that eyeball to eyeball, they blinked first." The same
evening Kennedy received two messages from Khrushchev, the first
repeating the original offer and the second demanding in addition
the removal of American missiles from Turkey. The two messages
probably reflected divided counsels in the Kremlin. Ironically,
Kennedy had already ordered removal of the outmoded missiles in
Turkey, but he refused now to act under the gun. Instead he followed Robert Kennedy's suggestion that he respond favorably to the

first letter and ignore the second. On Sunday, October 28, Khrushchev agreed to remove the missiles and added a conciliatory invitation: "We should like to continue the exchange of views on the prohibition of atomic and thermonuclear weapons, general disarmament, and other problems relating to the relaxation of international tension."

In the aftermath of the crisis, the level of tension between the United States and Russia was quickly lowered. Kennedy, aware that Khrushchev had problems with his own hawks in the Kremlin, cautioned his associates against any gloating over the favorable settlement and began to explore in correspondence the opening provided by the premier's invitation. Several symbolic steps were taken to relax tensions: an agreement to sell Russia surplus wheat, the installation of a "hot line" between Washington and Moscow to provide instant contact between the heads of government, and the removal of obsolete missiles from Turkey, Italy, and Britain. On June 10, 1963, the president announced in a speech at American University that direct discussions with the Soviets would soon begin, and called upon the nation to reexamine its attitude toward peace, the Soviet Union, and the Cold War. Those discussions resulted in a treaty with Russia and Britain to stop nuclear testing in the atmosphere. The treaty, ratified in September 1963, did not provide for on-site inspection nor did it ban underground testing, which continued, but it promised to end the dangerous pollution of the atmosphere with radioactivity. The treaty was an important symbolic and substantive move toward détente. As Kennedy put it: "A journey of a thousand miles begins with one step."

KENNEDY AND VIETNAM   In Southeast Asia events were moving toward what would become within a decade the greatest American foreign policy calamity of the century. During John Kennedy's "thousand days" in office the turmoil of Indochina never preoccupied the public mind for any extended period, but it dominated international diplomatic debates from the time the administration entered office.

The landlocked kingdom of Laos, along with neighboring Cambodia, had been declared neutral in the Geneva Accords of 1954, but had fallen into a complex struggle for power between the Communist Pathet Lao and the Royal Laotian Army. There matters stood when Eisenhower left office and told Kennedy: "You might have to go in there and fight it out." The chairman of the Joint Chiefs of Staff argued in favor of a stand against the Pathet Lao, even at the cost of direct intervention. After a lengthy consideration of alternatives, Washington decided to favor a neutralist coalition which would preclude American military involvement in Laos, yet prevent a Pathet Lao victory. The Soviets, who were extending aid to the Pathet Lao, indicated a readiness to negotiate, and in May 1961 talks began in Geneva. After more than a year of tangled negotiations the three factions in Laos agreed to a neutral coalition. American and Russian aid to the opposing parties was supposed to end, but both countries continued covert operations, while North Vietnam kept open the Ho Chi Minh Trail through eastern Laos, over which it supplied its Vietcong allies in South Vietnam.

There the situation worsened under the leadership of Premier Ngo Dinh Diem, despite encouraging reports from the military commander of American "advisers" in South Vietnam. At the time the problem was less the scattered Communist guerrilla attacks than Diem's failure to deliver social and economic reforms and his inability to rally popular support. His repressive tactics, directed not only against Communists but also against Buddhists and other critics, played into the hands of his enemies. In 1961 White House assistant Walt Rostow and General Maxwell Taylor became the first in a long train of presidential emissaries to South Vietnam's capital, Saigon. Focusing on the military situation, they proposed a major increase in the American military presence. Kennedy refused, but continued to dispatch more "advisers" in the hope of stabilizing the situation: when he took office there had been 2,000; by the end of 1963 there were 16,000, none of whom had been officially committed to battle.

South Vietnamese troops in combat with Vietcong guerrillas in the Mekong River delta, 1961.

By 1963 sharply divergent reports were coming in from the South Vietnamese countryside. Military advisers, their eyes on the inflated "kill ratios" reported by the Army of the Republic of Vietnam (ARVN), drew optimistic conclusions. On-site political reporters like David Halberstam of the *New York Times*, watching the reactions of the Vietnamese people, foresaw continued deterioration without the promised political and economic reforms. By mid-year growing Buddhist demonstrations made the discontent in South Vietnam more plainly visible. The spectacle of Buddhist monks immolating themselves in protest brought from Diem's sister-in-law only sarcasm about "barbecued monks." By the fall of 1963 the Kennedy administration had decided that Diem was a lost cause. When dissident generals proposed a coup d'état, American ambassador Henry Cabot Lodge assured them that Washington would not stand in the way. On November 1 they seized the government and murdered Diem, though without American approval. But the generals provided no more stability than earlier regimes, as successive coups set the country spinning from one military leader to another.

KENNEDY'S ASSASSINATION Kennedy seemed to be facing up to the intractability of the situation in Vietnam by the fall of 1963. In September he declared of the South Vietnamese: "In the final analysis it's their war. They're the ones who have to win it or lose it. We can help them as advisers but they have to win it." And the following month he announced the administration's intention to withdraw United States forces from South Vietnam by the end of 1965. What Kennedy would have done has remained a matter of endless controversy among historians, endless because it is unanswerable and unanswerable because on November 22, 1963, while visiting Dallas, he was shot in the neck and head by Lee Harvey Oswald, whose motives remain unknown, and died almost immediately. Kennedy's death and then the murder of Oswald by Jack Ruby, a Dallas nightclub owner, were shown over and over again on television, the medium that had so helped Kennedy's rise to the presidency and that now captured his death and the moving funeral at Arlington Cemetery, thereby assuring his enshrinement in the public imagination as a martyred leader.

Shortly after the funeral Jacqueline Kennedy reminisced for a reporter about their family life. At night they would play records, and the song John Kennedy loved most came from a current Broadway hit, *Camelot*, based on the legends of King Arthur: " 'Don't let it be forgot, that once there was a spot, for one brief shining moment, that was known as Camelot'—and it will never be that way again." This "Camelot mystique" soon enshrouded the fallen president, magnifying his accomplishments and creating an aura of glamour and poignancy around his legacy. A Gallup poll in 1976 showed that a majority of Americans regarded Kennedy as the greatest of all American presidents.

LYNDON JOHNSON AND THE GREAT SOCIETY

Lyndon Johnson took the oath as president of the United States on board the plane that took John Kennedy's body back to Washington from Dallas. At age fifty-five he had spent twenty-six years on the Washington scene and had served nearly a decade as Democratic leader in the Senate, where he had displayed the greatest gift for compromise since Henry Clay. Johnson brought to the White House a marked change of style from Kennedy. A truly self-made man who through gritty determination and shrewd manipulation had worked his way out of a hardscrabble rural Texas background to become one of Washington's most powerful figures, Johnson had none of the Kennedy elegance or charisma. He was a rough-hewn, gregarious, and domineering man who craved both political power and public affection. The first southern president since Woodrow Wilson, he harbored always, like another southern president, Andrew Johnson, a sense of being the perpetual "outsider" despite his long experience with power. And indeed he was so regarded by Kennedy "insiders."

Kennedy's vice-president, Lyndon B. Johnson, takes the presidential oath as Air Force One *returns from Dallas with Jacqueline Kennedy* (right), *the presidential party, and the body of the assassinated president.*

Those who viewed Johnson as a stereotypical southern conservative reckoned without his long-standing admiration for Franklin
Roosevelt, the depth of his concern for humble people, and his
commitment to the cause of civil rights. "By political background, by
temperament, by personal preference," wrote one journalist, Johnson was "the riverboat man. He was brawny and rough and skilled
beyond measure in the full use of tricky tides and currents, in his
knowledge of the hidden shoals. He was a swashbuckling master of
the political midstreams—but only in the crowded, well-traveled
and familiar inland waterways of domestic politics." In foreign affairs he was, like Wilson, a novice.

POLITICS AND POVERTY   Quite naturally, domestic politics became
Johnson's first priority. He exploited the national grief after the
assassination by declaring that Kennedy's cabinet and advisers
would stay on and that his legislative program, stymied in several
congressional committees, would be passed. Given to ceaseless
work, fourteen hours or more a day, Johnson loved the kind of
political infighting and legislative detail that Kennedy loathed. "Not
a sparrow falls," reported one aide, "that he doesn't know about."
Recalcitrant congressmen and senators were brought to the White
House for what became famous as "the Johnson Treatment." A
journalist described the technique: "He moved in close, his face a
scant millimeter from his target, his eyes widening and narrowing,
his eyebrows rising and falling. From his pockets poured clippings,
memos, statistics. Mimicry, humor, and the genius of analogy made
the Treatment an almost hypnotic experience and rendered the
target stunned and helpless." The logjam in the Congress that had
blocked Kennedy's program broke under Johnson's forceful leadership and a torrent of legislation poured through. Virtually the entire
agenda of twentieth-century liberalism would be enacted.

Before the year 1963 was out Congress approved the pending
foreign aid bill and a plan to sell wheat to the Soviet Union. But
America's commitment to foreign aid pointed up its own people's
needs. In January 1964 the Council of Economic Advisers reported
that 9.3 million American families, about 20 percent of the population, were below the "poverty line" of $3,000 per year for a family
of four. "Unfortunately, many Americans live on the outskirts of
hope," Johnson told the Congress in his first State of the Union
message on January 8, 1964, "some because of their poverty and
some because of their color, and all too many because of both." At
the top of his agenda he put the stalled measures for tax reduction
and civil rights, then added to his "must" list a bold new idea which
bore the LBJ brand: "This Administration today, here and now,

declares unconditional war on poverty in America." The particulars were to come later, the product of an administration task force already at work before Johnson took office.

Americans had suddenly rediscovered poverty in the early 1960s when the social critic Michael Harrington published a powerful exposé entitled *The Other America* (1962). Brandishing an impressive array of statistics as well as convincing theories of social psychology, Harrington argued that while most Americans had been celebrating their rising affluence during the postwar era, some 40 million to 50 million people were mired in a "culture of poverty" hidden from view and passed on from one generation to the next. Unlike the upwardly mobile immigrant poor at the turn of the century, they were impervious to hope. "To be impoverished," he asserted, "is to be an internal alien, to grow up in a culture that is radically different from the one that dominates the society." Television only exacerbated the problem by accentuating the relative deprivation of the poor. They saw how different they were from middle-class Americans, leaving many fatalistic about their condition. Consequently the poor "tend to be hopeless and passive, yet prone to bursts of violence; they are lonely and isolated, yet often rigid and hostile. To be poor is not simply to be deprived of the material things of this world. It is to enter a fatal, futile universe, an America within an America, a twisted spirit."

President Kennedy read *The Other America* in 1963 and asked his advisers to investigate the problem and suggest a plan of attack. Upon taking office Johnson announced that he wanted an antipoverty package that was "big and bold that would hit the nation with real impact." When his advisers told him that their research was still incomplete, he declared that he was determined to act anyway. Money for the program would come from the revenues generated by the tax reduction of more than $10 billion passed in February 1964, which generated one of the longest sustained economic booms in American history. The lower taxes provoked a surge in capital investment and personal consumption, thus generating higher corporate profits which in turn led to an increase in tax revenues.

The administration's task force on poverty had its Economic Opportunity Bill ready to submit in March. The bill incorporated a wide range of programs: a Job Corps for inner-city youths aged sixteen to twenty-one, a Head Start program for disadvantaged preschoolers, work-study jobs for college students, grants to farmers and rural businesses, loans to those willing to hire the chronically unemployed, the Volunteers in Service to America (VISTA, a "domestic Peace Corps"), and the Community Action Program, which would provide "maximum feasible participation" of the poor in directing programs designed for their benefit. Speaking at Ann Arbor, Michigan, in May 1964, Johnson called for a "Great Society" resting on "abundance and liberty for all. The Great Society demands an end to poverty and racial injustice, to which we are fully committed in our time."

THE 1964 ELECTION   In the Republican party, a new frenzy of activity was developing on the right. For years the conviction had grown within the party that it had fallen into the hands of an "Eastern Establishment" that had given in to the same internationalism and big-government policies as liberal Democrats. Ever since 1940, so the theory went, the party had nominated "me-too" candidates who merely promised to run more efficiently the programs that Democrats designed. Offer the voters "a choice, not an echo," they reasoned, and a conservative majority would assert itself. The Republican right thus began to drift toward varieties of dogmatic conservatism, ranging from a kind of "aristocratic" intellectual "new conservatism" which found voice in the *National Review*, edited by William F. Buckley, Jr., to the John Birch Society, founded by Robert Welch, a New England candy manufacturer given to accusing such distinguished citizens as Eisenhower, Dulles, and Chief Justice Warren of supporting a Communist conspiracy.

By 1960 Arizona senator Barry Goldwater, a millionaire department-store magnate from Phoenix, had begun to emerge as the leader of the Republican right. In his book *The Conscience of a Conservative* (1960), Goldwater proposed abolition of the income tax, sale of the TVA, and a drastic overhaul of social security. Almost from the time of Kennedy's victory in 1960 a movement to draft Goldwater began, mobilizing right-wing activists to capture party caucuses and contest primaries. In 1964 they took an early lead, and after sweeping the all-important California primary, Goldwater's forces controlled the Republican convention when it gathered in Los Angeles. "I would remind you," Goldwater told the delegates, "that extremism in the defense of liberty is no vice."

By the end of the campaign Goldwater had achieved a position of splendid isolation on the far right of the political spectrum. He had an unusual gift for frightening voters. Accusing the administration of waging a "no-win" war in Vietnam, he urged wholesale bombing of North Vietnam and left the impression of being trigger-happy. He savaged Johnson's War on Poverty and the entire New Deal tradition. At one stop he called LBJ the "Santa Clause of the free lunch." In Tennessee he proposed the sale of the Tennessee Valley Authority; in St. Petersburg, Florida, a major retirement community, he questioned the value of social security. He was on record as opposing

*Many voters feared that the Republican candidate for president
in 1964, Arizona senator Barry Goldwater, was trigger-happy.
In this cartoon he wields his book,* The Conscience of a
Conservative, *in one hand and a hydrogen bomb in the other.*

both the nuclear test ban and the Civil Rights Act. To Republican
campaign buttons that claimed "In your heart, you know he's right,"
Democrats responded "In your guts you know he's nuts."

Johnson, on the other hand, appealed to the great consensus that
spanned most of the political spectrum. Conceded the Democratic
nomination from the start, he chose as his running mate Hubert
Humphrey from Minnesota, a prominent liberal senator who had
long promoted the cause of civil rights. In contrast to Goldwater's
bellicose rhetoric on Vietnam, Johnson pledged: "We are not about
to send American boys nine or ten thousand miles from home to do
what Asian boys ought to be doing for themselves"—a statement
reminiscent of the assurance which Johnson's idol, Franklin Roosevelt, voiced regarding the European war in 1940.

The result was a landslide. Johnson polled 61 percent of the total
votes; Goldwater carried only Arizona and five states in the Deep
South, where race remained the salient issue. Vermont went Democratic for the first time ever in a presidential election. Johnson won
the electoral vote by a whopping 482 to 52. In the Senate the Democrats increased their majority by two (68 to 32) and in the House by
thirty-seven (295 to 140). But LBJ was aware that a mandate such as
he had received could quickly erode. He shrewdly told aides, "every
day I'm in office, I'm going to lose votes. I'm going to alienate
somebody. . . . We've got to get this legislation fast. You've got to get
it during my honeymoon."

LANDMARK LEGISLATION   Johnson flooded the new Congress with Great Society legislation that, he promised, would end poverty, revitalize the decaying central cities, provide every young American with the chance to attend college, protect the health of the elderly, enhance the cultural life of the nation, clean up the air and water, and make the highways safer. The scope of Johnson's legislation was unparalleled since Franklin Roosevelt's Hundred Days.

Priority went to health insurance and aid to education, proposals that had languished since President Truman advanced them in 1945. For twenty years the proposal for a comprehensive plan of medical insurance had been stalled by the American Medical Association. But now that Johnson had the votes, the AMA joined Republicans in boarding the bandwagon for a bill serving those over age sixty-five. The AMA proposed, in addition to hospital insurance, a program for payment of doctor bills and drug costs with the government footing half the premium. The act that finally emerged went well beyond the original program. It not only incorporated the new proposal into the Medicare program for the aged, but added another program, dubbed Medicaid, for federal grants to states that would help cover medical payments for the indigent. President Johnson signed the bill on July 30, 1965, in Independence, Missouri, with eighty-one-year-old Harry Truman looking on.

Five days after he submitted his Medicare program, Johnson sent to Congress his proposal for $1.5 billion in federal aid to elementary and secondary education. Such proposals had been ignored since the 1940s, blocked alternately by issues of segregation or separation of church and state. The first issue had been laid to rest, legally at least, by the Civil Rights Act of 1964. Now the Congress devised a means of extending aid to "poverty-impacted" school districts regardless of their public or parochial character. This measure Johnson signed in the dilapidated one-room schoolhouse he had first attended, with his first-grade teacher looking on.

The momentum generated by the progress of these measures had already begun to carry others along, and the momentum continued through the following year. Before the Eighty-ninth Congress adjourned, it had established a record in the passage of landmark legislation unequaled since the time of the New Deal. Altogether the tide of Great Society legislation had carried 435 bills through the Congress. Among them was the Appalachian Regional Development Act of 1966, which provided $1.1 billion for programs in remote mountain coves. The Housing and Urban Development Act of 1965 provided aid for construction of 240,000 units of housing and $2.9 billion for urban renewal. Funds for rent supplements for low-income families followed in 1966, and in that year a new Department of Housing and Urban Development appeared, headed by Robert C.

Weaver, the first black cabinet member. Johnson had, in the words of one Washington reporter, "brought to harvest a generation's backlog of ideas and social legislation."

Little noticed among the stream of legislation flowing from the Congress was a major new immigration bill that had originated in the Kennedy White House. In collaboration with the Anti-Defamation League, John Kennedy had written a pamphlet in 1958 entitled "A Nation of Immigrants" in which he celebrated the role played by immigration in shaping the United States and emphasized the need for revising the immigration regulations. In 1963 he sent to Congress a new immigration bill, but it was languishing in committee when he was assassinated. Johnson used his 1964 State of the Union address to endorse immigration reform in general and the Kennedy bill in particular. A modified version finally passed the Congress in the fall of 1965.

President Johnson signed the Immigration Act of 1965 in a ceremony held at Liberty Island in New York Harbor, with Ellis Island in the background. In his speech, Johnson stressed that the new law would redress the wrong done to those "from southern and eastern Europe" and the "developing continents" of Asia, Africa, and Latin America. It did so by abolishing the discriminatory quotas based on national origins that had governed immigration policy since the 1920s. The old system had favored immigrants from Britain and western Europe and had effectively shut the door to most people from eastern Europe and Asia. The new law, whose provisions were to take full effect in 1968, treated all nationalities and races equally. In place of national quotas it created hemispheric ceilings on visas issued: 170,000 for persons from outside the Western Hemisphere, 120,000 for persons from within. It also stipulated that no more than 20,000 people could come from any one country each year. The new act allowed the entry of immediate family members of American residents without limit. For others, the immigration bill provided a revised system of preferences used to decide which applicants qualified for admission. Most of the annual visas were to be given on a first-come-first-served basis to "other relatives" of American residents and only a small proportion (about 10 percent) were allocated to those with special talents or job skills.

The Immigration Act of 1965 passed with so little opposition in part because no one expected it to generate profound change. Attorney-General Robert Kennedy told the Senate that perhaps as many as 5,000 Asians might come the first year, "after which immigration from that source would virtually disappear." But he was wrong. During the prosperous sixties, few western Europeans sought to emigrate to the United States; those living in Communist-controlled eastern Europe could not leave. But Asians and Latin Americans flocked to American consulates in search of visas. And within a few years the new arrivals in turn used the family-preference system to bring their family members as well. This so-called chain immigration quickly filled the annual quotas for nations such as the Philippines, Mexico, Korea, and the Dominican Republic, and Hispanics and Asians became the largest contingent of new Americans.

The Great Society programs included several genuine success stories. The Highway Safety Act and the Traffic Safety Act (1966) established safety standards for automobile manufacturers and highway design, and the scholarships provided for college students under the Higher Education Act (1965) were quite popular. Many Great Society initiatives aimed at improving the health, nutrition, and education of poor Americans, young and old, made some headway against these problems. So, too, did federal efforts to clean up air and water pollution. But several ambitious programs were hastily designed and ill-conceived, others were vastly underfunded, and many were mismanaged. Medicare, for example, removed any incentives for hospitals to control costs, and medical bills skyrocketed. Often funds appropriated for various programs never made it through the tangled bureaucracy to the needy. Widely publicized cases of welfare fraud became a powerful weapon in the hands of those opposed to liberal social programs. By 1966 middle-class resentment over the cost and waste of the Great Society programs helped generate a conservative backlash.

From Civil Rights to Black Power

THE CIVIL-RIGHTS MOVEMENT   Among the successes of the Great Society were several landmark pieces of civil-rights legislation. After Kennedy's death President Johnson, who had maneuvered through the Senate the Civil Rights Acts of 1957 and 1960, called for passage of a new civil-rights bill as a memorial to the fallen leader. With bipartisan support he finally broke the Senate filibuster mounted by a diminishing band of bitter-enders. "Nothing," said Republican Senate leader Everett Dirksen, quoting the French writer Victor Hugo, "is so powerful as an idea whose time has come."

On July 2 Johnson signed the Civil Rights Act of 1964, the most far-reaching civil-rights measure ever enacted by the Congress. The act outlawed discrimination in hotels, restaurants, and other public accommodations. It required that literacy tests for voting be administered in writing, and defined as literate anybody who had finished the sixth grade. The attorney-general could now bring suits for school desegregation, relieving parents of a painful necessity. Federally assisted programs and private employers alike were required to eliminate discrimination. An Equal Employment Opportunity Commission (the old Fair Employment Practices Committee reborn) administered a ban on job discrimination by race, religion, national origin, or sex.

Early in 1965 King announced a drive to register the 3 million blacks in the South who had not registered to vote. In Selma, Alabama, the focus at the outset, he found in Sheriff Jim Clark a foil as perfect as Birmingham's police chief. On March 7 civil-rights protesters began a march to Montgomery, about 50 miles away, only to be violently dispersed by state troopers and a mounted posse. A federal judge agreed to allow the march, and President Johnson provided protection with National Guardsmen and army military police. By March 25, when the demonstrators reached Montgomery, some 35,000 people were with them, and King delivered a rousing address from the steps of the state capitol.

Several days before the march President Johnson went before Congress with a moving plea which reached its climax when he slowly intoned the words of the movement's hymn: "And we shall overcome." The resulting Voting Rights Act of 1965, passed to ensure all the right to vote, rejected the old case-by-case procedures and authorized the attorney-general to dispatch federal examiners to

President Johnson congratulates Martin Luther King, Jr., at the ceremonial signing of the 1965 Voting Rights Act.

register voters. In states or counties where fewer than half the adults had voted in 1964, the act suspended literacy tests and other devices commonly used to defraud citizens of the vote. By the end of the year some 250,000 blacks were newly registered.

"BLACK POWER" But in the midst of this success the civil-rights movement began to fragment. On August 11, 1965, less than a week after the passage of the Voting Rights Act, Watts, a predominantly black and poor community in Los Angeles, exploded in a frenzy of riots and looting. When the uprising ended, there were 34 dead, almost 4,000 rioters in jail, and property damage exceeding $35 million. Liberal commentators were both stunned and surprised, as the riots occurred in the wake of the greatest legislative victories for black Americans since Reconstruction. Moreover, Watts was not an outrageous slum. The national Urban League in fact had rated Los Angeles as the most prosperous and desirable city for black urban residents in the United States.

But events did not stand still to await white liberal comprehension. Chicago and Cleveland, along with forty other American cities, suffered racial riots in the summer of 1966. The following summer Newark and Detroit burst into flames. Detroit provided the most graphic example of urban violence, as tanks rolled through the streets and soldiers from the 101st Airborne used machine guns to deal with snipers in the tenements. *Pravda*, the official Soviet newspaper, ran the story with accompanying pictures of the carnage on its front page. Firemen who tried to put out the flames in several of the urban riots were showered by bricks and bottles thrown by the very people whose houses were burning.

In retrospect, it was predictable that the civil-rights movement would focus on the plight of urban blacks. By the middle 1960s about 70 percent of America's black population lived in metropolitan areas, most of them in central-city ghettos that had been bypassed by the postwar prosperity. And again it seemed clear, in retrospect, that the nonviolent tactics which had worked in the rural South would not work in the northern cities. In the North the problems were *de facto* segregation resulting from residential patterns, not *de jure* segregation amenable to changes in law, and northern white ethnic groups did not have the cultural heritage which southern whites shared with blacks. "It may be," wrote a contributor to *Esquire*, "that looting, rioting and burning . . . are really nothing more than radical forms of urban renewal, a response not only to the frustrations of the ghetto but the collapse of all ordinary modes of change, as if a body despairing of the indifference of doctors sought to rip a cancer out of itself." A special Commission on Civil Disorders noted that, unlike

A *National Guardsman on patrol in Detroit during the summer 1967 riots.*

earlier race riots, the urban upheavals of the middle 1960s were initiated by blacks themselves; earlier riots had been started by whites, which had then provoked black counterattacks. Now blacks visited violence and destruction on themselves in an effort to destroy what they could not stomach and what civil-rights legislation seemed unable to change.

By 1966 "black power" had become the new rallying cry. Radical members of the SNCC had become estranged from Martin Luther King's theories of militant nonviolence. As King became the center of attention from the white media, SNCC members began to refer to him cynically as "de Lawd." When Stokely Carmichael, a twenty-five-year-old graduate of Howard University, became head of the SNCC in May 1966, the separatist philosophy of black power became official and whites were ousted from the organization. "We reject an American dream defined by white people and must work to construct an American reality defined by Afro-Americans," said a SNCC position paper. H. Rap Brown, who succeeded Carmichael as head of the SNCC in 1967, even urged blacks to "get you some guns" and "kill the honkies." Meanwhile Carmichael had moved on to the Black Panther party, a self-professed group of urban revolutionaries founded in Oakland, California, in 1966 and headed by Huey P. Newton and Eldridge Cleaver. Under their leadership the Black Panthers echoed the separatist demands of Marcus Garvey in the late 1910s and early 1920s, terrified the public by wearing bandeleros and carrying rifles, but eventually fragmented in spasms of violence.

The most articulate spokesman for black power was one of the earliest, Malcolm X (formerly Malcolm Little, with the "X" denoting his lost African surname). Malcolm had risen from a ghetto childhood of narcotics and crime to become the chief disciple of Elijah Muhammad, the Black Muslim prophet who rejected Christianity as "the religion of white devils." "Yes, I'm an extremist," Malcolm acknowledged in 1964. "The black race in the United States is in extremely bad shape. You show me a black man who isn't an extremist and I'll show you one who needs psychiatric attention." By 1964 Malcolm had broken with Elijah Muhammad and founded his own organization, which was committed to the establishment of alliances between African-Americans and the nonwhite peoples of the world. But just after the publication of his *Autobiography* in 1965, Malcolm was gunned down in the Audubon Ballroom in Harlem by assassins representing a rival faction of Black Muslims. With him went the most effective voice for urban black militancy since Marcus Garvey.

Black power was a slogan more than a philosophy. The conclusion of the Commission on Civil Disorders was harsh but accurate: "Black Power rhetoric and ideology actually expresses a lack of power. . . . Powerless to make any fundamental changes in the life of the masses . . . many advocates of Black Power have retreated into an unreal world, where they see an outnumbered and poverty-

Malcolm X, influential spokesman for the Black Muslim movement.

stricken minority organizing itself independently of whites and creating sufficient power to force white Americans to grant its demands." But if Lyndon Johnson's Great Society encountered harsh realities in American cities, it was running into even grimmer realities in the Vietnamese countryside.

THE TRAGEDY OF VIETNAM

DIMENSIONS OF A WAR   At the time of President Kennedy's death there were 16,000 American military "advisers" in Vietnam. Johnson inherited a commitment to prevent a Communist takeover in South Vietnam along with a reluctance to assume the military burden for fighting the war. Ever since Truman, one president after another did just enough to avoid the prospect of being charged with having "lost" Vietnam. Such an outcry, Johnson feared, would undermine his influence and endanger his Great Society programs in Congress.

Therefore he found himself drawn inexorably deeper into intervention in Asia. During the presidential campaign of 1964 Johnson had opposed the use of American combat troops and had privately described Vietnam as "a raggedy-ass fourth-rate country" not worthy of American blood and money. Nevertheless, by the end of 1965 there were 184,000 American troops in Vietnam; in 1966 the troop level reached 385,000; and by 1969, the height of the American presence, 542,000. By the time the last American troops left in March 1973, 58,000 Americans had died and another 270,000 had been wounded. The war had cost the American taxpayers $150 billion, generated economic dislocations that destroyed many Great Society programs, produced 570,000 draft offenders and 563,000 less-than-honorable discharges from the service, toppled Johnson's administration, and divided the country as no event in American history had since the Civil War.

ESCALATION   The official sanction for "escalation"—a Defense Department term coined in the Vietnam era—was the Tonkin Gulf Resolution, voted by Congress on August 7, 1964. Johnson told a national television audience that two American destroyers, the U.S.S. *Maddox* and *C. Turner Joy*, had been attacked by North Vietnamese vessels on August 2 and 4 in the Gulf of Tonkin off the coast of North Vietnam. Although Johnson described the attack as unprovoked, in truth the destroyers had been monitoring South Vietnamese attacks against two North Vietnamese islands—attacks planned by American advisers. The Tonkin Gulf Resolution authorized the president to "take all necessary measures to repel any armed attack against the forces of the United States and to prevent further aggression." Only Senator Wayne Morse of Oregon and Senator Ernest Gruening of Alaska voted against the resolution, which Johnson thereafter interpreted as equivalent to a congressional declaration of war.

Soon after Johnson's landslide victory over Goldwater in 1964, the crucial decisions that shaped American policy in Vietnam for the next four years were made. On February 5, 1965, the Vietcong (Communist-led guerrillas fighting in South Vietnam) killed 8 and wounded 126 Americans at Pleiku. Further attacks on Americans later that week led Johnson to order operation "Rolling Thunder," the first sustained bombings of North Vietnam, which were intended to stop the flow of soldiers and supplies into the south. Six months later a task force conducted an extensive study of the bombing's effects on the supplies pouring down the Ho Chi Minh Trail from North Vietnam through Laos. It concluded that there was "no way" to stop the traffic.

In March 1965 the new American army commander in Vietnam, General William C. Westmoreland, requested and received the first installment of combat troops, who waded ashore at Da Nang. By the summer American forces were engaged in "search-and-destroy" operations, thus ending the fiction that American soldiers were only "advisers." And as combat operations increased, so did the mounting list of American casualties, announced each week on the nightly news along with the "body count" of alleged Vietcong dead. "Westy's War," although fought with helicopter gunships, chemical defoliants, and napalm, became like the trench warfare of World War I—a war of attrition.

U.S. Marines under fire after landing at Da Nang, March 1965.

THE CONTEXT FOR POLICY   Johnson's decision to "Americanize" the war, so ill-starred in retrospect, was consistent with the foreign policy principles pursued by all American presidents after World War II. The version of the containment theory articulated in the Truman Doctrine, endorsed by Eisenhower and Dulles throughout the 1950s, and reaffirmed by Kennedy, pledged United States opposition to the advance of communism anywhere in the world. "Why are we in Vietnam?" Johnson asked rhetorically at Johns Hopkins University in 1965. "We are there because we have a promise to keep. . . . To leave Vietnam to its fate would shake the confidence of all these people in the value of American commitment." Secretary of State Dean Rusk repeated this rationale before countless congressional committees, warning that Thailand, Burma, and the rest of Southeast Asia would fall to communism if American forces withdrew. American military intervention in Vietnam was not an aberration, but a logical culmination of the assumptions widely shared by the foreign policy establishment and leaders of both political parties since the early days of the Cold War.

If Vietnam was not an aberration, the "Pentagon Papers" subsequently made clear that the United States did not "stumble into a quagmire." Undersecretary of State George Ball consistently warned of disaster: "Once on the tiger's back we cannot be sure of picking the place to dismount." It was also clear to Johnson and his advisers from the start that American military involvement must not reach levels that would provoke the Chinese or Soviets into direct intervention. And this meant, in effect, that military victory in any traditional sense of the term was never possible. "It was startling to me to find out," said the new secretary of defense, Clark Clifford, in 1968, "that we have no military plan to end the war." The goal of the United States was not to win the war in any traditional sense, but to prevent the North Vietnamese and Vietcong from winning. This meant that America would have to maintain a military presence as long as the enemy retained the will to fight.

As it turned out, American support for the war eroded faster than the will of the North Vietnamese leaders to tolerate devastating casualties. Systematic opposition to the war on college campuses began in 1965 with "teach-ins" at the University of Michigan. And in January 1966 Senator J. William Fulbright of Arkansas, chairman of the Senate Foreign Relations Committee, began congressional investigations into American policy. George Kennan, the founding father of the containment doctrine, told Fulbright's committee that the doctrine was appropriate for Europe, but not Southeast Asia. And a respected general testified that Westmoreland's military strategy had no chance of achieving victory. By 1967 opposition to the

war had become so pronounced that antiwar demonstrations in New York and at the Pentagon attracted massive support. Nightly television accounts of the fighting—Vietnam was the first war to receive extended television coverage, and hence has been dubbed "the living room war"—made official optimism appear fatuous. By May 1967 even Secretary of Defense McNamara was wavering: "The picture of the world's greatest superpower killing or injuring 1,000 noncombatants a week, while trying to pound a tiny backward nation into submission on an issue whose merits are hotly disputed, is not a pretty one."

In a war of political will, North Vietnam had the advantage. Johnson and his advisers never came to appreciate the tenacity of the North Vietnamese commitment to unify Vietnam and expel the United States. Ho Chi Minh had warned the French in the 1940s that "You can kill ten of my men for every one I kill of yours, but even at those odds, you will lose and I will win." He predicted that the Vietnamese Communists would win a war of attrition, for they were willing to sacrifice all for their cause. Indeed, just as General

Westmoreland was assuring Johnson and the American public that the American war effort in early 1968 was on the verge of gaining the upper hand, the Communists again displayed their tenacity.

THE TURNING POINT On January 31, 1968, the first day of the Vietnamese New Year (Tet), the Vietcong defied a holiday truce to launch assaults on American and South Vietnamese forces throughout South Vietnam. The old capital city of Hue fell to the Communists and Vietcong units temporarily occupied the grounds of the American embassy in Saigon. General Westmoreland proclaimed the Tet offensive a major defeat for the Vietcong, and most students of military strategy later agreed with him. But while Vietcong casualties were enormous, the impact of the events on the American public was more telling. *Time* and *Newsweek* soon ran antiwar editorials urging American withdrawal. Walter Cronkite, the dean of American television journalists, confided to his viewers that he no longer believed the war was winnable. "If I've lost Walter," Johnson was reported to say, "then it's over. I've lost Mr. Average Citizen." Polls showed that Johnson's popularity declined to 35 percent, lower than any president since Truman's darkest days. Civil-rights leaders and social activists felt betrayed as they saw federal funds earmarked for the war on poverty siphoned off by the expanding war. In 1968 the

During the 1968 Tet offensive Vietcong units temporarily took the grounds of the American embassy in Saigon. Here, American military police lead a captured Vietcong guerrilla away from the embassy.

The President Shows His Scar.
*Pointing to a postsurgical scar in the
shape of Vietnam, LBJ in this
cartoon seems to be indicating the
wound from which he never
recovered.*

United States was spending $322,000 on every Communist killed in
Vietnam; the poverty programs at home received only $53 per per-
son.

During 1968 Johnson grew increasingly embittered and isolated.
Clark Clifford, the new secretary of defense, reported to Johnson
that a task force of prominent soldiers and civilians saw no prospect
for a military victory. Robert Kennedy was reportedly considering a
run for the presidency in order to challenge Johnson's Vietnam policy. And Senator Eugene McCarthy of Minnesota had already made
the decision to oppose Johnson in the Democratic primaries. With
antiwar students rallying to his candidacy, McCarthy polled 42 percent of the vote to Johnson's 48 percent in New Hampshire's March
primary. It was a remarkable showing for a little-known senator,
even though the president was a write-in candidate. Each presidential primary now promised to become a referendum on Johnson's
Vietnam policy. In Wisconsin, scene of the next primary, Johnson's
political advisers forecast a humiliating defeat: "We sent a man [to
campaign for Johnson] and all we've heard from him since is a few
faint beeps, like the last radio signals from the Bay of Pigs."

Despite Johnson's troubles in the conduct of foreign policy, he
remained a master at reading the political omens. On March 31 he
went on national television to announce a limited halt to the bombing of North Vietnam and fresh initiatives for a negotiated cease-fire.
Then he added a dramatic postscript: "I have concluded that I
should not permit the Presidency to become involved in the partisan
divisions that are developing in this political year. Accordingly, I
shall not seek, and I will not accept the nomination of my party for
another term as your President." Although American troops would
remain in Vietnam for five more years and the casualties would

The Vietnam War sapped the spirit of Lyndon Johnson, who decided not to run for reelection in 1968.

continue, the quest for military victory had ended. Now the question was how the most powerful nation in the world could extricate itself from Vietnam with a minimum of damage to its prestige.

Sixties Crescendo

A TRAUMATIC YEAR   History moved at a fearful pace throughout the 1960s, but 1968 was a year of extreme turbulence even for that tumultuous decade. On April 4, only four days after Johnson's announced withdrawal, Martin Luther King was gunned down while standing on the balcony of his motel in Memphis, Tennessee. The assassin, James Earl Ray, had expressed hostility toward blacks, but debate still continues over whether he was a pawn in an organized conspiracy. King's death set off an outpouring of grief among whites and blacks. It also ignited riots in over sixty American cities, with the most serious occurring in Chicago and Washington, D.C.

Two months later, on June 6, Robert Kennedy was shot in the head by a young Palestinian, Sirhan Sirhan, who resented Kennedy's strong support of Israel. Kennedy's death occurred at the end of the day on which he had convincingly defeated Eugene McCarthy in the California primary, thereby assuming leadership of the antiwar forces in the race for the Democratic nomination for president. David Halberstam thought back to the assassinations of John Kennedy and Malcolm X, then the violent end of King, the most influential black leader of the twentieth century, and then Robert Kennedy, the heir to leadership of the Kennedy clan. "We could make a calendar of the decade," Halberstam wrote, "by marking where we were at the hours of those violent deaths."

CHICAGO AND MIAMI   In August 1968 Democratic delegates gathered inside the convention hall at Chicago to nominate Hubert Humphrey, while 24,000 police and National Guardsmen and a small army of television reporters stood watch over an eclectic gathering of protesters herded together miles away in a public park. The liberal tradition represented by the Democratic party was clearly in disarray, a fact that gave heart to the Republicans who gathered in Miami to nominate Richard Nixon. Only six years earlier, after he had lost the California gubernatorial race, Nixon had told reporters, "You won't have Nixon to kick around anymore, because, gentlemen, this is my last press conference." But by 1968 he had become a preeminent spokesman for all the values of "Middle America." The novelist Norman Mailer, who covered both conventions to gather material for a book on American politics, likened the convention in Miami to a Rotarian gathering in a cemetery. But Nixon and the Republicans were offering a vision of stability and order that a majority of Americans—soon to be called "the silent majority"—wanted desperately.

George Wallace, the Democratic governor of Alabama who had made his reputation as a defender of segregation, became a third candidate in the campaign on the American Independent party ticket. Wallace moderated his position on the race issue, but appealed even more candidly than Nixon to the fears generated by protesters, the welfare system, and the growth of the federal government. Wallace's reactionary candidacy generated considerable ap-

Vice-President Hubert Humphrey, the 1968 Democratic presidential nominee, shows his scar in this cartoon: the legacy of Johnson and Vietnam.

peal outside his native South, especially among white working-class communities, where resentment against Johnson's Great Society liberalism flourished. Although never a possible winner, Wallace did pose the possibility of denying Humphrey or Nixon an electoral majority and thereby throwing the choice into the House of Representatives, which would have provided an appropriate climax to a chaotic year.

NIXON AGAIN   It did not happen that way. Nixon enjoyed an enormous lead in the polls, which narrowed as the election approached. Wallace's campaign was hurt by his running mate, retired air force general Curtis LeMay, who favored expanding the war in Vietnam and spoke approvingly of using nuclear weapons. (It was reported that LeMay was the model for the deranged general in the 1964 film *Doctor Strangelove: Or, How I Learned to Stop Worrying and Love the Bomb*.) In October 1968 Humphrey announced that he would stop bombing North Vietnam "as an acceptable risk for peace." Eugene McCarthy, who had been strangely silent and had even spent some time cloistered in a Benedictine monastery, eventually came out in support of Humphrey. "I believe the Vice-President is a man who can be relied on to tell the difference between the pale horse of death and the white horse of victory," said McCarthy. "I am not sure Nixon can make that distinction."

Nixon and Governor Spiro Agnew of Maryland, his running mate, eked out a narrow victory by about 800,000 votes, a margin of about

Richard Nixon (right) *and Spiro Agnew, victors in the 1968 election.*

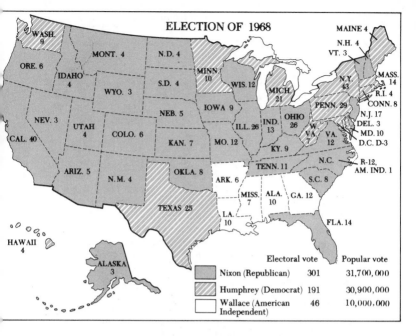

ELECTION OF 1968

	Electoral vote	Popular vote
Nixon (Republican)	301	31,700,000
Humphrey (Democrat)	191	30,900,000
Wallace (American Independent)	46	10,000,000

one percentage point. The electoral vote was more decisive, 301 to 191. Wallace received 10 million votes, 13.5 percent of the total, for the best showing by a third-party candidate since Robert La Follette in 1924. All but one of Wallace's 46 electoral votes were from the Deep South. Nixon swept all but four of the states west of the Mississippi. Humphrey's support came almost exclusively from the Northeast.

And so at the end of a turbulent year near the end of a traumatic decade, power passed peacefully to a president who was associated with the complacency of the 1950s. A nation that had seemed on the verge of consuming itself in spasms of violence looked to Richard Nixon to provide what he had promised in the campaign: "peace with honor" in Vietnam and a middle ground on which a majority of Americans, silent or otherwise, could come together.

FURTHER READING

For the context of the Camelot years, consult first James L. Sundquist's *Politics and Policy: The Eisenhower, Kennedy, and Johnson Years* (1968).° For the 1960 campaign see Theodore H. White's *The Making of the President 1960* (1961).° Herbert Parmet traces the influence of Kennedy in two volumes, *Jack: The Struggle of John Fitzgerald Kennedy* (1980) and

°These books are available in paperback editions.

JFK: The Presidency of John Fitzgerald Kennedy (1983). Favorable memoirs from White House staffers include Arthur M. Schlesinger, Jr.'s *A Thousand Days: John F. Kennedy in the White House* (1965)° and Theodore C. Sorensen's *Kennedy* (1965). Less favorable assessments come from Henry Fairlie's *The Kennedy Promise* (1973) and Bruce Miroff's *Pragmatic Illusions: The Presidential Politics of John F. Kennedy* (1976). For details of the assassination, see William Manchester's *The Death of the President* (1967).°

There are fewer works about Kennedy's successor, but many are solidly detailed. Lyndon Johnson's own *The Vantage Point: Perspectives on the Presidency, 1963–1969* (1971),° can be balanced with Doris Kearns's *Lyndon Johnson and the American Dream* (1976).° Also helpful is Merle Miller's *Lyndon: An Oral Biography* (1980).° Eric Goldman's *The Tragedy of Lyndon Johnson* (1969)° is critical of Johnson's Vietnamese escalation. Ronnie Dugger's *The Politician: The Life and Times of Lyndon Johnson* (1982) depicts in detail Johnson's early career, as does the first volume of Robert Caro's biography, *The Years of Lyndon Johnson* (1982).° See also the second volume of Caro's LBJ biography, *The Path to Power* (1990).°

Among the works that interpret the policy of the liberals are W. W. Rostow's *The Diffusion of Power, 1957–1972* (1972) and Robert Lekachman's *The Age of Keynes* (1966).° Also helpful is the memoir of a leading Keynesian, John Kenneth Galbraith, *A Life in Our Times* (1981).° Very helpful for background on the formation of policy is James T. Patterson's *America's Struggle against Poverty, 1900–1980* (1981).

On foreign policy, see Richard Walton's *Cold War and Counter-revolution: The Foreign Policy of John F. Kennedy* (1972),° and *Kennedy's Quest for Victory: American Foreign Policy, 1961–1963* (1989), edited by Thomas G. Paterson. To learn more about Kennedy's problems in Cuba, see Haynes Johnson's *The Bay of Pigs* (1964). For the Alliance of Progress, see Jerome Levinson and Juan de Onis's *The Alliance That Lost Its Way* (1970).

Policy in Vietnam has received voluminous treatment from all political perspectives. For an overview, see Larry Berman's *Planning a Tragedy: The Americanization of the War in Vietnam* (1982) and *Lyndon Johnson's War: The Road to Stalemate in Vietnam* (1989), as well as Stanley Karnow's *Vietnam: A History* (1983).° Three of the most popular critical accounts of the struggle are Chester L. Cooper's *The Lost Crusade* (1970), Frances Fitzgerald's *Fire in the Lake: The Vietnamese and the Americans in Vietnam* (1972),° and David Halberstam's *The Best and the Brightest* (1972).° Works which see American policy in a favorable light include Norman Podhoretz's *Why We Were in Vietnam* (1982), Guenter Lewy's *America in Vietnam* (1978),° and Leslie Gelb and Richard Bett's *The Irony of Vietnam: The System Worked* (1979).° The life of the common soldier is depicted in Robert Pisor's *The End of the Line: The Siege of Khe Sanh* (1982).

Many scholars have dealt with various aspects of the civil-rights movement and race relations of the 1960s. Studies of the national politics of civil rights include Carl Brauer's *John F. Kennedy and the Second Reconstruction* (1977)° and Lee Rainwater and William L. Yancey's *The Moynihan Report and the Politics of Controversy* (1967). These studies of Martin Luther King, Jr., are helpful: David Garrow's *Bearing the Cross* (1986), Adam Fairclough's *To Redeem the Soul of America: The Southern Christian Leadership Conference and Martin Luther King, Jr.* (1987), and David Lewis's *King: A Critical Biography* (1970).° David Garrow also has two specialized studies of King, *Protest at Selma* (1978)° and *The FBI and Martin Luther King, Jr.: From "Solo" to Memphis* (1981).° King is also enlightening in his own book *Why We Can't Wait* (1964).° Other personalities in the civil-rights movement are studied in Charles F. Kellogg's *NAACP* (1967), August Meier and Elliott Rudwick's *CORE* (1973),° and Howard Zinn's *SNCC: The New Abolitionists* (1964). For legal turns the civil-rights movement took during the 1960s, see J. Harvie Wilkinson's *From Brown to Bakke: The Supreme Court and School Integration, 1954–1978* (1978). William Chafe's *From Civilities to Civil Rights: Greensboro, North Carolina, and the Black Struggle for Freedom* (1980)° details the original sit-ins. The reaction of one government agency is examined in Kenneth O'Reilly's *"Racial Matters": The FBI's Secret File on Black America, 1960–1972* (1989).

For race relations subsequent to the Civil Rights Act, consult Theodore Draper's *The Rediscovery of Black Nationalism* (1970). Important books by blacks during the period include *The Autobiography of Malcolm X*, edited by Alex Haley (1965),° Eldridge Cleaver's *Soul on Ice* (1967),° George Jackson's *Soledad Brother* (1970),° and Stokely Carmichael and Charles Hamilton's *Black Power* (1967).° Claude Brown's *Manchild in the Promised Land* (1975)° explores the world of ghetto life.

For the tumultuous events of the 1968 campaign, start with Theodore White's *The Making of the President 1968* (1969).° Less favorable to Nixon is Joe McGinnis's *The Selling of the President* (1969).° Arthur M. Schlesinger, Jr.'s *Robert Kennedy and His Times* (1978)° and Marshall Frady's *Wallace* (1976)° report the campaign from the viewpoint of other candidates.

35

REBELLION AND REACTION: THE NIXON YEARS

THE ROOTS OF REBELLION

As Richard Nixon entered the White House he faced a nation whose social fabric was in tatters. Everywhere, it seemed, traditional institutions and notions of authority were coming under attack. The turbulent events of 1968 revealed how deeply divided American society had become and how difficult a task Nixon faced in carrying out his pledge to restore social harmony. Not surprisingly, the stability he promised proved to be elusive. His policies and combative temperament served to heighten rather than reduce the tensions wracking the nation. Those tensions had been long in developing and reflected profound fissures in the postwar consensus promoted by Eisenhower and inherited by Kennedy and Johnson. What had caused such a seismic breakdown in social harmony? Ironically, many of the same forces that had promoted the flush times of the Eisenhower years helped generate the social upheavals of the 1960s.

YOUTH REVOLT By the 1960s the "baby-boomers" were maturing. Now young adults, they differed from their elders in that they had experienced neither economic depression nor a major war, and had been surrounded by the homogenizing effects of a flourishing consumer culture and television. Moreover, they were aware of the Cold War primarily as a battle of words and gestures without immediate consequences for them. Record numbers of these young people were attending American colleges and universities during the 1960s: college enrollment quadrupled between 1945 and 1970. At the same time many universities had become gigantic institutions dependent on research contracts from huge corporations and the federal government. As these "multiversities" grew more bureaucratic and hierarchical, they unknowingly invited resistance from a generation of students wary of involvement in what Eisenhower had labeled the "military-industrial complex."

The success of the Greensboro sit-ins in 1960 not only precipitated a decade of civil-rights activism; it also signaled an end to the supposed apathy that had enveloped college campuses and social life during the 1950s. Although most immediately concerned with the rights and status of black people, the sit-ins, marches, protests, principles, and sacrifices associated with the civil-rights movement provided the model and inspiration for other estranged and excluded groups who demanded justice, freedom, and equality as well.

During 1960–1961 a small but significant number of white students joined African-Americans in the sit-in movement. They and many others were also inspired by President Kennedy's direct appeals to their youthful idealism. Thousands enrolled in the Peace Corps and VISTA (Volunteers in Service to America, the domestic version of the Peace Corps), and others continued to participate in civil-rights demonstrations. But as it became clear that politics mixed with principle in the president's position on civil rights, and later, as criticism of escalating American involvement in Vietnam mounted, more and more young people grew disillusioned with the government as well as other institutional bastions of the status quo. Folksinger Bob Dylan translated the ferment of rebellion into these lyrics in 1963:

> Come mothers and fathers,
> Throughout the land
> And don't criticize
> What you can't understand
> Your sons and your daughters
> Are beyond your command
> There's a battle
> Outside and it's ragin'
> It'll soon shake your windows
> And rattle your walls
> For the times they are a-changin'.

Indeed there was a growing feeling that something was fundamentally wrong not just with the political system but with the entire structure of American life and values. By the mid-1960s a full-fledged youth revolt had broken out on campuses across the country.

Rebellious students began to flow into two distinct, yet frequently overlapping, movements: the New Left and the counterculture.

THE NEW LEFT   The explicitly political strain of the youth revolt had its official origin when Tom Hayden and Al Haber, two University of Michigan students, formed the Students for a Democratic Society (SDS) in 1960. Hayden, a wayward Jesuit, had during his college years been inspired by Jack Kerouac's *On the Road* and Jean-Jacques Rousseau's notion of participatory democracy. As an ardent critic of American society, Hayden was both charismatic and convincing. A Marxist radical who heard him speak in 1962 rushed home and told his wife, "I've just seen the next Lenin."

In June 1962 Hayden and Haber convened a meeting of sixty activists at Port Huron, Michigan. After four days of intense discussion and a final all-night session, Hayden drafted what became known as the Port Huron Statement: "We are the people of this generation, bred in at least moderate comfort, housed in universities, looking uncomfortably to the world we inherit." Hayden's earnest manifesto focused on the absence of individual freedom in modern American life. The country, he insisted, was dominated by huge organizational structures—governments, corporations, unions, universities—all of which conspired to oppress and alienate the individual. Enlightened and energized by the example of black activism in the South, Hayden declared that students had the power to restore "participatory democracy" to American life by wresting "control of the educational process from the administrative bureaucracy" and then forging links with other dissident movements. He and others soon adopted the term "New Left" to distinguish their efforts at grass-roots democracy from the Old Left of the 1930s which had espoused an orthodox Marxism and had embraced Stalinism.

In the fall of 1964 students at the University of California at Berkeley took Hayden's program to heart. Many of them had returned to the campus after spending the summer working with hundreds of other students in the SNCC voter registration project in Mississippi. It had been a revealing as well as a traumatic experience. Three volunteers had been killed, dozens shot, and nearly a thousand arrested. The Berkeley student activists returned to school with mixed emotions—exhilarated, frustrated, and embittered. Clark Kerr, the university chancellor, had no idea how combustible student sentiments had become. He still viewed the state of the campus essentially as he had in 1958, when he observed: "I find the three major administrative problems on a campus are sex for the students, athletics for the alumni, and parking for the faculty." Times had changed. When Kerr announced in October 1964 that political demonstrations would no longer be allowed at the Telegraph Avenue street corner traditionally used for such activity, several hundred students staged a sit-in at the scene. Soon thereafter over 2,000 more joined in. After a tense thirty-two-hour standoff the administration relented. Student groups then formed the Free Speech Movement (FSM).

Led by Mario Savio, a philosophy major and compelling public speaker, the FSM was initially a protest on behalf of student rights. But it quickly escalated into a more general criticism of the modern university and what Savio called the "depersonalized, unresponsive bureaucracy" infecting American life. In December 1964 Savio made an impassioned speech on the steps of the main administration building in which he asserted that there comes "a time when the operation of a machine becomes so odious, makes you so sick at heart, that you can't take part—you can't even passively take part, and you've got to put your bodies upon the gears and upon the wheels, upon the levers, upon all the apparatus and you've got to make it stop." When he finished, hundreds of students rushed into the building and organized a sit-in. In the early-morning hours 600 policemen, dispatched by the governor, moved in and arrested the protesters. Jerry Rubin, one of the young demonstrators, later observed: "The war against Amerika [*sic*] in the schools and the streets by white middle-class kids thus commenced."

The program and tactics of the FSM and the SDS soon spread to

Mario Savio, leader of the Free Speech Movement at the University of California, Berkeley, 1964.

colleges throughout the country. The initial focal point of protest was the quality of campus life. Students at the huge state universities chanted "I am a student. Do not fold, spindle, or mutilate." As the atmosphere of rebellion spread, however, issues large and small became the subject of student protest: unpopular tenure decisions, mandatory ROTC programs, dress codes, curfews, dormitory regulations, appearances by Johnson administration officials. Michigan students rallied against higher movie prices; at Fairleigh Dickinson they marched for no particular reason but as "an expression of general student discontent."

But escalating American involvement in Vietnam soon changed the student agenda. With the dramatic expansion of the draft after 1965 millions of young American men faced the grim prospect of being drafted to fight in a more and more unpopular war. In fact, however, the Vietnam conflict, like virtually every other American war, was primarily a poor man's fight. Deferments enabled college students to postpone military service until they received their degree or reached the age of twenty-four; in 1965–1966 they made up only 2 percent of all military inductees. In 1966, however, the Selective Service System modified the provisions so as to make those students at the lower levels of their academic class eligible for the draft. As the war dragged on and opposition sentiment grew, students and others developed sophisticated ways to avoid, evade, or resist the draft. Some 200,000 young men simply refused to obey their draft notices, and some 4,000 of those served prison sentences. Those on college campuses or in urban areas took advantage of draft counseling centers that provided legal advice, and hundreds of young men instituted court challenges to the draft. One result was a much broader interpretation of the term "conscientious objector" so as to allow exemptions for those with moral and ethical objections to war rooted in secular rather than spiritual principles. Some 56,000 men qualified for conscientious-objector status during the Vietnam War compared with 7,600 during the Korean conflict. Still others left the country altogether—several thousand fled to Canada or Sweden—to avoid military service. The most popular way to avoid the draft was to flunk the physical examination. Many gorged themselves so as to exceed the weight limit; others raised their blood pressure by drinking excessive amounts of coffee; some pretended to be drug addicts or alcoholics; a few feigned homosexuality. Whatever the preferred method, many students succeeded in avoiding military service. Of the 1,200 men in the Harvard class of 1970, only fifty-six served in the military, and just two of those went to Vietnam.

During the spring of 1965 faculty members sympathetic to the growing student radicalism staged "teach-ins" at many universities.

At these informal gatherings professors would declare their own opposition to the Vietnam War and encourage student resistance. The mushrooming radical student movement also began to organize underground newspapers and radio stations. At the same time the number of antiwar demonstrations across the country soared. "Yesterday's ivory tower," observed the president of Hunter College, "has become today's foxhole."

In the spring of 1967, 500,000 war protesters of all ages converged on Manhattan's Central Park, chanting "Hey, hey, LBJ, how many kids did you kill today?" Dozens ceremoniously burned their draft cards, and the so-called resistance phase of the antiwar movement was born. Thereafter a coalition of draft-resistance groups around the country sponsored draft-card-burning rallies and sit-ins which led to numerous arrests. Meanwhile some SDS leaders were growing even more militant. Inspired by the rhetoric and revolutionary violence of Black Power spokesmen such as Stokely Carmichael, Rap Brown, and Huey Newton, Tom Hayden abandoned his earlier commitment to participatory democracy and passive civil disobedience. "If necessary," he now could "shoot to kill." Rap Brown told the white radicals to remember the heritage of John Brown: "Take up a gun and go shoot the enemy." Not only did the SDS become more militant; it also grew more centralized and authoritarian. Rousseau was now replaced by Lenin as the organization's prophet, and capitalist imperialism replaced university bureaucracy as the primary foe.

Throughout 1967 and 1968 the antiwar movement mushroomed at the same time that inner-city ghettos were seething with tension and exploding into flames. "There was a sense everywhere, in 1968," the journalist Garry Wills wrote, "that things were giving. That man had not only lost control of his history, but might never regain it." At the end of March Lyndon Johnson announced that he would not run for reelection and in early April Martin Luther King was murdered.

During that eventful spring campus unrest spread across the country. Over 200 major demonstrations took place. The turmoil reached a climax with the disruption of Columbia University. There on April 23 Mark Rudd, leader of the SDS chapter, who had earlier thrown pies at the faces of Selective Service officials and disrupted speeches at the campus memorial service for King, led a small cadre of radicals in occupying the president's office and classroom buildings. They also kidnapped a dean—all in protest of the university's insensitive decision to displace neighboring black housing in order to build a new gymnasium. During the next week more buildings were commandeered, faculty and administrative offices were ransacked, and classes were canceled. University officials finally called in the New

A student rally on the campus of Columbia University, calling for the resignation of the university's president, April 1968.

York City police. In the process of arresting the protesters, the police injured a number of innocent bystanders. Their excessive force aroused the anger of many heretofore unaligned students, and they staged a strike which shut down the university for the remainder of the semester.

The militants were buoyed by the whole affair. Tom Hayden announced: "We are moving toward power." Similar clashes between students, administrators, and eventually police occurred at Harvard, Cornell, and San Francisco State. At Berkeley, Governor Ronald Reagan dispatched a small army of police to evict 5,000 students and activists who had turned a vacant lot into a "people's park." In the melee one student was killed and another blinded.

At the August 1968 Democratic convention in Chicago the polarization of American society reached a tragic and bizarre climax. While inside the tightly guarded convention hall Democrats were nominating Lyndon Johnson's faithful vice-president, Hubert Humphrey, on Chicago's streets were gathered the whole spectrum of antiwar dissenters, from the earnest supporters of Eugene McCarthy through the Resistance and the SDS to the nihilistic Yippies, members of the new Youth International party. The Yippies were determined to provoke anarchy in the streets of Chicago. Abbie Hoffman, one of their leaders, explained that they were "revolutionary artists. Our conception of revolution is that it's fun." The Yippies distributed a leaflet at the convention calling for the immediate legalization of marijuana and all psychedelic drugs, the abolition of money, student-run schools, and free sex.

Yet the boorish behavior of the Yippies did not justify the unrestrained response of Mayor Daley and his army of 12,000 police. As a horrified television audience watched, many of the police went berserk, clubbing and gassing demonstrators as well as bystanders caught up in the chaotic scene. The spectacle lasted three days and seriously damaged Humphrey's candidacy by generating a wave of anger among many middle-class Americans, anger that Richard Nixon and the Republicans shrewdly exploited at their convention in Miami. At the same time, the Chicago riots helped to fragment the antiwar movement. Those groups committed to nonviolent protest, while castigating the reactionary policies of Mayor Daley and the police, also felt betrayed by the actions of the Yippies and other anarchistic militants.

In 1968 the SDS began to break up into rival factions, the most extreme of which was the Weathermen, a term derived from one of Bob Dylan's lyrics: "You don't need a weatherman to know which way the wind is blowing." These hardened young activists, mesmerized by the radical chic of Third World guerrillas such as Cuba's Che Guevara, decided that revolutionary terrorism was the only appropriate strategy. So during 1969 they embarked on a rampage of violence and disruption, fire-bombing university buildings and killing innocent people—as well as several of themselves. Government forces responded in kind, arresting most of the Weathermen and sending the rest underground. Tom Hayden finally broke with the

The violence at the 1968 Democratic National Convention in Chicago seared the nation.

group, declaring that it was "not the conscience of its generation, but more like its id." By 1971 the New Left was dead as a political movement. In large measure it had committed suicide by abandoning the democratic and pacifist principles that had originally inspired participants and given the movement moral legitimacy. The larger antiwar movement also began to fade. There would be a wave of student protests against the Nixon administration in 1970, but then campus unrest virtually disappeared.

If the social mood was changing during the Nixon years, still a large segment of the public continued the quest for personal fulfillment *and* social justice. The burgeoning environmental and consumer movements attested to the continuity of sixties idealism. A *New York Times* survey of college campuses in 1969 revealed that many students were transferring their attention from the antiwar movement to the environment. This ecological conscience would blossom in the 1970s into one of the most compelling items on the nation's social agenda.

THE COUNTERCULTURE   The numbing events of 1968 led other disaffected activists away from radical politics altogether and toward another manifestation of the sixties youth revolt: the "counterculture." Long hair, blue jeans, tie-dyed shirts, sandals, mind-altering drugs, rock music, and cooperative living arrangements were more important than revolutionary ideology to the "hippies," the direct descendants of the Beats of the 1950s and the romantic utopians of the 1830s. These advocates of the counterculture were, like their New Left peers, primarily affluent, well-educated young whites alienated by the Vietnam War, racism, political and parental demands, runaway technology, and a crass corporate mentality that equated goodness with goods. In their view, a bland materialism and smug complacency had settled over urban and suburban life. But they were uninterested in or disillusioned with organized political action. Instead they eagerly embraced the tantalizing credo outlined by the Harvard professor Timothy Leary: "Tune in, turn on, drop out."

For some the counterculture entailed the study and practice of Oriental mysticism. For many it meant the use of hallucinogenic drugs. These were deemed necessary to strip away what the historian Theodore Roszak, a friendly chronicler of the counterculture, called "the myth of objective consciousness." Collective living in urban enclaves such as San Francisco's Haight-Ashbury district, New York's East Village, or Atlanta's Fourteenth Street was the rage for a time among the hippies, until conditions grew so crowded, violent, and depressing that residents migrated elsewhere. Rural communes also attracted many of the bourgeois rebels. During the 1960s and early 1970s thousands of young and inexperienced romantics flocked to the countryside, eager to be liberated from parental and institutional restraints, to live in harmony with nature, and to coexist in an atmosphere of love and openness.

But only a handful of these utopian homesteads survived more than a few months. Commune dwellers were frequently the victims of their own liberationist philosophy and their affluent backgrounds. Disgusted by the modern work ethic, they tended to exchange the materialistic hedonism of the consumer culture for the sexual and sensory hedonism of the counterculture. Rooted in the pleasure principle, the rustic hippies often produced more babies than bread. One such "flower child" confessed that "we are so stupid, so unable to cope with anything practical. Push forward, smoke dope. But maintain? Never. We don't know how." Initially intent upon rejecting conventional society, many found themselves utterly dependent on it, and they were soon panhandling on street corners or lined up at government offices, collecting welfare, unemployment compensation, and food stamps to help them survive the rigors of natural living. They had hoped to create a self-sustaining "lifestyle which unites a generation in love and laughter," but instead saw increasing friction among themselves. Drifters, runaways, addicts, and crazies soon crowded into the hippie settlements scattered across the country. A participant at Paper Farm in northern California said of its residents: "They had no commitment to the land—a big problem. All would take food from the land, but few would tend it. . . . We were entirely open. We did not say no. We felt this would make for a more dynamic group. But we got a lot of sick people."

Huge outdoor rock music concerts were also a popular source of community for the hippies. The largest of these was the Woodstock Music Festival. In August 1969 over 400,000 young people converged on a 600-acre farm near the tiny rural town of Bethel, New York. The musicians—including Joan Baez; Jimi Hendrix; Crosby, Stills, Nash, and Young; Santana; and Richie Havens—were a real attraction. But so too was the easy availability of drugs. For three days the assembled flower children reveled in good music, cheap marijuana, and free love. "Everyone swam nude in the lake," a journalist reported. He added that the country had never "seen a society so free of repression."

But the Woodstock karma was short-lived. When promoters tried to repeat the scene four months later, this time at Altamont, California, the counterculture was invaded by the criminal culture. The Rolling Stones hired Hell's Angels motorcycle gang members to provide the "security" for their show. In the midst of Mick Jagger's

The Woodstock festival drew nearly half a million people to a New York farm in August 1969.

WOODSTOCK
3 DAYS OF PEACE
AND MUSIC...AND LOVE

performance of "Sympathy for the Devil," the drunken white motorcyclists proceeded to beat to death a black man in front of the stage. Three other spectators were accidentally killed that night; much of the vitality and innocence of the counterculture died with them.

After 1969 the hippie phenomenon clearly began to wane. "It was good for a time," drug guru Timothy Leary lamented; "then we went so far that we lost it." The counterculture had become counterproductive. Thousands of young teenage runaways had joined the movement, bringing with them plenty of adolescent idealism but no historical consciousness of the roots of cultural rebellion or the practical consequences of bohemian living. The counterculture also soon developed both faddish and fashionable overtones, and much of the movement's original idealism was coopted by commercialization. Entrepreneurs were quick to see profits in protest. Retailers developed a banner business in faded blue jeans, surplus army jackets, beads, incense, and sandals. Health-food stores and "head" shops appeared in shopping malls alongside Nieman Marcus and Sears, and *Playboy* magazine featured a hippie playmate on its cover. Rock music groups, for all their lyrical protests against the "system," made millions. As one wit recognized, the "difference between a rock king and a robber baron [was] about six inches of hair." Many of the flower children themselves grew tired of their riches-to-rags existence and returned to school to become lawyers, doctors, politicians, and accountants. The search on the part of alienated youth for a better society and a good life was strewn with both comic and tragic aspects, and it reflected the deep social ills that had been allowed to fester throughout the post–World War II period.

FEMINISM The logic of liberation that spread during the sixties helped accelerate the emergence of a powerful women's-rights crusade which aggressively challenged the cult of domesticity that had become so firmly entrenched during the 1950s. Like the New Left, the new feminism drew much of its inspiration and tactics from the civil-rights movement.

The mainstream of the women's movement was led by Betty Friedan. Her immensely influential book, *The Feminine Mystique* (1963), launched the new phase of female protest on a national level. Friedan, a Smith College graduate, had married in 1947 and during the 1950s raised three children in a New York suburb. She was politically active but socially domestic. She mothered her children, pampered her husband, "read *Vogue* under the hair dryer," and occasionally did some free-lance writing. In 1957 she conducted a poll of her fellow Smith alumnae and discovered that despite all the rhetoric about the happy suburban housewife during the fifties, many—too many—were in fact miserable. This revelation led to more research which culminated in the publication of *The Feminine Mystique*.

Women, Friedan wrote, had actually lost ground during the years after World War II, when many left wartime assembly lines and

Betty Friedan, author of The Feminine Mystique.

settled down in suburbia. They were encouraged to do so by the propaganda campaign engineered by advertisers and women's magazines which created the "feminine mystique" of blissful domesticity. This notion that women were "gaily content in a world of bedroom, kitchen, sex, babies, and home" thus served to imprison women. In Friedan's view, the American middle-class home had become "a comfortable concentration camp" where women suffocated in an atmosphere of mindless consumption and affluent banality.

Friedan's book was an immediate best-seller. The book raised the consciousness of many women who had long suffered from a feeling of being trapped in a rut with no way out. A mother of four from Florida explained in a letter to Friedan: "I have been trying for years to tell my husband of my need to do something to find myself—to have a purpose. All I've ever achieved was to end up feeling guilty about wanting to be more than a housewife and mother." Friedan also discovered that there were far more women working outside the home than the pervasive "feminine mystique" suggested. Many of her correspondents were working women frustrated by the demands of holding "two full-time jobs instead of just one—underpaid clerical worker and unpaid housekeeper."

Such letters convinced Friedan that there was a movement waiting to be organized. In 1966 she and a small group of other spirited activists founded the National Organization for Women (NOW). Soon regarded as the NAACP of the women's movement, NOW grew rapidly. Its immediate objective was the end of discrimination in the workplace on the basis of sex. NOW spearheaded efforts to end job discrimination, to legalize abortion, and to obtain federal and state support for child-care centers.

In the early 1970s Congress and the Supreme Court advanced the cause of sexual equality. Under Title IX of the Educational Amendments Act of 1972, colleges were required to institute "affirmative-action" programs to ensure equal opportunity for women; in the same year Congress overwhelmingly approved the Equal Rights Amendment, which had been bottled up in a House committee for almost half a century. In 1973 the Supreme Court, in *Roe v. Wade*, struck down state laws forbidding abortions during the first three months of pregnancy. Meanwhile the educational bastions of male segregation, including Yale and Princeton, led a new movement for coeducation that swept the country. "If the 1960s belonged to blacks," said one feminist, "the next ten years are ours."

By the end of the 1970s, however, continuing divisions between moderate and radical feminists within the women's movement, as well as the movement's failure to broaden its appeal much beyond the confines of the middle class, caused reform efforts to stagnate. The Equal Rights Amendment, which had once seemed a straightforward assertion of equal opportunity ("Equality of rights under the law shall not be denied or abridged by the United States or by any State on account of sex") and assured of ratification, was stymied in several state legislatures. Despite a congressional extension of the normal time allowed for ratification, by 1982 it died several states short of passage. And the very success of NOW's efforts to change abortion laws generated a powerful reaction, especially among Catholics and fundamentalist Protestants, who mounted a potent "right-to-life" crusade.

But the success of the women's movement seemed likely to endure despite setbacks and long after the militant rhetoric had evaporated. For in fact women were not another minority group pursuing the traditional path of liberal reform. They were a majority: they constituted 51 percent of the population. Their political power, only partially mobilized in the 1970s, had enormous potential for achieving social change. Moreover their growing presence in the labor force assured women of a greater share of economic and political influence. In the year of the bicentennial over half the married women in America and nine of ten women college graduates were employed outside the home, a development that one economist called "the single most outstanding phenomenon of this century." Many career women did not regard themselves as feminists; they took jobs because they and their families needed the money to survive or to achieve higher levels of material comfort. Whatever their motives, traditional sex roles and childbearing practices were being changed to accommodate the two-career family. Indeed the two-career family had replaced the established pattern of male breadwinner and female housekeeper as the new American norm. "The classic differences between masculinity and femininity are disappearing," observed one sociologist, "as both sexes in the adult generation take on the same roles in the labor market." This quiet revolution continued apace into the 1990s.

MINORITIES The activism that fired the student revolt, the civil-rights movement, and the women's-rights crusade soon spread to include ethnic minorities, the poor, homosexuals, and the elderly. The nation's fastest-growing minority group in the 1960s, the Hispanics, for example, began to organize for political and economic action under the effective leadership of Cesar Chavez, who almost single-handedly founded the United Farm Workers (UFW) in California, then launched a series of strikes for an increase in the wages and benefits of migrant workers. By 1970 the UFW had won recognition from California's grape growers and national visibility for the plight of Hispanic farm laborers through well-publicized boycotts of table grapes and lettuce.

But the chief strength of the Hispanic movement lay less in the duplication of civil-rights strategies than in the sheer growth of the Hispanic population. In 1960 Hispanics had numbered slightly more than 3 million; by 1970 they had increased to 9 million, and by 1990 they numbered 22.4 million, making them the largest minority in America after African-Americans. The most numerous among them were Mexican-Americans, or Chicanos, who were concentrated in California and the Southwest. Next came the Puerto Rican population, most of whom lived in New York City and the Connecticut Valley. Finally there were the Cubans, many of them refugees from Castro's regime, who were concentrated in southern Florida.

Although affluent Hispanics became influential in Miami, Houston, and Los Angeles, the vast bulk of the Hispanic population were poor, deprived, and often isolated from the mainstream of American life by the language barrier. Bilingualism—the belief that Hispanics were entitled to schooling in Spanish as well as English—divided the

Cesar Chavez (left) *leading a line of striking grape pickers, December 1965. Their aim was to win recognition of their national farm-workers union.*

Hispanic community between those who wished to cultivate their heritage and those who feared that failure to adopt English as their primary language would block their social advance. By 1980, however, aspiring presidential candidates were openly courting the Hispanic vote, promising support for urban renewal projects in New York and amnesty programs for illegal immigrants in Texas, and delivering rousing anti-Castro speeches in Miami. The voting power of Hispanics and their concentration in states with key electoral votes had helped give the Hispanic point of view political clout.

American Indians—many of whom now called themselves Native Americans—also emerged as a new political force in the late 1960s. Two conditions combined to make Indian rights a priority: first, white Americans felt a deep and persistent sense of guilt for the destructive policies of their ancestors toward a people who had, after all, been here first; second, the plight of the Indian minority was more desperate than that of any other minority group in the country. Indian unemployment was ten times the national rate, their life expectancy was twenty years lower than the national average, and the suicide rate was a whopping one hundred times higher than the rate for whites. If blacks had extracted a deserved promise of compensation for past injustices from whites in the 1960s, Indians felt that they had an even more compelling claim on white consciences.

At first the Indian militants copied the tactics of civil-rights and black power activists. In 1968 the American Indian Movement (AIM) was founded on the promise of advancing "red power." The leaders of AIM occupied Alcatraz Island in San Francisco Bay in 1969, claiming the site "by right of discovery." And in 1972 an Indian "sit-in" at the Bureau of Indian Affairs in Washington attracted national attention to their cause. Soon Indian protesters discovered a more effective tactic than direct action and "sit-ins." They went into federal courts armed with copies of old treaties and demanded that these become the basis for restitution. In Alaska, Maine, South Carolina, and Massachusetts they won significant settlements that provided legal recognition of their tribal rights and financial compensation at levels that upgraded the standard of living on several reservations.

NIXON AND VIETNAM

The numerous liberation movements of the 1960s fundamentally changed the tone and texture of American social life. But by the early 1970s there were signs that the pendulum of national mood was swinging back. The election of Richard Nixon and Spiro Agnew in 1968 and the rise of George Wallace as a serious political force reflected the emergence of the "silent majority"—those predominantly white working-class and middle-class citizens who were determined to regain control of a society they felt had become awash in permissiveness, anarchy, and minority tyranny.

Large as the gap was between the "silent majority" and the forces of dissent, both sides agreed that the Vietnam War remained the dominant event of the time. Until the war was ended and all American troops had returned home, the nation would find it difficult to achieve the equilibrium and moderation that the new president had promised. In his State of the Union message of 1970 President Nixon called on Americans to pursue "the lift of a driving dream," a memorable phrase that reporters asked him to define. "Well, before we can get the lift of a driving dream," Nixon explained, "we have to get rid of the nightmares we inherited. One of the nightmares is a war without end."

GRADUAL WITHDRAWAL   During the campaign of 1968 Nixon had claimed to have a secret plan that would bring "peace with honor" in Vietnam. But peace was long in coming and not very honorable. Although Henry Kissinger, the professor of international relations at Harvard who became Nixon's special assistant for national security affairs, insisted that the war in Indochina was a mere "sideshow" of considerably less significance than American interests in Europe and the Middle East, American withdrawal from Vietnam was agonizingly slow nonetheless. Like several preceding administrations, the Nixon administration, even while withdrawing American forces, held to a policy that it was contrary to the national interest to let the North Vietnamese dominate Indochina. When a settlement was finally reached in 1973, another 20,000 Americans had died, the morale of the American army was shattered, millions of additional Asians were killed or wounded, and fighting in fact continued in Southeast Asia. In the end, Nixon's policy gained nothing he could not have accomplished in 1969.

The new Vietnam policy of the Nixon administration moved along three separate fronts. First, American negotiators in Paris insisted on the withdrawal of Communist forces from South Vietnam and the preservation of the American-supported regime of President Nguyen Van Thieu. The North Vietnamese and Vietcong negotiators insisted on the retention of a military presence in the south and the reunification of the Vietnamese people under a government dominated by the Communists. There was no common ground on which to come together. It required months before the parties could even agree on the shape of the table around which they would meet.

Richard Nixon (left) *with his special assistant for national security affairs, Henry Kissinger.*

Second, Nixon tried to quell domestic unrest over the war. He reduced the number of American troops in Vietnam, justifying the reduction as the natural result of "Vietnamization"—the equipping and training of the South Vietnamese to assume the burden of ground combat in place of Americans. From a peak of 540,000 in 1969, American combat troops were withdrawn at a gradual and steady pace that matched almost precisely the pace of the American buildup from 1965 to 1969. By 1973 only 50,000 American troops remained in Vietnam. In December 1969 Nixon also established a draft lottery system that eliminated many inequities and clarified the likelihood of being drafted—only those nineteen-year-olds with low lottery numbers would have to go—and in 1973 he did away with the draft altogether by creating an all-volunteer military. Nixon was more successful in achieving the goal of reducing antiwar activity than at forcing concessions from the North Vietnamese in Paris.

Third, while reducing the number of American combat troops, Nixon and Kissinger actually expanded the air war in an effort to persuade the enemy to come to terms. On March 18, 1969, American planes began a fourteen-month-long bombing campaign aimed at Communist sanctuaries in Cambodia. Congress did not learn of these secret raids until 1970, although the total tonnage of bombs dropped was four times that dropped on Japan during World War II. Then on April 30, 1970, Nixon announced what he called an "incursion" into "neutral" Cambodia by United States troops to "clean

Even as the Nixon administration began a phased withdrawl of American troops, the war took a heavy toll on Vietnamese and Americans alike.

out" North Vietnamese staging areas. The head of Cambodia's government for two decades, Prince Norodom Sihanouk, had previously objected to such American raids into his country, but Sihanouk had been replaced in a coup by General Lon Nol earlier in the spring, clearing the way for the American invasion.

DIVISIONS AT HOME   The effect of America's gradual withdrawal on the morale and reputation of the American military was devastating. "No one wants to be the last grunt to die in this lousy war," said one soldier. In May 1969 the newspaper *GI Says* offered a bounty of $10,000 for the murder of the officer who ordered the assault on "Hamburger Hill," where 476 American soldiers had died to capture a position which was abandoned the following day. Between 1969 and 1971 there were 730 reported "fragging" incidents, efforts to kill or injure officers, usually with fragmentation grenades. Even the old marching chants became cynical, as troops shouted, "If I die in a combat zone, box me up and ship me home," while keeping cadence. Drug abuse became a major problem. In 1971 four times as many American troops were hospitalized for drug abuse as for combat-related wounds. "In Vietnam," one officer wrote, the army "is numbly extricating itself from a nightmare war . . . foisted on them by bright civilians who are now back on campus writing books about the folly of it all."

And back on the home front the public learned of previously suppressed events in Vietnam that caused even the staunchest supporters of the war to wince. Late in 1969 the story of the My Lai massacre broke in the press and plunged the country into two years of exposure to the gruesome tale of Lieutenant William Calley, who ordered the murder of over 200 civilians in My Lai village in March 1968. Twenty-five army officers were charged with complicity in the massacre and subsequent cover-up, but only Calley was convicted; Nixon soon granted him parole.

Perhaps the loudest public outcry against Nixon's Indochina policy occurred in the wake of the Cambodian "incursion." Nixon's television speech of April 30, 1970, sounded the tocsin: "we will not be defeated. . . . If, when the chips are down, the world's most powerful nation . . . acts like a pitiful, helpless giant, the forces of totalitarianism and anarchy will threaten free nations and free institutions throughout the world." Campuses across the country exploded in what the president of Columbia University called "the most disastrous month of May in the history of American higher education." Hundreds of colleges and universities closed down. At Kent State University the Ohio National Guard was called in to quell rioting in which the campus Reserve Officer Training Corps (ROTC) building was burned. The young Guardsmen panicked and opened fire on the demonstrators, killing four student bystanders. Eleven days later, on May 15, Mississippi highway patrolmen riddled a dormitory at Jackson State College with bullets, killing two black students. Although an official investigation of the Kent State episode condemned the "casual and indiscriminate shooting," polls indicated that the American public supported the actions by the National Guard; students had "got what they were asking for." In New York City, antiwar demonstrators who gathered to protest the deaths at Kent State and the invasion of Cambodia were attacked by "hard-hat" construction workers, who forced the student protesters to disperse and then marched on City Hall to raise the flag that had been lowered to half-staff in mourning for the Kent State victims.

The following year, in June 1971, the *New York Times* began publishing excerpts from *The History of the U.S. Decision Making Process in Vietnam*, a secret Defense Department study commissioned by Robert McNamara before his resignation as secretary of defense in 1968. The so-called Pentagon Papers leaked to the press by a former Defense Department official, Daniel Ellsberg, confirmed

"Son . . . !" "Dad . . . !" *The Vietnam War caused vehement divisions between "hawks" and "doves," old and young, even parents and children.*

what many critics of the war had long suspected: Congress and the people had not received the full story on the Gulf of Tonkin incident of 1964, and contingency plans for American entry into the war were being drawn up while Johnson was promising the American people that combat troops would never be sent to Vietnam. Moreover, there was no plan for bringing the war to an end so long as the North Vietnamese persisted. Although the Pentagon Papers dealt with events up to 1965, the Nixon administration attempted to block their publication, arguing that they endangered national security and that their publication would prolong the war. On June 30, by a vote of 6 to 3, the Supreme Court ruled against the government. Newspapers throughout the country began publication the next day.

WAR WITHOUT END   The mounting social divisions at home and the approach of the 1972 presidential elections combined to produce a shift in the American negotiating position in Paris. In the summer of 1972 Henry Kissinger again began meeting privately with Le Duc Tho, the North Vietnamese negotiator, and dropped his insistence on the removal of all North Vietnamese troops from the south before the withdrawal of American troops. On October 26, only a week before the American presidential election, Kissinger announced: "Peace is at hand." But this was a cynical play to win votes. Several days earlier the Thieu regime in South Vietnam had rejected the plan for a cease-fire, fearful that the presence of North Vietnamese troops in the south virtually guaranteed an eventual Communist victory. The talks broke off on December 16 and two days later the president ordered the saturation bombing of Hanoi and Haiphong, the two largest cities in North Vietnam. These so-called Christmas bombings by B-52s, and the simultaneous mining of North Vietnamese harbors, aroused worldwide protest. "Civilized man will be horrified," read a *New York Times* editorial. Fifteen of the giant B-52s were shot down, and captured American pilots and crew were paraded before television cameras in Hanoi to "express regret" at the civilian deaths and carnage.

But the bombings also made the North Vietnamese more flexible at the negotiating table. The "Christmas bombings" stopped on December 29, and the resumption of talks in Paris soon followed. On January 27, 1973, the United States signed an "agreement on ending the war and restoring peace in Vietnam." While Nixon and Kissinger both claimed that the bombing had brought North Vietnam to its senses, in truth the North Vietnamese never altered their basic stance; they kept troops in the south and remained committed to the reunification of Vietnam under one government. What had changed since the previous fall was the willingness of the South Vietnamese to accept these terms, albeit reluctantly, on the basis of Nixon's promise that the United States would respond "with full force" to any violation of the agreement.

On March 29, 1973, the last American combat troops left Vietnam. And on that same day the last of several hundred American prisoners of war, most of them downed pilots, were released from Hanoi. Within a period of months, however, the cease-fire in Vietnam ended, the war between north and south resumed, and the military superiority of the Communist forces soon became evident. In Cambodia (renamed Kampuchea after it fell to the Communists) and Laos, where fighting had been more sporadic, Communist victory also seemed inevitable. In March 1975 the North Vietnamese

Henry Kissinger (glasses) *confers with Le Duc Tho, North Vietnam's special envoy, during peace talks in Paris, November 1972.*

launched a full-scale armored invasion against the south, and Thieu appealed to Washington for assistance. Congress refused. The much-mentioned "peace with honor" had proved to be, in the words of one CIA official, only a "decent interval"—enough time for the United States to extricate itself from Vietnam before the collapse of the South Vietnamese government. On April 30 Americans watched on television as North Vietnamese tanks rolled into Saigon, soon to be renamed Ho Chi Minh City, and helicopters lifted the officials in the American embassy to ships waiting offshore. In those last desperate moments, crying South Vietnamese fought to get on the helicopters as they took off; a sign in the embassy courtyard read "Turn off the light at the end of the tunnel when you leave."

The longest war in American history was over, leaving in its wake a bitter legacy. During the period of American involvement in the fighting, almost 2 million combatants and civilians were killed on both sides. North Vietnam absorbed incredible losses—some 600,000 soldiers and countless civilians killed. More than 58,000 Americans died in Vietnam, 300,000 were wounded, 2,500 were declared missing, almost 100,000 returned without one or more limbs, and over

As Saigon falls to the North Vietnamese, frantic South Vietnamese scale the fourteen-foot wall of the U.S. embassy to reach helicopters for evacuation, April 30, 1975.

150,000 combat veterans suffered drug or alcohol addiction or severe psychological disorders. To be sure, most of the Vietnam veterans readjusted well to civilian life, but even they carried for years the stigma of a "lost war." As a government official observed, the "men who came home from World War II were heroes, but the Vietnam vets were different. The public either felt that they were suckers to have gone, or that they were the kids who lost the war."

And so the war designed to serve as a showcase for American military power instead eroded respect for the military so thoroughly that many young Americans came to regard military service as corrupting and ignoble. The war, described as a noble crusade on behalf of democratic ideals, instead suggested that democracy was not easily transferable to Third World regions which lacked any historical experience with liberal values and representative government. The war fought to show the world that the United States was united in its commitment to containing the spread of communism instead sapped the national will and fragmented the national consensus that had governed foreign affairs since 1947. It also changed the balance of power in domestic politics. Not only did the war cause the downfall of Lyndon Johnson's presidency; it also created enduring fissures in the Democratic party. Said antiwar senator and 1972 Democratic presidential candidate George McGovern: "The Vietnam tragedy is at the root of the confusion and division of the Democratic party. It tore up our souls."

Little wonder that the dominant reaction to the war's end was the urge to "put Vietnam behind us" and forget. Although subsequent debates over American foreign policy in the Middle East, Africa, and Latin America frequently involved recourse to "the lessons of Vietnam," the phrase was used by different factions for diametrically opposed purposes, ranging from refusal to commit American troops and resources in El Salvador and Nicaragua to an insistence on massive military commitments unfettered by any diplomatic restrictions that might preclude outright victory. "In the end, then," one journalist wrote concerning the Vietnam era, "there was no end at all."

NIXON AND MIDDLE AMERICA

Richard Nixon had been elected in 1968 as the representative of "Middle America," those middle-class citizens fed up with the liberal politics and promises of the 1960s. The Nixon cabinet and White House staff reflected their values. The chief figures were John Mitchell, the gruff attorney-general who had made his fortune as a municipal bond lawyer in Nixon's old firm; H. R. Haldeman and John Ehrlichman, advisers on domestic policy whose major experience before their association with the Nixon campaign had been in advertising; William Rogers, the secretary of state, an oldtime Nixon friend whose control over foreign policy was quickly preempted by Henry Kissinger; and Melvin Laird, the secretary of defense, who also found his influence undercut by Kissinger's access to the White House. The cabinet was all white, all male, all Republican. "There are no blooded patricians in the lot," said *Time* magazine, "just strivers who have acted out the middle-class dream."

DOMESTIC AFFAIRS   If a balanced assessment of the Kennedy foreign policy is only now becoming possible, a detached evaluation of the Nixon administration's domestic record remains out of reach, in part because the Watergate scandal affixed a stigma on Nixon's administration that colors all judgments, in part because the major legislative achievements happened largely in spite of rather than because of Nixon's efforts. Nixon was the first new president since 1849 to confront a Congress in which both houses were under the control of the opposition party. It followed that he focused his energies on foreign policy, where presidential initiatives were less encumbered and where he, in tandem with Kissinger, achieved several stunning

In July 1969, a program begun by President Kennedy reached its goal: putting a man on the moon.

breakthroughs. The domestic front became a holding action in which Nixon, like Eisenhower before him, found it difficult to stop the march of liberal programs.

Despite the efforts of the Nixon administration, the civil-rights legislation enacted during the Johnson years continued to take effect. "There are those who want instant integration and those who want segregation forever," said Nixon in September 1969. "I believe we need to have a middle course between these extremes." In practice this "middle course" took the shape of a concerted effort in 1970 to block congressional renewal of the Voting Rights Act and to delay implementation of court orders requiring the desegregation of school districts in Mississippi. "For the first time since Woodrow Wilson," said the head of the NAACP, "we have a national administration that can be rightly characterized as anti-Negro." Sixty-five lawyers in the Justice Department signed a letter of protest against the administration's stance. Congress then extended the Voting Rights Act over Nixon's veto. The Supreme Court, in the first decision made under the new chief justice, Warren Burger—a Nixon appointee— ordered the integration of the Mississippi schools. In *Alexander v. Holmes County Board of Education* (1969) a unanimous Court ordered a quick end to segregation. Fifteen years after the original school desegregation cases, the standard of "all deliberate speed" no longer applied. During Nixon's first term more schools were desegregated than in all the Kennedy-Johnson years combined.

Nixon's attempts to block desegregation efforts in urban areas also failed. The Burger Court ruled unanimously in *Swann v. Charlotte-Mecklenburg Board of Education* (1971) that cities must bus students out of their neighborhoods if this was necessary to achieve integration. As it happened, one little-noticed result was that the change caused shorter bus trips, on average, for Charlotte-Mecklenburg students. Protest over desegregation now began to manifest itself more in the North than in the South as white families in Boston, Denver, and other cities denounced the destruction of "the neighborhood school," and angry parents in Pontiac, Michigan, fire-bombed school buses.

Sensing the anxieties that many parents felt about the busing issue, Nixon asked Congress to impose a moratorium on all busing orders by the federal courts. The House of Representatives, equally attuned to voter outrage at busing, went along. But a Senate filibuster blocked the president's antibusing bill. Busing opponents won a limited victory when the Supreme Court ruled, in *Milliken v. Bradley* (1974), that desegregation plans in Detroit requiring the transfer of students from the inner city to the suburbs were unconstitutional. This landmark decision, along with the *Bakke v. Board of*

Regents of California (1978) decision which restricted the use of quotas to achieve racial balance, marked the transition of desegregation from an issue of simple justice to a more tangled thicket of conflicting group and individual rights.

Fate and the aging of the justices on the Warren Court gave Nixon the chance to make four new appointments. His first, Warren Burger, caused no dissent. But Nixon's next two nominations generated opposition in the Senate. Clement F. Haynsworth, a federal appeals court judge from South Carolina, had the support of the American Bar Association but drew fire from civil-rights groups and labor unions for his conservative record. There was no question of Haynsworth's integrity, but the Senate rejected him when it learned that he had heard a case involving a subsidiary of a corporation in which he owned a small amount of stock.

The nomination of G. Harrold Carswell, a judge of the Florida appeals court, created far more trouble. Carswell had not only been an out-and-out defender of white supremacy, but he was acknowledged by all parties to be singularly lacking in distinction. By a vote of 51 to 45 the Senate rejected Carswell. Nixon condemned the Senate rejection as "an act of regional discrimination." But he took care thereafter to nominate jurists of stature for the Supreme Court: Harry Blackmun, a compatriot of Burger's from Minnesota; Lewis F. Powell, Jr., a respected conservative judge from Virginia; and William Rehnquist, an articulate, conservative lawyer in the Justice Department. None encountered serious opposition in the Senate. And none, save perhaps Rehnquist, would consistently support Nixon's interpretation of the Constitution.

Nixon had also promised to "get tough on crime," a promise hard to fulfill because criminal statutes were local and state concerns. In July 1969, however, he proposed a crime bill for the District of Columbia designed to clarify his administration's tough stance and thereby assume symbolic leadership as "the nation's number one cop." The bill empowered judges to jail suspects for sixty days before trial ("preventive detention") and allowed police to break into houses with a "no-knock" warrant. Senator Samuel J. Ervin, Jr., of North Carolina called it "A bill to repeal the fourth, fifth, sixth and eighth amendments to the Constitution." Afraid of appearing "soft" on crime, Congress passed the bill, but its influence on state and local laws proved negligible.

The single most innovative piece of domestic legislation proposed by the administration was the Family Assistance Plan, a proposal to overhaul the welfare system and cut out several layers of the bureaucracy created by Great Society programs. Daniel Patrick Moynihan, head of the Council on Urban Affairs, drafted the plan, which called for direct grants of $1,600 to poor families: in short, a guaranteed income floor. The idea had support among a wide range of experts, including some conservatives, but the plan's constituency had little political clout. The Family Assistance Plan went down to defeat in the Congress, in part because Nixon had insisted that it was "workfare and not welfare." In truth the plan was unadulterated welfare—a guaranteed income—but liberals in Congress, befuddled by Nixon's characterization of the plan, or miffed that it did not go far enough, joined with conservatives in a strange alliance to kill the bill.

Nixon invented several names for his domestic program. At one point it was called the "New Federalism," which would "start resources and power flowing back from Washington to the people." To that end, in 1972 he pushed through Congress a five-year revenue-sharing plan which would distribute $30 billion of federal revenues to the states for use as they saw fit. At another point Nixon called for a "New American Revolution" to revive traditional values. These catchphrases never caught on, as had the "New Frontier" or the "Great Society," because Nixon's domestic program was mostly defensive and negative.

In the fall of 1969 Nixon sent Vice-President Spiro Agnew on a national speaking tour to assault and demean the opposition. Agnew and a clutch of White House speechwriters described war protesters as "anarchists and ideological eunuchs" and the liberal news media as "an effete corps of impudent snobs" and "nattering nabobs of negativism." It was time, said Agnew, "to rip away the rhetoric and divide on authentic lines. . . . When the president said 'bring us together,' he meant the functioning, contributing portions of the American citizenry."

But while Agnew turned phrases, the Democratic Congress moved forward with new legislation: the right of eighteen-year-olds to vote in national elections (1970), and in all elections under the Twenty-sixth Amendment (1971); increases in social security benefits indexed to the inflation rate and a rise in food-stamp funding; the Occupational Safety and Health Act (1970), the Clean Air Act (1970), new bills to control water pollution (1970 and 1972), and the Federal Election Campaign Act (1972), which modified the rules of campaign finance. These measures accounted for a more rapid rise in spending on social programs than Johnson's Great Society programs had.

ECONOMIC MALAISE   The economy continued to prove troublesome. The inflation rate began to rise in 1967, when it was 3 percent. By 1973 it was at 9 percent; a year later it was at 12 percent, and it remained in double digits for most of the 1970s. The Dow-Jones average of major industrial stocks fell by 36 percent between November 1968 and May 1970, its steepest decline in over thirty years. In 1970 real gross national product (adjusted for inflation) declined for the first time since 1958, and the following year American imports exceeded exports for the first time since 1893. Meanwhile unemployment, at a low of 3.3 percent when Nixon took office, climbed to 6 percent by the end of 1970 and threatened to keep rising. Somehow the American economy was undergoing a recession and inflation at the same time. Economists coined the term "stagflation" to describe the syndrome which defied the orthodox laws of economics.

The economic malaise had at least three deep-rooted causes. First, the Johnson administration had attempted to pay for both the Great Society and the war in Vietnam without a major tax increase, generating larger federal deficits, a major expansion of the money supply, and price inflation. Second, and more important, by the late 1960s American goods faced stiff competition in international markets from West Germany, Japan, and other emerging industrial powers. No longer was American technological superiority unquestioned. Third, the American economy had depended heavily on cheap sources of energy; no nation was more dependent on the automobile and the automobile industry, and no nation was more careless in its use of fossil fuels in factories and homes.

Just as domestic petroleum reserves began to dwindle and dependence on foreign sources increased, the Organization of Petroleum Exporting Countries (OPEC) combined to use their oil as a political and economic weapon. In 1973, when the United States sent massive aid to Israel after a devastating Syrian-Egyptian attack during Yom Kippur, the holiest day in the Jewish calendar, OPEC announced in October that it would not sell oil to nations supporting Israel and that it was raising its prices by 400 percent. Motorists faced long lines at gas stations, schools and offices closed down, factories cut production, and the inflation rate took off as if fueled by all the oil not being delivered to the United States.

Another condition leading to stagflation was the flood of new workers—mainly baby-boomers and women—entering the labor market. From 1965 to 1980 the work force grew by 40 percent, almost 30 million workers, a number greater than the total labor force of France or West Germany. The number of new jobs could not keep up, leaving many unemployed. At the same time worker productivity declined, pushing up inflation in the face of rising demand.

Stagflation posed a new set of economic problems, but Nixon responded erratically and ineffectively with old remedies for a new

The lineup of cars at a California gas station during the fuel shortage.

problem. First, he tried to reduce the federal deficit by raising taxes and cutting the budget. When the Democratic Congress refused to cooperate with this approach, he followed the advice of Milton Friedman, the conservative economist at the University of Chicago, and encouraged the Federal Reserve Board to reduce the money supply by raising interest rates. The stock market immediately collapsed and the economy plunged into the "Nixon recession."

In 1969, when asked about wage and price controls, Nixon had been unequivocal: "Controls. Oh, my God, no! I was a lawyer for the OPA [Office of Price Administration] during the war and I know about controls. . . . We'll never go to controls." But on August 15, 1971, he reversed himself. He froze all wages and prices for ninety days and announced that the United States would no longer convert dollars into gold for foreign banks. This ended an era that had begun in 1944 with the international agreement to set up the World Bank and the International Monetary Fund, reached at Bretton Woods, New Hampshire. The United States had made the dollar convertible to gold at $35 an ounce, thereby setting a firm standard by which other currencies were measured. Now the dollar, its link to gold cut, drifted lower on world currency exchanges. After ninety days Nixon established mandatory guidelines for subsequent wage and price increases under the supervision of a federal agency. Still the economy floundered. When administration economists kept predicting an imminent upturn, journalists recalled General Westmoreland's predictions of victory in Vietnam. By 1973 the wage and price guidelines were made voluntary, and therefore almost entirely ineffective.

ENVIRONMENTAL PROTECTION The widespread recognition that America faced limits to economic growth fueled the sudden emergence of broad support for environmental protection in the early

An Earth Day demonstration dramatizing the dangers of air pollution, April 1972.

1970s. The realization that cities and industrial development were damaging the physical environment and altering the earth's ecology was not new: Rachel Carson's *Silent Spring* (1962) had sounded the warning years earlier. But in Nixon's first term the Democratic-controlled Congress took concerted action, passing several acts to protect and clean up the environment, and blocking support for development of the supersonic transport (SST) plane on grounds that its sonic boom would disrupt the atmosphere. The administration at the same time created by executive order the Environmental Protection Agency, a consolidation of existing agencies, to oversee federal guidelines for air pollution, toxic wastes, and water quality.

The energy crisis that struck home after the Arab oil boycott and the OPEC price increase heightened public awareness that natural resources were not infinitely expendable. "Although it's positively un-American to think so," said one sociologist, "the environmental movement and energy shortage have forced us all to accept a sense of our limits, to lower our expectations, to seek prosperity through conservation rather than growth."

Although the environmental movement cut across class, racial, and ethnic lines by appealing to the collective interests of all Americans in clean air and water, it simultaneously aggravated the competition between regional vested interests. In Texas, where the oil lobby resented controls on gas prices and speed limits, bumper stickers read: "Drive fast, freeze a Yankee." In Tennessee, where a federal dam project was halted because it threatened the snail darter—a species of fish—with extinction, local developers took out ads asking residents to "tell the government that the size of your wallet is more important than some two-inch-long minnow."

As stagflation persisted into the middle and late 1970s, corporate criticism that environmental regulations were cutting into jobs and profit margins began to sound more persuasive, especially when the staggering cost of cleaning up accumulated toxic wastes became known. "Why worry about the long run," said one unemployed steelworker in 1976, "when you're out of work right now." Polls showed that protection of the environment remained a high priority among a majority of Americans, but that few were willing to suffer a cutback in their standard of living to achieve that goal. "It was," bemoaned one journalist, "as if passengers knew they were boarding the *Titanic,* but preferred to jostle with one another for first class accommodations so they might enjoy as much of the voyage as possible."

NIXON TRIUMPHANT

CHINA If the ailments of the economy proved more than Nixon could remedy, in foreign policy his administration managed to diagnose and improve American relations with the major powers of the Communist world—China and the Soviet Union—and to shift fundamentally the pattern of the Cold War. In July 1971 Henry Kissinger made a secret trip to Peking to explore the possibility of American recognition of China. Since 1949, when Mao Tse-tung's revolutionary movement established control in China, the United States had refused to recognize Communist China, preferring to regard Chiang

President Nixon and the chairman of the
Chinese Communist party, Mao Tse-tung,
February 1972.

Kai-shek's exiled regime on Taiwan as the legitimate government of China. In one simple but stunning stroke, Nixon and Kissinger ended two decades of diplomatic isolation for the People's Republic of China and drove a wedge between the two chief bastions of communism in the world.

In February 1972 Americans watched on television as their president visited famous Chinese landmarks, which had been invisible to Americans for over two decades, and drank toasts with Premier Chou En-lai and Mao Tse-tung. The United States and China agreed to scientific and cultural exchanges, steps toward the resumption of trade, and the eventual reunification of Taiwan with the mainland. A year after the Nixon visit, "liaison offices" were established in Washington and Peking that served as unofficial embassies, and in 1979 diplomatic recognition was formalized. Richard Nixon, the former anti-Communist crusader who had condemned the State Department for "losing" China in 1949, accomplished a diplomatic feat his more liberal predecessors could not.

DÉTENTE   In truth, China welcomed the breakthrough in relations with the United States because its rivalry with the Soviet Union, with which it shared a long border, had become more bitter than its rivalry with the West. The Soviet leaders, troubled by the Sino-American agreements, were also anxious for an easing of tensions now that they had, as the result of a huge arms buildup following the Cuban missile crisis, achieved virtual parity with the United States in nuclear weapons. Once again the president surprised the world, by announcing that he would visit Moscow in May 1972 for discussions with Leonid Brezhnev, the Soviet premier. The high theater of the China visit was repeated in Moscow, with toasts and elegant dinners between world leaders who had previously regarded each other as incarnations of evil.

What became known as "détente" with the Soviets offered the promise of a more orderly and restrained competition between the two superpowers. Nixon and Brezhnev signed agreements reached at the Strategic Arms Limitation Talks (SALT) which negotiators had been working on since 1969 in Helsinki and Vienna. The SALT agreement did not end the arms race, but it did limit both the number of intercontinental ballistic missiles (ICBMs) and the construction of antiballistic missile systems (ABMSs). In effect the Soviets were allowed to retain a greater number of missiles with greater destructive power while the United States retained a lead in the total number of warheads. No limitations were placed on new weapons systems, though each side agreed to work toward a permanent freeze on all nuclear weapons. The Moscow summit also produced new trade agreements, including an arrangement whereby the United States sold almost one-quarter of its wheat crop to the Soviets at a favorable price. American farmers rejoiced, since the wheat deal assured them a high price for their crop, but domestic critics grumbled that the deal would raise food prices in the United States and rescue the Russians from troublesome economic problems.

SHUTTLE DIPLOMACY The Nixon-Kissinger initiatives in the Middle East were less dramatic and conclusive than the China or Russia agreements, but did show that America recognized Arab power in the region and its own dependence on the oil from Islamic states fundamentally opposed to Israel. After the Six-Day War of 1967, in which Israeli forces routed the armies of Egypt, Syria, and Jordan, Israel seized territory from all three Arab nations. Moreover, the Palestinian refugees, many of them homeless since the creation of Israel in 1948, were made much more numerous by the Israeli victory in 1967. When Israel recovered from the initial shock of the surprise Yom Kippur War of 1973, Kissinger negotiated a cease-fire and exerted pressure to prevent Israel from taking additional Arab territory. American reliance on Arab oil led to closer ties with Egypt and its president, Anwar el-Sadat, and more restrained support for Israel. Kissinger, whose "shuttle diplomacy" among the capitals of the Middle East won acclaim from all sides, failed to find a comprehensive formula for peace in the troubled region and ignored altogether the Palestinian problem, but did lay groundwork for the subsequent accord between Israel and Egypt in 1977.

THE 1972 ELECTION Nixon's foreign policy achievements allowed him to stage the campaign of 1972 as a triumphal procession. At the Republican convention Nixon's nomination was a foregone conclusion. Film stars who symbolized the certitudes of an earlier era— John Wayne, Jimmy Stewart, Glenn Ford—delivered patriotic endorsements. The main threat to Nixon's reelection came from George Wallace, who had the potential as a third-party candidate to deprive the Republicans of conservative votes and thereby throw the election to the Democrats or the Democratic-controlled Congress. But on May 15, 1972, Wallace was shot and left prematurely paralyzed below the waist by a white midwesterner anxious to achieve a grisly brand of notoriety. Wallace was forced to withdraw from the campaign.

Meanwhile the Democrats were further ensuring Nixon's victory by nominating Senator George S. McGovern of South Dakota, a crusading liberal who embodied antiwar and social welfare values associated with the turbulence of the 1960s. At the Democratic convention in Miami Beach McGovern's nomination was made easier by party reforms that increased the representation of women, blacks, and minorities, but which alienated party regulars. Mayor Richard Daley of Chicago was actually ousted from the convention, and the AFL-CIO refused to endorse the Democratic candidate. McGovern also suffered from his handling of the crisis that developed when it was revealed that his running mate, Senator Thomas Eagleton of Missouri, had undergone shock treatments for emotional disturbances. McGovern first announced complete support for Eagleton, then bowed to critics and dropped him, leaving an impression of vacillation and indecisiveness.

The campaign was an exercise in futility for McGovern, while Nixon made only a few formal political trips and cast himself in the role of "global peacekeeper." Nixon won the greatest victory of any Republican presidential candidate in history, winning 520 electoral votes to only 17 for McGovern. The popular vote was equally decisive: 46 million to 28 million, a proportion of the total vote (60.8 percent) that was second only to Johnson's victory over Goldwater in 1964.

During the course of the campaign McGovern complained about the "dirty tricks" of the Nixon administration, most especially the curious incident in which a group of burglars was caught red-handed breaking into the Democratic National Committee headquarters in the Watergate apartment complex in Washington. McGovern's accusations seemed shrill and biased at the time, the lamentations of an obvious loser. Nixon and his staff made plans for "four more years" as the investigation of the fateful Watergate break-in proceeded apace.

WATERGATE

Under the relentless prodding of Judge John J. Sirica, one of the burglars began to tell the full story of the Nixon administration's complicity in the Watergate episode. James W. McCord, a former CIA agent and security chief for the Committee to Re-elect the President (CREEP), was the first in a long line of informers and penitents in a melodrama which unfolded over the next two years and which mixed the special qualities of soap opera and Machiavellian intrigue. It ended in the first resignation of a president in American history, the conviction and imprisonment of twenty-five officials of the Nixon administration, including four cabinet members, and the most serious constitutional crisis since the impeachment trial of President Andrew Johnson.

UNCOVERING THE COVER-UP The trail of evidence pursued first by Judge Sirica, then by a grand jury, and then by a Senate investigation committee headed by Senator Samuel J. Ervin, Jr., of North Carolina led directly to the White House. Senator Howard Baker of Tennessee, a member of the Ervin Committee, put the crucial questions succinctly: "What did the President know and when did he know it?" There was never any evidence that Nixon ordered the break-in or that he was aware of plans to burglarize the Democratic National Committee. But from the start Nixon was personally involved in the cover-up of the incident, he used his presidential powers to discredit and block the investigation, and, most alarming, the Watergate burglary was merely one small part of a larger pattern of corruption and criminality sanctioned by the Nixon White House.

The White House had become committed to illegal tactics in May 1970 when the *New York Times* broke the story of the secret bombings in Cambodia. Nixon had ordered illegal telephone taps on several newsmen and government employees suspected of leaking the story. The covert activity against the press and critics of Nixon's Vietnam policies increased in 1971 during the crisis generated by the publication of the Pentagon Papers, when a team of burglars under the direction of White House adviser John Ehrlichman had broken into a psychiatrist's office in an effort to obtain damaging information on Daniel Ellsberg. By the spring of 1972 Ehrlichman commanded a team of "dirty tricksters" who performed various acts of sabotage against prospective Democratic candidates for the presidency, including falsely accusing Hubert Humphrey and Senator Henry Jackson of sexual improprieties, forging press releases, setting off stink-bombs at Democratic rallies, and associating the opposition candidates with racist remarks. By the time of the Watergate break-in, the money to finance such "pranks" was being illegally collected through the Committee to Re-elect the President and placed under the control of the White House staff.

The cover-up unraveled further in April 1973 when L. Patrick Gray, acting director of the FBI, resigned after confessing that he had confiscated and destroyed several incriminating documents. On April 30 Ehrlichman and Haldeman resigned, together with Attorney-General Richard Kleindienst. A few days later the president nervously assured the public in a television address, "I am not a crook." But then John Dean, whom Nixon had dismissed as counsel to the president because of his cooperation with prosecutors, told the Ervin Committee that there had been a cover-up and that Nixon had approved it. In another "bombshell" disclosure a White House aide told the committee that Nixon had installed a taping system in the White House and that many of the conversations about Watergate had been recorded.

Senator Sam Ervin (D, N.C.), chairman of the Senate Watergate Committee, swears in the ex–White House counsel John Dean, whose testimony linked President Nixon to the cover-up.

A year-long battle for the "Nixon tapes" began. The Harvard law professor Archibald Cox, who had been appointed by Nixon as special prosecutor to handle the Watergate case, took the president to court in October 1973 in order to obtain the tapes. Nixon, pleading "executive privilege," refused to release the tapes and ordered Cox fired. In what became known as the "Saturday Night Massacre," Attorney-General Elliot Richardson and Deputy Attorney-General William Ruckelshaus resigned rather than execute the order. Solicitor-General Robert Bork finally fired Cox. Cox's replacement as special prosecutor, Leon Jaworski, proved no more pliable than Cox, and also took the president to court. On July 24, 1974, the Supreme Court ruled unanimously that the president must surrender the tapes. No sooner were the tapes handed over than investigators learned that sections of certain recordings were missing, including eighteen minutes of a key conversation during which Nixon first mentioned the Watergate burglary. The president's loyal secretary tried to accept blame for the erasure, claiming she accidentally pushed the wrong button. But experts later concluded that the missing segments had been intentionally deleted.

A few days later the House Judiciary Committee dramatically

voted to recommend three articles of impeachment: obstruction of justice through the payment of "hush money" to witnesses and the withholding of evidence; using federal agencies to deprive citizens of their constitutional rights; and defiance of Congress by withholding the tapes. But before the House of Representatives could meet to vote on impeachment, Nixon handed over the complete set of White House tapes. On August 9, 1974, fully aware that the evidence on the tapes implicated him in the cover-up, Richard Nixon resigned from office, the only president ever to do so.

EFFECTS OF WATERGATE   Nixon was not succeeded by Spiro Agnew because Agnew himself had been forced to resign in October 1973 when it became known that he had accepted bribes from contractors before and during his term as vice-president. In a plea bargain with prosecutors he agreed to a single charge of tax evasion. The vice-president at the time of Nixon's resignation was Gerald Ford, the former House minority leader whom Nixon had appointed, with the approval of Congress, under provisions of the Twenty-fifth Amendment. Ratified in 1967, the amendment provided for the appointment of a vice-president when the office became vacant. Ford insisted that he had no intention of pardoning Nixon, who was still liable for criminal prosecution. "I do not think the public would stand for it," said Ford. But a month after Nixon's resignation the

Having resigned his office, Richard Nixon waves farewell outside the White House, August 9, 1974.

new president did issue the pardon, explaining that it was necessary to end the national obsession with the Watergate scandals.

Many suspected that Nixon and Ford had made a deal, though there was no evidence to confirm the speculation. President Ford testified personally to a congressional committee: "There was no deal, period." But Watergate spawned a wave of cynicism. In the spring of 1974 polls showed that a majority of Americans believed that Nixon was lying about his complicity, but that four out of five judged him as no more guilty of wrongdoing than his presidential predecessors. The Watergate scandals and Nixon's resignation seemed to justify the most distrustful appraisals of American leaders and political institutions; little wonder that barely half the eligible electorate would vote in the next presidential election. Apart from Nixon's illegal action, the language used in the White House and made public in the tapes stripped away the veils of mystery surrounding national leaders and left even the die-hard defenders of presidential authority shocked at the crudity and duplicity of Nixon and his subordinates. If there was a silver lining in this dark cloud, it was the vigor and resiliency of the institutions that had brought a president down—the press, Congress, the courts, and an aroused public opinion.

Although many observers attributed Watergate to the idiosyncrasies of one man, Richard Nixon, whose entire political career revealed an obsession with routing out hidden enemies, Congress responded to the revelations of Watergate with several pieces of legislation designed to curb executive power in the future. Already nervous about possible efforts to renew American military assistance to South Vietnam, the Democratic-led Congress passed the War Powers Act (1973), which required the president to consult with Congress before sending American troops into combat abroad and to withdraw troops after sixty days unless Congress specifically approved their stay. In an effort to correct abuses of campaign funds, Congress enacted legislation in 1974 that set new ceilings on contributions and expenditures. And in reaction to the Nixon claim of "executive privilege," Congress strengthened the 1966 Freedom of Information Act to require prompt responses to requests for information from government files and to place on government agencies the burden of proof for classifying information.

The nation had weathered a profound constitutional crisis, but the aftershock of the Watergate episode produced a deep sense of disillusionment with the so-called imperial presidency. Coming on the heels of the erosion of public confidence generated by the Vietnam War, the Watergate affair renewed public cynicism toward a government that had systematically lied to the people and violated their civil liberties. Said one bumper sticker of the day: "Don't vote. It only encourages them."

Nixon's resignation thus pleased his critics but also initiated a prolonged crisis of confidence. A poll taken in 1974 asked people how much faith they had in the executive branch of government. Only 14 percent answered "a great deal"; 43 percent said "hardly any." Restoring credibility and respect thus became the primary challenge facing Nixon's successors. Unfortunately a new array of economic and foreign crises would make that task doubly difficult.

FURTHER READING

Engaging overviews of the cultural trends of the 1960s include William L. O'Neill's *Coming Apart* (1972)° and Godfrey Hodgson's *America in Our Time* (1976).° The scholarly literature on the New Left and the antiwar movement continues to grow. A good starting point is Irwin Unger's *The Movement: A History of the American New Left* (1974).° Another lively survey is Milton Viorst's *Fire in the Streets: America in the 1960s* (1970).° On the evolution and eventual destruction of the Students for a Democratic Society, see Kirkpatrick Sale's *SDS* (1973) and Allen J. Matusow's *The Unraveling of America* (1984).° The story of the pivotal confrontation at Columbia is told in James Kunen's *The Strawberry Statement* (1968). For a fascinating analysis of the role of the media in the street politics of the 1960s, see Todd Gitlin's *The Whole World Is Watching* (1980).° Two illuminating sociological studies of the hippies and student radicals are, respectively, Kenneth Keniston's *The Uncommitted* (1965) and *The Young Radicals* (1968).

Two contemporary and influential assessments of the counterculture by sympathetic researchers are Theodore Roszak's *The Making of a Counterculture* (1969) and Charles Reich's *The Greening of America* (1970).° The best examination of the motives behind the alienated youth remains Philip Slater's *The Pursuit of Loneliness* (1970).° The relationship of hallucinogenic drugs to the counterculture is a feature of Tom Wolfe's *The Electric Kool-Aid Acid Test* (1969).° Stanley Booth examined the relationship of rock music to the youth culture in *Dance with the Devil: The Rolling Stones and Their Times* (1984). On the communal movement, see Keith Melville's *Communes in the Counter Culture* (1972).

There is a wealth of good books dealing with the women's liberation movement. Among the most powerful accounts are those by participants. See Shulamith Firestone's *The Dialectic of Sex* (1972), Betty Friedan's *It Changed My Life: Writings on the Women's Movement* (1985),° Kate Millett's *Sexual Politics* (1971), and *Sisterhood Is Powerful* (1970),° edited by Robin Morgan. Sara Evans explained the ambivalent relationship of feminism with the civil-rights movement in *Personal Politics: The Roots of*

°These books are available in paperback editions.

Women's Liberation in the Civil Rights Movement and the New Left
(1980).° For the background of the movement in the 1960s and 1970s, see
Nancy Cott's *The Grounding of Modern Feminism* (1987) and Cynthia
Harrison's *On Account of Sex: The Politics of Women's Issues, 1945–1968*
(1988).

The organizing efforts of Cesar Chavez are detailed in Ronald Taylor's
Chavez and the Farm Workers (1975).° See also Feliciano Rivera's *The
Chicanos* (1972). The struggles of Native Americans for recognition and
power are sympathetically described in Stan Steiner's *The New Indians*
(1968). On the shifting cultural mood of the 1970s, see Christopher Lasch's
controversial and influential jeremiad, *The Culture of Narcissism* (1978).°
Other critiques of the social mood of the decade include Peter Carroll's *It
Seemed Like Nothing Happened: The Tragedy and Promise of America in
the 1970s* (1982)° and Edwin Schur's *The Awareness Trap: Self-Absorption
instead of Social Change* (1976).° Tom Wolfe gave the decade its enduring—
and misleading—tag in his "The 'Me' Decade and the Third Great Awakening," *New York,* 9 (1976):26–40. Peter Clecak convincingly questions the
stereotypic notion of the seventies as an age of apathy and narcissism in
America's Quest for the Ideal Self (1983).°

A good start for the events of the Nixon years is the former president's
memoirs: *RN: The Memoirs of Richard Nixon* (1978).° On Nixon himself,
see Roger Morris's *Richard Milhous Nixon: The Rise of an American Politician* (1990) and Stephen Ambrose's *Nixon: The Triumph of a Politician,
1962–1972* (1989). A study of Nixon at the time of his resurgence to power
is Garry Wills's *Nixon Agonistes* (1970).° James David Barber's *The Presidential Character* (1972)° insightfully compares Nixon to his predecessors in
the White House.

For a solid overview of the Watergate scandal, see Stanley Kutler, *The
Wars of Watergate* (1990).° The works of the two *Washington Post* reporters
involved, Robert Woodward and Carl Bernstein, recount their role in the
events; follow *All the President's Men* (1974)° with *The Final Days* (1976).°
Arthur M. Schlesinger, Jr.'s *The Imperial Presidency* (1973)° looks for the
scandal's cause in the growing power of the president to conduct foreign
affairs. Other views of Watergate can be found in Theodore H. White's
Breach of Faith (1975),° Jonathan Schell's *The Time of Illusion* (1976),° and
Anthony Lukas's *Nightmare* (1976).

For the way the Republicans handled affairs abroad, consult Tad Szulc's
The Illusion of Power: Foreign Policy in the Nixon Years (1978). Secretary
of State Henry Kissinger recounts his role in policy formation in *The White
House Years* (1978). A less favorable report of the Kissinger role appears in
Seymour M. Hersh's *The Price of Power: Kissinger in the Nixon White
House* (1983). Also helpful is Lloyd C. Gardner's *The Great Nixon Turn-
around* (1975), for background on Nixon's relations with Russia and China.

The loss of Vietnam and the end of American involvement are traced in
A. E. Goodman's *The Lost Peace: America's Search for a Negotiated Settle-
ment of the Vietnam War* (1978) and Gareth Porter's *A Peace Denied: The
United States, Vietnam and the Paris Agreement* (1975). William Shaw-

cross's *Sideshow: Kissinger, Nixon, and the Destruction of Cambodia* (1978)°
deals with the broadening of the war, while Larry Berman's *Planning a
Tragedy: The Americanization of the War in Vietnam* (1982)° assesses the
final impact of American involvement.

For the domestic side of the Nixon years, see Daniel P. Moynihan's *The
Politics of a Guaranteed Income: The Nixon Administration and the Family
Assistance Plan* (1973).°

36

RETRENCHMENT: FORD AND CARTER

An Unelected President

During Richard Nixon's last year in office the Watergate crisis so dominated the Washington scene that major domestic and foreign problems received little executive attention. The perplexing combination of inflation and recession worsened, as did the oil crisis. At the same time, Henry Kissinger, who assumed virtually complete control over the management of foreign policy, watched helplessly as the South Vietnamese forces began to crumble before North Vietnamese attacks, attempted with limited success to establish a framework for peace in the Middle East, and supported a CIA role in overthrowing Salvador Allende, the popularly elected Marxist president of Chile. Allende was subsequently murdered and replaced by General Augusto Pinochet, a military dictator supposedly friendly to the United States.

THE FORD YEARS   Gerald Ford inherited these simmering problems when he assumed office after Nixon's resignation. An amiable, honest man, Ford candidly admitted upon becoming vice-president, "I am a Ford, not a Lincoln." He enjoyed widespread popular support for only a short time. His pardon of Nixon on September 8, 1974, generated a storm of criticism. And as president he soon adopted the posture he had developed as a conservative minority leader in the House: nay-saying leader of the opposition who believed that the federal government exercised too much power over domestic affairs. In his fifteen months as president Ford vetoed thirty-nine

bills, thereby outstripping Herbert Hoover's veto record in less than
half the time. By resisting congressional pressure to reduce taxes and
increase federal spending, he succeeded in plummeting the economy
into the deepest recession since the Great Depression. Unemployment jumped to 9 percent in 1975 and the federal deficit hit a record
$60 billion the next year. When New York City announced that it
was near bankruptcy, unable to meet its payrolls and bond payments, Ford vowed "to veto any bill that has as its purpose a federal
bailout." The headline in the New York *Daily News* was: "Ford to
New York: Drop Dead." But the president relented after the Senate
and House banking committees voted to guarantee a loan; New York
was saved from insolvency. Ford rejected wage and price controls to
curb inflation, preferring voluntary restraints which he tried to bolster by passing out "WIN" buttons, symbolizing his campaign to
"Whip Inflation Now." The WIN buttons instead became a national
joke and a popular symbol of Ford's ineffectiveness in the fight
against stagflation.

In foreign policy, Ford retained Henry Kissinger as secretary of
state and attempted to pursue Nixon's goals of stability in the Middle
East, rapprochement with China, and détente with the Soviet Union.
Late in 1974 Ford met with Soviet leader Leonid Brezhnev at Vladivostok in Siberia and accepted the framework for another arms-
control accord that was to serve as the basis for SALT II. Meanwhile
Kissinger's tireless shuttling between Cairo and Tel Aviv produced
an agreement: Israel promised to return to Egypt most of the Sinai
territory captured in the 1967 war, and the two nations agreed to

President Gerald Ford, May 1975.

rely on negotiations rather than force to settle future disagreements. These limited but significant achievements should have enhanced Ford's image, but they were drowned in the sea of criticism and carping that followed the collapse of South Vietnam in May 1975.

Not only had a decade of American effort in Vietnam proved futile, but the Khmer Rouge, the Cambodian Communist movement, had also won a resounding victory, plunging that country into a fanatical bloodbath. And the OPEC oil cartel was threatening another boycott while other Third World nations denounced the United States as a depraved and declining imperialistic power. Daniel Patrick Moynihan, the new American ambassador to the United Nations, attempted to answer these shrill accusations with his own unique blend of passion and stridency, but succeeded in further aggravating American relations with the developing countries. Ford also lost his patience, sending in the marines to rescue the crew of the American merchant ship *Mayaguez*, which had been captured by the Cambodian Communists in May 1975. This vigorous move won popular acclaim until it was disclosed that the Cambodians had already agreed to release the captured Americans: the forty-one Americans killed in the operation had died to no purpose.

THE 1976 ELECTION   In the midst of such turmoil, the Democrats could hardly wait for the 1976 election. At the Republican convention Ford managed to fend off a powerful challenge for the nomination from the former California governor and Hollywood actor, Ronald Reagan, whose robust appearance belied his sixty-five years. Since even the Republicans were divided over Ford's leadership, and since Ford's failure to solve the economic and energy problems was beyond dispute, the Democratic nominee seemed a shoo-in for the presidency. "We could run an aardvark this year and win," predicted one Democratic leader.

The Democrats chose an obscure former naval officer turned peanut farmer who had served one term as governor of Georgia. Jimmy Carter campaigned harder than any of the other Democratic hopefuls; he capitalized on the post-Watergate cynicism by promising "I will never tell a lie to the American people" and by citing his inexperience in the byways of Washington politics as an asset. With the help of a skilled Atlanta advertising executive, and by dint of full-time campaigning for over a year, the Georgian outdistanced his better-known rivals and sewed up the nomination before the convention. Facing the prospect of the first president from the Deep South since 1849, and the first ever born and bred in that particular briar patch, the media gorged themselves on "southern fried chic." Reporters marveled at a Baptist candidate who claimed to be "born-again," and began to speculate that Carter's native region harbored some forgotten virtues after all.

To the surprise of many pundits Carter revived the New Deal coalition of southern whites, blacks, urban labor, and ethnic groups to win 41 million votes to Ford's 39 million, and a narrow electoral majority of 297 to 241. A heavy turnout of blacks in the South enabled Carter to sweep every state in the region but Virginia. Carter also benefited from the appeal of Walter F. Mondale, his liberal running mate and a favorite among blue-collar workers and the urban poor. He lost most of the trans-Mississippi West, but no other Democratic candidate had made much headway there since Harry Truman in 1948. The big story of the election was the low voter turnout. "Neither Ford nor Carter won as many votes as Mr. Nobody," said one reporter, commenting on the fact that almost half the eligible voters, apparently alienated by Watergate and the lackluster candidates, chose to sit out the election.

THE CARTER INTERREGNUM

POLICY STALEMATE   During the televised debates between the presidential candidates in 1976, Jimmy Carter had chided Ford by telling voters, "Anything you don't like about Washington, I suggest you blame on him." Once in office, Carter suffered the fate of all American presidents since Kennedy: after an initial honeymoon, during which Carter displayed folksy charms by walking down Pennsylvania Avenue after his inauguration rather than riding in a limousine, and wearing cardigan sweaters during televised "fireside chats," his popularity and political effectiveness waned. Soon *Newsweek* was referring to the "corn bread-and-cardigan atmospherics," and television journalists were noting that, during one "fireside chat," the fire actually went out. The truth was that, like Ford before him, Carter faced an almost insurmountable set of domestic and international problems. He was expected to cure the economic recession and inflation at a time when all industrial economies were shaken by a shortage of energy and confidence. He was expected to reassert America's global power at a time of waning respect for America's international authority. And he was expected to do this, as well as buoy the national spirit, through a set of political institutions in which many Americans had lost faith. In short, Carter was predestined to fail at an impossible task.

Yet during the first two years of his term Carter enjoyed several successes, most reflecting the values of moderate liberalism. His administration included more blacks and women than ever before;

his appointment of Andrew Young, a former protégé of Martin Luther King, as ambassador to the United Nations attracted the most attention. Carter created a federal task force to study the problem of Vietnam-era draft evaders and eventually offered amnesty to the thousands of young Americans who had fled the country rather than serve in Vietnam. He reformed the civil service to provide rewards for merit, and he created new cabinet-level Departments of Energy and Education. He also pushed several significant environmental bills through Congress, including a bill to establish controls over strip mining, a "superfund" of $1.6 billion to clean up chemical waste sites, and a proposal to protect over 100 million acres of Alaskan land from development.

But success was short-lived. Carter's political predicament surfaced in the protracted debate over energy policy. Borrowing a phrase from the turn-of-the-century philosopher William James, the president declared that solving the energy problem must become for the nation "the moral equivalent of war," and he presented the Congress with what he called "a comprehensive energy program"

President Jimmy Carter and wife, Roslynn, forgo the traditional limousine and walk down Pennsylvania Avenue after the inauguration, January 20, 1977.

that would ensure victory. Carter, like Hoover, served at a time of diminishing resources, and like that other engineer-businessman, he had a distaste for stroking legislators or wheeling and dealing to get legislation through. The energy bill passed in August 1978 was a gutted version of the original, reflecting the power of both conservative and liberal special-interest lobbies. One Carter aide said that the energy bill looked like it had been "nibbled to death by ducks." The clumsy political maneuvers that plagued Carter and his inexperienced aides repeatedly frustrated his sincere desire to create a moral presidency.

Carter also urged the coupling of deregulation of the oil industry, which would increase prices and encourage domestic oil discovery, with a "windfall-profits tax" on the oil companies, whose profits would skyrocket as a result of deregulation. Liberals resented deregulation because it meant higher prices for consumers. Conservatives opposed the windfall-profits tax. The resulting bill made no one happy. With party discipline in the Congress a shambles and each special-interest group clamoring for its own program, the White House was forced to create what one Carter aide described as a "roll-your-own majority" for each presidential proposal. And Carter, unlike Wilson, FDR, and LBJ, was ill-equipped to maneuver his proposals around congressional obstacles. By early 1979, Carter's aides sensed a crisis of leadership. One told the president: "No one seems to be in charge. We still seem at times to have two or more foreign policies. Cabinet members contradict one another on major policy and it is never made clear who is speaking for the administration. People get reprimanded from time to time but *no one ever gets fired*. There is the feeling that you cannot provide strong leadership to the country because you don't yet have control of your own administration." Events soon brought this crisis of confidence to a head.

In the summer of 1979, when renewed violence in the Middle East produced a second fuel shortage, motorists were again forced to wait in long lines for limited supplies of gas that they regarded as excessively expensive. Opinion polls showed Carter with an approval rating of only 26 percent, lower than Nixon during the worst moments of the Watergate crisis. During July Carter called his advisers to an extraordinary retreat at Camp David, Maryland, and emerged ten days later proclaiming a "crisis of confidence" and a need for "a rebirth of the American spirit." He also called for a "new and positive energy program." But motorists in the gas lines traded jokes about Carter's "born-again energy theology" and Congress only partially funded the major feature of his new plan—a federal agency to encourage development of synthetic fuels.

Several of Carter's early foreign policy initiatives also got caught in political crossfires. Soon after his inauguration Carter vowed that "the soul of our foreign policy" should be the defense of human rights abroad. But the human-rights campaign provoked attack from two sides: those who feared it sacrificed a detached appraisal of national interest for high-level moralizing, and those who pointed to the administration's inconsistency in applying the standard. But foreign policy always turns on multiple considerations, and the Carter policy was a reaffirmation of American ideals which heartened many around the world.

Similarly, Carter's successful negotiation of treaties to turn over control of the Panama Canal to the government of Panama generated intense criticism. Republican Ronald Reagan claimed that the Canal Zone was sovereign American soil purchased "fair and square" in Theodore Roosevelt's administration. (In the congressional debate one senator quipped, "We stole it fair and square, so why can't we keep it?") Carter argued that the limitations on American influence in Latin America, and the deep resentment toward American colonialism in Panama, left the United States with no other choice. The Senate ratified the treaties by a paper-thin margin (68 to 32, two votes more than the required two-thirds), but conservatives lambasted Carter for surrendering American authority in a strategically critical part of the world. The Canal Zone would revert in stages to Panama by 1999. Finally, Carter completed the restoration of diplomatic relations with China, a process that had begun under Nixon. But because the Sino-American agreement of December 1978 required the United States to sever diplomatic relations with Taiwan, conservative critics condemned the agreement as a "sellout" of the Taiwanese and another instance of American international withdrawal from past commitments.

THE CAMP DAVID ACCORDS   Carter's crowning foreign policy achievement, which even his most devoted critics applauded, was the arrangement of a peace agreement between Israel and Egypt. In November 1977 President Anwar el-Sadat flew to Tel Aviv at the invitation of Israeli prime minister Menachem Begin. Sadat's bold act, and his accompanying announcement that Egypt was now willing to recognize the legitimacy of the Israeli state, opened up diplomatic opportunities that Carter and Secretary of State Cyrus Vance quickly pursued.

In September 1978 Carter invited Sadat and Begin to the presidential retreat at Camp David for two weeks of difficult negotiations. The first part of the eventual agreement called for Israel to return all land in the Sinai in exchange for Egyptian recognition of Israel's sovereignty. This agreement was successfully implemented in April

1982 when the last Israeli settler vacated the Sinai. But the second part of the agreement, calling for Israel to negotiate with Sadat to resolve the Palestinian refugee dilemma, began to unravel soon after the Camp David summit.

By March 26, 1979, when Begin and Sadat returned to Washington to sign the formal treaty, Begin had already made clear his refusal to block new Israeli settlements on the West Bank of the Jordan River, which Sadat had regarded as a prospective homeland for the Palestinians. In the wake of the Camp David accords most of the Arab nations condemned Sadat as a traitor to their Islamic cause. Still, Carter and Vance were responsible for a dramatic display of high-level diplomacy that, whatever its limitations, made an all-out war between Israel and the Arab world less likely in the foreseeable future.

MOUNTING TROUBLES Carter's crowning failure, which even his most avid supporters acknowledged, was his management of the economy. In effect he inherited a bad situation and left it worse. Carter employed the same economic policies as Nixon and Ford to fight stagflation, but he reversed the order of the federal "cure," preferring first to fight unemployment with a tax cut and increased public spending. Unemployment declined slightly, from 8 to 7 percent in 1977, but inflation soared; at 5 percent when he took office,

Egyptian president Anwar Sadat (left), Jimmy Carter, and Israeli prime minister Menachem Begin at the announcement of the Camp David accords, September 1978.

it reached 10 percent in 1978 and kept going. During one month in 1980 it measured an annual rate of no less than 18 percent. Like previous presidents, Carter then reversed himself to fight the other side of the economic malaise. By midterm he was delaying tax reductions and vetoing government spending programs that he had proposed in his first year. The result, however, was the worst of both possible worlds—a deepened recession with unemployment at 7.5 percent in 1980, mortgage rates at 15 percent, and interest rates at an all-time high of 20 percent; and a runaway inflation averaging between 12 and 13 percent.

The conclusion of a new Strategic Arms Limitation Treaty (SALT) with the Soviets put Carter's leadership to the test just as the mounting economic problems made him the subject of biting editorial cartoons nationwide. Like SALT I, the new agreement did not do much to slow down the nuclear arms race. It placed a ceiling of 2,250 bombers and missiles on each side and set limits on the number of warheads and new weapons systems. In order to quell his conservative critics, who charged that SALT II would give the Soviets a decided advantage in the number and destructive power of land-based missiles, Carter announced that the United States would build a new missile system, called the MX, that would be housed in a vast maze of underground tunnels connected by railroad, creating a sort of "nuclear shell game" that would prevent Soviet planners from knowing where to strike. Liberal critics called the MX plan "a combination of Disney World and Armageddon" and criticized the SALT II agreement as "a step sideways rather than backwards in the arms race." Conservatives questioned the whole idea of détente, arguing that the Soviets would never have signed the agreement if it did not guarantee them nuclear superiority. Whether or not SALT II would pass the Senate became an open question.

The question became moot in December 1979 when the Soviet army invaded Afghanistan in order to rescue the faltering Communist government there, which was being challenged by Muslim rebels. Carter immediately shelved SALT II, suspended grain shipments to the Soviet Union, and began a campaign for an international boycott of the 1980 Olympics, which were to be held that summer in Moscow. Zbigniew Brzezinski, Carter's hard-line national security adviser, won out over Cyrus Vance in the behind-the-scenes shuffling for influence and persuaded the president that the Soviet invasion of Afghanistan was only the first step in a Soviet scheme to dominate the oil-rich Persian Gulf. Calling the Soviet invasion "the gravest threat to world peace since World War II," Carter proclaimed that the United States would oppose by force any further Soviet advances in the Middle East. Military experts claimed that the United States lacked the military capability to block a Soviet move into the region, but Carter was determined to assert American power, even though, as one congressman put it, "the act of fighting for the oil would undoubtedly destroy all the oil fields, if not lead to thermonuclear war."

IRAN Then came the Iranian crisis, a year-long cascade of unwelcome events that epitomized the inability of the United States to control world events. The crisis began with the fall of the shah of Iran in January 1979. The revolutionaries who toppled the shah rallied around Ayatollah Ruhollah Khomeini, a Muslim religious leader who symbolized the Islamic values the shah had tried to replace with Western ways. Khomeini's hatred of the United States dated back to the CIA-sponsored overthrow of Iran's Mossadegh government in 1953. Nor did it help the American image that the CIA had trained SAVAK, the shah's ruthless secret police force. Late in October 1979 the exiled shah was allowed to enter the United States in order to undergo treatment for cancer. A few days later, on November 4, a frenzied mob stormed the American embassy in Teheran and seized the diplomats and staff inside. Khomeini endorsed the mob action and demanded the return of the shah along with all his wealth in exchange for the release of the fifty-three American hostages. In the meantime the Iranian militants staged daily demonstrations for the benefit of worldwide news and television coverage in which the American flag and effigies of the American president were burned and otherwise desecrated.

Indignant Americans demanded a military response to such outrages, but Carter's range of options was limited. He appealed to the United Nations, protesting what was a clear violation of diplomatic immunity and international law. Khomeini scoffed at U.N. requests for the release of hostages. Carter then froze all Iranian assets in the United States and appealed to American allies for a trade embargo of Iran. The trade restrictions were only partially effective—even America's most loyal European allies did not want to lose their access to Iranian oil—so a frustrated and besieged Carter authorized a risky rescue attempt by American commandos in April 1980. Secretary of State Vance resigned in protest against the rescue attempt, and against Carter's sharp turn toward a more hawkish foreign policy. The commando raid was aborted because of helicopter failures, and ended with eight fatalities when another helicopter collided with a transport plane in the desert.

Nightly television coverage of the taunting Iranian rebels generated widespread popular craving for action, cries of "Let's nuke the whole damn Iranian country" from angry Americans, and a near

The year-long Iranian hostage crisis damaged America's prestige and President Carter's chances for reelection.

obsession with the falling fortunes of the United States and the fate of the hostages. The end came after 444 days of captivity when Carter, in his last act as president, released several billion dollars of Iranian assets to ransom the kidnapped hostages. A plane carrying them left Teheran for Algiers moments after Ronald Reagan finished his inaugural address. Carter then flew to Wiesbaden, West Germany, as the new president's envoy to greet the released hostages at an American base. Few noted the irony that Algiers was one of the Barbary states that had extorted tribute from the early republic by holding American prisoners until 1815.

THE REAGAN REVOLUTION

THE MAKING OF A PRESIDENT   Ronald Reagan seemed at first a more remote presidential possibility than Carter, if longer in the public eye as a screen and television personality. A small-town boy from Dixon, Illinois, with a gift for gab, he became a radio sports announcer after graduation in 1932 from Eureka College. In Davenport and Des Moines, Iowa, he spun out play-by-play accounts of baseball games from bare-bones telegraph reports.

In 1937 he went west to cover the Chicago Cubs' spring camp and wangled a screen test, the start of a career mostly in B movies. His most memorable roles were as George Gipp ("the Gipper," a legendary Notre Dame football player) in *Knute Rockne—All American* and as Drake McHugh in *King's Row,* his finest role. In the climactic scene the hapless Drake, his inheritance lost to an embezzler and his legs to a sadistic surgeon, woke up to ask: "Where's the rest of me?" The line later became the title of Reagan's autobiography.

King's Row might have led to major stardom, but World War II intervened. Commissioned in the U.S. Army Air Force but consigned to limited service because of myopia, Reagan served out the war at "Fort Roach," the old Hal Roach studio in Culver City converted to make films for the army.

At first a New Dealer, like his father who headed the relief program in Dixon, Reagan became in Hollywood what he later called a "hemophilic liberal," and served as president of the Screen Actors Guild from 1947 to 1952 and 1959 to 1960. In 1950 when Helen Gahagan Douglas challenged Richard Nixon for a Senate seat from California, her aides played down Reagan's support because of his "leftist" reputation.

Reagan kept his Rooseveltian rhetoric but in less than a decade he had bounced to the far right on the political spectrum. Various reasons for the change have been adduced by Reagan and others. Repelled by Communist infiltrators in liberal groups, he said, "I was beginning to see the seamy side of liberalism"—although some groups he left (Americans for Democratic Action, the American Veterans Committee, and others) rejected the Communists, the "East wing" looked to Moscow for guidance. His transformation also may have been a rerun of an old story: the newly rich who resent taxes. Reagan's developing conservative views were reinforced, after his divorce from screen star Jane Wyman, by his new in-laws when he married starlet Nancy Davis in 1952.

President Ronald Reagan, "the Great Communicator."

From a dwindling film career Reagan eased into television as host of the "General Electric Theater" (1954–1962). He toured the country delivering conservative homilies to G. E. employees, practicing and perfecting what came to be known as "the Speech." He moved on to be host and actor in the weekly "Death Valley Days" (1962–1965). Meanwhile he campaigned for both Eisenhower (1952, 1956) and Nixon (1960), switched his registration to Republican in 1962, then achieved political stardom in 1964 when he delivered "the Speech" on national television in behalf of Barry Goldwater.

The Republican right had a new idol, whose appeal survived the Goldwater debacle. Those who discounted him as a minor actor and a mental midget underrated the importance of his years in front of the camera. Politics had always been a performing art, the more so in an age of television, and few, if any, others in public life had Reagan's stage presence. He had, moreover, a contagious zest for life and a genuine instinct for the funny bone, for the one-liner, often cribbed from old movies. Drawn by wealthy admirers into the campaign for governor of California in 1966, Reagan moderated his rawest rhetoric, quit calling the graduated income tax "spawned of Marx," and swamped Democratic incumbent Edmund G. (Pat) Brown.

He appealed especially to middle-class and lower-middle-class voters resentful of taxes, welfare for the dependent, the "neurotic vulgarities" of university students running wild, crime in the streets, and challenges to traditional values in general. In the forefront of the counterculture, California was in the forefront of reaction against it as well.

Much of Reagan's rhetoric, therefore, became a symbolic exploitation of social and cultural resentments. He arrived in Sacramento with no clear program for the state and with an entourage of what one aide called "novice amateurs." He had promised to reduce taxes, but found that state responsibilities mandated under law required higher taxes. During his term the state budget went from $4.6 billion to $10.2 billion. He railed against abortions, but signed a law that permitted them in cases of rape or incest, or where childbirth would gravely endanger the physical or mental health of the mother—a sizable loophole. During his first term the welfare rolls in the state nearly doubled. During his second, welfare reform reduced the numbers marginally, but greatly increased the payments to those remaining.

Still, Reagan left the impression that he had passed a miracle by reducing taxes and big government. He ran for reelection like an outsider challenging the government he had headed for nearly four years. He practiced "the politics of symbolism," one historian wrote.

"Matters of substance are less important than rhetoric and appearances."

From the start of his gubernatorial term Reagan had his eye on the presidency, but in the mid-1970s his rhetoric still seemed too extreme for the mainstream and his "back-to-basics" speeches provoked barbed jokes from journalists: "Ronald Reagan wants to take us back to the fifties," wrote one reporter, "back to the 1950s in foreign policy and back to the 1850s in economic and domestic policy."

THE MOVE TO REAGAN By the eve of the 1980 election, however, Reagan had become the beneficiary of two developments that made his conservative vision of America more than a harmless flirtation with nostalgia. First, the 1980 census revealed that the nation's population of 226,505,000 was aging, and was moving to the "Sunbelt" states of the South and West. This dual development—an increase in the numbers of senior citizens and the steady transfer of population to regions of the country where hostility to "big government" was endemic—meant that demographics were carrying the United States toward Reagan's position.

Second, in the 1970s the country experienced a major revival of evangelical religion, not unlike the Great Awakenings of the eighteenth and nineteenth centuries. No longer a local or provincial phenomenon that could be easily dismissed, Christian evangelicals now owned their own television and radio stations and operated their own schools and universities. A survey in 1977 revealed that more than 70 million Americans described themselves as born-again Christians who had a direct, personal relationship with Jesus.

The new fundamentalism emerged with a political agenda far broader than the war on Darwinism. During the previous two decades widely publicized Supreme Court decisions had stirred fundamentalist indignation and thus unwittingly helped arouse a political backlash. Among these were rulings for abortion (up to a point), against prayer in public schools, for the right to teach Darwinism, and for narrower definitions of pornography.

The Reverend Jerry Falwell's "Moral Majority" (later the Liberty Lobby) expressed the sentiments of countless other groups in a new religious political right: the economy should operate without "interference" by the government, which should be reduced in size; the Supreme Court decision in *Roe v. Wade* (1973) legalizing abortion should be reversed; evolution should be replaced in schoolbooks by the biblical story of creation; and Soviet expansion should be opposed as a form of pagan totalitarianism. "Our task is not to Christianize America," said Falwell, "but to bring about a moral and conservative revolution." By not focusing on divisive theological questions, he and others sought to use "traditional morality" to create an interdenominational political force drawing upon millions of evangelical Christians. To that end, Falwell formed Moral Majority, Inc. in 1979, describing it as a "nonpartisan political organization to promote morality in public life and to combat legislation that favors the legalization of immorality." The moralistic zeal and financial resources of the religious right made them formidable opponents of liberal political candidates and programs. Within a year Falwell claimed over 4 million members, including 72,000 ministers, priests, and rabbis. The Moral Majority's base of support was in the South and was strongest among Baptists, but its appeal extended across the country.

A curiosity of the 1980 campaign was that the Religious Right opposed Jimmy Carter, a self-professed born-again Christian, and supported Ronald Reagan, a man who denied such a profession and was neither conspicuously pious nor even often in church. His divorce and remarriage, once an almost automatic disqualification for the office, got little mention. So did the fact that as governor he had signed one of the most permissive abortion laws in the country. That Ronald Reagan became the Messiah of the Religious Right, God's man for the hour, was a tribute both to the force of social issues and the candidate's political skills. Later, during his first week in office, he gave the anti-abortion March for Life a well-publicized presidential audience. When a reporter asked an unnamed presidential aide what the administration wanted to give the Moral Majority, the aide responded: "Symbolism."

By 1980 Reagan also benefited from the failing fortunes of Jimmy Carter, whose campaign was beset by the frustrations of the Iranian hostage crisis, by a desperately sick economy, and by party divisions remaining from Edward M. Kennedy's failed quest for the Democratic nomination. Voters had rallied around the president early in the Iranian hostage crisis, and it seems plausible that a successful rescue of the hostages might have carried him to reelection.

Reagan, who had lost a last-minute try for the Republican nomination in 1968 and had failed to wrest it from Gerald Ford in 1976, emerged as the early front-runner in 1980. After losing ground to George Bush in Iowa's January caucus, he won the New Hampshire primary and had an insurmountable lead by March. The key event in the nomination race may have occurred in Nashua, New Hampshire, when Reagan invited other candidates to a scheduled one-to-one debate with Bush. When Bush objected and the sponsor threatened to shut off the audio system, Reagan angrily said, "I am paying for this microphone, Mr. Green." (Reagan cribbed this zinger from a Spencer Tracy line in the 1948 movie *State of the Union*.) Despite some later victories, notably in Pennsylvania, Bush dropped out late in May. Speculation at the convention turned on the vice-presidential choice. After a flurry of rumors that it would go to Gerald Ford, Reagan's choice fell upon Bush.

Reagan's acceptance speech, however, dumbfounded the assembled Republicans as the Republican conservative took to quoting Franklin D. Roosevelt, paragraph after paragraph, and calling upon the convention to fulfill FDR's promise. But it was a brilliant stroke—Reagan's personal admiration for Roosevelt was deep-seated, and he very much needed to reach out to Democratic voters, who were in the majority.

Forming a Reagan coalition proved no easy task. Reagan stumbled several times early in the campaign with impromptu remarks that ruffled certain voting blocs. He spoke of the Vietnam War as "a noble cause" and urged the nation never again to ask "young men to fight and possibly die in a war the government is afraid to win." He told a press conference that fascism was the inspiration for the New Deal. At a fundamentalist meeting in Dallas he endorsed the teaching of creationism. On Labor Day he wrongly called Tuscumbia, Alabama, where Carter opened his campaign, "the city that gave birth to . . . the Ku Klux Klan." Aside from being historically wrong, the attempt to link Carter with the Klan seemed more than a shade contrived.

Reagan's managers thereafter convinced him to stick to the script and limited his contacts with the press, "trying to protect him from himself," as one reporter said. Carter balanced Reagan's missteps by attacking the grandfatherly Reagan as a racist and warmonger, and complaining of the "stirrings of hate" in the campaign. Much of the campaign hinged on television, and in that medium Reagan was the champion. Television, moreover, offered frequent reminders of "America Held Hostage," with screaming anti-American mobs in Teheran, and a daily count of days held hostage that mounted to 365 by election day.

Yet the two candidates remained about even in the polls just before the television debate in Cleveland, on October 28. There Carter repeatedly attacked Reagan's positions only to be met with bland accusations of misstatement. When Carter attacked Reagan's record on Medicare, Reagan simply said, "There you go again"—and went on to pose to the audience the most telling question of the campaign: "Are you better off than you were four years ago?" In the end the voters took the candidate who breathed optimism over the candidate who had talked of a "crisis of confidence."

On November 4, before the polls had closed on the West Coast,

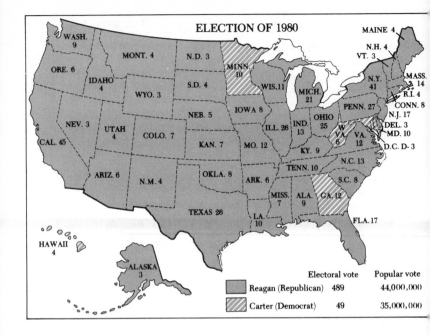

ELECTION OF 1980

	Electoral vote	Popular vote
Reagan (Republican)	489	44,000,000
Carter (Democrat)	49	35,000,000

Carter conceded the election. Reagan won a bare majority (50.7 percent) of the popular vote, but that was well ahead of Carter's 41 percent. John Anderson, a liberal Republican congressman running as an independent, got most of the rest. In the electoral college, Reagan's victory was more overwhelming—489 to 49. Carter carried only six states and the District of Columbia. More than a victory for the conservative policies Reagan championed, the outcome may have reflected the triumph of what one political scientist called the "largest mass movement of our time"—non-voting. Almost as striking as Reagan's one-sided victory was the fact that his vote total represented only 28 percent of the potential electorate. Only 53 percent of eligible voters cast ballots in the 1980 election; in western European countries such as France and Germany, voter participation hovered at 85 percent in national elections during the 1970s.

Where had all the voters gone? Political analysts noted that most of the non-voters were working-class Democrats in the major urban centers. Voter turnout was lowest in poor inner-city neighborhoods such as New York's Bedford-Stuyvesant district, which had a 19 percent voter participation rate. Turnout was highest, by contrast, in the affluent suburbs of large cities, areas where the Republican party was experiencing a dramatic surge in popularity. Such trends meant that American officeholders were being selected during the 1970s by an electorate increasingly dominated by middle- and upper-class voters.

Explanations for the high levels of voter apathy among working-class Americans vary. Some argue that they reflected the continuing sense of disillusionment with government itself growing out of the Watergate affair. Pollster Daniel Yankelovich saw a marked trend "from trust to mistrust. In the course of a single generation Americans have grown disillusioned about the relation of the individual to his government." Many Americans had come to believe that all politicians were essentially the same. When asked why people no longer voted in her community, one office worker replied: "Because it doesn't make any difference." Another widespread perception influencing voting behavior was that the Democratic party had turned its back on its traditional blocs of support among common folk. Democratic leaders no longer spoke eloquently on behalf of those at the bottom of America's social scale. By embracing a fiscal conservatism indistinguishable from the Republicans', as Carter had done, Democrats lost their appeal among blue-collar workers and ghetto dwellers. And so the largest group of non-voters in the 1980 election were former Democrats who had decided that neither party served their interests. When viewed in this light, Ronald Reagan's victory represented less a resounding victory for conservative Republicans than a self-inflicted defeat by a fractured Democratic party. But for the moment, at least, such results were masked by the Republicans' euphoric victory celebrations. Flush with a sense of power and destiny, Ronald Reagan headed toward Washington with a blueprint for dismantling the welfare state.

FURTHER READING

For additional views of politics during the 1970s, consult Henry S. Parmet's *The Democrats: The Years after FDR* (1976).° Gerald Ford's memoir, *A Time to Heal: The Autobiography of Gerald R. Ford* (1979), is illuminating on the post-Watergate years. See also Richard Reeve's *A Ford, Not a Lincoln* (1975).

To examine the rise of Jimmy Carter, consult Betty Glad's *Jimmy Carter: In Search of the Great White House* (1980) and James T. Wooten's *Dasher: The Roots and the Rise of Jimmy Carter* (1978). A work critical of the Carter administration is Haynes Johnson's *In the Absence of Power: Governing America* (1980). Gaddis Smith's *Morality, Reason, and Power* (1986) provides an overview of American diplomacy in the Carter years. Zbigniew Brzezinski's *Power and Principle: Memories of the National Security Advisor, 1977–1981* (1983) and Cyrus Vance's *Hard Choices: Critical Years in America's Foreign Policy* (1983) lend insight to the Carter approach to foreign policy. Background on how the Middle East came to dominate much

°These books are available in paperback editions.

of American policy is found in William B. Quandt's *Decade of Decision: American Policy toward the Arab-Israeli Conflict, 1967–1976* (1977).° What followed in the Camp David accords is handled best by Jimmy Carter in *Keeping Faith: The Memoirs of a President* (1982).° Background on the SALT controversy is provided in Harold B. Moulton's *From Superiority to Parity: The United States and the Strategic Arms Race, 1961–1972* (1973).

For an overview of politics during these years, see Walter Karp's *Liberty Under Siege* (1988). Peter Steinfel's *The Neoconservatives* (1979) heralded the election of conservatives in 1980.

For works on the Reagan presidency, see the Further Reading section at the end of Chapter 37.

37 ✐

A NEW GILDED AGE

REAGAN'S FIRST TERM

INAUGURATION The installation of the first professional actor to become chief executive was a triumph of opulence and show-biz spectacle as far removed as one could imagine from Jeffersonian simplicity or from Carter's gesture of walking down Pennsylvania Avenue four years before. At Carter's inauguration no ticket for any event cost more than $25. At Reagan's, nine balls cost $250 each, dinners went for $500 a plate, a gala for $50 and up, and a good seat at the parade cost $75. One observer calculated that tickets for all major events would cost at least $2,000 per person. "Ostentatious," said Senator Barry Goldwater, looking out at one glitzy inaugural party. "I've seen seven of them. And I say when you've got to pay $2,000 for a limousine for four days, $7 to park, and $2.50 to check your coat, at a time when most people in this country can't hack it, that's ostentatious."

The inaugural address, made up largely of recycled campaign speeches, promised "a new beginning." The "tax system which penalizes successful achievement and keeps us from maintaining full productivity" was the central point of attack, along with deficits "mortgaging our future and our children's future for the temporary convenience of the present. To continue this long trend is to guarantee tremendous social, cultural, political, and economic upheavals. . . . We must act today in order to preserve tomorrow. And let there be no misunderstanding—we are going to begin to act beginning today."

The ceremony was held for the first time on the West Front of the Capitol, facing the Mall, and the new president seized the occasion to point in turn to the great monuments of the past: the Washington Monument, the Jefferson and Lincoln Memorials, and finally, Arlington National Cemetery. Citing the sacrifices of those who lay buried there, he called upon Americans "to believe in ourselves and to believe . . . that together we can and will resolve the problems which confront us." He finished with a rhetorical question: "And after all, why shouldn't we believe that? We are Americans." It was vintage Reagan, the Reagan of "the Speech."

REAGANOMICS   Shortly after Reagan's nomination, *Newsweek* pronounced him the "incarnation of what a more worldly politician once called nostalgia for the future. He was brought up with much of his generation to venerate Franklin D. Roosevelt and now cheerfully proposes to govern like Calvin Coolidge." After invoking Roosevelt repeatedly, Reagan gave symbolic confirmation of *Newsweek*'s judgment when he had a portrait of Harry Truman removed from the Cabinet Room and replaced by a picture of Coolidge.

To promote Coolidge programs with a Rooseveltian flourish was mind-boggling, but Ronald Reagan brought it off with élan. "Reagan is probably taking us down the wrong road," noted a *New York Times* columnist, "but he's doing it with the style and grace and 'don't-look-back' bravado that the job requires." Reagan's inaugural address evoked the spirit of Roosevelt's first inaugural in its focus on "an economic affliction of great proportions" and its call for a "new beginning."

Reagan's "new beginning," however, was full-strength conservative medicine for the decade-long stagflation. "Government is not the solution to our problem," Reagan insisted; "government is the problem." His "supply-side" economics, soon dubbed "Reaganomics," derived from a group of economists who challenged the Keynesian doctrine that the problems of the economy were mainly on the demand side. Supply-siders contended, to the contrary, that these problems resulted from governmental intrusions into the marketplace and from excessive taxes that hampered incentives to work, save, and invest.

One of Reagan's first steps was to abandon price controls on oil; another was to call off the embargo on wheat exports to Russia. But the administration's energies focused on the tax plan advanced during the election campaign. Reagan had become entranced by the idea of the "Laffer curve," named for economist Arthur Laffer of the University of Southern California. Derived from the truism that neither a tax of 0 nor a tax of 100 percent would produce revenue, the theory held that somewhere in between tax rates reached a point beyond which they began to reduce the incentive to seek more income.

Reagan, who according to one aide "registers anecdotes rather than concepts," remembered the disincentives under World War II top rates of 91 percent on annual incomes above $5 million. A film star, he said, felt little push to go beyond, say, four films a year because he had by then reached a level at which most additional income went to pay taxes.

In the campaign Reagan proposed to cut taxes and domestic spending, increase military spending, and reduce the deficit with the increased revenues that would flow in from a rejuvenated economy. It was "voodoo economics," George Bush had said before he joined the Reagan team. It would have to be done with "blue smoke and mirrors," John Anderson, the independent candidate, said.

For a while, during his first two months in office, Reagan's popularity declined in the polls and doubts arose that he could get his economic program through a Democratic House. Then on March 30, 1981, a tragic event, an attempted assassination, fortuitously worked to the support of Reagan's program. The troubled young assailant, obsessed by the hope of impressing a movie actress, got off several shots as Reagan's party emerged from a speech in a Washington hotel. He hit Reagan in the chest, inflicted permanent brain damage on Press Secretary James A. Brady, and wounded a policeman and a Secret Service agent. At the hospital Reagan's first reported words to his wife were: "Honey, I forgot to duck" (a line first used by the boxer Jack Dempsey after a knockout in the 1920s). Reagan's show of wit and will aroused universal admiration for his courage.

Reagan's economic program gained ground along with his recovery. Enough Democrats—sympathetic southern "boll weevils" or centrists and liberals frightened by his popularity—went along to pass it by overwhelming majorities. On August 4, 1981, Reagan signed the Economic Recovery Tax Act, which cut personal income taxes 25 percent across the board over thirty-three months, lowered the maximum rate from 70 to 50 percent for 1982, cut the capital-gains tax from a 28 percent maximum to 20 percent, and offered a broad array of other tax concessions.

The "new beginning" advanced an old idea, its hour come round again: it was Alexander Hamilton's principle that more cash in the hands of the rich would benefit society at large, since the rich would invest their money productively. A closer parallel lay in the 1920s. Reaganomics amounted to Mellonomics warmed over. Like Coolidge's treasury secretary Andrew Mellon, Reagan offered some tax relief to all, but rolled back mainly the upper brackets. On this point the parallel was precise. Reagan's first tax reduction in 1981, like Mellon's in 1921, brought the maximum rate down to 50 percent. Both had greater reductions in mind.

Budget Director David A. Stockman, a young, former two-term

congressman trained in theology, crunched the numbers through his computers. He soon affirmed the parallel with what in the Hoover years had been denounced as the "trickle-down" theory—help the rich and benefits will trickle down to the rest. In conversations with a reporter, Stockman confided that the promise of an across-the-board reduction "was always a Trojan horse to bring down the top rate. It's kind of hard to sell 'trickle-down,' " he explained, "so the supply-side formula was the only way to get a tax policy that was really 'trickle down.' " Surprisingly, after a presidential show of taking Stockman "to the woodshed" for chastisement, Stockman stayed on for a time as budget director.

Reaganomics departed from the Coolidge record mainly in its mounting deficits and in their major cause—growing expenditures for the armed forces. This category of spending was considered untouchable, unless it was to be increased. While Republican administrations of the 1920s had steadily reduced the national debt by holding the line on government expenditures, the Republican administration of the 1980s built ever-larger deficits. Many expected them, but few foresaw that the new administration would soon run up debts larger than those under all its predecessors put together.

Whatever the administration's preference, it soon became clear that most items other than defense were also politically inviolable. The biggest category in the projected $700 billion budget involved payments to individuals: social security checks, pension checks, reimbursements for Medicare and Medicaid services, veterans' checks, and welfare checks. About 48 cents of every dollar the government spent thus went to social groups capable of capturing attention in Congress. Defense accounted for about 25 cents; interest payments for another 10 cents. Of the remaining 17 cents, about 9 cents went to entrenched operations like the Foreign Service, the FBI, the national parks, and the Weather Bureau, while the other 8 cents went for highways, services to the handicapped, and the like.

In trying to cut the budget, Stockman and his staff were practically limited to that last 17 cents in the dollar. There was not enough waste and fraud to make the cuts that had been so easily promised in the campaign. "It means," Stockman said, "I've got to cut the highway program. It means I've got to cut milk-price supports . . . Social Security student benefits . . . education and student loans . . . manpower training and housing. . . . I've got to shut down the synfuels program and a lot of other programs."

BUDGET CUTS   The administration was as good as its word. Along with the 1981 tax cuts went budget cuts of $35.2 billion, while defense spending in 1982 went up $12.3 billion. Budget cuts were aimed at educational programs, along with health, housing, urban aid, food stamps, school meals, the National Endowments for the Arts and Humanities, and the Corporation for Public Broadcasting. Synthetic-fuel projects were completely canceled as oil imports continued to rise.

Reagan promised to retain a "safety net" for the "truly needy." This spelled a departure from the task of encouraging welfare recipients to seek work while keeping them on the rolls. The new approach was to target for aid only those who could not work because of disability or child care. This, in fact, had been the original purpose of New Deal welfare, but during the New Deal the government had provided WPA jobs for those able to work.

In 1981 the administration put across its position that support from Aid for Dependent Children (AFDC) should last only four months after one joined the working poor, and that every dollar earned should reduce one's welfare payments by that amount. As a consequence more than 400,000 people lost AFDC coverage, many of whom also lost the benefits of Medicaid. The administration argued that the working poor would keep working despite the loss of AFDC-Medicaid, and studies confirmed this in many cases. Still, a determination to work proved costly. Many working mothers, however eager to be self-reliant, refused to penalize their children and returned to welfare full time. "I tried to do it the good old American way," the *Los Angeles Times* quoted one working mother as saying in 1983, "but I got my hands slapped because I was contributing to society." She went back on welfare.

Cuts in programs for the disadvantaged, added to problems in the private economic sector, raised the percentage of persons under the poverty level from 11.7 in 1979 to 15.3 in 1983. By 1984 one of five Americans was at or below 125 percent of the poverty level. Edwin Meese III, counselor to the president and later attorney-general, nevertheless commented that he had seen no "authoritative evidence" of hunger, only "anecdotal evidence." People went to soup kitchens "because the food is free." The president expressed a similar skepticism.

Wall Street, perversely fearful that a rising public debt would send interest rates up, responded to the most pro-business president in years with sagging bond and stock markets. A business slump and rising unemployment carried through most of 1982. In the fiscal year 1982 the deficit nearly doubled to $110.6 billion, and the total national debt went above $1 trillion for the first time. Government economic policy was strangely out of sync, a combination of fiscal stimulus (tax cuts) and monetary restraint (interest rates kept high by an independent Federal Reserve to control inflation).

"Oh, Me, Too —Why, When We're at the Ranch, I Just Love Camping Out!" *This cartoon suggests that behind President Reagan's cuts in social programs lay a callous attitude toward the needy.*

Aides persuaded the president that to reassure the public about deficits and the threat of inflation the government needed "revenue enhancements," a fine euphemism for tax increases. With Reagan lending support, Congress and the administration cobbled together the Tax Equity and Fiscal Responsibility Bill of 1982, signed by the president on September 3, which would raise an estimated $98.3 billion by reversing some of the previous year's concessions to business, by closing such "loopholes" as speedier depreciation of equipment, and by raising excise taxes such as those on cigarettes, telephone service, and airline tickets. The new law would become effective on January 1, 1983, once the fall elections were safely out of the way.

Having turned around on taxation, Reagan proceeded in the midterm elections to pursue the rhetoric of supply-side economics. "Stay the course" was his slogan. Perseverance would give the tax cuts time to work their magic. But it was the economic slump that persevered through November, with unemployment standing at 10.4 percent. The Republicans experienced the usual, if moderate, midterm losses. The Democrats gained 26 seats in the House for a margin of 269 to 166, but in the Senate there remained a Republican margin of 54 to 46.

Over the next two years, the administration adopted further tax increases, never as such but under some euphemism, and in forms less visible than income-tax rates. The Social Security Amendment of 1983, signed on April 20, counted social security benefits as taxable income for the first time. A previously scheduled social security tax increase was put into effect a year early. The Deficit Reduction Act of 1984, quietly signed by the president while the spotlight was on the Democratic National Convention, raised taxes an estimated $50 billion, again through complex and not highly visible means. Altogether, however, these increases ran behind the earlier reductions, Band-Aids hardly adequate to stanch the revenue hemorrhage begun in 1981.

NEW PRIORITIES   Like Coolidge and Harding in the 1920s, Reagan named to government posts people who were less than sympathetic to the regulatory functions for which they were responsible, rendering such regulation less than effective. The most visible early example was Interior Secretary James Watt, who had a gift for provocative denunciations of environmentalists. A Colorado champion of the "Sagebrush Rebellion," which proposed to turn public lands over to the states, he breezily proposed to encourage commercial development of public resources because the end of the world was near. He was finally forced out of office by the uproar over an offensive remark about affirmative-action appointments.

From the start the administration betrayed a failure to comprehend potential conflicts of interest in offices of public trust, and a dangerous insensitivity to borderline ethics and outright scandals which one pundit soon labeled the "sleaze factor." Secretary of Labor Raymond Donovan, for instance, was pursued by allegations of payoffs and other crimes that involved his New Jersey construction firm. Donovan finally had to leave the cabinet in 1984 under indictment, but was later acquitted of defrauding the New York City Transit Authority.

Anne Gorsuch Burford had to resign as administrator of the Environmental Protection Agency (EPA) after the disclosure of favors to industrial polluters who were former clients. Rita Lavelle, chief of toxic waste cleanup, the "Superfund" at the EPA, was accused of favoritism to polluters. She was fired and later convicted of perjury before a congressional committee. In 1982 William J. Casey, despite his access to classified information as director of the CIA, traded personal oil and computer stocks worth $3 million, and until 1983 refused to put his assets into a blind trust.

Shadows also hung over two of the president's three chief advisers. Edwin Meese got loans on favorable terms from California cronies who later turned up with federal appointments. Michael Deaver, the president's deputy chief of staff, obtained a sweetheart loan from a person who later became an officeholder. Once he left office in 1985, he, like presidential aide Lyn Nofziger earlier, set up a profitable counseling business which traded on his connections. Both eventually wound up under indictment for their activities.

In April 1984 the *New Republic* printed the names of forty-five Reaganites so tainted, although nothing to that point offered muck-raking journalists such raw meat as Teapot Dome or Watergate had. The president himself remained so totally untouched by hints of impropriety that Representative Patricia Schroeder (D, Colo.) tagged the Reagan reign the "Teflon Presidency," where the buck never stopped because the blame never stuck.

As in the 1920s organized labor encountered severe setbacks during the Reagan years. Nearly half of all union members, entranced by Reagan's personality and showmanship, had voted for him against the advice of their leaders. Reagan himself made much of being the only president to have headed a national union (the Screen Actors Guild), but his appointees to the National Labor Relations Board tended to favor management. In 1981, early in his term, Reagan himself set the anti-labor tone of industrial relations for the decade by firing members of the Professional Air Traffic Controllers who went on strike. The union, ironically, had been among the few to support Reagan's election, but that did not prevent its total destruction by the president.

Feminists were offended by Reagan's opposition to the Equal Rights Amendment and abortion on demand, by the cuts in welfare that aggravated the "feminization" of poverty, and by his opposition to the cause of equal pay for jobs of comparable worth, a practice which remained confined mainly to highly paid executives. Women in opposition were little mollified by his naming the first woman justice to the Supreme Court, Sandra Day O'Connor. Polls consistently reported a "gender gap" in opinion on Reagan, who had less support among women than among men.

Blacks and other minorities shared with women aggravation at the administration's limited support for affirmative-action programs in employment. In the administration itself the Civil Rights Commission reported in 1982 that only 8 percent of its appointments had gone to females and 8 percent to minorities, in contrast to 12 and 17 percent, respectively, under Carter. Because of the commission's criticisms the president in 1983 fired three members and tried to fire two more.

Funds for civil-rights enforcement were among those targeted for reduction, and the Equal Employment Opportunity Commission's staff was sharply reduced. The administration supported in the courts the action of its Internal Revenue Service in granting tax exemptions to fundamentalist schools which practiced racial segregation. On that it was overruled by the Supreme Court, 8 to 1.

THE DEFENSE BUILDUP   Reagan's conduct of foreign policy was governed by the idea that trouble in the world stemmed mainly from Moscow. He believed that Americans had overlearned the lessons of Vietnam and forgotten the lessons of Munich. He speeded the arms race with a major buildup of nuclear and conventional weapons, to close the gap that he claimed had developed between Soviet and American forces. It was reminiscent of John F. Kennedy's "missile gap"—and equally groundless. While preaching retrenchment in everything else, Reagan had promised in the campaign an increase in defense appropriations of 7 percent after inflation. He insisted on sticking to that goal, thus creating a bonanza for defense contractors.

Defense Secretary Caspar Weinberger, who had earned the name "Cap the Knife" as Nixon's budget director, now seemed hard-put to meet a weapon he did not like. The B-1 bomber, halted by Carter because of doubts as to its effectiveness, went back into production. The MX missiles were brought back and placed in hardened silos. So much money poured into Pentagon coffers as to strain the craft of weapons makers in thinking up exotic and costly hi-tech devices. Less skill if more brass went into Pentagon bills for $659 ashtrays, $750 toilet seats, $7,600 coffee brewers, and $9,600 wrenches. Congressional revelations of overcharges in 1985 raised a question of whether the least truly needy "welfare mother" on the government payroll might be General Dynamics or General Electric.

One deputy undersecretary of defense told a reporter that the United States could recover from a nuclear war. People simply needed to evacuate to the country, dig holes, and cover each with two doors and three feet of dirt. "It's the dirt that does it," he said. Such bellicose talk backfired when it set off massive protests calling for a "freeze" on all nuclear weapons development and a declaration of "no first use" in Europe, where Allied nuclear weapons offset a Soviet advantage in conventional forces.

Reagan recovered the rhetoric of John Foster Dulles and the Kennedy inaugural to express American resolve in the face of "Communist aggression anywhere in the world." At his first news conference he pronounced the Soviet rulers men who "reserved unto themselves the right to commit any crime, to lie, to cheat." Some day, however, the West would "transcend Communism," leaving it "a sad, bizarre chapter in human history whose last pages are even now being written." But, as yet, he said in February 1981, they still sought "world domination through world rule of Communist states."

The massive demonstration against nuclear weapons, New York City, June 12, 1982.

THE AMERICAS Reagan's ruling passion, however, seemed to be Central America. Like Reaganomics at home, policies there replicated some old themes. From time to time since the Monroe Doctrine in 1823 Central America had been a bone of contention between great powers. The United States had feared revolutionary anarchy at its doorstep, whether as cause or result of foreign influence. But American fears of Spanish, British, French, or now Russian imperialism had so far proved overblown because these powers always had deeper involvements and higher priorities elsewhere.

In the month of Reagan's 1981 inauguration an endemic guerrilla war in El Salvador intensified. It was, his State Department declared, a textbook case of indirect armed aggression by the Soviets. Many of the weapons reaching the Salvadoran rebels were American arms earlier seized in Vietnam and Ethiopia. The administration therefore abandoned Jimmy Carter's efforts to promote a compromise and sent in more arms and advisers to help the government of President José Napoleon Duarte. The fighting persisted on through the 1980s, but after elections in 1982 showed heavy turnouts in support of moderate candidates, Duarte's government gained a tenuous stability, but one still threatened from both the left and right.

Jimmy Carter had confronted another trouble spot in Nicaragua. Carter had decided that a rebel victory over the corrupt regime of dictator Anastasio Somoza was inevitable, even though Cuban-sponsored "Sandinistas" were part of the rebel National Liberation Front (FSLN). America's best hope was to help democratic elements in the Front, but the Sandinistas gradually emerged dominant once Somoza's government fell.

The Reagan State Department claimed that the Sandinista government in Nicaragua was funneling Soviet and Cuban arms to Salvadoran rebels. The administration's response was to set the CIA and the American ambassador in Honduras to mobilizing guerrilla bands of disgruntled Nicaraguans, soon tagged "Contras." Along with outcast Miskito Indians and disillusioned democratic elements in Nicaragua, the CIA embraced cadres of experienced former National Guardsmen and other supporters of Somoza. United States and Honduran forces engaged in joint maneuvers just over the Nicaraguan border. The administration's hidden agenda, it soon became clear, was not only to interdict arms for El Salvador but to overthrow the Sandinistas, to make them "cry uncle," in Reagan's words.

Critics of Reagan's anti-Sandinista policy argued that American involvement ensured the Marxist forces in Central America would emerge as victorious representatives of local nationalism against Yanqui imperialism. Supporters countered by warning that American failure to act would allow for a repeat of Communist victories in Nicaragua, and that Honduras, Guatemala, and other neighboring countries would eventually enter the Communist camp.

U.S.-backed Contra rebels at a camp in southern Nicaragua.

Fearing a military tinderbox in Central America, neighboring countries pressed for a negotiated settlement. Representatives of Mexico, Panama, Colombia, and Venezuela began the Contadora Process (after the Panamanian island where they first met). By October 1983 the Contadora countries had advanced the first of many proposals for a compromise peace, the withdrawal of foreign advisers, and an end to imports of foreign arms. Drawn into the talks, the Reagan administration raised so many technical objections as to suggest that it would settle for nothing less than an overthrow of the Sandinistas.

THE MIDDLE EAST   The Middle East has so often violated American expectations as to be a maddening enigma for policy-makers, yet an all-too-likely tinderbox for world war. The region has proven intractable to more than one president. It consumed the Carter administration not long after Carter had scored perhaps his greatest triumph by making peace between Egypt and Israel.

No peaceable end seemed possible for the prolonged, bloody Iran-Iraq war, entangled as it was with the passions of Islamic fundamentalism. In 1984 both sides began to attack oil tankers in the Persian Gulf, a major source of the world's oil. (The main international response was the sale of arms to both sides.) Nor was any settlement in sight for Afghanistan, where the Russians had bogged down as badly as the Americans had in Vietnam.

American governments continued to see Israel as the strongest and most reliable ally in the region, all the while seeking to encourage moderate Arab groups. But the forces of moderation were dealt a blow during the mid-1970s when Lebanon, long an enclave of peace despite its ethnic complexity, collapsed into an anarchy of warring groups. The capital, Beirut, became a battleground of Sunni and Shi'ite Muslims, the Druze, the Palestine Liberation Organization (PLO), Arab Christians, Syrian invaders cast as peacekeepers, and Israelis responding to PLO attacks across the border.

Israel's aim in the area was to establish peaceful borders; America's, to prevent Russian involvement that might come through its close ties with Syria. As a key to long-term peace the United States pressed upon Israel the need for a Palestinian homeland on the West Bank of the Jordan River, preferably under the control of the Jordanian government. It was to no avail, but the administration surmised that the Israelis might become more amenable if the PLO could be eliminated as a fighting force. The Israelis then got the impression, rightly or not, that a speech by Secretary of State Alexander Haig calling for "international action" to end the anarchy in Lebanon was a signal to move.

In June 1982 Israeli forces pushed the PLO out of southern Lebanon all the way north to Beirut. The United States neither endorsed nor condemned the invasion, but sent a special ambassador, Philip Habib, to negotiate a settlement. That August Israel began heavy shelling of PLO strongholds in Beirut, and horrified American reactions led to the replacement of Secretary Haig with George Shultz.

Habib finally arranged an agreement for French, Italian, and American troops to supervise the withdrawal of PLO troops from Beirut. The administration tried to build a broad international settlement, with a homeland for the Palestinians and a guarantee of Israel's borders by its Arab neighbors—a hopeful goal, but one defeated by Middle Eastern passions. Israeli troops then moved into Beirut and, while they looked the other way, Christian militiamen took revenge for the murder of their president by slaughtering women and children left in Palestinian refugee camps.

French, Italian, and American forces moved back into Lebanon as "peacekeepers," but in such small numbers as to become only targets. Angry Muslims kept them under constant harassment. American warships and planes responded by shelling and bombing Muslim positions in the highlands behind Beirut, which only increased Mus-

A terrorist bomb attack devastated U.S. Marine headquarters near Beirut International Airport, October 23, 1983—241 marines were killed, and 80 wounded, in the attack.

lim resentment. On October 23, 1983, a truck laden with explosives burst into the U.S. Marine quarters at Beirut airport and exploded, leaving 241 Americans dead. Reagan declared that a continued American presence was "central to our credibility," but soon began preparations to pull out. On February 7, 1984, he announced that the marines would be "redeployed" to warships offshore. The Israelis pulled back to southern Lebanon, while the Syrians remained in eastern Lebanon. And bloody anarchy remained a way of life in a long-peaceful country.

GRENADA Fortune, as it happened, presented Reagan the chance for an easy triumph closer to home, a "rescue mission" which eclipsed news of the debacle in Lebanon. On the island of Grenada, the smallest independent country in the Western Hemisphere, a leftist government under Prime Minister Maurice Bishop had admitted Cuban workers to build a new airfield and signed military agreements with Communist countries. In October 1983 General Hudson Austin and an even more radical military council seized power and killed Bishop.

Appeals from the governments of neighboring islands led Reagan to order 1,900 marines to invade the island, depose Austin, and evacuate a small group of American students at Grenada's medical school. Grenadan troops and Cuban workers had little chance of holding on—although later reports suggested shockingly poor coordination of American forces.

The U.N. General Assembly condemned the action and many Latin Americans saw it as a revival of gunboat diplomacy, but it was popular among Grenadans and their neighbors, and immensely popular in the United States. The action made Reagan look decisive, although it was a lopsided affair, and served notice on Latin American revolutionaries to beware of American force.

REAGAN'S SECOND TERM

THE ELECTION OF 1984 The Reagan luck, running low in 1982, returned in force two years later. Contradictory policies of fiscal stimulus (tax cuts and heavy expenditures for defense) and monetary restraint (high interest rates) brought at least in the short run an economic recovery without inflation. The gradual unraveling of the OPEC cartel and resultant decline in oil prices was the greatest stroke of luck for Reagan and the economy.

Republican strategy for the presidential election worked on the old principle that if you have a good thing you should stick with it.

Reagan, the consummate practitioner of politics as performing art, appeared before the camera in carefully staged and rehearsed situations. He delivered prepared lines in front of enthusiastic crowds and posed before scenic backdrops.

By contrast the nominee of the Democrats, former vice-president Walter Mondale, never quite got his act together. Endorsed by the AFL-CIO, by the National Organization for Women, and by many blacks despite a serious challenge from Jesse Jackson, Mondale was tagged the candidate of the "special interests"—a curious turn-around of a term which once implied fat cats. Mondale set a precedent by choosing as his running mate New York representative Geraldine Ferraro. Unhappily for the Democratic campaign, she was quickly placed on the defensive by the need to explain her spouse's complicated finances, something no male candidate had been called upon to do. One politician observed that "the pioneers take all the arrows." The attention focused on her husband's finances made it awkward for Democrats to use the administration's "sleaze factor" as an issue.

Mondale further complicated his campaign by a fit of frankness in his acceptance speech. "Mr. Reagan will raise taxes, and so will I," he told the convention. "He won't tell you. I just did." Remembered as a political blunder, it was a brilliant opportunity missed. Although it was reported in the *San Francisco Chronicle,* Mondale seemed unaware that just the previous day, while attention was focused on the Democratic convention, Mr. Reagan had quietly signed a bill that raised taxes $50 billion, the Deficit Reduction Act of 1984. Nor did he mention that Reagan had signed tax increases in each of the

The Democratic ticket in 1984: Walter Mondale and Geraldine Ferraro.

two previous years. Reagan responded by vowing never to approve a tax increase, and by chiding Mondale for his candid stand.

Mondale never caught up. The closest he came was in the first of two televised debates when Reagan used an old one-liner once too often: "There you go again." Mondale reminded him that the last time had been in response to Carter's warning that Reagan would propose reductions in social security, which he had done right after entering office. For once Reagan became rattled and responded to a final question incoherently. In the second debate, however, he recovered with a new zinger. Responding to a question about the issue of age, the seventy-three-year-old president said: "I'm not going to exploit for political purposes my opponent's youth and inexperience."

In the end, Reagan took 58.8 percent of the popular vote and lost only Minnesota and the District of Columbia. His coattails were not as strong, however. Republicans had a net gain of only fifteen seats in the House, and lost two in the Senate.

THE LANDSLIDE SYNDROME   Reagan's overwhelming victory brought him to a testing time between his charmed life and the malevolent fate which seems to pursue presidents who win such prodigious electoral victories. Victimized most recently were Richard Nixon, who met his Watergate soon after winning reelection in a landslide, and Lyndon Johnson, who got stuck in the Vietnam quagmire.

Entering his second term, Reagan had a goodly share of political time bombs ticking away. They were planted around the world from Nicaragua to Afghanistan. At home there were the episodes of borderline ethics and outright scandals that had emerged during his first term. Strains seemed bound to arise as well in a coalition of the indulgent rich and the ultra-righteous.

Post-election changes in the administration raised distant early warning signals—especially the departure of his first-term management team: Michael Deaver for a private consulting business soon accused of influence peddling, Edwin Meese for the Justice Department, and Chief-of-Staff James Baker for the Treasury in an unusual job swap with former secretary Donald Regan. Regan, however, lacked any background in politics. He may have met a payroll, one cliché had it, but he had never carried a precinct, and his forceful management style ruffled the feathers of politicos. Not long after this reshuffling, in March 1985 a much younger, more vigorous, and clearly abler new leader emerged in the Soviet Union, Mikhail Gorbachev.

Still, the Reagan luck held out. OPEC continued to lower oil prices, sending inflation down and the stock market up. In his State of the Union message, Reagan called for "a Second American Revolution of hope and opportunity." He dared Congress to raise taxes. His veto pen was ready: "Go ahead and make my day," he said in echo of yet another movie line.

TAX REFORM Through much of 1985 the president was back on the campaign trail, this time drumming up support for a tax simplification which would eliminate loopholes and set only two or three brackets. It was a retreat from the principle of a progressive tax which levied higher rates on high incomes, but that principle had long since been eroded by a variety of complex tax dodges within the reach mainly of the rich.

After long and vigorous debate that ran nearly two years, Congress passed, and in September 1986 the president finally signed, a comprehensive Tax Reform Act. The new measure would by 1988 reduce the number of tax brackets from fourteen to two, and reduce rates from the maximum of 50 percent to 15 and 28 percent—the lowest since Coolidge. Tax shelters were sharply limited. Economists were cautious about predicting the effects of the tax "simplification." One pundit noted that the tax law remained a good bit longer than the Constitution and a good bit harder to understand.

ARMS CONTROL Meanwhile Reagan, for all his bluff talk about Russia's being an "evil empire," seemed unwilling to go out as the first president since World War II to arrive at no agreement on arms with the Soviets. Presidents as a rule, it seems, begin to think more about their places in history as their terms advance, and all would like to go down as peacemakers. In November 1985 for the first time in six years an American president met with the leader of the Soviet Union. After much preliminary maneuvering, Reagan and Gorbachev met in Geneva on November 19 for a series of talks. On November 21 they signed six agreements on cultural and scientific exchanges and other matters.

They also issued statements, but reached no agreements, on arms limitations. A major stumbling block seemed to be Reagan's refusal to consider any restrictions on his pursuit of the Strategic Defense Initiative (often called "Star Wars"), which he had announced in 1983. An elaborate dream of building a shield in space against incoming missiles, the SDI seemed a consummation devoutly to be wished, a release from the threat of planetary destruction. The plan involved a combination of computers, satellites, mirrors in space, nuclear devices, and laser beams far beyond present capabilities. In the opinion of many, if not most, scientists, it was technologically beyond reach in the foreseeable future. To some, SDI stirred memories of the impenetrable French Maginot Line which the Nazis sim-

Soviet premier Mikhail Gorbachev (left) *and U.S. president Ronald Reagan during a light moment at the Geneva summit, November 1985.*

ply outflanked in 1940. And the necessary experiments raised questions of violating the Anti-Ballistic Missile Treaty of 1972.

Nearly a year later, on sudden notice and with limited preparation, Gorbachev and Reagan met in Reykjavik, Iceland, for two days. Hopes leaped high on reports that the two were on the verge of major decisions for the extensive limitation of nuclear weapons. Reagan said later that the United States put forward the "most sweeping and generous arms-control proposal in history," but the talks collapsed on disagreement over SDI. Gorbachev insisted that the ABM Treaty forbade any experiments in space for another ten years; Reagan refused to accept that interpretation and the talks collapsed, but without slamming the door on further exploration. Gorbachev would later hold out at least the possibility of eliminating short-range nuclear missiles from Europe.

THE IRAN-CONTRA AFFAIR   The year 1986 opened with a terrible tragedy on January 28 when the space shuttle *Challenger* exploded minutes after liftoff, killing its seven crew members, including a teacher. Later investigations revealed evidence of startling failures at NASA to heed warnings about the danger of launch at low temperatures. But the revelations there had little effect on the ratings of a president whose responsibility was remote and whose "Teflon shield" seemed indestructible.

Then came a double blow on November 4, 1986. In the midterm elections the Senate went from a Republican majority of 53 to 47 to Democratic control by 55 to 45. Senators elected in 1980 on Reagan's coattails lacked that advantage this time. All seven Senate races in the South went to Democrats. Farm problems in the Midwest damaged Republicans there. The Democrats picked up only six seats in the House, but they increased their already comfortable margin there to 259 to 176. For his last two years as president Reagan would face an opposition Congress.

What was worse, on election day one of the administration's political time bombs went off. Reports arrived from an obscure publication in Beirut that the United States had been secretly selling arms to Iran in hope of securing the release of American hostages held in Lebanon by extremist groups sympathetic to Iran. Such actions contradicted Reagan's repeated public insistence that his administration would never negotiate with terrorists. The disclosures angered America's allies as well as many Americans who vividly remembered the 1979 Iranian takeover of their country's embassy in Teheran.

Yet there was more to the sordid story. Over the next several months, a series of revelations reminiscent of the Watergate affair disclosed a more complicated and even more incredible series of covert activities carried out by administration officials. At the center of the Iran-Contra affair was the much-decorated Marine Lieutenant-Colonel Oliver North. A swashbuckling aide to the National Security Council who specialized in counterterrorism, North had been running secret operations from the basement of the White House involving many governmental, private, and foreign individuals. His most farfetched scheme sought to use the profits gained from the secret sale of military hardware to Iran to subsidize the Contra rebels fighting in Nicaragua, at a time when Congress had voted to ban such aid.

North's activities, it turned out, had been approved by National Security Adviser Robert McFarlane, his successor Admiral John Poindexter, and CIA Director William Casey. Secretary of State George Shultz and Secretary of Defense Caspar Weinberger both criticized the arms sale to Iran, but their objections were ignored and they were thereafter kept in the dark about what was going on. Later, on three occasions, Shultz threatened to resign over the continuing operation of the "pathetic" scheme. As information about the secret (and illegal) dealings surfaced in the press, McFarlane attempted suicide, Poindexter resigned, North was fired, and Casey, who denied any connection, left the CIA for health reasons. Casey died shortly thereafter from a brain tumor.

The White House, meanwhile, assumed a siege mentality as the president's popularity plummeted. "The Presidency is paralyzed," declared one Republican senator. Under increasing criticism and amid growing doubts of his own credibility and ability, Reagan appointed both an independent counsel and a three-man commission led by former Republican senator John Tower to investigate the spreading scandal. The Tower Commission issued a devastating report early in 1987 which placed much of the responsibility for the bungled Iran-Contra affair on Reagan's loose management style. The report portrayed the president as uninformed and forgetful, a leader detached from the inner workings of his own administration.

Worse was yet to come. During the spring and summer of 1987, a joint House-Senate investigating committee began holding televised hearings into the Iran-Contra affair. The sessions dominated public attention for months and revealed a tangled web of inept financial and diplomatic transactions, the shredding of incriminating government documents, crass profiteering, and misguided patriotism. With the special prosecutor on their heels, Poindexter and North initially invoked the Fifth Amendment and refused to testify; they relented after being granted limited immunity from prosecution. North's four-day appearance before the committee in a uniform festooned with medals and ribbons was a bravura performance composed of patriotic rhetoric, self-righteous preaching, skillful evasion, and beguiling sincerity. For a few days his passionate defense of his actions won over the hearts of many Americans, and he became the poster boy of the American right. But his sudden popularity could not obscure the clumsiness and utter naiveté of the Iran-Contra affair. The hearings confirmed Reagan's insistence that he had not known about the diversion of funds to the Contras, but testimony also contradicted his earlier claim that the sale of arms to Iran was intended to open up new diplomatic channels rather than buy the freedom of American hostages.

The Iran-Contra affair left support for the Nicaraguan Contras badly eroded in the Congress, and it undermined much of Reagan's popularity. One Democratic senator said that the president had "become a kindly old relative that you don't have to pay much attention to. He's just run his course." The investigations of the independent counsel led to six indictments in 1988. A Washington jury found Oliver North guilty of three relatively minor charges but innocent of nine more serious counts, apparently reflecting the jury's reasoning that he acted as an agent of higher-ups. Of those involved in the affair, only John Poindexter got a jail sentence—six months for his conviction on five felony counts of obstructing and lying to Congress.

CENTRAL AMERICA The Iran-Contra affair showed the lengths to which members of the Reagan administration would go to support the rebels fighting the ruling Sandinistas in Nicaragua. Fearing heightened Soviet and American involvement in Central America, neighboring countries pressed during the mid-1980s for a negotiated settlement to the unrest in Nicaragua. In 1987 Costa Rican president Oscar Arias received the Nobel Peace Prize for designing an ambitious new regional peace plan signed by five Central American presidents. The agreement, signed on August 7, called for cease-fires in all countries and actions to reduce tensions, promote democratic reforms, and begin negotiations. Outside aid to combatants—including American assistance to the Nicaraguan Contras—was to be suspended. But by the end of the year, the plan's implementation continued to be hampered by posturing, foot-dragging, and finger-pointing among the parties concerned. In January 1988 Daniel Ortega, the Nicaraguan president, pledged to negotiate directly with the Contra rebels.

In the spring of 1988 these negotiations produced a cease-fire agreement, ending nearly seven years of fighting in Nicaragua. Secretary of State George Shultz called the pact an "important step forward," but the settlement surprised and disappointed hardliners within the Reagan administration who saw in it a Contra surrender. The Contra leaders themselves, aware of the eroding support for their cause in the United States Congress, saw the truce as their only chance for tangible concessions such as amnesty for political prisoners, the return of the Contras from exile, and "unrestricted freedom of expression."

In neighboring El Salvador, the Reagan administration's attempt to shore up the centrist government of José Napoléon Duarte through economic and military aid was dealt a body blow when the far-right ARENA party scored an upset victory at the polls during the spring of 1988. Further embarrassment to the administration's Latin America policies occurred when a federal grand jury in Miami indicted Panama's military ruler, General Manuel Antonio Noriega, for drug trafficking. After Noriega refused to resign, the Reagan administration applied economic sanctions in the hope of provoking a domestic rebellion, only to see Noriega turn to Cuba for military aid and tighten his iron-fisted control of the country. Explained one frustrated White House official: "We announced the result—that Noriega must go—and then started thinking about how to make it happen. That's completely backwards." Everywhere in Central

America, it seemed in 1988, events conspired to highlight the limits of American power and the ineptness of administration initiatives.

LBOs AND S&Ls   Throughout the 1980s, social commentators repeatedly bemoaned the virus of greed and self-absorbed materialism that seemed to infect the nation. One prominent symptom was the largest outbreak of corporate mergers and acquisitions ever to befall the economy. Hijacking corporations was nothing new, but by the mid-1980s an innovative technique had come into play: leveraging the value of the company itself as a means of taking it over. The corporate "raiders" would buy out the target company's public stockholders with borrowed money, to be repaid from the future earnings of the company. They then used its value to underwrite voluminous "junk bonds"—speculative issues which drew investors into risky investments with the promise of very high returns. Given this magic act, no company was out of reach now, no matter how big. In the largest leveraged buyout of the decade, the investment firm of Kohlberg, Kravis, Roberts & Co. engineered the takeover of RJR-Nabisco Company in 1988 at a value of $24.9 billion.

The charm of the device was that the takeover targets got stuck with the debts, while stockholders could bail out at handsome prices driven up by the acquisition. Commonly, although not always, the company was then broken up and sold piece by piece on the principle that components could be sold off separately for more than the whole. A character in a popular movie of 1990 likened the process to stealing cars and selling the parts.

Beginning in 1978, Michael Milken ran a bustling junk-bond shop in Beverly Hills, far removed from his parent firm of Drexel, Burnham, Lambert in New York. In an MBA thesis at the Wharton School of Business, the future "junk king" had argued that interest on low-rated bonds had gone so high that the potential gain for investors outweighed the risk. Acting on his theory, he generated low-rated junk bonds and leveraged buyouts (LBOs) in massive lots.

Milken himself was a bundle of contradictions. The ultimate workaholic and health nut, he was in his office by 4:15 A.M., and abstained from alcohol, coffee, and other stimulants, even soft drinks. He generously endowed philanthropies for the have-nots. Yet his annual meeting for the high-rollers at the Beverly Hilton came to be known as "the Predators' Ball."

Defenders of the buyouts claimed that junk bonds raised long-term venture capital for innovators the conservative banks avoided. Milken, for example, helped finance MCI, a new long-distance telephone service, and Turner Broadcasting, which built a clutch of cable TV networks, including the worldwide Cable News Network.

High levels of debt, moreover, were said to discipline management to better performance in order to pay the interest they owed. The business writer Peter Drucker noted, however, that fear of corporate raiders was "the largest single cause for the increasing tendency of American companies to manage for the short term and let the future go hang." By the end of the 1980s, about one-fourth of the cash flow of American corporations was going to pay debt—incurred in some cases to ward off takeovers, a strategy known as taking the "poison pill."

In the quick profits the LBOs afforded stockholders who sold out at inflated prices lay one of the greatest temptations to criminal abuse of the system: "risk arbitrage." Simple arbitrage involved spotting small price discrepancies between markets, buying a stock or commodity low on one, and selling high on another—almost a sure thing with computers to detect the spreads and close the deals quickly. Risk arbitrage, on the other hand, meant buying stock in hope of profit from a later takeover—not so sure a thing, unless you had the inside scoop. But trading on inside information was a felony, and evidence of such crimes led to the discovery of yet others in what one financier called "the casino society."

In May 1986 the Securities and Exchange Commission charged a trader at Drexel, Burnham, Lambert on multiple counts of insider dealing. His case in turn led to others at several financial houses, where these "masters of the universe" (in the novelist Tom Wolfe's phrase) were arrested at their desks and led out in manacles. A bigger catch came in November 1986 with the arrest of Ivan Boesky, one of the more visible risk arbitrageurs, for trading on inside information. In 1985 Boesky had proclaimed to students at the University of California, Berkeley, "Greed is healthy. . . . You can be greedy and still feel good about yourself." Now Boesky struck a deal with the government to reduce his fine and imprisonment if he would finger informants, who included Michael Milken and others at Drexel, Burnham, Lambert.

The climax of the disclosures came in an SEC investigation of Drexel, which agreed in 1988 to pay the government $650 million to settle inside-trader charges, and to operate for three years under an administrative probation that held the appointment of high officers subject to SEC approval. By February 1990, however, the firm— founded in 1838—declared bankruptcy and began to liquidate. In the predators' fall, Milken took the deepest plunge. Indicted on ninety-six counts early in 1989, he pleaded guilty to six felonies, including conspiracy, security fraud, and helping Boesky file a false statement with the SEC. On November 21, 1990, a federal judge ended an era of financial mania when she sentenced Milken to ten years in prison plus three years of probation and 5,400 hours of community service.

Milken's shenanigans were not unusual during the 1980s. Other financial buccaneers saw quick profits to be made within the "thrift institutions"—the savings and loan banks (S&Ls) designed at first to serve aspiring homeowners. With variations, the business had long operated on what was called the 3–6–3 principle: take in deposits at 3 percent interest, lend the money at 6, and leave for the golf course at 3 o'clock. In 1934, to encourage home ownership, the New Deal set up the Federal Savings and Loan Insurance Corporation (FSLIC) to insure depositors and regulate the industry.

The system worked reasonably well until the mid-1960s, when inflation began to lift interest rates. The interest cost of deposits went up, but the prevailing belief in widespread home ownership kept legal ceilings on mortgage rates. Caught in the squeeze, the S&Ls turned to Congress for help, and by the early 1980s government began easing restrictions on the industry. In 1980 Congress raised the interest rates S&Ls could pay on deposits in an effort to make them more competitive with banks. But the mortgage rates they could offer remained frozen, which forced the S&Ls to pay higher interest than they could collect. At the same time Congress raised insurance ceilings from $40,000 to $100,000 per deposit.

Then in 1982 Congress "hit a home run" (in President Reagan's words) by permitting S&Ls to invest up to 40 percent of their assets in nonresidential real estate. High-rise office buildings began to clutter the landscape. California, not to be outdone, then permitted state-chartered thrifts to invest 100 percent of their assets in any venture, and other states followed suit. From a conservative industry designed to encourage homeowning, many of the S&Ls joined the high-rollers. They became major customers for Milken's junk bonds, among other risky ventures.

The opportunities for outrageous profits, with regulators and Congress reducing capital reserve requirements and looking the other way, brought hustlers flocking into the business, often with borrowed capital. The best way to rob a bank, an old saying has it, is to own one. Vernon Savings and Loan, which served a town of 12,000 in Texas, at one time kept a fleet of six jets; company funds also bought expensive homes for its head, and provided $5.5 million to decorate the walls.

At the peak of the S&L frenzy, Charles Keating of the Lincoln Savings and Loan Association in Irvine, California, paid himself $3.2 million a year, and at least $34 million in all to family members. Like others in the S&L crowd, he might have been able to keep a fairly low profile but for his generous donations to a group of influential senators, the "Keating Five," who were chastised by the Senate Ethics Committee for the appearance of impropriety. And Keating himself was arrested and hauled into court, to become, along with Michael Milken, one of the symbols of a corrupt age.

The looting extended beyond corporations into the federal treasury itself. The most conspicuous case in point was the Wedtech Corporation, a federal contractor in New York that raised 95 percent of its revenues from no-bid federal contracts won through Washington connections that reached directly into the White House. In all, more than two dozen people were convicted of Wedtech crimes, including members of Congress and the executive branch. One department—Housing and Urban Development (HUD)—had become, according to its former inspector-general, a "dumping ground" for political appointees by the White House. HUD secretary Samuel "Silent Sam" Pierce was a functionary whose department was so low on the administration's list of priorities that at one social occasion the president did not know who he was. The problems at the department remained invisible until 1989, when the new secretary, Jack Kemp, began to notice irregularities, and congressional committees began investigating millions of dollars in consulting fees paid to prominent Republicans for using influence with department officials. An internal audit showed that the dubious arrangements centered in a program designed to supply housing for low-income families. The administration had tried to eliminate the program, but instead it was bent to the wants of high-income contractors. Former interior secretary James Watt collected $400,000 as a consultant to housing developers, although he admitted to no expertise in housing. He just knew the right people. One senator's hometown got a $1 million swimming pool out of the program; Biloxi, Mississippi, got a fancy marina. Escrow agents who collected proceeds on sales of foreclosed houses often pocketed the money. One agent admitted to stealing about $5.5 million, but told the committee she had given much of it to the poor. The media tagged her "Robin HUD."

THE END OF THE 1980s   The gaining and spending of more and more money was a pervasive concern throughout the 1980s. Debt, all kinds of debt—personal, corporate, and governmental—increased dramatically during the decade. Whereas in the 1960s Americans on average saved 10 percent of their income, in 1987 the figure was less than 4 percent. The Reagan budget deficits also reached record levels as legislators reluctant to offend constituents by raising taxes or cutting popular programs engaged in talk and symbolic action with a president ideologically resistant to taxes. In 1985 three senators sponsored a measure, the Gramm-Rudman-Hollings Act, through which an irresolute Congress would impose on itself automatic spending cuts of $11.7 billion annually until a balanced budget was reached in fiscal year 1991. Although the measure easily passed both houses, Congress and the president found various dodges, such as raising excise taxes (less visible than the income tax), passing social programs on to the states, making unrealistic estimates of revenues, or placing certain expenditures "off budget." The federal debt nearly tripled from $908 billion in 1980 to $2.9 trillion at the end of the fiscal year, September 30, 1989.

Then, on October 19, 1987, the bill collector suddenly arrived at the nation's doorstep. On that "Black Monday," Wall Street, already buffeted by sharp declines the previous week, experienced a tidal wave of selling reminiscent of the 1929 crash, as the Dow Jones industrial average plummeted 508 points, or an astounding 22.6 percent. In the midst of the panic selling, one broker yelled: "This is going to make '29 look like a kiddie party." He was right. The market plunge was almost double the record 12.8 percent fall on October 28, 1929. Almost $560 billion in paper value disappeared, an amount larger than the gross national product of France. The chairman of the New York Stock Exchange employed a haunting nuclear metaphor to describe the market collapse, noting that it was the "nearest thing to a meltdown that I ever want to see." With cyclonic suddenness the nation's financial mood went from boom to gloom

An exhausted New York Stock Exchange trader at the close of "Black Monday," October 19, 1987.

during the fall of 1987. Several smaller brokerage houses went under amid the speculative whirlpool, thousands of investment bankers and stockbrokers were fired, consumer confidence took a beating, a few distraught traders committed suicide, and one irate customer murdered his broker and then killed himself. Wall Street's selling frenzy reverberated throughout the capitalist world, sending stock prices plummeting in Tokyo, London, Paris, and Toronto.

What caused the goring of the bull market? Some analysts argued that the runaway market of the 1980s had become artificially high, driven by excessive greed and hope rather than by the economy's actual performance. Others blamed new computerized trading programs that distorted market activity. But most agreed that the fundamental problem was the nation's spiraling indebtedness and chronically high trade deficits. Americans were consuming more than they were producing, importing the difference, and paying for imported goods with borrowed money and a dollar sharply declining in value. Foreign investors had lost confidence in Reaganomics and were no longer willing to finance America's spending binge. One economist recognized that there "is nobody in the world left to lend money to the U.S. That's what the market crash is telling us." The editors of *Business Week* declared, "The message of the Crash is clear: Americans have spent too much, borrowed too much, and imported too much. Now it has to stop."

In the aftermath of the calamitous selling spree on Black Monday, President Reagan tried to reassure the nation. He insisted that the "underlying economy remains sound," an unsettling echo of Herbert Hoover's equally sunny assurances in 1929. Few observers actually feared a depression of the magnitude of the 1930s; there were too many safeguards built into the system to allow that. But there was real concern of an impending recession, and this led business leaders and economists to attack the president for glossing over such a profound warning signal. Within a few weeks the White House did begin to take tepid and grudging action. Reagan agreed to work with Congress in developing a deficit-reduction package, and for the first time indicated that he was willing to include increased taxes in such a package. But the eventual compromise plan was so modest that it did little to restore investor confidence. As one Republican senator lamented, "There is a total lack of courage among those of us in the Congress to do what we all know has to be done."

If, as political scientist Harold D. Lasswell once put it, politics is about "who gets what, when, how," then people of the upper-income groups benefited most in a material way from the public policies of the 1980s. Jim Hightower, Democratic agriculture commissioner of Texas, said in 1987 that the Reagan years "produced one of the quickest and most regressive redistributions of wealth in American history." Congressional Budget Office data showed that from 1977 to 1987 (in 1987 dollars) after-tax family income of the lower 10 percent fell 10.5 percent; the average for the upper 10 percent of families rose 24.4 percent; and the highest 1 percent went up by 74.2 percent.

Against the picture that the president's supporters envisioned of roaring prosperity, burgeoning new technology, and 19 million new jobs in the Reagan years could be set the picture of uncounted beggars in the streets and homeless people sleeping in doorways, in cardboard boxes, and on heat grates—street scenes once associated with Calcutta. A variety of causes could be adduced for the shortage of low-cost housing: government had given up on building public housing; with the best of intentions, urban renewal had demolished blighted areas but provided no housing for the displaced; and owners had abandoned unprofitable buildings in poor neighborhoods or converted them into expensive condominiums. The last was called "gentrification." Other causes of homelessness included family disorganization, and the de-institutionalization of the mentally ill on the prospect of community mental health services which failed to materialize—a program started under President Kennedy but never adequately funded. By the summer of 1988, the *New York Times* estimated, more than 45.3 percent of the city's residents over sixteen constituted an underclass totally outside the labor force for lack of skills, lack of motivation, drug use, and other problems.

Still another group cast aside were those suffering from a terrifying new disease known as AIDS (acquired immune deficiency syndrome). At the beginning of the decade, public health officials began to report a strange new malady that primarily struck gay men and intravenous drug users. Those infected with the virus showed signs of fatigue, developed a strange combination of infections, and eventually died. Frustrated by a lack of federal funds, researchers struggled to discern the origins of the new malady. Eventually they linked it to a virus originating in Africa that was most likely spread to the United States via Haiti. People contracted it by coming into contact with the blood or body fluids of an infected person. One reason the Reagan administration showed little interest in AIDS was that it initially was viewed as a "gay" disease. Patrick Buchanan, the conservative spokesman who served as White House director of communications, said that homosexuals had "declared war on nature, and now nature is extracting an awful retribution." By 1991, however, AIDS had claimed over 106,000 American lives and was spreading rapidly among the larger population. Nearly 2 million Americans were estimated to be carrying the deadly virus. The potential for

A quilt commemorating the deaths of many thousands of Americans from AIDS, displayed before the White House in October 1988.

exponential spread of the virus, owing to the very long incubation period before the onset of symptoms, provoked the surgeon general to launch a controversial public education program that included encouraging "safe sex" through the use of condoms. With no prospect for an early cure and with skyrocketing treatment costs, AIDS has emerged as one of the nation's most horrifying and intractable dilemmas.

A HISTORIC TREATY   In the midst of a weak, unpredictable economic situation, the main prospect for positive achievement before the end of Reagan's second term seemed to lie in arms-reduction agreements with the Soviet government. Under Mikhail Gorbachev, the Soviets pursued renewed détente in order to free their energies to address pressing domestic problems. The logjam that had impeded arms negotiations since the summit at Reykjavik suddenly broke in February 1987, when Gorbachev announced that he was willing to deal separately on a medium-range missile treaty. After nine more months of strenuous, highly technical negotiations, Reagan and Gorbachev met amid much fanfare in Washington on December 9, 1987, and signed a treaty to eliminate intermediate-range (300–3,000 miles) nuclear forces (INF). It was an epochal event, not only because it marked the first time that the two nations had agreed to destroy a whole class of weapons systems but because it represented a key first step toward the eventual end of the arms race altogether. Under the terms of the treaty, the United States would destroy 859 missiles, and the Russians would eliminate 1,752. Provisions were also made for on-site inspections by each side to verify compliance. Still, this winnowing would represent only 4 percent of the total nuclear missile count on both sides. Arms-control advocates thus looked toward a second and more comprehensive treaty dealing with long-range strategic missiles.

But virtually all Kremlin watchers were heartened by continuing evidence that General Secretary Gorbachev was successfully liberalizing Soviet domestic life and aggressively improving East-West foreign relations. The Soviets suddenly began stressing cooperation with the West in dealing with "hot spots" around the world. They urged the Palestine Liberation Organization to recognize Israel's right to exist and advocated a greater role for the U.N. in the volatile Persian Gulf. Perhaps the most dramatic symbol of a thawing Cold War was the phased withdrawal of 115,000 Soviet troops from Afghanistan, which began in May 1988.

THE REAGAN LEGACY   Looking back over 1987, Nancy Reagan described the year as "Terrible. Next year has got to be better." She was wrong. As the Reagan presidency neared its end, its public image was rocked by dissension and scandal within the administration itself. As indictments were handed up in the spring of 1988 against Oliver North, John Poindexter, and two other conspirators involved in the Iran-Contra affair, President Reagan provoked criticism by continuing to label North "a hero" and by insisting that North was innocent even before seeing the evidence. Rumors that he would pardon his former aides also dogged the president. Continuing allegations of shady financial dealings involving Attorney-General Edwin Meese, perhaps the president's closest friend and confidant, led to a year-long investigation by an independent counsel. In July 1988 the counsel issued a report that accused Meese of three separate legal violations but did not call for criminal indictments. The besieged attorney-general, claiming he had been exonerated, thereupon resigned.

Even more embarrassing to the Reagan administration were revelations contained in several best-selling books written by former White House aides and Reagan family members. Their composite portrait was of a president passionately committed to a few key issues, a man capable of being a superb public spokesman and projecting a genial, sunny disposition, yet privately aloof and essentially devoid of intellectual curiosity and energy. Reports surfaced that Nancy Reagan was a "manipulative" First Lady who told her husband whom to fire and regularly consulted a San Francisco astrologer in planning her husband's itinerary. Equally damaging was a revelation by one of Reagan's former press secretaries that the president's newspaper reading focused on the comics and that, as press secretary, he had occasionally made up quotes which he had attributed to the president during press briefings.

As Ronald Reagan prepared to leave office after eight years, his legacy remained problematic. Would he be remembered as the architect of revitalized military spending, lower tax rates, sharply reduced inflation and unemployment, a prolonged economic recovery, and an unprecedented arms-reduction treaty? Or would history find an administration rife with corruption and policies that had weakened American credibility abroad and bequeathed an economic time bomb for the 1990s?

Only time would tell, but the herd of aspiring Democratic candidates for the 1988 election thought they knew the answer. Said Jesse Jackson, "We must fundamentally reject the lie of Reaganomics." He and other aspirants knew that history was on their side. Few two-term presidents had left office with greater popularity than when they entered it. The stage was set for a tempestuous campaign year.

THE 1988 ELECTION   Scenting victory in November, a gaggle of eight Democratic presidential candidates entered a wild scramble for their party's nomination. As the primary season progressed, however, it soon became a two-man race between Massachusetts governor Michael Dukakis and Jesse Jackson, the charismatic civil-rights activist who had been one of Martin Luther King, Jr.'s chief lieutenants. Dukakis eventually won out, and managed a difficult reconciliation with the Jackson forces that left the Democrats unified and confident as the fall campaign began. As in 1960, they envisioned a popular president and his tired presidency giving way to a cool, poised politician from Massachusetts.

The bushy-browed son of Greek immigrants, noted for his earnest frugality and simple living, Dukakis expressed his ethnic sensitivity by speaking perfect Spanish in his convention address. In addition, he trumpeted his pragmatic management skills by noting that he had successfully balanced the Massachusetts state budget every year of his administration, implying that he would do the same with the hemorrhaging federal budget. He adopted liberal positions on several explosive issues: he opposed the death penalty and called for compulsory health insurance, gun-control legislation, and an end to nuclear power plants. In the area of defense policy, Dukakis promised to curtail the "Star Wars" program and cancel several other expensive nuclear missile systems. And in foreign affairs he repeated his opposition to military aid for the Nicaraguan Contras. But he insisted that the election was not really about such issues: "This election is not about ideology; it's about competence."

At their convention in New Orleans in August, the Republicans nominated Reagan's two-term vice-president, George Bush, who after a bumpy start had easily cast aside his rivals in the primaries. As Reagan's handpicked heir, Bush claimed credit for the administration's successes, but like all dutiful vice-presidents, he also faced the challenge of defining and asserting his own political identity. Although a veteran government official, having served as a Texas congressman, envoy to China, ambassador to the U.N., and head of the CIA, Bush projected none of Reagan's charisma or rhetorical skills. Cartoonists caricatured the patrician vice-president, the son of a rich Connecticut senator, schooled at Andover and Yale, as a well-heeled "wimp," and one Democrat described him as a man born "with a silver foot in his mouth." Early polls showed Dukakis with a surprisingly wide lead.

Yet Bush, a genuinely decent and honorable man with a distinguished record of heroism in World War II, delivered a surprisingly forceful convention address that sharply enhanced his stature. Although pledging to continue the Reagan agenda, he also recognized that "things aren't perfect" in America, an admission his boss rarely acknowledged. Bush promised to use the White House to fight bigotry, illiteracy, and homelessness. His conservatism, he insisted, was guided by humane sympathies. "I want a kinder, gentler nation," Bush said softly in his acceptance speech. But the most memorable line was a defiant statement on taxes: "Congress will push me to raise taxes, and I'll say no, and they'll push, and I'll say no, and they'll push again. And all I can say to them is, read my lips: *no new taxes.*"

Bush's convention performance gave his heretofore sluggish campaign a jump-start. The Republicans also enjoyed two real advantages. In 1988 the United States basked in peace and prosperity, and the Republican party benefited from its continuing demographic advantages. During the 1980s, population growth was most rapid in the Republican-dominated Sunbelt states. And throughout the nation, population during the decade had continued to shift from Democratic cities to Republican suburbs. In addition, the leftward tilt of the Democratic party in 1984 had led many moderate and conservative Democrats as well as the growing number of "independents" to vote for Reagan.

George Bush (right) *at the 1988 Republican National Convention with his newly chosen running mate, Dan Quayle.*

In a campaign given over to mud-slinging, Bush and his strategists fastened on an effective strategy: they attacked Dukakis as a camouflaged liberal in the mold of McGovern, Carter, and Mondale who would increase federal spending, raise taxes, gut the defense program, refuse to intervene against Communist aggression abroad, oppose the pledge of allegiance to the flag, and support furloughs for convicted murderers. Dukakis chose not to respond to the Republican attacks. Studiously informed on the issues, he had a Jimmy Carter-like trust in the force of sweet reason. Dukakis was, in Bush's words, "the Iceman," cool, rational, in control of his emotions, blind to the emotional power that trivial issues could exert.

Dukakis—who had chosen Texas senator Lloyd Bentsen as his running mate—did hone in on Bush's choice of Senator J. Danforth Quayle of Indiana. Dan Quayle, born to a wealthy newspaper publisher, had done little to distinguish himself academically or politically. His ultra-conservative background might have reassured right-wing Republicans, but it emerged in a television interview that during the Vietnam War he had joined the National Guard, perceived at the time as a way to avoid service overseas. After an early public flap on his record and qualifications, he was consigned to obscure campaign events subject to little more than local notice.

The Republican onslaught, engineered by Bush's campaign manager Lee Atwater and his media consultant Roger Ailes, took its toll

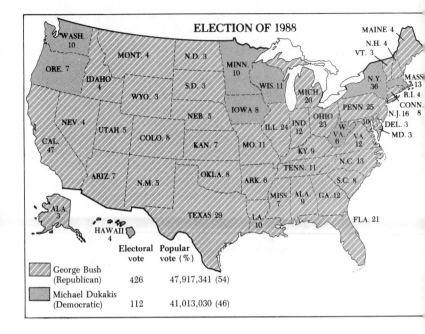

ELECTION OF 1988

	Electoral vote	Popular vote (%)
George Bush (Republican)	426	47,917,341 (54)
Michael Dukakis (Democratic)	112	41,013,030 (46)

against the less organized, less focused Dukakis campaign. As he slipped hopelessly behind in the polls, Dukakis set out in the closing weeks of the campaign to revive traditional Democratic liberalism, identifying himself by the "L-word," which he had previously avoided. "I'm on your side," he told growing, enthusiastic crowds. But the new tack, if effective, came too late. Dukakis took ten states plus the District of Columbia, with clusters in the Northeast, Midwest, and Northwest. Bush carried the rest, with a margin of about 54 percent to 46 percent in the popular vote and 426 to 111 in the electoral college—one Democratic elector voted for Bentsen for president.

THE BUSH YEARS

Although Bush's inaugural address lacked specific calls to action, it did invite national unity and bipartisan harmony. The American people had a purpose, he said, "to make kinder the face of the nation and gentler the face of the world." The new president acknowledged the homeless, "the children who have nothing," the addicted, the unwed mothers, but pleaded: "We have a deficit to bring down. We have more will than wallet, but will is what we need." In short, he looked to voluntary associations and individuals, the "thousand points of light" of which he spoke in the campaign.

During eight years as vice-president, Bush had loyally embraced the Reaganism he had once called "voodoo economics." His own administration, one commentator now said, would be "déjà voodoo." But there would be subtle differences. Whereas Reagan had hung Coolidge's portrait in place of Truman's on a White House wall, Bush now installed one of Theodore Roosevelt. The symbolism suggested two things. An eastern patrician with a Western patina, like Teddy Roosevelt, "Poppy" Bush would preside over an administration less arriviste than Reagan's. His appointees were more often from the upper crust or career public servants. And in foreign policy he would go much further than TR in wielding the big stick. The parallels vanished, though, in Bush's lack of interest in domestic policy, noted by *Time* magazine when it named the president its "Men of the Year" for 1990, attributing to him a double image: "a foreign policy profile that was a study in resoluteness and mastery, the other a domestic visage just as strongly marked by wavering and confusion."

THE BAILOUT AND THE BUDGET   The Reagan administration left some issues that demanded immediate attention from the Bush White House. In February 1989 Bush tackled the most pressing of these, the savings and loan crisis, with a rescue plan to close or sell ailing thrifts, and bail out the depositors. Congress responded the following August by consolidating the insurance fund for savings and loan deposits with the fund covering banks, the Federal Deposit Insurance Corporation (FDIC). A new agency, the Resolution Trust Corporation (RTC), was created to sell off failed thrifts—or at least their assets. At the time, the cost to taxpayers of the bailout was put at $300 billion over thirty years, although in July 1990 the General Accounting Office estimated the cost at $500 billion.

The biggest hangover from the binge years of the 1980s was the national debt, which stood at $2.6 trillion by the time Bush was elected, nearly three times its 1980 level. Bush's taboo on tax increases (meaning, mainly, income taxes) and his insistence upon lowering capital-gains taxes—on profits from the sales of stocks and other property—made it more difficult to reduce the deficit or trim the debt. But Bush did not get the capital-gains cut, while continued differences with Congress delayed adoption of a new budget. Finally in October the Gramm-Rudman plan triggered automatic cuts of $16.1 billion in the federal budget. Not until November was the budget tangle straightened out, after a fashion, by certain cuts across the board and accounting gimmicks that brought the budget in line with Gramm-Rudman. "We're getting a reconciliation bill that's written in Egyptian," said Republican senator Alan Simpson of Wyoming. "It doesn't mean a damn thing."

By 1990, according to political writer Elizabeth Drew, the country faced "a horrendous fiscal mess." Bipartisan budget talks between administration and congressional leaders, begun in May, were characterized by "rancorous partisanship [and] deep divisions within the two parties." Democrats feared an administration trap: knowing that only higher taxes could solve the deficit problem, the Republicans wished to maneuver Democrats into putting a plan on the table, and then charge them once more with being the high-tax party. The Democrats determined to hold fast and flush out the president. Eventually, on June 26, Bush issued a statement: "It seems clear to me that both the size of the deficit problem and the need for a package that can be enacted" required a number of measures, including "tax revenue increases." Then he put the word out that he had been forced by the Democrats into accepting such language, a message that did not convey strong leadership. These elaborate partisan dances continued through the summer, until a budget plan was announced on September 30, 1990.

With midterm elections coming in November, the political timing was about the worst possible for reasoned dialogue in Congress, and a rebellion erupted on the floor of the House led by conservative Republican Newton Gingrich of Georgia. A majority of both parties ended up voting against the budget bill. After adopting two stopgap measures to extend government operations pending a final budget, the Congress reacted to mounting public anger at the continued indecision and approved a settlement, although most Republicans still opposed it.

Through a combination of tax hikes and spending cuts, the measure promised to reduce the budget deficit by $43.1 billion in 1991 and by $331.4 billion in 1991–1995. The top tax rate was 31 percent on incomes over $78,400; for incomes below that amount the existing 15 and 28 percent brackets remained in effect, and capital gains remained at the 28 percent level. On incomes above $100,000 exemptions were phased out. Excise taxes went up on gasoline, cigarettes, alcohol, and a number of luxury items: planes, expensive boats and cars, furs, and jewelry. Corporate tax deductions were reduced. Spending cuts hit a number of government programs, including Medicare and the military. In a few cases, tax breaks were extended to the poor and to companies involved in oil and gas exploration.

Aside from the S&L bailout and the limited response to deficit reduction, two domestic initiatives stand out during the early Bush years: the minimum-wage bill of November 1989, and the Clean Air Act of October 1990. Agreement on a higher minimum wage was reached after an earlier Bush veto of an attempt to raise the hourly minimum from $3.35, where it had remained since 1981, to $4.55. The November agreement set the minimum at $3.80 on April 1, 1990, and $4.25 a year later. At that time a full-time worker at the minimum wage would still fall $1,400 below the federal poverty line for a family of four.

The Clean Air Act of 1990, described at the time as the most comprehensive environmental act ever passed by Congress, set the goal of reducing sulfur dioxide emissions by 12 million to 14 million tons annually. It applied specific emission standards to hundreds of utilities, and beyond that granted extensive powers to the Environmental Protection Agency to set and enforce acceptable levels for toxics. Among many other provisions, cities were called upon to establish new low levels of carbon monoxide in the atmosphere.

SOCIAL ISSUES These solid achievements were surrounded by symbolic acts. In June 1989, the Supreme Court ruled by a 5–4 vote that burning an American flag as a form of protest amounted to an expression of opinion, protected as free speech under the First Amendment of the Constitution. A great hullabaloo followed and Bush, who had made a campaign issue of the pledge of allegiance, called for a constitutional amendment to permit laws against desecrating the flag. Congress instead overwhelmingly passed legislation to make it a crime to desecrate the flag by burning or defacing it. When the high court struck down that law too, in 1990, the call for an amendment was renewed, but Congress again declined to tinker with the Bill of Rights on the eve of its 200th anniversary.

There was more symbolism on the deadly matter of drug abuse. During the 1980s, cocaine addiction spread through sizable segments of American society, luring those with money to spend and—in its smokeable form, known as crack—those with little money to spare. Bush vowed to make drug abuse his number-one domestic priority, and appointed William J. Bennett, former education secretary, as "drug czar" or head of a new Office of National Drug Control Policy, with cabinet status but no department. President Bush's first nationally televised speech, delivered in September 1989, laid out a broad plan to combat illegal drugs. Total outlays in the war would amount to $7.9 billion in fiscal 1990, although only $716 million represented new spending. The money would support better law enforcement, treatment of addicts, education, and prevention. Democrats attacked the program as too focused on law enforcement, with too little money going toward treatment, education, and prevention. Bush's speech indirectly revealed a consistent theme in his domestic policy: "To win the war . . . will take more than just a Federal strategy. It will take a national strategy, one that reaches into every school, every workplace, involving every family." The message, on this and on education, housing, and other social problems, was that more of the burden should fall on state and local authorities.

"THE COLD WAR IS NOW BEHIND US" Replacing the portrait of Coolidge with Teddy Roosevelt's signified most clearly Bush's affinity with TR's "big stick" diplomacy—his conviction that America's manifest destiny was to become a world power. Bush entered the White House with more foreign policy experience than most presidents, and he found the spotlight of the world stage more congenial than wrestling with the intractable problems of the inner cities or the deficit. And within two years of his inauguration, George Bush would lead the United States into two wars, a record unequaled by any of his predecessors. Throughout most of 1989, however, he merely had to sit back and observe the dissolution of one totalitarian or authoritarian regime after another. For the first time in years, democracy was suddenly on the march in a sequence of mostly bloodless revolutions that took most of the world by surprise.

Although a suddenly risen democracy movement in China came to a tragic end in June 1989 when government forces mounted a deadly assault on demonstrators in Peking's Tiananmen Square, eastern Europe had an entirely different experience. The fall of Communist regimes there resembled the collapse of the "wonderful one-hoss shay" in Oliver Wendell Holmes's poetic satire on Puritanism—it was built "in such a logical way," no part weaker than any other, that when it finally fell apart everything crumbled all at once.

Not without preliminary shivers, of course. With a rigid economic system failing to deliver the goods to the Soviet peoples, Mikhail Gorbachev responded with policies of "perestroika" (restructuring) and "glasnost" (openness), a loosening of central economic planning and censorship. His foreign policy sought rapprochement with the West, to encourage trade and relieve the Soviet economy of burdensome military costs.

Gorbachev backed off from Soviet imperial ambitions. Early in 1989, Soviet troops left Afghanistan, after nine years bogged down in civil war there, and at Paris, in July, Gorbachev repudiated the "Brezhnev doctrine" asserting the right of the Soviet Union to intervene in the internal affairs of Communist countries. The days when Soviet tanks rolled through Warsaw and Prague were over, and hard-line leaders in the East-bloc countries found themselves beset by demands for reform. With opposition strength building, the old regimes fell in rapid order, and with surprisingly little bloodshed. Communist party rule ended first in Poland and Hungary, then in hard-line Czechoslovakia and in Bulgaria. In Romania, the year of peaceful revolution ended in a bloodbath when the Romanian people in December were joined by the army in a bloody uprising against the brutal dictator Nicolae Ceausescu. He and his wife were captured, tried, and then executed on Christmas Day. But lacking experienced opposition leaders, a problem in all the eastern European countries, the new government fell under the control of members of the old Communist establishment.

The most spectacular event in the collapse of the Soviet empire in eastern Europe came on November 9, when the chief symbol of the Cold War—the Berlin Wall—succumbed to popular pressures for change in East Germany. With the borders to the West fully open, the Communist government of East Germany collapsed, a freely elected government followed, and on October 3, 1990, the five states of East Germany were united with the West. The German nation remained in NATO, and the Warsaw Pact alliance was dissolved.

By the time President Bush had his first summit meeting with the Soviet leader, at Malta in December 1989, the revolutions in the Communist world were already far advanced. The meeting resulted in no substantive agreements, but the presidents discussed further treaties on arms reductions as well as the question of German reunification. The world, Bush said, was at the "threshold of a brand new era of U.S.-Soviet relations." Six months later, in late May 1990,

West Germans chipping away at the Berlin Wall on November 11, 1989, two days after all crossings between East and West Germany were opened.

Gorbachev visited Washington, where on June 1 he and Bush signed more than a dozen documents. These included an agreement to reduce long-range nuclear weapons to a limit of 1,600 delivery rockets and 6,000 warheads; another agreement requiring both countries to give up the manufacture of chemical weapons; and a treaty that would loosen trade restrictions between the countries. A few days later, speaking at Stanford University, Gorbachev said: "The Cold War is now behind us. Let us not wrangle over who won it."

The democratic movement reached other parts of the world. During 1990, the Communist party of Mongolia—strategically located on the borders of the Soviet Union and China—voted to give up its monopoly on power, and in Nicaragua, where the ruling Sandinista party avowed Marxism, President Daniel Ortega was defeated in a presidential election in February. Even in isolated Albania, the ruling party yielded to demands for an election in 1991.

Democratic change overtook authoritarian regimes of a different stripe as well. In Chile, Augusto Pinochet, who had become military dictator in a bloody coup of 1973, yielded to a popular vote in 1988 against continuing him in office, and was defeated in presidential elections the following year. And in South Africa, to which the U.S. Congress had applied trade sanctions in protest of its apartheid (racial segregation) policies since 1986, a new prime minister, Frederik W. DeKlerk, came to office in August 1989, released in early 1990 black nationalist Nelson Mandela from twenty-seven years in prison, and announced plans gradually to abandon apartheid.

The reform impulse that Gorbachev helped unleash in the East-bloc countries began to grow beyond his control at home. Gorbachev proved unusually adept at political restructuring, yielding the Communist monopoly of government but building a new presidential system which gave him, if anything, increased powers. His skills in the Byzantine politics of the Kremlin, though, did not extend to an antiquated economy that resisted change. The revival of old ethnic allegiances added to the instability. Although Russia proper included slightly over half the Soviet Union's population, it was only one of fifteen constituent republics, most of which began actively to seek autonomy, if not independence. Along the fringes of the Russian republic, to the west and south, lay a jigsaw puzzle of about a hundred nationalities and languages.

Gorbachev's popularity shrank in the Soviet Union as it grew abroad. It especially eroded among the Communist hard-liners who saw in his reforms the unraveling of their bureaucratic and political empire. Once the genie of freedom was released from the Communist lamp, however, it took on a momentum of its own. On August 18, 1991, a cabal of political and military leaders suddenly tried to

Mikhail Gorbachev and Boris Yeltsin before the Soviet parliament in the days following the failed coup of late August 1991.

seize the reins of power. They accosted Gorbachev at his vacation retreat in the Crimea and demanded that he sign a decree proclaiming a state of emergency and transferring his powers to them. He replied: "Go to hell," whereupon he was placed under house arrest. Twelve hours later the Soviet news agency reported to the world that Gorbachev was ill and had temporarily transferred his powers to his vice-president and an eight-member emergency committee. Political parties were suspended, newspapers were silenced, a curfew was announced, and street demonstrations were banned. Tanks and armored vehicles surrounded strategic installations and government buildings in Moscow. The new leadership promised to end the "chaos and anarchy" they claimed was bedeviling the country.

But the coup was doomed from the start. Poorly planned and clumsily implemented, it lacked effective coordination. Its leaders were bureaucrats, not revolutionaries, and they lacked the brutal decisiveness required of successful takeovers. The plotters failed to arrest popular leaders such as Boris Yeltsin, the populist president of the Russian republic, and they neglected to close the airports or cut off telephone and television communications. They also took for granted the unified support of the military and the KGB, only to discover that many units and key commanders opposed the coup. But most important, the putschists failed to recognize the strength of the democratic idealism unleashed by Gorbachev's reforms. Upon learning of the attempted overthrow, tens of thousands of Muscovites poured into the streets outside Yeltsin's headquarters to act as human shields against efforts to arrest him. Three were killed in the process.

A crescendo of indignation welled up from foreign leaders around the world. On August 20 President Bush, after a day of indecision, responded favorably to Yeltsin's request for support and convinced world leaders to join him in refusing to recognize the legitimacy of the new government. Siberian coal miners went on strike to oppose the coup. The next day word began to seep out that the plotters had given up and were fleeing. Several committed suicide, and a newly released Gorbachev ordered the others arrested. But his freedom did not bring a restoration of his power. By courageously clambering atop a menacing tank and publicly defying the conspirators, calling them a "gang of bandits," Yeltsin had emerged as the most popular political figure in the country. Gorbachev reclaimed the title of president, but was forced to resign as head of the Communist party and admit that he had made a grave mistake in appointing the men who had turned against him.

What began as a reactionary coup turned into a powerful accelerant for stunning new changes in the Soviet Union, or the Soviet Disunion, as one wag termed it. No sooner had the plotters been arrested than most of the fifteen republics proclaimed their independence, with the Baltic republics of Latvia, Lithuania, and Estonia regaining the status of independent nations. The Communist party apparatus was dismantled, prompting celebrating crowds to topple statues of Lenin and other mythic Communist heroes. A chastened Gorbachev could only acquiesce in the breakup of the Soviet empire. The man who had put reform into motion was now buffeted by the whirlwind of change. But new leaders voiced real concerns about the uncontrolled disintegration of the union, and the likelihood of ethnic violence. Moreover, the systemic problems burdening the Soviet Union before the coup remained intractable. The economy was stagnant, languishing between the promise of free-market principles and the gridlock of state collectivism. Food and coal shortages loomed on the horizon, and consumer goods remained scarce. It would take decades before the moribund economies of the fifteen republics would approach Western standards of production and efficiency. The reformers had won, but they had yet to establish deep roots in a country with no democratic tradition. Leaping into the unknown, they faced years of hardship and uncertainty ahead.

The aborted coup also accelerated Soviet and American efforts to reduce the stockpiles of nuclear weapons. In late September 1991

President Bush stunned the world by announcing that the United States would destroy all its tactical nuclear weapons on land and at sea in Europe and Asia, take its long-range bombers off twenty-four-hour alert status, and initiate discussions with the Soviet Union for the purpose of instituting sharp cuts in ICBMs with multiple warheads. Bush explained that the prospect of a Soviet invasion of western Europe was "no longer a realistic threat," and this presented an unprecedented opportunity for reducing the threat of nuclear holocaust. President Gorbachev responded by announcing reciprocal Soviet cutbacks.

PANAMA Despite the hopes of many, the end of the Cold War did not spell the end of international tensions and conflict. Indeed, before the end of 1989, American troops were engaged in battle in Panama, where a petty tyrant provoked the first of America's military engagements under George Bush. Two years after the death of Panama's previous dictator in a mysterious plane crash in 1981, General Manuel Noriega maneuvered himself into the leadership of the Panamanian Defense Forces—which made him head of government in fact if not in title. Earlier, as chief of intelligence, Noriega had developed a profitable business of supplying information on the region to the CIA, including the period when Bush headed the agency. Noriega also became an agent of Colonel North's secret activities. At the same time, he was developing avenues in the region for drug smuggling and gun-running, laundering the money through Panamanian banks. For a time, American intelligence looked the other way, regarding him as too useful a contact, but eventually he became too great an embarrassment. In June 1987 a rejected associate published charges of his drug activities, and accused him further of rigged elections and political assassination.

In February 1988, federal grand juries in Miami and Tampa indicted Noriega and fifteen others on drug charges. Another associate went public with charges of Noriega's dealings with Castro and Oliver North, and the CIA connections began to leak. The Panamanian president tried to fire Noriega, but the National Assembly ousted the president instead. The United States in March 1988 froze Panamanian assets and restrained banks from transferring cash to Panama, where the American dollar was the local currency. Panama's economy continued to deteriorate over the next year, and in May 1989, when an opposition candidate for president won in a landslide, Noriega simply voided the election and continued to rule.

Exploiting the anti-American feeling present in Latin America, Noriega had his pliable Assembly name him "maximum leader" and proclaimed that Panama "is declared to be in a state of war" with

Panamanian refugees held in an air force hangar after their houses were destroyed by bombs during the U.S. invasion, December 20, 1989.

the United States. The next day, December 16, 1989, four off-duty American servicemen were stopped at a roadblock, and as they tried to go on one marine was shot and killed. President Bush responded by ordering a Panama invasion with the purpose of capturing Noriega for trial on the American indictments and installing a government headed by President Guillermo Endara and other leaders who presumably had been chosen in the May election nullified by Noriega.

The 12,000 American military personnel in Panama were quickly joined by 12,000 more, and in the early morning of December 20, five military task forces struck at strategic targets in the country. They quickly disabled and seized the headquarters of the Panamanian Defense Forces, but Noriega vanished. Hit-and-run attacks by the Panamanian Defense Forces continued, but resistance collapsed when Noriega took refuge in the Vatican embassy on Christmas Eve. After intense negotiations among American, Vatican, and Panamanian diplomats, Noriega surrendered to American forces a week later. Twenty-three American servicemen were killed in the action, and estimates of Panamanian casualties ranged up to 4,000, including many civilians caught in the crossfire. Noriega languished in a federal jail well over a year after his surrender, his case a tangle of legal technicalities.

THE GULF WAR   Months after Panama had moved to the background of public attention, another former American client, Saddam Hus-

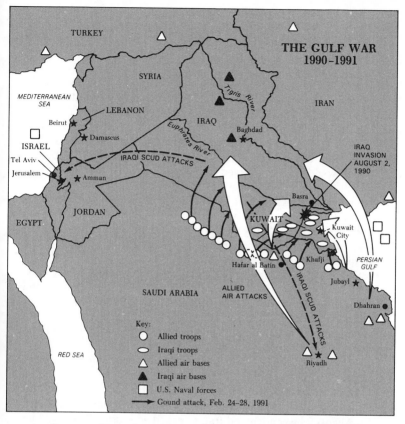

sein, dictator of Iraq, focused attention on the Middle East when his
army suddenly fell upon his tiny, wealthy neighbor Kuwait on August 2, 1990. A decade earlier, when Saddam attacked Iran hoping
to exploit its revolutionary turmoil for territorial concessions, the
United States and most of Saddam's Arab neighbors "tilted" toward
Iraq as a regional buffer against Iran, which was then holding American diplomats hostage. From 1985 to 1990, Iraq received about $500
million worth of American technology—advanced computers, lasers,
and specialized machine tools related to the development of missiles.

Saddam's war against Iran meanwhile bogged down in a bloody
stalemate, until the U.N. finally arranged a truce on August 8, 1988.
The very next day the neighboring oil-rich enclave of Kuwait raised
its production of oil contrary to agreements with the Organization of
Petroleum Exporting Countries (OPEC). The resultant drop in oil
prices offended Saddam, deep in debt and heavily dependent on oil
revenues. Complaining of "economic aggression" against Iraq, he
demanded that Kuwait reduce its production and, with Saudi Arabia, cancel Iraqi debts of $30 million. He also revived boundary
disputes that had simmered since the post–World War I settlement

that had created the current map of the Gulf region. Saddam seemed to nurture hopes of unifying the Arab lands and dominating the region's oil resources.

As tensions intensified, American officials remained focused on events in Europe and on Iraq's value as a counterweight to Iran. A meeting on July 25, 1990, between Saddam Hussein and the American ambassador to Iraq, April Glaspie, failed to resolve the mounting crisis. A text of the meeting later released by Iraq pictured Glaspie as deferential and conciliatory, assuring Saddam that the United States would not get involved in a dispute between Arab neighbors. Glaspie, a career expert on the Middle East and fluent in Arabic, later testified to Congress: "I told him orally we would defend our vital interests, we would support our friends in the Gulf, we would defend their sovereignty and integrity." The main American mistake, she said, was not to "realize he was stupid." On August 2, the Iraqi army occupied Kuwait.

Saddam did not expect the sudden storm he would stir. The U.N. Security Council quickly voted 14–0 to condemn the invasion and demand withdrawal. On August 3, Secretary of State James Baker and Soviet foreign minister Edouard Shevardnadze issued a joint statement of condemnation. On August 6, the Security Council endorsed Resolution 661, an embargo on trade with Iraq, by a vote of 13–0, with Cuba and Yemen abstaining. Such unanimity, of course, would have been unlikely during the Cold War.

One cannot say precisely when President Bush decided for war, although what is known so far suggests a rapid hardening of attitude. On August 2 he condemned Iraq's "naked aggression," and said he was not ruling any options out. On August 3 the president called the "integrity of Saudi Arabia" a vital American interest. Two days later he vowed to reporters: "This aggression will not stand." Asked how it would be undone, he replied: "Just wait, watch, and learn." On August 6–7, the United States dispatched planes and troops to Saudi Arabia on a "wholly defensive" mission—to protect Saudi Arabia. British forces soon joined in, as did Arab troops from Egypt, Morocco, Syria, Oman, the United Arab Emirates, and Qatar. On August 22, Bush began to order the mobilization of American reserve forces for the operation now dubbed "Desert Shield." Later in September, after meeting with Gorbachev in Helsinki, Bush told Congress that dictators could no longer find comfort in East-West divisions, and proclaimed a "New World Order," which he described as "A world where the strong respect the rights of the weak."

Very early on the Pentagon was putting together plans for offensive military action. Although Colin Powell, chairman of the Joint Chiefs of Staff, favored sticking with the U.N. trade embargo against

Iraq, which he believed would work over time, Bush declared it politically unfeasible. On October 1, large majorities in both houses of Congress approved the actions taken to that point.

In public comments the president began to speak of "senseless suffering" and "ghastly atrocities" in Kuwait, and said of Saddam that he was like "Hitler revisited." On November 8, two days after midterm elections in which the Democrats scored small gains, Bush announced that he was doubling American forces in the Middle East from about 200,000 to 400,000, to build up "an adequate offensive military capability." Bush asserted that he already had authority to take such action under the Security Council resolutions.

The Congress erupted in debate, with many arguing that the embargo should have a chance to work, and that it would be ill-advised to go to war without formal congressional support. Bush's position was strengthened on November 29 by U.N. Resolution 678, which authorized the use of force to dislodge Iraq from Kuwait, and set a deadline for Iraqi withdrawal of January 15, 1991.

A flurry of peace efforts sent diplomats scurrying all over, but without result. Saddam refused to yield, and declined even to meet with Secretary of State Baker until January 12, three days before the U.N. deadline. On January 10 Congress began to debate a resolution authorizing the use of U.S. armed forces. Senate Majority Leader George Mitchell (D, Me.) warned, "A grave decision for war is being made prematurely. There has been no clear rationale, no convincing explanation for shifting American policy from one of sanctions to one of war." Others insisted on the need to present a united front behind the president. The outcome was uncertain to the end, but on January 12 the resolution for the use of force passed the House by 250–183, and the Senate by 52–47.

By January 1991, a twenty-eight-nation allied force was committed to Operation Desert Shield. Some nations sent only planes, ships, or support forces, but sixteen committed ground combat forces, ten of these Islamic countries. Desert Shield became Operation Desert Storm when the first missiles and planes began to hit Iraq at about 2:30 A.M., January 17, Baghdad time, or about 6:30 P.M., January 16, Washington time. The Persian Gulf War, the "mother of all battles" in Saddam Hussein's words, was intense and deadly, ending with an allied cease-fire just six weeks later, and leaving consequences to be played out far into the future.

War has long been a popular spectator sport, alas, in the age of television literally so, and Americans derived their impressions of the Gulf conflict largely from that source. According to the polls, a great majority of Americans approved of the practice already followed in Grenada and Panama—a reaction to the "Vietnam syndrome"—of forming reporters into pools to be fed information primarily through official briefings either at the Pentagon or at Central Command headquarters in Riyadh, Saudi Arabia. There Commanding General H. Norman Schwarzkopf proved both telegenic and deft at handling questions. He became an instant public hero. Reporters could venture into the field only with military escorts who controlled what and whom they saw. Those reporters who ventured out on their own were quickly reined in.

The greatest wonder of the briefings was the television footage of "smart bombs"—missiles guided by laser beams precisely to their targets. One missile penetrated the center of the roof on Baghdad's telephone and communications center, and others could be seen going down the air shafts and into the doors of other strategic targets. Only later did it emerge that just 7 percent of the tonnage dropped had been "smart bombs," or about 6,520 tons out of 88,500. B-52s carrying conventional bombs from as far away as Britain and Spain delivered a heavy battering to Saddam's elite Republican Guard, many of them lined up along the Kuwait border behind the less trained and less experienced conscripts on the front lines.

With the allies in control of the air from the beginning, Saddam's only recourse was to fire off lumbering Soviet-made SCUD missiles, which he aimed from the first day into Israel with the hope of provoking Israeli retaliation and undermining the coalition against him. But the resulting damage and casualties were light, and the Israelis showed remarkable restraint in the face of the continuing attacks. The Israelis gained a measure of protection from Patriot missiles installed and operated by American crews; the Patriots had considerable success in taking out or altering the course of incoming SCUDs. The Iraqis responded also with desperation moves, which did more damage to the environment than to enemy forces: releasing oil into the Persian Gulf from tankers and loading platforms in Kuwait—and setting fire to Kuwaiti oil wells, in wholesale numbers at the end.

Saddam's key strategy of digging in and prolonging the war into a costly land struggle, as he did in his war with Iran, never had a chance. Saddam concentrated his forces in Kuwait—into a bag, as Schwarzkopf put it—and expected an allied attack northward into Kuwait and a landing on the coast. But the Iraqis were outflanked when 200,000 allied troops, largely American, British, and French, vanished with much of their heavy armor and turned up on the undefended border with Saudi Arabia 100–200 miles to the west. The allied ground assault began on February 24, and lasted only four days. Republican Guard tanks were smashed in the largest armored battle, probably, since the Battle of the Bulge. Iraqi soldiers offered themselves for surrender in wholesale lots, and there was a quick breakthrough into Kuwait. Iraqi soldiers and civilians fleeing Ku-

H. Norman Schwarzkopf, commanding general of the allied force committed to Desert Storm.

wait, in some cases with hostages rounded up in large numbers, were caught in a traffic jam which provided what one naval pilot dubbed a "turkey shoot."

On February 28, President Bush called for a cease-fire, the Iraqis accepted, and the shooting ended. American fatalities were 137. The lowest estimates of Iraqi fatalities, civilian and military, were around 100,000. The coalition forces occupied about one-fifth of Iraq. In late March, after a quick survey, a U.N. official reported: "Bombing had wrought near apocalyptic results upon the infrastructure of what had been, until January 1991, a rather highly urbanized and mechanized society." The U.N. Children's Fund director called for a crash program of immunization to ward off epidemics. For all the destruction, Saddam Hussein remained in power.

Conditions got worse when the Gulf War dissolved into civil war, in both the south and the north. Iraq was in fact something of an artificial entity, cobbled together by the British after World War I out of three provinces of the former Ottoman Empire and named by them what in Arabic meant "well-rooted country." In the south, a large minority of Arabs belonging to the Shi'ite sect of Islam—the prevailing group in Iran—rose in rebellion; in the north a larger minority of Kurds—Sunni Muslims, but a people of distinct identity and language since ancient times—sought release from Saddam's despotic rule. Although they had been promised an independent Kurdistan after World War I, they remained minorities in five different countries.

One unidentified official said that the president wanted to sign a cease-fire and "get the hell out of there." As a presidential spokes-

Kurdish refugees from Iraq desperate for relief supplies in the aftermath of the Gulf war.

man explained, "It is good for the stability of the region that [Iraq] maintain its territorial integrity." And so with American troops already returning home to crowds of flag-waving celebrants, Iraqi forces held in reserve or newly escaped from the allied trap proceeded to put down first the Shi'ite rebellion in the south, and then the Kurds in the north. Apparently the administration would have preferred a palace coup against Saddam Hussein, but now held forth a policy of not interfering in the internal affairs of Iraq. American troops on the southern shore of the Euphrates had to stand by and watch as the rebels were brutally suppressed.

In the south, refugees flooded into Iran, the Kuwait border zone, and the region controlled by the allies. In the north they made the dangerous and painful climb into the highlands along the Turkish and Iranian borders. On the Turkish frontier, American television broadcast to audiences back home pathetic scenes of people without even basic necessities, huddling on snow-flecked hillsides or in camps without food, shelter, or adequate clothing. With the coalition victory seeming to turn sour, the administration launched a military relief effort, "Operation Provide Comfort," with the help of British, French, and Dutch forces in the region.

The Middle East, as it had for centuries, still resisted any quick fix. The Persian Gulf War was far from a reprise of Vietnam, but it ended with what conceivably could turn into a longer hangover. There was an understanding—details to be worked out—that the United States would maintain a military presence in the Persian Gulf. Secretary of State Baker succeeded in organizing a conference to address the tough problems between Israel and its Arab neighbors, but any settlement remained far off. It was, ironically, an American missionary who said to one of the British planners carving up the former Ottoman territory after World War I: "You are flying in the face of four millenniums of history." The words retain their haunting quality.

AMERICA'S CHANGING FACE: THE 1990 CENSUS

AGE, GENDER, RACE   At the same time that American military forces were converging on the Persian Gulf during Operation Desert Shield, an army of census workers was roaming the streets and byways of the United States, counting heads and accumulating data about the American people. The preliminary results of the 1990 census revealed several dramatic changes in the country's demographic profile. During the 1980s the nation's population grew by 10 percent, or some 23 million people, boosting the total to almost 250 million. The median age of the quarter-billion Americans rose from thirty to thirty-three, and the much-discussed "baby-boom" generation—the 43 million people born between 1946 and 1964—entered middle age. Because of its disproportionate size, the baby-boom generation magnifies changes in American society as it moves through the life cycle. As one demographer noted, it resembles a "pig in a python." Political analysts suggested that this generation's maturation and preoccupation with practical concerns such as raising families and buying houses helped explain the surge of political conservatism during the 1980s. Surveys revealed that baby-boomers wanted stronger family and religious ties in the eighties and promoted a greater respect for authority. Yet having come to maturity during the turbulent sixties and early seventies, the baby-boomers also displayed more tolerance of social and cultural diversity than their parents.

The census revealed that the fastest-growing age groups, however, were the oldest ones. Americans in their nineties more than doubled during the 1980s, and those over a hundred grew by 77 percent. In 1991, over 57,000 Americans were centenarians. This "graying of America" was both a blessing and a burden. It demonstrated that Americans were healthier than ever, and helped erode the cultural stigma attached to the aged and aging, but it also posed a stiff challenge to public officials. How was the nation to care for so many old people? Corporations found their pension costs soaring. In 1967 the ratio of General Motors workers to pensioners—what demographers call the dependency ratio—was 10 to 1. In 1990 it was approaching 1 to 1. "We're building one hell of a burden for our future workers," warned a personnel manager. The same burden was straining the social security system. To finance an ever-growing group of retirees, American workers had to contribute an ever-higher portion of their paycheck to the social security system. During the 1980s, social security payroll taxes increased 24 percent.

The 1990 census described a nation on the move, as the "Sunbelt" states of the South and West continued to lure residents from the Midwest and Northeast. Fully 90 percent of the nation's total population growth during the 1980s came in southern or western states. California gained more people than any other state during the eighties, boosting its total to 29.8 million, 5 million more than in 1980. Texas and Florida each added more than 3 million new residents, while West Virginia, Iowa, and the District of Columbia experienced a net loss of residents. The Northeast became the least populous region of the country. These population shifts forced a massive redistricting of the House of Representatives, with Florida and California gaining three more seats each and Texas two, while states such as New York lost seats.

As they moved during the 1980s, Americans tended to settle in larger and larger communities. Almost 90 percent of the decade's population growth occurred in large metropolitan areas. The number of cities with 100,000 people or more increased by 29 to a total of 195, with 18 of the new metropolises in California alone. In 1990 some 78 percent of the population lived in a metropolitan urban area and, for the first time, a majority of Americans lived in cities of a million or more people. "We are a country not only of city dwellers," said a Census Bureau analyst, "but of large-city dwellers, a country of metropolitan-dwellers." This move to the cities largely reflected trends in the job market, as the economy continued to shift from manufacturing to professional service industries, particularly those specializing in telecommunications and information-processing.

The 1990 census also showed that women continued to enter the work force in large numbers. Indeed, one of the most significant sociological developments in American life since 1970 was the accelerated entry of women into the world of work outside the home. In 1970, 38 percent of the work force was female; in 1990 the figure was almost 50 percent. Women workers accounted for 60 percent of labor force growth since 1980, and fully 58 percent of all adult women were gainfully employed. A third of the new medical doctors during the eighties were women (4 percent in 1970); 40 percent of new lawyers were female (8.4 percent in 1970); and 22.6 percent of new dentists were women (less than 1 percent in 1970). Such advances in the professions indicated that women were also better educated than ever. During the 1980s the educational gap between men and women continued to narrow. Among people aged forty-five to fifty-four, the share of men with college degrees was ten points higher than the share of women. But among people aged twenty-five to thirty-four the difference was less than 1 percent.

The decline of the traditional family unit—two parents with children—continued during the 1980s. The proportion of the nation's households in that category declined from 31 percent in 1980 to 26 percent in 1990. And more people were living alone than ever before, largely as a result of high divorce rates or a growing practice of delaying marriage until well into the twenties. One out of every four households in 1990 was made up of a person living alone, a 26 percent increase over 1980. The number of single mothers increased 35 percent during the decade. The rate was much higher for African-Americans: in 1990 less than 38 percent of black children lived with both parents, down from 67 percent in 1960.

Young blacks burdened by the absence of one or both parents also faced shrinking economic opportunities in the 1980s. The 1990 census documented a slight decline in the proportion of Americans living in poverty, but a substantially heightened inequality in the distribution of income. Roughly 13 percent of the American people in 1990 were living at or below the official poverty level, pegged at $12,675 in annual income for a family of four. The urban poor were particularly victimized by a developing underclass culture, with young black males suffering the most. In 1990, the leading cause of death among black males between the ages of fifteen and twenty-four was homicide. Twenty-five percent of black males aged twenty to twenty-nine were in prison, on parole, or on probation while only 4 percent were enrolled in college. Forty percent of black adult males were functionally illiterate.

THE NEW IMMIGRANTS   The Census Bureau reports also revealed that the racial and ethnic composition of the country changed more during the 1980s than at any other time in the twentieth century, with nearly one in every four Americans claiming African, Asian, Hispanic, or American Indian ancestry. Among an overall population of 250 million, blacks represented 12 percent of the total, Hispanics 9 percent, Asians about 3 percent, and American Indians almost 1 percent. The rate of increase among those four groups was twice as fast as it had been during the 1970s.

The primary cause of this dramatic change in the nation's ethnic mix was a surge of immigration. During the 1980s, legal immigration into the United States totaled almost 6 million people, 30 percent higher than the previous decade and more than in any other decade except 1901–1910. If the hundreds of thousands of illegal aliens, mostly Mexicans and Haitians, were added to the totals, the figure would surpass the 8.8 million newcomers of the first decade of the century. In 1990 the United States welcomed more than twice as

RESIDENT POPULATION DISTRIBUTION FOR THE UNITED STATES BY RACE AND HISPANIC ORIGIN: 1990 AND 1980

	1990		1980		% Change
	Number	%	Number	%	
Total population	248,709,873	100.0	226,545,805	100.0	9.8
White	199,686,070	80.3	188,371,622	83.1	6.0
Black	29,986,060	12.1	26,495,025	11.7	13.2
American Indian, Eskimo, or Aleut	1,959,234	0.8	1,420,400	0.6	37.9
Asian or Pacific Islander	7,273,662	2.9	3,500,439	1.5	107.8
Other race	9,804,847	3.9	6,758,319	3.0	45.1
Hispanic origin	22,354,059	9.0	14,608,673	6.4	53.0

Source: Bureau of the Census, 1991.

many immigrants as all other countries in the world put together. The magnetic attraction of the United States to foreigners during the 1980s was vividly revealed in 1987 when the Immigration Service opened a special "visa lottery" for citizens in those countries historically shortchanged by annual immigration quotas. Officials allotted 10,000 such visas and assumed that would meet the demand, but 1.4 million people applied.

Even more significant than the overall number of newcomers were their places of origin. For the first time in the nation's history, the majority of immigrants came not from Europe but from other parts of the world. The percentage of European immigrants to the United States declined from 53 percent of the total in the 1950s to 12 percent in the 1980s. Asian-Americans were the fastest-growing segment of the population in the eighties, with numbers increasing by 80 percent, a rate seven times as great as the general population. Among the legal immigrants during the decade, Mexicans made up the largest share, averaging about 60,000 a year. The second-highest number came from the Philippines (46,000), and immigrants from mainland China, Taiwan, and Hong Kong totaled 45,000 annually. The next largest groups were Vietnamese and Koreans, followed by Dominicans, Asian Indians, Jamaicans, Iranians, Cubans, Cambodians, and Laotians.

Heightening the social impact of these new immigrants was their tendency to cluster in a handful of states and cities. Most of them gravitated to New York, Illinois, and New Jersey, as well as Florida, Texas, Hawaii, California, and other Sunbelt states. By 1990, California harbored 64 percent of the Asian-Americans in the country, and 34 percent of the Hispanics. The population of Miami, Florida, was 64 percent Hispanic, and San Antonio, Texas, boasted 55 percent. Los Angeles contained 2 million Mexican-Americans, more than any other city except Mexico City itself. Preferring their own ethnic enclaves and bringing with them distinctive languages, cuisine, clothes, dress, and folkways, the immigrants from Asia, Latin America, and the Caribbean quickly became an insistent cultural presence. "It's fascinating," remarked New York governor Mario Cuomo, himself the son of Italian immigrants. "For those of us who have been in the city for fifty years, it's wonderful to see the faces on the street now. Our diversity level has gone up." When asked to assess the overall impact of the new immgration trends, he replied: "Plus, plus, plus."

Others were equally enthusiastic about the benefits of America's distinctive cultural pluralism. The theme even emerged in General

IMMIGRANTS ADMITTED BY TOP 15 COUNTRIES OF BIRTH IN FISCAL YEAR 1990

Country of Birth	1990
Total	**656,111**
Mexico	56,549
Philippines	54,907
Vietnam	48,662
Dominican Republic	32,064
Korea	29,548
China (mainland)	28,746
India	28,679
Soviet Union	25,350
Jamaica	18,828
Iran	18,031
Taiwan	13,839
United Kingdom	13,730
Canada	13,717
Poland	13,334
Haiti	11,862
Other	248,265

Source: U.S. Immigration and Naturalization Service, 1991.

Schwarzkopf's address to Congress upon his return from the Persian Gulf. The Allied forces in the Gulf, he emphasized, "were Protestants and Catholics and Jews and Muslims and Buddhists . . . fighting for a common and just cause. . . . We were black and white and yellow and brown and red, and we noticed when our blood was shed in the desert, it didn't separate by race but it flowed together."

But battlefield experiences proved to be more bonding than the day-to-day encounters between ethnic groups back home. What New York City mayor David Dinkins liked to characterize as America's "gorgeous mosaic" of racial and ethnic groups seemed to be losing its cohesion during the century's last decade. The wave of new immigration brought rising conflict between old and new ethnics. African-American leaders such as the Reverend Calvin Butts of the Abyssinian Baptist Church in Harlem worried that the newcomers were gaining an economic foothold at the expense of poor blacks. And many native whites resented the influx of newcomers into their communities. When a Miami radio talk-show host invited listeners to share their feelings about continuing Cuban immigration into south Florida, one suggested that they "be shot before they land." In Texas, Louisiana, and Florida, angry white fishermen joined with local chapters of the Ku Klux Klan in harassing and assaulting Vietnamese shrimpers. A group of laid-off Detroit auto workers vented their frustration against imported Japanese cars by beating to death an Asian passerby who, it turned out, was a Chinese-American. California witnessed a violent gang war between Hispanic and Cambodian residents, two immigrant groups with little in common except the desire to build a new life in the same neighborhood.

Such clashes recall earlier chapters in American immigrant history, a story marked from the start by ambivalence about the nation's tradition of inclusiveness. With rhetoric reminiscent of the nativist movement a century earlier, critics of the new tide of immigration charged that America was being "overrun" with foreigners; they questioned whether Hispanics and Asians could be "assimilated" into American culture. "We should start reducing quotas before we become a Third World country," argued David Duke, a former Klan member elected as Republican state legislator in Louisiana. Others made the same ethnocentric point. "As whites see their power and control over their lives declining," asked Dr. John Tanton, co-founder of a nativist group called US English, "will they simply go quietly into the night? Or will there be an explosion?" Tanton vowed to fight, and he led a campaign for the repeal of bilingual education programs and for a federal law mandating English as the official national language. In 1986 California voters passed a referendum ending bilingual education. Florida soon followed suit.

The bitter irony of this new nativism was that it targeted recent immigrants for bringing with them to the United States virtues long prized by Americans—hope, energy, persistence, and an aggressive work ethic. Like most of their predecessors who braved tremendous hardships to make their way to America, they toiled long and hard for a slice of the American dream, and most economic studies concluded that their presence was beneficial to the nation. They created more wealth than they consumed, and many of them compiled an astonishing record of achievement. The median household income of Asian-Americans, for example, exceeded every other group, including native whites, and Asian-Americans were disproportionately represented in the nation's most prestigious colleges and universities. Although constituting only 1.6 percent of the total population in 1985, Asian-Americans made up over 11 percent of Harvard's freshman class and almost 20 percent at Berkeley and the California Institute of Technology. Yet the very success of the new immigrants contributed to the resentment they encountered from other groups.

Distrust and bitterness between native blacks and whites soared as well, issuing in a series of violent incidents—white police brutally beating a black suspect in Los Angeles, a gang of black youths raping a white woman jogging in New York's Central Park—that both symbolized and aggravated the tensions. Demagogues of both races seized upon such incidents to fan racial hatreds, while politicians used the debate over affirmative-action hiring policies to play upon white prejudices. Even college campuses, the seedbed of the civil-rights movement, witnessed recurring incidents of racial bigotry.

In this turbulent atmosphere of mounting ethnic strife and political confrontation, some observers worried that the social fabric was being stretched to the breaking point. The nation seemed awash in "special-interest groups," highly organized, well-financed, and politically savvy organizations designed to promote single issues: corporate tax breaks, gun ownership, prayer in schools, abortion, animal rights, and environmentalism, to name just a few. It was becoming increasingly difficult to recognize the common good. Said a prominent law professor: "We are witnessing a gradual decline in the legal and social significance of community interests."

Many critics of this eroding sense of commonality blamed the influx of foreigners. Yet as a 1991 editorial in the *Los Angeles Times* pointed out, the immigrants of the eighties were not primarily responsible for the fragmentation of cultural consensus: immigrants arrived in a country that was already losing its sense of collective unity. "Conformity is no longer the norm because there is nothing to conform to, no single national norm of culture, behavior, religion. In these circumstances, to blame immigrants for being different is to miss the point." Indeed the most potent challenge facing Americans during the 1990s came not from abroad but from within: how could they find a "common ground" of shared civic values that nourished both cultural pluralism and individual rights? How could Americans live up to their national motto—*E pluribus unum*, One out of many? The dream of pluralistic unity survives, and in its resilient imperative Americans continued to find both challenge and hope.

FURTHER READING

For further insight into Reagan and his policies see the memoirs of members of his administration, such as Donald Regan's *For the Record: From Wall Street to Washington* (1988), Peggy Noonan's *What I Saw at the Revolution: A Political Life in the Reagan Era* (1990), or Terrel Bell's *The Thirteenth Man: A Reagan Cabinet Memoir* (1988).

Robert B. Reich's *The Next American Frontier* (1981)° examines the nation's recent industrial crisis. On Reaganomics, see David Stockman's *The Triumph of Politics: How the Reagan Revolution Failed* (1986) and Robert Lekachman's *Greed Is Not Enough: Reaganomics* (1982). On the issue of arms control, see Strobe Talbott's *Deadly Gambits: The Reagan Administration and the Stalemate in Nuclear Arms Control* (1984).°

For Reagan's foreign policy in Central America, see James Chace's *Endless War: How We Got Involved in Central America and What Can Be Done* (1984)° and Walter LaFeber's *Inevitable Revolutions: The United States in Central America* (rev. ed., 1984).° Shirley Christian's *Nicaragua: Revolution in the Family* (1985)° is a good account of affairs in that troubled country. Broader views of Reagan's foreign policy are offered in Alexander M. Haig, Jr.'s *Caveat: Realism, Reagan, and Foreign Policy* (1984) and Caspar W. Weinberger's *Fighting for Peace: Seven Critical Years in the Pentagon* (1990).

Elizabeth Drew's *Campaign Journal: The Political Events of 1983–1984* (1985) covers the events of the election of 1984, as does Jack W. Germond and Jules Witcover's *Wake Us When It's Over: Presidential Politics of 1984* (1985). Geraldine A. Ferraro and Linda B. Francke's *Ferraro: My Story* (1985)° is about America's first major female vice-presidential candidate.

On Reagan's second term, see Jane Mayer and Doyle McManus's *Landslide: The Unmaking of the President, 1984–1988* (1988) and Jane Hunter et al.'s *The Iran-Contra Connection* (1987). For a masterful work on the Iran-Contra affair, see Theodore Draper's *A Very Thin Line* (1991). Several books of essays collect varying assessments of the Reagan years. Among these are *The Reagan Revolution* (1988), edited by B. B. Kymlicka and Jean V. Matthews; *The Reagan Presidency: An Incomplete Revolution* (1990), edited by Dilys M. Hill et al.; and *Looking Back on the Reagan Presidency* (1990), edited by Larry Berman. The best overview thus far on the Reagan years is Lou Cannon's *The Role of a Lifetime* (1991).

°These books are available in paperback editions.

APPENDIX

THE DECLARATION OF
INDEPENDENCE

When in the course of human events, it becomes necessary for one people to dissolve the political bands which have connected them with another, and to assume the Powers of the earth, the separate and equal station to which the Laws of Nature and of Nature's God entitle them, a decent respect to the opinions of mankind requires that they should declare the causes which impel them to the separation.

We hold these truths to be self-evident, that all men are created equal, that they are endowed by their Creator with certain unalienable rights, that among these are Life, Liberty, and the pursuit of Happiness. That to secure these rights, Governments are instituted among Men, deriving their just powers from the consent of the governed. That whenever any Form of Government becomes destructive of these ends, it is the Right of the People to alter or to abolish it, and to institute new Government, laying its foundation on such principles and organizing its powers in such form, as to them shall seem most likely to effect their Safety and Happiness. Prudence, indeed, will dictate that Governments long established should not be changed for light and transient causes; and accordingly all experience hath shown, that mankind are more disposed to suffer, while evils are sufferable, than to right themselves by abolishing the forms to which they are accustomed. But when a long train of abuses and usurpations, pursuing invariably the same Object evinces a design to reduce them under absolute Despotism, it is their right, it is their duty, to throw off such Government, and to provide new Guards for their future security.—Such has been the patient sufferance of these Colonies; and such is now the necessity which constrains them to alter their former Systems of Government. The history of the present King of Great Britain is a history of repeated injuries and usurpations, all having in direct object the establishment of an absolute Tyranny over these States. To prove this, let Facts be submitted to a candid world.

He has refused his Assent to Laws, the most wholesome and necessary for the public good.

He has forbidden his Governors to pass Laws of immediate and pressing importance, unless suspended in their operation till his Assent should be obtained; and when so suspended, he has utterly neglected to attend to them.

He has refused to pass other Laws for the accommodation of large districts of people, unless those people would relinquish the right of Representation in the Legislature, a right inestimable to them and for midable to tyrants only.

He has called together legislative bodies at places unusual, uncomfortable, and distant from the depository of their public Records, for the sole purpose of fatiguing them into compliance with his measures.

He has dissolved Representative Houses repeatedly, for opposing with manly firmness his invasions on the rights of the people.

He has refused for a long time, after such dissolutions, to cause others to be elected; whereby the Legislative powers, incapable of Annihilation, have returned to the People at large for their exercise; the State remaining in the mean time exposed to all dangers of invasion from without, and convulsions within.

He has endeavoured to prevent the population of these States; for that purpose obstructing the Laws of Naturalization of Foreigners; refusing to pass others to encourage their migrations hither, and raising the conditions of new Appropriations of Lands.

He has obstructed the Administration of Justice, by refusing his Assent to Laws for establishing Judiciary powers.

He has made Judges dependent on his Will alone, for the tenure of their offices, and the amount and payment of their salaries.

He has erected a multitude of New Offices, and sent hither swarms of Officers to harass our People, and eat out their substance.

He has kept among us, in times of peace, Standing Armies without the Consent of our legislature.

He has affected to render the Military independent of and superior to the Civil Power.

He has combined with others to subject us to a jurisdiction foreign to our constitution, and unacknowledged by our laws; giving his Assent to their Acts of pretended Legislation:

For quartering large bodies of armed troops among us:

For protecting them, by a mock Trial, from Punishment for any Murders which they should commit on the Inhabitants of these States:

For cutting off our Trade with all parts of the world:

For imposing taxes on us without our Consent:

For depriving us of many cases, of the benefits of Trial by jury:

For transporting us beyond Seas to be tried for pretended offences:

For abolishing the free System of English Laws in a neighbouring Province, establishing therein an Arbitrary government, and enlarging its Boundaries so as to render it at once an example and fit instrument for introducing the same absolute rule into these Colonies:

For taking away our Charters, abolishing our most valuable Laws, and altering fundamentally the Forms of our Governments:

For suspending our own Legislatures, and declaring themselves in vested with Power to legislate for us in all cases whatsoever.

He has abdicated Government here, by declaring us out of his Protection and waging War against us.

He has plundered our seas, ravaged our Coasts, burnt our towns, and destroyed the lives of our people.

He is at this time transporting large armies of foreign mercenaries to compleat the works of death, desolation, and tyranny, already begun with circumstances of Cruelty & perfidy scarcely paralleled in the most barbarous ages, and totally unworthy the Head of a civilized nation.

He has constrained our fellow Citizens taken Captive on the high Seas to bear Arms against their Country, to become the executioners of their friends and Brethren, or to fall themselves by their Hands.

He has excited domestic insurrections amongst us, and has endeavoured to bring on the inhabitants of our frontiers, the merciless Indian Savages, whose known rule of warfare, is an undistinguished destruction of all ages, sexes, and conditions.

In every stage of these Oppressions We have Petitioned for Redress in the most humble terms: Our repeated Petitions have been answered only by repeated injury. A Prince, whose character is thus marked by every act which may define a Tyrant, is unfit to be the ruler of a free people.

Nor have We been wanting in attention to our British brethren. We have warned them from time to time of attempts by their legislature to extend an unwarrantable jurisdiction over us. We have reminded them of the circumstances of our emigration and settlement here. We have appealed to their native justice and magnanimity, and we have conjured them by the ties of our common kindred to disavow these usurpations, which, would inevitably interrupt our connections and correspondence. They too must have been deaf to the voice of justice and of consanguinity. We must, therefore, acquiesce in the necessity, which denounces our Separation, and hold them, as we hold the rest of mankind, Enemies in War, in Peace Friends.

WE, THEREFORE, the Representatives of the UNITED STATES OF AMERICA, in General Congress, Assembled, appealing to the Supreme Judge of the world for the rectitude of our intentions, do, in the Name, and by Authority of the good People of these Colonies, solemnly publish and declare, That these United Colonies are, and of Right ought to be FREE AND INDEPENDENT STATES; that they are Absolved from all Allegiance to the British Crown, and that all political connection between them and the State of Great Britain, is and ought to be totally dissolved; and that as Free and Independent States, they have full Power to levy War, conclude Peace, contract Alliances, establish Commerce, and to do all other Acts and Things which Independent States may of right do. And for the support of this Declaration, with a firm reliance on the Protection of Divine Providence, we mutually pledge to each other our Lives, our Fortunes, and our sacred Honor.

The foregoing Declaration was, by order of Congress, engrossed, and signed by the following members:

John Hancock

NEW HAMPSHIRE
Josiah Bartlett
William Whipple
Matthew Thornton

MASSACHUSETTS BAY
Samuel Adams
John Adams
Robert Treat Paine
Elbridge Gerry

RHODE ISLAND
Stephen Hopkins
William Ellery

CONNECTICUT
Roger Sherman
Samuel Huntington
William Williams
Oliver Wolcott

NEW YORK
William Floyd
Philip Livingston
Francis Lewis
Lewis Morris

NEW JERSEY
Richard Stockton
John Witherspoon
Francis Hopkinson
John Hart
Abraham Clark

PENNSYLVANIA
Robert Morris
Benjamin Rush
Benjamin Franklin
John Morton
George Clymer
James Smith
George Taylor
James Wilson
George Ross

DELAWARE
Caesar Rodney
George Read
Thomas M'Kean

MARYLAND
Samuel Chase
William Paca
Thomas Stone
*Charles Carroll, of
  Carrollton*

VIRGINIA
George Wythe
Richard Henry Lee
Thomas Jefferson
Benjamin Harrison
Thomas Nelson, Jr.
Francis Lightfoot Lee
Carter Braxton

NORTH CAROLINA
William Hooper
Joseph Hewes
John Penn

SOUTH CAROLINA
Edward Rutledge
Thomas Heyward, Jr.
Thomas Lynch, Jr.
Arthur Middleton

GEORGIA
Button Gwinnett
Lyman Hall
George Walton

Resolved, That copies of the Declaration be sent to the several assemblies, conventions, and committees, or councils of safety, and to the several commanding officers of the continental troops; that it be proclaimed in each of the United States, at the head of the army.

ARTICLES OF CONFEDERATION

To ALL TO WHOM these Presents shall come, we the undersigned Delegates of the States affixed to our Names send greeting.

Whereas the Delegates of the United States of America in Congress assembled did on the fifteenth day of November in the Year of our Lord One Thousand Seven Hundred and Seventy-seven, and in the Second Year of the Independence of America agree to certain articles of Confederation and perpetual Union between the States of Newhampshire, Massachusetts-bay, Rhodeisland and Providence Plantations, Connecticut, New York, New Jersey, Pennsylvania, Delaware, Maryland, Virginia, North-Carolina, South-Carolina and Georgia in the Words following, viz.

Articles of Confederation and perpetual Union between the States of Newhampshire, Massachusetts-bay, Rhodeisland and Providence Plantations, Connecticut, New-York, New-Jersey, Pennsylvania, Delaware, Maryland, Virginia, North-Carolina, South-Carolina and Georgia.

ARTICLE I. The stile of this confederacy shall be "The United States of America."

ARTICLE II. Each State retains its sovereignty, freedom and independence, and every power, jurisdiction and right, which is not by this confederation expressly delegated to the United States, in Congress assembled.

ARTICLE III. The said States hereby severally enter into a firm league of friendship with each other, for their common defence, the security of their liberties, and their mutual and general welfare, binding themselves to assist each other, against all force offered to, or attacks made upon them, or any of them, on account of religion, sovereignty, trade or any other pretence whatever.

ARTICLE IV. The better to secure and perpetuate mutual friendship and intercourse among the people of the different States in this Union, the free inhabitants of each of these States, paupers, vagabonds and fugitives from justice excepted, shall be entitled to all privileges and immunities of free citizens in the several States; and the people of each State shall have free ingress and regress to and from any other State, and shall enjoy therein all the privileges of trade and commerce, subject to the same duties, impositions and restrictions as the inhabitants thereof respectively, provided that such restrictions shall not extend so far as to prevent the removal of property imported into any State, to any other State of which the owner is an inhabitant; provided also that no imposition, duties or restriction shall be laid by any State, on the property of the United States, or either of them.

If any person guilty of, or charged with treason, felony, or other high misdemeanor in any State, shall flee from justice, and be found in any of the United States, he shall upon demand of the Governor or Executive power, of the State from which he fled, be delivered up and removed to the State having jurisdiction of his offence.

Full faith and credit shall be given in each of these States to the records, acts and judicial proceedings of the courts and magistrates of every other State.

ARTICLE V. For the more convenient management of the general interests of the United States, delegates shall be annually appointed in such manner as the legislature of each State shall direct, to meet in Congress on the first Monday in November, in every year, with a power reserved to each State, to recall its delegates, or any of them, at any time within the year, and to send others in their stead, for the remainder of the year.

No State shall be represented in Congress by less than two, nor by more than seven members; and no person shall be capable of being a delegate for more than three years in any term of six years; nor shall any person, being a delegate, be capable of holding any office under the United States, for which he, or another for his benefit receives any salary, fees or emolument of any kind.

Each State shall maintain its own delegates in a meeting of the States, and while they act as members of the committee of the States.

In determining questions in the United States, in Congress assembled, each State shall have one vote.

Freedom of speech and debate in Congress shall not be impeached or questioned in any court, or place out of Congress, and the members of Congress shall be protected in their persons from arrests and imprisonments, during the time of their going to and from, and attendance on Congress, except for treason, felony, or breach of the peace.

ARTICLE VI. No State without the consent of the United States in Congress assembled, shall send any embassy to, or receive any embassy from, or enter into any conference, agreement, alliance or treaty with any king, prince or state; nor shall any person holding any office of profit or trust under the United States, or any of them, accept of any present, emolument, office or title of any kind whatever from any king, prince or foreign state; nor shall the United States in Congress assembled, or any of them, grant any title of nobility.

No two or more States shall enter into any treaty, confederation or alliance whatever between them, without the consent of the United States in Congress assembled, specifying accurately the purposes for which the same is to be entered into, and how long it shall continue.

No State shall lay any imposts or duties, which may interfere with any stipulations in treaties, entered into by the United States in Congress assembled, with any king, prince or state, in pursuance of any treaties already proposed by Congress, to the courts of France and Spain.

No vessels of war shall be kept up in time of peace by any State, except such number only, as shall be deemed necessary by the United States in Congress assembled, for the defence of such State, or its trade; nor shall any body of forces be kept up by any State, in time of peace, except such number only, as in the judgment of the United States, in Congress assembled, shall be deemed requisite to garrison the forts necessary for the defence of such State; but every State shall always keep up a well regulated and disciplined militia, sufficiently armed and accoutred, and shall provide and constantly have ready for use, in public stores, a due number of field pieces and tents, and a proper quantity of arms, ammunition and camp equipage.

No State shall engage in any war without the consent of the United States in Congress assembled, unless such State be actually invaded by enemies, or shall have received certain advice of a resolution being formed by some nation of Indians to invade such State, and the danger is so imminent as not to admit of a delay, till the United States in Congress assembled can be consulted: nor shall any State grant commissions to any ships or vessels of war, nor letters of marque or reprisal, except it be after a declaration of war by the United States in Congress assembled, and then only against the kingdom or state and the subjects thereof, against which war has been so declared, and under such regulations as shall be established by the United States in Congress assembled, unless such State be infested by pirates, in which case vessels of war may be fitted out for that occasion, and kept so long as the danger shall continue, or until the United States in Congress assembled shall determine otherwise.

ARTICLE VII. When land-forces are raised by any State of the common defence, all officers of or under the rank of colonel, shall be appointed by the Legislature of each State respectively by whom such forces shall be raised, or in such manner as such State shall direct, and all vacancies shall be filled up by the State which first made the appointment.

ARTICLE VIII. All charges of war, and all other expenses that shall be incurred for the common defence or general welfare, and allowed by the United States in Congress assembled, shall be defrayed out of a common treasury, which shall be supplied by the several States, in proportion to the value of all land within each State, granted to or surveyed for any person, as such land and the buildings and improvements thereon shall be estimated according to such mode as the United States in Congress assembled, shall from time to time direct and appoint.

The taxes for paying that proportion shall be laid and levied by the authority and direction of the Legislatures of the several States within the time agreed upon by the United States in Congress assembled.

ARTICLE IX. The United States in Congress assembled, shall have the sole and exclusive right and power of determining on peace and war, except in the cases mentioned in the sixth article—of sending and receiving ambassadors—entering into treaties and alliances, provided that no treaty of commerce shall be made whereby the legislative power of the respective States shall be restrained from imposing such imposts and duties on foreigners, as their own people are subjected to, or from prohibiting the exportation or importation of and species of goods or commodities whatsoever—of establishing rules for deciding in all cases, what captures on land or water shall be legal, and in what manner prizes taken by land or naval forces in the service of the United States shall be divided or appropriated—of granting letters of marque and reprisal in times of peace—appointing courts for the trial of piracies and felonies committed on the high seas and establishing courts for receiving and determining finally appeals in all cases of captures, provided that no member of Congress shall be appointed a judge of any of the said courts.

The United States in Congress assembled shall also be the last resort on appeal in all disputes and differences now subsisting or that hereafter may arise between two or more States concerning boundary, jurisdiction or any other cause whatever; which authority shall always be exercised in the manner following. Whenever the legislative or executive authority or lawful agent of any State in controversy with another shall present a petition to Congress, stating the matter in question and praying for a hearing, notice thereof shall be given by order of Congress to the legislative or executive authority of the other State in controversy, and a day assigned for the appearance of the parties by their lawful agents, who shall then be directed to appoint by joint consent, commissioners or judges to constitute a court for hearing and determining the matter in question: but if they cannot agree, Congress shall name three persons out of each of the United States, and from the list of such persons each party shall alternately strike out one, the petitioners beginning, until the number shall be reduced to thirteen; and from that number not less than seven, nor more than nine names as Congress shall direct, shall in the presence of Congress be drawn out by lot, and the persons whose names shall be so drawn or any five of them, shall be commissioners or judges, to hear and finally determine the controversy, so always as a major part of the judges who shall hear the cause shall agree in the determination: and if either party shall neglect to attend at the day appointed, without reasons, which Congress shall judge sufficient, or being present shall refuse to strike, the Congress shall proceed to nominate three persons out of each State, and the Secretary of Congress shall strike in behalf of such party absent or refusing; and the judgment and sentence of the court to be appointed, in the manner before prescribed, shall be final and conclusive; and if any of the parties shall refuse to submit to the authority of such court, or to appear or defend their claim or cause, the court shall nevertheless proceed to pronounce sentence, or judgment, which shall in like manner be final and decisive, the judgment or sentence and other proceedings being in either case transmitted to Congress, and lodged among the acts of Congress for the security of the parties concerned: provided that every commissioner, before he sits in judgment, shall take an oath to be administered by one of the judges of the supreme or superior court of the State where the case shall be tried, "well and truly to hear and determine the matter in question, according to the best of his judgment, without favour, affection or hope of reward:" provided also that no State shall be deprived of territory for the benefit of the United States.

All controversies concerning the private right of soil claimed under different grants of two or more States, whose jurisdiction as they may respect such lands, and the states which passed such grants are adjusted, the said grants or either of them being at the same time claimed to have originated antecedent to such settlement of jurisdiction, shall on the petition of either party to the Congress of the United States, be finally determined as near as may be in the same manner as is before prescribed for deciding disputes respecting territorial jurisdiction between different States.

The United States in Congress assembled shall also have the sole and exclusive right and power of regulating the alloy and value of coin struck by their own authority, or by that of the respective States—fixing the standard of weights and measures throughout the United States—regulating the trade and managing all affairs with the Indians, not members of any of the States, provided that the legislative right of any State within its own limits be not infringed or violated—establishing and regulating post-offices from one State to another, throughout all of the United States, and exacting such postage on the papers passing thro' the same as may be requisite to defray the expenses of the said office—appointing all officers of the land forces, in the service of the United States, excepting regimental officers—appointing all the officers of the naval forces, and commissioning all officers whatever in the service of the United States—making rules for the government and regulation of the said land and naval forces, and directing their operations.

The United States in Congress assembled shall have authority to appoint a committee, to sit in the recess of Congress, to be denominated "a Committee of the States," and to consist of one delegate from each State; and to appoint such other committees and civil officers as may be necessary for managing the general affairs of the United States under their direction—to appoint one of their number to preside, provided that no person be allowed to serve in the office of president more than one year in any term of three years; to ascertain the necessary sums of money to be raised for the service of the United States, and to appropriate and apply the same for defraying the public expenses—to borrow money, or emit bills on the credit of the United States, transmitting every half year to the respective States an account of the sums of money so borrowed or emitted,—to build and equip a navy—to agree upon the number of land forces, and to make requisitions from each State for its quota, in proportion to the number of white inhabitants in such

State; which requisition shall be binding, and thereupon the Legislature of each State shall appoint the regimental officers, raise the men and cloath, arm and equip them in a soldier like manner, at the expense of the United States; and the officers and men so cloathed, armed and equipped shall march to the place appointed, and within the time agreed on by the United States in Congress assembled: but if the United States in Congress assembled shall, on consideration of circumstances judge proper that any State should not raise men, or should raise a smaller number of men than the quota thereof, such extra number shall be raised, officered, cloathed, armed and equipped in the same manner as the quota of such State, unless the legislature of such State shall judge that such extra number cannot be safely spared out of the same, in which case they shall raise officer, cloath, arm and equip as many of such extra number as they judge can be safely spared. And the officers and men so cloathed, armed and equipped, shall march to the place appointed, and within the time agreed on by the United States in Congress assembled.

The United States in Congress assembled shall never engage in a war, nor grant letters of marque and reprisal in time of peace, nor enter into any treaties or alliances, nor coin money, nor regulate the value thereof, nor ascertain the sums and expenses necessary for the defence and welfare of the United States, or any of them, nor emit bills, nor borrow money on the credit of the United States, nor appropriate money, nor agree upon the number of vessels to be built or purchased, or the number of land or sea forces to be raised, nor appoint a commander in chief of the army or navy, unless nine States assent to the same: nor shall a question on any other point, except for adjourning from day to day be determined, unless by the votes of a majority of the United States in Congress assembled.

The Congress of the United States shall have power to adjourn to any time within the year, and to any place within the United States, so that no period of adjournment be for a longer duration than the space of six months, and shall publish the journal of their proceedings monthly, except such parts thereof relating to treaties, alliances or military operations, as in their judgment require secresy; and the yeas and nays of the delegates of each State on any question shall be entered on the Journal, when it is desired by any delegate; and the delegates of a State, or any of them, at his or their request shall be furnished with a transcript of the said journal, except such parts as are above excepted, to lay before the Legislatures of the several States.

ARTICLE X. The committee of the States, or any nine of them, shall be authorized to execute, in the recess of Congress, such of the powers of Congress as the United States in Congress assembled, by the consent of nine States, shall from time to time think expedient to vest them with; provided that no power be delegated to the said committee, for the exercise of which, by the articles of confederation, the voice of nine States in the Congress of the United States assembled is requisite.

ARTICLE XI. Canada acceding to this confederation, and joining in the measures of the United States, shall be admitted into, and entitled to all the advantages of this Union: but no other colony shall be admitted into the same, unless such admission be agreed to by nine States.

ARTICLE XII. All bills of credit emitted, monies borrowed and debts contracted by, or under the authority of Congress, before the assembling of the United States, in pursuance of the present confederation, shall be deemed and considered as a charge against the United States, for payment and satisfaction whereof the said United States, and the public faith are hereby solemnly pledged.

ARTICLE XIII. Every State shall abide by the determinations of the United States in Congress assembled, on all questions which by this confederation are submitted to them. And the articles of this confederation shall be inviolably observed by every State, and the Union shall be perpetual; nor shall any alteration at any time hereafter be made in any of them; unless such alteration be agreed to in a Congress of the United States, and be afterwards confirmed by the Legislatures of every State.

And whereas it has pleased the Great Governor of the world to incline the hearts of the Legislatures we respectively represent in Congress, to approve of, and to authorize us to ratify the said articles of confederation and perpetual union. Know ye that we the undersigned delegates, by virtue of the power and authority to us given for that purpose, do by these presents, in the name and in behalf of our respective constituents, fully and entirely ratify and confirm each and every of the said articles of confederation and perpetual union, and all and singular the matters and things therein contained: and we do further solemnly plight and engage the faith of our respective constituents, that they shall abide by the determinations of the United States in Congress assembled, on all questions, which by the said confederation are submitted to them. And that the articles thereof shall be inviolably observed by the States we respectively represent, and that the Union shall be perpetual.

In witness thereof we have hereunto set our hands in Congress. Done at Philadelphia in the State of Pennsylvania the ninth day of July in the year of our Lord one thousand seven hundred and seventy-eight, and in the third year of the independence of America.

THE CONSTITUTION OF
THE UNITED STATES

WE THE PEOPLE OF THE UNITED STATES, in order to form a more perfect Union, establish Justice, insure domestic Tranquility, provide for the common defence, promote the general Welfare, and secure the Blessings of Liberty to ourselves and our Posterity, do ordain and establish this Constitution for the United States of America.

ARTICLE. I.

Section. 1. All legislative Powers herein granted shall be vested in a Congress of the United States, which shall consist of a Senate and House of Representatives.

Section. 2. The House of Representatives shall be composed of Members chosen every second Year by the People of the several States, and the Electors in each State shall have the Qualifications requisite for Electors of the most numerous Branch of the State Legislature.

No Person shall be a Representative who shall not have attained to the Age of twenty five Years, and been seven Years a Citizen of the United States, and who shall not, when elected, be an Inhabitant of that State in which he shall be chosen.

Representatives and direct Taxes shall be apportioned among the several States which may be included within this Union, according to their respective Numbers, which shall be determined by adding to the whole Number of free Persons, including those bound to Service for a Term of Years, and excluding Indians not taxed, three fifths of all other Persons. The actual Enumeration shall be made within three Years after the first Meeting of the Congress of the United States, and within every subsequent Term of ten Years, in such Manner as they shall by Law direct. The Number of Representatives shall not exceed one for every thirty Thousand, but each State shall have at Least one Representative; and until such enumeration shall be made, the State of New Hampshire shall be entitled to chuse three, Massachusetts eight, Rhode-Island and Providence Plantations one, Connecticut five, New-York six, New Jersey four, Pennsylvania eight, Delaware one, Maryland six, Virginia ten, North Carolina five, South Carolina five, and Georgia three.

When vacancies happen in the Representation from any state, the Executive Authority thereof shall issue Writs of Election to fill such Vacancies.

The House of Representatives shall chuse their Speaker and other Officers; and shall have the sole Power of Impeachment.

Section. 3. The Senate of the United States shall be composed of two Senators from each State, chosen by the legislature thereof, for six Years; and each Senator shall have one Vote.

Immediately after they shall be assembled in Consequence of the first Election, they shall be divided as equally as may be into three Classes. The Seats of the Senators of the first Class shall be vacated at the Expiration of the second Year, of the second Class at the Expiration of the fourth Year, and of the third Class at the Expiration of the sixth Year, so that one third maybe chosen every second Year; and if Vacancies happen by Resignation, or otherwise, during the Recess of the Legislature of any State, the Executive thereof may make temporary Appointments until the next Meeting of the Legislature, which shall then fill such Vacancies.

No Person shall be a Senator who shall not have attained to the Age of thirty Years, and been nine Years a Citizen of the United States, and who shall not, when elected, be an Inhabitant of that State for which he shall be chosen.

The Vice President of the United States shall be President of the Senate, but shall have no Vote, unless they be equally divided.

The Senate shall chuse their other Officers, and also a President pro tempore, in the Absence of the Vice President, or when he shall exercise the Office of President of the United States.

The Senate shall have the sole Power to try all Impeachments. When sitting for that Purpose, they shall be on Oath or Affirmation. When the President of the United States is tried, the Chief Justice shall preside: And no Person shall be convicted without the Concurrence of two thirds of the Members present.

Judgment in Cases of Impeachment shall not extend further than to removal from Office, and disqualification to hold and enjoy any Office of honor, Trust or Profit under the United States: but the Party convicted shall nevertheless be liable and subject to Indictment, Trial, Judgment and Punishment, according to Law.

Section. 4. The Times, Places and Manner of holding Elections for Senators and Representatives, shall be prescribed in each State by the Legislature thereof; but the Congress may at any time by Law make or alter such Regulations, except as to the Places of chusing Senators.

The Congress shall assemble at least once in every Year, and such Meeting shall be on the first Monday in December, unless they shall by Law appoint a different Day.

Section. 5. Each House shall be the Judge of the Elections, Returns and Qualifications of its own Members, and a Majority of each shall constitute a Quorum to do Business; but a smaller Number may adjourn from day to day, and may be authorized to compel the Attendance of absent Members, in such Manner, and under such Penalties as each House may provide.

Each House may determine the Rules of its Proceedings, punish its Members for disorderly Behaviour, and, with the Concurrence of two thirds, expel a Member.

Each House shall keep a Journal of its Proceedings, and from time to time publish the same, excepting such Parts as may in their Judgment require Secrecy; and the Yeas and Nays of the Members of either House on any question shall, at the Desire of one fifth of those Present, be entered on the Journal.

Neither House, during the Session of Congress, shall, without the Consent of the other, adjourn for more than three days, not to any other Place than that in which the two Houses shall be sitting.

Section. 6. The Senators and Representatives shall receive a Compensation for their Services, to be ascertained by Law, and paid out of the Treasury of the United States. They shall in all Cases, except Treason, Felony and Breach of the Peace, be privileged from Arrest during their Attendance at the Session of their respective Houses, and in going to and returning from the same; and for any Speech or Debate in either House, they shall not be questioned in any other Place.

No Senator or Representative shall, during the Time for which he was elected, be appointed to any civil Office under the Authority of the United States, which shall have been created, or the Emoluments whereof shall have been encreased during such time; and no Person holding any Office under the United States, shall be a Member of either House during his Continuance in Office.

Section. 7. All Bills for raising Revenue shall originate in the House of Representatives; but the Senate may propose or concur with Amendments as on other Bills.

Every Bill which shall have passed the House of Representatives and the Senate shall, before it become a Law, be presented to the President of the United States; If he approve he shall sign it, but if not he shall return it, with his Objections to that House in which it shall have originated, who shall enter the Objections at large on their Journal, and proceed to reconsider it. If after such Reconsideration two thirds of that House shall agree to pass the Bill, it shall be sent, together with the Objections, to the other House, by which it shall likewise be reconsidered, and if approved by two thirds of that House, it shall become a Law. But in all such Cases the Votes of both Houses shall be determined by yeas and Nays, and the Names of the Persons voting for and against the Bill shall be entered on the Journal of each House respectively. If any Bill shall not be returned by the President within ten Days (Sundays excepted) after it shall have been presented to him, the Same shall be a Law, in like Manner as if he had signed it, unless the Congress by their Adjournment prevent its Return, in which Case it shall not be a Law.

Every Order, Resolution, or Vote to which the Concurrence of the Senate and House of Representatives may be necessary (except on a question of Adjournment) shall be presented to the President of the United States; and before the Same shall take Effect, shall be approved by him, or being disapproved by him, shall be repassed by two thirds of the Senate and House of Representatives, according to the Rules and Limitations prescribed in the Case of a Bill.

Section. 8. The Congress shall have Power To lay and collect Taxes, Duties, Imposts and Excises, to pay the Debts and provide for the common Defence and general Welfare of the United States; but all Duties, Imposts and Excises shall be uniform throughout the United States;

To borrow Money on the credit of the United States;

To regulate Commerce with foreign Nations, and among the several States, and with the Indian Tribes;

To establish an uniform Rule of Naturalization, and uniform Laws on the subject of Bankruptcies throughout the United States;

To coin Money, regulate the Value thereof, and of foreign Coin, and fix the Standard of Weights and Measures;

To provide for the Punishment of counterfeiting the Securities and current Coin of the United States;

To establish Post Offices and Post Roads;

To promote the Progress of Science and useful Arts, by securing for limited Times to Authors and Inventors the exclusive Right to their respective Writings and Discoveries;

To constitute Tribunals inferior to the supreme Court;

To define and punish Piracies and Felonies committed on the high Seas, and Offences against the Law of Nations;

To declare War, grant Letters of Marque and Reprisal, and make Rules concerning Captures on land and Water;

To raise and support Armies, but no Appropriation of Money to that Use shall be for a longer Term than two Years;

To provide and maintain a Navy;

To make Rules for the Government and Regulation of the land and naval Forces;

To provide for calling forth the Militia to execute the Laws of the Union, suppress Insurrections and repel Invasions;

To provide for organizing, arming, and disciplining, the Militia, and for governing such Part of them as may be employed in the Service of the United States, reserving to the States respectively, the Appointment of the Officers, and the Authority of training the Militia according to the discipline prescribed by Congress.

To exercise exclusive Legislation in all Cases whatsoever, over such District (not exceeding ten Miles square) as may, by Cession of Particular States, and the Acceptance of Congress, become the Seat of the Government of the United States, and to exercise like Authority over all Places purchased by the Consent of the Legislature of the State in which the Same shall be, for the Erection of Forts, Magazines, Arsenals, dock-Yards, and other needful Buildings;—And

To make all Laws which shall be necessary and proper for carrying into

Execution the foregoing Powers, and all other Powers vested by this Constitution in the Government of the United States, or in any Department or Officer thereof.

Section. 9. The Migration or Importation of such Persons as any of the States now existing shall think proper to admit, shall not be prohibited by the Congress prior to the Year one thousand eight hundred and eight, but a Tax or duty may be imposed on such Importation, not exceeding ten dollars for each Person.

The Privilege of the Writ of Habeas Corpus shall not be suspended, unless when in Cases of Rebellion or Invasion the public Safety may require it.

No Bill of Attainder or ex post facto Law shall be passed.

No Capitation, or other direct, Tax shall be laid, unless in Proportion to the Census or Enumeration herein before directed to be taken.

No Tax or Duty shall be laid on Articles exported from any State.

No Preference shall be given by any Regulation of Commerce or Revenue to the Ports of one State over those of another: nor shall Vessels bound to, or from, one State, be obliged to enter, clear, or pay Duties in another.

No Money shall be drawn from the Treasury, but in Consequence of Appropriations made by Law; and a regular Statement and Account of the Receipts and Expenditures of all public Money shall be published from time to time.

No Title of Nobility shall be granted by the United States: And no Person holding any Office of Profit or trust under them, shall, without the Consent of the Congress, accept of any present, Emolument, Office, or Title, of any kind whatever, from any King, prince, or foreign State.

Section 10. No State shall enter into any Treaty, Alliance, or Confederation; grant Letters of Marque and Reprisal; coin Money; emit Bills of Credit; make any Thing but gold and silver Coin a Tender in Payment of Debts; pass any Bill of Attainder, ex post facto Law, or Law impairing the Obligation of Contracts, or grant any Title of Nobility.

No State shall, without the Consent of the Congress, lay any Imposts or Duties on Imports or Exports, except what may be absolutely necessary for executing it's inspection Laws: and the net Produce of all Duties and Imposts, laid by any State on Imports or Exports, shall be for the Use of the Treasury of the United States; and all such Laws shall be subject to the Revision and Controul of the Congress.

No State shall, without the Consent of Congress, lay any Duty of Tonnage, keep Troops, or Ships of War in time of Peace, enter into any Agreement or Compact with another State, or with a foreign Power, or engage in War, unless actually invaded, or in such imminent Danger as will not admit of delay.

ARTICLE. II.

Section. 1. The executive Power shall be vested in a President of the United States of America. He shall hold his Office during the term of four Years, and, together with the Vice President, chosen for the same Term, be elected, as follows

Each State shall appoint, in such Manner as the Legislature thereof may direct, a Number of Electors, equal to the whole Number of Senators and Representatives to which the State may be entitled in the Congress: but no Senator or Representative, or Person holding an Office of Trust or Profit under the United States, shall be appointed an Elector.

The Electors shall meet in their respective States, and vote by Ballot for two Persons, of whom one at least shall not be an Inhabitant of the same State with themselves. And they shall make a List of all the Persons voted for, and of the Number of Votes for each; which List they shall sign and certify, and transmit sealed to the Seat of the Government of the United States, directed to the President of the Senate. The President of the Senate shall, in the Presence of the Senate and House of Representatives, open all the Certificates, and the Votes shall then be counted. The Person having the greatest Number of Votes shall be the President, if such Number be a Majority of the whole Number of Electors appointed; and if there be more than one who have such Majority, and have an equal Number of Votes, then the House of Representatives shall immediately chuse by Ballot one of them for President; and if no Person have a Majority, then from the five highest on the List the said House shall in like Manner chuse the President. But in chusing the President, the Votes shall be taken by States, the Representation from each State having one Vote; A quorum for this Purpose shall consist of a Member or Members from two thirds of the States, and a Majority of all the States shall be necessary to a Choice. In every Case, after the Choice of the President, the Person having the greatest Number of Votes of the Electors shall be the Vice President. But if there should remain two or more who have equal Votes, the Senate shall chuse from them by Ballot the Vice President.

The Congress may determine the Time of chusing the Electors, and the Day on which they shall give their Votes; which Day shall be the same throughout the United States.

No Person except a natural born Citizen, or a Citizen of the United States, at the time of the Adoption of this Constitution, shall be eligible to the Office of President; neither shall any Person be eligible to that Office who shall not have attained to the Age of thirty five Years, and been fourteen Years a Resident within the United States.

In Case of the Removal of the President from Office, or of his Death, Resignation, or Inability to discharge the Powers and Duties of the said Office, the Same shall devolve on the Vice President, and the Congress may by Law provide for the Case of Removal, Death, Resignation or Inability, both of the President and Vice President, declaring what Officer shall then act as President, and such Officer shall act accordingly, until the Disability be removed, or a President shall be elected.

The President shall, at stated Times, receive for his Services, a Compensation, which shall neither be encreased or diminished during the Period for which he shall have been elected, and he shall not receive within that Period any other Emolument from the United States, or any of them.

Before he enters on the Execution of his Office, he shall take the following Oath or Affirmation:—"I do solemnly swear (or affirm) that I will faithfully execute the Office of President of the United States, and will to the best of my Ability, preserve, protect and defend the Constitution of the United States."

Section. 2. The President shall be Commander in Chief of the Army and Navy of the United States, and of the Militia of the several States, when called into the actual Service of the United States; he may require the Opinion, in writing, of the principal Officer in each of the executive Departments, upon any Subject relating to the Duties of their respective Offices, and he shall have Power to grant Reprieves and Pardons for Offences against the United States, except in Cases of Impeachment.

He shall have Power, by and with the Advice and Consent of the Senate, to make Treaties, provided two thirds of the Senators present concur; and he shall nominate, and by and with the Advice and Consent of the Senate, shall appoint Ambassadors, other public Ministers and Consuls, Judges of the supreme Court, and all other Officers of the United States, whose Appointments are not herein otherwise provided for, and which shall be established by Law; but the Congress may by Law vest the Appointment of such inferior Officers, as they think proper, in the President alone, in the Courts of Law, or in the Heads of Departments.

The President shall have Power to fill up all Vacancies that may happen during the Recess of the Senate, by granting Commissions which shall expire at the End of their next Session.

Section. 3. He shall from time to time give to the Congress Information of the State of the Union, and recommend to their Consideration such Measures as he shall judge necessary and expedient; he may, on extraordinary Occasions, convene both Houses, or either of them, and in Case of Disagreement between them, with Respect to the Time of Adjournment, he may adjourn them to such Time as he shall think proper; he shall receive Ambassadors and other public Ministers; he shall take Care that the Laws be faithfully executed, and shall Commission all the Officers of the United States.

Section. 4. The President, Vice President and all civil Officers of the United States, shall be removed from Office on Impeachment for, and Conviction of, Treason, Bribery, or other high Crimes and Misdemeanors.

ARTICLE. III.

Section. 1. The judicial Power of the United States, shall be vested in one supreme Court, and in such inferior Courts as the Congress may from time to time ordain and establish. The Judges, both of the supreme and inferior Courts, shall hold their Offices during good Behavior, and shall, at stated Times, receive for their Services, a Compensation, which shall not be diminished during their Continuance in Office.

Section. 2. The judicial Power shall extend to all Cases, in Law and Equity, arising under this Constitution, the Laws of the United States, and Treaties made, or which shall be made, under their Authority;—to all Cases affecting Ambassadors, other public Ministers and Consuls;—to all Cases of admiralty and maritime Jurisdiction;—the Controversies to which the United States shall be a Party;—to Controversies between two or more States;—between a State and Citizens of another State;—between Citizens of different States;—between Citizens of the same State claiming Lands under Grants of different States, and between a State, or the Citizens thereof, and foreign States, Citizens or Subjects.

In all cases affecting Ambassadors, other public Ministers and Consuls, and those in which a State shall be Party, the supreme Court shall have original Jurisdiction. In all the other Cases before mentioned, the supreme Court shall have appellate Jurisdiction, both as to Law and Fact, with such Exceptions, and under such Regulations as the Congress shall make.

The Trial of all Crimes, except in Cases of Impeachment, shall be by Jury; and such Trial shall be held in the State where the said Crimes shall have been committed; but when not committed within any State, the Trial shall be at such Place or Places as the Congress may by Law have directed.

Section. 3. Treason against the United States, shall consist only in levying War against them, or in adhering to their Enemies, giving them Aid and Comfort. No Person shall be convicted of Treason unless on the Testimony of two Witnesses to the same overt Act, or on Confession in open Court.

The Congress shall have Power to declare the Punishment of Treason, but no Attainder of Treason shall work Corruption of Blood, or Forfeiture except during the Life of the Person attainted.

ARTICLE. IV.

Section. 1. Full Faith and Credit shall be given in each State to the public Acts, Records, and judicial Proceedings of every other State. And the Congress may by general Laws prescribe the Manner in which such Acts, Records and Proceedings shall be proved, and the Effect thereof.

Section. 2. The Citizens of each State shall be entitled to all Privileges and Immunities of Citizens in the several States.

A Person charged in any State with Treason, Felony, or other Crime, who shall flee from Justice, and be found in another State, shall on Demand of the executive Authority of the State from which he fled, be delivered up, to be removed to the State having Jurisdiction of the Crime.

No Person held to Service or Labour in one State, under the Laws thereof, escaping into another, shall, in Consequence of any Law or Regulation therein, be discharged from such Service or Labour, but shall be delivered up on Claim of the Party to whom such Service or Labour may be due.

Section. 3. New States may be admitted by the Congress into this Union; but no new State shall be formed or erected within the Jurisdiction of any other State; nor any State be formed by the Junction of two or more States, or Parts of States, without the consent of the Legislatures of the States concerned as well as of the Congress.

The Congress shall have Power to dispose of and make all needful Rules and Regulations respecting the Territory or other Property belonging to the United States; and nothing in this Constitution shall be so construed as to Prejudice any Claims of the United States, or of any particular States.

Section. 4. The United States shall guarantee to every State in this Union a Republican Form of Government, and shall protect each of them against Invasion; and on Application of the Legislature, or of the Executive (when the Legislature cannot be convened) against domestic Violence.

ARTICLE. V.

The Congress, whenever two thirds of both Houses shall deem it necessary, shall propose Amendments to this Constitution, or, on the Application of the Legislatures of two thirds of the several States, shall call a Convention for proposing Amendments, which, in either Case, shall be valid to all Intents and Purposes, as Part of this Constitution, when ratified by the Legislatures of three fourths of the several States, or by Conventions in three fourths thereof, as the one or the other Mode of Ratification may be proposed by the Congress; Provided that no Amendment which may be made prior to the Year One thousand eight hundred and eight shall in any Manner affect the first and fourth Clauses in the Ninth Section of the first Article; and that no State, without its Consent, shall be deprived of its equal Suffrage in the Senate.

ARTICLE. VI.

All Debts contracted and Engagements entered into, before the Adoption of this Constitution, shall be as valid against the United States under this Constitution, as under the Confederation.

This Constitution, and the Laws of the United States which shall be made in Pursuance thereof; and all Treaties made, or which shall be made, under the Authority of the United States, shall be the supreme Law of the Land; and the Judges in every State shall be bound thereby, any Thing in the Constitution or Laws of any State to the Contrary notwithstanding.

The Senators and Representatives before mentioned, and the Members of the several State Legislatures, and all executive and judicial Officers, both of the United States and of the several States, shall be bound by Oath or Affirmation, to support this Constitution; but no religious Test shall ever be required as a Qualification to any Office or public Trust under the United States.

ARTICLE. VII.

The Ratification of the Conventions of nine States, shall be sufficient for the Establishment of this Constitution between the States so ratifying the Same.

Done in Convention by the Unanimous Consent of the States present the Seventeenth Day of September in the Year of our Lord one thousand seven hundred and Eighty seven and of the Independence of the United States of America the Twelfth. In witness thereof We have hereunto subscribed our Names,

G^o. WASHINGTON—Presd^t.
and deputy from Virginia.

New Hampshire	John Langdon Nicholas Gilman		Geo: Read Gunning Bed-
Massachusetts	Nathaniel Gorham Rufus King	Delaware	ford jun John Dickinson Richard Bassett
Connecticut	Wm Saml Johnson Roger Sherman		Jaco: Broom
New York: . . .	Alexander Hamilton	Maryland	James McHenry Dan of St Thos Jenifer Danl Carroll
New Jersey	Wil: Livingston David A. Brearley. Wm Paterson. Jona: Dayton	Virginia	John Blair— James Madison Jr.
Pennsylvania	B Franklin Thomas Mifflin Robt Morris Geo. Clymer Thos FitzSimons Jared Ingersoll James Wilson Gouv Morris	North Carolina	Wm Blount Richd Dobbs Spaight. Hu Williamson
		South Carolina	J. Rutledge Charles Cotesworth Pinckney Charles Pinckney Pierce Butler.
		Georgia	William Few Abr Baldwin

AMENDMENTS TO THE CONSTITUTION

ARTICLES IN ADDITION TO, and Amendment of the Constitution of the United States of America, proposed by Congress, and ratified by the Legislatures of the several States, pursuant to the fifth Article of the original Constitution.

AMENDMENT I.

Congress shall make no law respecting an establishment of religion, or prohibiting the free exercise thereof; or abridging the freedom of speech, or of the press; or the right of the people peaceably to assemble, and to petition the Government for a redress of grievances.

AMENDMENT II.

A well regulated Militia, being necessary to the security of a free State, the right of the people to keep and bear Arms, shall not be infringed.

AMENDMENT III.

No Soldier shall, in time of peace be quartered in any house, without the consent of the Owner, nor in time of war, but in a manner to be prescribed by law.

AMENDMENT IV.

The right of the people to be secure in their persons, houses, papers, and effects, against unreasonable searches and seizures, shall not be violated, and no Warrants shall issue, but upon probable cause, supported by Oath or affirmation, and particularly describing the place to be searched, and the persons or things to be seized.

AMENDMENT V.

No person shall be held to answer for a capital, or otherwise infamous crime, unless on a presentment or indictment of a Grand Jury, except in cases arising in the land or naval forces, or in the Militia, when in actual service in time of War or public danger; nor shall any person be subject for the same offence to be twice put in jeopardy of life or limb; nor shall be compelled in any criminal case to be a witness against himself, nor be deprived of life, liberty, or property, without due process of law; nor shall private property be taken for public use, without just compensation.

AMENDMENT VI.

In all criminal prosecutions, the accused shall enjoy the right to a speedy and public trial, by an impartial jury of the State and district wherein the crime shall have been committed, which district shall have been previously ascertained by law, and to be informed of the nature and cause of the accusation; to be confronted with the witnesses against him; to have compulsory process for obtaining witnesses in his favor, and to have the Assistance of Counsel for his defence.

AMENDMENT VII.

In Suits at common law, where the value in controversy shall exceed twenty dollars, the right of trial by jury shall be preserved, and no fact tried by a jury, shall be otherwise re-examined in any Court of the United States, than according to the rules of the common law.

AMENDMENT VIII.

Excessive bail shall not be required, nor excessive fines imposed, nor cruel and unusual punishments inflicted.

AMENDMENT IX.

The enumeration in the Constitution, of certain rights, shall not be construed to deny or disparage others retained by the people.

AMENDMENT X.

The powers not delegated to the United States by the Constitution, nor prohibited by it to the States, are reserved to the States respectively, or to the people. [The first ten amendments went into effect December 15, 1791.]

AMENDMENT XI.

The Judicial power of the United States shall not be construed to extend to any suit in law or equity, commenced or prosecuted against one of the United States by Citizens of another State, or by Citizens or Subjects of any Foreign State. [January 8, 1798.]

AMENDMENT XII.

The Electors shall meet in their respective states, and vote by ballot for President and Vice-President, one of whom, at least, shall not be an inhabitant of the same state with themselves; they shall name in their ballots the person voted for as President, and in distinct ballots the person voted for as Vice-President, and they shall make distinct lists of all persons voted for as President, and of all persons voted for as Vice President, and of the number of votes for each, which lists they shall sign and certify, and transmit sealed to the seat of the government of the United States, directed to the President of the Senate;—The President of the Senate shall, in the presence of the Senate and House of Representatives, open all the certificates and the votes shall then be counted;—The person having the greatest number of votes for

President, shall be the President, if such number be a majority of the whole number of Electors appointed; and if no person have such majority, then from the persons having the highest numbers not exceeding three on the list of those voted for as President, the House of Representatives shall choose immediately, by ballot, the President. But in choosing the President, the votes shall be taken by states, the representation from each state having one vote; a quorum for this purpose shall consist of a member or members from two-thirds of the states, and a majority of all the states shall be necessary to a choice. And if the House of Representatives shall not choose a President whenever the right of choice shall devolve upon them, before the fourth day of March next following, then the Vice-President shall act as President, as in the case of the death or other constitutional disability of the President.—The person having the greatest number of votes as Vice-President, shall be the Vice-President, if such number be a majority of the whole number of Electors appointed, and if no person have a majority, then from the two highest numbers on the list, the Senate shall choose the Vice-President; a quorum for the purpose shall consist of two-thirds of the whole number of Senators, and a majority of the whole number shall be necessary to a choice. But no person constitutionally ineligible to the office of President shall be eligible to that of Vice-President of the United States. [September 25, 1804.]

Amendment XIII.

Section 1. Neither slavery nor involuntary servitude, except as a punishment for crime whereof the party shall have been duly convicted, shall exist within the United States, or any place subject to their jurisdiction.

Section 2. Congress shall have power to enforce this article by appropriate legislation. [December 18, 1865.]

Amendment XIV.

Section 1. All persons born or naturalized in the United States, and subject to the jurisdiction thereof, are citizens of the United States and of the State wherein they reside. No State shall make or enforce any law which shall abridge the privileges or immunities of citizens of the United States; nor shall any State deprive any person of life, liberty, or property, without due process of law; nor deny to any person within its jurisdiction the equal protection of the laws.

Section 2. Representatives shall be apportioned among the several States according to their respective numbers, counting the whole number of persons in each State, excluding Indians not taxed. But when the right to vote at any election for the choice of electors for President and Vice President of the United States, Representatives in Congress, the Executive and Judicial officers of a State, or the members of the Legislature thereof, is denied to any of the male inhabitants of such State, being twenty-one years of age, and citizens of the United States, or in any way abridged, except for participation in rebellion, or other crime, the basis of representation therein shall be reduced in the proportion which the number of such male citizens shall bear to the whole number of male citizens twenty-one years of age in such State.

Section 3. No person shall be a Senator or Representative in Congress, or elector of President and Vice President, or hold any office, civil or military, under the United States, or under any State, who, having previously taken an oath, as a member of Congress, or as an officer of the United States, or as a member of any State legislature, or as an executive or judicial officer of any State, to support the Constitution of the United States, shall have engaged in insurrection or rebellion against the same, or given aid or comfort to the enemeis thereof. But Congress may by a vote of two-thirds of each House, remove such disability.

Section 4. The validity of the public debt of the United States, authorized by law, including debts incurred for payment of pensions and bounties for services in suppressing insurrection or rebellion, shall not be questioned. But neither the United States nor any State shall assume or pay any debt or obligation incurred in aid of insurrection or rebellion against the United States, or any claim for the loss or emancipation of any slave; but all such debts, obligations and claims shall be held illegal and void.

Section 5. The Congress shall have power to enforce, by appropriate legislation, the provisions of this article. [July 28, 1868.]

AMENDMENT XV.

Section 1. The right of citizens of the United States to vote shall not be denied or abridged by the United States or by any State on account of race, color, or previous condition of servitude—

Section 2. The Congress shall have power to enforce this article by appropriate legislation.—[March 30, 1870.]

AMENDMENT XVI.

The Congress shall have power to lay and collect taxes on incomes, from whatever source derived, without apportionment among the several States, and without regard to any census or enumeration. [February 25, 1913.]

AMENDMENT XVII.

The Senate of the United States shall be composed of two senators from each State, elected by the people thereof, for six years; and each Senator shall have one vote. The electors in each State shall have the qualifications requisite for electors of the most numerous branch of the State legislature.

When vacancies happen in the representation of any State in the Senate, the executive authority of such State shall issue writs of election to fill such vacancies: *Provided,* That the legislature of any State may empower the executive thereof to make temporary appointments until the people fill the vacancies by election as the legislature may direct.

This amendment shall not be so construed as to affect the election or term of any senator chosen before it becomes valid as part of the Constitution. [May 31, 1913.]

Amendment XVIII.

After one year from the ratification of this article, the manufacture, sale, or transportation of intoxicating liquors within, the importation thereof into, or the exportation thereof from the United States and all territory subject to the jurisdiction thereof for beverage purposes is hereby prohibited.

The Congress and the several States shall have concurrent power to enforce this article by appropriate legislation.

This article shall be inoperative unless it shall have been ratified as an amendment to the Constitution by the legislatures of the several States, as provided in the Constitution, within seven years from the date of the submission thereof to the States by Congress. [January 29, 1919.]

Amendment XIX.

The right of citizens of the United States to vote shall not be denied or abridged by the United States or by any State on account of sex.

The Congress shall have power by appropriate legislation to enforce the provisions of this article. [August 26, 1920.]

Amendment XX.

Section 1. The terms of the President and Vice-President shall end at noon on the twentieth day of January, and the terms of Senators and Representatives at noon on the third day of January, of the years in which such terms would have ended if this article had not been ratified; and the terms of their successors shall then begin.

Section 2. The Congress shall assemble at least once in every year, and such meeting shall begin at noon on the third day of January, unless they shall by law appoint a different day.

Section 3. If, at the time fixed for the beginning of the term of the President, the President-elect shall have died, the Vice-President-elect shall become President. If a President shall not have been chosen before the time fixed for the beginning of his term, or if the President-elect shall have failed to qualify, then the Vice-President-elect shall act as President until a President shall have qualified; and the Congress may by law provide for the case wherein neither a President-elect nor a Vice-President-elect shall have qualified, declaring who shall then act as President, or the manner in which one who is to act shall be selected, and such person shall act accordingly until a President or Vice-President shall have qualified.

Section 4. The Congress may by law provide for the case of the death of any of the persons from whom the House of Representatives may choose a President whenever the right of choice shall have devolved upon them, and for the case of the death of any of the persons from whom the Senate may choose a Vice-President whenever the right of choice shall have devolved upon them.

Section 5. Sections 1 and 2 shall take effect on the 15th day of October following the ratification of this article.

Section 6. This article shall be inoperative unless it shall have been ratified as an amendment to the Constitution by the legislatures of three-fourths of the several States within seven years from the date of its submission. [February 6, 1933.]

AMENDMENT XXI.

Section 1. The eighteenth article of amendment to the Constitution of the United States is hereby repealed.

Section 2. The transportation or importation into any State, Territory or possession of the United States for delivery or use therein of intoxicating liquors, in violation of the laws thereof, is hereby prohibited.

Section 3. This article shall be inoperative unless it shall have been ratified as an amendment to the Constitution by convention in the several States, as provided in the Constitution, within seven years from the date of the submission thereof to the States by the Congress. [December 5, 1933.]

AMENDMENT XXII.

Section 1. No person shall be elected to the office of the President more than twice, and no person who has held the office of President, or acted as President, for more than two years of a term to which some other person was elected President shall be elected to the office of the President more than once. But this Article shall not apply to any person holding the office of President when this Article was proposed by the Congress, and shall not prevent any person who may be holding the office of President, or acting as President, during the term within which this Article becomes operative from holding the office of President or acting as President during the remainder of such term.

Section 2. This article shall be inoperative unless it shall have been ratified as an amendment to the Constitution by the legislatures of three-fourths of the several states within seven years from the date of its submission to the States by the Congress. [February 27, 1951.]

AMENDMENT XXIII.

Section 1. The District constituting the seat of government of the United States shall appoint in such manner as the Congress may direct:

A number of electors of President and Vice-President equal to the whole number of Senators and Representatives in Congress to which the District would be entitled if it were a State, but in no event more than the least populous State; they shall be in addition to those appointed by the States, but they shall be considered, for the purposes of the election of President and Vice-President, to be electors appointed by a State; and they shall meet in the District and perform such duties as provided by the twelfth article of amendment.

Section 2. The Congress shall have the power to enforce this article by appropriate legislation. [March 29, 1961.]

AMENDMENT XXIV.

Section 1. The right of citizens of the United States to vote in any primary or other election for President or Vice President, for electors for President or Vice President, or for Senator or Representative in Congress, shall not be denied or abridged by the United States or any State by reason of failure to pay any poll tax or other tax.

Section 2. The Congress shall have power to enforce this article by appropriate legislation. [January 23, 1964.]

AMENDMENT XXV.

Section 1. In case of the removal of the President from office or of his death or resignation, the Vice President shall become President.

Section 2. Whenever there is a vacancy in the office of Vice President, the President shall nominate a Vice President who shall take office upon confirmation by a majority vote of both Houses of Congress.

Section 3. Whenever the President transmits to the President pro tempore of the Senate and the Speaker of the House of Representatives his written declaration that he is unable to discharge the powers and duties of his office, and until he transmits to them a written declaration to the contrary, such powers and duties shall be discharged by the Vice President as Acting President.

Section 4. Whenever the Vice President and a majority of either the principal officers of the executive departments or of such other body as Congress may by law provide, transmit to the President pro tempore of the Senate and the Speaker of the House of Representatives their written declaration that the President is unable to discharge the powers and duties of his office, the Vice President shall immediately assume the powers and duties of the office as Acting President.

Thereafter, when the President transmits to the President pro tempore of the Senate and the Speaker of the House of Representatives his written declaration that no inability exists, he shall resume the powers and duties of his office unless the Vice President and a majority of either the principal officers of the executive departments or of such other body as Congress may by law provide, transmit within four days to the President pro tempore of the Senate and the Speaker of the House of Representatives their written declaration that the President is unable to discharge the powers and duties of his office. Thereupon Congress shall decide the issue, assembling within forty-eight hours for that purpose if not in session. If the Congress, within twenty-one days after receipt of the latter written declaration, or, if Congress is not in session, within twenty-one days after Congress is required to assemble, determines by two-thirds vote of both Houses that the President is unable to discharge the powers and duties of his office, the Vice President shall continue to discharge the same as Acting President; otherwise, the President shall resume the powers and duties of his office. [February 10, 1967.]

AMENDMENT XXVI.

Section 1. The right of citizens of the United States, who are eighteen years of age or older, to vote shall not be denied or abridged by the United States or by any State on account of age.

Section 2. The Congress shall have power to enforce this article by appropriate legislation [June 30, 1971.]

PRESIDENTIAL ELECTIONS

Year	Number of States	Candidates	Parties	Popular Vote	% of Popular Vote	Electoral Vote	% Voter Participation
1864	36	ABRAHAM LINCOLN	Republican	2,206,938	55.0	212	73.8
		George B. McClellan	Democratic	1,803,787	45.0	21	
1868	37	ULYSSES S. GRANT	Republican	3,013,421	52.7	214	78.1
		Horatio Seymour	Democratic	2,706,829	47.3	80	
1872	37	ULYSSES S. GRANT	Republican	3,596,745	55.6	286	71.3
		Horace Greeley	Democratic	2,843,446	43.9		
1876	38	RUTHERFORD B. HAYES	Republican	4,036,572	48.0	185	81.8
		Samuel J. Tilden	Democratic	4,284,020	51.0	184	
1880	38	JAMES A. GARFIELD	Republican	4,453,295	48.5	214	79.4
		Winfield S. Hancock	Democratic	4,414,082	48.1	155	
		James B. Weaver	Greenback-Labor	308,578	3.4		
1884	38	GROVER CLEVELAND	Democratic	4,879,507	48.5	219	77.5
		James G. Blaine	Republican	4,850,293	48.2	182	
		Benjamin F. Butler	Greenback-Labor	175,370	1.8		
		John P. St. John	Prohibition	150,369	1.5		
1888	38	BENJAMIN HARRISON	Republican	5,477,129	47.9	233	79.3
		Grover Cleveland	Democratic	5,537,857	48.6	168	
		Clinton B. Fisk	Prohibition	249,506	2.2		
		Anson J. Streeter	Union Labor	146,935	1.3		

Year	No. States	Candidates	Parties	Popular Vote	% Popular	Electoral Vote	% Turnout
1892	44	**GROVER CLEVELAND** Benjamin Harrison James B. Weaver John Bidwell	Democratic Republican People's Prohibition	5,555,426 5,182,690 1,029,846 264,133	46.1 43.0 8.5 2.2	277 145 22	74.7
1896	45	**WILLIAM McKINLEY** William J. Bryan	Republican Democratic	7,102,246 6,492,559	51.1 47.7	271 176	79.3
1900	45	**WILLIAM McKINLEY** William J. Bryan John C. Wooley	Republican Democratic; Populist Prohibition	7,218,491 6,356,734 208,914	51.7 45.5 1.5	292 155	73.2
1904	45	**THEODORE ROOSEVELT** Alton B. Parker Eugene V. Debs Silas C. Swallow	Republican Democratic Socialist Prohibition	7,628,461 5,084,223 402,283 258,536	57.4 37.6 3.0 1.9	336 140	65.2
1908	46	**WILLIAM H. TAFT** William J. Bryan Eugene V. Debs Eugene W. Chafin	Republican Democratic Socialist Prohibition	7,675,320 6,412,294 420,793 253,840	51.6 43.1 2.8 1.7	321 162	65.4
1912	48	**WOODROW WILSON** Theodore Roosevelt William H. Taft Eugene V. Debs Eugene W. Chafin	Democratic Progressive Republican Socialist Prohibition	6,296,547 4,118,571 3,486,720 900,672 206,275	41.9 27.4 23.2 6.0 1.4	435 88 8	58.8
1916	48	**WOODROW WILSON** Charles E. Hughes A. L. Benson J. Frank Hanly	Democratic Republican Socialist Prohibition	9,127,695 8,533,507 585,113 220,506	49.4 46.2 3.2 1.2	277 254	61.6

Year	Number of States	Candidates	Parties	Popular Vote	% of Popular Vote	Electoral Vote	% Voter Participation
1920	48	**WARREN G. HARDING**	Republican	16,143,407	60.4	404	49.2
		James M. Cox	Democratic	9,130,328	34.2	127	
		Eugene V. Debs	Socialist	919,799	3.4		
		P.P. Christensen	Farmer-labor	265,411	1.0		
1924	48	**CALVIN COOLIDGE**	Republican	15,718,211	54.0	382	48.9
		John W. Davis	Democratic	8,385,283	28.8	136	
		Robert M. La Follette	Progressive	4,831,289	16.6	13	
1928	48	**HERBERT C. HOOVER**	Republican	21,391,993	58.2	444	56.9
		Alfred E. Smith	Democratic	15,016,169	40.9	87	
1932	48	**FRANKLIN D. ROOSEVELT**	Democratic	22,809,638	57.4	472	56.9
		Herbert C. Hoover	Republican	15,758,901	39.7	59	
		Norman Thomas	Socialist	881,951	2.2		
1936	48	**FRANKLIN D. ROOSEVELT**	Democratic	27,752,869	60.8	523	61.0
		Alfred M. Landon	Republican	16,674,665	36.5	8	
		William Lemke	Union	882,479	1.9		
1940	48	**FRANKLIN D. ROOSEVELT**	Democratic	27,307,819	54.8	449	62.5
		Wendell L. Willkie	Republican	22,321,018	44.8	82	
1944	48	**FRANKLIN D. ROOSEVELT**	Democratic	25,606,585	53.5	432	55.9
		Thomas E. Dewey	Republican	22,014,745	46.0	99	
1948	48	**HARRY S. TRUMAN**	Democratic	24,179,345	49.6	303	53.0
		Thomas E. Dewey	Republican	21,991,291	45.1	189	
		J. Strom Thurmond	States' Rights	1,176,125	2.4	39	
		Henry A. Wallace	Progressive	1,157,326	2.4		

Year	States	Candidates	Party	Popular Vote	% Popular	Electoral Vote	% Participation
1952	48	**DWIGHT D. EISENHOWER**	Republican	33,936,234	55.1	442	63.3
		Adlai E. Stevenson	Democratic	27,314,992	44.4	89	
1956	48	**DWIGHT D. EISENHOWER**	Republican	35,590,472	57.6	457	60.6
		Adlai E. Stevenson	Democratic	26,022,752	42.1	73	
1960	50	**JOHN F. KENNEDY**	Democratic	34,226,731	49.7	303	64.0
		Richard M. Nixon	Republican	34,108,157	49.5	219	
1964	50	**LYNDON B. JOHNSON**	Democratic	43,129,566	61.1	486	61.7
		Barry M. Goldwater	Republican	27,178,188	38.5	52	
1968	50	**RICHARD M. NIXON**	Republican	31,785,480	43.4	301	60.6
		Hubert H. Humphrey	Democratic	31,275,166	42.7	191	
		George C. Wallace	American Independent	9,906,473	13.5	46	
1972	50	**RICHARD M. NIXON**	Republican	47,169,911	60.7	520	55.5
		George S. McGovern	Democratic	29,170,383	37.5	17	
		John G. Schmitz	American	1,099,482	1.4		
1976	50	**JIMMY CARTER**	Democratic	40,830,763	50.1	297	54.3
		Gerald R. Ford	Republican	39,147,793	48.0	240	
1980	50	**RONALD REAGAN**	Republican	43,901,812	50.7	489	53.0
		Jimmy Carter	Democratic	35,483,820	41.0	49	
		John B. Anderson	Independent	5,719,722	6.6		
		Ed Clark	Libertarian	921,188	1.1		
1984	50	**RONALD REAGAN**	Republican	54,451,521	58.4	525	52.9
		Walter F. Mondale	Democratic	37,565,334	41.6	13	
1988	50	**GEORGE H. BUSH**	Republican	47,917,341	54.0	426	48.6
		Michael Dukakis	Democratic	41,013,030	46.0	112	

Candidates receiving less than 1 percent of the popular vote have been omitted. Thus the percentage of popular vote given for any election year may not total 100 percent.

Before the passage of the Twelfth Amendment in 1804, the Electoral College voted for two presidential candidates; the runner-up became vice-president.

ADMISSION OF STATES

Order of Admission	State	Date of Admission	Order of Admission	State	Date of Admission
1	Delaware	December 7, 1787	26	Michigan	January 26, 1837
2	Pennsylvania	December 12, 1787	27	Florida	March 3, 1845
3	New Jersey	December 18, 1787	28	Texas	December 29, 1845
4	Georgia	January 2, 1788	29	Iowa	December 28, 1846
5	Connecticut	January 9, 1788	30	Wisconsin	May 29, 1848
6	Massachusetts	February 7, 1788	31	California	September 9, 1850
7	Maryland	April 28, 1788	32	Minnesota	May 11, 1858
8	South Carolina	May 23, 1788	33	Oregon	February 14, 1859
9	New Hampshire	June 21, 1788	34	Kansas	January 29, 1861
10	Virginia	June 25, 1788	35	West Virginia	June 30, 1863
11	New York	July 26, 1788	36	Nevada	October 31, 1864
12	North Carolina	November 21, 1789	37	Nebraska	March 1, 1867
13	Rhode Island	May 29, 1790	38	Colorado	August 1, 1876
14	Vermont	March 4, 1791	39	North Dakota	November 2, 1889
15	Kentucky	June 1, 1792	40	South Dakota	November 2, 1889
16	Tennessee	June 1, 1796	41	Montana	November 8, 1889
17	Ohio	March 1, 1803	42	Washington	November 11, 1889
18	Louisiana	April 30, 1812	43	Idaho	July 3, 1890
19	Indiana	December 11, 1816	44	Wyoming	July 10, 1890
20	Mississippi	December 10, 1817	45	Utah	January 4, 1896
21	Illinois	December 3, 1818	46	Oklahoma	November 16, 1907
22	Alabama	December 14, 1819	47	New Mexico	January 6, 1912
23	Maine	March 15, 1820	48	Arizona	February 14, 1912
24	Missouri	August 10, 1821	49	Alaska	January 3, 1959
25	Arkansas	June 15, 1836	50	Hawaii	August 21, 1959

POPULATION OF THE UNITED STATES

Year	Number of States	Population	% Increase	Population per Square Mile
1790	13	3,929,214		4.5
1800	16	5,308,483	35.1	6.1
1810	17	7,239,881	36.4	4.3
1820	23	9,638,453	33.1	5.5
1830	24	12,866,020	33.5	7.4
1840	26	17,069,453	32.7	9.8
1850	31	23,191,876	35.9	7.9
1860	33	31,443,321	35.6	10.6
1870	37	39,818,449	26.6	13.4
1880	38	50,155,783	26.0	16.9
1890	44	62,947,714	25.5	21.1
1900	45	75,994,575	20.7	25.6
1910	46	91,972,266	21.0	31.0
1920	48	105,710,620	14.9	35.6
1930	48	122,775,046	16.1	41.2
1940	48	131,669,275	7.2	44.2
1950	48	150,697,361	14.5	50.7
1960	50	179,323,175	19.0	50.6
1970	50	203,235,298	13.3	57.5
1980	50	226,504,825	11.4	64.0
1985	50	237,839,000	5.0	67.2
1990	50	250,122,000	5.2	70.6

IMMIGRATION TO THE UNITED STATES, FISCAL YEARS 1820–1990

Year	Number	Year	Number	Year	Number	Year	Number
1820–1989	55,457,531	1871–80	2,812,191	1921–30	4,107,209	1971–80	4,493,314
1820	8,385	1871	321,350	1921	805,228	1971	370,478
1821–30	143,439	1872	404,806	1922	309,556	1972	384,685
1821	9,127	1873	459,803	1923	522,919	1973	400,063
1822	6,911	1874	313,339	1924	706,896	1974	394,861
1823	6,354	1875	227,498	1925	294,314	1975	386,194
1824	7,912	1876	169,986	1926	304,488	1976	398,613
1825	10,199	1877	141,857	1927	335,175	1976, TQ	103,676
1826	10,837	1878	138,469	1928	307,255	1977	462,315
1827	18,875	1879	177,826	1929	279,678	1978	601,442
1828	27,382	1880	457,257	1930	241,700	1979	460,348
1829	22,520	1881–90	5,246,613	1931–40	528,431	1980	530,639
1830	23,322	1881	669,431	1931	97,139	1981–90	7,338,062
1831–40	599,125	1882	788,992	1932	35,576	1981	596,600
1831	22,633	1883	603,322	1933	23,068	1982	594,131
1832	60,482	1884	518,592	1934	29,470	1983	559,763
1833	58,640	1885	395,346	1935	34,956	1984	543,903
1834	65,365	1886	334,203	1936	36,329	1985	570,009
1835	45,374	1887	490,109	1937	50,244	1986	601,708
1836	76,242	1888	546,889	1938	67,895	1987	601,516
1837	79,340	1889	444,427	1939	82,998	1988	643,025
1838	38,914	1890	455,302	1940	70,756	1989	1,090,924
1839	68,069	1891–1900	3,687,564	1941–50	1,035,039	1990	1,536,483
1840	84,066	1891	560,319	1941	51,776		
1841–50	1,713,251	1892	579,663	1942	28,781		
1841	80,289	1893	439,730	1943	23,725		
1842	104,565	1894	285,631	1944	28,551		
		1895	258,536	1945	38,119		
		1896	343,267	1946	108,721		

Year	Number	Year	Number	Year	Number
1843	52,496	1897	230,832	1947	147,292
1844	78,615	1898	229,299	1948	170,570
1845	114,371	1899	311,715	1949	188,317
1846	154,416	1900	448,572	1950	249,187
1847	234,968				
1848	226,527	**1901–10**	**8,795,386**	**1951–60**	**2,515,479**
1849	297,024	1901	487,918	1951	205,717
1850	369,980	1902	648,743	1952	265,520
		1903	857,046	1953	170,434
1851–60	**2,598,214**	1904	812,870	1954	208,177
1851	379,466	1905	1,026,499	1955	237,790
1852	371,603	1906	1,100,735	1956	321,625
1853	368,645	1907	1,285,349	1957	326,867
1854	427,833	1908	782,870	1958	253,265
1855	200,877	1909	751,786	1959	260,686
1856	200,436	1910	1,041,570	1960	265,398
1857	251,306				
1858	123,126	**1911–20**	**5,735,811**	**1961–70**	**3,321,677**
1859	121,282	1911	878,587	1961	271,344
1860	153,640	1912	838,172	1962	283,763
		1913	1,197,892	1963	306,260
1861–70	**2,314,824**	1914	1,218,480	1964	292,248
1861	91,918	1915	326,700	1965	296,697
1862	91,985	1916	298,826	1966	323,040
1863	176,282	1917	295,403	1967	361,972
1864	193,418	1918	110,618	1968	454,448
1865	248,120	1919	141,132	1969	358,579
1866	318,568	1920	430,001	1970	373,326
1867	315,722				
1868	138,840				
1869	352,768				
1870	387,203				

Source: U.S. Immigration and Naturalization Service, 1991.

IMMIGRATION BY REGION AND SELECTED COUNTRY OF LAST RESIDENCE, FISCAL YEARS 1820–1989

Region and Country of Last Residence[1]	1820	1821–30	1831–40	1841–50	1851–60	1861–70	1871–80	1881–90
All countries	8,385	143,439	599,125	1,713,251	2,598,214	2,314,824	2,812,191	5,246,613
Europe	7,690	98,797	495,681	1,597,442	2,452,577	2,065,141	2,271,925	4,735,484
Austria-Hungary	—[2]	—[2]	—[2]	—[2]	—[3]	7,800	72,969	353,719
Austria	—[2]	—[2]	—[2]	—[2]	—[3]	[3,7]7,124	63,009	226,038
Hungary	—[2]	—[2]	—[2]	—[2]	—[3]	[3]484	9,960	127,681
Belgium	1	27	22	5,074	4,738	6,734	7,221	20,177
Czechoslovakia	—[4]	—[4]	—[4]	—[4]	—[4]	—[4]	—[4]	—[4]
Denmark	20	169	1,063	539	3,749	17,094	31,771	88,132
France	371	8,497	45,575	77,262	76,358	35,986	72,206	50,464
Germany	968	6,761	152,454	434,626	951,667	787,468	718,182	1,452,970
Greece	—[5]	20	49	16	31	72	210	2,308
Ireland[5]	3,614	50,724	207,381	780,719	914,119	435,778	436,871	655,482
Italy	30	409	2,253	1,870	9,231	11,725	55,759	307,309
Netherlands	49	1,078	1,412	8,251	10,789	9,102	16,541	53,701
Norway-Sweden	3	91	1,201	13,903	20,931	109,298	211,245	568,362
Norway	—[6]	—[6]	—[6]	—[6]	—[6]	—[6]	95,323	176,586
Sweden	—[6]	—[6]	—[6]	—[6]	—[6]	—[6]	115,922	391,776
Poland	5	16	369	105	1,164	2,027	12,970	51,806
Portugal	35	145	829	550	1,055	2,658	14,082	16,978
Romania	—[7]	—[7]	—[7]	—[7]	—[7]	—[7]	11	6,348
Soviet Union	14	75	277	551	457	2,512	39,284	213,282
Spain	139	2,477	2,125	2,209	9,298	6,697	5,266	4,419
Switzerland	31	3,226	4,821	4,644	25,011	23,286	28,293	81,988
United Kingdom[5,8]	2,410	25,079	75,810	267,044	423,974	606,896	548,043	807,357
Yugoslavia	—[9]	—[9]	—[9]	—[9]	—[9]	—[9]	—[9]	—[9]
Other Europe	—	3	40	79	5	8	1,001	682

Asia	6	30	55	141	41,538	64,759	124,160	69,942
China[10]	1	2	8	35	41,397	64,301	123,201	61,711
Hong Kong	1	8	39	36	43	69	163	269
India	—[12]	—[12]	—[12]	—[12]	—[12]	—[12]	—[12]	—[12]
Iran	—[13]	—[13]	—[13]	—[13]	—[13]	—[13]	—[13]	—[13]
Israel	—[14]	—[14]	—[14]	—[14]	—[14]	—[14]	149	—[14]
Japan	—[15]	—[15]	—[15]	—[15]	—[15]	186	—[15]	2,270
Korea	—[16]	—[16]	—[16]	—[16]	—[16]	—[16]	—[16]	—[16]
Philippines	—[16]	—[16]	—[16]	—[16]	—[16]	—[16]	—[16]	—[16]
Turkey	1	20	7	59	83	131	404	3,782
Vietnam	—[11]	—[11]	—[11]	—[11]	—[11]	—[11]	—[11]	—[11]
Other Asia	3	—	1	11	15	72	243	1,910
America	387	11,564	33,424	62,469	74,720	166,607	404,044	426,967
Canada & Newfoundland[17,18]	209	2,277	13,624	41,723	59,309	153,878	383,640	393,304
Mexico[18]	1	4,817	6,599	3,271	3,078	2,191	5,162	1,913[19]
Caribbean	164	3,834	12,301	13,528	10,660	9,046	13,957	29,042
Cuba	—[12]	—[20]	—[20]	—[20]	—[20]	—[20]	—[12]	—[12]
Dominican Republic	—[20]	—[20]	—[20]	—[20]	—[20]	—[20]	—[20]	—[20]
Haiti	—[20]	—[20]	—[20]	—[20]	—[20]	—[20]	—[20]	—[20]
Jamaica	—[21]	—[21]	—[21]	—[21]	—[21]	—[21]	—[21]	—[21]
Other Caribbean	164	3,834	12,301	13,528	10,660	9,046	13,957	29,042
Central America	2	105	44	368	449	95	157	404
El Salvador	—[20]	—[20]	—[20]	—[20]	—[20]	—[20]	—[20]	—[20]
Other Central America	2	105	44	368	449	95	157	404
South America	11	531	856	3,579	1,224	1,397	1,128	2,304
Argentina	—[20]	—[20]	—[20]	—[20]	—[20]	—[20]	—[20]	—[20]
Colombia	—[20]	—[20]	—[20]	—[20]	—[20]	—[20]	—[20]	—[20]
Ecuador	—[20]	—[20]	—[20]	—[20]	—[20]	—[20]	—[20]	—[20]
Other South America	11	531	856	3,579	1,224	1,397	1,128	2,304
Other America	—[22]	—[22]	—[22]	—[22]	—[22]	—[22]	—[22]	—[22]
Africa	1	16	54	55	210	312	358	857
Oceania	1	2	9	29	158	214	10,914	12,574
Not specified[22]	300	33,030	69,902	53,115	29,011	17,791	790	789

Source: U.S. Immigration and Naturalization Service, 1991.

Region and Country of Last Residence[1]	1891–1900	1901–10	1911–20	1921–30	1931–40	1941–50	1951–60	1961–70
All countries	3,687,564	8,795,386	5,735,811	4,107,209	528,431	1,035,039	2,515,479	3,321,677
Europe	3,555,352	8,056,040	4,321,887	2,463,194	347,566	621,147	1,325,727	1,123,492
Austria-Hungary	592,707[2,3]	2,145,266[2,3]	896,342[2,3]	63,548	11,424	28,329	103,743	26,022
Austria	234,081[3]	668,209[3]	453,649	32,868	7,861	24,860[2,4]	67,106	20,621
Hungary	181,288[3]	808,511[3]	442,693	30,680	4,817	3,469	36,637	5,401
Belgium	18,167	41,635	33,746	15,846	12,189	18,575	9,192	
Czechoslovakia	—[4]	—[4]	3,426[4]	102,194	14,393	8,347	918	3,273
Denmark	50,231	65,285	41,983	32,430	2,559	5,393	10,984	9,201
France	30,770	73,379	61,897	49,610	12,623	38,809	51,121	45,237
Germany	505,152[2,3]	341,498[2,3]	143,945[2,3]	412,202	114,058[2,4]	226,578[2,4]	477,765	190,796
Greece	15,979	167,519	184,201	51,084	9,119	8,973	47,608	85,969
Ireland[5]	388,416	339,065	146,181	211,234	10,973	19,789	48,362	32,966
Italy	651,893	2,045,877	1,109,524	455,315	68,028	57,661	185,491	214,111
Netherlands	26,758	48,262	43,718	26,948	7,150	14,860	52,277	30,606
Norway-Sweden	321,281	440,039	161,469	165,780	8,700	20,765	44,632	32,600
Norway	95,015	190,505	66,395	68,531	4,740	10,100	22,935	15,484
Sweden	226,266	249,534	95,074	97,249	3,960	10,665	21,697	17,116
Poland	96,720[2,3]	—[3]	4,813[2,3]	227,734	17,026	7,571	9,985	53,539
Portugal	27,508	69,149	89,732	29,994	3,329	7,423	19,588	76,065
Romania	12,750	53,008	13,311	67,646	3,871	1,076	1,039	2,531
Soviet Union	505,290[2,3]	1,597,306[2,3]	921,201[2,3]	61,742	1,370	571	671	2,465
Spain	8,731	27,935	68,611	28,958	3,258	2,898	7,894	44,659
Switzerland	31,179	34,922	23,091	29,676	5,512	10,547	17,675	18,453
United Kingdom[5,8]	271,538	525,950	341,408	339,570	31,572	139,306	202,824	213,822
Yugoslavia	—[9]	—[9]	1,888[9]	49,064	5,835	1,576	8,225	20,381
Other Europe	282	39,945	31,400	42,619	11,949	8,486	16,350	11,604

Asia	74,862	323,543	247,236	112,059	16,595	37,028	153,249	427,642
China[10]	14,799	20,605	21,278	29,907	4,928	16,709	9,657	34,764
Hong Kong	—[11]	—[11]	—[11]	—[11]	—[11]	—[11]	15,541[11]	75,007
India	—[12]	4,713	2,082	1,886	496	1,761	1,973	27,189
Iran	—[13]	—[12]	—[12]	241[12]	195	1,380	3,388	10,339
Israel	—[13]	—[13]	—[13]	—[13]	—[13]	476[13]	25,476	29,602
Japan	25,942	129,797	83,837	33,462	1,948	1,555	46,250	39,998
Korea	—[15]	—[15]	—[15]	—[15]	—[15]	107[15]	6,231	34,526
Philippines	—[16]	—[16]	—[16]	—[16]	528[16]	4,691	19,307	98,376
Turkey	30,425	157,369	134,066	33,824	1,065	798	3,519	10,142
Vietnam	—[11]	—[11]	—[11]	—[11]	—[11]	—[11]	335[11]	4,340
Other Asia	3,628	11,059	5,973	12,739	7,435	9,551	21,572	63,369
America	38,972	361,888	1,143,671	1,516,716	160,037	354,804	996,944	1,716,374
Canada & Newfoundland[17,18]	3,311	179,226	742,185	924,515	108,527	171,718	377,952	413,310
Mexico[18]	971[19]	49,642	219,004	459,287	22,319	60,589	299,811	453,937
Caribbean	33,066	107,548	123,424	74,899	15,502	49,725	123,091	470,213
Cuba	—[12]	—[20]	—[12]	15,901[12]	9,571	26,313	78,948	208,536
Dominican Republic	—[20]	—[20]	—[20]	—[20]	1,150[20]	5,627	9,897	93,292
Haiti	—[20]	—[20]	—[20]	—[20]	191[20]	911	4,442	34,499
Jamaica	—[21]	—[21]	—[21]	—[21]	—[21]	—[21]	8,869[21]	74,906
Other Caribbean	33,066	107,548	123,424	58,998	4,590	16,874	20,935[21]	58,980
Central America	549	8,192	17,159	15,769	5,861	21,665	44,751	101,330
El Salvador	—[20]	—[20]	—[20]	—[20]	673[20]	5,132	5,895	14,992
Other Central America	549	8,192	17,159	15,769	5,188	16,533	38,856	86,338
South America	1,075	17,280	41,899	42,215	7,803	21,831	91,628	257,954
Argentina	—[20]	—[20]	—[20]	—[20]	1,349[20]	3,338	19,486	49,721
Colombia	—[20]	—[20]	—[20]	—[20]	1,223[20]	3,858	18,048	72,028
Ecuador	—[20]	—[20]	—[20]	—[20]	337[20]	2,417	9,841	36,780
Other South America	1,075	17,280	41,899	42,215	4,894	12,218	44,253	99,425
Other America	—[22]	—[22]	—[22]	31[22]	25	29,276	59,711	19,630
Africa	350	7,368	8,443	6,286	1,750	7,367	14,092	28,954
Oceania	3,965	13,024	13,427	8,726	2,483	14,551	12,976	25,122
Not specified[22]	14,063	33,523[23]	1,147	228	—	142	12,491	93

Region and Country of Last Residence[1]	1971–80	1981–89	1984	1985	1986	1987	1988	1989	Total 170 Years 1820–1989
All countries	4,493,314	5,801,579	543,903	570,009	601,708	601,516	643,025	1,090,924	55,457,531
Europe	800,368	637,524	69,879	69,526	69,224	67,967	71,854	94,338	36,977,034
Austria–Hungary	16,028	20,152	2,846	2,521	2,604	2,401	3,200	3,586	4,338,049
Austria	9,478	14,566	2,351	1,930	2,039	1,769	2,493	2,845	1,825,172[3]
Hungary	6,550	5,586	495	591	565	632	707	741	1,666,801[3]
Belgium	5,329	6,239	787	775	843	859	706	705	209,729
Czechoslovakia	6,023	6,649	693	684	588	715	744	526	145,223
Denmark	4,439	4,696	512	465	544	515	561	617	369,738
France	25,069	28,088	3,335	3,530	3,876	3,809	3,637	4,101	783,322
Germany	74,414	79,809	9,375	10,028	9,853	9,923	9,748	10,419	7,071,313
Greece	92,369	34,490	3,311	3,487	3,497	4,087	4,690	4,588	700,017
Ireland[3]	11,490	22,229	1,096	1,288	1,757	3,032	5,121	6,983	4,715,393
Italy	129,368	51,008	6,328	6,351	5,711	4,666	5,332	11,089	5,356,862
Netherlands	10,492	10,723	1,313	1,235	1,263	1,303	1,152	1,253	372,717
Norway–Sweden	10,472	13,252	1,455	1,557	1,564	1,540	1,669	1,809	2,144,024
Norway	3,941	3,612	403	386	367	372	446	556	800,672[6]
Sweden	6,531	9,640	1,052	1,171	1,197	1,168	1,223	1,253	1,283,097[6]
Poland	37,234	64,888	7,229	7,409	6,540	5,818	7,298	13,279	587,972
Portugal	101,710	36,365	3,800	3,811	3,804	4,009	3,290	3,861	497,195
Romania	12,393	27,361	2,956	3,764	3,809	2,741	2,915	3,535	201,345
Soviet Union	38,961	42,898	3,349	3,532	1,001	1,139	1,408	4,570	3,428,927
Spain	39,141	17,689	2,168	2,278	2,232	2,056	1,972	2,179	282,404
Switzerland	8,235	7,561	795	980	923	964	920	1,072	358,151
United Kingdom[5,8]	137,374	140,119	16,516	15,591	16,129	15,889	14,667	16,961	5,100,096
Yugoslavia	30,540	15,984	1,404	1,521	1,915	1,793	2,039	2,464	133,493
Other Europe	9,287	7,324	611	719	771	708	785	741	181,064

Asia	1,588,178	2,416,278	247,775	255,164	258,546	248,293	254,745	296,420	5,697,301
China[10]	124,326	306,108	29,109	33,095	32,389	32,669	34,300	39,284	873,737
Hong Kong	113,467	83,848	12,290	10,795	9,930	8,785	11,817	15,257	287,863[11]
India	164,134	221,977	23,617	24,536	24,808	26,394	25,312	28,599	426,907
Iran	45,136	101,267	11,131	12,327	12,031	10,323	9,846	13,027	161,946[12]
Israel	37,713	38,367	4,136	4,279	5,124	4,753	4,444	5,494	131,634[13]
Japan	49,775	40,654	4,517	4,552	4,444	4,711	5,085	5,454	455,813[14]
Korea	267,638	302,782	32,537	34,791	35,164	35,397	34,151	33,016	611,284[15]
Philippines	354,987	477,485	46,985	53,137	61,492	58,315	61,017	66,119	955,374[16]
Turkey	13,399	20,028	1,652	1,690	1,975	2,080	2,200	2,538	409,122
Vietnam	172,820	266,027	25,803	20,367	15,010	13,073	12,856	13,174	443,522[11]
Other Asia	244,783	557,735	55,998	55,595	56,179	51,793	53,717	74,458	940,099
America	1,982,735	2,564,698	208,111	225,519	254,078	265,026	294,906	672,639	12,017,021
Canada & Newfoundland[17,18]	169,939	132,296	15,659	16,354	16,060	16,741	15,821	18,294	4,270,943
Mexico[18]	640,294	975,657	57,820	61,290	66,753	72,511	95,170	405,660	3,208,543
Caribbean	741,126	759,416	68,368	79,374	98,527	100,615	110,949	87,597	2,590,542
Cuba	264,863	135,142	5,699	17,115	30,787	27,363	16,610	9,523	739,274[13]
Dominican Republic	148,135	209,899	23,207	23,861	26,216	24,947	27,195	26,744	468,000[20]
Haiti	56,335	118,510	9,554	9,872	12,356	14,643	34,858	13,341	214,888[20]
Jamaica	137,577	184,481	18,997	18,277	18,916	22,430	20,474	23,572	405,833[21]
Other Caribbean	134,216	111,384	10,911	10,249	10,252	11,232	11,812	14,417	762,547
Central America	134,640	321,845	27,626	28,447	30,086	30,366	31,311	101,273	673,385
El Salvador	34,436	133,938	8,753	10,093	10,881	10,627	12,043	57,628	195,066[20]
Other Central America	100,204	187,907	18,873	18,354	19,205	19,739	19,268	43,645	478,319
South America	295,741	375,026	38,636	40,052	42,650	44,782	41,646	59,812	1,163,482
Argentina	29,897	21,374	2,287	1,925	2,318	2,192	2,556	3,766	125,165[20]
Colombia	77,347	99,066	10,897	11,802	11,213	11,482	10,153	14,918	271,570[20]
Ecuador	50,077	43,841	4,244	4,601	4,518	4,656	4,736	7,587	143,293[20]
Other South America	138,420	210,745	21,208	21,724	24,601	26,452	24,201	33,541	623,454
Other America	995	458	2	2	2	11	9	3	110,126
Africa	80,779	144,096	13,594	15,236	15,500	15,730	17,124	22,485	301,348
Oceania	41,242	38,401	4,249	4,552	4,352	4,437	4,324	4,956	197,818
Not specified[22]	12	582	295	12	8	63	72	86	267,009

[1]Data for years prior to 1906 relate to country whence alien came; data from 1906–79 and 1984–89 are for country of last permanent residence; and data for 1980–83 refer to country of birth. Because of changes in boundaries, changes in lists of countries, and lack of data for specified countries for various periods, data for certain countries, especially for the total period 1820–1989, are not comparable throughout. Data for specified countries are included with countries to which they belonged prior to World War I.

[2]Data for Austria and Hungary not reported until 1861.

[3]Data for Austria and Hungary not reported separately for all years during the period.

[4]No data available for Czechoslovakia until 1920.

[5]Prior to 1926, data for Northern Ireland included in Ireland.

[6]Data for Norway and Sweden not reported separately until 1871.

[7]No data available for Romania until 1880.

[8]Since 1925, data for United Kingdom refer to England, Scotland, Wales, and Northern Ireland.

[9]In 1920, a separate enumeration was made for the Kingdom of Serbs, Croats, and Slovenes. Since 1922, the Serb, Croat, and Slovene Kingdom recorded as Yugoslavia.

[10]Beginning in 1957, China includes Taiwan.

[11]Data not reported separately until 1952.

[12]Data not reported separately until 1925.

[13]Data not reported separately until 1949.

[14]No data available for Japan until 1861.

[15]Data not reported separately until 1948.

[16]Prior to 1934, Philippines recorded as insular travel.

[17]Prior to 1920, Canada and Newfoundland recorded as British North America. From 1820 to 1898, figures include all British North America possessions.

[18]Land arrivals not completely enumerated until 1908.

[19]No data available for Mexico from 1886 to 1893.

[20]Data not reported separately until 1932.

[21]Data for Jamaica not collected until 1953. In prior years, consolidated under British West Indies, which is included in "Other Caribbean."

[22]Included in countries "Not specified" until 1925.

[23]From 1899 to 1919, data for Poland included in Austria-Hungary, Germany, and the Soviet Union.

[24]From 1938 to 1945, data for Austria included in Germany.

[25]Includes 32,897 persons returning in 1906 to their homes in the United States.

—represents zero.

NOTE: From 1820 to 1867, figures represent alien passengers arrived at seaports; from 1868 to 1891 and 1895 to 1897, immigrant aliens arrived; from 1892 to 1894 and 1898 to 1989, immigrant aliens admitted for permanent residence. From 1892 to 1903, aliens entering by cabin class were not counted as immigrants. Land arrivals were not completely enumerated until 1908. For this table, fiscal year 1843 covers 9 months ending September 1843; fiscal years 1832 and 1850 cover 15 months ending December 31 of the respective years; and fiscal year 1868 covers 6 months ending June 30, 1868.

PRESIDENTS, VICE-PRESIDENTS, AND SECRETARIES OF STATE

President	Vice-President	Secretary of State
17. Andrew Johnson, Unionist 1865		W. H. Seward 1865
18. Ulysses S. Grant, Republican 1869	Schuyler Colfax, Republican 1869 Henry Wilson, Republican 1873	E. B. Washburne 1869 H. Fish 1869
19. Rutherford B. Hayes, Republican 1877	William A. Wheeler, Republican 1877	W. M. Evarts 1877
20. James A. Garfield, Republican 1881	Chester A. Arthur, Republican 1881	J. G. Blaine 1881
21. Chester A. Arthur, Republican 1881		F. T. Frelinghuysen 1881
22. Grover Cleveland, Democratic 1885	T. A. Hendricks, Democratic 1885	T. F. Bayard 1885
23. Benjamin Harrison, Republican 1889	Levi P. Morton, Republican 1889	J. G. Blaine 1889 J. W. Foster 1892
24. Grover Cleveland, Democratic 1893	Adlai E. Stevenson, Democratic 1893	W. Q. Gresham 1893 R. Olney 1895
25. William McKinley, Republican 1897	Garret A. Hobart, Republican 1897 Theodore Roosevelt, Republican 1901	J. Sherman 1897 W. R. Day 1897 J. Hay 1898

	President	Vice-President	Secretary of State
26.	Theodore Roosevelt, Republican 1901	Chas. W. Fairbanks, Republican 1905	J. Hay 1901 E. Root 1905 R. Bacon 1909
27.	William H. Taft, Republican 1909	James S. Sherman, Republican 1909	P. C. Knox 1909
28.	Woodrow Wilson, Democratic 1913	Thomas R. Marshall, Democratic 1913	W. J. Bryan 1913 R. Lansing 1915 B. Colby 1920
29.	Warren G. Harding, Republican 1921	Calvin Coolidge, Republican 1921	C. E. Hughes 1921
30.	Calvin Coolidge, Republican 1923	Charles G. Dawes, Republican 1925	C. E. Hughes 1923 F. B. Kellogg 1925
31.	Herbert Hoover, Republican 1929	Charles Curtis, Republican 1929	H. L. Stimson 1929
32.	Franklin D. Roosevelt, Democratic 1933	John Nance Garner, Democratic 1933 Henry A. Wallace, Democratic 1941 Harry S. Truman, Democratic 1945	C. Hull 1933 E. R. Stettinius, Jr. 1944
33.	Harry S. Truman, Democratic 1945	Alben W. Barkley, Democratic 1949	J. F. Byrnes 1945 G. C. Marshall 1947 D. G. Acheson 1949
34.	Dwight D. Eisenhower, Republican 1953	Richard M. Nixon, Republican 1953	J. F. Dulles 1953 C. A. Herter 1959

President	Vice-President	Secretary of State
35. John F. Kennedy, Democratic 1961	Lyndon B. Johnson, Democratic 1961	D. Rusk 1961
36. Lyndon B. Johnson, Democratic 1963	Hubert H. Humphrey, Democratic 1965	D. Rusk 1963
37. Richard M. Nixon, Republican 1969	Spiro T. Agnew, Republican 1969 Gerald R. Ford, Republican 1973	W. P. Rogers 1969 H. A. Kissinger 1973
38. Gerald R. Ford, Republican 1974	Nelson Rockefeller, Republican 1974	H. A. Kissinger 1974
39. Jimmy Carter, Democratic 1977	Walter Mondale, Democratic 1977	C. Vance 1977 E. Muskie 1980
40. Ronald Reagan, Republican 1981	George Bush, Republican 1981	A. Haig 1981 G. Schultz 1982
41. George Bush, Republican 1989	J. Danforth Quayle, Republican 1989	J. A. Baker 1989

CHRONOLOGY OF
SIGNIFICANT EVENTS

1865	Freedmen's Bureau established
1865	Assassination of President Lincoln
1866–1868	Fourteenth Amendment passed and ratified
1867	First Reconstruction Act
1867–1877	Congressional Reconstruction of the South
1867	United States purchases Alaska
1868	Impeachment of President Andrew Johnson
1869	Completion of first transcontinental railroad
1869	National Woman Suffrage Association founded
1870	Standard Oil Company of Ohio established by John D. Rockefeller
1873	Crédit-Mobilier Scandal
1876	Battle of the Little Big Horn
1876	Telephone invented by Alexander Graham Bell
1877	*Munn v. Illinois*
1878	Bland-Allison Act
1879	Terence Powderly becomes president of Knights of Labor
1879	Incandescent bulb invented by Thomas Edison
1881	Helen Hunt Jackson's *A Century of Dishonor*
1882	Chinese Exclusion Act
1883	Pendleton Act

1883	Brooklyn Bridge completed
1884	Mark Twain's *The Adventures of Huckleberry Finn*
1885	Josiah Strong publishes *Our Country*
1886	Haymarket Riot
1886	American Federation of Labor founded
1887	Interstate Commerce Act
1887–1889	National Farmers' Alliance founded
1888	Edward Bellamy's *Looking Backward*
1889	Hull House founded by Jane Addams
1890	Battle of Wounded Knee
1890	Sherman Anti-Trust Act
1890	Jacob Riis's *How the Other Half Lives*
1892	Homestead Massacre
1892	Populist party founded
1893	Panic of 1893
1893	Stephen Crane's *Maggie: A Girl of the Streets*
1893	Chicago World's Fair
1894	Pullman Strike
1895	Booker T. Washington's Atlanta Exposition Speech
1896	*Plessy v. Ferguson*
1898	Spanish-American War
1899–1900	"Open Door" Notes
1899	Thorstein Veblen's *The Theory of the Leisure Class*
1900	Theodore Dreiser's *Sister Carrie*
1900–1917	"Ash Can" school of painting
1901–1917	Progressive movement
1903	Orville and Wilbur Wright's first flight
1903	William E. B. DuBois's *Souls of Black Folk*
1904	*Northern Securities Company v. U.S.*
1904–1905	Roosevelt corollary to Monroe Doctrine
1905	Roosevelt mediates end to Russo-Japanese War
1906	Upton Sinclair's *The Jungle*
1906–1914	Construction of the Panama Canal
1908	Gentlemen's Agreement with Japan
1909	First Model T automobile produced by Henry Ford
1909	National Association for the Advancement of Colored People founded
1909–1910	Ballinger/Pinchot dispute

1910	President Taft's "dollar diplomacy" in Nicaragua
1912	Woodrow Wilson elected president
1913	Underwood-Simmons Tariff Act
1913	Federal Reserve Act
1913–1917	Revolt in Mexico and U.S. intervention
1914	Clayton Anti-Trust Act
1914	Outbreak of World War I
1915	German submarine sinks *Lusitania*
1915	Albert Einstein's general theory of relativity
1917	Russian Revolution
1917	United States enters the war against Germany
1918	Wilson announces Fourteen Points
1919	Treaty of Versailles signed
1919	Boston Police Strike
1919	Volstead Act (Prohibition)
1919	Sherwood Anderson's *Winesburg, Ohio*
1919–1920	United States rejects treaty over League of Nations
1919–1920	Red Scare
1920–1930	Harlem Renaissance
1921	Marcus Garvey's African Zionist Movement
1922	T. S. Eliot's *The Waste Land*
1922	Washington Conference on Disarmament
1924	Harding administration scandals
1924	McNary-Haugen Bill
1925	Scopes trial
1925	F. Scott Fitzgerald's *The Great Gatsby*
1926	Ernest Hemingway's *The Sun Also Rises*
1927	Charles Lindbergh's solo flight to Paris
1927	Sacco and Vanzetti executed
1927	Babe Ruth hits 60 home runs
1928	Kellogg-Briand Peace Pact
1929	William Faulkner's *The Sound and the Fury*
1929	Stock market crash
1929–1933	Great Depression
1932	Bonus Army march on Washington
1932	Franklin Delano Roosevelt elected president
1933	Emergency Banking Act
1933	Unemployment Relief Act
1933	Agricultural Adjustment Act
1933	Tennessee Valley Authority Act
1933	National Industrial Recovery Act

1933	Hitler comes to power in Germany
1935–1936	Second New Deal
1935	National Labor Relations Act
1935	Social Security Act
1935	*Schechter v. United States*
1936	Spanish Civil War
1937	Supreme Court "packing" fight
1938	Munich Conference
1939	Germany annexes Czechoslovakia and invades Poland
1939	John Steinbeck's *The Grapes of Wrath*
1940	Battle of Britain
1940	Richard Wright's *Native Son*
1941	Lend-Lease aid to Allies
1941	Atlantic Charter
1941	Japanese attack on Pearl Harbor
1941	United States enters World War II
1944	Allied invasion of Normandy
1945	Atomic bombs dropped on Hiroshima and Nagasaki
1945	Germany surrenders; Japan surrenders
1945	Yalta Conference
1945	Potsdam Conference
1946	Benjamin Spock's *Baby and Child Care*
1947	Taft-Hartley Labor-Management Relations Act
1947	Truman Doctrine
1947	Marshall Plan
1947	Jackie Robinson becomes first black in major-league baseball
1949	North Atlantic Treaty Organization (NATO) founded
1949	Arthur Miller's *Death of a Salesman*
1950	Internal Security Act
1950–1953	Korean War
1950–1954	McCarthyism
1950	David Riesman's *The Lonely Crowd*
1952	Ralph Ellison's *Invisible Man*
1952	Norman Vincent Peale's *The Power of Positive Thinking*
1954	*Brown v. Board of Education of Topeka*
1954	Geneva Conference on Indochina
1955	Montgomery bus boycott
1955	Dr. Jonas Salk's polio vaccine

1956	Suez crisis
1956	Alan Ginsberg's *Howl*
1957	Dispute over integration in Little Rock, Arkansas
1957	Eisenhower Doctrine
1957	Jack Kerouac's *On the Road*
1957	USSR launches Sputnik satellite
1959	Fidel Castro leads revolution in Cuba
1960	U-2 incident
1960	"Sit-in" movement begins in Greensboro, N.C.
1960	Students for a Democratic Society founded
1961	Bay of Pigs invasion
1962	Cuban missile crisis
1962	Michael Harrington's *The Other America*
1962	Rachel Carson's *Silent Spring*
1963	Nuclear Test Ban Treaty
1963	Assassination of President John F. Kennedy
1963	March on Washington for civil rights
1963	Betty Friedan's *The Feminine Mystique*
1964	Gulf of Tonkin Resolution
1964, 1965	Civil Rights Acts
1965	President Lyndon Johnson's Great Society
1965	U.S. troop buildup begins in Vietnam
1965	Ralph Nader's *Unsafe at Any Speed*
1966	National Organization for Women founded
1967	Arab-Israeli War
1968	Tet Offensive in Vietnam
1968	Martin Luther King assassinated
1968	Robert Kennedy assassinated
1968	Violence at Democratic National Convention in Chicago
1969	Woodstock Festival for Music and Peace
1969	My Lai massacre
1969	Neil Armstrong becomes first man on moon
1970	Violence at Kent State and Jackson State Universities
1972	Earth Day demonstrations
1972	President Nixon visits China
1972–1974	Watergate scandal
1973	Vietnam Peace Agreement
1973–1974	Arab oil embargo
1975	Fall of South Vietnam
1978	Camp David accords between Egypt and Israel

1979	Three Mile Island nuclear accident
1979	SALT II Agreement
1979–1981	Iranian hostage crisis
1983	American marines killed in Lebanon
1986	Tax Reform Act
1986	Iran-Contra affair
1987	Scandals in politics and evangelical movement
1987	Congressional hearings on Iran-Contra affair
1987	Controversy over air traffic safety
1987	"Black Monday" on Wall Street
1987	INF treaty with Soviet Union
1988–1989	S & L crisis and bailout
1989	End of Communist Party rule in East-bloc nations
1989	Fall of the Berlin Wall
1989–1990	U.S. military action in Panama
1990–1991	Persian Gulf crisis
1991	U.S. military action against Iraq
1991	Failed coup in the Soviet Union

ILLUSTRATION CREDITS

CHAPTER 18 694 / Library of Congress. 695 / Library of Congress. 696 / Library of Congress. 697 / Library of Congress. 701 / Library of Congress. 704 / Harper's Weekly. 705 / (left) Library of Congress; (right) National Archives. 707 / The Warder Collection. 709 / Library of Congress. 713 / National Archives. 716 / Chicago Historical Society. 719 / Library of Congress. 723 / Library of Congress. 725 / Library of Congress. 728 / Library of Congress.

CHAPTER 19 736 / The Warder Collection. 738 / Brown Brothers. 741 / The Granger Collection. 746 / New York Public Library. 748 / Library of Congress. 749 / The Warder Collection. 751 / Denver Public Library. 754 / Library of Congress. 756 / Library of Congress. 757 / Colorado Historical Society. 759 / (left) South Dakota State Historical Society; (right) National Archives. 760 / The Smithsonian Institution. 761 / The Smithsonian Institution. 763 / Oklahoma Historical Society. 765 / Kansas State Historical Society. 767 / Solomon D. Butcher Collection, Nebraska State Historical Society. 770 / University of Oklahoma Library.

CHAPTER 20 775 / Southern Pacific Transportation Company. 776 / Union Pacific Railroad Museum Collection. 779 / New-York Historical Society. 780 / National Archives. 782 / U.S. Department of the Interior, National Park Service, Edison National Historic Site. 784 / Drake Well Museum. 785 / The Warder Collection. 786 / Carnegie Library, Pittsburgh. 789 / The Pierpont Morgan Library. 790 / R. W. Johnston, Carnegie Library, Pittsburgh. 792 / Chicago Historical Society. 794 / Carnegie Library, Pittsburgh. 797 / Chicago Historical Society. 799 / Chicago Historical Society. 801 / The Warder Collection. 804 / The Archives of Labor and Urban Affairs, Wayne State University. 807 / The Archives of Labor and Urban Affairs, Wayne State University.

CHAPTER 21 813 / Library of Congress. 815 / Chicago Historical Society. 816 / Library of Congress. 817 / New York Public Library. 819 / Museum of the City of New York. 821 / (top and bottom) New York Public Library. 823 / Lewis W. Hine, International Museum of Photography at George Eastman House. 826 / Historical Pictures Service, Chicago. 827 / California Historical Society Library. 829 / Kansas State Historical Society. 830 / Library of Congress. 832 / Schlesinger Library, Radcliffe College. 834 / Library of Congress. 836 / American Museum of Natural History. 837 / The Warder Collection. 838 / Brown University Library. 840 / (left) Harvard University Archives; (right) New York Public Library. 842 / Mark Twain Memorial, Hartford, Connecticut. 844 / (left) The Warder Collection; (right) Library of Congress. 849 / The Salvation Army. 851 / New York Public Library. 853 / Schlesinger Library, Radcliffe College. 856 / Museum of the City of New York.

CHAPTER 22 861 / Library of Congress. 863 / Library of Congress. 867 / Library of Congress. 870 / The Warder Collection. 872 / The Warder Collection. 874 / The Warder Collection. 877 / Library of Congress. 880 / The Warder Collection. 883 / Library of Congress. 887 / Library of Congress. 893 / Library of Congress.

CHAPTER 23 899 / U.S. Signal Corps photo, National Archives. 901 / Public Archives of Hawaii. 903 / National Archives. 907 / Brown Brothers. 909 / Library of Congress. 913 / National Archives. 915 / Library of Congress. 918 / National Archives. 922 / National Archives. 925 / Drake, in the *New York Times*. 929 / National Archives. 930 / Library of Congress.

CHAPTER 24 938 / AP / Wide World Photos. 942 / National Archives. 944 / The Bettmann Archive, Inc. 947 / Library of Congress. 950 / The Warder Collection. 952 / Schlesinger Library, Radcliffe College. 953 / The Warder Collection. 955 / Library of Congress. 959 / Library of Congress. 963 / Library of Congress. 968 / The Warder Collection. 970 / Historical Pictures Services, Chicago. 972 / Brandeis University.

CHAPTER 25 979 / The Warder Collection. 980 / Library of Congress. 983 / Harding, in the Brooklyn *Eagle*, The Warder Collection. 986 / The *New York Times*. 990 / United Press International Photo. 994 / National Archives. 995 / Library of Congress. 997 / National Archives. 1000 / National Archives. 1001 / National Archives. 1003 / National Archives. 1004 / National Archives. 1005 / The Warder Collection. 1007 / National Archives. 1008 / National Archives. 1012 / Library of Congress. 1014 / Library of Congress. 1017 / The Bettmann Archive, Inc. 1019 / Chicago Historical Society. 1020 / New York Public Library.

CHAPTER 26 1024 / Collection of the Museum of Modern Art, New York; gift of Abby Aldrich Rockefeller. Tempera on paper over composition board, $10\frac{1}{2} \times 14\frac{1}{2}''$. 1027 / UPI / Bettmann Newsphotos. 1029 / Looking Back at Tennessee Collection, Tennessee State Library and Archives, Courtesy of Mrs. Frances Robinson Gabbert. 1031 / UPI / Bettmann Newsphotos. 1033 / Chicago Historical Society. 1036 / Library of Congress. 1038 / State Historical Society of Wisconsin. 1039 / National Archives. 1041 / University of Chicago Press. 1042 / The Warder Collection. 1045 / The Bettmann Archive, Inc. 1048 / Ramsey Archive. 1050 / Metropolitan Museum of Art, bequest of Gertrude Stein, 1946. 1051 / Brown Brothers. 1053 / The Warder Collection. 1054 / National Archives. 1056 / AP / Wide World Photos. 1059 / University of Virginia. 1061 / Library of Congress.

CHAPTER 27. 1067 / Library of Congress. 1070 / Library of Congress. 1072 / Brown Brothers. 1075 / Museum of Modern Art / Film Stills Archive. 1076 / National Archives. 1077 / National Archives. 1079 / The Henry Ford Museum. 1082 / Library of Congress. 1087 / International News / Herbert Hoover Presidential Library. 1089 / Historical Association of Southern Florida. 1091 / AP / Wide World Photos. 1093 / Library of Congress. 1094 / Museum of History and Industry, Seattle. 1096 / State Historical Society of Wisconsin. 1097 / N.Y. *Daily News* Photo.

CHAPTER 28 1103 / Wide World Photos. 1109 / Franklin D. Roosevelt Library Collection. 1112 / Library of Congress. 1115 / Library of Congress. 1118 / National Archives. 1120 / UPI / Bettmann Newsphotos. 1122 / Library of Congress. 1124 / Library of Congress. 1126 / New York Public Library. 1127 / UPI / Bettmann Newsphotos. 1131 / Library of Congress. 1133 / George Meany Memorial Archives. 1135 / *Life* magazine, © 1965, Time, Inc. 1137 / National Archives.

CHAPTER 29 1146 / AP / Wide World Photos. 1148 / New York Public Library. 1151 / The Granger Collection. 1152 / National Archives. 1155 / The Warder Collection. 1157 / (left) Shoemaker, © the Chicago *Daily News,* used with permission of the Chicago *Sun-Times,* Inc. 1988; (right) Hutton in the Philadelphia *Inquirer.* 1159 / Imperial War Museum, London. 1162 / The *Daily Mail,* London. 1164 / Wide World Photos. 1166 / UPI / Bettmann Newsphotos. 1172 / (top) National Archives; (bottom) National Archives.

CHAPTER 30 1176 / The Warder Collection. 1179 / Library of Congress. 1181 / Library of Congress. 1183 / National Archives. 1184 / National Archives. 1186 / National Archives. 1189 / National Archives. 1194 / UPI / Bettmann Newsphotos. 1195 / Bill Mauldin and Wil-Jo Associates, Inc. 1197 / Library of Congress. 1198 / National Archives. 1204 / National Archives. 1205 / National Archives. 1207 / National Archives. 1209 / National Archives. 1211 / TASS from Sovfoto. 1213 / National Archives. 1216 / National Archives.

CHAPTER 31 1222 / University of Louisville Photographic Archives. 1223 / Library of Congress. 1226 / New York Public Library. 1227 / George Meany Memorial Archives. 1230 / United Nations Photo. 1232 / U.S. Army Signal Corps Photo. 1234 / Library of Congress. 1236 / Wide World Photos. 1239 / U.S. Information Agency. 1240 / The Hartford *Courant.* 1243 / UPI / Bettmann Newsphotos. 1244 / AP / Wide World Photos. 1245 / United Press International Photo. 1247 / Eastfoto. 1251 / AP / Wide World Photos. 1252 / Roche in the Buffalo *Courier Express.* 1255 / United Press International Photo.

INDEX

under Bourbon rule, 743
of buses and trains, 743, 745–47,
1312–14, 1335, 1337
constitutionality of, 745–46
in defense industries, 1184–85
judicial actions on, 1043, 1310–12, 1313,
1314
in military, 1184
NAACP campaigns against, 1043–44
of schools, 1310–12, 1314, 1337,
1338–39, 1353–54, 1395
"separate but equal" rubric in, 746,
1311–12
in suburbs, 1268
see also African-Americans; civil rights
movement
Seidel, Emil, 805
Seize the Day (Bellow), 1281, 1282
Selective Service Act (1917), 994–95
Selective Service System, 1374
Senate, U.S., 1155
see also Congress, U.S.
Senate Ethics Committee, 1455
Senate Foreign Relations Committee,
1235, 1360
Senate War Investigating Committee, 1187
Seneca Falls Convention (1848), 1037
Sennett, Max, 1076
Serbia, 981, 1010
servants, indentured (redemptioners), 799
Servicemen's Readjustment Act (1944),
1223
settlement houses, 851–52, 941
Seven Years' War, *see* French and Indian
War
Seward, William H., 708
assassination attempt on, 700
in foreign affairs, 898–99
sex, 1035, 1036, 1047
AIDS and, 1458–59
Freudian theories on, 1035
obsession with, in roaring twenties,
1035
premarital, 1036
Seymour, Horatio, 722
Shahn, Ben, 1061
Shame of the Cities, The (Steffens), 937
Share Croppers Union, 1096
sharecropping, 738–39
Share Our Wealth program, 1119
Shaw, Anna Howard, 853
Sheen, Fulton, J., 1273
Shepard, Alan B., Jr., 1320
Shepard, Morris, 1032
Sheridan, Philip, H.
in Indian wars, 758
Sherman, John, 774, 878, 880
Sherman, William Tecumseh, 702, 712
in march to sea, 695
Sherman Anti-Trust Act (1890), 786,
880–81, 941, 969, 1136

prosecutions under, 736, 946, 948
strikes as violations of, 804
Sherman Silver Purchase Act (1890), 880,
885, 892
Shevardnadze, Edvard, 1475
Shipping Board, U.S., 988, 996
shopping, 1264–65
Shrine of the Little Flower, 1120
Shultz, George, 1449, 1451
shuttle diplomacy, 1403, 1413–14
"Significance of the Frontier in American
History, The" (Turner), 769–70
silent majority, 1386
Silent Spring (Carson), 1400
Silliman, Benjamin, Jr., 783
silver, ratio of gold to, 884–85, 890
silver coinage, 826, 890, 892–95, 925
legislation on, 868–69, 881, 884–85, 892
see also currency
silver rushes, 755
silver standard, 885, 889
Simmons, William J., 1026
Simpson, Alan, 1465
Simpson, "Sockless Jerry," 889
Sims, William S., 994
Sinclair, Harry, 1071
Sinclair, Upton, 951
Singal, Daniel J., 1047
"single-tax" concept, 846–47
Sino-Japanese War (1894–1895), 921
Sioux Indians, 755, 756–59, 760
Sioux War (1860s-1870s), 757
Sirhan, Sirhan, 1364
Sirica, John J., 1404
Sister Carrie (Dreiser), 846
Sitting Bull, chief of Sioux, 759, 761
Sitzkrieg, 1161
Six-Day War (1967), 1403
Six-Power Consortium, 978
Slater, John F., Fund, 741
slavery, 843
constitutional amendment on, 693
recreated by Black Codes, 704
see also antislavery movements;
African-Americans; emancipation;
freedmen; Fugitive Slave Act;
Kansas-Nebraska Act; Missouri
Compromise
slaves:
emancipation of, 693, 695, 696–97,
703
Slavic-Americans, 824
Slovak-Americans, 824
Small, Albion W., 839
Smith, Adam, 792
Smith, Alfred, E., 1085–86, 1102, 1119,
1330
Smith, "Cotton" Ed, 1138
Smith Act (1940), 1254, 1256, 1299
Smith and Wesson Arms Company, 996
Smith College, 831